A Vigorous Spirit of Enterprise

A Vigorous Spirit of Enterprise

Merchants and Economic Development in Revolutionary Philadelphia

Thomas M. Doerflinger

Published for the
Institute of Early American
History and Culture
Williamsburg, Virginia
by the University of
North Carolina Press
Chapel Hill and London

The Institute of
Early American History and Culture
is sponsored jointly by
The College of William and Mary and
The Colonial Williamsburg Foundation.

Manufactured in the United States of America

Library of Congress Cataloging in Publication Data

Doerflinger, Thomas M.
A vigorous spirit of enterprise.

"Published for the Institute of Early American History and Culture, Williamsburg, Virginia."
Bibliography: p.
Includes index.
1. Businessmen—Pennsylvania—Philadelphia—History—18th century. 2. Philadelphia (Pa.)—Commerce—History—18th century. 3. Philadelphia (Pa.)—Economic conditions. I. Institute of Early American History and Culture (Williamsburg, Va.) II. Title.
HC108.P5D64 1985 380.1'09748'11 84-28036
ISBN 0-8078-1653-1

Portions of Chapter 2 appeared in *Business History Review*, LVII (1983), 20–49, and are reprinted here by permission. Portions of Chapter 4 appeared in the *William and Mary Quarterly*, 3d Ser., XL (1983), 197–226.

For my parents:
William Main Doerflinger
Anne Homer Doerflinger

Acknowledgments

Research for this book began when I was an undergraduate at Princeton University, where I particularly benefited from the instruction of Robert Darnton, James Banner, Jr., and the late Wesley Frank Craven. Donald Fleming, David Landes, and Stephan Thernstrom influenced the study as it assumed the shape of a doctoral dissertation at Harvard University, and I owe a special debt to the incisive counsel of my thesis adviser, Bernard Bailyn. A year spent as an Andrew W. Mellon Fellow at the Philadelphia Center for Early American Studies, then directed by Richard Dunn, afforded a fine opportunity to share my research with other students of eighteenth-century Philadelphia, and a fellowship at the Institute of Early American History and Culture provided a superb environment for turning the dissertation into a book. I owe a great deal to Thad Tate, John Selby, Michael McGiffert, Drew McCoy, and other members of the Institute staff. I am especially indebted to Norman Fiering and Gil Kelly of the Institute; their painstaking editorial work improved the study immeasurably. Jacob Price and Richard Ryerson also read a draft of the book and saved me from many errors, and I learned much from discussions with Fred Anderson, Jules Boymel, Rachel Klein, John McCusker, Kenneth Morgan, Philip Morgan, Thomas Purvis, Sharon Salinger, Carole Shammas, Daniel Vickers, Conrad Wright, and other colleagues too numerous to mention. Finally my wife, Janet Doerflinger, provided invaluable assistance of every description.

The archival backbone of this book is the spectacularly rich manuscript collections of the Historical Society of Pennsylvania, one of the finest libraries in the world for the study of the Atlantic community in the eighteenth century. I am most grateful to Peter Parker and his staff in the manuscript room for their generous assistance over the years, and likewise to the farsighted Philadelphians who have been contributing family papers to the Society for many generations. Ward Childs of the Philadelphia City Archives was unfailingly helpful in making available to me the City's records. I am no less indebted to the librarians of Princeton University, Harvard University, the University of Pennsylvania, the College of William and Mary, Columbia University, the Philadelphia City Archives, the American Philosophical Society, the National Archives, the Library of Congress, the Massachusetts Historical Society, the American Jewish Historical Society, the Bucks County Historical Society, the Eleutherian Mills Historical Library, Morristown National Historical Park, the New York Historical Society, the New York Public Library, the Pennsylvania Historical and Museum Commission, and the University of North Carolina.

Contents

Illustrations

PLATES

MAPS

FIGURES

Tables

APPENDIX

A Vigorous Spirit of Enterprise

The Spirit of Enterprize has seized most people & they are making or trying to make Fortunes. Their Attempt will probably have the happy Effect of procuring us many Supplies that we stand in need off.

Robert Morris to William Bingham, Philadelphia, October 20, 1776

The inhabitants of the trading towns of America, possessed of a vigorous spirit of enterprize, that has hitherto surmounted a variety of difficulties & disadvantages, have notwithstanding carried its Commerce to so flourishing an extent, that our enemies have been astonished at its progress, whilst every State in the Union has most sensibly experienced its beneficial effects.

Petition of Philadelphia Merchant Community to the Continental Congress, April 1782

That unequalled spirit of enterprise, which signalises the genius of the American Merchants and Navigators . . . is in itself an inexhaustible mine of national wealth.

Alexander Hamilton, Federalist 11, 1787

Introduction

In 1834 a nineteen-year-old lad on leave from Harvard College boarded the Boston ship *Pilgrim*, bound for California. After a perilous, exhilarating voyage around Cape Horn he was put to work on the deserted beaches near Santa Barbara, stacking heavy cowhides on his head, wading barefoot into the Pacific surf, loading the hides onto a small boat, and ferrying them out to the *Pilgrim*, anchored three miles offshore. The work was demanding and the hours were long, but not too long to prevent this Brahmin deckhand from spending his Sundays touring California's mainland. What he found was a land of paradox. It was a country of unparalleled resources—"four or five hundred miles of seacoast, with several good harbors; with fine forests in the north; the waters filled with fish, and the plains covered with thousands of herds of cattle; blessed with a climate than which there can be no better in the world; free from all manner of disease whether epidemic or endemic; and with a soil in which corn yields from seventy to eighty fold." Yet of actual *wealth* there was little: the villages were mean, dirty, and poor, inhabited by Mexicans and Indians who were content to support themselves with a minimum of effort. More energy seemed to be devoted to fighting and gaming than to expanding the local economy. Might not a more enterprising people make something of California's natural abundance? Probably not, he decided, for English and American settlers to the region were likely, by the second generation at least, to contract "the 'California fever' (laziness)."[1]

Whatever his shortcomings as a futurist, Richard Henry Dana's ruminations on the development of California probed an intriguing question, one that has been too often overlooked by historians and economists. The rapid economic development of the United States is frequently taken for granted, treated as a nonproblem that requires little formal analysis. To many historians, American prosperity is simply a logical extension of natural abundance: as conquerors of a huge continent, Americans had the good fortune of being able to found their economy on an unrivaled foundation of natural resources that made them, in the apt phrase of David Potter, a "people of plenty."[2] In fact, however, abundant resources

1. Richard Henry Dana, Jr., *Two Years before the Mast: A Personal Narrative* (Boston, 1883), 199–200.

2. David M. Potter, *People of Plenty: Economic Abundance and the American Character* (Chicago, 1954).

are neither a necessary nor a sufficient condition for national prosperity. Many nations with plentiful resources have failed to build strong and vital economies, while other lands enjoying few natural advantages, including Holland, Japan, England, and New England, have prospered mightily.

The task of unraveling this paradox, of discerning why certain nations at certain times have achieved superior economic performance, is an enduring challenge for the economic historian. The solution to the problem requires a comprehensive approach, because economic development is, at bottom, not merely a physical achievement but a cultural expression and a social process, a distinctive manifestation of the values of a people. As such, it is a problem that the discipline of pure economics is poorly equipped to tackle. Economists have little patience with the irritating variability of human nature and therefore tend to ignore it, conveniently assuming that people devote their lives to maximizing monetary income. Such an assumption may be useful when analyzing the workings of a particular market or industry, but when applied to far-reaching questions of social and economic change, it does violence to historical reality. For the mechanically rational, compulsively acquisitive individuals of classical economic theory are parodies of human beings, systematic distortions of social reality whose utility lies in the fact that they permit mathematical analysis of economic affairs. Historical explanations that rely on the fiction of "economic man" must ignore the complex relationship between national character and economic development. Indeed, in general the imposition of a priori behavioral assumptions often gives economic analysis a simplistic, unreal quality. One practitioner of the dismal science has observed: "Economists have traditionally tried to infer business behavior by deductive logic. They start out by assuming that people running a business think just like economists do. Then they conjure up a set of very simple conditions, again assuming that all businesses face those conditions. Finally, they try to figure out what businessmen might do following the economists' type of thinking—under the assumed conditions. All this without ever leaving the office."[3]

This deductive approach leads economists to assume the presence of a key condition of economic success that actually needs to be explained, namely, that the inhabitants of certain countries at certain times have systematically devoted themselves to making much more money than they need for survival. Far from being inherently rational, such behavior may be thought of, in fact, as being rather bizarre. In world history as a

3. Barbara R. Bergmann, "The Failures of a Chair-Bound Science," *New York Times*, Dec. 12, 1982.

whole, it has been far more common for men of means to concentrate on religious, military, intellectual, and political affairs—all more noble and interesting pursuits than the dull and dangerous task of accumulating a fortune in trade or industry. The behavior that Adam Smith observed in the countinghouses of Glasgow and London and wrote about in *The Wealth of Nations* was much less in evidence in seventeenth-century Paris or eighteenth-century Madrid or, for that matter, in twentieth-century London. Indeed, relatively few countries have been seized by a spirit of enterprise, a driving compulsion to swiftly develop a powerful, dynamic economy. Fifteenth-century Florence, seventeenth-century Holland, eighteenth-century Britain, twentieth-century Japan—all of these countries have been distinguished by a strong commitment to economic success that enabled them to outperform their rivals by wide margins.

Into this category falls the northern half of the United States during the century and a half after 1775. Despite its sparse population and vast wilderness tracts, the region plunged into the Industrial Revolution as rapidly as possible. As early as 1825, according to one authority, the "revolutionary phase" of the Industrial Revolution in America was completed.[4] Technological advances were so impressive during the period that by the 1850s Englishmen were crossing the Atlantic to inspect the factories of their former colonies.

To understand the origins of this extraordinary economic progress, we must reconstruct the mentality of its engineers. The present study contributes to this effort by examining Philadelphia's merchant community during the period 1750–1791. The largest port in America by 1760, Philadelphia was the leading financial, political, and intellectual center of Revolutionary America. Although the city's foreign trade declined rapidly after 1815, Philadelphia was the foremost industrial city in the United States during the first half of the nineteenth century and served as the nation's banking center until the 1840s. Much of the credit for this economic success must go to Philadelphia's merchants, who not only established its flourishing eighteenth-century commerce—the foundation for later economic advances—but also spearheaded the diversification into industry and finance.

By understanding the outlook of these Pennsylvania traders, we can learn a good deal about the entrepreneurial origins of American economic development as a whole. For although there were important differences between the major ports of the northeastern United States, the similarities were far more striking: Philadelphia traders were broadly

4. Thomas C. Cochran, *Frontiers of Change: Early Industrialism in America* (New York, 1981), 78.

representative of their counterparts in Boston, New York, and Baltimore. Since the Industrial Revolution in the United States took hold first in the Boston-Baltimore corridor and was led in no small degree by merchants, an understanding of the region's mercantile communities will help to clarify and bring out the social foundations of its economic success.

Part I of this study depicts the general character of the merchant community. Chapter 1 analyzes the social structure of the merchant group, paying particular attention to the recruitment of new commercial talent. Chapter 2 describes how trade was organized in Philadelphia and shows how the merchant community became not only much wealthier between 1750 and 1791 but also more highly differentiated. Chapter 3 analyzes the mentality of Philadelphia's traders, emphasizing the heavy risks they faced and examining the effect of a climate of risk on their character as businessmen.

Part II analyzes the experience of the merchants during the American Revolution. Chapter 4 explores why so many merchants approached the Revolutionary movement of the years 1764–1776 with great ambivalence and ultimately opposed Independence. Chapter 5 describes the actual wartime experience of the merchants, a particularly important but poorly documented subject. And Chapter 6 analyzes the political legacy of the Revolution, arguing that the hyperinflation and general disorder of the war years encouraged merchants to become active Federalists during the 1780s. From the merchants' perspective, the Constitution was indeed an economic document.

Part III traces the role of Philadelphia's traders in diversifying the American economy and proposes that their behavior was broadly representative of mercantile behavior in the period 1775–1860. Chapter 7 describes how, during the period 1776–1791, Philadelphia's traders aggressively seized the opportunities available during the war and moved into such unfamiliar fields as commercial banking, the tobacco trade, the China trade, securities speculation, and textile manufacturing. Taken together, these innovations dramatically advanced the economic sophistication of the port and laid the groundwork for both the upsurge in overseas trade between 1790 and 1812 and the industrialization of the Delaware Valley. Chapter 8 places these developments in a national context by showing that merchants in other ports behaved similarly and that American merchants, as a group, played an important role in the nation's industrial revolution.

The final section of Chapter 8 illuminates the distinctive economic contribution of northeastern merchants by contrasting their behavior with that of planters in the American South, particularly Virginia. Because southern businessmen based their operations on America's most abundant factor of production, land, they were extremely successful for a time. But this very success, coupled with the social stability characteristic of landed societies, ultimately made southern planters less flexible and adaptive, less aggressively acquisitive, than northern merchants. The southern pattern undeniably had certain advantages, and southern society was spared much of the avarice that pervaded northern ports. But the attendant cost was a considerably slower pace of economic development. Such broad comparisons are always dangerous, and this discussion is intended to be forward-looking and provocative. It will serve its purpose if it illustrates the dangers of reducing intersectional comparisons of economic performance to the single issue of labor systems. There is something narrow and anachronistic about adopting the perspective of the abolitionists and viewing the planter simply as an owner of slaves. He was, of course, much more than that: he was a businessman firmly committed to agricultural production, and this fact, in and of itself, caused him to behave very differently from the merchants of Philadelphia and other northern ports. The divergent course of economic development in the North and the South cannot be understood until these differing styles of entrepreneurship are explicitly delineated.

Part I
The Character of the Merchant Community

1
Social Structure and Recruitment

When he came to Philadelphia in 1776, Stephen Girard was another disreputable foreigner—blind in one eye, unable to speak polite English, alienated from his father, and in debt to businessmen in his native Bordeaux. A mariner by training, he did have some useful business skills and connections, but that was about all: no sizable capital, no apprenticeship with a major firm. Girard did not shake off such disadvantages easily. For six chaotic years during the Revolution he traded in the middle states and the Caribbean with no great success. In 1782 his total net worth amounted to only £2,280, about enough to buy one good ship. But during the 1780s, while many neighboring merchant houses reeled and broke in the unsettled business climate, Girard effectively employed his modest capital by smuggling provisions into Haiti and making a few shrewd shipments of foodstuffs to famine-devastated France. By the end of 1790 he was worth over £20,681, by 1794 his fortune was £55,211, and by 1812 he was one of the richest men in America, wealthy enough to set up, with only a part of his fortune, a major commercial bank that could successfully compete with joint-stock banks owned by hundreds of stockholders.[1]

Girard's career was propelled by a nimble mind, ferocious energy, and an aloof, despotic personality. One time he squabbled with a fellow entrepreneur, Jacob Ridgway, about a piece of property. "I could buy & sell you," exclaimed Ridgway. Responded Girard coolly, "I could buy you, Mr. Ridgway, but I do not think that I could sell you again." Girard

1. John Bach McMaster, *The Life and Times of Stephen Girard, Mariner and Merchant*, 2 vols. (Philadelphia, 1918), I, 1–48; Stephen Girard Ledger, 1780–1783, accounts for Feb. 18, 1782, Stephen Girard Papers, 3d Ser., Reel 48; Stephen Girard Journal, 1788–1790, entry for Dec. 31, 1790, Girard Papers, 3d Ser., Reel 44; Stephen Girard Journal, 1791–1794, 258, Girard Papers, 3d Ser., Reel 113. All references to the Girard Papers are to the microfilm collection in the American Philosophical Society (hereafter cited as APS). Donald R. Adams, Jr., *Finance and Enterprise in Early America: A Study of Stephen Girard's Bank, 1812–1831* (Philadelphia, 1978).

stood apart from Philadelphia's social scene, feuded viciously with his brother, fired his ship captains regularly, and resolutely refused to assist his indigent mother-in-law. Even when laid up in bed with a serious head wound, Girard insisted on conducting his banking business himself; he only regretted not being able to supervise his rental properties while sick: "I know that the rascals cheat me," he explained. He developed a similar attitude toward his first wife, who gradually went insane as Girard grew rich: "I hate her like the devil and note with pleasure that this feeling increases daily." The resulting disruption in his sex life was remedied by forming "the acquaintance of a young Quakeress, tailoress by trade, with whom I amuse myself at very little expense and when I have time."

Yet Girard was more than a callous plutocrat. When yellow fever ravaged the city late in the summer of 1793, nearly every Philadelphian who could afford to do so fled, leaving behind the blacks and the poor to care for the sick, bury the dead, and die themselves. Yet Girard had the courage to direct the establishment of a hospital in a mansion outside of Philadelphia and committed his days and nights, in a scene of putrid devastation, to nursing the victims.[2]

George Dunlope and William Glenholme came to Philadelphia from Ireland in the 1760s with far better prospects than did Stephen Girard. Together with their partner Andrew Orr, who was left behind in Dublin, they had ample financial resources, in the form of a generous line of credit supplied by their fathers, excellent trading contacts in Ireland and the West Indies, and two solid brigantines suitable for the flaxseed trade with Ireland. They even owned an expensive racehorse with which they hoped to earn substantial sums in prize money.

The firm's prospects were excellent, and it was soon inundated with business. By 1767, in addition to the managing of its own two ships, it was overseeing the construction of two vessels for foreign firms and dispatching several other ships on commission. All this demanded the execution of dozens of disparate tasks; there were deals to make with shipwrights and chandlers, flaxseed to buy from farmers and merchants, captains and seamen to hire. Most of these activities required cash expenditures rather than credit purchases, and because the rental demand for cargo space was low in the mid-1760s, the firm had to buy especially large amounts of flaxseed to make up cargoes. Consequently the com-

2. Thomas P. Cope, *Philadelphia Merchant: The Diary of Thomas P. Cope, 1800–1851*, ed. Eliza Cope Harrison (South Bend, Ind., 1978), 394–395; Benjamin Rush to John Adams, June 2, 1812, in L. H. Butterfield, ed., *Letters of Benjamin Rush*, 2 vols. (Princeton, N.J., 1951), II, 1136; Girard to John Girard, Mar. 21, Apr. 28, 1787, Girard Papers, 2d Ser., Reel 121; J. H. Powell, *Bring out Your Dead: The Great Plague of Yellow Fever in Philadelphia in 1793* (Philadelphia, 1949), 140–172.

PLATE I. Stephen Girard (1750–1831). By Bass Otis. Oil on panel.
Stephen Girard Collection. Girard College, Philadelphia

pany suffered severe pressure on its supply of ready money. Wrote one partner, "You actually cannot perceive how Cash goes away at this season of the year for many things that I cannot now mention having four vessels now on hand that for one thing or another they run away with a vast sight of money."[3] At precisely this inopportune juncture, when flaxseed had to be shipped out of port in time for the planting season in Ireland, and before the Delaware froze up, Glenholme took sick with a "nervous fever" so serious that for a while the doctors had given up on him. Glenholme managed to recover, but on the very day that he was back on his feet, Dunlope went numb in the limbs while walking home from dinner and expired before soldiers could carry him into his house.

So Glenholme was alone in Philadelphia with four vessels to rush out of port. By freely drawing bills of exchange (equivalent to checks) on his merchant banker in Europe, he effectively managed this crisis. The financial pressure continued to increase throughout 1768, however, as his business commitments grew. He dispatched eight vessels in that year, but the demand for freight was still weak, and one of the syndicates that had ordered the construction of a vessel refused to pay for it. This meant that Glenholme had to cover much of its cost out of his own pocket. More ominous still, his banker in Dublin refused to pay some of his drafts. Then there was the minor irritation of a mutiny that cost the lives of four crew members and—far more serious in Glenholme's view—threatened the success of a voyage. He also found himself in danger of being outwitted by his slave, who had taken advantage of the death of Dunlope to put it out around town that he was not a slave at all, but merely a bond servant who would be free in several years. The cumulative weight of all this financial and personal pressure was too much for the young Irishman to bear, and in the spring of 1769—just as the demand for freight was finally beginning to improve—Orr, Dunlope, and Glenholme went bankrupt. An advertisement in the *Pennsylvania Gazette* offered for sale "feather beds, mahogany chairs and tables, a mahogany desk and bookcase, looking-glasses" as well as "a very likely Negro boy," and "the famous horse NORTHUMBERLAND."

In 1722 Thomas Clifford was born into the undistinguished middling ranks of Bucks County's Quaker community.[4] Most of his relatives were tradesmen—millers, coopers, silk dyers, and the like—who lived in the

3. O., D., and G. to Andrew Orr, Dec. 16, 1767, Orr, Dunlope, and Glenholme Letterbook, 1767–1769, Historical Society of Pennsylvania, Philadelphia (hereafter cited as HSP). The entire account of the firm is based on this volume. *Pennsylvania Gazette* (Philadelphia), Mar. 23, 1767.

4. Grace Hutchison Larsen, "Profile of a Colonial Merchant: Thomas Clifford of Pre-Revolutionary Philadelphia" (Ph.D. diss., Columbia University, 1955), 1–47.

PLATE 1. Stephen Girard (1750–1831). By Bass Otis. Oil on panel. *Stephen Girard Collection. Girard College, Philadelphia*

pany suffered severe pressure on its supply of ready money. Wrote one partner, "You actually cannot perceive how Cash goes away at this season of the year for many things that I cannot now mention having four vessels now on hand that for one thing or another they run away with a vast sight of money."[3] At precisely this inopportune juncture, when flaxseed had to be shipped out of port in time for the planting season in Ireland, and before the Delaware froze up, Glenholme took sick with a "nervous fever" so serious that for a while the doctors had given up on him. Glenholme managed to recover, but on the very day that he was back on his feet, Dunlope went numb in the limbs while walking home from dinner and expired before soldiers could carry him into his house.

So Glenholme was alone in Philadelphia with four vessels to rush out of port. By freely drawing bills of exchange (equivalent to checks) on his merchant banker in Europe, he effectively managed this crisis. The financial pressure continued to increase throughout 1768, however, as his business commitments grew. He dispatched eight vessels in that year, but the demand for freight was still weak, and one of the syndicates that had ordered the construction of a vessel refused to pay for it. This meant that Glenholme had to cover much of its cost out of his own pocket. More ominous still, his banker in Dublin refused to pay some of his drafts. Then there was the minor irritation of a mutiny that cost the lives of four crew members and—far more serious in Glenholme's view—threatened the success of a voyage. He also found himself in danger of being outwitted by his slave, who had taken advantage of the death of Dunlope to put it out around town that he was not a slave at all, but merely a bond servant who would be free in several years. The cumulative weight of all this financial and personal pressure was too much for the young Irishman to bear, and in the spring of 1769—just as the demand for freight was finally beginning to improve—Orr, Dunlope, and Glenholme went bankrupt. An advertisement in the *Pennsylvania Gazette* offered for sale "feather beds, mahogany chairs and tables, a mahogany desk and bookcase, looking-glasses" as well as "a very likely Negro boy," and "the famous horse NORTHUMBERLAND."

In 1722 Thomas Clifford was born into the undistinguished middling ranks of Bucks County's Quaker community.[4] Most of his relatives were tradesmen—millers, coopers, silk dyers, and the like—who lived in the

3. O., D., and G. to Andrew Orr, Dec. 16, 1767, Orr, Dunlope, and Glenholme Letterbook, 1767–1769, Historical Society of Pennsylvania, Philadelphia (hereafter cited as HSP). The entire account of the firm is based on this volume. *Pennsylvania Gazette* (Philadelphia), Mar. 23, 1767.

4. Grace Hutchison Larsen, "Profile of a Colonial Merchant: Thomas Clifford of Pre-Revolutionary Philadelphia" (Ph.D. diss., Columbia University, 1955), 1–47.

vicinity of either Warwick, England, or Bristol, Pennsylvania, eighteen miles to the north of Philadelphia. Trained as a cooper, Clifford was orphaned at the age of fifteen but inherited some land from his father. When he married, he probably received little in the way of a dowry, for his father-in-law was poor enough to merit financial assistance from the Philadelphia monthly meeting. There was, in short, little in his background, training, or financial resources to prepare Thomas Clifford for a life as a Philadelphia merchant. Shortly after his marriage in 1743, Clifford nevertheless moved to Philadelphia, set himself up as a cooper, and used the earnings and knowledge acquired in this occupation to trade with the West Indies. His financial ascent was remarkably rapid. By 1750, at an age when many merchants would still be living in a boardinghouse, Clifford could afford to rent not only a house but stores and a wharf besides. In the late 1750s he invested heavily in vessels to take advantage of the strong demand for cargo space during the Seven Years' War. Clifford evidently prospered during the conflict, for in 1760 he bought a choice promontory jutting into the Delaware, not far from his birthplace, as a site for a country seat.

These sketches illustrate several key features of the social structure of Philadelphia's merchant community in the second half of the eighteenth century. As the breadbasket to the expanding population of the Atlantic community, the Delaware Valley economy was growing, and Philadelphia's commerce grew with it. Business organization was far too unstructured for a coterie of insiders to engross this expanding trade; it was easy for businessmen from many foreign quarters to sail up the Delaware and compete with merchants from local families. Quakers and Anglicans of English extraction predominated in the community, but there were also Scots, Irishmen, Germans, Frenchmen, Dutchmen, and Jews. Outsiders of limited means, like Thomas Clifford and Stephen Girard, could break into the merchant group and prosper. They were the exception, however, not the rule. For every Stephen Girard there were two other firms like Orr, Dunlope, and Glenholme that crumbled in the intense competition and several other companies that failed to amass large capitals. The merchant community, therefore, was not a tight commercial elite of merchant princes, but a large occupational group embracing both wealthy traders and many petty capitalists who lived no more sumptuously than a successful cooper or grocer. The combination of ethnic diversity, rapid growth, considerable turnover of personnel, and an unequal distribution of wealth prevented the merchant community from attaining a high degree of social cohesion. It was amorphous, divided, unorganized.

Hence, it is misleading to refer to a "merchant aristocracy," as many historians have done. The belief that "on the basis of fortunes accumulated in overseas trade, the Quaker merchants of Philadelphia reared a structure of aristocratic living comparable to that of the Virginia planters, the landed gentry of the Hudson Valley, and the Puritan merchant princes of Boston" is largely inaccurate. Nor is it true that "the Quaker mercantile class possessed to a surprising degree the typical attributes of aristocracy."[5] There existed no simple congruence between the city's aristocracy and its merchant community. Instead, one can identify three distinct groups, with somewhat overlapping memberships. First, there was the city's *merchant community*, a large and diverse occupational group consisting of all Philadelphia wholesalers. A second, much smaller occupational group, largely separate from the merchant community, consisted of *independently wealthy gentlemen*, the true aristocrats of Philadelphia society, who lived off their rents and loans and devoted their lives to public service and genteel amusements. These gentlemen were far too few to constitute by themselves a distinct social stratum. Consequently, they combined with most of the city's other wealthy citizens, including roughly the top 15 percent of the merchant community, to form Philadelphia's social elite, or *upper class*. This elite was divided into Quaker and non-Quaker wings, but each segment was united by a complex web of genealogical and organizational ties. It is to this religiously bifurcated but otherwise cohesive social group that historians typically refer when they write of the "merchant aristocracy." In fact, however, about 50 percent of its members were not merchants, and fully 85 percent of the city's merchants were not part of this social elite.

The great bulk of Philadelphia's wholesalers were part of the city's large middle stratum. This fundamental feature of the trading community was reciprocally linked, as both cause and effect, to the fact that entry into the merchant community was not inordinately difficult. An ambitious person possessing modest capital, proper contacts, or commercial talent had a fair chance of becoming a merchant, although it was far less easy to become actually wealthy. As a result, a great many merchants were upwardly mobile strivers—intense entrepreneurs who were tough, grasping, and willing to take large risks. Even many of the wealthiest traders fitted this description, for they too were arrivistes whose fortunes were not large by the wider standards of the Atlantic community. The merchants of the Delaware Valley, in sum, were remarkably dynamic and creative entrepreneurs, who displayed little of the complacent caution that has often characterized groups of securely established businessmen.

5. Frederick B. Tolles, *Meeting House and Counting House: The Quaker Merchants of Colonial Philadelphia, 1682–1763* (Chapel Hill, N.C., 1948), 109, 117; Carl Bridenbaugh, *Cities in Revolt: Urban Life in America, 1743–1776* (New York, 1955), 282–284.

These central characteristics of the merchant group did not change radically during the second half of the eighteenth century. Indeed, several of the major features of the group, including its large size, ethnic diversity, unequal distribution of wealth, and high rate of turnover of personnel, were actually intensified by the American Revolution. It cannot be said, certainly, that the development of the merchant community in the course of the century eliminated opportunity for upward mobility from the middle stratum because of a concentration of economic power in Philadelphia society. Though such opportunity was never notably great for the typical shopkeeper or artisan, it was no harder to become a merchant in 1770 or 1790 than it had been in 1750.

To the twentieth-century reader, a grocer sells food, a shopkeeper runs a fairly small store, and a merchant is anyone engaged in commerce. In the eighteenth century these and other occupational terms had quite different and much more precise meanings. Merchants were wholesalers who—in America, at least—were typically active in foreign markets; shopkeepers were general retailers who obtained their goods from merchants; and grocers were purveyors, usually at retail, of imported foods such as coffee, cocoa, wine, lemons, and pepper. A miscellany of less numerous distributors were also to be found in the shops and stores of eighteenth-century cities, including ironmongers, chandlers, tobacconists, and others. Naturally, the business operations of certain individuals did not easily fit into a single classification, but these distinctions were real and generally recognized by, among others, Philadelphia's tax assessors, census takers, and compilers of city directories. From their imperfect efforts we can estimate with a fair degree of accuracy what the size of the merchant community was at four points between 1756 and 1791. There were about 230 merchants in the city in 1756, 320 in 1774, 514 in 1785, and 440 in 1791.[6] All of these figures may be too high or too low by as much as 15 percent, but the orders of magnitude that they imply certainly are not misleading. Although the exceptionally high fig-

6. Hannah Benner Roach, comp., "Taxables in the City of Philadelphia, 1756," *Pennsylvania Genealogical Magazine*, XXII (1961–1962), 3–41; Transcript of the Assessment for the 1774 Provincial Tax for the City and County of Philadelphia, Pennsylvania Historical and Museum Commission (hereafter cited as PHMC) (microfilm copy at HSP); Francis White, *The Philadelpia Directory* (Philadelphia, 1785); Clement Biddle, ed., *The Philadelphia Directory* (Philadelphia, 1791). Figures for 1756 and 1774 are estimates because occupational designations in the documents covering those years are incomplete. The enumeration for 1774 was supplemented by County Tax Duplicates, 1773–1775, Philadelphia City and County, in Philadelphia City Archives, Philadelphia City Hall; and by Transcript of the Assessment for the 1772 Provincial Tax for the City and County of Philadelphia (microfilm copy at HSP).

ure for 1785 may seem anomalous and therefore suspect, it accords well with what we know of Philadelphia's business cycle. After the Revolution, newcomers rushed into the city to sell cloth and other manufactures, but in the ensuing depression many left or shifted to other occupations.

These wholesalers to some extent formed a coherent social group. Because of the common demands of business, mercantile transactions were facilitated by standard rules concerning such matters as commissions charged for various services, the correct manner of negotiating bills of exchange, and procedures for settling insurance claims. Naturally, the merchants had many common concerns about which to gossip during long, convivial sessions in William Bradford's London Coffee House or the more elegant City Tavern. A favorite topic of discussion was the relative merits of the merchants' various English suppliers. The price and quality of their wares and the terms on which they were exported to America were intently examined and compared. The fortunes of fellow traders, rumors of war, and market trends throughout the Atlantic world were other staples of conversation. The merchants also had strong financial incentives for getting to know their peers: they were continually sizing up one another, trying to determine who was and who was not a good credit risk. In such appraisals the man and the merchant were inseparable. Not only were the liquidity and net worth of a trader taken into account but also many details about his business and private life. Does he keep a clean, well-organized store? Does he have good business connections in the backcountry? Is his wife a big spender? Does his father or father-in-law have much money? Most important of all, is he known for "punctuality and prudence"? These terms had fairly precise meanings to the eighteenth-century merchant. Every trader tried to have as much ready cash as possible, available for investment in new ventures that would generate profits. If one of his trading partners failed to pay a debt on time—that is, "punctually"—he reduced his creditor's capital base and profit potential. Involvement with a merchant inclined to "slow pay" could thus be a costly mistake. If a debtor was prone to commit the further transgression of speculating with his creditor's money, he was a grave risk indeed. A merchant who acquired a reputation for such "unmerchantable" behavior did so at his peril; fellow traders would be loath to deal with him except on very unfavorable terms. And should he go bankrupt, he would be particularly susceptible to the wrath of his creditors.[7]

7. The William Pollard Letterbook, 1772–1774, HSP, contains many assessments of Philadelphia traders. See, for example, Pollard to Benjamin and John Bowers, Feb. 25, 1773, 161.

There were, however, definite limits to the cohesion of the merchant community. For one thing, no institutional links existed to strengthen the informal business ties we have observed. There was nothing comparable, for example, to a modern professional association. Significantly enough, one attempt to establish a chamber of commerce produced meager results. Far more successful was the Bank of North America, founded in 1781, which counted about 120 merchants as stockholders and dozens of others as customers. But this institution also failed truly to unite the merchants socially, for it was controlled by a narrow clique of rich Anglican merchants whom the Quakers, among others, distrusted. Competition further dampened the fellow feeling of the merchants, for the trader who was too open and honest could lose an advantage. "Most of our trading people here," one Philadelphian observed, "are complaisant sharpers; and that maxim in trade, to think every man a knave, until the contrary evidently appears, would do well to be observed." John Reynell admonished an apprentice: "In doing business, be a little on the Reserve, and Observe well the Person thou has to do with. . . . Keep thy Business to thy self, and don't let it be known, who thou dost Business for, or what Sorts of goods thou Ships off. Some will want to know both, perhaps with a Design to Circumvent thee." Similarly Stephen Girard advised his brother to "use on every occasion a great deal of secret observation and coolness." Illegal trade required particular caution. "You are to keep thos Directions as Secrate as Death," commanded one smuggler to his captain.[8]

Finally, the specific organization of trade in Philadelphia did little to enhance the feeling of mutuality within the merchant community. Many traders operated alone, very few firms had more than three partners, and there was little need for extensive cooperation among companies. Cartels were unknown, except in the highly specialized iron industry, and large projects or investment syndicates requiring the joint efforts of more than a few firms were likewise rare. Even the largest investments of most Philadelphia firms, an oceangoing vessel, were carried alone or owned in partnership with, at most, one or two Philadelphia firms, the captain of the ship, and a foreign firm situated in the port to which the ship regularly sailed. As for the more important activity of buying and selling

8. Jacob E. Cooke, *Tench Coxe and the Early Republic* (Chapel Hill, N.C., 1978), 73; Lawrence Lewis, Jr., *A History of the Bank of North America: The First Bank Chartered in the United States* (Philadelphia, 1882), 133–147; Alexander Graydon, *Memoirs of a Life Chiefly Passed in Philadelphia, within the Last Sixty Years* (Harrisburg, Pa., 1811), 6; Tolles, *Meeting House and Counting House*, 60; Girard to John Girard, May 15, 1784, Girard Papers, 2d Ser., Reel 121; Riche to Peter Spence, n.d. (ca. Apr. 22, 1760), Thomas Riche Letterbook, 1748–1764, Thomas Riche Papers, HSP.

commodities, firms varied considerably in how much they traded with other local merchants. A few firms that specialized as commodity brokers dealt simultaneously with a great many merchants. The natural customers of most merchants, however, were local retailers or foreign correspondents, not other Philadelphia wholesalers, and a merchant needed to trade with only a modest fraction of the entire merchant community. Thus there was a considerable degree of anonymity in the merchant group. In 1757 Thomas Willing remarked that he was not personally acquainted with the wealthy Irish merchant John McMichael, who had come to the city several years before. Joseph Turner, who had been in Philadelphia for many years, claimed that he did not know one member of the prominent Wharton family from another and had not exchanged more than ten words with still another well-known merchant.[9]

Merchant Princes and Paupers

If the organization of commerce did not strongly unite the mercantile body into a cohesive group, a number of other factors conspired to divide the merchants. One was the important matter of social class, for, like the trees in the forest, the merchants were of widely diverse importance. There were vulnerable saplings, numerous but insignificant, and a few giant oaks that dominated the landscape. Of 503 merchants present in Philadelphia at some time between 1756 and 1775, the top 50 alone bought about half of all the shipping tonnage purchased by merchants. Just eleven firms handled over a quarter of all the shipping not consigned to captains during a ten-year period before the Revolution. And only fifty-seven firms (a total of about 76 merchants, with all partners included) imported 54 percent of the goods entering Philadelphia during a three-year period in the 1780s. Unfortunately, neither these facts nor any other single quantitative index can measure the economic importance of every trader residing in the Quaker City at a particular time. The data on imports are, at best, approximations. Still, after adjusting for the presence of wholesalers who were not overseas traders, we can estimate that about 52 traders, organized into thirty-seven firms, were the great oaks of Philadelphia's merchant community. The hundreds of lesser merchants who labored in their shadow were bona fide

9. T. Willing to Thomas Pennington and Son, July 1, 1757, Willing and Morris Letterbook, 1754–1761, 293, HSP; Turner to David Barclay and Sons, Nov. 29, 1759, Joseph Turner Letterbook, 1753–1774, HSP.

wholesalers, rather than shopkeepers or grocers, but they operated on a much smaller scale.[10]

Perhaps a more meaningful way to convey the stratification of the merchant community is to analyze the fortunes, incomes, and living styles of the various strata of merchants. At the pinnacle of the mercantile pyramid were the great men of the Delaware whose fortunes were sufficiently large to enable them to emulate, if not quite duplicate, the lives of the lesser gentry of England. They generally lived in the heart of the city in three-story town houses that were graced by high ceilings, elaborate trim in the main parlors and dining room, and a fine garden in the back. In designing these residences the merchants favored elegance over size. Although they expected to accommodate many guests, sizable household staffs, large families, and sometimes business quarters as well, the town houses usually had only two or three medium-sized public rooms, with the balance of the floorspace given over to bedrooms, kitchen, and pantry. But the parlors and the dining rooms of the finest town houses were indeed magnificent. Lavish carving around the windows, doorways, mantelpieces, and cornices depicted all sorts of natural and unnatural objects. One gentleman received a bill for a "carved freeze, folded flowers, birds, etc.," "two dragons for the pediments," a "large flower & ribbon down the corners of the chimney," and "eighteen square flowers in pediments," among many other adornments. A chandelier hanging from an ornate ceiling illuminated expensive mirrors and portraits of the master and his family, and the smooth mahogany and walnut furnishings set off porcelain figurines and locally crafted silver. Imported carpets and drapes completed the effect.[11]

10. On the distribution of incoming shipping, see Tonnage Duties on Incoming Vessels, Nov. 1, 1765–Aug. 30, 1775, 3 vols., Cadwalader Collection, Thomas Cadwalader Section, HSP (hereafter cited as Tonnage Duty Book). A small additional fragment of this document is the Register of Tonnage Duties, 1775–1776, Record Group 4, PHMC. On patterns of vessel ownership, see Ship Register of Pennsylvania, 1726–1776, HSP; and Declarations of British Registry, 1727–1776, 12 vols., Record Group 41, PHMC (hereafter cited as the Pennsylvania Ship Register). The portion of the ship register in the HSP, which contains an important gap covering 1762, 1763, and 1764, is contained, with certain other records, in John J. McCusker, comp., "Ships Registered at the Port of Philadelphia before 1776: A Computerized Listing," HSP. Although based on the originals, my data were checked with this valuable and accurate list, and I am very grateful to Professor McCusker for allowing me to use it. On the distribution of incoming cargoes, Registers of Duties Paid on Imported Goods, 1781–1787, 6 vols., Record Group 4, PHMC. For further discussion of these items, see the Bibliography.

11. Nicholas B. Wainwright, *Colonial Grandeur in Philadelphia: The House and Furniture of General John Cadwalader* (Philadelphia, 1964), esp. 21. See also Bridenbaugh,

PLATE 2. The Blackwell Parlor. Circa 1764. *Courtesy of The Henry Francis du Pont Winterthur Museum*

Because these elegant chambers overlooked dusty streets strewn with noxious refuse from the waterfront and marketplace, rich Philadelphians found it convenient to spend the summer months in country seats beyond the city limits. Although the finest of these summer residences were grand indeed and cost as much as a good town house, merchants more often elected to build relatively simple structures. Frequently they were built in stages, as the money for construction became available. Thomas Clifford, David Deshler, William Coleman, and Richard Peters all followed this pattern, and the first stage tended to be a fairly modest cottage of two or three rooms. Even Mount Pleasant, a magnificent Palladian structure considered by many to be the finest surviving country seat in Philadelphia, is not particularly large. Though dictated by financial constraints, such simplicity had the positive effect of focusing attention on the splendid sites on which many of the buildings were constructed. Promontories overlooking the Schuylkill and Delaware rivers were favorite locations. Thomas Clifford's residence was situated at the end of an avenue, lined with cherry trees, that extended for a quarter of a mile to the Delaware. From here one had "a most extensive view up and down the river and in the Jerseys for miles."[12]

Whether in their town houses or at their country seats, the wealthy merchants and their families enjoyed a wide array of luxuries. The more serious-minded of them acquired libraries that typically had a preponderance of works on religion, commerce, and history. As well-connected importers, they could set their tables with the finest wines, rum, fruits, and spices that the Atlantic world had to offer. The merchants were not sparing in their purchases of such delicacies. Thomas Fitzsimons's liquor

---

Cities in Revolt, 334–340; and George B. Tatum, *Philadelphia Georgian: The City House of Samuel Powel and Some of Its Eighteenth-Century Neighbors* (Middletown, Conn., 1976). More valuable still is actual inspection of the Powel House, 244 South Third Street; the Hill-Keith-Physick House, 321 South Fourth Street; the Bishop White House, 309 Walnut Street; and the exteriors of the Abercrombie and Neave Houses at 268 and 272–274 South Second Street. For a complete inventory of 18th-century city dwellings that are still standing, see Richard J. Webster, *Philadelphia Preserved: Catalog of the Historic Buildings Survey* (Philadelphia, 1976), 1–110.

12. Larsen, "Thomas Clifford," 16, 17. Surviving country seats include the Deshler-Morris House, 5442 Germantown Avenue; Stenton, corner of Courtland and Eighteenth streets; Cliveden, 6401 Germantown Avenue; and the following mansions in Fairmount Park: Mount Pleasant, Lemon Hill, Woodford, the Cliffs, Randolph Mansion, and Solitude. For short descriptions of these buildings and their histories, see Webster, *Philadelphia Preserved*, 227–264, 276–277; Esther M. Klein, *Fairmount Park: A History and a Guidebook* (Bryn Mawr, Pa., 1974), 72–76, 81–83, 85, 89; *Antiques*, LXXXII (1962), 508–537; and Margaret B. Tinkcom, "Cliveden: The Building of a Philadelphia Countryseat, 1763–1767," *Pennsylvania Magazine of History and Biography*, LXXXVIII (1964), 2–36.

PLATE 3. The Cliffs, Country Seat of Joshua Fisher. Built between 1770 and 1773. *Reproduced from the Collections of the Library of Congress*

budget for 1784 was large enough to support two artisan families comfortably. About a third of the rich merchants could obtain fresh milk from their own cows, and about half owned at least one horse. This could be hitched to a phaeton or chariot for summer touring or for city visiting during the busy social season that set in after Christmas. As for larger vehicles, light, four-wheel carriages had to suffice, for only three or four traders were rich enough to afford the extravagance of a coach. Like all the other menial chores of the household, the task of driving the carriage was left to a servant who was likely to be a slave or bond servant. This abundance of luxury left the merchant with little to do but eat, drink, and make money, and if he did so to fatal excess, he would go to his grave in a "Mahogany Coffin, with Inscription plate, Handles, Cherrubs &c."[13]

13. Thomas Fitzsimons Journal, 1781–1785, HSP; Larsen, "Thomas Clifford," 20–26; Robert F. Oaks, "Big Wheels in Philadelphia: Du Simitière's List of Carriage Owners,"

PLATE 4. The Parlor of the Cliffs. *Reproduced from the Collections of the Library of Congress*

What was the exact cost of such genteel elegance? Three excellent studies of individual Philadelphia mansions, together with evidence culled from ledgers, tax lists, and probate records, allow us to determine fairly accurately the cost of the trappings of wealth. A good town house sold for about £4,000; a serviceable but not magnificent country seat cost £2,000; a houseful of furniture was worth over £500; and a good phaeton could not be obtained for less than £120. Thus the material rewards of commercial success were worth approximately £6,620. Just how high this figure was, in contemporary values, can be appreciated by realizing that most wealthy merchants had a net worth of between

PMHB, XCV (1971), 351–362; David Evans, "Excerpts from the Day-Books of David Evans, Cabinet-Maker, Philadelphia, 1774–1811," *PMHB*, XXVII (1903), 49–55.

£15,000 and £35,000. This means that a very sizable proportion of a wealthy capitalist's fortune—between a third and a fifth in most cases—would have to be tied up not in vessels, merchandise, and commercial credits, but in articles of consumption if he was to live in the grand style commonly associated with the merchant prince.[14]

Although Philadelphia's leading merchants were among the richest people in the northern colonies, it is obvious that they were not particularly rich by modern standards or by the standards of eighteenth-century Europe. Their town houses were large but not huge, their country seats would barely qualify as substantial outbuildings for the great country houses of England, and coaches were normally out of their reach. The meaning of a thin pocketbook was brought home to one prominent merchant who, for his new house, had intended to use grey stone as trim. "But Ive found after tryal," he wrote, "our grey stone comes so very dear, when wrot[t] that Ive laid aside all thoughts of putting any rustick work about it. or even as Sils or Arches for the Windows & Doors."[15] The effect upon entrepreneurial activity of such financial constraints was great, for the perennial shortage of money created the incentive to take risks. Every commercial success permitted a perceptible improvement in one's style of living, not merely the swelling of one's financial net worth. The rewards of successful risk taking were real, not abstract, and therefore the more worth taking.

An excellent example of this phenomenon appears in the behavior of Robert Morris and two of his associates, John Ross and William Bing-

14. All money is expressed in Pennsylvania currency unless stated otherwise (£167 Pennsylvania currency = £100 sterling). For the prices of fine town houses, see William West Ledger, 1770–1777, 37, 91, William West Account Books, 1769–1804, HSP; Thomas Wharton Ledger, 1765–1784, 123, 141, Leonard T. Beale Collection, HSP; Henry Drinker Journal, 1776–1791, 18, Henry Drinker Papers, HSP; Chaloner to Wadsworth and Carter, Sept. 26, 1783, John Chaloner Letterbook, 1782–1784, 180, Chaloner and White Collection, box 4, HSP; Tatum, *Philadelphia Georgian*, 6; Thomas Lea Will no. 343, 1793, Office of the Recorder of Wills, Philadelphia City Hall; Wainwright, *Colonial Grandeur*, 58–59. For the prices of country seats, see Tinkcom, "Cliveden," *PMHB*, LXXXVIII (1964), 34; Turner to William Allen, Dec. 9, 1763, Turner Letterbook, 1753–1774; Walter Goodman Will no. 193, 1782, Office of the Recorder of Wills, Philadelphia City Hall; Thomas Wharton Ledger, 1765–1784, 17; Samuel and Miers Fisher Journal, 1792–1795, 98, HSP. It should be noted that the cost of housing rose considerably during the second half of the 18th century. The value of household furniture is based on probate records; the top 23 of a group of 85 merchants had furniture worth £501 or more, and this figure is confirmed by manuscript evidence. See, for example, Henry Drinker Journal, 1776–1791, 2; Wastebook of John Reynell Estate, 1784–1791, 1, Coates and Reynell Collection, HSP; Girard Journal, 1788–1790, entries for Dec. 31, 1790, Girard Papers, 3d Ser., Reel 44. On carriage prices, see Oaks, "Big Wheels," *PMHB*, XCV (1971), 355, 356. The net worth of merchants is discussed in chap. 2, below.

15. C. Willing to John Wallis, Nov. 6, 1754, Willing and Morris Letterbook, 40.

PLATE 5. The William Bingham Mansion on Third Street. Built between 1786 and 1788. *From W. Birch and Son,* The City of Philadelphia . . . As It Appeared in 1800. *Courtesy of The Historical Society of Pennsylvania*

ham. All three were wealthy merchants by the time of the Revolution but became far richer during the war. With a part of their fortunes each of these magnates set about building rather tasteless, outsized dwellings on a far grander scale than most of their peers could manage. John Ross's town house was nearly twice the size of the standard large, city dwelling, and when he purchased a country seat in 1783 that had once belonged to one of Philadelphia's richest pre-Revolutionary traders, he substantially expanded both the mansion and surrounding acreage. William Bingham somehow found the need for two country seats, and his city house was even more imposing than Ross's: "Consuming almost an entire city square and set in landscaped and ornamented grounds, it boasted great iron gates, a wide carriage drive, large octagonal bays, conservatory and greenhouses containing numerous exotic plants."[16]

16. Ethel Elise Rasmusson, "Capital on the Delaware: The Philadelphia Upper Class in Transition, 1789–1801" (Ph.D. diss., Brown University, 1962), 72; "Memoir of John Ross, Merchant, of Philadelphia," *PMHB*, XXIII (1899), 77–85; Margaret L. Brown, "Mr. and

PLATE 6. The Powel House. Built 1765–1766. *Photograph by Cortlandt V. D. Hubbard. Courtesy of the owners and operators, The Philadelphia Society for the Preservation of Landmarks*

PLATE 7. The Bishop White House. Built 1786–1787. *Photo by Tom Davies. Courtesy of Independence National Historical Park Collection*

What makes Bingham, Ross, and Morris so significant is that they were not exceptions to the conventional mores of the city's post-Revolutionary upper class, but were widely emulated social leaders. Together with his neighbor and close friend George Washington, Robert Morris stood at the very center of the Republican court that took shape in Philadelphia during the 1790s, and his closest rival for social preeminence in the city was his former partner, William Bingham. Other prominent merchants were also obsessed with wealth and the social status it brought. In 1786 a visitor reported that the "war has introduced a spirit of Dissipation & exteriour emulation," and a French traveler claimed that "the homage paid to wealth is a worship in which all sects unite." He went on to describe how "the rich man loves to shew the stranger his splendid furniture, his fine English glass, and exquisite china. But when the stranger has once viewed the parade in a ceremonious dinner, he is dismissed for some other new-comer, who has not yet seen the magnificence of the house nor tasted the old Madeira that has been twice or thrice to the East Indies. And then, a new face is always more welcome than an old one to him who has little to say to either." Spirited competition among the wives of such men gave rise to exhausting winter social seasons featuring sumptuous banquets and splendid balls, in addition to innumerable afternoon teas and evening card games.[17]

But what portion of Philadelphia's entire merchant group did these aristocratic merchants represent? A rough answer to this problem, and indeed a general conception of the social configuration of the merchant group, emerges from an analysis of the 1789 tax list, which indicates the value of the house that every merchant householder owned or rented.[18] For the 80 percent of the merchants who were not living in a boardinghouse or in the home of a parent or friend, we can determine the value of the houses in which they lived. These values are of little significance in themselves, but they take on vivid meaning when matched with dwellings still standing near the waterfront. We know, for instance, that the restored Powel House on Third Street was rated at £2,000, the Bishop White House on Walnut Street was valued at £1,500, the Todd House several doors away at £600, and the still simpler dwellings in Elfriths Alley at only £150–£200 (see plates 6–9). Comparisons of the value of

---

Mrs. William Bingham of Philadelphia," *PMHB*, LXI (1937), 286–324. The Ross House is still standing at the southeast corner of Second and Pine streets. On Robert Morris's new home, see Thompson Westcott, *The Historic Mansions and Buildings of Philadelphia . . .* (Philadelphia, 1877), 351–366.

17. Rasmusson, "Capital on the Delaware," 66, 80, and chap. 4. I have relied heavily on Rasmusson's exceptionally fine portrait of Philadelphia during the 1780s and 1790s.

18. County Tax Assessment Ledgers, for City and County of Philadelphia, 1789, Philadelphia City Archives, Philadelphia City Hall.

housing of 251 merchants with both these structures and the value of housing of a random sample of 632 Philadelphia residents allow us to fix the social level, or style of life, of the city's merchants quite accurately.

Authorities on colonial Philadelphia's social elite have generally fixed their attention on five town houses, comparable to the Powel House, that were rated at two thousand pounds or more in 1789, and they have implied that such houses were numerous. Nicholas B. Wainwright, for example, states that "scores" of such houses were to be found in the city.[19] But the tax list demonstrates that this estimate is far off the mark: there were only twenty-six residences in the Quaker City rated at two thousand pounds or more. If we move the cutoff point down to fifteen hundred pounds in order to include such dwellings as the small, ornate Stamper-Blackwell House (sixteen hundred pounds) and the large but modestly decorated Bishop White House (fifteen hundred pounds), there were eighty-two grand town houses in the city. In 1789 only thirty-four of these were owned by active traders, and another sixteen by retired merchants. Thus at most only 50—one-ninth—of Philadelphia's 450 merchants lived in houses of a quality traditionally associated with the city's mercantile aristocracy. Similarly, in 1774 perhaps no more than 40 merchants owned a country seat.[20] These two findings powerfully support the conclusion that Philadelphia's traders as a group could not easily afford to live in an elegant style. For most, this was a distant goal, not a reality to be taken for granted.

It would be a mistake, however, to claim definitely that only about forty of Philadelphia's active traders were part of the city's socioeconomic elite. Many wealthy traders of social distinction either could not afford to or did not elect to live in sumptuous town houses. Just how many people fall into this category is difficult to say. One careful attempt to identify the members of the city's social elite by their participation in prominent civic and political organizations concluded that on the eve of the Revolution the social elite included forty-three merchants.[21] These men constituted about half of the entire elite group, but less than 15

19. The preserved town houses of Samuel Powel and Henry Hill were rated at £2,000 and £2,200, respectively; the Cadwalader house studied by Wainwright was rated at £2,000; and the urban counterparts of two well-known country seats were also rated at this level. Wainwright, *Colonial Grandeur*, vii, 96; Tinkcom, "Cliveden," *PMHB*, LXXXVIII (1964), 2–36; and Frederick B. Tolles, "Town House and Country House: Inventories from the Estate of William Logan, 1776," *PMHB*, LXXXII (1958), 397–410.

20. Transcript of the Assessment for the 1774 Provincial Tax for the City and County of Philadelphia, PHMC, shows 34 merchants owning country seats but excludes seats located in New Jersey.

21. Stephen James Brobeck, "Changes in the Composition and Structure of Philadelphia Elite Groups, 1756–1790" (Ph.D. diss., University of Pennsylvania, 1973), chap. 5, 308, 309, 325, 326.

PLATE 8. The Todd House. Built circa 1783. *Courtesy of Independence National Historical Park Collection*

percent of the total merchant community. It is quite clear, then, that the ubiquitous term "merchant aristocracy" is misleading insofar as it suggests a congruence between the merchant group and Philadelphia's upper class. While it is true that merchants composed a substantial portion of the city's elite, the converse proposition—that most merchants were aristocrats—does not hold.

If only a small proportion of the merchant community were outstandingly rich, it is true nonetheless that most merchants were in the upper part of the city's amorphous middle class. We can enter their well-ordered world by stepping into the Todd House (plate 8) which stands at the corner of Walnut and Fourth streets (map 1). This building falls near the middle of the distribution of houses owned by the lower three-quarters of the merchant community's householders. We enter from Fourth Street. To our right is the merchant's office, which has a separate entrance from Walnut; to our left is a family room for eating and day-to-day living, and behind it a kitchen. Taking three steps through the little hallway and climbing the steep, winding staircase, we find on the second floor a formal parlor, situated over the office, and two of the dwelling's four bedrooms. If we had just left the town house of a great merchant,

PLATE 9. Houses in Elfriths Alley. *Courtesy of City Archives of Philadelphia*

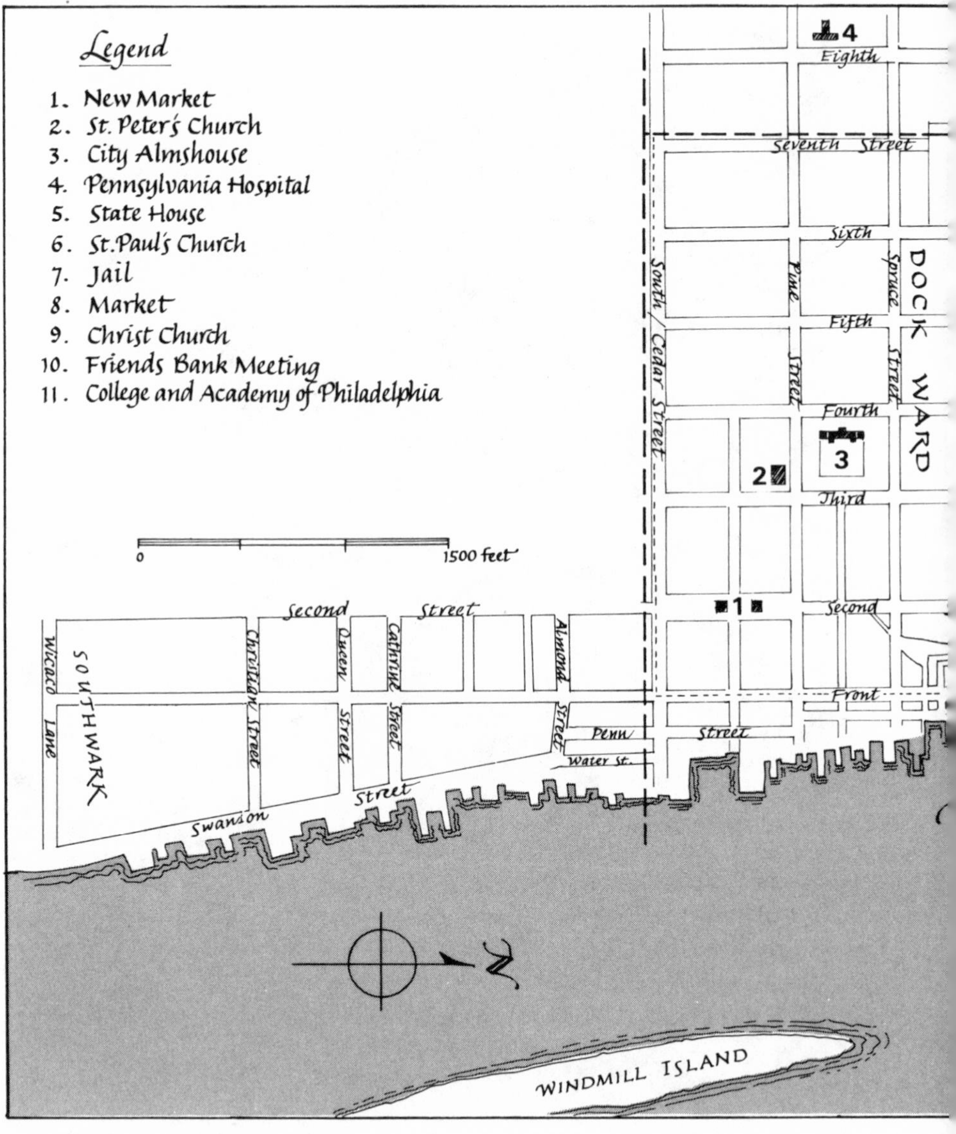

MAP 1. Philadelphia, 1774. *After Lester J. Cappon et al., eds.,* Atlas of Early American History: The Revolutionary Era, 1760–1790 *(Princeton, N.J., 1976), 10. Drawn by Richard Stinely*

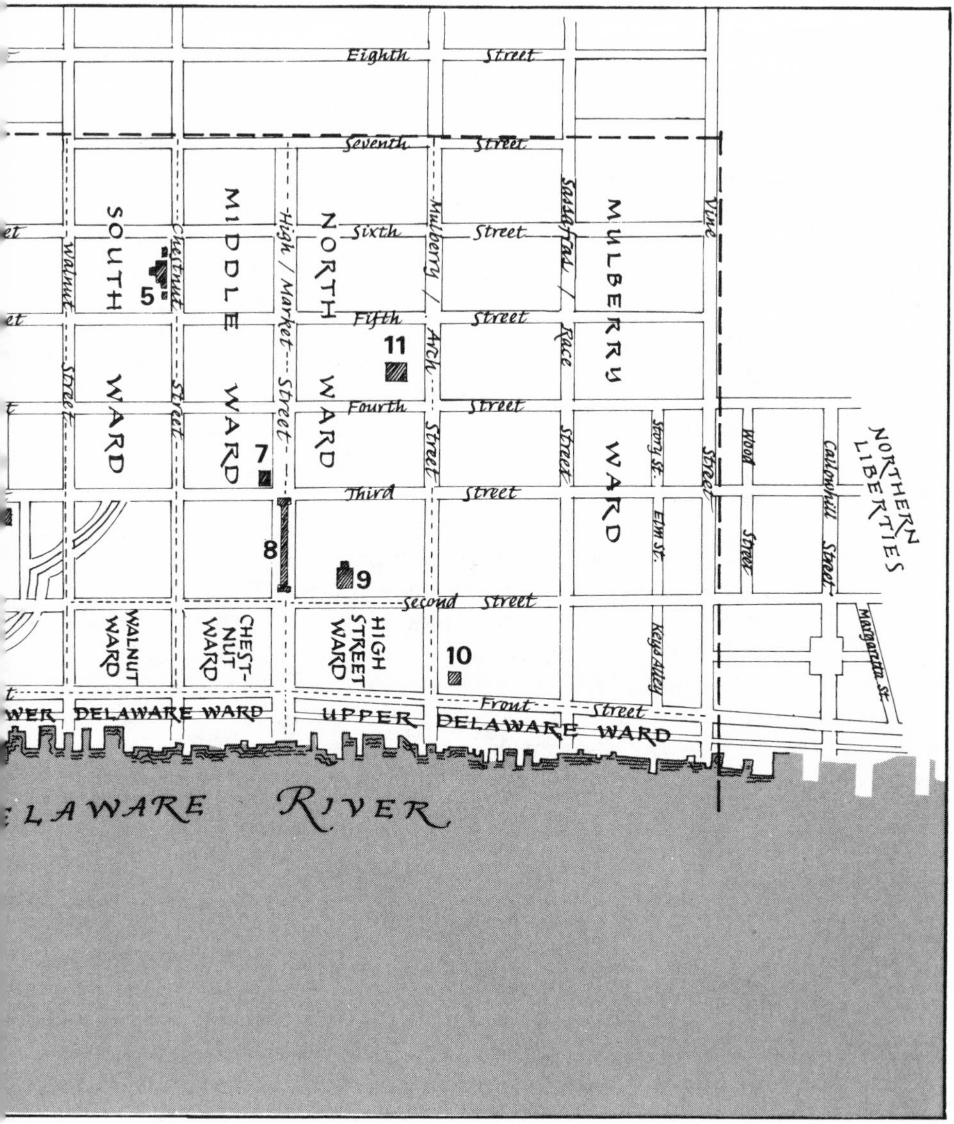
Eighth Street
Seventh Street
Sixth Street
Fifth Street
Fourth Street
Third Street
Second Street
Front Street
SOUTH WARD
MIDDLE WARD
NORTH WARD
MULBERRY WARD
NORTHERN LIBERTIES
WALNUT WARD
CHEST-NUT WARD
HIGH STREET WARD
DELAWARE WARD
UPPER DELAWARE WARD
Walnut Street
Chestnut Street
High / Market Street
Mulberry / Arch Street
Sassafras / Race Street
Vine Street
Story St.
Elm St.
Keys Alley
Wood Street
Callowhill Street
Margaretta St.
DELAWARE RIVER
5
7
8
9
10
11

such as the Powel House, several things would impress us by contrast. The ceilings in the Todd House are lower, and there is an absence of such ornamentation as decorative carving, wallpaper, chandeliers, and expensive carpets. Furthermore, the house lacks privacy; not only is it situated on a street corner with the windows four feet above the sidewalk, but it has no sizable private garden. Again unlike the Powel House, this structure was built not for entertaining, but for the needs of family and business. There are no grand hallway and no dining room, and since the logical place for the parlor is occupied by an office, visitors must negotiate the steep and narrow stairs to find the sitting room. Obviously, a house like this was no place to hold the sort of grand entertainments to which members of the Continental Congress were regularly treated. It would even be difficult for the owner of such a house to accommodate a single business associate. William Pollard once apologetically wrote a friend that because the lot next door was being built upon, he had to bring some of his merchandise indoors, with the result that there was no room for a guest.

The vast social distance between a middling merchant like Pollard and a merchant prince is suggested by Pollard's comment that William Bingham "has treated me with greater hauteur than I ever was treated by my Master during my youthfull apprenticeship."[22] But men living in buildings resembling the Todd House were far from poor. Their household expenditures were likely to be in the range of three hundred to five hundred pounds, roughly half as much as the expenses of wealthy merchants but still enough to provide many of the marks of gentility denied the common man. Slaves, servants, cows, horses, and silver plate were all owned by substantial fractions of these middling traders, and by the 1780s quite a few also owned light carriages known as chairs. These luxuries were less commonly part of the property of ordinary merchants, the fifth or so of the traders who did not even own a private home, but instead lived in a boardinghouse or the home of a parent. Such merchants might live on as little as two hundred pounds per year.[23]

22. Pollard to Charles Startin, Sept. 2, 1772, Pollard Letterbook, 1772–1774, 73. Pollard to Nicholson, Jan. 13, 1793, John Nicholson Papers, PMHC.

23. On ownership of various types of property, see Appendix, tables A-14–A-18. On the living expenses of wealthy merchants, which tended to be at least £600 per year, see William West Ledger, 68, 94, 123, William West Account Books; Joshua Fisher and Sons Ledger, 1769–1773, 105, 166, 203, HSP; Fitzsimons Journal, 91–151; Levi Hollingsworth Journal F, 1781–1782, 390, Hollingsworth Papers, HSP. The moderately wealthy merchant Benjamin Fuller said in 1772 that a small family could live "genteely" for £500, but for considerably less a decade earlier, when luxuries were fewer. William Pollard wrote in the same year that he needed at least £334 to support his small family, and a committee of merchants allowed the bankrupt John Mitchell a salary of £300 to support his family.

Merchants, Artisans, and Gentlemen

Heavy emphasis on the aristocratic segment of the trading community has led some writers to imply that the entire merchant community was positioned above the city's artisan population. "The merchant aristocracy may have dominated the economic life of Philadelphia," one analyst writes, "but it goes without saying that they comprised only a small minority of the city's population. Beneath them in the social scale were the city's artisans, who comprised about half the population of Philadelphia. . . . masters and journeymen—men who possessed a skill, owned their own tools and had usually served an apprenticeship—were clearly distinguished both from merchants and professionals above them and from the pre-industrial, pre-proletariat class of sailors and laborers below."[24] In fact, however, the typical merchant did not live well above the level of all mechanics. A successful artisan or shopkeeper could live in a house comparable to that of many merchants. About 28 percent of the merchants lived in houses assessed in the range of £501–£750, but of the houses in this category only a quarter were inhabited by merchants (table 1). The remaining three-quarters were inhabited by people of many occupations, including shopkeepers, ironmongers, coachmakers, blockmakers, and tailors. From an occupational breakdown of the residents of dwellings rated at between £250 and £750, a class in which 52 percent of the merchant householders lived, we can conclude that fully three-quarters of the merchant householders lived in houses of a type inhabited mainly by nonmerchants, and better than half of all Philadelphians in 1789 lived in dwellings perfectly suitable for merchants (see table 2). In short, the overlap in living style between the merchant group and the general population, though far from complete, was very considerable. Instead of looking down on the successful artisan or shopkeeper, many merchants lived on a par with him.

It is important not to exaggerate this overlap, however. Because they used their brains instead of their hands to make money, merchants had higher status than artisans. And age is important; relatively young merchants probably could afford to live in houses that a mechanic could

---

However, the young merchants Charles Wharton and Robert Henderson had annual expenses of £158 and £150–£200, respectively. Fuller to John Scott, Dec. 26, 1772, Benjamin Fuller Letterbook, 1762–1781, Benjamin Fuller Papers, 1762–1799, HSP; Pollard to Bowers, Dec. 21, 1772, Oct. 28, 1773, Pollard to John Woolman, Dec. 28, 1772, Pollard Letterbook, 1772–1774, 129, 287, 139; Charles Wharton Daybook, 1768–1772, Wharton Papers, HSP; Robert Henderson Daybook, 1790–1791, Robert Henderson Receipt Book, 1781–1791, Robert Henderson Papers, HSP.

24. Eric Foner, *Tom Paine and Revolutionary America* (New York, 1976), 28.

TABLE 1. *Value of Dwellings of Merchants and General Population of Philadelphia, 1789*

	Proportion of Occupancy				
	Value of Dwelling				
	0–£250	£251–£500	£501–£750	£751–£1,000	£1,001+
Sample of general population (N=632)	45.9%	30.7%	12.5%	5.7%	5.2%
Merchants (N=251)	4.4	22.3	27.4	18.3	27.1
Approximate share of value class inhabited by merchants	[a]	[a]	25	40	50

Source: County Tax Assessment Ledger, 1789, Philadelphia City Archives.
Note 1. The 29.7% of the general population and 19.0% of the merchant population who did not own or rent their own house are not figured into this table.
Note 2. Deviations from 100.0% in totaling are due to rounding.
[a]These values well below 25%.

acquire only after years of saving. Furthermore, the functional and symbolic core of the merchant community—the group of men whom outsiders, whether historians or contemporary Philadelphians, viewed as the heart and backbone of the merchant group—were not the dozens of minor merchants who lived in the style of successful mechanics, but the great men of commerce. It was not just that the merchant princes lived in prominent town houses, owned their own wharves and warehouses, and drove through town in fine phaetons. They also had direct, tangible financial power that reverberated through the ranks of the city's middling classes. A big shipping firm like Willing and Morris dispatched over twenty vessels a year, and nearly every one of them needed the services of blacksmiths, sailmakers, caulkers, carpenters, and the like.[25] Similarly, the forty top importers had far more extensive dealings with the city's retailers than did four times as many minor dry goods importers. One must remember, too, that over half of Philadelphia's citizens lived in cramped little houses, of the type found in Elfriths Alley, which almost no merchants would deign to inhabit. And below them were sailors, servants, and slaves who usually had no houses of their own. The

25. Based on an analysis of the Tonnage Duty Book.

TABLE 2. *Occupations of Residents of Houses Rated at £250–£750 in 1789*

Occupation (*N*=242)	Proportion
Merchant	20%
Retailer	18
Artisan	37
Professional and retired	14
Proprietor of boarding house and miscellaneous	11

Source: County Tax Assessment Ledger, 1789, Philadelphia City Archives.
Note: Data based on High, Middle, and Dock wards.

gap between such workers as these and even a lesser merchant was indeed enormous. Consider, for example, the finances of Philadelphia's hundreds of indentured servants. If they had had at their point of embarkation for Philadelphia only about ten pounds—3 percent of the annual expenses of a fairly representative merchant—they could have paid their way to America with cash, instead of signing away four years of their life.

In social position the merchants were neither conspicuously separate nor equably intermixed with the generality of Philadelphians, and we find the same pattern in the location of their residences. Considering the sights, sounds, and especially the smells that they chose to live with, the merchants were remarkably urban creatures. Their Philadelphia stretched for about two miles along the Delaware River but was only two or three blocks wide at most points. Only along Market Street could one walk six blocks away from the river and still find contiguous houses lining the street. Wealthy merchants, it appears, could easily have lived on a salubrious, well-landscaped, two-acre lot ten blocks from the river and walked each morning to their stores along the waterfront. Such an arrangement would have spared them the necessity of living on cramped lots backing onto alleys piled high with garbage.[26] With few exceptions, however, the merchants lived in the heart of the city, often in its busiest sections. John Ross, for example, in 1791 chose to build his imposing

26. The alley running behind the house of Bishop White, for instance, was said to be so full of garbage that a wagon could not pass through it. The waterfront area was similarly strewn with refuse. See Powell, *Bring out Your Dead*, 11, 12.

mansion next to the market on Second Street, a site that must have reeked of discarded entrails and horse manure and echoed with the shouts of hawkers and the clatter of heavy wagons banging over the cobblestones.

Although they were naturally most numerous along the waterfront, the merchants did not congregate in any particular part of Philadelphia, and traders of all levels of wealth were to be found in every ward in the city. On the other hand, they were not spread evenly throughout the population. Merchants tended to avoid the northern and southern fringes of the city, which were packed with members of the city's lower classes (see table 3). Although 53 percent of Philadelphia taxables lived in Mulberry Ward, Southwark, and the Northern Liberties in 1774, only 15 percent of the merchants did. This pattern reveals a choice not to live in the outlying sections, for as the city grew between 1756 and 1774, the general population and the merchant group expanded into different areas. In 1756 the merchants were heavily concentrated along the waterfront, 53 percent of them living in wards contiguous to the Delaware. As the city's population grew, it expanded north and south along the water, and given the commercial utility of a "water lot," one would expect the merchants to have led this waterfront expansion. Instead, however, the merchants moved inland, away from the water, as the riverfront became built up. The proportion of merchants in the city proper who lived in Middle, North, and South wards increased from 12 percent in 1756 to 27 percent in 1789, while relatively few merchants, as we have seen, chose to live in Southwark and the Northern Liberties. Thus although the merchants were in no sense concentrated in a single area, they did choose their neighborhoods quite purposively. They also preferred to live on particular types of streets. Whether for business reasons or comfort and status, the merchants did not live on the minor lanes and alleys that ran through the major blocks of the city. Of 505 people known to have lived on such secondary streets in 1790 whose occupations can be determined, only 9 were merchants.[27] This may explain why so few merchants are listed in the 1789 tax list as living in houses rated at under £250, for most such dwellings were probably on the side streets.

As we have seen, even well-informed students have likened Philadelphia's merchants to the gentry of tidewater Virginia and the Hudson River valley. This questionable confusion results from focusing attention on the meetinghouse, town house, and country seat, where

27. Based on an analysis of lanes and alleys listed in United States Bureau of the Census, *Heads of Families at the First Census of the United States Taken in the Year 1790: Pennsylvania* (Washington, D.C., 1908), 208–245.

TABLE 3. *Distribution of Philadelphia Merchants among Wards and Liberties, 1756, 1774, 1789*

	Excluding Northern Liberties and Southwark			Including Northern Liberties and Southwark	
	1756	1774	1789	1774	1789
Waterfront					
Upper Delaware	16.4%	10.7%	7.3%	9.8%	6.8%
Lower Delaware	11.9	10.3	8.3	9.5	7.7
Dock	24.9	28.8	27.4	26.4	25.4
Total	53.2	49.8	43.0	45.7	39.9
Core					
High	4.5	5.5	6.6	5.1	6.1
Chestnut	11.9	5.9	5.9	5.4	5.5
Walnut	7.9	7.4	4.2	6.8	3.9
Total	24.3	18.8	16.7	17.3	15.5
Western Wards					
North	3.4	11.8	9.4	10.9	8.7
Middle	2.8	5.9	11.1	5.8	10.3
South	5.6	5.9	6.3	5.4	5.8
Total	11.8	23.6	26.8	22.1	24.8
North and South Peripheries					
Northern Liberties				4.7	3.9
Mulberry Ward	10.7	7.7	13.5	6.8	12.5
Southwark				3.4	3.5
Total				14.9	19.9

Sources: Hannah Benner Roach, comp., "Taxables in the City of Philadelphia, 1756," *Pennsylvania Genealogical Magazine*, XXII (1961–1962), 3–41; Transcript of the Assessment for the 1774 Provincial Tax for the City and County of Philadelphia, Pennsylvania Historical and Museum Commission; County Tax Assessment Ledger, 1789, Philadelphia City Archives.

PLATE 10. Looking East on Arch Street. *From W. Birch and Son,* The City of Philadelphia . . . As It Appeared in 1800. *Courtesy of The Historical Society of Pennsylvania*

money was spent, rather than on the countinghouse, where money was made. For although the styles of life of the highly successful merchant and the leisured gentleman were quite similar, their careers and their social outlook were not. The richest merchants in the city were second to none in influence and weight, but they held their position in society by dint of hard labor and the taking of very real risks. With few exceptions they did not have a truly genteel education; instead, they were brought up in countinghouses on a concentrated diet of bookkeeping and letter writing, and their early years of adulthood were consumed with the task of building a fortune. They tended, as a result, to be narrow and materialistic, with politics of secondary interest, except as it impinged on trade. If their commercial ventures were successful, such merchants could retire to the life of the country gentleman, but this new circumstance could not change their basic outlook: they were still retired merchants, not born-and-bred gentlemen.

Philadelphia's true aristocrats—the Logans, Norrises, Dickinsons, Allens, Hamiltons, Tilghmans, and others—had two distinguishing characteristics: they were born rich, and their money was invested in relatively safe investments, rather than in trade. As young men they could afford to go to the College of Philadelphia and take the grand tour of Europe, perhaps picking up some professional training along the way. Such an education was not expected to be arduous. Samuel Powel reported home: "Your two friends have been lolling in the lap of ease. Italia, nurse of the softer arts, has detained them from mixing with the turbulent throng. The pleasures and entertainments she affords have rendered our time most pleasing." For men like Powel, wealth was a condition of life, not a goal to be achieved through scrambling and gambling in the marketplace. Such gentlemen in Philadelphia, like their counterparts in Virginia, were likely to turn their attention to politics and civic affairs at an early age.[28]

The career of John Cadwalader is not atypical.[29] Born in 1742, he was educated at the College of Philadelphia and was probably sent on the grand tour. In 1760 his father helped him and his brother to enter trade by sending £1,000 to England to establish the brothers' credit with a London dry goods house. Many poorer merchants' sons would have envied his excellent beginning in commerce, but Cadwalader grew tired of ledgers and manifests rather quickly. He could afford to do so, for in 1768 he married the heiress of a very wealthy Maryland planter whose health, conveniently enough, was failing rapidly. The young bride was worth £11,000 at the time of the marriage and stood to inherit much more when her father died. Cadwalader did not long hesitate to invest his wife's money; in 1768 he purchased the home of a leading real estate operator for the considerable sum of £2,650 and during the next three years spent an additional £6,350 turning it into one of the most opulent houses in the city. He owned a coach and "all sorts" of other carriages, kept a large retinue of retainers (including seven slaves), and was not only an accomplished equestrian and hunter but also one of the two best skaters in Philadelphia. Cadwalader did not shirk his public responsibilities, however; during the Revolution he was a brigadier general in the Pennsylvania militia and distinguished himself in the battles of Trenton and Princeton. At one point he dueled, and nearly killed, Thomas Conway of the Conway Cabal.

Cadwalader's ostentation may have been somewhat unusual for a Philadelphia gentleman, but his aversion to trade was not. Searching the careers of second- and third-generation members of Philadelphia's aristo-

28. Sketch of the Powel family by Frank Willing Leach for the *North American*, one of a series of such genealogical sketches by Leach collected in three volumes at the HSP.

29. Wainwright, *Colonial Grandeur*, 1–36, 58, 59; Turner to David Barclay and Sons, Aug. 19, 1763, Turner Letterbook, 1753–1774.

cratic families, one finds strikingly few prominent traders. Lawyers, doctors, and country gentlemen are present in abundance, but merchants—despite their greater proportion of Philadelphia's entire upper class—are rare. This fact is hardly surprising. Trade was less interesting and more precarious than a genteel profession, and gentlemen who had the resources to get a first-class European education were exceptionally well situated to become doctors or lawyers.

So it was with George Logan, who, beginning his career as an apprentice for the tough old Quaker merchant John Reynell, found trade distasteful and decided to go to Scotland to train for the medical profession.[30] Upon returning to America after the Revolution, however, he lived off the family estate and occupied himself primarily by promoting agricultural improvements. In 1798, he made a disastrous personal diplomatic mission to France. The family fortune that underwrote these activities, as with several other prominent families, was based on shrewd investments by an early and well-connected settler in Pennsylvania, George Logan's grandfather James Logan, who was secretary to William Penn. But, in general, Pennsylvania in its early years, unlike Maryland, Virginia, and South Carolina, was not a particularly good place to found a fortune; it is not surprising, therefore, to find that a substantial proportion of the great families of the province, including the Hamiltons, Dickinsons, Chews, Cadwaladers, Tilghmans, Pleasantses, and Galloways, had kinship ties with the Chesapeake.

To appreciate fully the distinctive position of the aristocratic gentleman, as contrasted with the life of a merchant, one must understand that commerce in eighteenth-century Philadelphia was a brutally demanding and financially dangerous occupation. It required steady nerves, hard work, and an optimistic vigilance more common in ambitious traders from the middling classes than in the sons of polished gentlemen. Examples are plentiful of well-born gentlemen who, despite starting with many advantages, failed to prosper in trade. The ill-fated Irish firm described at the beginning of this chapter falls in this category; and George Clymer, who inherited six thousand pounds from his uncle, disliked commerce so deeply that he persuaded his children to pursue noncommercial careers. A colleague explained Clymer's aversion to trade: "He disliked it from its peculiar precariousness, and the necessary dependence

30. Frederick B. Tolles, *George Logan of Philadelphia* (New York, 1953), 3–59. An analysis of the prominent members of the Chew, Tilghman, Dickinson, Galloway, Allen, Shippen, Peters, Hamilton, Cadwalader, Norris, and Logan families present in Philadelphia after 1750 turns up 6 merchants as against 26 professionals. A systematic study, described later in this chapter, which traced the careers of hundreds of merchants, found only 3 who were professionals at some time during their careers.

which the merchant must place in the honor and integrity of others, thereby removing to a certain degree, the conduct of his affairs beyond his control." Tench Coxe was likewise born into a prominent family but found trade little to his liking. Not inclined to remain an "anxious slave" to his "laborious profession," Coxe abandoned trade in favor of politics and land speculation. Here too he ran into trouble and more than once was saved from bankruptcy by an indulgent father with a deep pocket. Samuel Meredith was still another wealthy heir who failed to capitalize on his head start in trade and, in fact, spent the last years of his life in virtual poverty. Naturally, this pattern did not apply to all well-born merchants—Thomas Willing, William Bingham, and Tench Coxe's own brother are conspicuous exceptions—but it is prevalent enough in the records to demonstrate that many Philadelphia gentlemen kept clear of commerce.[31]

How to Become a Merchant

The pronounced stratification of the merchant community was a direct consequence of its competitive structure. Instead of being able to divide up markets and monopolize various segments of business in Philadelphia, the established merchants of the city had to compete with—because they could not exclude—hundreds of traders who entered the merchant community both from outside the city and from other occupational groups in Philadelphia. Since many of the newcomers were men with little capital, this phenomenon gave rise to an unequal distribution of wealth within the merchant group, a pattern that was further intensified by the presence in the city of many veteran traders who had never managed to build up sizable capital. We must not make the common error, however, of confusing stratification with rigidity and lack of mobility; minor traders were in a good position to supplant wealthy ones if they made the right moves.

It may well be asked why traders worth twenty or thirty thousand pounds could not freeze out of Philadelphia's commerce those traders worth only a hundredth as much. Part of the reason is that despite this great difference in wealth there was relatively little qualitative difference in their businesses. The wealthy trader did not have at his command any

31. Jerry Grundfest, "George Clymer, Philadelphia Revolutionary, 1739–1813" (Ph.D. diss., Columbia University, 1973), 35 n. 54, 236; Cooke, *Tench Coxe*, 332–333, 338, 410–411; Coxe to Nalbro Frazier, Jan. 1, 1787, Tench Coxe Papers, Reel 49. All references to the Coxe Papers are to the microfilm collection, available in the HSP and various other libraries, of the original Coxe Papers in the HSP.

special patents, capital sources, brand names, or sources of supply that were unavailable to the small merchant, and he did not control a trading network that was decisively better than what a small merchant could construct in two or three years. A large dry goods importer might import ten times as much cloth and hardware as a small trader, but he obtained these products and sold them in exactly the same way that his smaller competitor did. Consequently, a successful minor merchant could generate considerable capital very rapidly. Stephen Girard increased his fortune by a factor of nine in seven years, while Levi Hollingsworth's net worth rose by 600 percent in just five years. Cadwallader Colden, the dyspeptic lieutenant governor of New York, claimed that during the Seven Years' War a number of Manhattan traders "rose suddenly from the lowest Rank of the People to considerable Fortunes."[32]

The distinctiveness of Philadelphia's competitive structure becomes clearer when it is compared with that prevailing in other, more developed ports. In eighteenth-century Glasgow three groups of firms alone controlled over half of the port's large tobacco trade, because they had developed extensive chains of stores in the Chesapeake region and could afford enormous capital advances to their customers in the New World. Glasgow was, in effect, the exact opposite of Philadelphia: "Transatlantic trade was not a sector in which the *arriviste* adventurer whose only assets were cool nerves and business skill could easily or quickly prosper." Similarly, England's extensive trade with the Near East during the eighteenth century was dominated by "a small group of rich men." Because it often took over two years to send out a shipment of woolen cloth and receive a return cargo of silk, only businessmen of great wealth could enter the trade. The Levant trade during the 1730s was dominated by just five firms and family groups. The French slave trade, which also required that a merchant tie up his capital in long voyages, was similarly dominated by a small group of firms. And by the nineteenth century, American merchant communities had also become more stratified and less open to upward mobility. John Jacob Astor by 1830 had managed virtually to monopolize America's fur trade by setting up an elaborate trading network in the wilderness of Canada and the American West. At this time it was said that only four firms controlled seven-eighths of America's entire China trade by virtue of their large capital and excellent contacts in Canton. And Alexander Brown and Sons, a Baltimore-based

32. See Girard manuscripts cited in n. 1, above; Hollingsworth Ledger E, 1780–1781, 208, 209; Hollingsworth Journal, 1784–1785, 377–398, Hollingsworth Papers; Robert A. East, "The Business Entrepreneur in a Changing Colonial Economy, 1763–1795," *Journal of Economic History*, VI, Supplement (1946), 20 n. 13.

firm with partners in New York, Philadelphia, and Liverpool, managed to engross at least one-eighth of the United States foreign exchange market by the 1850s. Although merchants in the Quaker City were also beginning to specialize in particular branches of commerce by the 1780s, almost none of them had built up comparably strong competitive positions.[33]

From the biographies and business records of ninety-one Philadelphia merchants and evidence drawn from a mobility study of hundreds of merchants who can be traced through city directories and tax lists, it is possible to identify four main career paths through which the city's merchants might move. Although the relative frequency of these patterns cannot be determined precisely, the sample is large enough to make one confident that these patterns are representative.

The first of these career paths is that of a young man of fortune. The son of a rich Philadelphia merchant or gentleman, he would enter the prominent firm of his father or commence trading on his own account with enough capital to fund and operate a half or a third of a good-sized ship. Such young merchants were the sons of wealthy traders worth at least twenty thousand pounds who occupied roughly the top seventh of the merchant community. Thomas Willing, Tench Coxe, William Bingham the younger, and George Morgan are prominent Anglicans who fit this description, while the sons of such Quaker merchants as Thomas Clifford, Jeremiah Warder, Joshua Fisher, and William Fisher are also good examples. These well-placed traders stepped into Philadelphia commerce at its top echelon, handled thousands of pounds of imported dry goods annually, and sent out big shipments of provisions to Europe and the Caribbean. If they traded effectively and made no disastrous mistakes, they were in a good position to become wealthy in ten or fifteen years. Those who started their careers with a business interest worth four thousand pounds and achieved, after deduction of household

33. T. M. Devine, *The Tobacco Lords: A Study of the Tobacco Merchants of Glasgow and Their Trading Activities, c. 1740–1790* (Edinburgh, 1975), 3–17, 72–81; Ralph Davis, *Aleppo and Devonshire Square: English Traders in the Levant in the Eighteenth Century* (London, 1967), esp. 60. Robert Louis Stein, *The French Slave Trade in the Eighteenth Century: An Old Regime Business* (Madison, Wis., 1979), 152–158; Kenneth Wiggins Porter, *John Jacob Astor: Business Man*, 2 vols., Harvard Studies in Business History, I (Cambridge, Mass., 1931), II, 770–771; Foster Rhea Dulles, *The Old China Trade* (Boston, 1930), 113; Carl Seaburg and Stanley Paterson, *Merchant Prince of Boston: Colonel T. H. Perkins, 1764–1854* (Cambridge, Mass., 1971), 155–166; Edwin J. Perkins, *Financing Anglo-American Trade: The House of Brown, 1800–1880* (Cambridge, Mass., 1975), 149.

expenses, a compound annual return of 12 percent would in ten years be worth over twelve thousand pounds and in fifteen years nearly twenty-two thousand pounds.[34]

Though constituting a prominent group in the merchant community, these young men of fortune were nevertheless a distinct minority, especially before 1760 or so, when relatively fewer older traders had built up large businesses that could be shared with their sons. Moreover, these favored young men usually did not begin their careers with notably large fortunes. Consider the case of Joshua Fisher and his three sons. In 1770 the net worth of their firm amounted to £31,225; if the father had owned only half of the total business, his sons would each have possessed a share worth £5,204. The son of another wealthy merchant started his business with £1,400, which proved an insufficient sum to support himself and his family when they moved to Bristol, England; and the son of still another rich merchant received as a legacy £8,530. A fourth example is Thomas Willing, arguably the bluest of Philadelphia's blue-blooded traders. His father was twice mayor of the Quaker City, and rich enough in the mid-1750s to own three vessels—two ships more than most firms possessed at the time of the Revolution. Yet when his father died in 1754, the sum total of Thomas Willing's assets, including both his legacies and the capital built up over five years of active participation in the family business, amounted to £10,000.[35]

A second group of entrants into the merchant community, whom contemporaries were careful to distinguish from "young Men of very wealthy families, and under the best Patronage," were those young traders who were "of good family but . . . slender capitals." Members of this group had little trouble entering the commercial world, but they had to live cheaply and nurture their businesses cautiously. Although their actual capital might amount to only a few hundred pounds, such well-connected but impecunious Philadelphians still benefited in many ways from their personal ties with the local merchant community. Credit, local patronage, apprenticeships, and jobs as supercargoes all came fairly easily to such men. For example, Benjamin Fuller helped advance the career of a young merchant stationed in Saint Eustatius by helping him find Philadelphia customers while continually lending him money. When

34. For examples, see Jacob Harman Will no. 297, 1780; Robert Morton Will no. 223, 1786; Hugh Roberts Will no. 208, 1786; Jeremiah Warder Will no. 222, 1783, all in the Office of the Recorder of Wills, Philadelphia City Hall.

35. Joshua Fisher and Sons Ledger, 1769–1773, 104; Thomas Clifford, Jr., to Thomas Clifford, Dec. 21, 1784, Clifford Correspondence, 1778–1785, VII, 167, HSP; Jeremiah Warder Will no. 222, 1783; Eugene R. Slaski, "Thomas Willing: Moderation during the American Revolution" (Ph.D. diss., Florida State University, 1971), 43.

the wealthy merchant Thomas Riche sent his younger brother on a voyage as supercargo (business agent for the voyage), he made the purpose of the assignment quite explicit: "I recommend Ceare Prudence. & dilligence in the Transacting of this affair to you as it is the first Voyage which is the Greatis Diffickility you are to Surmount. you Cannot think anuff of it, if you have amine to push your self in the world." Apparently young John took this advice, for thirteen years later his older brother, rudely chastened by commercial disasters that had drained his fortune of eleven thousand pounds, was offering counsel of a distinctly different cast: "You must by this time [have] accumulated enough for your small Family and remember you have a Sould to be saved. if you should Gain all the world & luse your own Sould it would profit you nothing."[36]

Still another way for an established merchant to assist a beginner was to recommend him to a dry goods house in England, which would then send out a modest shipment of manufactured goods on twelve months' credit. Finally, a merchant of limited funds could place his son as an apprentice in a major firm, hoping that he would eventually become a partner. Robert Morris followed this route to the top, and in the 1780s Morris himself granted John Swanwick, a clerk of obscure social origins, a partnership in his firm. This pattern was rare, however, because Quaker City firms generally had at most three partners, who preferred to reserve spaces for their sons or other close relatives. But even if an apprentice did not rise within the firm, he could form valuable connections by working in a prestigious countinghouse. William Pollard placed a lad with the firm of Coxe and Furman, hoping he would form a connection with "a young Gentleman Apprentice with them of a most amiable Character & as steady as a Man of 40 Y:rs of Age, he is one of the first Families in this Town & of a very pretty Fortune."[37]

Patronage from family and friends was far from mandatory for entry into Philadelphia's mercantile ranks, however. A third substantial minority of the city's traders began their careers in lesser occupations. We can observe this mobility by tracing the careers of individuals through tax lists and city directories that are available for various years during the

36. Collins to Harrison, Ansley, and Co., Nov. 17, 1784, Stephen Collins Papers, LXI, 114, Library of Congress; Collins to William Neate, Aug. 1, 1772, Collins Papers, LVII; Charles Wharton Daybook, 1768–1772; Benjamin Fuller and James Craig, Jr., to Henry Ash and Jedediah Snowden, Apr. 18, 1785, and Fuller to Jedediah Snowden, Aug. 27, 1785, Fuller Letterbook, 1784–1787, 96, 126; Thomas Riche and Co. to John Riche, Aug. 5, 1758, Riche Letterbook, 1748–1764, and T. Riche to J. Riche, June 17, 1771, Riche Letterbook, 1764–1771.

37. Pollard to Dr. William McDonnald, Oct. 2, 1773, Pollard Letterbook, 1772–1774, 299.

second half of the eighteenth century. Unfortunately, this procedure is hampered by the fact that many traders were immigrants who spent only part of their career in Philadelphia and by the failure of tax lists to indicate the occupation of every individual listed. For these reasons we cannot figure a precise rate of occupational mobility into the merchant group. But it can be demonstrated that it was not an uncommon phenomenon. Of 66 people who were merchants in 1774, 22 were retailers, mariners, artisans, or of a miscellaneous occupation in 1756; of 140 people who were merchants in 1785, 51 were in one of these other occupations in 1774 (see table 4). Of 256 merchants who can be traced from the 1799 city directory to the 1791 directory—only eight years—fully 35 percent were earlier in one of the occupations listed above. These figures are hardly surprising, for as we have seen, many retailers and artisans could afford to live in the same type of house that lesser merchants used. The converse of this fact, of course, is that by becoming merchants such people did not necessarily increase their income. They did, however, put themselves in a position to become quite wealthy, a feat that a number of them actually accomplished.

These occupationally mobile merchants most commonly moved into wholesaling after being mariners, artisans, grocers, or shopkeepers. It is possible to identify twenty-one merchants active in Philadelphia in the decade before 1776 who had formerly been captains. A captain could amass the capital and skills necessary for trade while directing the vessel, for business affairs were often among his duties, and he was likely to own a share of the vessel under his command. Fully 21 percent of the vessels entering Philadelphia from other American ports in 1773 were consigned to a captain rather than a merchant, and 42 percent of the vessels registered in the port before the Revolution were owned in part by captains. Experienced ship captains probably had more firsthand experience with foreign markets than most sedentary merchants, and if they saved their earnings, they seemingly could enter trade without much difficulty. Thus in 1763 Capt. Samuel Bunting asked James and Drinker to recommend him to a leading British export firm. Although the dry goods trade was in disarray, James and Drinker willingly endorsed Bunting's entry into wholesaling, for in addition to being an "Industrious prudent young man" the mariner had influential friends and was worth three thousand pounds.[38]

38. The figure of 21 captains was calculated by matching the names of people listed as merchants in tax lists and city directories with shipmasters listed in the Tonnage Duty Book. The figure for 1773 is based on this document, and the information on ownership of vessels is a mean of the figures appearing in Simeon John Crowther, "The Shipbuilding Industry and the Economic Development of the Delaware Valley, 1681–1776" (Ph.D. diss.,

TABLE 4. *Previous Occupations of Philadelphia Merchants*

	Base Year as Merchant				
	1774	1785	1785	1791	1791
	Retrospective Year				
Previous Occupation	1756	1756	1774	1756	1774
N	66	36	140	22	73
Merchant	44 (66.7%)	22 (61.1%)	83 (59.3%)	11 (50.0%)	46 (63.0%)
Professional gentleman or government	0	0	6 (4.3%)	0	2 (2.7%)
Retailer	4 (6.1%)	0	16 (11.4%)	0	10 (13.7%)
Artisan	11 (16.7%)	10 (27.8%)	22 (15.7%)	8 (36.4%)	11 (15.1%)
Mariner	5 (7.6%)	3 (8.3%)	6 (4.3%)	2 (9.1%)	3 (4.1%)
Miscellaneous	2 (3.0%)	1 (2.8%)	7 (5.0%)	1 (4.5%)	1 (1.4%)

Sources: Hannah Benner Roach, comp., "Taxables in the City of Philadelphia, 1756," *Pennsylvania Genealogical Magazine*, XXII (1961–1962), 3–41; Transcript of the Assessment for the 1774 Provincial Tax for the City and County of Philadelphia, Pennsylvania Historical and Museum Commission; Francis White, *The Philadelphia Directory* (Philadelphia, 1785); Clement Biddle, ed., *The Philadelphia Directory* (Philadelphia, 1791).

Successful artisans also gained experience that was transferable into wholesaling. As independent businessmen they often kept a set of books and were continually making deals with suppliers and customers that took account of current supply and demand for their service. For example, when a war was in the offing, ship carpenters greatly increased their rates. During the period 1785–1787 no fewer than thirty-five artisan firms had businesses of sufficient volume to necessitate importations

University of Pennsylvania, 1970), 205. James and Drinker to Neate and Pigou, Oct. 9, 1763, James and Drinker Letterbook, 1762–1764, 174, Drinker Papers. For an example of a merchant-mariner, see Enoch Hobart Papers, New York Historical Society, New York.

from foreign ports valued at £300 or more, and many of these business activities were of direct relevance to trade. The major shipping firm of James and Drinker relied heavily on their cooper to judge the quality of an outward cargo, and, of course, coopers learned a great deal about the various grades of staves and headings, which were major items of export from the Delaware Valley. One artisan who used such knowledge effectively was William Forbes. Before the Revolution Forbes was the cooper for his next-door neighbor, Reese Meredith, a great shipping merchant reputedly worth £80,000. From Meredith alone—he may have had other customers as well—Forbes received about £240 per year, and during the Revolution he became a merchant. He was prominent during the 1780s as a dealer in various types of groceries, and by the end of that decade Forbes owned a dwelling and three very valuable waterfront stores. Forbes was not alone in his ability to parlay manual skills into a mercantile career during the Revolution; we know of five men who changed their occupation from carpenter to board merchant during the conflict. Samuel Wetherill became a clothmaker during the Revolution after working as a carpenter for twenty years, and later in the 1780s he became a wholesaler of imported drugs.[39]

Retailers of two types, grocers and shopkeepers, were also in a good position to become merchants if their trade was successful. Grocers, who traded imported foodstuffs, could evidently build up very sizable businesses, for we find them buying goods in large quantities from provision merchants during the 1780s and borrowing heavily from the Bank of North America. It was a simple matter for such large operators to buy a ship and start obtaining their groceries directly from foreign ports. The grocers Samuel and Josiah Coates, for instance, not only dealt in locally procured goods but also regularly sold mackerel, rum, and other products consigned to them by correspondents in New England. They were as much shipping merchants as grocers.[40]

Similar, too, were the businesses of the small dry goods importer and the ambitious shopkeeper. The ideal business arrangement between these two groups was for the merchant to import cloth and hardware on

39. James and Drinker to John Clitherall, July 4, 1772, James and Drinker Foreign Letterbook, 1772–1785, 2, Drinker Papers; William Forbes Account Book, 1768–1780, HSP; County Tax Assessment Ledgers, for City and County of Philadelphia, 1789, Lower Delaware Ward. Miriam Hussey, *From Merchants to "Colour Men": Five Generations of Samuel Wetherill's White Lead Business* (Philadelphia, 1956).

40. Josiah and Samuel Coates Papers, in Coates and Reynell Collection, HSP (see especially Bills of Lading, 1786–1791; Daybook, 1783–1785; Journal, 1785–1789; and Letterbook, 1784–1790). On the place of grocers in Philadelphia's commercial system, see chap. 2, below. For an example of a shipping syndicate involving a grocer, a shopkeeper, and a mariner, see William Bell Clark, *Gallant John Barry, 1745–1803: The Story of a Naval Hero of Two Wars* (New York, 1938), 16–26.

twelve months' credit and sell the merchandise on several months' credit to shopkeepers, who retailed the goods to the final consumer. Credit was the key, and it was held ultimately in England. Much to the disgust of the established merchants of the Quaker City, aggressive English houses freely extended credit to marginal importers. So long as they sent out the goods and received payment within a year, the English exporters did not care who their Philadelphia customers were. Consequently, it was not very difficult for a well-established shopkeeper to become, first, a retailer of directly imported goods and then, if business went well, a wholesaler of them: that is, a merchant.

Clearly this was not an uncommon phenomenon. One importer wrote to his London supplier in 1750, "I shall also take the liberty to inform you that your supplying the shopkeepers at all is more harm than good to you." When the firm of James and Drinker was serving as agent to a major London dry goods supplier, it had occasion to review the credit standing of the London firm's Philadelphia accounts and was appalled to find that some of them were not bona fide wholesalers: "No 105 J——c——b is an indistrious young man and supposed to be with money. We never knew that the other had any pretension by himself to import goods on credit. He was our clerk some time." "No. 106 ought not to have goods sent him unless he sends the cash, for it is such as him that we get our living by selling to." Likewise with another customer, Samuel Caruthers: "Not but we esteem him an honest man and one to whom we give a credit, but he is only a retailer." James and Drinker had less to say about several other firms because they were so insignificant: "We know no more than thee does." Shortly before the Revolution the Philadelphia agent for a Manchester firm encouraged the advancing of credit to two retailers, and in 1790 and 1791 the ironmonger Samuel Dilworth imported hardware from Liverpool, Bristol, and Birmingham to the amount of £978. Over a period of thirty-two months during the 1780s, at least twenty-eight Philadelphia retailers received shipments of foreign goods worth three hundred pounds or more. As one dry goods importer snorted in 1789, "Credit is as *cheap* this year as it was in 1784—The Manchester folks have made all the retail *Shopkeepers*, & merchants *apprentices* Importers!"[41]

We must not suppose, however, that importations on credit automati-

41. Marc Matthew Egnal, "The Pennsylvania Economy, 1748–1762: An Analysis of Short-Run Fluctuations in the Context of Long-Run Changes in the Atlantic Trading Community" (Ph.D. diss., University of Wisconsin, 1974), 125, 241, 242; Pollard to Benjamin Bowers, Mar. 9, May 16, 1774, Pollard Letterbook, 1772–1774, 357, 419; Samuel Dilworth Invoice Book, 1788–1792, HSP; Registry of Imports and Exports, 1781–1787; David Cay to Andrew Clow, May 31, 1789, Andrew Clow and Co. Papers, 1784–1836, Eleutherian Mills Historical Library.

cally transformed a shopkeeper into a merchant. Many retailers probably used such purchases merely to supplement an inventory provided primarily by local wholesalers. At least two retailers found to their sorrow that a line of credit from London could become a noose, for they were unable to make remittances and went bankrupt. But for enterprising retailers such as Thomas Armat, contact with England was an important element in their business advancement. Judging from the messiness of his books and the inability of his brother to pay for even a transatlantic passage, Armat was not of genteel background. The city directories for 1785 and 1791 describe him as a shopkeeper. Nevertheless, his business activities were impressively diversified and demonstrate the opportunities available to retailers. In 1781 Armat's capital stock was only £660, but in 1783 and 1784 he imported goods from England to the amount of at least £1,888. Unlike many Philadelphians, Armat had little trouble repaying his English suppliers, and this access to English credit may have been instrumental in allowing him to raise his stock to £2,606 by the end of 1784. Buttressing this slender capital with funds borrowed from a widow and with frequent discounts at the Bank of North America, Armat seems to have prospered during the 1780s. He dabbled in both urban and frontier real estate and by the end of the decade was doing a high-volume retail business which involved purchasing goods from a variety of Philadelphia merchants and selling them to a large clientele situated both in the city and in outlying areas. He even set up a special arrangement with a shopkeeper in Chestertown, Maryland, to supply his complete inventory, a deal involving sales of £2,500 per year. In 1789 Armat resumed ordering from English suppliers and reported, "Some of our neighbours have made an ungenerous attempt to prevent us in procuring our goods immediately from the manufactories." If these neighbors were local merchants, their fears were quite justified, for by 1795, according to the city directory, they had lost a major customer and gained a competitor.[42]

What this analysis suggests is that the chance for entry into the merchant group was widely distributed through Philadelphia society, but

42. Egnal, "Pennsylvania Economy," 114. Thomas Armat to William Armat, Oct. 1789, T. Armat to John Lorain, Aug. 28, 1789, T. Armat to Holy and Newbold, June 10, 1791, Thomas Armat Letterbook, 1781–1794. Armat Ledger, 1784–1790, esp. 5, 45, 78, 98, 102, 215; Armat Ledger, 1781–1784, 1, 141; "Invoice of sundry goods . . . forwarded by Russels and Smith . . . ," Jan. 12, 1784, and Account Current of Champion and Dickason and Thomas Armat, Dec. 31, 1784, in box 1, Thomas Armat Papers, in Loudoun Papers, HSP. Although he possessed no inherited wealth, Charles Thomson imported goods from England in 1760 after resigning a teaching post that paid £200 per year. See J. Edwin Hendricks, *Charles Thomson and the Making of a New Nation, 1729–1824* (Rutherford, N.J., 1979), 55, 56.

that relatively few individuals achieved that end. Both points bear emphasis. In assessing the career of the wealthy Boston merchant Thomas Hancock, son of a minister and apprentice to a bookseller, one historian has commented that Hancock enjoyed "cumulative advantages bestowed by social class and childhood training" that gave him a far better opportunity to advance commercially than a "mason, shipwright, or ropemaker."[43] The evidence for Philadelphia does not particularly support such a distinction. The successful mechanic was no less of a businessman than a shopkeeper was, for both types of tradesmen needed some knowledge of bookkeeping and the marketplace. Since retailers, artisans, brokers, and mariners constituted 59 percent of Philadelphia's occupational population, it is misleading to maintain that class strictures limited the number of possible entrants into the merchant group.[44] They did, of course, but only within rather broad limits. What does deserve emphasis, however, is that very few of the people in this universe of potential wholesalers actually became merchants in the stratified social structure that Philadelphia, like most unregulated capitalist societies, possessed. The situation may be illustrated by the following oversimplified model: if merchants made up 8 percent of the work force and one-third of them were recruited from a group of artisans and retailers who themselves made up 60 percent of the occupational structure, then only one in twenty-two of these tradesmen would actually become a wholesaler.

A fourth and final path into the Philadelphia merchant group was through foreign contacts and experience. Of ninety-one merchants whose biographies and manuscripts were studied, at least thirty-one were immigrants from Ireland, Scotland, France, Holland, or, especially, England. Not unlike native-born traders, most of these foreigners started with more contacts and credit than solid capital. Some of them knocked around the Atlantic world for quite a while before settling in Philadelphia. Cropley Rose came to Philadelphia via London and Madeira, where he had been victimized—if we can believe his account—by the treachery of his partner and the collusion of sharp-trading Scots. John Reynell sailed to Philadelphia from Jamaica because his Quaker sensibilities could not brook the godlessness of the Caribbean isle—"the Wickedest Place I ever beheld with my Eyes." Stephen Girard also came to the Delaware after a sojourn in the Caribbean, but one doubts whether religious scruples had anything to do with the move. At least Rose, Rey-

43. James A. Henretta, *The Evolution of American Society, 1700–1815: An Interdisciplinary Analysis*, Civilization and Society: Studies in Social, Economic, and Cultural History (Lexington, Mass., 1973), 98.

44. Jacob M. Price, "Economic Function and the Growth of American Port Towns in the Eighteenth Century," *Perspectives in American History*, VIII (1974), 177–183.

nell, and Girard migrated voluntarily; in 1692 Isaac Norris had left Jamaica for what he thought would be a business trip to Philadelphia, but while he was gone, a cataclysmic earthquake literally dumped his hometown of Port Royal into the sea, wiping out his business and family. After returning to view the wreckage, he decided to return permanently to Philadelphia.[45]

But such dramas were rare. The most common route into the Philadelphia merchant community for immigrants—as for many shopkeepers—was via the vigorous stream of commercial credit that flowed into Philadelphia from the great dry goods houses of London, Bristol, and Manchester. Throughout the eighteenth century these firms were in the habit of granting credit to young English merchants and sending them across the Atlantic. For the British trader of limited means, emigration was a logical choice, for his paltry resources went further in the provinces than in the empire's wealthy and expensive metropolis. His reception in the New World could be chilly, however, for he presented still more competition to the established merchants of the Delaware. Wrote one crusty Philadelphian to a major London firm: "I am in hopes for the time to Come you will be more Carefull to whom you trust[.] those young fellows may appear brisk & Industryus & appear to be thankfull for your trusting them but on there arrival here are soon seized with the Distemper that our Climate is so Subject too Viz. upstarts." These "upstarts" were not strictly agents of the English firm, but, rather, independent credit customers who, like all small Philadelphia dry goods merchants, were heavily dependent on their English supplier of merchandise and capital. If their patron sent defective merchandise, capriciously demanded repayment exactly when it was due, or failed to send goods promptly when ordered, the young Englishman's career could be injured. William Pollard claimed that the perfidy of John Woolman in Yorkshire had crippled his career, which had started out promisingly a decade before. For the first ten years of his life in Philadelphia, John Kidd depended heavily on the London firm of Neate and Neave, one of only two houses with which he traded, and both William Gough and Stephen Carmault were also sponsored by this firm. Of course, not all foreign traders were capital-poor when they came to Philadelphia. In the early 1760s the Irish firm of McMichael and Scott engaged heavily in shipping management from the moment it entered the port, but like the affluent

45. Cropley Rose Letterbook, 1779–1781, HSP; Carl Leroy Romanek, "John Reynell, Quaker Merchant of Colonial Philadelphia" (Ph.D. diss., Pennsylvania State University, 1969), 15, 16; William T. Parsons, "Isaac Norris, II, The Speaker" (Ph.D. diss., University of Pennsylvania, 1955), 1–7.

Irish firm described earlier in this chapter, it went bankrupt in a couple of years.[46]

It should be clear by now that it was not very difficult to enter Philadelphia's merchant community if one had contacts, capital, or experience. Not only the offspring of local commercial families but also hundreds of immigrants and occupationally mobile Philadelphians became merchants. Such an influx of commercial talent, if it were not offset by departures to various nonmercantile quarters, would, of course, have enormously swollen the ranks of the merchant group. To some extent, this swelling occurred; the merchant community more than doubled in size between 1750 and 1791, accommodating the careers of hundreds of successful traders. Nevertheless, many other merchants withdrew from the community by one of four routes. Because the mortality rate in Philadelphia was relatively high, we can be confident that quite a few died; manuscript sources provide two examples of traders who died in the midst of their careers and of a great many other merchants who were seriously ill for long periods of time. Other traders left the field because they had piled up substantial capital stocks which they wished to protect from the unlimited liability of eighteenth-century trade. In a society where the title of gentleman still carried great weight, trade was not so much a way of life as a way to get rich; if one could do this in a decade or so, there was no good reason to slave away for another quarter of a century. Had not Poor Richard himself retired from the printing business at the age of forty-two? Retirement was certainly financially feasible for the successful merchant, for he could invest his capital in judiciously selected lots, houses, and farms that would appreciate rapidly in capital value while paying a good rent as well. The merchants William Allen and Joseph Turner began to curtail their business when they were in their early fifties; Israel Pemberton abandoned commerce at age thirty-five after becoming rich in King George's War; and Henry Drinker quit the "busy scenes of life" when only forty-two years old. Of 109 people who were merchants in 1774, over a quarter had become "gentlemen" or "esquires" by 1791—in part, no doubt, because trade was relatively unremunerative during the 1780s.

46. Turner to David Barclay and Son, Sept. 10, 1757, Turner Letterbook, 1753–1774; Pollard to Thomas Simpson, July 1, 1772, Pollard Letterbook, 1772–1774, 48; John Kidd Letterbook, 1749–1763, HSP; Gough and Carmault Letterbook, 1757–1761, HSP. Benjamin Fuller, John Chaloner, and Robert Henderson are other examples of British emigrants who became Philadelphia merchants. See their respective papers in HSP, as well as Henderson's papers in the New York Public Library.

A third group of merchants left the trading community not through death or retirement, but simply because they left Philadelphia, and a fourth group stayed within the city but assumed occupations other than merchant. A significant proportion of the people in these two classes were bankrupts or near-bankrupts; we can identify a minimum of 108 traders who went broke, and downward occupational mobility was also a fairly common phenomenon. Of 266 people who were merchants in 1785 and can be traced to 1791, 45 had assumed what appear to be lower occupations by the latter year.[47]

This analysis implies that a considerable degree of mobility was built into the merchant community, and we can calculate typical rates of movement from tax lists and city directories. These rates seem relatively stable over time, except for the chaotic decade after 1775. If we assume, for example, that there were 300 merchants in Philadelphia in 1774—a figure reasonably close to the actuality—about 195 (65 percent) of them would not have been in the city at all seventeen years before. Of the remaining 105 merchants, whose roots did go back to before 1757, about 39 of them were not merchants at the earlier date. In other words, only about 20 percent of the merchants in Philadelphia in 1774 had been merchants in the city seventeen years earlier. The mobility evidenced by these figures is also apparent when one looks into the future from 1774. Of the 300 merchants present then, nearly half (46 percent) would be gone by 1791.

This mobility in and out of the merchant group was matched by considerable geographical movement within the city. A substantial majority of the merchants—65 percent in 1774 and 60 percent in 1789—were renters, so it is not surprising to find that the merchants shifted frequently from ward to ward. Thirty-six percent of merchants in 1774, for example, had lived in a different ward seven years earlier.[48]

Friends and Churchmen

The formation of a unified mercantile group in Philadelphia was inhibited not only by the sharp economic stratification, by the con-

47. See Appendix. Turner to John and William Halliday, June 1757, Turner Letterbook, 1753–1774. Theodore Thayer, *Israel Pemberton, King of the Quakers* (Philadelphia, 1943), 3–24; Drinker to John and Robert Barclay and Co., May 20, 1783, James and Drinker Foreign Letterbook, 1772–1785, 346, Drinker Papers. Some gentlemen remained active capitalists, involved in land speculation, iron manufacture, or other activities, as were William Allen, Henry Drinker, and William Bingham the younger.

48. On spatial mobility, see Appendix. The rather awkward time span of 17 years was dictated by the spacing of the surviving evidence.

stant arrival of new commercial talent from many parts of the world, and by population turnover in general. It was inhibited also by religious and ethnic divisions. In general, social and business connections coincided with ethnic identity, and nowhere was this more evident than in the formation of firms. The 40 percent of the merchants who did not operate alone obviously selected their partners very carefully. One had to cooperate closely day after day with a partner, and a bad partner could easily cause the ruin of a firm. It is not surprising that partners were often close relatives, and almost always of the same ethnic group. The very name of a firm often indicated its ethnicity—Keppelle and Steinmetz, Levy and Franks, Cunningham and Nesbitt, Girard and Hourquebie. Each of these companies tended to have its own circle of close contacts and customers within the merchant community, and these were often of the same background as the firm itself. The city's small, tightly intermarried group of Jewish merchants, for instance, cooperated closely in the specialized field of Indian trading. Stephen Girard during his early years in Philadelphia traded quite heavily with his fellow French merchants, while Charles Wharton counted many Quaker traders among his most important customers. The Irishman Benjamin Fuller seems to have played a prominent role in the affairs of his countrymen. We find him acting as executor for at least five Irish merchants, while managing the bankruptcies of several others. After the Revolution, even recently arrived Englishmen counted themselves a special social group that had to take care of its own. When the wealthy young merchant James Cramond was in New York, he made the acquaintance of an English gentleman who had "lost his money in vice" and been forced in consequence to spend a week at a tavern. Cramond paid off the man's debts and sent him on to his Philadelphia friend David Cay, a recent immigrant from Manchester, with the suggestion that his passage to Europe be "privately raised by subscription by our countrymen."[49]

The most evident social division in the trading body was that between Quakers and Anglicans, for both groups were numerous and included many powerful traders. Certainly the gulf between them was great, especially before 1770 or so. At critical junctures they feuded viciously in politics as well. The correspondence of the Willings in the 1750s excoriated the "Vile Broadbrims," and Joseph Turner decried the "obstinate Shocking" behavior of the Quaker-dominated Pennsylvania legislature.

49. Imports and Exports, 1781–1787; Edwin Wolf 2d and Maxwell Whiteman, *The History of the Jews of Philadelphia from Colonial Times to the Age of Jackson*, 2d ed. (Philadelphia, 1975), 23–75; Girard Papers; Charles Wharton Daybook, 1768–1772; Fuller to John Mitchell, Dec. 2, 1784, Fuller Letterbook, 1784–1787, 55; James Cramond to David Cay, Mar. 5, 1789, Andrew Clow and Co. Papers, Gratz Collection, HSP.

Anglicans and Quakers also tended to maintain separate civic organizations. Friends, for example, dominated the Pennsylvania Hospital and the Library Company, while churchmen were prominent in the Dancing Assembly, the First Troop, and the Bank of North America. Strict Quakers also strived self-consciously to stand aloof from worldly affairs, as this statement by a leading Friend attests: "As to being on a footing of intimacy with either Hamilton or Jefferson, it never was so & that it never was so lays a good deal with myself—My path in life don't naturally lead to an assimilation with Great Men or at least with those so held in worldly estimation—It is true . . . I have met one over a dish of Tea & the other at his particular request I breakfasted with." Quakers were not permitted to marry out of the faith, and even the trading styles of the two groups were different in important respects. Quakers were forbidden to engage in privateering, smuggling, trading with the enemy, and military contracting. Despite some notable lapses, Friends do seem to have respected these interdictions, notwithstanding the loss of trading opportunities that they suffered. It is sometimes asserted that Quakers were exceptionally cautious, prudent traders who consequently enjoyed excellent credit ratings. Though there undoubtedly is some truth to this generalization, Quaker reliability has been exaggerated by historians. One can point to many Quaker merchants, including Abel James, Clement Biddle, Elias Bland, and Owen Jones, who went bankrupt partly as a result of overtrading, and one can find little evidence that religion was an important consideration in gauging creditworthiness.[50]

The divergent religious beliefs and mores of Quaker and Anglican did lead to certain significant differences in social and business conduct, however. Quakers valued highly the bourgeois virtues of industry, frugality, and economy that marked the way to wealth, yet deemphasized the social distinctions that wealth itself created. Though far from being ascetics, wealthy Quaker merchants shunned the expensive carriages and opulent dress of rich Anglicans. At the same time, strict Friends placed great emphasis on the importance of maintaining the purity and numerical strength of their sect. For the Quakers, therefore, in comparison to Anglicans, religion was a greater social bond than economic class. All of this put the ambitious, devout Quaker artisan in a relatively better position for upward mobility than his Anglican counterpart. Instead of being harshly confronted by the sheer wealth of his betters, he found within the

50. C. Willing and Son to Thomas Willing, n.d., Willing and Morris Letterbook, 28; Turner to David Barclay and Sons, Sept. 20, 1755, Turner Letterbook, 1753–1774, 1; Brobeck, "Philadelphia Elite Groups," 76–178, 329–330; Henry Drinker to George Joy, Dec. 24, 1791, Henry Drinker Letterbook, 1790–1793, 251, Drinker Papers; Rasmusson, "Capital on the Delaware," 164–168, 173–176, 180–182.

meeting wealthy men who did not flaunt their riches and who positively valued the sober virtues of the aspiring tradesman. These men could be both excellent role models and sources of business support. This may explain why the Quaker merchant Joseph Wharton preferred to be called a "cooper" even after he had grown rich and why tradesmen were far more prominent as leaders in the Quaker than in the Anglican church of Philadelphia. These characteristics of Quaker life also suggest why there seems to have been an especially large number of Quaker merchants who began their careers as artisans, and why the sons of wealthy Quakers often became successful traders.[51]

It has often been emphasized by historians that the economic usefulness of religious and family ties extended beyond the water's edge. New England merchants in the seventeenth century preferred to deal with overseas relatives, and this pattern was still common in the Atlantic world a century later. As David Landes has stressed, young merchants in particular relied on family contacts to form their initial trading links. Even so independent a figure as Stephen Girard wrote maudlin letters to his father in Bordeaux celebrating his filial loyalty and suggesting that it ought to be rewarded with commissions. Girard's first successful trading relationship was with his brother in Cap-Français, Hispaniola.[52]

Although Girard's experience was duplicated time and again by other Philadelphians, by the second half of the eighteenth century this pattern was no longer the norm.[53] Not surprisingly, commercial networks had advanced far beyond the tentative, fragile links fashioned by the first English traders who settled in America, and these new networks depended far less on kinship. The English dry goods trade is the best example. By the late colonial period, the thousands of pounds of manufactured goods that entered Philadelphia every year were supplied in the main by roughly twenty large English suppliers. These great houses had hundreds of customers in Philadelphia and other cities, and it is obvious that the English partners of these firms were not related by blood or religion to every one of their customers. Frequently the English firms knew nothing more about a customer than that he was reputed to be safe

51. Brobeck, "Philadelphia Elite Groups," 271, 272, 286, 287, 288. The sons of Abel James, Joshua Fisher, William Fisher, Thomas Clifford, Joseph Wharton, Jeremiah Warder, and Samuel Sansom were all energetic traders. Significantly, wealthy Quakers who wished to become fashionable gentlemen tended to switch to the Anglican church.

52. Bernard Bailyn, *The New England Merchants in the Seventeenth Century* (Cambridge, Mass., 1955), 34–36; Alfred D. Chandler, Jr., *The Visible Hand: The Managerial Revolution in American Business* (Cambridge, Mass., 1977), 18; McMaster, *Stephen Girard*, I, 16–18.

53. Robert A. Davison, *Isaac Hicks: New York Merchant and Quaker, 1767–1820* (Cambridge, Mass., 1964), 13–23; Romanek, "John Reynell," 1–12.

and had so far paid off his debts promptly. In one case, even the Philadelphia agent of a major Quaker firm in London was not a Friend. The firm of Parr and Bulkeley, situated in Lisbon, handled the business of a large number of Philadelphia merchants, including Quakers, Anglicans, and Germans.[54]

Divided along economic, ethnic, and religious lines, fragmented by extensive migration, and atomized by the competition of trade itself, Philadelphia's merchant community did not constitute a "class," an "aristocracy," or a cohesive social group of any other description. Although "community" is serviceable as a label, we are really dealing not with a cohesive commercial elite, but, rather, with a specific occupational group engaged in the business of wholesaling. The merchants had a common economic function which set them apart from retailers on the one hand and leisured gentlemen on the other. But these wholesalers were a diverse and divided lot. Some were wealthy members of the city's social elite, while many others had little or no capital. Some were of old families, but others had been in the city for only two or three years. Some were Quakers; others were Anglicans, Frenchmen, Jews, or Irishmen. Little in the organization of Philadelphia commerce knitted these diverse individuals together. They were basically competitors and distrustful of one another, motivated to cooperate closely with only a restricted group of associates.

The fragmented and open character of the merchant community affected the economic and social character of the city as a whole. As an expanding city on the periphery of the empire, Philadelphia constantly attracted new business talent and possessed an exceptionally fluid, competitive, and materialistic social environment that strongly encouraged aggressive entrepreneurship. Its entrepreneurial ranks were exceptionally deep: in addition to the true commercial elite, comprising perhaps fifty individuals at any one time, there was a pool of small but capable capitalists—minor merchants, shopkeepers, grocers, and others—waiting like sharks to snatch any opportunities that opened up. The majority of these merchants, aristocrats as well as petty traders, were men on the move—ambitious, competitive, and intensely acquisitive. Many were immigrants, others were upwardly mobile within Philadelphia's occupational structure, and even the sons of established local families received only a good start from their social background, rather than a secure career. To such men, risk and change, not stability and caution, were the

54. Turner Letterbook, 1753–1774, documents Allen and Turner's relationship with David Barclay and Son. On Parr and Bulkeley, see Jasper Yates Brinton Collection, box 2, HSP.

norm: they were psychologically prepared to move to a new city or undertake a new enterprise in order to advance their fortunes.

In such efforts these men were spurred on by their mediocre social credentials. They were nouveaux riches whose position in society was principally the result of their own material success and not a gift of birth. To secure their position in the competitive social environment of Philadelphia, they gave ever more lavish balls, banquets, and receptions. But such frivolity meant huge expenditures, and the merchants were not particularly wealthy by contemporary standards. They therefore labored strenuously to augment their fortunes, forever scheming and projecting with an intensity that would have seemed quite alien to the socially secure squires of Maryland and Virginia. Thus the marquis de Chastellux remarked during the Revolution, "Philadelphia is, so to speak, the great sink wherein all the speculation of America terminates and mingles." Eighteen years later another visitor to the Quaker City wrote, "It is a nation of Merchants, always alive to their interests; & therefore almost wholy engrossed with the thoughts of it; keen in the pursuit of wealth in all the various modes of acquiring it." Even the more conventional forms of business carried on by the merchants entailed a great deal of risk. It is hardly surprising, therefore, that when new, potentially lucrative investment media became available during and after the Revolution, these ambitious arrivistes plunged in.[55]

The social fluidity of the merchant community may seem surprising in view of the discovery by historical researchers that economic stratification in American cities was increasing during the eighteenth century. Pointing to the ever more unequal distribution of wealth, as measured by probate inventories and tax lists, analysts have concluded that economic power was becoming concentrated in the hands of an elite. According to one study, this "social transformation" was wrought by the "consolidation of wealth" "apparent in the augmentation of power in the hands of merchants, lawyers, and land speculators." "The chances of success at any level of society below the upper class seem to have been considerably less in the eighteenth century than before."[56] As another historian

55. Marquis de Chastellux, *Travels in North America in the Years 1780, 1781, and 1782*, trans. Howard C. Rice, Jr., 2 vols. (Chapel Hill, N.C., 1963), I, 181; Henretta, *Evolution of American Society*, 99. See chap. 3, below, for a discussion of the heavy business risks that the merchants faced.

56. Gary B. Nash, "Urban Wealth and Poverty in Pre-Revolutionary America," *Journal of Interdisciplinary History*, VI (1975–1976), 545–584. See also James A. Henretta, "Economic Development and Social Structure in Colonial Boston," *William and Mary Quarterly*, 3d Ser., XXII (1965), 75–92; Allan Kulikoff, "The Progress of Inequality in Revolutionary Boston," *WMQ*, 3d Ser., XXVIII (1971), 375–412.

has said, "Impersonal market forces disrupted traditional social and economic relationships, led to an increasingly unequal distribution of wealth, and restructured urban society along rigid class lines."[57]

If this schema is correct, opportunities for artisans, shopkeepers, or petty merchants to become successful wholesalers would have declined radically between 1740 and 1790. Was this in fact the case? We know very little about the business activities of the artisans, retailers, and other small businessmen who composed Philadelphia's amorphous middle class—let alone how these activities changed during the century—but the evidence available on the merchant community does not suggest a marked contraction in the rate of upward mobility into the mercantile ranks. This rate was never high in absolute terms, when measured as a percentage of all the people in the middle class, but there is no reason to suppose that it was radically reduced by a transformation of the business system or social structure.

Because of the many deficiencies of probate documents for measuring wealth distribution, discussion of Philadelphia's evolving class structure has centered on the distribution of taxable wealth.[58] Unfortunately, tax assessments also do not provide a very accurate measure of economic power, and they certainly are not precise enough to measure the transfer of economic leverage from one decile of the population to another. The reason is straightforward: taxable wealth did not include the types of property that most readily confer economic power in a port city. In Philadelphia, assessed wealth consisted primarily of servants, slaves, livestock, public offices, and real estate (dwellings, acreage, shops, houses rented out, and ground rents). Excluded from the rolls were most forms of commercial wealth, including business inventories, vessels, notes and bonds, cash, and book debts. Also missing, of course, were intangible forms of human capital, including mechanical and commercial skills,

57. Robert E. Shalhope, "Republicanism and Early American Historiography," *WMQ*, 3d Ser., XXXIX (1982), 340, summarizing a finding of Gary B. Nash, *The Urban Crucible: Social Change, Political Consciousness, and the Origins of the American Revolution* (Cambridge, Mass., 1979).

58. The primary deficiencies of Philadelphia probate documents for this purpose are the following: (1) they generally do not list land; (2) they usually do not list the total assets and debts of decedents; and (3) they are skewed toward the elderly and wealthy. Of 97 probate documents examined for the present study, reliable nonland net worth figures could be calculated for only 16. It is significant that Jacob M. Price, in studying New York, wrote, "An experimental analysis of those [wills] for the years 1771–1776 shows them to misrepresent grossly (as one might expect) the relative weight of the wealthier inhabitants of the city, particularly merchants." Price, "American Port Towns," *Perspectives in Am. Hist.*, VIII (1974), 131. For further discussion of probate records, see Bibliography.

commercial contacts, and business franchises.[59] If Philadelphia had been an agricultural community, its tax assessments would offer a fairly accurate measure of individual economic power and social status, because in a rural setting land, servants, and livestock are the primary generators of income and the determinants of social position. In a port city populated by small businessmen, however, such assets are not so clearly related to income and economic power.

If Philadelphia were in the process of economic transformation led by an elite, the tax lists do not reveal it. Many of the men appearing at the top of the tax list were not dynamic capitalists who were rapidly engrossing wealth and reshaping the economy. Of the forty-one Philadelphians rated at over three hundred pounds, only nine were active merchants, while the remaining thirty-two were primarily economically passive "gentlemen" of various descriptions: retired merchants (thirteen), gentlemen or wealthy professionals (eleven), retired carpenters (two), and others (six).[60] Only five of the forty-one were among the twenty-three top shipowners in colonial Philadelphia.[61]

This apparent paradox is explained by the strong bias inherent in the tax list toward the favorite property of the idle rich—land. By contrast, active merchants invested most of their wealth in commercial ventures that were not taxed, rather than in real estate. It was only towards the end of a merchant's career, when he converted his liquid assets into urban real estate, that he became a major taxpayer, joining such wealthy gentlemen as John Dickinson, Joseph Galloway, Samuel Powel, and William Logan.[62] Although some of these heavily taxed Philadelphians were shrewd real estate entrepreneurs, most were passive rentier investors who were no longer in the forefront of economic change in Philadelphia, if

59. For an analysis of these sources, see Bibliography.

60. Active merchants: Joshua Fisher, Thomas Willing, James Pemberton, Reese Meredith, John Pemberton, Jerse Warder, Edward Stiles, Thomas Lawrence, William Moore. Retired merchants: John Stamper, Israel Pemberton, William Allen, Owen Jones, Jonathan Mifflin, Walter Goodman, William Coates, Luke Morris, Joseph Wharton, Joseph Turner, Mary Bingham, Reynold Keene, Richard Hockley. Gentlemen and professionals: Samuel Powel, Ben Franklin, Samuel Preston Moore, William Shippen, Lynford Lardner, John Dickinson, James Hamilton, James Tilghman, Benjamin Chew, John Lawrence, Thomas Pryor. Retired carpenters: Samuel Rhoads, Joseph Fox. Others: George Emlen, Anthony Morris (brewer), Benjamin Loxley (carpenter), Joseph Potts (ironmaker), Wm ——— (goldsmith), Samuel Emlen (not categorized).

61. See Simeon J. Crowther, "The Shipbuilding Output of the Delaware Valley, 1722–1776," American Philosophical Society, *Proceedings*, CXVII (1973), 103. Three of these five were retired.

62. On the reasons for this life cycle in the structure of estates see below, chap. 2.

they ever had been. Such gentlemen were particularly prominent on the tax roll because they were most likely to hold provincial offices that were heavily taxed.[63]

The paradoxes are no less apparent at the opposite extreme of the tax list. If the tax assessments truly reveal the economic power of individuals, we would not expect to find many merchants rated at £10 or less. In fact, however, 45 percent of the city's merchants, including a number of major traders, are among these apparently lowly taxpayers.[64] Rated at only £10 in 1774, William Pollard might seem to be a member of Philadelphia's emerging proletariat, but despite recent reverses he was receiving an annual salary of £334 and earning significant commission income.[65] Also rated at £10 was Moore Furman, a partner in a successful shipping firm. George Meade and Thomas Fitzsimons, leading provision merchants and prominent speculators during the Revolution, were rated at £9 and £10, respectively. Even Philadelphia's most dynamic merchant, Robert Morris, while purchasing massive quantities of wheat for export to Europe, was rated at only £9 in 1769, although his assessment had risen to a more respectable £116 by 1774. Of eighty-three merchants who handled over one thousand measured tons of shipping in the prewar decade, twenty-nine (35 percent) were assessed at less than £21.[66] Though relatively wealthy, these people simply did not own land in Philadelphia. Clearly, tax assessments are not a very accurate or faithful measure of economic power in Philadelphia.

A more subtle difficulty that arises from using tax lists to measure economic power is that the procedure ignores the actual competitive structure of the economy. Economic power is roughly synonymous with competitive advantage and is thus finite: one individual can gain economic power only at the expense of his competitors. It has been said that

63. Eleven of the 41 taxpayers owning estates of over £300 in 1774 had offices with a mean assessed value of £210. A very small portion of the total group of taxpayers, or even of merchant taxpayers, had offices.

64. The distribution of merchants in the provincial tax list for 1774 was as follows:

Taxable Wealth	*Proportion of Merchants*
£ 0–10	45%
11–20	9
21–40	10
41–100	18
101+	18

Transcript of the Assessment for the 1774 Provincial Tax for the City and County of Philadelphia, PHMC.

65. William Pollard to B. and J. Bowers, Dec. 21, 1772, Pollard Letterbook, 1772–1774, 129.

66. Based on Tonnage Duty Book, 1774 Provincial Tax for Philadelphia.

the share of taxable wealth, and thus economic power, controlled by the top twentieth of Philadelphians expanded greatly during the eighteenth century, at the expense of the remaining 95 percent.[67] We are implicitly invited to interpret such data as analogous to the market shares of various firms competing with each other in a given industry: as one firm grows bigger, relative to its competitors, it also becomes stronger and more difficult to compete with.

The trouble with this implicit model is that Philadelphia was not one big industry. It was a complex, segmented society composed of many skilled craftsmen and specialized traders, serving particular markets and executing distinct economic functions. Operators in separate trades were not direct competitors, and the transfer of capital and entrepreneurship from one trade to another was not always possible. There was, for example, a fairly clear division between most mechanical crafts and mercantile pursuits. Although the wealth of successful merchants increased greatly during the eighteenth century, these expanded resources were generally invested in international commerce, banking, securities speculation, and land speculation, a process that did not economically injure workingmen.[68] A certain amount of capital went into ironmaking, flour milling, sugar refining, brewing, and cotton cloth production, but very little was directed into such crafts as baking, shipbuilding, ropemaking, needlecrafts, house construction, and coopering. It cannot even be said that the prosperity of wholesalers led to the dispossession of retail business, for few wholesalers attempted to integrate backward into retailing.

The segmentation of the economy meant that the competitive threat of big money was often an unrealized danger to lesser businessmen. When a successful shipping merchant ordered a large new vessel to be built by ship carpenters, the carpenters in turn employed boatbuilders, caulkers, blockmakers, sailmakers, mastmakers, and other artisans. The estates of these mechanics probably were not growing as rapidly as the capital of the merchants they worked for, but their livelihood was hardly endangered. The merchants had no intention of operating their own shipyards, and they therefore remained customers, rather than competitors, of the artisans. It is quite possible that certain trades in Philadelphia did in fact undergo marked shifts in economic power in favor of the largest firms, but the voluminous information on the merchants provides little evidence that mercantile capital was transforming the competitive structure of most mechanical and retailing activities.

67. Nash, "Urban Wealth and Poverty," *Journal of Interdisciplinary History*, VI (1975–1976), 550.

68. See chap. 7, below.

It is true that social distance was increasing in eighteenth-century Philadelphia, and many tradesmen clearly resented the growing ostentation and hauteur of their social betters.[69] But tradesmen were prospering along with the capitalists, and their position in the economy was fairly stable. By the 1830s, to be sure, things had changed. The transportation revolution and technological innovations made it possible for merchants to reorganize traditional manufacturing activities along capitalist lines. Master craftsmen protested bitterly as their wages shrank and they descended into the ranks of the semiskilled. This was a development of the nineteenth century, however, not the eighteenth.

Finally, it should be noted that the actual facts on social mobility cannot be derived from analysis of wealth distribution. Lorenz curves and gini coefficients provide only a static profile of the social pyramid: they show how high it was and how steeply graded, but not how freely people moved up and down it. The presumption has been that if the pyramid becomes steeper, it becomes more difficult to climb, but this is merely a supposition, not a documented fact. So far as the merchant community is concerned, one can think of several reasons why the rate of movement into the merchant group did indeed decline. Ships became larger and more expensive, the use of banks and commercial paper made business methods more difficult to master, certain merchants developed sophisticated trading networks that were not easily duplicated, and the wealth of major firms increased.

Yet counterbalancing these developments were four other factors that encouraged a constant influx of new talent into the merchant group. For one thing the rate of bankruptcy for established merchants was high in the second half of the century; so new positions in the trading community were continually arising.[70] The rapid expansion of the merchant community generally throughout this period created new slots for potential climbers, and the frequent wars of the period 1744–1815 continually agitated the commercial world, creating new opportunities for nimble traders.[71] In addition, it must be remembered that the key to social mobility was commercial credit, which was controlled not primarily by wealthy Philadelphians, but by English merchants. Study after study has shown that aggressive English exporters were generously extending credit not only to wealthy merchants but also to minor merchants, shopkeepers, vendue masters, and others in a fairly broad spectrum of Phila-

69. The growth of a wealthy landlord class, discussed below, is one example of this phenomenon.

70. See below, chap. 2.

71. For examples of mobility during the Revolution, see chap. 5.

delphia society.[72] The continual immigration of foreign merchants into the port was another, hitherto overlooked, conduit of trading capital into the city. Commercial credit, unlike land, is an expandable resource, transferable through a simple entry in a ledger. For this reason credit extended from England was about as easy for rich Philadelphians to monopolize as sunlight. Nor could any merchant group prevent successful grocers, mariners, and artisans from becoming wholesalers. The unabated influx of newcomers into the merchant community helps to explain the chronic complaints about the glutted dry goods market and also explains the steady growth of the trading community, the fairly frequent bankruptcies of prominent traders, and the large number of secondary merchants who were able to operate in the city. One indication of the stiff competition that major traders faced is the fact that the amount of shipping handled by the great provision merchants of Philadelphia—James and Drinker, Reese Meredith, Samuel Smith, and others—actually dropped, both absolutely and as a proportion of the total, between 1766 and 1775.[73] Moreover, fully two-fifths of the traders present in 1799 who can be traced back to 1791 had not been merchants in the earlier year.[74] One historical researcher has found that the upper 40 percent of decedents, and not merely a narrow elite, possessed increasingly larger probated estates during the eighteenth century.[75] While the rich assuredly did become richer during the century, they were not able, in the highly competitive, relatively fluid business environment of a growing port, to seal off the opportunities available to their lesser competitors.

72. Marc Egnal and Joseph A. Ernst, "An Economic Interpretation of the American Revolution," *WMQ*, 3d Ser., XXIX (1972), 15–18; Harry D. Berg, "The Organization of Business in Colonial Philadelphia," *Pennsylvania History*, X (1943), 159–160; William S. Sachs, "The Business Outlook in the Northern Colonies, 1750–1775" (Ph.D. diss., Columbia University, 1957), 53–61, 253–254.

73. The number of shipping firms handling over 1,250 measured tons dropped from 13 in 1766 to 4 in 1774, although the total tonnage entering port rose from 59,728 tons to 68,793 tons (Tonnage Duty Book).

74. Derived from tracing individuals from the 1799 Philadelphia city directory to the 1791 directory.

75. Nash, "Urban Wealth and Poverty," *Journal of Interdisciplinary History*, VI (1975–1976), 572.

2 The Articulation of the Merchant Community

In 1775 Philadelphia's overseas trading area described a wide arc, sweeping through the Atlantic from the Caribbean to the Azores and Madeira, on to the Iberian Peninsula, then northward to England and Ireland, and finally back across the ocean to New England. The massive tropical archipelago known as the West Indies was a botanical gold mine worked by adventurers from many nations—England, France, Spain, Holland, and Denmark. Here black slaves and their white masters had hacked out of the jungle valuable fields planted with sugar, coffee, cocoa, cochineal, and other crops. These exotic commodities were far too lucrative for planters to waste much land and labor on the production of foodstuffs and lumber, so these products were imported from Europe and North America. The plantations were virtually self-contained factories, complete with quarters for slaves and overseer, sugar mills for grinding cane, sugarhouses for boiling down the juice, and distilleries for producing rum. The Africans who actually operated these factories were killed off by a debilitating regimen of planting, weeding, cutting, and milling, while the small group of resident planters enjoyed unbounded luxury on their lush estates.[1]

The islands were numerous—Philadelphia ships visited no fewer than twenty-five in 1774 alone—and in size and degree of development they were diverse. The smaller islands that had long been colonized were completely settled, whereas the interiors of the largest ones remained thickets of mountainous jungle. Nor were the islands uniformly productive. Newer, fresher fields could produce sugar more cheaply, and by the last quarter of the eighteenth century the French possessions of Saint

1. Tonnage Duties on Incoming Vessels, Nov. 1, 1765–Aug. 30, 1775, 3 vols., Cadwalader Collection, Thomas Cadwalader Section, Historical Society of Pennsylvania (hereafter referred to as Tonnage Duty Book).

Domingue, Martinique, and Guadeloupe undersold on world markets the key British islands, Barbados and Jamaica.[2]

Four thousand miles to the northeast, eighteenth-century Madeira resembled a giant vineyard ingeniously planted on the steep slopes of the mountainous island. Too steep for horses, Madeira's roads were traversed primarily by mules, and since the roads became rivers during the violent rainy season, they were carefully paved. To one outsider the island's population seemed to be a mixture of beggars and businessmen, the latter living in flea-ridden apartments above their countinghouses. Since the island's population was small, imports were of secondary importance: the main object of these resident merchants was to export the prized wine that was a staple of genteel taverns throughout the Atlantic.[3]

Madeira was a possession of Portugal, which together with Spain became a major market of Philadelphia during the eighteenth century. The Iberian landscape was intermittently flat and hilly, fertile and barren, and featured fine fields of grain complemented by olive trees, cork trees, and vineyards. Since the signing of the Methuen Treaty in 1703, Portugal had become a commercial vassal of England, which maintained trading factors in the major ports. Traditionally, Portuguese wine was exchanged for English cloth, and British merchants also supplied the country with grain when Iberian crops were disappointing. However, as British grain production fell short of domestic demand, the kingdom relinquished its role as granary to the Iberian Peninsula, and North American merchants seized the market. Philadelphia vessels traveled to many Iberian ports, including Cádiz, Barcelona, Oporto, and El Ferrol, but the most important destination was Lisbon. Although this splendid port, looming above the Tagus River, had been devastated by an earthquake in 1755, a modern city, constructed of white stone, was rising out of the dirty, dilapidated old city that dated back to the Moorish occupation.[4]

In commercial affairs as in everything else, the sun of the imperial solar system was London, a sprawling, brawling metropolis of seven hundred thousand in 1775—an "overgrown monster" that hugged both

2. Richard S. Dunn, *Sugar and Slaves: The Rise of the Planter Class in the English West Indies, 1624–1713* (Chapel Hill, N.C., 1972), 188–201; [Janet Schaw], *Journal of a Lady of Quality; Being the Narrative of a Journey from Scotland to the West Indies, North Carolina, and Portugal, in the years 1774 to 1776*, ed. Evangeline Walker Andrews and Charles McLean Andrews (New Haven, Conn., 1923), 73–143.

3. Samuel W. Woodhouse, Jr., "Log and Journal of the Ship *United States* on a Voyage to China in 1784," *Pennsylvania Magazine of History and Biography*, LV (1931), 236–238.

4. [Schaw], *Journal of a Lady of Quality*, 216–254; William Dalrymple, *Travels through Spain and Portugal, in 1774: with a Short Account of the Spanish Expedition against Algiers, in 1775* (Dublin, 1777), 18–33, 123–173, 186–195.

sides of the Thames for ten miles. Shrouded in smog generated by coal fires in thousands of hearths—residential, commercial, and industrial—the city was divided between the grimy, narrow, crime-ridden streets of the East End and the expansive squares and streets of the fashionable West End. Virtually anything could be purchased in this mammoth emporium. It was a center for the distribution of linen cloth imported from Holland, Germany, and Russia; the home of the declining trades with Portugal and the Levant; and a major mart for such colonial commodities as sugar and tobacco. Thousands of bushels of grain changed hands each day at the great Corn Exchange, and mountains of hay were sold at four separate markets. Operating from its headquarters on Leadenhall Street, the East India Company from 1765 increasingly governed India as an unforeseen byproduct of its business of importing tea, cottons, and silk. Over two thousand vessels could at times be sighted in the harbor of this stupendous shipping center, apart from the ships in His Majesty's fleet. And London was also the financial center of the empire—the headquarters of the Bank of England, Lloyd's insurance exchange, and the great private bankers that financed commercial expansion.[5]

London's commercial hegemony was weakened, though hardly threatened, by the astonishing growth of new industrial towns in the north during the century. The great aristocrats, powerful court bankers, and colonial nabobs returned from Jamaica or Bombay, commonly seen in London, were not much in evidence in these northern cities that formed the seedbed of the Industrial Revolution. These towns were the domain of substantial bourgeois manufacturers, many of them dissenters, who were in "easy and flourishing circumstances, rather than very rich or affluent." The towns were austere and businesslike, inhabited by workers who were "diminutive in size, and sickly in their appearance, from their sedentary employment." Each locality tended to specialize in a particular trade: Birmingham in hardware, Sheffield in cutlery, the five towns of Staffordshire in pottery, and Manchester in cotton cloth. Yorkshire in the north was a primary center for woolens, a product that had been a mainstay of English industrial strength since the Middle Ages. Before the American Revolution, much of this industrial output was still exported by way of London, but the closer, more convenient port of Liverpool was rapidly gaining in importance.[6]

5. Asa Briggs, comp., *How They Lived*, III, *An Anthology of Original Documents Written between 1700 and 1815* (New York, 1969), 54–57; M. Dorothy George, *London Life in the Eighteenth Century* (London, 1925), chap. 2; George Rudé, *Hanoverian London, 1714–1808* (London, 1971), 1–81.

6. Briggs, *How They Lived*, III, 69–75 (quotations on 70); David MacPherson, *Annals of Commerce, Manufactures, Fisheries, and Navigation* . . . , 4 vols. (New York, 1972 [orig. publ. London, 1805]), III, 324–325.

Across the Irish sea, long-suffering Ireland possessed an extraordinarily unequal social structure. Impoverished tenants and laborers were treated little better than slaves—gentlemen routinely knocked them down with their canes—yet they flourished demographically on a diet of potatoes and milk, and Ireland's population doubled during the century. To the joy of English mercantilists, who frowned on the importation of linen cloth from Europe, Ireland developed a flourishing linen industry that was centered in the north. Using seed imported from North America, Irish peasants grew flax, which was soaked in pools of water for a week or two, and then separated into fibers. These fibers were spun into thread, which in turn was woven into cloth. After it was bleached, the cloth was shipped from Belfast, Newry, and Londonderry to England and America. In years when the linen industry was slack, many Irish Presbyterians were inclined to migrate to America as indentured servants, substituting the hardships of the frontier for the degradation of a conquered land.[7]

England's virtuous, querulous colony of Massachusetts was still another important market for Philadelphia flour, for although the province was thickly settled and relatively prosperous, it could not feed itself. By midcentury, Boston had become a poor and crowded town, blighted by a destructive series of wars and fires. Impressive enough when viewed at a distance, it was a congested hodgepodge of architectural forms, ranging from medieval to Georgian, that was partly surrounded by mudflats at low tide. This unlucky capital had to vie for commercial prominence with a series of smaller coastal towns, including Lynn, Marblehead, Ipswich, Salem, and Newburyport. Although much of the land around these towns was "little better than a rocky, bare and frightful desert, with patches of soil here and there," the inhabitants wrung a good living out of the sea by fishing, whaling, shipping, trading, and distilling rum from imported molasses. Beyond the coast the rocky hills of Massachusetts sustained indifferent crops and fine herds of cattle, and a dense carpet of pine trees stretched northward to Canada, supporting a prolific shipbuilding industry.[8]

7. Arthur Young, *A Tour in Ireland, with General Observations on the Present State of that Kingdom Made in the Years 1776, 1777 and 1778*, ed. Constantia Maxwell (Cambridge, 1925), esp. 40, 190, 192; Kenneth Hugh Connell, *The Population of Ireland, 1750–1845* (Oxford, 1950), 25.

8. Carl Bridenbaugh, *Cities in the Wilderness: The First Century of Urban Life in America, 1625–1742* (New York, 1938), 17, 18; Patrick M'Robert, "Patrick M'Robert's Tour Through Part of the North Provinces of America," ed. Carl Bridenbaugh, *PMHB*, LIX (1935), 164–167; Robert Honyman, *Colonial Panorama, 1775: Dr. Robert Honyman's Journal for March and April*, ed. Philip Padelford (San Marino, Calif., 1939), 42–58 (quotation on 45); marquis de Chastellux, *Travels in North America in the Years 1780, 1781, and 1782*, trans. Howard C. Rice, Jr., 2 vols. (Chapel Hill, N.C., 1963), II, 483–493.

These far-flung overseas markets were balanced by Philadelphia's hinterland—the territory that furnished the city with flour, pork, beef, and lumber for export and consumed the cloth, hardware, wine, sugar, and other products imported by the city's merchants. Travelers bound northward from Virginia often entered the Philadelphia hinterland by sailing up Chesapeake Bay on a sloop or schooner. Looking off the starboard bow, they could see the low, level banks of Maryland's Eastern Shore, which was broken by dozens of inlets and creeks. Although living in a region famous for tobacco, planters on the Eastern Shore had been growing large quantities of wheat since the 1730s, and by the 1760s much of this grain was exported via Philadelphia. So strong was this commercial link that one Philadelphia newspaper was more widely read on the Eastern Shore than in Bucks County, Pennsylvania.[9]

Reaching the northern extremity of the Chesapeake, at Head of Elk, a traveler would usually hire a horse or carriage to complete the journey to Philadelphia. As he set out, the land was "hilly & full of rocks & not well cleared," but presently the appearance of the countryside improved. The well-tended fields of wheat, corn, and barley; the bountiful orchards and meadows; and the excellent inns and genteel country seats reminded more than one visitor of the public roads leading to London. Along the way the traveler encountered a series of towns—Christiana, Wilmington, Chester, and Darby—devoted to trading and milling. Particularly impressive was the cluster of eight stone gristmills, three stories high, that were built by Quaker entrepreneurs along the Brandywine Creek, near Wilmington. The broad expanse of the lower Delaware was visible from the road much of the way, and it was alive with boats of many types—small shallops heading upriver with Maryland wheat, schooners carrying provisions to Jamaica and Massachusetts, impressive three-masted snows transporting flour to Lisbon or mahogany and iron to London. Across the river was southern New Jersey, a barren land of sandy soil, scrubby pine trees, and deep, narrow rivers made reddish by the bog iron deposits along their banks. The area was sparsely settled and important chiefly as a source of firewood and a center of iron production.[10]

9. Andrew Burnaby, *Travels Through the Middle Settlements in North-America. In the Years 1759 and 1760. With Observations Upon the State of the Colonies*, 2d ed. (Ithaca, N.Y., 1960 [orig. publ. London, 1775], 51; Lester J. Cappon *et al.*, eds., *Atlas of Early American History: The Revolutionary Era, 1760–1790* (Princeton, N.J., 1976), 35. John Flexer Walzer, "Transportation in the Philadelphia Trading Area, 1740–1775" (Ph.D. diss., University of Wisconsin, 1968), 15–17, 20.

10. Honyman, *Colonial Panorama*, 12, 13 (quotation on 12); M'Robert, "Tour," *PMHB*, LIX (1935), 164–167; Cappon *et al.*, eds., *Atlas of Early American History*, 23; Peter C. Welsh, "Merchants, Millers, and Ocean Ships: The Components of an Early American Industrial Town," *Delaware History*, VII (1956), 319–336; and "The Brandywine Mills: A Chronicle of an Industry, 1762–1816," *Del. Hist.*, VII (1956), 20–21.

As one crossed the Schuylkill River at Gray's Ferry, the unmistakable prosperity of the region was accentuated by a view of Woodlands, the white Palladian mansion belonging to Pennsylvania's provincial secretary. Once in the city, the traveler who had no time to linger in a tavern over oysters and madeira might proceed in several directions. One possibility was to continue northward along the Delaware, passing the important milling center of Frankford and the town of Bristol, Pennsylvania. Across the river from Bristol was Burlington, a town as famous for its excellent pork as for its former status as capital of West Jersey. If he was headed toward New York City, the traveler would take a ferry across the river to Trenton, a sizable settlement of over one hundred houses, and continue on for ten miles to Princeton. This college town was on the border of Philadelphia's trading area, and its shopkeepers traded with both New York and Philadelphia wholesalers. Situated about thirty miles north of Philadelphia, Trenton marked the extremity of deepwater navigation on the Delaware, but riverboats able to negotiate rapids could continue upriver an additional seventy miles. Later in the century, loggers as far north as the New York border contrived to float lumber down the Delaware to Philadelphia.[11]

The traveler who proceeded northwest by road from Philadelphia, through the Schuylkill River valley, soon came to Germantown, a group of buildings unimaginatively strung along the road for two miles. The town had eight mills and was well known for its extensive manufactures, including butchering, tanning, stocking-weaving, carriage-making, and coopering. Proceeding further up the Schuylkill (which like the Delaware was navigable for riverboats), one entered iron country. Nestled in the valleys of Berks County were many large ironworks, which smelted the local ore into pig iron and produced wrought iron in water-powered forges. At night the incandescent glow of the furnace and the insistent thumping of the forge hammer gave these lonely industrial sites a hellish aspect, and because they were voracious consumers of charcoal, much of Berks County had been stripped of trees by 1775. But the local German farmers put the clear land to good use, growing crops that were sold in Reading.[12]

11. Martin P. Snyder, comp., *City of Independence: Views of Philadelphia before 1800* (New York, 1975), 71; Burnaby, *Travels*, 67; Honyman, *Colonial Panorama*, 13; Chastellux, *Travels*, I, 129; M'Robert, "Tour," *PMHB*, LIX (1935), 167; Walzer, "Philadelphia Trading Area," 99–134, esp. 113; Henry Drinker to Samuel Preston, Nov. 15, Dec. 15, 1791, Henry Drinker Letterbook, 1790–1793, 235, 241, Henry Drinker Papers, Historical Society of Pennsylvania (hereafter identified as HSP).

12. Stephanie Grauman Wolf, *Urban Village: Population, Community, and Family Structure in Germantown, Pennsylvania, 1683–1800* (Princeton, N.J., 1976), 23–39, 96–126; Johann David Schoepf, *Travels in the Confederation [1783–1784]* trans. and ed. Alfred J. Morrison, 2 vols. (Philadelphia, 1911), 196–202; Walzer, "Philadelphia Trading Area,"

The traveler who headed west from Philadelphia would find the road rutted and muddy, thanks to heavy use by hundreds of Conestoga wagons loaded with produce. The farms near Philadelphia were principally owned by men of English and Welsh descent, many of them Quakers, but as one crossed the line into Lancaster County, Germans became numerous. The thrift and industry of the Palatine immigrants had produced in Lancaster County "one of the most lovely and luxuriant regions in the country," "delightfully diversified with waving hills, pleasant dales, adorned by lovely scenery, and highly cultivated farms." With a population of thirty-three hundred in 1775, the town of Lancaster was the largest inland settlement in North America, and it was graced with paved streets and wooden houses grouped around a large brick courthouse. Ubiquitous gardens and fruit trees made Lancaster resplendent in the spring. Thirteen miles further west one came to the Susquehanna River—broad, shallow, and swift—which could be crossed with some difficulty by ferryboat. Pennsylvania west of the Susquehanna was the domain of the Scotch-Irish (transplanted peasants from the linen-and-potatoes economy of northern Ireland) who were as rough and obdurate as the wilderness they were attempting to subdue. Now the road became stony and steep. Log houses were a common sight, and the infrequent taverns were stinking fleabags often as not. Nevertheless, there were pleasant market towns at Carlisle and York, and the traveler who pressed on for two hundred miles over the rugged passes of the Allegheny Mountains came to Fort Pitt, staging ground for the assault by white settlers on the wilderness of the Ohio Valley.[13]

Simply put, the essential economic function of Philadelphia's merchant community was to link the city's hinterland with its overseas markets. It was the merchants who shipped flour to Lisbon, lumber to London, flaxseed to Belfast; and it was they who imported vast amounts of cloth and hardware from London and the outports. How, exactly, was this vital economic activity organized? A vast historical literature on the early American merchant has argued, in essence, that it was not organized: in the crude economic environment of eighteenth-century America, it has been suggested, commercial specialization was impossible, and mer-

33–37; Linda McCurdy, "The Potts Family Iron Industry in the Schuylkill Valley" (Ph.D. diss., Pennsylvania State University, 1974), 167, 168.

13. Jerome H. Wood, Jr., *Conestoga Crossroads: Lancaster, Pennsylvania, 1730–1790* (Harrisburg, Pa., 1979), 47–62 (quotation on 51); "John Penn's Journal of a Visit to Reading, Harrisburg, Carlisle, and Lancaster, in 1788," *PMHB*, III (1879), 290–295; "Mrs. Mary Dewees's Journal from Philadelphia to Kentucky, 1787–1788," *PMHB*, XXVIII (1904), 183–185.

chants had to be jacks-of-all-trades.[14] An implicit corollary of this belief is that the structure of merchant communities did not much change before 1815. Only after this date, it is assumed, was the all-purpose merchant of the colonial era superseded by more specialized traders. Although perhaps applicable to certain American ports during the eighteenth century, this formulation does not accurately describe the situation in Revolutionary Philadelphia. As the port grew and matured between 1750 and 1790, the merchant community became ever more sophisticated in at least three respects. In the first place, individual merchants became increasingly specialized during the period, and by the 1790s the community was much more clearly differentiated than it had been at midcentury. Second, the trading capitals of the merchants also grew considerably in this period. And, third, the growing sophistication of Philadelphia's financial institutions made it possible for merchants to mobilize their expanding fortunes more effectively, thereby conducting more business with the same amount of capital. The first and second of these important developments are discussed in the present chapter, and the third is discussed in Chapter 7.

Patterns of Commercial Specialization

Philadelphia's merchants, as a group, traded throughout the North Atlantic, but few individual merchants traded in more than one or two markets. Commercial activity, in short, was geographically specialized. This specialization was not, however, equally typical of all segments of the merchant community: the larger a firm's operations, the less geographically specialized it was likely to be. Small firms were usually forced to concentrate on only one or two markets, whereas large firms could command enough capital and credit to trade simultaneously with many parts of the world.[15]

Specialization did not follow only geographical lines, however. There were in fact two separate and parallel distribution systems in the port, each with a distinct organization and financial structure and with its peculiar relationship to the shipping industry. One of these was the dry goods network, which moved manufactures of all kinds—cloth, buttons,

14. For an introduction to this problem, see Stuart Bruchey, ed., *The Colonial Merchant: Sources and Readings* (New York, 1966), esp. 169–173.

15. For a more detailed discussion of this subject, see Thomas M. Doerflinger, "Commercial Specialization in Philadelphia's Merchant Community, 1750–1791," *Business History Review*, LVII (1983), 20–49.

hardware, and so on—from England to Philadelphia and its extensive rural trading area. These goods were purchased from English suppliers on twelve months' credit by a Philadelphia importer who then sold them to retailers on several months' credit. Thus, the dry goods trade was a major conduit of commercial credit throughout the Delaware Valley. Since Philadelphia had few products suitable for the English market, this trade consisted primarily of importation. And because manufactures were not bulky in relation to their value, the dry goods trade did not require much shipping space.

The second major branch of the commercial community, the provision trade, specialized not in the importation of manufactures, but in the exportation of bread, flour, meat, lumber, and flaxseed to various parts of the Atlantic world, particularly the West Indies and southern Europe. Because such products were bulky, major provision merchants usually operated their own vessels, and extensive shipping was necessary. Moreover, since the trade did not involve the British Empire's financial heart, London, it did not operate on long-term credit. The provision trade was also more complicated than the dry goods trade and included three types of merchants: shippers who employed their capital in importing and exporting, flour merchants and lumber merchants who supplied these shippers with outward cargoes, and distributors who sold in the hinterland the shippers' inward cargoes of rum, molasses, wine, coffee, and other groceries.

Not every firm in Philadelphia can be neatly placed in the dry goods or provision trade, and merchants shifted their functions during the course of their careers. Nevertheless, by the 1780s specialization was sufficiently advanced to squeeze out of the distribution system many of the inefficiencies that still characterized trade at midcentury. Shippers no longer had to wrangle directly with farmers and millers to construct a cargo, storage facilities could be designed for particular types of goods, and traders developed expertise in the one or two markets in which they traded.

The simplest way to determine the degree of geographical specialization of the merchants' businesses is to divide Philadelphia's trading area into regions—say, Great Britain, the North American coast, the West Indies, and continental Europe—and ask the following question: What percentage of a given merchant's total trade was claimed by the most important sector that he traded with? For a highly specialized merchant who did nothing, for example, but import cloth from England, the answer would be 100 percent, because all his trade involved only one region. By contrast, a perfectly unspecialized trader who dealt equally with all four regions would have a score of only 25 percent, since each region claimed a quarter of his trade. By using this simple but powerful approach, we can measure quite precisely how hundreds of Philadelphia firms organized their trade. The method can be applied both to shipping records, available for the period 1772–1775, which list every vessel that entered Philadelphia; and to customs records covering the years 1785–1787, which show the value of the goods entering Philadelphia.[16]

This methodology suggests a very considerable degree of geographical specialization during the Revolutionary period. For all firms mentioned in the prewar shipping records, an average of 86 percent of the tonnage handled came from only one of the four geographical sectors. For merchant firms alone, the figure is 82 percent. (For the size distribution of this figure, among merchant and nonmerchant firms, see table 5.) Refinement of these data is vital, however, since not all firms were of equal importance. Some firms handled twenty vessels per year, others only one, and the larger firms tended to be less specialized. When we take this factor into account by computing an average percentage for all the firms, weighted by the tonnage handled by each firm, the result is 72 percent. Over a four-year period, nearly three-quarters of the tonnage received by the average firm came from one of four possible sectors. The customs records for the 1780s provide even more striking evidence of geographical specialization. For all Philadelphia firms, both merchant and nonmerchant, the average share claimed by the largest sector was 90 percent, and the average when weighted by the volume of imports of the firm was 78 percent.

Because business historians have long emphasized that the eighteenth-century wholesaler was an all-purpose merchant, this compelling evidence of geographical specialization seems most surprising. Yet the paradox is easily resolved by comparing the degree of specialization of large and small firms. An analysis of the shipping and customs records reveals a striking pattern: larger firms were consistently less specialized than smaller operators (see tables 6, 7). The reason for this pattern is clear. The large firms had substantial amounts of capital that could be simultaneously deployed in several different markets; the smaller firms, by contrast, were forced to concentrate their limited resources in only one or two markets. Since the typical Philadelphia firm was fairly small, it

16. Tonnage Duties on Incoming Vessels, Nov. 1, 1765–Aug. 30, 1775, 3 vols., Cadwalader Collection, Thomas Cadwalader Section, HSP (hereafter cited as Tonnage Duty Book); Registers of Duties Paid on Imported Goods, 1781–1787, 6 vols., Record Group 4, Pennsylvania Historical and Museum Commission.

TABLE 5. *Geographical Specialization of Firms by Proportion of Tonnage, 1772–1775*

	Percentage of Firms Receiving Shipping Tonnage from Largest of 4 Sectors						
Type of Firm	0–50%	50–60%	60–70%	70–80%	80–90%	90–100%	Overall
Merchant (*N*=134)	10.4	11.2	11.2	9.7	9.0	48.5	100.0
Nonmerchant (*N*=77)	1.3	2.6	5.2	5.2	3.9	81.8	100.0
Unknown status (*N*=9)	22.2	0.0	0.0	0.0	0.0	77.8	100.0

Source: Tonnage Duties on Incoming Vessels, November 1, 1765–August 30, 1775, 3 vols., Cadwalader Collection, Thomas Cadwalader Section, Historical Society of Pennsylvania.

was also quite specialized. Business historians have not recognized this fact, however, because they have trained their attention on exceptionally wealthy traders, such as Thomas Hancock, Stephen Girard, Robert Oliver, and Thomas Clifford.

Small and middling traders were often specialists who concentrated on a limited number of activities until a war, a change in markets, or a financial setback caused them to shift their strategy. They had too little to do, not too much, for their trading stocks were severely limited. For precisely this reason they focused a great deal of energy and care on each transaction. For instance, the Scottish immigrant Robert Henderson imported small, unprofitable shipments of dry goods and shipped flour to a Charleston correspondent in return for indigo. Although it provided a large share of his income, this latter operation was on a remarkably small scale: it amounted to the equivalent of only one full cargo in each direction each year.[17] Many young merchants adopted similar strategies: they imported dry goods on credit or traded commodities domestically,

17. Robert Henderson Ledger, 1781–1794, and Robert Henderson Invoice Book, 1784–1793, 46–55, Robert Henderson Papers, HSP. The flour and indigo were worth £1,322 and £874, respectively, in 1790, and £1,869 and £1,837, respectively, in 1791.

TABLE 6. *Geographical Specialization of Firms by Amount of Tonnage, 1772–1775*

Tonnage Received by Firm	No. of Firms	Mean Proportion from Largest of 4 Sectors
1–100	70	99%
101–400	68	88
401–1,000	34	80
1,001–2,000	26	77
2,001 +	22	63
Overall	220	86
Overall, weighted by tonnage received	220	72

Source: Tonnage Duties on Incoming Vessels, November 1, 1765–August 30, 1775, 3 vols., Cadwalader Collection, Thomas Cadwalader Section, Historical Society of Pennsylvania.

TABLE 7. *Geographical Specialization of Firms by Value of Imports, May 1785–December 1787*

Total Imports Received by Firm	No. of Firms	Proportion of Merchant Firms in Group	Mean Proportion of Imports from Largest of 5 Sectors
0–£500	293	81%	94%
£501–£2,000	261	45	92
£2,001–£8,000	152	68	86
£8,001–£30,000	90	92	80
Over £30,000	19	100	68
Overall	815	64	90
Overall, weighted by total imports	815	64	78

Source: Registers of Duties Paid on Imported Goods, 1781–1787, 6 vols., Record Group 4, Pennsylvania Historical and Museum Commission.

but avoided large, risky, long-term adventures. Vessel ownership was beyond their reach. Somewhat richer merchants could, with the help of a partner, afford to operate one—and only one—vessel, which would normally trade with a single port or part of the world.[18] Although merchants of these two classes had great latitude and could trade wherever they wished, they frequently elected to concentrate on only one or two markets. In all we can identify about fifteen firms that fit this description. By contrast, the really rich firms had the means simultaneously to operate three vessels, import a large assortment of dry goods, and carry out a variety of commissions for overseas correspondents. They were indeed all-purpose merchants and continued to play an important role in the economy.

The Division between the Dry Goods and Provision Trades

One dimension of the advance in specialization was the gradual dissociation of the functions of foodstuff exporting and dry goods importing. During the 1750s and early 1760s a number of firms whose main concern was shipping flour to the West Indies and elsewhere felt disposed or even compelled to import English dry goods as well. At this time the seasoned smuggler Thomas Riche was feverishly engaged in shipping provisions to the French West Indies, yet he also maintained an active dry goods trade. Charles Willing and Son, another big shipping firm concerned in the West Indies trade, scorned dry goods as a waste of capital when more lucrative opportunities were offered; they likened backcountry credit sales to "throwing Your Money on the surface of the Water." The Willings nevertheless felt obliged to import manufactures in 1754 and 1755 in order to "keep an assortment" of goods in their store.[19] We can identify seven other provision firms that likewise sold dry goods before 1765.[20] Apparently Joseph Turner was correct when he wrote in 1764, "I can see Little other means, or ways, for a Merchant, to

18. An analysis of the Tonnage Duty Book indicates that in 1769, 53 firms owned one vessel, 23 owned two, and 9 owned three, four, or five.

19. C. Willing and Son to Robert Hibbert, July 30, 1754, Willing and Morris Letterbook, 1754–1761, 10, HSP; T. Willing to David Barclay and Sons, May 22, 1755, Willing and Morris Letterbook, 97.

20. Baynton, Wharton, and Morgan Journal A, 1763–1766, Baynton, Wharton, and Morgan Papers, Reel 8. All references to these papers are to the microfilm edition, available in various libraries, of the originals in the Pennsylvania Historical and Museum Com-

employ himself then partly with Dry goods."[21] By the 1780s, however, a fairly clear division between shippers had emerged. Of 107 firms that imported goods worth at least eight thousand pounds during a three-year period, only about 21 percent of the firms maintained a rough balance between imports from Great Britain and from other sectors. The vast majority, 79 percent, concentrated on one type of trade or the other. This dichotomy is confirmed in the records of several individual businesses.[22]

One can also demonstrate quantitatively a dissociation between shipping and trading by measuring what segment of the merchant community earned income from shipping. Such earnings could come in one of two ways: a merchant could own all or part of a vessel and either use it for his own trade or rent it for freight, or he could manage a vessel consigned to him by its owner in another part of the world. In the latter case he would earn a sizable commission for rendering such services as collecting freight money and having the vessel repaired, provisioned, and sent back out to sea. We can measure the size of the merchant group engaged in these activities by compiling a roster of all merchants who appeared in pre-Revolutionary tax lists and matching them with people mentioned in two documents: the Tonnage Duty Book (described above) and the Pennsylvania Ship Register. The Duty Book lists all firms that received a vessel from overseas between 1766 and 1775; the Ship Register lists, for about forty years before the Revolution, all owners of vessels built in Philadelphia or using the city as their home port.[23] For

mission (hereafter cited as PHMC). James and Drinker Letterbook, 1756–1759, Henry Drinker Papers, HSP; John and Peter Chevalier Daybook, 1760–1766, HSP; Daniel Clark Letterbook, 1759–1762, HSP; Grace Hutchison Larsen, "Profile of a Colonial Merchant: Thomas Clifford of Pre-Revolutionary Philadelphia" (Ph.D. diss., Columbia University, 1955), chaps. 2, 4; John Greeves Ledger, 1753–1757, HSP; Thomas Wharton Daybook, 1758–1762, Leonard T. Beale Collection, HSP.

21. Turner to John Gibson, July 8, 1764, Joseph Turner Letterbook, 1753–1774, HSP.

22. Registers of Duties Paid; Stephen Girard Journals, 1780–1794, 5 vols., Girard Papers, 3d Ser., Reels 44, 113. All references to the Girard Papers are to the microfilm collection in the American Philosophical Society (hereafter cited as APS). James and John Cox Ledger, 1788–1802, Thomas A. Biddle Collection, HSP; Benjamin Fuller Journal, 1782–1789, William West Account Books, 1769–1804, HSP; Francis and John West Letterbooks, 1783–1788, 2 vols., West Account Books; Thomas Fitzsimons Journal, 1781–1785, HSP. For still another example of a Philadelphia shipping firm, see Joseph A. Goldenberg, "The *William* and *Favorite*: The Post-Revolutionary Voyages of Two Philadelphia Ships," *PMHB*, XCVIII (1974), 325–338.

23. Ship Register of Pennsylvania, 1726–1776, HSP; and Declarations of British Registry, 1727–1776, 12 vols., Record Group 41, PHMC (hereafter cited as Pennsylvania Ship Register). For analyses of this document, see John J. McCusker, "Sources of Investment Capital in the Colonial Philadelphia Shipping Industry," *Journal of Economic History*,

TABLE 8. *Participation by Philadelphia Merchant Groups in Vessel Investment and Management*

Total Merchant Population		Merchant Population Active in Shipping			
Year(s)	No.	Period	Role	No.	Proportion of Merchant Population
1756	177	before 1761	investment	110	62.1%
1774	296	1766–1775	investment	146	49.3
1756–1775	503	before 1776	investment	296	58.8
1765–1775	402	1766–1775	management	176	43.8
1765–1775	402	1766–1775	management, investment	221	55.0

Sources: For management: Tonnage Duties on Incoming Vessels, November 1, 1765–August 30, 1775, 3 vols., Cadwalader Collection, Thomas Cadwalader Section. For investment: Ship Register of Pennsylvania, 1726–1776, Historical Society of Pennsylvania; Declarations of British Registry, 1727–1776, 12 vols., Record Group 41, Pennsylvania Historical and Museum Commission. Philadelphia tax lists, 1756–1774 (see Bibliography).

Note: Vessels managed by a firm might or might not be owned by that firm.

the relevant period, all Philadelphia merchants who invested in shipping would appear in the Ship Register, while all those who managed shipping for a fee would appear in the Duty Book. By determining what fraction of all the merchants in Philadelphia appear in one, both, or neither of these documents, we can determine the percentage that owned or managed vessels.[24]

XXXII (1972), 146–157; and "The Pennsylvania Shipping Industry in the Eighteenth Century," 1973, manuscript in HSP. Simeon J. Crowther, "The Shipbuilding Output of the Delaware Valley, 1722–1776," American Philosophical Society, *Proceedings*, CXVII (1973), 90–104; and "The Shipbuilding Industry and the Economic Development of the Delaware Valley, 1681–1776" (Ph.D. diss., University of Pennsylvania, 1970).

24. Since many firms owned or managed small amounts of shipping, this method yields an *upper bound* to the degree of mercantile involvement in the shipping industry. Of 375 merchant investors appearing in the Pennsylvania Ship Register, 71 purchased 30 tons or less, while of 238 firms that, according to the Tonnage Duty Book, received a vessel between 1766 and 1775, 76 received 3 or less.

Two basic conclusions emerge from analysis of the two documents (see table 8). For long periods of time a clear majority of merchants earned money from shipping: 62 percent of the merchants present in the city in 1756 had by 1761 invested in a vessel, and 59 percent of those present before 1776 had invested in one. At least 55 percent of the merchants present in the period 1765–1774 are in the Duty Book or the Ship Register, or both, and for certain technical reasons this figure may actually be somewhat higher. Thus it is correct to say that over the course of their careers merchants *usually* owned their own vessels or managed ships for others. However, not one of these figures is much above 60 percent. It is apparent that a significant fraction of traders earned nothing from shipping for decades at a time.

When we scrutinize the Ship Register and Tonnage Duty Book more closely, a second aspect of this specialization emerges: a relatively small group of Philadelphia firms provided a large proportion of the shipping services for the city. In the pre-Revolutionary decade, just twenty-two firms, containing roughly 6 percent of the merchants in Philadelphia, managed 38 percent of the tonnage entering the port that was not consigned to captains. Of 375 merchants who owned shipping before the Revolution, only 50 (13.3 percent) owned half of the tonnage registered by merchants. Although simple wealth stratification partially explains this pattern, it appears that some wealthy merchants did not invest heavily in shipping, while others did. John Head, one of the wealthiest men in the city, chose to manage just one vessel, which sailed twice a year to London.[25] By contrast, the big shipping firms handled between fifteen and twenty-five vessels per year. They achieved this high volume not only by investing heavily in shipping but also by attracting more vessels on consignment than other firms.[26]

The Dry Goods Trade

A merchant in Philadelphia could establish credit with a dry goods house in England either through the recommendation of a mutual contact or by sending a bill of exchange to demonstrate his financial

25. Tonnage Duty Book; John Head Will no. 128, 1792, Office of the Recorder of Wills, Philadelphia City Hall. Data from tax lists suggest that much of Head's fortune was earned before the Revolution.

26. Analysis of the Tonnage Duty Book shows that of the top 17 shipping firms, 47% owned more than 75% of the shipping they handled. Of the 127 next smaller firms, 59% owned more than 75% of the shipping they handled.

capacity.[27] The Philadelphian would then order a shipment of merchandise—woolens, canvas, glass, hardware, china, and so forth—worth several times the value of the bill of exchange. The English house would expect to receive payment for the balance due within twelve months of the date of the invoice of the exported goods. These would normally be shipped across the Atlantic as freight in one of the large, solid vessels that shuttled between Philadelphia and England. Thus, the Philadelphia importer normally had nothing to do with the ownership or management of vessels. His interest was in the goods.

Once the Philadelphia importer received his bales of cloth and boxes of hardware, he set about selling them. This task was usually easy enough; the trick was receiving payment, for the goods were normally sold to craftsmen and retailers not on a cash basis, but on several months' credit. Not infrequently, several months' credit stretched into several years. Once the importer had finally rounded up cash from at least some of his customers, he would normally purchase bills of exchange and send them to England to pay off his supplier. These bills were drafts on English houses by planters and merchants in the New World who had funds lodged with the English firms, funds earned by shipping across the Atlantic tobacco, wheat, sugar, or other agricultural staples. The bills were to be found in Philadelphia not because merchants there had shipped foodstuffs directly to England—the mother country had little need for imported food in this age of the agricultural revolution—but because provision exporters had shipped flour to southern Europe, the Chesapeake region, the Carolinas, and the West Indies and had been paid in English bills of exchange. The price of such bills in Philadelphia fluctuated with the supply and demand for them, and this price constituted the exchange rate. If the exchange rate went very high, a Philadelphia importer could try to round up some hard money to send to England instead of bills, but the supply of specie was limited and easily exhausted. As a last resort he could try to send some product to England as a remittance, but the Delaware Valley produced few really suitable remittances except iron, which was difficult to obtain.

During the late-colonial period the dry goods trade with Philadelphia was dominated by a restricted group of English export firms. Ledger after ledger in Philadelphia countinghouses contained the names of the

27. Of the vast documentary literature on the dry goods trade, several particularly helpful sources are the William Pollard Letterbook, 1772–1774, HSP; the Turner Letterbook, 1754–1763; and the Stephen Collins Papers, Library of Congress. See also Arthur L. Jensen, *The Maritime Commerce of Colonial Philadelphia* (Madison, Wis., 1963), 87–106.

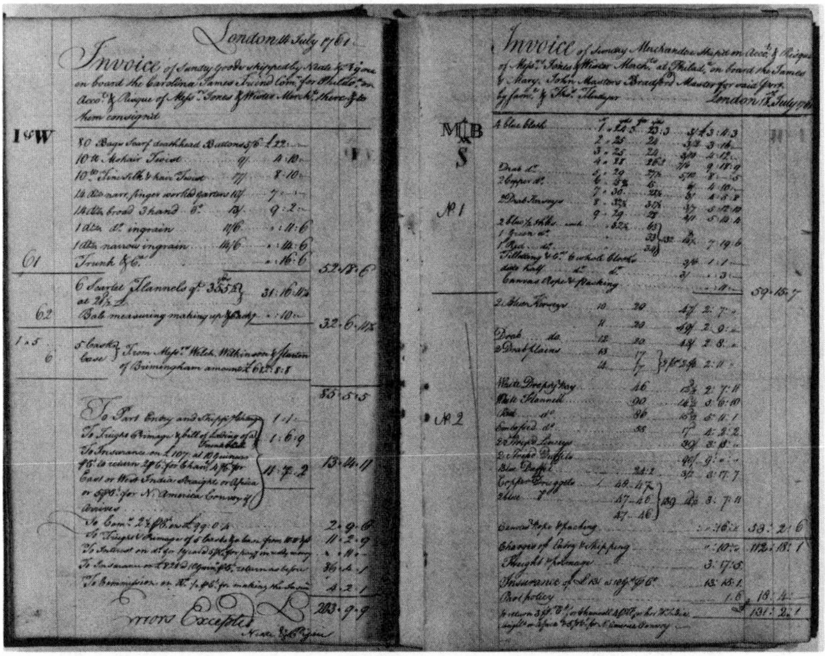

PLATE 11. Invoices of London Merchants. *From Jones and Wister Invoice Book, 1759–1762. Courtesy of The Historical Society of Pennsylvania*

same group of English suppliers to whom money was owed: Elias Bland, Neate and Neave, Mildred and Roberts, Hyde and Hamilton—perhaps twenty in all at any one time.[28] Some of these suppliers were great London merchants who doubled as bankers for their American correspondents, while others were smaller houses in Manchester and the outports who produced some of the goods they exported. Their basic function, however, was not finance or production, but, rather, buying goods from many English manufacturers on the best terms possible and sending them to their American correspondents. They tended to concentrate on a particular category of wares and charged a 2.5 percent commission for their services. To represent their interest in the New World, they retained American mercantile firms, which filed suits, advised on credit risks, and attempted to placate disgruntled customers.

28. For representative listings, see Jones and Wister Invoice Book, 1759–1762, HSP; and John Reynell Invoice Book, 1758–1772, Coates and Reynell Collection, HSP. After the Revolution many new British firms entered the trade.

On the actions of these English houses much depended. They could unilaterally alter the business climate of Philadelphia by withholding or generously extending credit to the dozens of entrepreneurs, big and small, who wished to sell dry goods. They tended to be generous, excessively so. From 1749 to 1790 the constant cry in Philadelphia, broken only by a few brief pauses, was that the city was glutted with dry goods, that cloth was cheaper in Philadelphia than in Manchester, and that dozens of importers were about to go broke. There is no question that these complaints, though exaggerated, had a real basis in fact. It is harder to determine why the English exporters persisted in flooding the Delaware Valley with goods. One hypothesis was advanced by the Philadelphia importer Stephen Collins:

> The merchants in England are such Fools that if they can Possibly get Credit for the good they will be Shiped so long as the People are Roges anough here to write for them when they know they cant pay for them, and be assurd we shall not cease to have enough of such Rogues, so you see between the Folley of England & the vilinay of this cuntry we are all likely to be ruined.[29]

Such cataclysmic prognoses as this must not be accepted uncritically, however. Although easy credit sharpened competition for established importers like Collins, it also, as we have seen, launched the career of many aspiring traders.

If the dry goods business in Philadelphia was relatively easy to break into, the case was otherwise with the carrying trade for dry goods. The vessels that brought in manufactured items from England carried enormously valuable and fragile cargoes worth many times the typical cargo of flour and lumber. To attract freight, such vessels had to be large and well built, and only well-established firms could afford to operate them. The competitors for transatlantic dry goods freight were rich merchants, such as the Quaker merchants James and Drinker, Joshua Fisher and Sons, and John Head.

A large number of Philadelpha wholesalers—at least 250 in the mid-1780s—regularly imported European dry goods, and increasingly, as we have seen, certain firms tended to specialize in this activity. The long-term specialist in the dry goods trade could gain a competitive edge over the fly-by-night importer in a number of ways. He could own or rent a house well suited to the trade, such as John Chaloner rented when he

29. Stephen Collins to David Knox, Mar. 8, 1785, Collins Papers, LXI, 158.

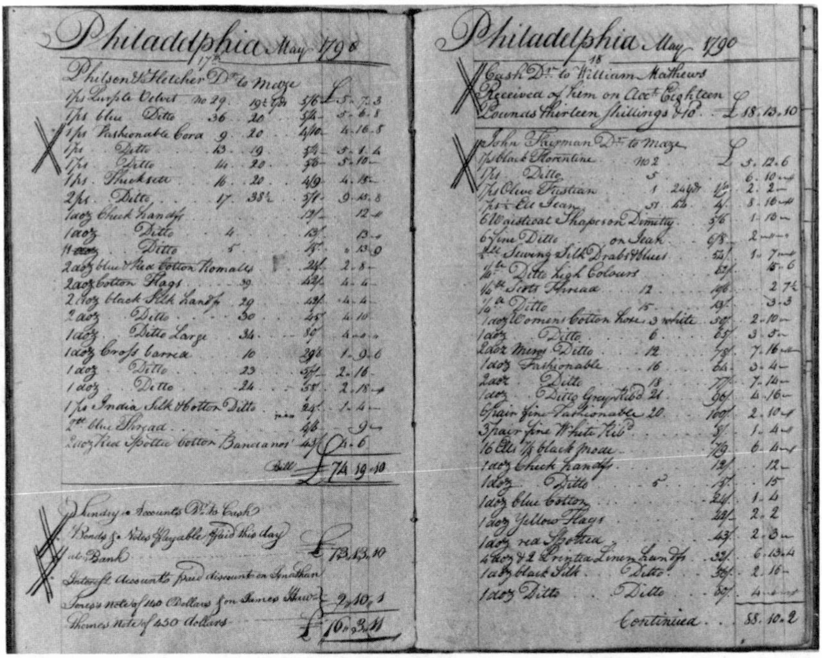

PLATE 12. Daybook of a Philadelphia Merchant. *From Owen Jones and Company Daybook, 1789–1791. Courtesy of The Historical Society of Pennsylvania*

decided to become an importer in 1784. Chaloner announced to a potential supplier, "I have taken the large & commodious house & stores next door to me formerly occupied by Mr Joseph Hillborne . . . my situation affords me not only a great plenty of Store room but every other convenience requisite, which the convenience of my Landlord (who pursued the business many years) dictated to him."[30] The importer could also build a trading network that might include five or ten suppliers in England and a large number of customers scattered through Philadelphia's extensive hinterland. The volume of sales to this group of customers varied widely, both from firm to firm and from year to year. In 1764 William Pollard wrote that he needed sales of at least £3,670 per year to stay in business, but major firms sold over £40,000 in a good year.

30. Chaloner to Theodore Hopkins, Apr. 22, 1784, John Chaloner Letterbook, 1782–1784, 279, Chaloner and White Collection, box 4, HSP.

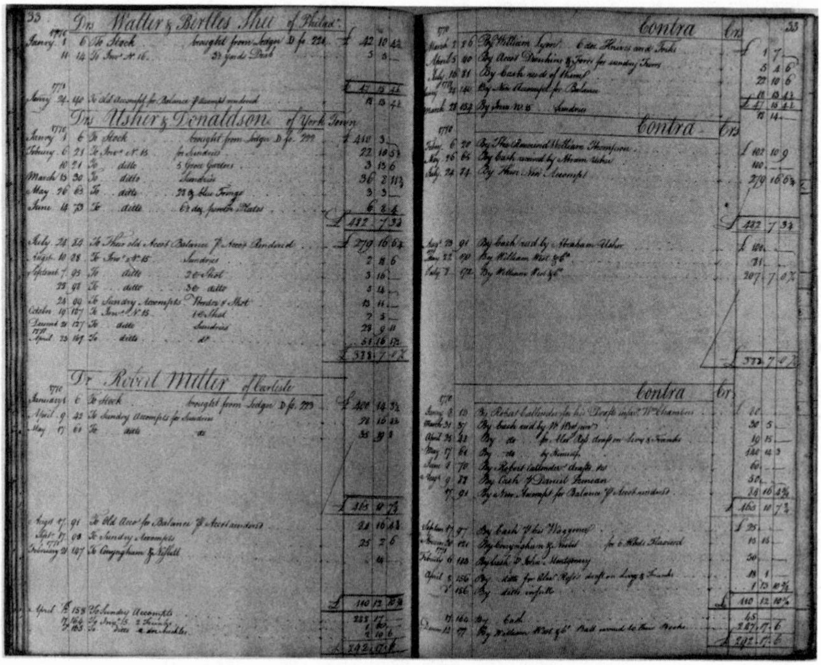

PLATE 13. Ledger of a Philadelphia Merchant. *From William West Ledger, 1770–1777. Courtesy of The Historical Society of Pennsylvania*

Annual sales of £6,500 were an acceptable volume for a middling firm in the late-colonial period.[31]

Roughly a tenth of these sales would be made for cash, while the balance were on credit. Most dry goods wholesalers made credit sales to between 50 and 150 customers per year, but many of these customers made single purchases of only £5 or £10.[32] The wholesalers' bread and

31. William Pollard to John Woolmer, Aug. 18, 1764, William Pollard Letterbook, 1764–1768, 8, Montgomery Collection, Columbia University Library; Daniel Wister Ledger, 1762–1770, Wister Papers, HSP; Joshua Fisher and Sons Ledger, 1769–1773, fol. 110, HSP; Samuel and Miers Fisher Journal, 1792–1795, HSP. Stephen Collins, a successful but not opulent dry goods merchant, achieved sales of £2,504, £7,083, £3,221, £6,343, £18,817, and £3,973 in 1759, 1763, 1768, 1774, 1784, and 1788. Collins Papers, CXVII, CXVIII, CXIX, CXXXI, CXXXII. See Appendix, table A-10.

32. These generalizations are based on table A-10 and on an analysis of the business of Thomas Riche in 1758 and Thomas Wharton in 1761. See Collins Papers; Thomas Riche Journal, 1757–1761, Thomas Riche Papers, HSP; and Thomas Wharton Daybook, 1758–1762. Also informative are Joshua Fisher and Sons Ledger, 1769–1773; William West Ledger, 1770–1777, in William West Account Books, 1769–1804, HSP.

FOR LONDON,

THE SHIP

MARY and ELIZABETH,

NATHANIEL FALCONER,

MASTER,

TO ſail with all convenient Speed. For Freight or Paſſage, apply to JOHN HEAD, or the MASTER, on board the Ship, at Bickley's Wharff, or at the London Coffee-Houſe.

N. B. Said HEAD has imported in the above Ship, and other Veſſels from Briſtol, and now opening, a general Aſſortment of European GOODS. *Fifth-Month 2, 1774.*

FOR BRISTOL,

The SHIP CONCORD,

JOSEPH VOLANS,

MASTER,

A GOOD Ship, well fitted for the Seas, and expected to ſail early in next Month. For Freight or Paſſage, apply to JAMES and DRINKER, or to the Commander, at their Wharff.

Philadelphia, April 25, 1774.

N. B. Arrived in ſaid Ship, a Number of likely healthy SERVANTS, young Men and Boys, their Times of Service to be diſpoſed of, by applying as above.

FOR BRISTOL,

The SHIP SALLY,

A NEW Veſſel, well fitted for the Trade, will be provided with neat and convenient Accommodations for Paſſengers, and is intended to be diſpatched with the firſt Ship. For Freight or Paſſage, apply to

THOMAS CLIFFORD and SONS.

Juſt arrived in the Ship Betſey, Captain Hood, from Briſtol, a Number of indented SERVANTS, Men, Women and Boys, whoſe Times of Service are to be diſpoſed of by THOMAS CLIFFORD and SONS, who have imported in ſaid Ship, a great Variety of MERCHANDIZE.

TO BE SOLD.

PLATE 14. Advertisements of Vessels Bound for England. *Courtesy of The Library Company of Philadelphia*

butter was the core group of customers—10–30 for a medium-sized firm—whose annual purchases ran to between £75 and £250. A good set of reliable customers was invaluable; they could be depended upon to purchase goods year after year and, more important, to pay for them. William Pollard described with admiration a Baltimore merchant who was "a person of very little real, or landed estate, but he came there from the back part of the Country, where he knew every person from whom he has collected a most excellent Sett of Customers."[33] In Philadelphia also, some merchants based their inland trading networks on personal ties. Thomas Clifford had a large number of customers in the upper Delaware Valley, where he had grown up.[34] Joshua Fisher and Sons had many customers in their home base, the future state of Delaware, as did Thomas Wharton (see map 2). By contrast, German merchants like Daniel Wister and John Steinmetz were well established in the heavily German counties of Berks, Lancaster, and York. Wholesalers could hope to retain the loyalty of their clientele for many years; at least 14 of Stephen Collins's customers in 1774, who accounted for 19% of his sales in that year, had dealt with him eleven years earlier as well.[35] Specialized dry goods distributors also benefited from their knowledge of the particular tastes of rural consumers, ignorance of which doomed the efforts of many itinerant traders from Europe who swept into the American market in 1783 and 1784.[36]

A wide range of people, including shopkeepers, artisans, millers, shallopmen, tavernkeepers, and ironmasters, purchased goods from Philadelphia dry goods merchants. Most of these customers of the Philadelphia wholesalers had more than one supplier, an arrangement that provided them with flexibility and leverage in the market, and the bulk of their purchases were made in the spring (May and June) and fall (October and November). Retailing was a highly competitive activity in the towns and villages of the Philadelphia trading area, and consumers were very particular about quality, price, and credit terms. By charging exceptionally low prices in the 1760s, John Cameron of Lancaster was able to wipe out many rival shopkeepers.[37] The competitive strategy of a retailer in Reading relied on using groceries to lure traders into the store: "Sugar Tea Coffee & some other Trifling thing is only the one thing that Brings a

33. William Pollard to Ben. and Jn. Bowers, Feb. 25, 1773, Pollard Letterbook, 1772–1774, 161.

34. Larsen, "Thomas Clifford," 276–305.

35. Stephen Collins Ledger, 1761–1764; Stephen Collins Journal, 1773–1794, Collins Papers, CXVIII, CXXXI.

36. John Chaloner to Wadsworth and Carter, Nov. 1, 1783, Chaloner Letterbook, 1782–1784, 197.

37. Wood, *Conestoga Crossroads*, 100.

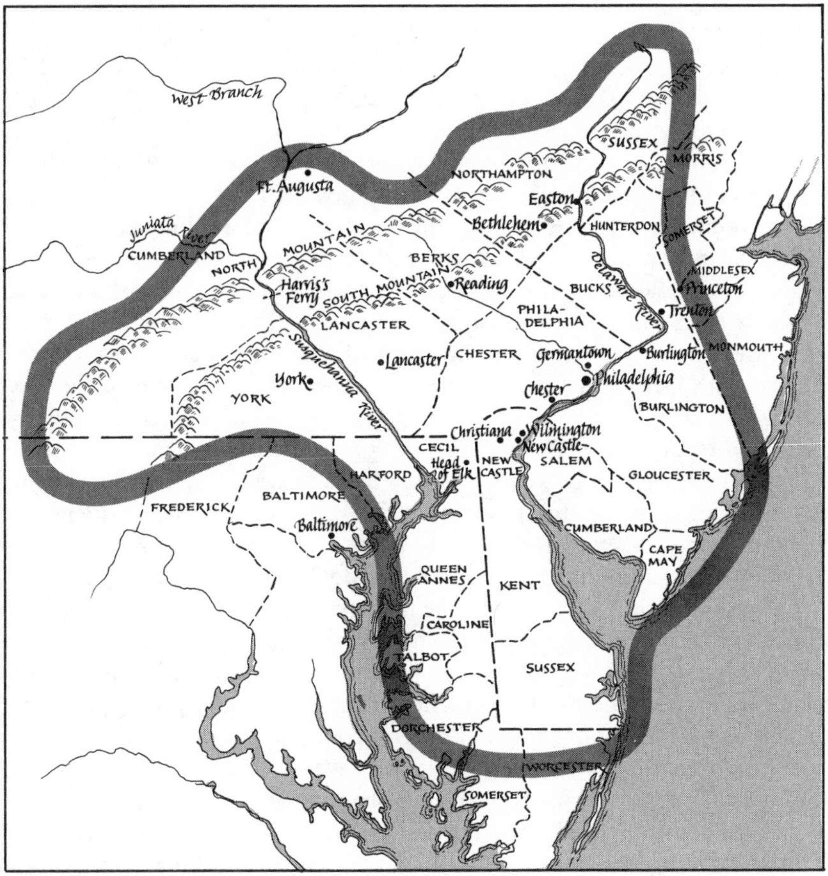

MAP 2. Philadelphia's Local Trading Area, circa 1760. *After John Flexer Walzer, "Transportation in the Philadelphia Trading Area, 1740–1755" (Ph.D. diss., University of Wisconsin, 1968), 3; and Lester J. Cappon* et al., *eds.*, Atlas of Early American History: The Revolutionary Era, 1760–1790 *(Princeton, N.J., 1976), 35. Drawn by Richard Stinely*

store Customers, Especially if we have good Sugar Tea & Coffee . . . Than we soon will have the Towns Custom & then whenever their Friends comes to Town and Wants to Buy Anything than they Always will Recommand [us]."[38] Credit terms were also important for attracting customers: "If I dont Trust some Farmers for Rum & other Articles till

38. Peter Anspach to John Mitchell, Feb. 14, 1773, John Mitchell Sequestered Papers, box 2, PHMC.

After Harvest dont think it will Be to the Advantage of the store as there is Many Able Farmers here has not Cash at this time of the Year."[39]

A glance at any of the long, monotonous lists of goods printed in Philadelphia newspapers reveals unmistakably that advertising was still an undeveloped art in the eighteenth century. Nevertheless, some progress was being made. In organizing a store in Virginia, Kuhn and Risberg made recommendations that obviously drew on their experience in the Philadelphia market. They printed up five hundred handbills announcing the opening of the store, which were to be distributed to customers and posted at warehouses and other public places. They endorsed the idea of retailing liquor in the store and recommended that the casks be placed near the windows. The different cases of groceries were to be clearly labeled with large letters, and it was also important "to *Display* the Dry Goods which is a matter very *essential to promote the Sales* as every Article is to be *in view*." The one exception to this rule was the white goods, which were to be kept in "small handy trunks" to avoid fading in the sunlight. As for some rum that had lost its color, Kuhn and Risberg recommended "a small Keg of colouring . . . for the purpose of giving the Spirits an additional tinge which will add much to the Sale."[40]

The risk of failure was high in the fiercely competitive dry goods trade. Philadelphia merchants were at the mercy of their English suppliers, who might ship off shoddy goods or send them too late in the selling season to get the best of the market. For larger firms with many suppliers, this danger was limited, but for small firms it could be a great worry. "I sweat with fear that they won't be in in time," wrote William Pollard of one shipment.[41] A second danger for wholesalers was that major debtors would go bankrupt without paying their debts: no part of a merchant's estate was more shaky than book debts "spread about the country."

39. John Taylor to John Mitchell, May 31, 1773, Mitchell Papers, box 2. Wood, *Conestoga Crossroads*, 97–112, esp. 97, suggests that there was a shrinkage in the number of shopkeepers in Lancaster and that those who remained, such as Paul Zantzinger, John Cameron, and Charles Hamilton, were large operators with excellent Philadelphia connections. Material from the Mitchell Papers cited here confirms this impression, as does Thomas Armat to John Lorain, Aug. 28, 1789, Thomas Armat Letterbook, 1781–1794, in Loudoun Papers, HSP, in which Armat, himself a large Philadelphia shopkeeper who imported some of his goods from England, discusses the financing of a country store with an inventory of £800: £200 in groceries and £600 in dry goods.

40. Kuhn and Risberg to William French, May 10, Oct. 17, 1785, Aug. 17, 1786, Kuhn and Risberg Letterbook, 1785–1788, Kuhn and Risberg Papers, Bucks County Historical Society.

41. William Pollard to Thomas Swaine, Aug. 28, 1764, Pollard Letterbook, 1764–1768, 12. For similar comments, see Gough and Carmault to William Neate, March 22, 1761, Gough and Carmault Letterbook, 1757–1761, HSP.

Major upheavals such as the Seven Years' War, Pontiac's Rebellion, or the American Revolution wiped out thousands of pounds in these paper assets.[42] The primitive monetary system of the Philadelphia area also posed threats to local wholesalers. A general downturn in the economy could strip the Philadelphia trading area of hard money and make it almost impossible for retailers to collect their debts and make payments to their Philadelphia suppliers. No complaint was more common in Philadelphia letterbooks than "scarcity of cash," a code phrase for slow sales and slower payments. William Pollard reported that "a merch[t] I am well acquainted with told me his Clark had been one Journey & he another in the country to collect 9000£ that had been out from 12 Mos. to three years & they did not both get so much as paid traveling expences."[43]

A fourth, more technical, factor affecting the profitability of the dry goods trade was exchange rate risk. It will be recalled that merchants paid for their dry goods by purchasing and sending to England bills of exchange, whose price fluctuated with the supply and demand for them. Thus, the effective price paid by the Philadelphia wholesaler of imported goods fluctuated with the price of bills (that is, the exchange rate). If the exchange rate happened to increase greatly during the eighteen-month period between the date when goods were ordered from England and the date they had to be paid for, the potential profit on a shipment could be partly wiped out. To see exactly how this might occur, consider the following case. If an importer sold goods worth £100 sterling in England for £195 currency and the exchange rate was £155, he would have to buy a £100 sterling bill of exchange at this price to pay his English supplier and would be left with a profit of £40 (£195 − £155). If, however, the exchange rate was £180, his profit would be only £15 (£195 − £180), or 63 percent less.

The individual elements of risk in the dry goods trade, troublesome enough when taken singly, became a deadly compound when combined in a general market crisis. Moreover, the dry goods trade by its nature was highly cyclical. In certain years dry goods imports ballooned to two or three times their normal level, and for the period 1751–1790, 30 percent of British imports entered Philadelphia in just five years. Typically, imports would sharply accelerate during or immediately after a war, as military spending enriched farmers and inflated demand. But once military spending ended, sales fell off precipitately, while incautious

42. Joseph Turner to David Barclay and Sons, Sept. 6, 1757, Turner Letterbook; on the impact of the Revolution on dry goods traders, see below, chap. 5.

43. William Pollard to Christopher Rawson, Aug. 28, 1764, Pollard Letterbook, 1764–1768, 15.

merchants continued to import goods for several months. Goods ordered six months earlier when sales were strong arrived in Philadelphia only to pile up on wholesalers' shelves. Worse still, many of these wares were particularly expensive because they had been acquired at a time of strong demand and bore the added costs of high wartime insurance and freight rates. Nor were they of the best quality; bought in a seller's market, when British manufacturers had more orders than they could handle, they were often shoddy. Loaded down with these high-priced, low-quality inventories, merchants would jam on the brakes, and imports would fall off sharply. But this did not solve their problems, for the Philadelphians still had to pay off their English suppliers within twelve months or pay 5 percent interest on the outstanding balance. And making remittances was extraordinarily difficult to do. As merchants bought up bills of exchange to pay their sterling debts, the price of bills would rise 10–15 percent. With bills so dear, merchants shipped off specie to London instead, thereby stripping the domestic economy of its circulating medium. For several years after the boom, the scarcity of cash made it impossible for retailers to collect debts from consumers, or for merchants to collect debts from retailers. This pattern of events characterized the depressions of the 1760s and the 1780s, which are discussed in later chapters.

Much of the boom-and-bust character of the dry goods trade may be ascribed to simple greed on the part of established local importers who ordered more goods than they could sell. However, this error in market timing was compounded by the ease of entry into the trade. When sales were quick and margins high, interlopers helped to overstock the market by rushing into Philadelphia to make a fast profit—not only little men handling £2,000 or £3,000 a year, but major foreign traders who added materially to the port's total imports. In 1784, for example, three foreign dry goods concerns failed for, respectively, £70,000, £130,000, and a "considerable amount."[44]

Local firms could be just as reckless. In the spring of 1759, two well-connected Philadelphia Quakers, Daniel Wister and Owen Jones, decided to cash in on the dry goods boom of the Seven Years' War by forming a firm with an initial capital of £4,340. They proceeded to fire off short, arrogant letters to major English suppliers in which, to secure credit, they dropped the names of prominent Philadelphia Friends and then demanded prompt delivery of large orders of goods. From twenty-three firms in six English cities Jones and Wister received during the next three years goods totaling £94,147. This equaled fully 4 percent of Penn-

44. Chaloner to Wadsworth and Church, July 3, 1784, Chaloner Letterbook, 325.

sylvania's total imports from Great Britain in 1759, 1760, and 1761. For a while sales kept pace—they amounted to £29,523 in 1760—but when the market soured in 1761, the firm desperately tried to countermand all orders. By then it was too late; Daniel Wister went bankrupt, and for the rest of the decade Owen Jones struggled to wind up the firm's affairs. Imperious orders for more goods on better terms were replaced by a complaint of a different type: "I wish many on your side of the water were more Careful how you have such large Credits to us on this Side."[45]

The Provision Trade

In marketing strategy, financial organization, and the nature of day-to-day operations, the provision merchant differed considerably from the dry goods distributor. While the importer of manufactures faced inland, the provision merchant looked out to sea. The axis of his risk was not only temporal, but spatial; not only did he have to gauge demand for some product six months hence, he had also to assess its relative profitability in Jamaica or London. Exporting, not importing, was the activity from which most provision traders made their greatest profits, and if they wished to have flexibility in the timing of their shipments, they had to own a vessel. The heavy involvement in shipping enormously complicated the finances of the provision trade, for ships were expensive to buy and operate. More burdensome still, both vessels and cargoes had to be financed with cash, not with long-term credits extended from London or Bristol. It was a risky, complicated, hazardous commerce demanding careful management of cash and shrewd selection among numerous options. But provision trading could also be lucrative, more so than the chronically overstocked dry goods trade.

Should he operate on commission or on his own account? This was one of four key choices confronting the provision merchant, and as with most mercantile decisions, capital and credit were key considerations. Partly out of custom and partly because London finance was not involved, this branch of commerce was managed on the basis of cash or short-term credit, rather than the twelve-month credit extended in the dry goods trade. Thus, it was not possible for the provision merchant to buy two thousand barrels of flour from a miller on six months' credit, send them to Jamaica and receive payment in five months, pay off the miller, and pocket the profit. Impecunious farmers and millers demanded cash on the spot. Shipping operated on the same terms: the shipbuilder

45. Owen Jones Letterbook, 1759–1781, and Owen Jones to Cooke, Lawrence, and Co., May 1, 1764; Jones and Wister Daybook A, 1759–1761, esp. entries for Apr. 20, 1759, both in Owen Jones Papers, HSP; Jones and Wister Invoice Book, 1759–1762, HSP.

PLATE 15. The Arch Street Ferry. *From W. Birch and Son,* The City of Philadelphia . . . As It Appeared in 1800. *Courtesy of The Historical Society of Pennsylvania*

and associated craftsmen had to be supplied with cash as their work progressed, for they did not have access to independent sources of financing. Consequently, a young merchant with limited resources who wished to take title to the goods he traded would have to start small. Unable to afford the cost of owning and operating even a small sloop or schooner, he would export, or "adventure," shipments of flour, staves, pork, and flaxseed in the holds of other merchants' vessels, paying the going freight rate for the privilege. Normally the goods would be received and sold in the foreign port by an agent who charged a commission for every service he rendered—selling, buying, making insurance, storage, and so on. The risk was, of course, that after deduction of all expenses, the sales price overseas would not exceed the purchase price in Philadelphia.

Instead of, or in addition to, trading on his own account, a merchant could himself act as a commission agent for merchants trading to Philadelphia. His major responsibilities would be to keep his correspondent constantly informed of market conditions, sell all consignments quickly and profitably, and remit the net sales promptly so that the consignor could make another investment with his money. At first glance, this was an excellent way for a merchant to conduct his business. There was no initial outlay in a cargo, and the risks remained with the consignor. Profits or no, the consignee charged his commission. The difficulty was that few consignors ever had enough cash, so there was a constant tug-of-war for ready money between the commission agent and his correspondent. In order to attract business, consignees were often obliged to send remittances for consignments they had not yet sold, which made them creditors of ("put them in advance to") their principals. This practice was particularly common when vessels were serviced for a commission, for ships had to be refitted, loaded, and sent back out to sea immediately, while their inward cargo might not sell for weeks. One merchant declared, "Ever Since Ive been in Bussiness I never knew one Instance where we have been able to dispose of an Inward Cargoe, or Receive one half the Cost of the outward One before we dispatch'd the Vessell, & have always been in advance." Thus even the commission merchant had to invest his own capital in trade, and this investment entailed real risk; if the consignor went bankrupt, he could lose part of his capital.[46]

A second decision facing the provision merchant was whether to own shipping. It was not essential to do so, but for two major reasons many traders did. Ships were invariably a headache, but if properly managed, they could be a lucrative investment. One or two highly successful voyages could garner enough freight earnings to cover the initial cost of a vessel. Shipowners usually preferred to rent out their vessels as carriers because this practice brought in precious cash with which to cover operating costs. When demand for carriers was slack, however, a shipowner was forced to fill his ship with his own cargoes. In consequence, every shipowner was, willy-nilly, a provision merchant. In addition to being valuable sources of income, vessels were useful trading tools, because they afforded the exporter latitude in the selection and timing of shipments. Although freight space for exports to most markets was usually available in abundance, it was likely to be most scarce and expensive at precisely those times when the most money was to be made in trade. When news of a war or of a crop failure in a foreign market reached the Quaker City, exporters scrambled to secure shipping, which rapidly drove up prices and depleted the supply.[47] On the other hand, the great

46. On the commission merchant and his problems, see Harry D. Berg, "The Organization of Business in Colonial Philadelphia," *Pennsylvania History*, X (1943), 157–177; Henderson Papers; Turner to John and William Halliday, June 1757, and Turner to David Barclay and Sons, Jan. 19, 1759, Turner Letterbook; 1753–1774; T. Willing to Coddrington Carrington, May 26, 1755, Willing and Morris Letterbook, 97.

47. Pollard to John Dorsius, Apr. 2, 1774, and Pollard to Thomas Earle, May 16, 1774, Pollard Letterbook, 1772–1774, 376, 423; J. and D. to Hillary and Scott, Feb. 25, 1757, James and Drinker Letterbook, 1756–1759, 94.

provision traders, such as Reese Meredith and Willing and Morris, owned several vessels and could reach any part of the Atlantic world where money was to be made.

Ships were expensive. A sloop or schooner could be obtained for five hundred pounds, but a good snow or ship, suitable for transatlantic trade, cost about two thousand pounds, and three times as much when demand for ships was high. Vessels had to be bought for cash, and few Philadelphia firms had this kind of money lying around their counting-houses. Even if they did, they usually did not care to take the risk of investing it in only one bottom. Most firms therefore coinvested in ships with one or more other firms, either local or foreign, as well as, in many cases, with the master of the ship. Such syndicates seldom had more than seven individual investors, and 87 percent of all the syndicates listed in the ship register had fewer than four. None of these partners was silent; each demanded a say about where the vessel was sent and how it was to be managed. Disagreements and disputes inevitably followed, and as the century wore on, wealthier firms, in order to minimize such friction, increasingly owned their ships outright. However they structured their holdings, few Philadelphia firms could own many vessels; at one point in 1769 62 percent owned only one ship, and only 11 percent possessed three or more.[48]

The expenses had only begun when the vessel was acquired, for it continued to be a voracious consumer of cash—for wages, repairs, provisions, and bribes. Routine costs of outfitting a ship could go as high as £250, major repairs might run to £900, and the cargoes themselves ranged in price from £500 to £3,000.[49] These charges were unpredict-

48. On the price of vessels, see Appendix, table A-4. The cost of £11 3s. per measured ton stated in McCusker, "Sources of Investment Capital," *Jour. Econ. Hist.*, XXXII (1972), 150, is too low for many vessels. On the makeup of shipping syndicates, see Crowther, "Shipbuilding Industry," 193. On disagreements among owners of vessels, see Fuller to Robert Totten, July 17, 1784, Benjamin Fuller Letterbook, 1784–1787, 26, Benjamin Fuller Papers, 1762–1799, HSP; Roberdeau to Charles and Alexander Stedman, Feb. 13, 1767, Daniel Roberdeau Letterbook, 1764–1771, 132, HSP. Figures for 1769 are based on the Tonnage Duty Book.

49. Merchants used the concept of disbursements, which referred to port charges, wharfage, wages of seamen and dockhands, as well as costs of repairing, provisioning, and otherwise making the vessel ready for its next voyage. See Pollard to Capt. William Williams, Oct. 28, 1772, and Pollard to Peter Holme, Nov. 11, 1772, July 10, Dec. 18, 1773, Pollard Letterbook, 1772–1774, 90, 104, 229, 342; James C. Fisher Journals, 1783–1787, 112, 167–168, 205–206, 296, Leonard T. Beale Collection, HSP; Samuel and Miers Fisher Journal, esp. 7–31, for disbursements of ship *Sussex*. On cargo size, see O., D., and G. to Oliver Birch and John Pooler, Mar. 29, 1768, and to Mussender Auld, Mar. 11, 1768, Orr, Dunlope, and Glenholme Letterbook, 1767–1769, HSP; J. and D. to Zachary Phillip Fonnereau and Sons, Nov. 27, 1772, James and Drinker Foreign Letterbook, 1772–1785, 64,

TABLE 9. *Shipping Activity from Geographical Sectors of Philadelphia Trade, 1773*

	Ships				Tonnage Entering	
Sector	No.	Mean Tonnage	Owned by Philadelphia Resident or Supercargo	Consigned to Shipmaster	No. of Tons	Portion of Total
West Indies	252	76.4	68.1%	8.5%	19,261	36.4%
Coastwise, north	117	56.9	18.1	63.2	6,661	12.6
Coastwise, south	143	48.7	51.0	24.4	6,963	13.2
Southern Europe	73	122.0	96.3	.9	8,908	16.9
England	52	147.9	71.7	4.5	7,691	14.6
Ireland	27	124.6	52.6	0.0	3,364	6.4

Source: Tonnage Duties on Incoming Vessels, November 1, 1765–August 30, 1775, 3 vols., Cadwalader Collection, Thomas Cadwalader Section, Historical Society of Pennsylvania.

Note: Covers only vessels for which a provenance is stated in document.

able and not easily postponed, for when a vessel entered port, it had to be dispatched as quickly as possible to minimize port charges. Under such circumstances, even a wealthy firm like Orr, Dunlope, and Glenholme, whose bankruptcy was described in the previous chapter, could not survive if it failed to protect its financial liquidity. To do just this, shipping merchants tied up much less of their capital in numerous backcountry accounts than did dry goods merchants. While large importers had well over 300 open accounts in all, the shippers Benjamin Fuller and Stephen Girard had 160 and 85, respectively. The partners in still another active shipping firm remarked that they could call in their debts rapidly, if necessary, a feat few importers could have achieved. This fi-

Henry Drinker Papers, HSP; Larsen, "Thomas Clifford," 105. Traders were often surprised by the cost of running a vessel. See F. and J. West to Munns West, Aug. 31, 1784, Francis and John West Letterbook, 1783–1786, 66, William West Account Books; Roberdeau to Meyler and Hall, Oct. 21, 1765, Roberdeau Letterbook; O., D., and G. to Andrew Orr, Dec. 16, 1767, Orr, Dunlope, and Glenholme Letterbook; Girard to John Girard, May 24, 1784, Girard Papers, 2d Ser., Reel 121.

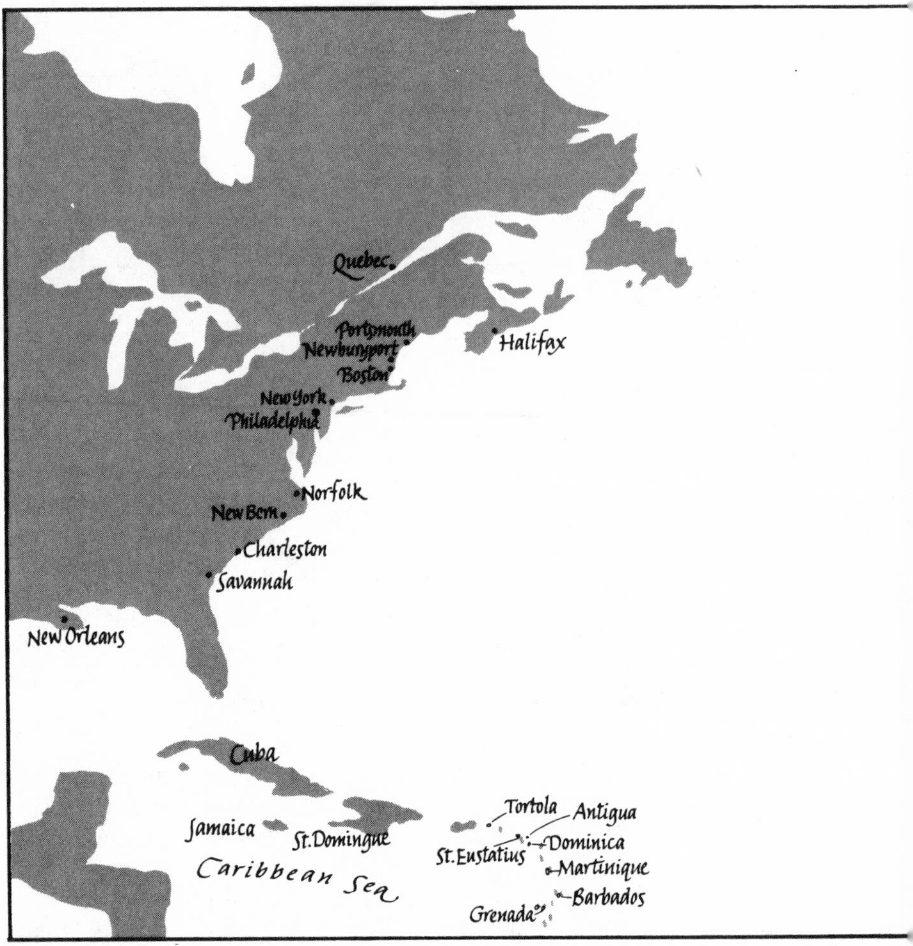

MAP 3. Philadelphia's Major Markets by Sea, 1750–1791.
Drawn by Richard Stinely

nancial structure reflected the fact that the provision merchant, preoccupied with dozens of details regarding his ships and cargoes, concentrated his affairs at the waterfront. As will be explained shortly, he left to other Philadelphia businessmen the onerous task of dealing with widely scattered millers, farmers, and shopkeepers.[50]

50. Joshua Fisher and Sons Ledger, 1769–1773, 1–111; William West Ledger, 1–66; Fuller Journal, 1782–1789, 360–363; Stephen Girard Journal, 1788–1790, entries for Dec. 31, 1790, Girard Papers, 3d Ser., Reel 44.

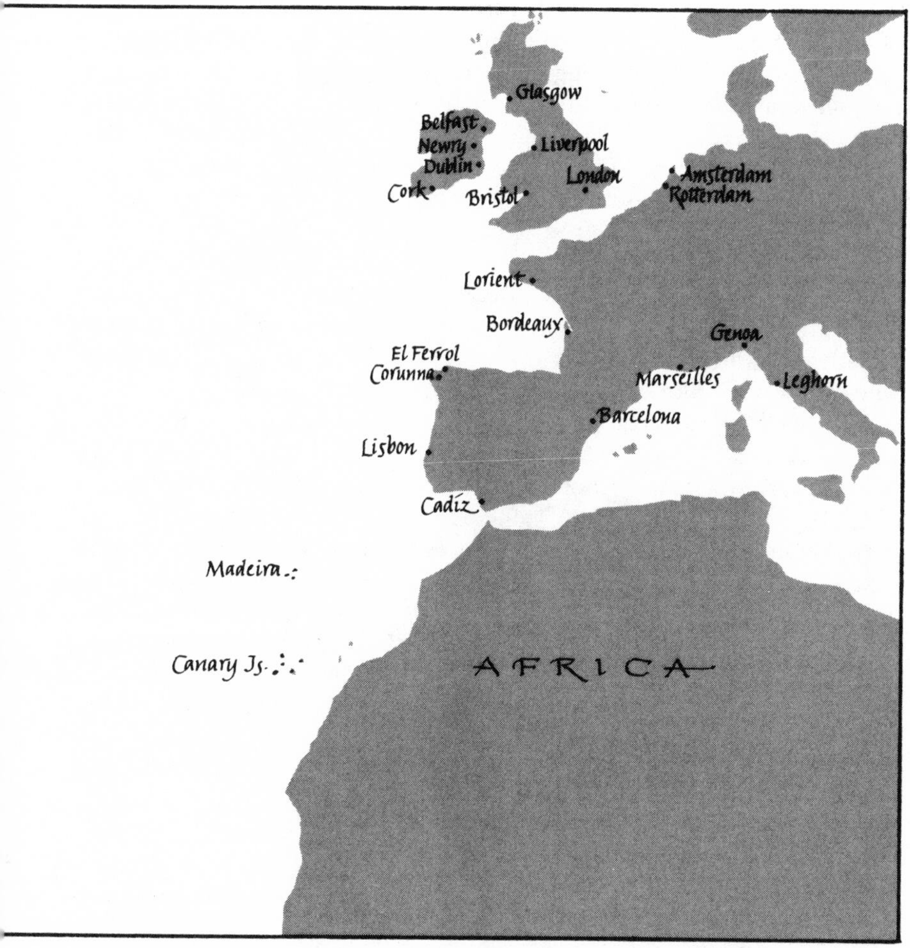

The third major problem confronting the Philadelphia provision merchant was the choice of market area in which to trade (see map 3 and table 9). Ireland, the North American coast, the West Indies, and southern Europe were all open to Philadelphia shipping, and each sector had a distinctive character. The Irish market was among the most specialized, for it focused on a single product—flaxseed—which sustained the burgeoning linen industry of northern Ireland.[51] An average of thirty large

51. On the Irish trade, see especially Orr, Dunlope, and Glenholme Letterbook; Clark Letterbook; Jensen, *Maritime Commerce*, 85–87. For a fine discussion of the trade from a New York perspective, see Philip L. White, *The Beekmans of New York in Politics and Commerce, 1647–1877* (New York, 1956), 235–264.

ships per year entered Philadelphia from Ireland during the third quarter of the eighteenth century, and the shipping volume was essentially stable in this period, neither growing nor declining significantly. Since the supply and demand for flaxseed was relatively predictable, this trade was primarily a source of freight earnings for Philadelphia merchants, rather than a potential source of large, speculative gains such as the flour trade with the West Indies and the Iberian Peninsula sometimes offered. The trade was in the hands of a restricted group of Irish merchants, many of them wealthy recent immigrants, who tended also to trade with the Caribbean and southern Europe. However, their flexibility to employ vessels in those markets was curtailed by the importance of having ships in Philadelphia during the few critical weeks in November and December when flaxseed had to be purchased and shipped off to Ireland.

Also troubling was the problem of what to bring back from Ireland. Linen was a possibility, but it had to touch in an English port before clearing for America.[52] Another possibility was indentured servants, a cargo that offered substantial gains but special problems, whether imported from Ireland, England, or Germany. Shipping merchants liked to deal in servants because in Philadelphia they could be sold for ready money—a powerful inducement for merchants spending large amounts of cash to operate their vessels. Unfortunately, servants were also a risky cargo because it took a long time to accumulate enough of them to justify a voyage, and there was always a danger that, failing to sell rapidly in Philadelphia, they would rapidly eat up the profit they were supposed to generate. In order to forestall this possibility, merchants were keen to import only high-quality servants who would command a quick and ready sale. Males were favored over females, Englishmen over Irishmen, young people over adults, and tradesmen of all kinds over common laborers. Because the cargo was mobile, it could be sent off to the country if it did not sell rapidly at the waterfront.[53]

Large and heterogeneous, Philadelphia's trade with the American coast was bifurcated into northern and southern regions. Trade to the north, chiefly involving the exportation of provisions to fill the food deficit of New England, was almost entirely in the hands of able Yankee capitalists. New Englanders themselves owned most of the shipping in

52. See Benjamin Fuller to John Scott, Aug. 26, 1768, Fuller Letterbook, 1762–1781.

53. On the servant trade with Ireland, England, and Germany, see the following: Daniel Clark to Edward Cochran, Nov. 23, Dec. 5, 1761, Clark Letterbook, 123, 129; Richard Neave, Jr., Account Book, HSP; Larsen, "Thomas Clifford," 110–124; Joseph Turner to Wolffindin and Birchinsha, Sept. 1756, and to Jacob Basanquart, Sept. 1756, Turner Letterbook, 1754–1763; Francis and John West to Munns West, Aug. 9, 12, 14, 31, Sept. 30, 1784, Francis and John West Letterbook, 1783–1786, 59, 61, 62, 66.

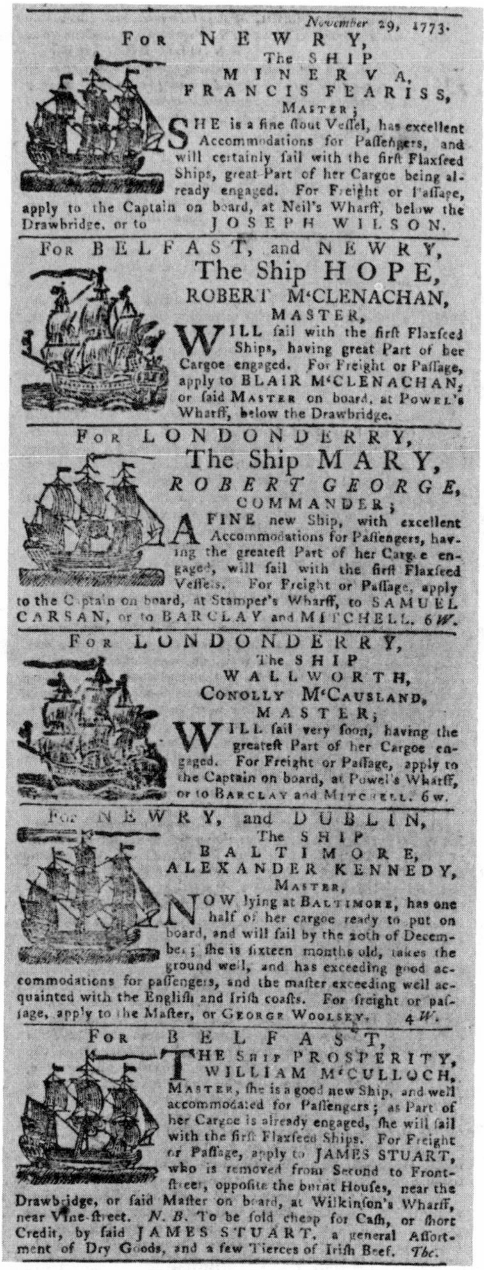

November 29, 1773.

FOR NEWRY,
The SHIP
MINERVA,
FRANCIS FEARISS,
MASTER;

SHE is a fine ſtout Veſſel, has excellent Accommodations for Paſſengers, and will certainly ſail with the firſt Flaxſeed Ships, great Part of her Cargoe being already engaged. For Freight or Paſſage, apply to the Captain on board, at Neil's Wharff, below the Drawbridge, or to JOSEPH WILSON.

FOR BELFAST, and NEWRY,
The Ship HOPE,
ROBERT M'CLENACHAN,
MASTER,

WILL ſail with the firſt Flaxſeed Ships, having great Part of her Cargoe engaged. For Freight or Paſſage, apply to BLAIR M'CLENACHAN, or ſaid MASTER on board, at POWEL'S Wharff, below the Drawbridge.

FOR LONDONDERRY,
The Ship MARY,
ROBERT GEORGE,
COMMANDER;

A FINE new Ship, with excellent Accommodations for Paſſengers, having the greateſt Part of her Cargoe engaged, will ſail with the firſt Flaxſeed Veſſels. For Freight or Paſſage, apply to the Captain on board, at Stamper's Wharff, to SAMUEL CARSAN, or to BARCLAY and MITCHELL. 6*W*.

FOR LONDONDERRY,
The SHIP
WALLWORTH,
CONOLLY M'CAUSLAND,
MASTER;

WILL ſail very ſoon, having the greateſt Part of her Cargoe engaged. For Freight or Paſſage, apply to the Captain on board, at Powel's Wharff, or to BARCLAY and MITCHELL. 6 w.

FOR NEWRY, and DUBLIN,
The SHIP
BALTIMORE,
ALEXANDER KENNEDY,
MASTER,

NOW lying at BALTIMORE, has one half of her cargoe ready to put on board, and will ſail by the 20th of December; ſhe is ſixteen months old, takes the ground well, and has exceeding good accommodations for paſſengers, and the maſter exceeding well acquainted with the Engliſh and Iriſh coaſts. For freight or paſſage, apply to the Maſter, or GEORGE WOOLSEY. 4 *W*.

FOR BELFAST,

THE SHIP PROSPERITY, WILLIAM M'CULLOCH, MASTER, ſhe is a good new Ship, and well accommodated for Paſſengers; as Part of her Cargoe is already engaged, ſhe will ſail with the firſt Flaxſeed Ships. For Freight or Paſſage, apply to JAMES STUART, who is removed from Second to Front-ſtreet, oppoſite the burnt Houſes, near the Drawbridge, or ſaid Maſter on board, at Wilkinſon's Wharff, near Vine-ſtreet. *N. B.* To be ſold cheap for Caſh, or ſhort Credit, by ſaid JAMES STUART, a general Aſſortment of Dry Goods, and a few Tierces of Iriſh Beef. *Tbc.*

PLATE 16. Advertisements of Vessels Bound for Ireland. *Courtesy of The Library Company of Philadelphia*

PLATE 17. View of Philadelphia from Kensington. *From W. Birch and Son,* The City of Philadelphia . . . As It Appeared in 1800. *Courtesy of The Historical Society of Pennsylvania*

the area's trade with Philadelphia, and since over half of the vessels sent to the Delaware from northern ports were consigned to the master of the ship, Philadelphia traders did not even pick up a commission for handling the vessel. The cargoes, too, were normally owned by the New England merchants. The earnings of the Philadelphia traders were thus restricted to a commission for assembling the outward cargoes of flour, bar iron, and other goods and selling the inward shipments of rum, fish, whale oil, and candles. A certain number of large firms, notably Samuel Smith, Francis Richardson, and Coates and Reynell, specialized in this activity and handled ten to twenty incoming vessels each year.[54]

In contrast to the New England trade, Philadelphians played a central

54. Jensen, *Maritime Commerce*, 70–76; Josiah and Samuel Coates Papers, Coates and Reynell Collection, HSP, esp. Bills of Lading, 1786–1791; James B. Hedges, *The Browns of Providence Plantations: The Colonial Years* (Cambridge, Mass., 1952), 155–174. The shipping activity of Samuel Smith and Francis Richardson may be followed in the Tonnage Duty Book.

role in trade with the South and, in fact, carried out certain entrepôt functions for the region.[55] This trade principally involved the importation of agricultural staples—indigo and rice from South Carolina, naval stores from North Carolina, tobacco from Virginia and Maryland—and the exportation to the South of European and local manufactures, Caribbean groceries, New England rum, and (to South Carolina) meat and flour. Philadelphia's role in the southern economies extended well beyond a simple exchange of commodities, however. Philadelphia merchants owned half of the shipping in the southern trade, they provided such financial services as making insurance and marketing bills of exchange, and they were increasingly involved in shipping to Europe the key southern staples—tobacco, wheat, and (to a lesser extent) rice. By the 1770s the northern Chesapeake region was becoming virtually a part of Philadelphia's hinterland, a process that was hastened by the disruption of the tobacco trade with England during the Revolution but was eventually cut short by the decisive rise of Baltimore during the last quarter of the eighteenth century.

Diverse in structure though it was, trade with Ireland, New England, and the southern coast shared one feature: it was not large and homogeneous enough for demand shifts in these markets to drive the business cycle of Philadelphia. By contrast, when the price of flour in the West Indies and Iberia soared, the demand for shipping in Philadelphia expanded, and so did the earnings of Delaware Valley farmers, whose purchases of dry goods rose accordingly. But though the West Indies and the Iberian Peninsula were both dynamic markets, they differed significantly. Trade with the Caribbean involved dozens of different islands, ranging in size from mere specks in the ocean to the large islands of Jamaica and Hispaniola (see map 4).[56] These islands regularly consumed large quantities of flour, bread, and lumber, but the price of these commodities was affected by several factors. For one thing, merchants from many North American ports shipped flour down to a given island, and thus these

55. Jensen, *Maritime Commerce*, 77–84; Pollard to Bowers, July 24, 1773, Pollard Letterbook, 1772–1774, 238; Levi Hollingsworth Ledger H, 1783–1784, 260, Hollingsworth Papers, HSP; Clement Biddle and Co. Letterbook, 1760–1770, Clement Biddle Papers, HSP; James and Drinker to John Clitherall, Jan. 1, Dec. 22, 1757, and to ———, Oct. 13, 1757, James and Drinker Letterbook, 1756–1759, 69, 208, 181.

56. On the West Indies trade, see Jensen, *Maritime Commerce*, 42–46; Richard Pares, *Yankees and Creoles: The Trade between North America and the West Indies before the American Revolution* (Cambridge, Mass., 1956); John Batho Letterbook, 1765–1768, HSP; Girard Papers, 2d Ser., Reel 121. William S. Sachs, "The Business Outlook in the Northern Colonies, 1750–1775" (Ph.D. diss., Columbia University, 1957), 64–96, provides a good discussion of how the West Indies trade was affected by the Seven Years' War. See also Willing and Morris Letterbook, and Turner Letterbook, 1753–1774.

small markets could be quickly glutted, even if the exports from Philadelphia alone were not excessive. But, on the other hand, hurricanes could swell the demand for foodstuffs and lumber. Imported foodstuffs had to compete with locally grown "ground provisions" such as yams and plantains. War, too, frequently transformed the West Indies market. During the Seven Years' War, the presence of British fleets in the Caribbean raised the demand for provisions there, and the French islands, cut off from the mother country, were willing to sell rum and molasses cheaply and to pay steep prices for North American produce. In addition, American merchants garnered windfall profits by purchasing French sugar and reexporting it to Europe.[57]

The classic pattern of the West Indies trade was for Philadelphia traders to adventure flour, bread, and lumber to the Caribbean on their own account and in their own ships.[58] Although it was quite practical to entrust the sale of the cargo to a captain or supercargo, most merchants employed an agent in the island who could make use of warehouse facilities to time the sale of a product more advantageously than a transient trader was able to do. The merchant hoped to earn his major gains on the outward cargo: the return shipment of sugar, rum, and molasses was chiefly important as a way of getting a quick return on his invested capital. So intent were the merchants on quickly getting their hands on their funds that they were willing to accept small losses on the return cargoes of groceries. Because Philadelphia's balance of trade with the Caribbean was favorable, the difference in value between outward and inward cargoes was made up by sending specie and bills of exchange northward. Never noted for high standards of business ethics, the West Indians' bills of exchange were not as highly valued as those written by merchants in southern Europe or the Chesapeake.

The Caribbean was gradually superseded as Philadelphia's most dynamic export market by Madeira, the Canaries, and the Iberian Peninsula, an area subsumed under the rubric "southern Europe." Tonnage clearing to this sector amounted to only 20 percent of West Indies tonnage during the 1750s, but by 1769, after a steady rise during the preceding decade, traffic to southern Europe exceeded clearances to the Caribbean.[59] Although the West Indies may have remained a somewhat larger market in most years, southern Europe was clearly a more lucra-

57. Sachs, "Business Outlook," 83–89.

58. See Marc Egnal's fine article, "The Changing Structure of Philadelphia's Trade with the British West Indies, 1750–1775," *PMHB*, XCIX (1975), 156–179.

59. Egnal, "Pennsylvania Economy," 328–329, lists the tonnage clearing to these two sectors. This listing understates the importance of southern Europe to Philadelphia during the 1760s and 1770s because many Philadelphia vessels collected cargoes of grain in the Chesapeake and shipped them directly across the Atlantic.

tive destination for Philadelphia provisions during the periods 1769–1775 and 1789–1792, when exports to the region boomed. The fundamental reasons for this trend were the demographic expansion and poor harvests in Europe, which together reduced the ability of the traditional provisioners of Portugal and Spain—England, Sicily, and the Levant—to meet the peninsula's needs.[60] Straitened by the stagnation of the West Indies trade, Philadelphia provision merchants eagerly took up the slack, extending the trade not only quantitatively but geographically. Still something of a novelty in 1760, trade with the ports beyond the Strait of Gibraltar—Leghorn, Barcelona, and Genoa—was commonplace by 1772 (see map 5).[61] Marseilles became a major port after the Revolution.

Although more research on the organization of the southern Europe trade is needed, it apparently consisted of three main commercial patterns. A small group of specialized merchants concentrated on the importation of wine from Madeira, Lisbon, and Tenerife and placed limited emphasis on the exportation of foodstuffs.[62] Far more important was the flour export trade to Lisbon, Cádiz, and other mainland ports, which was organized along the lines of the pre-1765 West Indies trade.[63] Using their own vessels and financial resources, Philadelphia merchants sent regular shipments of provisions across the Atlantic and accepted both the gains and losses of the market. This trade was heavily concentrated not only in the single port of Lisbon but in the hands of a single foreign firm, Parr and Bulkeley, which may have handled over half of all the Philadelphia shipping bound to Lisbon during the 1760s and 1770s.[64] In an indiscreet moment the firm boasted that it could manipulate the price of flour in Lisbon in order to enhance the profits of its correspondents.[65]

60. Sachs, "Business Outlook," 171–175; Jensen, *Maritime Commerce*, 64, 65.

61. Jensen, *Maritime Commerce*, 58.

62. See Cropley Rose Letterbook, 1779–1781, HSP; Daniel Roberdeau to John Sibbald, May 20, 1765, Roberdeau Letterbook; Orr, Dunlope, and Glenholme to Walter Marshall and Co., Sept. 23, 1767, Orr, Dunlope, and Glenholme Letterbook; Clymer-Meredith-Read Collection, New York Public Library.

63. See Jasper Yates Brinton Collection, box 2, HSP, concerning trade between Keppelle and Steinmetz of Philadelphia and Parr and Bulkeley of Philadelphia before the Revolution, and Charles Wharton Daybook, 1775–1785, Wharton Papers, HSP. See also James G. Lydon, "Fish and Flour for Gold: Southern Europe and the Colonial American Balance of Payments," *Business History Review*, XXXIX (1965), 171–183.

64. Parr and Bulkeley to Keppelle and Steinmetz, Apr. 3, 1772, Brinton Collection, box 2, mentions that the firm expects three vessels from major Philadelphia shipping merchants. Thomas Riche to Parr and Bulkeley, May 26, 1770, Thomas Riche Letterbook, 1764–1771, Riche Papers, mentions the large business of the Lisbon firm.

65. Parr and Bulkeley to Keppelle and Steinmetz, Aug. 6, 1772, Brinton Collection, box 2.

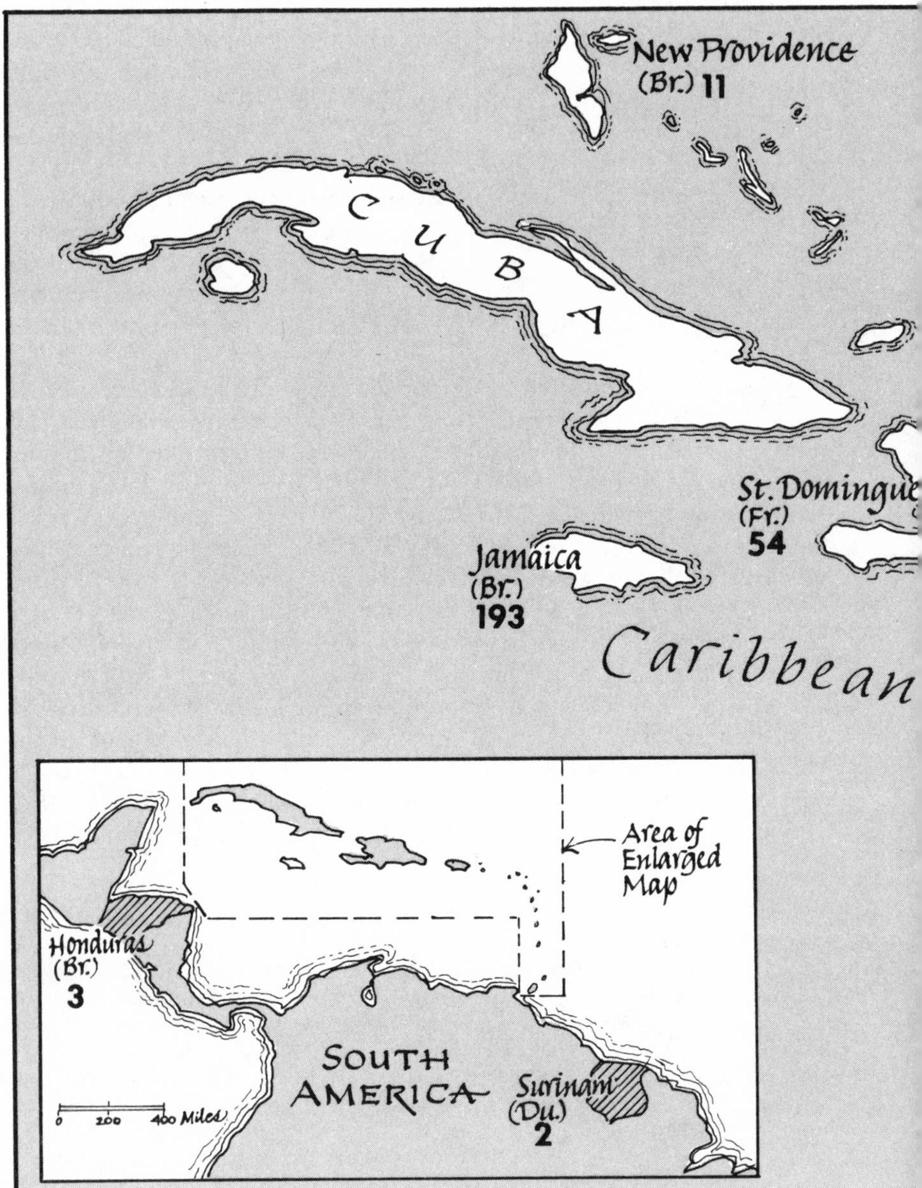

MAP 4. Vessels Entering Philadelphia from the West Indian Region, 1774. *After Lester J. Cappon* et al., *eds.*, Atlas of Early American History: The Revolutionary Era, 1760–1790 *(Princeton, N.J., 1976), 7.*
Drawn by Richard Stinely

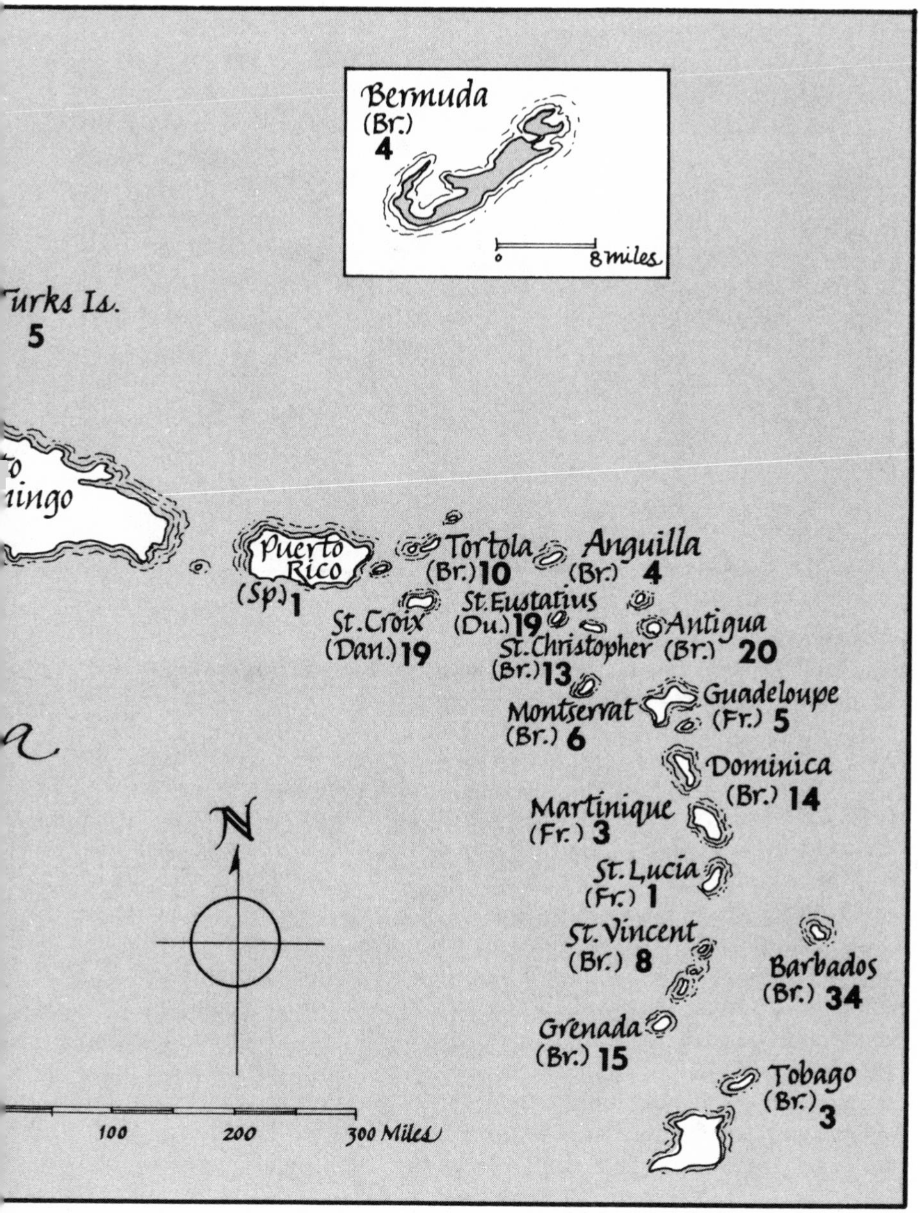
Bermuda
(Br.)
4
0
8 miles
Turks Is.
5
Puerto
Rico
(Sp.) 1
Tortola
(Br.) 10
Anguilla
(Br.) 4
St. Eustatius
(Du.) 19
St. Croix
(Dan.) 19
Antigua
(Br.) 20
St. Christopher
(Br.) 13
Montserrat
(Br.) 6
Guadeloupe
(Fr.) 5
Dominica
(Br.) 14
Martinique
(Fr.) 3
St. Lucia
(Fr.) 1
St. Vincent
(Br.) 8
Barbados
(Br.) 34
Grenada
(Br.) 15
Tobago
(Br.) 3
N
100
200
300 Miles

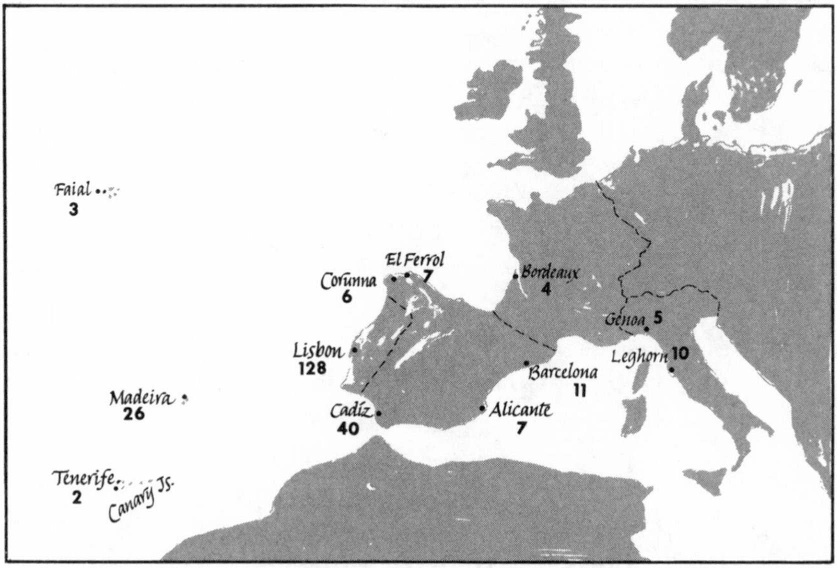

MAP 5. Vessels Entering Philadelphia from Southern Europe, 1772–1775. *Data from Tonnage Duties on Incoming Vessels, Nov. 1, 1765–Aug. 30, 1776, 3 vols., Cadwalader Collection, Thomas Cadwalader Section, Historical Society of Pennsylvania. Drawn by Richard Stinely*

A third part of the southern Europe trade, which might be termed the speculative wheat trade, flourished during periods of particularly strong demand for breadstuffs. In contrast to the regular flour trade with Lisbon, this commercial pattern typically involved a few large shipments of wheat (often obtained in Maryland or Virginia) to a British house in Cádiz, Lisbon, or Barcelona. Since a continuous trade between two ports was not contemplated, chartered vessels were frequently used, and the Philadelphia house commonly acted only as a factor, receiving a generous commission for arranging shipments worth two or three thousand pounds each. Whether he took a share of the cargo or only earned a commission, the Philadelphian financed the venture by drawing on the European houses for at least two-thirds of the value of the cargo.[66] More than one Philadelphia firm collapsed because the English house at the

66. See William Pollard to Peter Holme, July 20, 1772, Pollard Letterbook, 1772–1774, 53; Joshua Fisher and Sons Ledger, fol. 119; James and Drinker to Richard Forde and Co., Nov. 23, 1772, to Zachary Philip Fonnereau and Sons, Nov. 27, 1772, to Belli and Fonnereau, Nov. 27, 1772, to Zachary Philip Fonnereau and Sons, Jan. 4, 1773, James and Drinker Foreign Letterbook, 59, 64, 66, 88.

end of the voyage failed to honor the drafts.[67] The speculative wheat trade was by far the most dynamic part of the southern Europe trade. When favorable market reports and swollen orders hit the Philadelphia waterfront, the great shipping merchants swung into action, laying out thousands of pounds to purchase cargoes of wheat, corn, and flour and paying top prices to charter vessels. English merchants in 1790 described with amazement the fleet of ships clearing for southern Europe—four vessels dispatched by Thomas, Samuel, and Miers Fisher; three or four by James C. Fisher; six by Philip Nicklin; several more by John Vaughan and others. Operating on behalf of a firm in Marseilles, Stephen Girard shipped off provisions worth twenty-six thousand pounds in 1789 and 1790 alone.[68]

How could provision merchants obtain all of this wheat? Areas adjacent to Philadelphia could not fill the demand, and Philadelphia merchants were compelled to scour the Atlantic for new sources of exportable grain. In 1772 Willing and Morris reportedly sent six or seven ships to Quebec in order to secure grain, but the major sources were Virginia and Maryland. During the 1760s Philadelphia traders pushed into the Eastern Shore of Maryland, purchasing huge quantities of wheat and corn, which were either exported directly from Maryland or brought back to Philadelphia.[69] Philadelphia merchants evidently employed Maryland businessmen to purchase massive amounts of grain. One historian has estimated that a fifth of the wheat and flour and half of the corn exported from Philadelphia in 1774 came from the Eastern Shore of Maryland.[70] But Philadelphia influence in the Chesapeake

67. On the failure of Joseph Wharton, see Thomas Wharton to [Samuel Wharton], Nov. 7, 1774, and to Joseph Wharton, Jan. 18, 1775, Thomas Wharton Letterbook, 1773–1784, Wharton Papers, HSP; and John Warder to Jeremiah Warder, Feb. 2, 1777, John Warder Letterbooks, 1776–1778, HSP; Wm. Pollard to Thos. Hodgson, Oct. 27, 1767, Pollard Letterbook, 1764–1768, 401.

68. Girard Journal, 1786–1790, Girard Papers, 3d Ser., Reel 113; see also the correspondence between Girard and Samatan Freres of Marseilles in Girard Papers, 3d Ser., Reel 121. David Cay to Andrew Clow, July 13, 1789, Clow Papers, Franklin and Marshall Collection, HSP; ——— to Andrew Clow, May 31, 1789, and Patrick Morrogh and Co. to Andrew Clow and Co., June 29, 1790, Andrew Clow and Co. Papers, 1784–1836, Eleutherian Mills Historical Library.

69. William Pollard to Peter Holmes and Co., Sept. 23, 1773, Pollard Letterbook, 1772–1774, 271; Paul G. E. Clemens, *The Atlantic Economy and Colonial Maryland's Eastern Shore: From Tobacco to Grain* (Ithaca, N.Y., 1980), 126, 176–179, 203–204. For information on a Philadelphia flour merchant, owning a mill in Maryland that was supplied by the Lloyds, see Philadelphia Merchant Day Book, 1770–1788, AM 3081, HSP. This volume was kept by Thomas Canby.

70. Ronald Hoffman, *A Spirit of Dissension: Economics, Politics, and the Revolution in Maryland* (Baltimore, Md., 1974), 67.

extended beyond the Eastern Shore. In 1769 a relatively minor Philadelphia merchant, Clement Biddle, maintained a schooner in steady communication with two Potomac River towns, Georgetown and Alexandria.[71] Biddle worked closely with his correspondents on the Potomac, and the main activity of the three men was purchasing wheat, flour, and corn for export to the Iberian market, either directly or via Philadelphia. Biddle even arranged for flour to be ground at a mill near Winchester, Virginia, and sent down to Georgetown for shipment.[72]

Philadelphians like Biddle were torn between the alternatives of shipping produce across the Atlantic directly from the Chesapeake and sending it up to Philadelphia to be reshipped. It was ostensibly cheaper to send it directly from Virginia or Maryland; Biddle calculated that sending flour around to Philadelphia increased the total freight charges on one shipment by 17 percent and thus reduced the acceptable purchase price for flour from 5s. 3d. to 5s. per bushel.[73] This economy, however, was counterbalanced by the difficulties created by the dearth of port facilities and reliable agents in the Chesapeake. After receiving accounting statements of the sales of wheat shipped directly from the Chesapeake, many Philadelphia traders complained loudly about "a general Deficiency in the measurement [of wheat] and a considerable one" by their agents and about the "great detention of vessels" in Maryland.[74] More distressing still was the experience of a Philadelphia merchant who traveled to Maryland in order to arrange the purchase of a cargo of wheat for a vessel he expected from the West Indies.[75] He secured commitments from the farmers to deliver specified amounts of wheat on board the ship at a stipulated time and for a specific price, and he gave them advance payments in order to secure the bargain. But before the ship arrived, the price of wheat increased, and the farmers refused to sell the wheat at the lower price to which they had agreed. A second trip southward was necessary to get the vessel loaded, and the merchant had to bring suits against some of the farmers in order to recover the down payments he had made. Such were the hazards of engaging in the provi-

71. Clement Biddle and Co. Letterbook, 1769–1770, esp. Clement Biddle and Co. to Thomas Richardson, Aug. 15, Sept. 11, Nov. 5, 13, Dec. 12, 1769, Jan. 18, Feb. 24, Apr. 2, 1770.

72. Biddle to Thomas Richardson, Aug. 21, 1769, *ibid.*

73. Biddle to Thos. Richardson and Co., Jan. 18, 1770, *ibid.* For another example of a shipment to Europe from the Chesapeake, arranged by Philadelphians, see Girard to Samatan Freres, Sept. 17, 1789, Girard Papers, 2d Ser., Reel 121.

74. Pollard to Peter Holmes, July 20, 1772, Pollard Letterbook, 1772–1774, 53.

75. William Pollard to Thomas Hodgson, Oct. 27, 1767, Pollard Letterbook, 1764–1768, 401.

sion trade at a distance and without a port. The rise of Baltimore would solve this problem.

In the West Indies and southern European sectors, traders garnered their profits from exports. As we have noticed, imports seldom equaled exports in aggregate value, and traders were usually content to use them as a speedy means of receiving part of the net sales of the outward cargo. But it was extremely difficult to make money by the export of foodstuffs, Pennsylvania's chief export staple, because the merchant was nearly always in competition with local producers in the area to which he was shipping. The demand for exports was consequently highly dependent on local supplies; hurricanes, crop failures, wars, and other occurrences could shift foreign prices rapidly. And when crop shortages occurred, merchants from many ports rushed to fill the deficit. As a result of these various factors, commodity prices shifted drastically.[76] The merchants were handicapped in their efforts to react to this price volatility, for they were mired in a bog of stale information. Four months might elapse between the time a Lisbon merchant wrote to his Philadelphia correspondent with the information that flour prices were high and the moment that the flour shipment actually reached the shores of Portugal. Needless to say, in four months market conditions could have changed completely.[77] Market timing was so difficult that two different merchants concluded that the best way to time shipments was to act exactly *contrary* to the latest market advice.[78] Perhaps Benjamin Fuller wished in 1788 that he had followed this course when he toted up the results of fifty-one adventures to and from Saint Eustatius and Charleston over a three-year period. Despite a great deal of effort and a large outlay of capital, his twenty-nine losses outweighed his twenty-two gains by a margin of thirty pounds.[79]

Though wealthy traders enjoyed distinct competitive advantages, Philadelphia export markets offered real opportunities for lesser merchants. Even if one did not own a large vessel suitable for transatlantic

76. Sachs, "Business Outlook," 62, enumerates the reasons why the West Indies market was "constantly overstocked."

77. Jensen, *Maritime Commerce*, 63, writes, "The factors which made all eighteenth century commerce a risk were even more applicable, perhaps, to the south European trade. . . . In particular, the length of the ocean voyage made it impossible for information to be up-to-date."

78. Batho to Samuel Martin, June 6, 1766, Batho Letterbook; Parr and Bulkeley and Co. to Keppelle and Steinmetz, May 12, 1775, Brinton Collection, box 2. Egnal, "Trade with the British West Indies," *PMHB*, II (1975), 162–163, is more optimistic on the possibility of accurate market timing.

79. Fuller Journal, 1782–1789, front pages.

commerce, it was possible to make a small adventure of a few hundred pounds to southern Europe by renting freight space in a vessel bound for that market. In general, the coastal and Caribbean markets were so diverse that they contained many unexploited niches for the little man to fill. One could import smuggled tea from New York, as Charles Wharton did, or receive small loads of indigo from Charleston in the manner of Robert Henderson.[80] When dealing with a minor West Indies island, a small shipment of flour was actually preferable to a large one, which would flood the market. Customs records confirm the fact that small shipments were suitable for these markets. Participation in the coastal and Caribbean markets was much wider than in the southern Europe trade, and 58 percent of the total shipments received from them over a thirty-two-month period amounted to less than three hundred pounds.[81] In addition, trading in these sectors did not require the use of large, expensive vessels. The ships used in the coastal trade averaged fifty-two tons, and those in the Caribbean trade seventy-six tons, or about half the size of vessels typically employed in transatlantic routes (see table 9). Partly because the ships were smaller and more easily managed, a significant proportion of them (9 percent in the West Indies, and 43 percent in coastwise trade) were consigned to the master of the vessel, rather than a merchant or supercargo.

If he owned a vessel, a fourth key problem facing a provision merchant was deciding how best to deploy his shipping. It was once widely believed by historians that colonial American vessels generally followed triangular routes between three ports, or else tramped from port to port in a particular part of the world. Their routes were kept flexible and informal, it was said, because the shippers strived to secure full cargoes at all times instead of running a leg of the voyage in ballast. More modern research has brought out, however, that triangular routes were in fact quite rare and that most vessels followed a shuttle path, back and forth between two ports.[82] This conclusion is supported by my own analysis of shipping records. If firms had routinely sent out their vessels to many different ports, the patterns of geographical specialization documented earlier in this chapter would not have existed. Furthermore, a large body of manuscript evidence attests to the desire of merchants to, as they described it, "settle their vessel in a trade."

Merchants tried to follow this strategy in order to establish a stable,

80. Charles Wharton Daybook, 1768–1772; Henderson Invoice Book, 1784–1793.

81. Based on Registers of Duties Paid.

82. Gary M. Walton, "New Evidence on Colonial Commerce," *Jour. Econ. Hist.*, XXVIII (1968), 363–389.

secure modus operandi that turned a profit for them year after year. Their ideal was to build a vessel especially designed for a particular trade, regularly send it to a reliable correspondent (often a coowner), establish a solid reputation among potential customers for regularity and reliability, and achieve a steady income from freight earnings and trading profits. They were attracted to such an arrangement for several good reasons. Consider, for example, the degree of specialization involved necessarily in the ownership of a specific vessel. A vessel that was too large for a port would glut its market upon arriving. On the other hand, larger vessels were generally preferable because their running costs were proportionally lower, chiefly because of higher ton/crew ratios and lower port charges per ton. Furthermore, there were apparently gains in efficiency from having a vessel especially designed to carry a particular cargo, such as flour or lumber. The advantages of such specialization were naturally lost if a vessel regularly visited many different ports throughout the Atlantic.[83]

A ship that sailed regularly could also attract a clientele of merchants who used it frequently to send out their cargoes, in preference to owning their own vessel. To garner customers, at least one shipowner promised to leave port on a stipulated day, full freight or no, and many ships advertised the regularity of their sailings in their names: *Pennsylvania Packet*, *Charleston Packet*, *Jamaica Packet*, and so on.[84] Clearly, the concept of scheduled voyages, which became fully established in 1816 with the founding of New York's famous Blackball Line of Liverpool packets, had a long gestation period.

Regular sailings also cut costs by facilitating the difficult process of organizing a voyage. When the sailing pattern of a vessel was well established, not only the appropriate size and makeup of its cargo but also the approximate arrival time could be anticipated, and a return cargo could be kept waiting near the waterfront, ready to be stowed on board as quickly as possible. By reducing turnaround times at port, costs could be considerably cut. This fact was well understood by Stephen Girard, who early in his career acquired a waterfront warehouse in which to store the

83. O., D., and G. to William Beath and Co., Oct. 16, 1767, Orr, Dunlope, and Glenholme Letterbook; J. and D. to Lancelot Cowper, Oct. 29, 1773, James and Drinker Foreign Letterbook, 155; Girard to Girard and Hourquebie, Sept. 20, 1783, Girard Papers, 2d Ser., Reel 121; Riche to William Neate, July 29, 1760, Riche Letterbook, 1748–1764; McCusker, "Sources of Investment Capital," *Jour. Econ. Hist.*, XXXII (1972), 150.

84. Gough and Carmault to William Neate, Aug. 15, 1757, Gough and Carmault Letterbook. For an example of a merchant who regularly used vessels that shuttled between Philadelphia and Charleston, see Robert Henderson Receipt Book, 1781–1791, entries for 1790, 1791, Henderson Papers.

next outward cargo for Saint Domingue.[85] Methodical shipping paths also gave an owner maximum control of his shipping. Since transportation and communication speeds were equal in the eighteenth century, it was extremely difficult for a shipowner to direct the route of a vessel after it left port. Unless the path was planned in advance, much discretion had to be left to the captain and foreign correspondents who handled the ship. If their judgment was faulty, a vessel could sail around the Atlantic for over a year, tying up capital, running up losses, and all the while keeping the owners in the dark. For cash-poor traders obsessed with the problem of protecting their assets, such a situation was intolerable. It was far better to keep a vessel in a predictable path, managed by familiar agents who had a stake in the vessel.[86]

Yet it would be a mistake to suppose that efficient management could be achieved *only* by keeping a vessel in a shuttle pattern. Well-organized multilateral voyages were quite possible. For instance, English merchants who provided financing and marketing services for West Indies planters often sent their vessels to Philadelphia with dry goods, then on to the Caribbean with lumber and provisions, and then back to England loaded with sugar and other tropical produce. This plan obviated the necessity of running the westward leg of an England–West Indies shuttle route largely in ballast. The triangular route was not perfect, however. To get good freights of dry goods, a vessel had to be at the wharves of English ports at exactly the right time in spring and fall, for as we have seen, Philadelphia dry goods merchants demanded early shipment of their orders. But this requirement was not easily coordinated with the demands of West Indies planters, who needed their staves in the autumn in order to package the sugar crop. Despite these problems, several Philadelphians were involved in this commerce. In 1757 it was said that "many Vessels bound on an Annual Voyage to the West Indies do touch here & take a Cargoe of fret in their Way & often do very Well." For several years before the Revolution William Pollard received two or three vessels a year from Liverpool and sent them on to Jamaica. Thomas Clifford,

85. Girard to John Girard, Jan. 3, 1786, to Girard and Hourquebie, Sept. 20, 1783, Girard Papers, 2d Ser., Reel 121. Girard also rented a lot on the waterfront to facilitate loading. See Girard to John Girard, Apr. 14, 1785, Girard Papers, 2d Ser., Reel 121.

86. Larsen, "Thomas Clifford," 63–66; O., D., and G. to Andrew Orr, Nov. 9, 1767, Orr, Dunlope, and Glenholme Letterbook. For other examples of financial confusion in the management of vessels, see Roberdeau to William Hyndman, Dec. 7, 1765, and to Meyler and Hall, Oct. 21, 1765, Roberdeau Letterbook, 33, 71; Turner to John and William Halliday, June 1757, and to David Barclay and Sons, Feb. 23, 1759, Turner Letterbook, 1753–1774; Wharton to [Samuel Wharton], Oct. 25, 1774, Thomas Wharton Letterbook, 1773–1784.

Jeremiah Warder and Sons, and Miller and Emlen were also active in the Philadelphia–West Indies–England trade.[87]

Other exceptions to the merchants' predilection for planned, routine voyages may easily be found. Regular sailings were interspersed with speculative, experimental voyages or were sometimes disrupted by the sale or loss of a vessel. Frequently, the city's merchants found it unprofitable to deploy their ships in a way that led to the lowest operating costs in the long run. Nearly all of the traders were small businessmen who could not easily afford to run their vessels at a loss for many months in order to build a reputation and increase their share of the market. Even a rich merchant seldom had more than seven hundred pounds in cash on hand, and routine outfitting costs—to say nothing of major repairs—could equal a third of this sum. So when demand for freight space was slack and their vessels could not turn a profit in their settled routes, merchants naturally took advantage of the unique flexibility of their capital investment by using one of the many options that were available to them.[88] They transferred the ship to a different route, sold the vessel in Philadelphia, or sent it to a foreign port with orders to the captain to follow one of a variety of alternatives—sell the cargo but not the vessel, sell both cargo and vessel, send the vessel back to Philadelphia or steer it on to a third port, advertise for freight in the foreign port, or load it on the owners' account.[89]

87. Egnal, "Trade with the British West Indies," 160–179; Pollard to Peter Holme, May 16, Nov. 11, 1772, May 14, 1774, Pollard Letterbook, 1772–1774, 24, 104, 414. Similar problems faced the shipper who wished to use a vessel in triangular routes involving the seasonal flaxseed trade. See O., D., and G. to Andrew Orr, Sept. 23, 1767, Orr, Dunlope, and Glenholme Letterbook. T. Willing to Thomas Willing, July 1, 1757, Willing and Morris Letterbook, 295; Warder to George Noble, Nov. 16, 1776, Warder Letterbooks; Collins to William Neate, Apr. 30, 1772, Collins Papers, LVII.

88. For examples of merchants who found it difficult to employ vessels profitably or whose plans were affected by liquidity problems, see Fuller to Robert Totten, Feb. 16, 1785, Fuller Letterbook, 1784–1787, 79; F. and J. West to Haxall and West, Feb. 21, 1785, Francis and John West Letterbook, 1783–1786, 96; O., D., and G. to Andrew Orr, Nov. 9, 1767, Orr, Dunlope, and Glenholme Letterbook; John Reed to Standish Forde, May 7, 1788, Reed and Forde Letterbook, 1788–1790, 121, Reed and Forde Papers, HSP; Clement Biddle and Co. to Thomas Robinson, Aug. 25, 1770, Clement Biddle and Co. Letterbook, 1769–1770; Thomas Clifford, Jr., to John Clifford, Aug. 2, 1785, Clifford Correspondence, 1778–1785, VII, 250, HSP; Pollard to John Woolmer, July 1, 1772, Pollard Letterbook, 1772–1774, 46.

89. For examples of such contingency voyages, see Roberdeau to Robert and John Paisley, Nov. 30, 1765, Roberdeau Letterbook, 78; Fuller to Capt. John Fleming, Oct. 2, 1785, Fuller Letterbook, 1784–1787, 133; O., D., and G. to William Beath and George Anderson, Sept. 23, 1767, Orr, Dunlope, and Glenholme Letterbook; Girard to John Girard, Feb. 1786, Girard Papers, 2d Ser., Reel 121; Charles Wharton to Capt. John Osman, Sept. 8,

Ironically, this same flexibility could also be induced by exceptionally favorable market conditions: the profits from speculative voyages could be large enough to compensate for the risk and inconvenience of disrupting regular routes. One firm grossed £1,423 in freight on a single West Indies–England trip in 1773 and close to £3,000 on the same voyage three years later. Freights were so high during the American Revolution that vessels could be rented out for £334 per month, while Clement Biddle earned over £1,400 in freight on each of two trips to Philadelphia from Europe in 1783. And during the Seven Years' War, James and Drinker, after filling part of their vessel on their own account, still charged £1,677 in freight. On another occasion this firm sent a vessel from Bristol to a West Indies island on freight, there took on a cargo of manufactures that sold in Honduras at a profit of £411, and then loaded the vessel with mahogany that sold in Bristol at a profit of £1,872. Even after deducting the considerable running charges—wages, repairs, and the like—from these gross earnings, merchants were left with windfall profits that could repay the cost of a vessel in two or three voyages. Such gains fully justified experimental, one-time projects. One firm advised a correspondent:

> Freights are up here very high to the West Indies—10 [freights at] £12 p Ton—of Consequence shipping very Dear. Twice as much as when [Captain] Tree was here, so that if you can buy a good Vessel very Cheap, as they have been Sold with you of late, as we have been inform'd, and send her here for Sale, can't doubt thy making a a great hand of it.

Even if a merchant ignored such advice and steadfastly kept his vessel in a shuttle path, he was likely to find his operations disrupted by one of three mishaps: capture by privateers, shipwrecks, or ship sales caused by the disbanding of a firm.[90]

1785, Sarah A. G. Smith Collection, box 2, HSP; Turner to Capt. Hugh Wright, Sept. 9, 1753, Turner Letterbook, 1753–1774; J. and D. to William Bard, Sept. 1, 1757, James and Drinker Letterbook, 1756–1759, 168; Warder to Capt. John Cooke, Mar. 20, 1777, Warder Letterbooks; William Smith to Grant and Fine, July 4, 1775, William Smith Letterbook, 1771–1775, HSP; T. Willing to Robert Morris, Feb. 27, 1756, Willing and Morris Letterbook, 162; Riche and John Biddle to William Neate, Sept. 10, 1760, Riche Letterbook, 1748–1764.

90. Warder to George Noble, Nov. 16, 1776, to John Cross, Jr., Dec. 27, 1776, to Jeremiah Warder, Aug. 4, 1777, Warder Letterbooks; Clement Biddle Journal A, 1781–1784, 303–304, 307–308, Thomas A. Biddle Collection, HSP; J. and D. to Neate and Neave, Aug. 14, 1756, to Samuel Green, July 19, 1757, James and Drinker Letterbook,

For all of these reasons vessels often were not rigidly settled in a trade. They were part of a merchant's inventory, to be bought and sold, employed for freight earnings or to carry one's own cargo, or settled in a trade or switched from route to route as conditions dictated. They were handled flexibly, almost casually in some instances. "I had a ship in from Bristol belogg. to our late Compy." remarked one merchant "& intended her for your Market, but hearg. your Prices were low, & a Chap offerg. to Buy her, I preferred the Sale of the Ship, to a Voyage. I have another now bound to Lisbon, on her Return, if any Encouragement will send her to you in the spring."[91] During a period of low demand for shipping, one firm wrote, "Being quite tired of seeing the *Rebecca* at the Wharff, & no possibility of selling either at public or private Sale (Several Vessells having been put up and no bidders) we Concluded last Week to put the ship up for Lisbon."[92]

Precisely because of their elusive complexity, it is difficult to measure the number of irregular routes comprehensively with customs documents, but the papers of merchants are full of examples. It was the rare shipping firm that did not, in the course of two or three years, send a vessel out of its normal path. It is also clear that vessel sales were common and that firms moved in and out of shipping activities as market conditions changed. The Pennsylvania Ship Register contains 1,514 original registers for newly built vessels and 1,104 reregistrations made necessary in many cases by a change in ownership. The Tonnage Duty Book, which spans a decade, shows that 19 percent of the merchant firms received shipping in only one year, 61 percent in fewer than four years, and only 13 percent in all ten years. Two specific cases convey a similar impression of high vessel turnover combined with fairly frequent recourse to irregular routes. During the fourteen years that he worked for various firms associated with two families, Capt. John Ashmead operated six different vessels and made twenty voyages to the West Indies, two to Ireland, four to Lisbon, and one each to New York and Charleston. And Thomas Clifford, though he normally owned only two vessels at a time, bought twelve different ships over a twenty-year period. Of these twelve, three were captured, and two were lost at sea. One sturdy

1756–1759, 21, 146; Drinker to Robinson, Sandwith, and Co., Feb. 17, 1787, Henry Drinker Letterbook, 1786–1790, 139.

91. T. Willing to Whatley, Meyler, and Hall, Aug. 18, 1755, Willing and Morris Letterbook, 114.

92. Samuel and Israel Morris, Jr., to Caspar Wistar, Oct. 15, 1767, Samuel and Israel Morris, Jr., Letterbook, 1763–1775, Morris Family Papers, Eleutherian Mills Historical Library.

snow that remained in Clifford's fleet for a decade sailed to the West Indies for four years, to Bristol for two, to Lisbon for two, and then made successive trips to Saint Christopher, Lisbon, Liverpool, and Lisbon.[93]

In view of the many options available to the individual firm, Philadelphia's shipping industry at the aggregate level displayed a surprisingly stable pattern from one year to the next. Between 1766 and 1775 an average of nearly seven hundred vessels negotiated the treacherous shoals of the Delaware each year to unload a cargo at a Quaker City wharf. Over a fifth of these vessels, accounting for about 15 percent of the port's incoming tonnage, were consigned to ship captains, who owned roughly a third of this shipping. The remaining 85 percent of the incoming tonnage was consigned each year to about 160 different firms—100 merchant firms, plus 60 supercargoes and local nonmerchant traders. Although merchants were often active for only part of a decade, they tended as a group to be far less transient than the nonmerchants, and they were more likely to own the vessels they received.[94]

Suppliers and Distributors

We know that foodstuff exporters stuck close to the waterfront. It remains to be explained how they obtained the flour, bread, beef, flaxseed, and other provisions they shipped abroad and how their imports of coffee, sugar, rum, and other groceries were distributed to the hinterland. The main patterns of this process emerge in business records, tax lists, and city directories, and the evidence of specialization in this segment of Philadelphia's distribution system is unmistakable by the 1780s.

In the 1750s and earlier, exporters obtained their wheat and flour directly from millers and farmers, as the comments in the papers of several different merchants attest.[95] This arrangement worked well enough while the volume of foodstuffs exported by Philadelphia firms was limited. But as shipments increased in size and frequency, large-scale operators such as Baynton, Wharton, and Morgan continually had to

93. Tonnage Duty Book; Crowther, "Shipbuilding Industry," 68; William Bell Clark, "The John Ashmead Story, 1738–1818," *PMHB*, LXXXII (1958), 3–19; Larsen, "Thomas Clifford," 76, 106.

94. Tonnage Duty Book.

95. Larsen, "Thomas Clifford," 291–293; Romanek, "John Reynell," 92; Turner to Joshua Mauger, Feb. 25, 1759, Turner Letterbook, 1753–1774; T. Willing to Coddrington Carrington, May 26, June 10, 1755, Willing and Morris Letterbook, 97, 99.

turn to ten or fifteen suppliers to construct a cargo of wheat and lumber. Eventually, new middlemen called flour merchants and lumber merchants appeared in the Philadelphia commercial community to free the shipping merchants of this burden. Normally men with good hinterland connections, the flour merchants specialized in obtaining agricultural produce in the countryside, transporting it to Philadelphia in wagons and shallops, and selling it to exporters. The flour merchant Thomas Canby owned part of a grist mill on the Sassafras River, in Maryland, as well as a share of a sloop. In addition to selling his own flour, Canby sold the flour of Isaac Lloyd, a wealthy Maryland planter, on commission.[96]

Provision merchants were willing to purchase from these new middlemen for two reasons. The well-organized transportation systems of the middlemen put them in a position to get the staple to Philadelphia more cheaply than could provision merchants, engrossed as they were with dozens of details relating to the management of vessels.[97] Moreover, these flour merchants were experts. Close contact with farmers and, especially, millers gave them a detailed knowledge of the various types of flour, which by the 1780s were going by specific brand names, such as Red Clay, Morton, and Fisher.[98] This expertise was invaluable to a shipper, who might sink two thousand pounds into one large cargo of provisions. The importance of specialized knowledge in buying cargoes was literally underscored in one English merchant's advice to a young partner in Philadelphia: "I doubt not you will engage a person to purchase your grain &c who is a perfect judge of the article, as some Houses object to give their orders to general [*illeg.*] because they do not perfectly understand the quality."[99]

The emergence of the flour merchant is revealed clearly in Philadelphia tax lists and city directories. In 1774 there were only a few such merchants in the city. By 1785 there were fifteen. Already by the 1770s a firm like James and Drinker would depend on their "flour factor" to supply them when they shipped a large cargo to the Iberian Peninsula.[100] For the 1780s we can identify at least five provision merchants who

96. Philadelphia Merchant Day Book, 1770–1788.

97. Levi Hollingsworth's occupation was listed in a city directory as "Keeper of the stage boats twice a week to Christianna," and George Latimer also operated shallops. See Francis White, *The Philadelphia Directory* (Philadelphia, 1785), and Fitzsimons Journal, 116.

98. Fuller to John Mitchell, Sept. 30, 1785, Fuller Letterbook, 1784–1787, 132; Girard to John Girard, Oct. 27, 1789, Girard Papers, 2d Ser., Reel 121.

99. John Phillips to William Cramond, Oct. 7, 1789, Cramond and Phillips Papers, Gratz Collection, HSP.

100. J. and D. to Henry Trotman, Sept. 7, 1772, and to Zachery Philip Fonnereau and Sons, Aug. 3, 1773, James and Drinker Foreign Letterbook, 12, 126.

purchased foodstuffs for export mainly from flour merchants. In volume after volume the names of the same suppliers appear: Levi Hollingsworth, George Latimer, Thomas Canby, Joseph Russell, Wall and Flower.[101] Among them Levi Hollingsworth was probably the most successful. He developed an extensive network of contacts with about four hundred people in Pennsylvania, Delaware, Maryland, New Jersey, and Virginia, and his net worth of over twenty thousand pounds placed him among the major merchants of Philadelphia. It was the operations of people like Hollingsworth that allowed the provision merchant to concentrate his assets where he knew how to use them best—on the ocean—and to maintain running accounts with only several dozen people.

Specialized lumber merchants also emerged to serve the needs of the provision trader; there were twenty-four firms dealing in lumber, timber, or staves in 1785 and 1791. Lumber was a bulky and troublesome commodity to obtain from the backcountry. James and Drinker declared in 1773, "So many disappointments and difficulties have allways attended the procuring this Article, that scarcely any Comm^{s} would induce us to undertake obtaining a Cargo for others."[102] They reported that two other prominent firms were also thinking of giving up the shipment of oak because it was so difficult to obtain. By maintaining well-assorted inventories in their yards on the periphery of the city, lumber dealers were able to spare busy shippers this aggravation and to supply the city's construction industry as well. In fact, at least five lumber merchants were themselves former carpenters, and some lumber merchants were active real estate dealers.[103] John and Thomas Britton, for instance, evidently built many houses in the Northern Liberties; the 1774 tax list rated John for six new empty houses and Thomas for one, and fifteen years later they still had substantial property holdings in the district.[104] The resulting impression that some lumber merchants were men of considerable wealth is confirmed by other evidence. One had a business inventory of

101. Girard Journal, 1786–1790, 126, 137, 184, Girard Papers, 3d Ser. Reel 113; Josiah and Samuel Coates Journal, 1785–1789, 201, 239, 249, 263, 272, Coates and Reynell Collection, HSP; Henderson Ledger, 1781–1794, 2, Robert Henderson Papers; Benjamin Fuller Journal, 1782–1789, 317, 326; Coxe and Frazier Journal, 1783–1785, Tench Coxe Papers, Reel 20, HSP (all references to the Coxe Papers are to the microfilm collection, available in HSP and other libraries, of the original Coxe Papers in HSP); Fitzsimons Journal, 102, 125, 132, 211.

102. J. and D. to Lancelot Cowper, Apr. 30, 1773, James and Drinker Foreign Letterbook, 103.

103. Based on an analysis of Philadelphia tax lists and city directories for the years 1756–1791.

104. Lumber merchants Joseph Huddle, Daniel Richards, William Wayne, and Joseph Wetherill also owned significant amounts of urban property.

nearly eighteen hundred pounds when he died in 1793, while another firm bought lumber to the value of over eleven thousand pounds from one major supplier during the course of eight years.[105]

Although the matter demands more study, it is also clear that certain firms specialized in the collection and distribution of groceries imported by other firms from overseas. We know of three pre-Revolutionary firms that concentrated on this activity for fairly short periods of time. John Baynton in the 1750s purchased rum and wine from prominent merchants to sell in small quantities to retailers, and Samuel Neave bought sugar, coffee, spices, and other groceries from Philadelphia merchants and sold them to well over two hundred shopkeepers in Philadelphia and its hinterland.[106] Most of these sales were on his own account, but some were commission sales on the accounts of the big provision traders who supplied him. Mifflin and Massey in the early 1760s had a similar operation. Although they were themselves involved in trade with the West Indies, they bought a huge miscellany of goods—forty-seven commodities ranging from pepper to mahogany to mackerel to molasses—from provision merchants and other suppliers. These they sold to over one hundred customers in Philadelphia and its hinterland.[107] All three of these firms obtained the groceries they handled from shipping firms, and none of them handled dry goods extensively. However, unlike the flour and lumber merchants described above, they were not long-term specialists in this activity, but instead used it as a relatively low-risk entry into the mercantile world. They invested their profits from the distribution of groceries into overseas speculations, where the big money was to be made.

Provision merchants by the 1780s were regularly selling their incoming cargoes in fairly large lots to other Philadelphia merchants and to grocers. Far from doling out molasses by the gallon and tea by the pound, as the emphasis on the retail activity of eighteenth-century merchants would lead us to expect, they dealt in fairly large lots. The average sale of New England rum by Josiah and Samuel Coates, for instance, amounted to one hundred pounds during four months in 1786.[108] Thomas Fitzsimons, Benjamin Fuller, and Stephen Girard all tended to do this as well. They sold their imports in substantial amounts to a

105. Daniel Richards Will no. 294, 1793, Office of the Recorder of Wills, Philadelphia City Hall.

106. John Baynton Ledger B, 1754–1759, 14, 58, 82, Baynton, Wharton, and Morgan Papers, Reel 7; Samuel Neave Ledger, 1752–1756, HSP.

107. Mifflin and Massey Ledger, 1760–1763, HSP. For representative commodity accounts showing principal suppliers of the firm, see 4, 21, 25, 26, 28, 130, 184.

108. Josiah and Samuel Coates Journal, 1785–1789, 84–111.

number of merchants and grocers, rather than to dozens of retailers scattered throughout the hinterland.[109] Certain other firms evidently concentrated on the correlative activity of purchasing and reselling incoming cargoes of groceries, for they appear regularly in the journals of shippers. Wager and Habacker, William Forbes, McClaughlin and Taggart, and Ambrose Vasse were ubiquitous. Grocers were also important. The 1791 Philadelphia city directory describes five firms as "wholesale grocers," and a number of other grocers who purchased in large quantities from the shippers were probably also wholesalers who distributed goods to shopkeepers. Certainly they were large operators, for in 1791 and 1792 about thirty-six grocers were prominent discounters at the Bank of North America.[110]

Mercantile Fortunes

Whether he sold dry goods to rural customers or took his chances in overseas markets, the aim of the merchant was to build his fortune. In the realm of business, nothing was more important to a merchant than his net worth—the excess in value of his assets over his own debts. This was the measure of his worldly success; it was the lifeline that preserved him from bankruptcy and the leash that established the boundaries of his operations. But despite their central importance, we know little about the character of mercantile estates in the eighteenth century. Clearly the subject merits closer scrutiny.

To launch his career, a young trader would scrape together an initial capital, or "stock," from a variety of sources—personal savings, a wife's dowry, a gift from his father or an uncle. If the resulting sum was inadequate, it could be augmented by forming a partnership.[111] Small merchants could get started with as little as five hundred pounds, and a few

109. Fuller Journal, 1782–1789, 168–171, 184, 185, 203, 208, 215; Fitzsimons Journal, 113, 118, 174; Girard Ledger, 1783–1786, Girard Papers, 3d Ser., Reel 97; Coxe and Frazier Journal, entries for June, July 1787, Coxe Papers, Reel 20; James and John Cox Ledger, 16, 17, 20, 21, 22, 25, 32, 59, 89.

110. Of 88 firms identified as major borrowers in 1790 and 1791 whose occupation can be learned, about 50 were merchants, and 19 were grocers. See Bank of North America Discount Book, 1790–1792, Bank of North America Papers, HSP. A "major borrower" was defined as one who had at least one full page of discounts in the volume. The figure of 36 firms is an estimate based on this volume, which covers only the first half of the alphabet.

111. For examples of loans on bond from widows, see Mifflin and Massey Ledger, 1760–1763, fol. 38, HSP; indenture between Thomas Armat and Widow Hannah Hobart, Jan. 7, 1785, Thomas Armat Papers, box 1, Loudoun Papers.

firms began with more than four thousand pounds.[112] At this early stage in their careers, the difference between the rich and the poor merchant was not only the size of the trading capital but also the relationship between this sum and the trader's total estate. The young man of fortune was likely to have significant outside resources, such as a valuable piece of land or an expected inheritance, whereas in the case of the poor merchant his entire life savings could be tied up in business.[113] Whatever the initial capital, most merchants extended their equity capital by borrowing money. Perhaps because trade was so risky in America and the land market highly liquid, relatively little capital was borrowed on bond from widows and orphans. Far more important was credit obtained from European merchants, via the dry goods trade. After the Revolution the discounting of commercial paper at banks also augmented the initial stock.

Whether his initial stake was £500 or £5,000, the merchant tried to make his capital grow. Since the basic interest rate was 6 percent in America, merchants probably did not feel well compensated for the risks and trouble of trade if they consistently earned less than 10 percent. Fragmentary and inconclusive evidence suggests that a profit of 12 percent was not an unrealistic expectation.[114] The logic of capital accumu-

112. The starting capitals for selected firms were as follows: Mifflin and Massey, 1760, £2,819, Mifflin and Massey Ledger, 1760–1763, fols. 1, 3, 38; Owen Jones, Jr., 1789, £1,054, Owen Jones, Jr., Daybook A, 1789–1791, entry for Aug. 21, 1789, Owen Jones Papers; Stephen Girard, 1782, £2,280, Stephen Girard Ledger, 1780–1783, accounts opened Feb. 18, 1782, Girard Papers, 3d Ser., Reel 48; Coxe and Frazier, 1783, £4,000, Partnership Agreement between Nalbrough Frazier and Tench Coxe, Nov. 29, 1783, Coxe Papers, Reel 44; Thomas Armat, 1781, £660 (specie), Thomas Armat Ledger, 1781–1784, fol. 1, in Loudoun Papers; Charles Isaac and Samuel Norris, 1735, £5,332, in Berg, "Organization of Business," *Penn. Hist.*, X (1943), 158 n. 1; Jones and Wister £5,340, Jones and Wister Daybook A, 1759–1761, entry for Apr. 20, 1759; Morris and Miercken, Feb. 25, 1772–Jan. 8, 1773, £3,371; Morris and Miercken Sugar House Ledger, 1772–1775, fol. 1, Morris Family Papers, Hollingsworth Collection, HSP (an additional £3,400 was invested in the firm in 1773 and 1774).

113. William Pollard to Crow and Taylor, May 16, 1774, Pollard Letterbook, 1772–1774, 417, mentions a young man whose personal worth was £1,400, a "trifling" sum compared to his father's £20,000 sterling. Pollard makes it clear that the wealth of his father supported the young man's credit.

114. In 1769 and 1770, Joshua Fisher and Sons earned a rate of return on its capital of 10%, before deduction of household expenses. See Joshua Fisher and Sons Ledger, 1769–1773, fols. 104, 105, 149, 166. In the period 1788–1793 James and John Cox earned an average of £1,634, or 13%, on its initial stock of £12,594. See James and John Cox Ledger. John Wister's gross financial assets, before deduction of the debts that he owed but after deduction of "dubious" debts, grew by 22% per year between 1748 and 1757, but then stagnated for the next decade. See John Wister Ledger, 1747–1766, Wister Papers, HSP. I am grateful to Marianne Wokeck for bringing this information on John Wister to my attention.

lation centered on two principles: first, that a merchant's rate of return should exceed the basic interest rate of 6 percent, and, second, that this high rate should be earned on an expanded chunk of capital, equal to his initial capital plus borrowed funds. Six percent earned on a £1,000 stock would yield only £60—hardly enough to live on genteelly—but when an additional £2,000 was borrowed interest-free in the dry goods trade, and a 12 percent profit was earned on the entire £3,000, the merchant earned £360 per year, or six times as much. This financial strategy was risky, because profit or no, loans had to be paid off, and, as we have seen, the small merchant often did not diversify his operations. But the relationship between diversification and risk cut both ways: if they happened to be concentrated in a lucrative market, the tyro trader's limited assets could multiply much more rapidly than the broadly distributed assets of the wealthy merchant.[115] The dynamics of capital accumulation helps to explain why social mobility was a marked feature of the merchant community: because capital requirements were low, entry was not difficult, and it was *possible* for the small merchant, who borrowed outside funds and invested them wisely, to build a fortune with great rapidity.

How wealthy, then, could an aspiring Philadelphia trader reasonably hope to become? The most reliable answer to this question is derived not from the reports and rumors that circulated in trading circles or from the documents in probate records—which are usually incomplete—but from the merchants' own careful calculations of their net worth, as set down in journals and ledgers. Eleven such compilations show a range of estates from £5,384 to £35,559, and a mean of £17,681 (table 10). Perhaps because minor merchants felt less need to analyze their meager estates, these eleven observations are heavily weighted toward wealthy traders. It is probably safe to conclude that during the 1770s and 1780s wealthy Philadelphia merchants were worth between £20,000 and £35,000. A few traders were worth more, but only a few.

The majority of merchants were worth far less than £20,000. William Pollard once stated that he was worth £400 or £500, and one finds many other traders who at some point in their careers were worth less than £3,000.[116] It was said in 1757 that many young Philadelphians had so

115. Thus in Feb. 1781 Thomas Armat had a stock of £660, but by Dec. 1784 it had risen to £2,607. Armat Ledger, 1781–1784, fol. 1; Armat Ledger, 1784–1790, fol. 45. The gross financial assets of John Wister, valued at £4,522 on Jan. 1, 1748, grew by 51% in 1748 and 21% in 1749, or 83% in two years. Thereafter the rate declined. John Wister Ledger, back pages.

116. Pollard to Bowers, Nov. 16, 1772, Pollard Letterbook, 1772–1774, 108; Pollard to Christopher Rawson, Aug. 29, 1764, Pollard Letterbook, 1764–1768, 17; Romanek, "John Reynell," 40; Girard Ledger, 1780–1783, accounts opened Feb. 18, 1782, Girard Papers, 3d Ser., Reel 48; Hollingsworth Ledger D, 1779–1780, 221.

little money that they would bid up wheat to a "monstrous price" just to get a commission.[117] These impressions are confirmed by probate records, which in a limited number of cases—16 of 177 examined—provide enough information to determine the nonland net worth of decedents.[118] Probate records probably catch most merchants in the middle or later stages of the career cycle, after they have had time to amass an estate. For the 16 men, the mean estate was valued at £7,499 and the median at only £2,968. The distribution was as follows (in 1771–1773 prices).

Estate (in Pounds)	*No. of Men*
0– 2,000	5
2,001– 5,000	6
5,001–10,000	2
10,001–15,000	1
15,001–20,000	1
20,001 plus	1

If we guess that land composed a fifth of the average merchant's estate, then the mean total wealth of these traders was £8,999 and the median £3,562. Combining these data with the information from ledgers, we can estimate that nearly all merchants had estates of below £35,000, with half of the estates being worth less than £4,000. To keep these numbers in perspective, it should be remembered that a good-sized ship cost roughly £2,000 and a fine town house £3,000–£4,000.

As a merchant's estate grew in value, it generally became more diverse. After devoting all of his capital at first to merchandise, financial assets, and a few pieces of furniture, he would eventually buy a share in a vessel, a house to live in, one or two rental properties, and perhaps a few government bonds or shares of bank stock. If he was genuinely wealthy, a country seat or a share in an ironworks might be added to the estate. Because the character of the estate depended upon the age and wealth of the specific trader, it is impossible to describe a typical estate. Using tax lists, probate documents, and business records, however, we can analyze the five main types of property in most estates: furniture, merchandise, ships, financial assets, and real estate.

Thus merchants invested a median of £267 in furniture, plate, and other household goods (see table 11). Wealthy traders usually owned over £500 of such articles, but 59 percent of the merchants owned furniture worth between £51 and £500. By contrast, inventories of merchan-

117. Turner to David Barclay and Sons, Feb. 13, 1757, Turner Letterbook, 1753–1774.

118. For a discussion of the shortcomings of probate documents for determining total net worth, see Bibliography.

TABLE 10. *Net Worth of Selected Philadelphia Merchants*

Merchant	Year	Net Worth (in Pounds)
John Baynton	1754	5,384
Henry Drinker	1784	35,559
Joshua Fisher and Sons	1770	31,225
Benjamin Fuller	1789	15,844
Stephen Girard	1785	8,934
Stephen Girard	1790	20,681
Levi Hollingsworth	1782	10,915
Levi Hollingsworth	1785	22,430
Thomas Pratt	1754	8,404
Thomas Pratt	1758	13,251
William West	1770	22,828

Sources: John Baynton Journal B, 1754–1759, Baynton, Wharton, and Morgan microfilm, Reel 7, 1–3; Henry Drinker Ledger A, 1776–1792, 1, Henry Drinker Journal, 1776–1791, 18–20, Henry Drinker Papers; Joshua Fisher and Sons Ledger, 1769–1773, 104; Benjamin Fuller Journal, 1782–1789, 360–364, William West Account Books, Historical Society of Pennsylvania. Stephen Girard Journal, 1783–1786, Dec. 31, 1785, Girard Papers, 3d Ser., Reel 113; Stephen Girard Journal, 1788–1790, Dec. 31, 1790, Girard Papers, 3d Ser., Reel 44, American Philosophical Society. Levi Hollingsworth Journal, 1784–1785, 377–385, Hollingsworth Papers, Historical Society of Pennsylvania. Thomas Pratt Ledger, 1754, fols. 1, 19, Thomas Pratt Waste Book, 1758, Thomas Pratt Papers, New York Public Library. William West Ledger, 1770–1777, 1, William West Account Books, Historical Society of Pennsylvania.

dise were far more variable and, on balance, much larger than this (see table 12). While twelve of the thirty-five traders for whom we have probate evidence held business inventories of less than £500, six traders had business inventories valued at more than £3,000, and the median for all thirty-five was £942. Thus the merchants had considerably more money invested in the rough-hewn trunks and hogsheads stored in cellars and stores than in the grand mahogany highboys and clocks that adorned their parlors. They had still more wealth tied up in financial assets of all kinds—cash, notes receivable, debts owed by customers and correspondents. For thirty-six merchants the median value of such assets was £6,112. Usually less than £700 of this was in cash; the rest was tied up in dozens of separate debts, most of them fairly small.[119] If the trader owned a vessel, one of these debts was his share in the ship and was owed

119. The mean cash balance of 30 merchants was £445, and 23% of these balances were over £700. Office of the Recorder of Wills, Philadelphia City Hall.

TABLE 11. *Value of Household Goods of Merchants, 1750–1795*

Value (in 1771–1773 Prices)	No. of Merchants ($N = 85$)
£0–£50	3
£51–£100	12
£101–£300	31
£301–£500	16
£501–£700	11
£701–£1,000	12

Source: Wills and Administrations, City of Philadelphia, Office of the Recorder of Wills.
Note: Mean value of goods, £345; median value, £267.

to him by the shipping syndicate as a whole. On the eve of the Revolution this share was likely to be worth £920. After the Revolution a couple of shares of bank stock and some short-term bills and notes (normally IOUs of other local traders) were likely to be in the portfolio. The balance would be debts from overseas correspondents who handled his adventures and local customers who had purchased goods on credit.

It was vital for the merchant to be able to collect these debts in good time, because he himself owed to dozens of people money that (amid tremendous variation from trader to trader) equaled roughly half of his financial assets.[120] Thus, a merchant in possession of five hundred pounds in cash and fifty-five hundred pounds in debts receivable might himself owe three thousand pounds. This characteristic financial situation captures the essential vulnerability of the merchant. Although he had relatively little wealth tied up in fixed assets such as factories and buildings, he was not easily able to convert his wealth into cash on hand. As a trader who gave and received credit, most of his assets were not safely stored in his strongbox and warehouse. Rather, they were scattered throughout the Atlantic world and Philadelphia's own hinterland, committed to the "honor and integrity" of dozens of men whom he knew slightly, if at all.

The traders' most important fixed asset was land, an attractive holding that increased in value while generating income. Of these holdings we can learn a good deal from the 1774 tax list, which provides evidence on the landholdings in Philadelphia City and County of 296 traders. Only 36 percent chose to own their own town house, and only 12 percent owned a country seat in Philadelphia County. Twenty-three of

120. For 17 merchants, financial liabilities averaged 57% of financial assets. See *ibid.*

TABLE 12. *Gross Financial Assets and Business Inventories of Merchants, 1750–1795*

	No. of Merchants	
Value (in 1771–1773 Prices)	Gross Financial Assets (*N*=36)	Business Inventories (*N*=35)
£0–£500	1	12
£501–£1,000	1	9
£1,001–£3,000	8	8
£3,001–£5,000	7	3
£5,001–£10,000	9	2
£10,001–£20,000	6	1
£20,001–£40,000	3	0
£40,000+	1	0

Source: Wills and Administrations, City of Philadelphia, Office of the Recorder of Wills.
Note: Financial Assets: mean value, £9,291; median value, £6,112. Business Inventories: mean value, £1,682; median value, £942.

these homeowners possessed some acreage surrounding their dwelling or country seat, and 42 merchants owned land—usually less than sixteen acres—on the outskirts of the city. This acreage may have been used for grazing cows and horses or held for later construction. Since the merchants preferred to own income-producing property, the most popular properties were ground rents (akin to perpetual mortgages) and houses to rent out. Of the traders, 125 (42 percent) owned one or both of these types of real estate, and although the majority of traders owned fewer than four properties, 27 owned nine or more (see Appendix, tables A-11–A-13).

Wealthy but conservative merchants who were approaching the end of their career might build truly impressive real estate portfolios. In a will dated 1778, Joshua Fisher listed a lot and house on Second Street, a house on Dock Street, a fine town house on Front Street, two groups of waterfront stores with adjoining wharves, mills and land on the Brandywine Creek in Delaware, six pieces of land scattered throughout Philadelphia and its suburbs, a country seat and forty acres in the Northern Liberties, and lands in Delaware County. The real estate holdings of Henry Drinker were no less impressive by the time of the Revolution and were worth over £22,409. More striking still were the massive holdings of Israel Pemberton.[121] In 1774, after twenty-five years of retirement from trade, Pemberton owned seventy-seven properties—thirty-five ground rents and forty-two rental properties—that generated an income of about £1,500.

Taken together, the building of estates, big and small, by Philadelphia traders made a major contribution to the accumulation of capital in the city. In a growing port like Philadelphia, this process moved in two directions at the same time: vertically and horizontally. On the one hand, the width of the commercial pyramid expanded outward as the number of merchants more than doubled between 1750 and 1790, and this alone greatly increased the amount of capital available in the economy of the Delaware Valley. At the same time, the height of the commercial pyramid moved upward as the fortunes of the richest merchants—who controlled a very substantial percentage of the community's total resources—expanded. Scattered evidence suggests that before the Seven Years' War it was uncommon for a merchant to be worth more than £20,000, the net worth of Charles Willing when he died in 1754. Thomas Riche, one of only twenty-nine Philadelphians to own a carriage in 1761, lost £11,000 during the 1760s and had to leave the city to live as a sheep farmer.[122] If Riche's fortune had greatly exceeded £20,000, such a drastic change in life would not have been necessary, so he probably had a peak net worth of considerably less than that sum. In 1757, six merchants, of whom at least five were wealthy, formed an insurance company. Of the six founding partners, Robert Morris wrote, "Their stock can't be less than £80,000."[123] This averages out to just £13,333 per person.

By 1790, on the other hand, estates of £20,000 were commonplace; Stephen Girard and Levi Hollingsworth managed to establish fortunes of this size in the comparatively depressed decade of the 1780s, and Girard was worth £55,211 by 1794.[124] Another major Quaker trader was said

121. Joshua Fisher Will no. 207, 1783, *ibid.*; Henry Drinker Journal, 1776–1791, 1–4, 18, 218, 219, 230, Drinker Papers; Israel Pemberton Ledger, 1774–1790, HSP.

122. Riche to John Riche, June 17, 1770, Riche Letterbook, 1764–1771.

123. Quoted in Eugene R. Slaski, "Thomas Willing: Moderation during the American Revolution" (Ph.D. diss., Florida State University, 1971), 83.

124. On the growth of Girard's estate from £2,280 in 1782 to £20,681 in 1790 and £55,211 in 1794, see Girard Journal, 1780–1783, 62, 63, Girard Papers, 3d Ser., Reel 44; Girard Ledger, 1780–1783, accounts opened Feb. 18, 1783, Girard Papers, 3d Ser., Reel 48; Girard Journal, 1788–1790, accounts for Dec. 31, 1790, Girard Papers, 3d Ser., Reel 44; Girard Journal, 1791–1794, 258–261, Girard Papers, 3d Ser., Reel 113. On the growth of Levi Hollingsworth's estate from £3,767 in 1781 to £22,430 in 1785, see Hollingsworth Ledger E, 1780–1781, 208; and Hollingsworth Journal, 1784–1785, 377-398, Hollingsworth Papers. See also Henry Drinker Ledger A, 1776–1792, 1; Henry Drinker Journal, 1776–1791, 18–20; John Head Will no. 128, 1792. In addition to a considerable landed

to be worth £80,000 in 1772, a report which, if perhaps exaggerated, certainly exaggerated the truth.[125] Larger still were the estates of the great fortune builders of the Revolutionary war. William Bingham, for example, was reliably said to be worth £668,000 in the mid-1790s, when he was able to invest in a disastrous land project and survive to tell the tale.[126] With the number of traders more than doubling between 1750 and 1790 while the estates of the top traders jumped tenfold, the process of capital accumulation in Revolutionary Philadelphia was rapid indeed.

The evolution of Philadelphia's merchant community between 1750 and 1791 serves to remind us that the business history of eighteenth-century America, though lacking the dynamism of the next century, was far from static. Subtle but far-reaching changes were transforming the character of certain American trading communities, making them increasingly well articulated economic structures. In Philadelphia, the growth of markets and the general expansion of the economy concentrated unprecedented amounts of capital in the hands of certain entrepreneurs, while allowing many merchants to specialize in limited commercial functions. As a result, the power and sophistication of the merchant community dramatically increased, a fact that was underscored by the trauma of the American Revolution. For despite the shattering of normal economic activity and the immobilization of the highly important Quaker traders, the merchants responded creatively to the challenge of Independence and war, devising and financing an impressive range of new business institutions that advanced the economic development of the region.

---

estate, Head owned gold and silver valued at £26,402 and notes and bonds valued at £20,304. The debts of the estate were limited, and the executors distributed legacies to legatees worth £49,880, exclusive of real estate.

125. William Pollard to John Ramsden, Dec. 20, 1773, Pollard Letterbook, 1772–1774, 329.

126. Robert C. Alberts, *The Golden Voyage: The Life and Times of William Bingham, 1752–1804* (Boston, 1969), 283. Alexander Baring, an English financier who was closing a major deal with Bingham in 1796, wrote: "His property cannot be short of £4 or 500/M sterling, his expenses annually about £5,000 sterling. The houses he lives in with ground round it is estimated worth near £50/M sterling."

3
Enterprise and Adversity

The expanding wealth of the merchant community and the considerable opportunities available to newcomers that we have seen may easily create the impression that prosperity and success accompanied most mercantile careers. Indeed, such a view finds support in several prominent strains of historical analysis. Urban historians often write of the "rise" of Philadelphia, a noun that calls to mind the effortless ascension of a balloon or the skyward drifting of a plume of smoke. Social historians contrast the expanding fortunes of Philadelphia wholesalers with the modest resources of the average citizen and the near-destitution of the lower classes. Business historians in search of a significant biographical subject often select atypically successful traders who managed to build up substantial fortunes from meager beginnings. But these approaches obscure the tense reality of nearly every merchant's day-to-day life. Philadelphia traders, even the most successful, led demanding, nerve-racking lives in the intensely competitive, highly uncertain commercial climate of the Delaware Valley, and a large number of traders went bankrupt. In this respect the entrepreneurs of eighteenth-century Philadelphia were far from unique in the history of business. There were special reasons, however, why the merchants of Philadelphia and of all the northern colonies and states faced a particularly adverse environment. Thin markets, high wages, scarce capital, turbulent foreign exchange markets, and the difficulty of operating in an unfamiliar setting all conspired to heighten the risk of failure.

This fabric of adversity, while it drove many merchants to ruin, was of momentous importance to American economic development, for it induced many northern traders to venture into risky but potentially lucrative new markets, such as the Far East and the interior river valleys of North America. Even more important, the rigors of trade led them to experiment with such unfamiliar activities as manufacturing, banking, land speculation, public securities trading, and transportation improvement. Merchants were disposed to enter such new fields for two distinct reasons. A simple calculation of relative risks indicated that these unexplored areas could not be so much more dangerous than such familiar fields as the West Indies or the dry goods trade. Moreover, the harsh economic climate of northern ports forced the merchant to "use continuously every ounce of wit, imagination, patience, and perseverance which he possessed."[1] Tempered and toughened in the fire of adversity, traders were able to overcome the manifold difficulties that awaited them in novel spheres of enterprise. The merchants' imaginative, indeed reckless, response to adversity swallowed up many a mercantile fortune without yielding a penny in profit, but eventually it launched the Industrial Revolution in the North. That a comparable revolution did not occur in the South, where good profits were to be had from good agriculture, may in part be explained by the absence of such adversity.

The Fabric of Adversity

The fundamental economic condition shaping the experience of businessmen in eighteenth-century North America was the abundance of land and the shortage of capital and labor. This unusual combination of factor endowments gave America a comparative advantage over Europe in the production of agricultural staples and a relative disadvantage in manufacturing finished goods, which required greater inputs of labor and capital than did agriculture.[2] The consequences of this balance of factor endowments varied from one region to another. Businessmen in the South were able to take advantage of the abundance of land by producing staple crops for export—tobacco in Virginia and Maryland; indigo and rice in South Carolina; sugar, coffee, and cocoa in the West Indies. Because these commodities commanded a world market but had a limited growing region, they fetched sufficiently high prices to allow businessmen to buy up large amounts of land, secure slave or servant labor, and grow these commodities on a large scale. Northern businessmen, by contrast, were not able to base their businesses on the control of America's only plentiful factor of production. Fertile though much of it was, northern acreage was best suited to produce foodstuffs grown on the European continent. For such commodities, the West Indies, it is true, were a reasonably secure market for northern farmers, but also a small and fragmented one. As a result, the prices commanded by northern crops were never high enough to support the costs of buying both the land and the labor to work it. The owners of northern lands were, as a

1. Quotation of James B. Hedges in Stuart Bruchey, *The Roots of American Economic Growth: 1607–1861: An Essay in Social Causation* (New York, 1965), 54.

2. Richard E. Caves and Ronald W. Jones, *World Trade and Payments: An Introduction* (Boston, 1973), 138–205.

rule, the same people who tilled them: family farmers. Barred from the role of plantation owner, the businessmen of the North had to concentrate on exporting provisions and distributing manufactures imported from England to the interior.

In performing this function the merchants confronted a daunting array of problems. Their essential requirement was capital with which to buy, hold, and sell merchandise. But capital, unlike land, was in short supply in northern America and had to be imported from Europe at considerable trouble and expense. In addition, the northern merchant serviced relatively small and highly competitive markets. Though it was possible to make a living under such conditions, the North was no place to earn the big profits reaped by the primary producers of the South and the Caribbean. Philadelphia, as one trader lamented, was "more pleasant than profitable."[3]

The economic history of the North from 1630 to 1860 is essentially the story of the slow process by which impecunious entrepreneurs managed to break out of this economic vise by diversifying into other, potentially more lucrative, activities, such as banking and manufacturing. The northern entrepreneur, it must be emphasized, had no absolute economic advantage over the southerner in pursuing many of these activities. There was no geographical reason why the East India trade was centered in Salem rather than Norfolk, or why the early cotton mills were established in New England rather than in the Chesapeake region. What the North did have was a comparative advantage (vis-à-vis the South, but not Europe) in these activities, because it could not compete in the business of cash crop monoculture. The northerner, in short, was motivated to diversify by his comparative *dis*advantage in the field for which the English colonies as a whole were best suited, namely, agriculture. To understand the mentality of the northern entrepreneur, we must take the measure of the problems and pressures that constantly assaulted him.

Export Markets. Demand for Philadelphia products in Europe and the West Indies was sporadic and difficult to predict, and not infrequently cargoes were sold at a loss. That there were several different places to which produce could be sent did give the merchants valuable flexibility—if the Caribbean offered a poor market, there was the possibility of selling in Portugal or Charleston or Boston—but only the alert, enterprising trader, who constantly reviewed his opportunities, was able to take advantage of these options. To do so, moreover, required switch-

3. Arthur L. Jensen, *The Maritime Commerce of Colonial Philadelphia* (Madison, Wis., 1963), 115.

ing shipping from one route to another, which negated the possibility of settling a vessel in the single trade for which it was designed.

Import Markets. The dry goods market in eighteenth-century Philadelphia was almost chronically glutted. Capital for the trade was supplied by English exporters, who persisted in extending generous credits to both small and large interlopers. On the few occasions when profit margins were high, inexperienced new firms, backed by British credit, jumped into the market and quickly overstocked it. Only patient, cautious, skillful traders could regularly make money in this cutthroat market. Demand for dry goods, it is true, was growing rapidly, but so was the number of merchants. In any case, the imports had to be sold to people, not growth rates, and in 1760 the population of the area served by Philadelphia was only about 6 percent of that of England and Wales.[4]

Foreign Exchange Markets. The northern merchant faced a problem that the southern planter was spared: export cargoes were not directed to the same ports from which imports were received, a condition that created enormous problems with foreign exchange. England normally had no need for flour. Imports therefore had to be paid for with credits earned in third markets, a circumstance that forced northern merchants to participate in America's foreign exchange market. Because the supply of specie in the North was limited and easily exhausted and the market for bills of exchange was likewise thin, the price of foreign exchange in Philadelphia was much more volatile than in London.

Labor Markets. Commerce in the Delaware Valley was sufficiently taxing to propel a number of traders into various areas of manufacturing, particularly ironmaking. But here the entrepreneur faced the problem of high labor costs and a severe shortage of skilled workers.[5] Ironmasters sometimes had to wait at the wharves for cargoes of European servants who could be purchased as unskilled labor. Key skilled personnel often could be recruited only in Europe, and once assembled, a labor force had to be paid in good times and bad—even when the enterprise was not turning a profit—or the workers would drift away to other employers.

4. John Flexer Walzer, "Transportation in the Philadelphia Trading Area, 1740–1775" (Ph.D. diss., University of Wisconsin, 1968), 3, 4; Phyllis Deane and W. A. Cole, *British Economic Growth, 1688–1959: Trends and Structure*, University of Cambridge Department of Applied Economics Monographs, No. 8 (Cambridge, 1962), 103, 288.

5. Bruchey, *Roots of American Economic Growth*, 163.

Scaling the Learning Curve. Economists and common sense tell us that the efficiency of a business operation tends to increase as time goes by and participants gain in experience and knowledge. As immigrants to an alien continent, Philadelphia merchants were continually confronting novel investment possibilities and unfamiliar business terrain. Plenty of opportunities existed, but there were unimagined pitfalls as well. Whether they were testing a new market, constructing a slitting mill, digging a copper mine, or setting up a commercial bank, the merchants were accepting formidable but incalculable risks. One remarked, "Like all New Schemers & projecters of New Business [we] are Like to Suffer."[6]

Capital Scarcity. What made these risks particularly dangerous was that the capital of most merchants was too limited to allow them to absorb losses. The merchants of mainland America were, in effect, the proletarians of the Atlantic business world. In Philadelphia at the time of the Revolution a major merchant was worth only about £35,000, and anyone worth over £20,000 was considered rich; the majority possessed only a few thousand pounds. Before the Seven Years' War very few merchants had more than £20,000. By contrast, one *medium-sized* Jamaica sugar plantation (many planters owned two or more plantations) was worth about £32,000 in the 1770s. Major capitalists in eighteenth-century Glasgow were worth upwards of £150,000, and the magnates of London were worth between £150,000 and £800,000.[7] A careful analysis of 919 probate inventories demonstrates that even wealthy southerners were strikingly richer than their northern counterparts. The top tenth of southern decedents, for instance, owned physical wealth (land, effects, and slaves) worth £3,852 sterling, while those in the middle colonies and New England owned property worth £825 and £986, respectively.[8] The

6. Turner to George Rock, Nov. 1759, Joseph Turner Letterbook, 1753–1774, Historical Society of Pennsylvania (hereafter identified as HSP).

7. Richard B. Sheridan, *Sugar and Slavery: An Economic History of the British West Indies, 1623–1775* (Baltimore, Md., 1973), 229–332; T. M. Devine, *The Tobacco Lords: A Study of the Tobacco Merchants of Glasgow and Their Trading Activities, c. 1740–1790* (Edinburgh, 1975), 10, 23–24, 27, picture facing 29; Jacob M. Price, "Capital and Credit in the British-Chesapeake Trade, 1750–1775," in Virginia Bever Blatt and David Curtis Skaggs, eds., *Of Mother Country and Plantations: Proceedings of the Twenty-seventh Conference in Early American History* (Bowling Green, Ohio, 1971), 14–17; Louis Morton, *Robert Carter of Nomini Hall: A Virginia Tobacco Planter of the Eighteenth Century* (Williamsburg, Va., 1945).

8. Alice Hanson Jones, *American Colonial Wealth: Documents and Methods*, 2d ed., 3 vols. (New York, 1977), III, 2113–2115; see also 2096–2098, 2103–2108.

merchant who tried to augment his capital with loans would find that interest rates were about 50 percent higher in America than in Europe.[9]

This dearth of capital heightened the merchants' risk by making it more difficult for them to diversify. As we have seen, the smaller a firm's operations were, the greater the likelihood that it would operate in just one market. Lack of capital also made traders especially vulnerable to bankruptcy. In an emergency they had only small assets which might close the gap or serve as collateral for loans.

The Importance of Wars. The vicissitudes of armed conflict played a central role in the career of many successful northern merchants. When well-financed European armies and navies arrived, local demand was inflated, and sales volume jumped. At these times exceptional gains were also possible in war contracting, commerce with the enemy, and speculation in disrupted overseas markets. Risks and operating costs were also high during wars, but not high enough to discourage the hungry traders of the Delaware Valley.

Buffeted by this array of problems, merchants in Philadelphia did not consider themselves conquering capitalists or people of plenty, swiftly carving out fortunes from a bountiful continent. They were, in truth, undercapitalized provincials working on the outskirts of the Atlantic economy. What prosperity they did attain came by dint of hustling in an economic arena that was very risky and only modestly profitable. Writing of a correspondent firm, Stephen Girard remarked: "Their conduct shows the prudence that will risk nothing. As for me, I cannot do this; since I have not as much as I desire, it seems necessary to me to take some risks or to remain always poor." Another trader confessed that he was "Loaded with Ceare & Trouble," while Thomas Willing reflected that his father had lived a "life of care & Anxiety." And Stephen Collins, shaken by the news of a competitor's failure, sternly reminded his son that it was a "lessen every Day to learne by and shows the necessity of a strict oconomy[,] Frugality and Industry. . . . This is a hardharted Iron-Fisted & inhospitable world, and too many is caught in its snare."[10]

One person who fully shared this Hobbesian perspective was Benja-

9. Sidney Homer, *A History of Interest Rates*, 2d ed. (New Brunswick, N.J., 1977), 152–165, 274–279.

10. S. Girard to John Girard, Jan. 26, 1785, Stephen Girard Papers, 2d Ser., Reel 121. All references to the Girard Papers are to the microfilm collection in the American Philosophical Society (hereafter cited as APS). Riche to Abraham Judah, Jan. 6, 1759, Thomas Riche Letterbook, 1748–1764, Thomas Riche Papers, HSP; T. Willing to Mayne, Burne, and Mayne, Dec. 12, 1754, Willing and Morris Letterbook, 1754–1761, 49, HSP; Collins to Zachariah Collins, July 19, 1784, Stephen Collins Papers, LXI, 45, Library of Congress.

min Fuller, an Irishman of good family but meager capital who twice went bankrupt in Philadelphia, while his brother Joseph thrived in the homeland on an inherited income. Benjamin once wrote to his brother: "I coud not help smiling at your observation respecting my fatagueing myself with busyness—were it in my power I promise you I shoud like to take the World easy, & it gives me infinite satisfaction to find its in yours [power] to do it.—you know I like to live genteelly, tho' not extravagantly, and it takes all my industry to accomplish it, and with great fatague I have hitherto been able (thank God) to live well, but have not been able to lay up such a Stock, as would maintain me without dayly labour." In another letter Fuller explained why he had not been able to build up a large fortune: Pennsylvania was the "best Country in the World for Labourers & handycrafts, the worst for what may be called half bred Gentlemen, without some Capital—this observation I sensibly feel from past experiance, happy in a fortitude of Soul, that has (thank God) supported & carry'd me through many severe difficultys."[11]

Even the wealthiest merchant could not escape the "severe difficultys" that plagued Fuller's career. Among the prominent traders who went bankrupt were Robert Morris, George Meade, Abel James, John Scott, Thomas Fitzsimons, and John Ross. The situation in the 1770s of the six Wharton brothers is representative. One was a hatter, and another was just getting started in trade, while Thomas and Isaac were partners in a successful firm. Joseph Wharton was also successful for a time, but not so lucky; he was deceived by a correspondent in England and had to spend many years in Europe trying to right his affairs. The sixth Wharton brother, Samuel, was also in England, hiding from his American creditors after going bankrupt in an ambitious attempt to dominate the Indian trade in the Illinois country. Even for Thomas, solvent and successful, the strain of business was great; he complained, "The pressure I have had, owing to the close Attendance I have been obliged to give to B. W. and M. [*Baynton, Wharton, and Morgan*] affairs with some others have injured my health so much that I am often subject to a Pain in my breast."[12]

Hardly a year went by in the second half of the eighteenth century without at least one firm going bankrupt. A simple listing of failures mentioned in a wide variety of sources yields a total of 108 traders,

11. Fuller to Joseph Fuller, Dec. 3, 1768, July 8, 1769, Benjamin Fuller Letterbook, 1784–1787, Benjamin Fuller Papers, HSP.

12. William Wharton Ledger, 1761–1803; Charles Wharton Daybook, 1768–1772; Wharton to [Samuel Wharton], Oct. 4, 25, Nov. 7, Dec. 6, 1774, to Joseph Wharton, Nov. 6, 1774, Thomas Wharton Letterbook, 1773–1784, Wharton Papers, HSP; Max Savelle, *George Morgan, Colony Builder*, 2d ed. (New York, 1967), 53–110.

active between 1750 and 1791, who went bankrupt or became financially crippled for a time. Because it is highly incomplete, this figure cannot be used to calculate a rate of bankruptcy, but it is suggestive that of 60 merchants for whom we have substantive (though usually incomplete) biographical information, 21 went bankrupt. Far more comprehensive and precise information is available for the period 1784–1790, because in August 1785, in the midst of a commercial panic, the Pennsylvania legislature passed its first bankruptcy law, creating provisions for declaring bankruptcies.[13] Between 1786 and 1790, 171 people filed for bankruptcy under the law, of whom 126 were listed as Philadelphians, 84 of them Philadelphia merchants. This figure of 84 cannot be uncritically accepted as the total number of Philadelphia traders who went bankrupt during the depression of the 1780s, but it is close to the truth.[14] We may be certain that many others abandoned trade while they were still solvent.

"Bankruptcy" naturally had an imprecise meaning in the informal business world of the eighteenth century. It was common for firms to be tardy in paying their debts, and creditors, who normally were themselves debtors, tended to be patient in collecting them. However, if a creditor eventually sued for payment and the debtor could not meet his obligation, he would be forced to declare bankruptcy, reorganize his affairs, and pay as much as possible of each debt that he owed. Many hard-pressed firms stopped payment of their own accord, before their creditors took them to court. In either case a declaration of bankruptcy meant only that the firm did not have enough liquid assets—cash and property readily convertible into cash—to meet its current obligations. One reason why bankruptcies were common was that such liquid assets constituted a limited share of most merchants' estates. As we saw in the preceding chapter, landownership and book debts were typically of greater value. Frequently it was a merchant's inability to collect his debts that

13. James T. Mitchell and Henry Flanders, comps., *The Statutes at Large of Pennsylvania from 1682 to 1801*, 16 vols. (Harrisburg, Pa., 1896–1911), XII, 70–86; Bankruptcy File, in "Records of Pennsylvania's Revolutionary Governments, 1775–1790," Record Group 27, Pennsylvania Historical and Museum Commission (hereafter cited as PHMC). This file is conveniently abstracted in Harry E. Whipkey and Roland M. Baumann, eds., *Guide to the Microfilm of the Records of Pennsylvania's Revolutionary Governments, 1775–1790 (Record Group 27) in the Pennsylvania State Archives* (Harrisburg, Pa., 1978), 276–283.

14. On the one hand, the state's bankruptcy file used the term "merchant" rather indiscriminately; only 49 of the Philadelphia "merchants" in the file were described as merchants on tax lists and in city directories. On the other hand, many traders went bankrupt in 1784 and 1785, before the state file begins; fairly comprehensive manuscript evidence suggests that at least 19 traders fall in this category. When these 19 are added to the 49 known merchants in the bankruptcy file, it appears that 68 merchants, or 13% of the traders present in the city in 1785, went bankrupt in the 1780s.

made him unable to pay his own creditors. But this did not in every case mean that his *net worth*—his total assets minus total liabilities—was less than zero. A bankrupt trader who did manage to obtain payment for outstanding debts often was able to meet his own obligations in full. Conversely, foundering firms with negative net worths sometimes managed to keep their creditors at bay for long periods of time before finally stopping payment.

Bankruptcies often were handled not in the courts, but in formal discussions between the businessmen involved. The subtle negotiations in these meetings were shaped by the hopes, fears, and even the consciences of the interested parties. The main concern of the bankrupt himself was to get out of the mess with as much money and reputation as possible. If he appeared responsible and honorable, he could expect some leniency from his creditors and escape with enough capital and credit to begin again. For their part, the creditors were likely to consider three factors in deciding what to do. In the first place, they expected the debtor to stop payment as soon as necessary, while there were still some assets to distribute, instead of scrambling to right himself and squandering whatever assets remained. There was a tremendous difference between the bankrupt who was able to pay off fifteen shillings on the pound and the one who held out to the bitter end and was eventually able to pay off only two shillings on the pound.

A second concern of creditors was that no one of them be favored over any other by receiving full payment of his debt just before bankruptcy was declared. (Stephen Girard once did this by grabbing the Caribbean assets of a distressed Philadelphia firm shortly before it went out of business.) Finally, creditors gave thought to the causes of the failure: was it the product of mismanagement and extravagance, or simple bad luck? In the latter case they might be genuinely sympathetic. When Joseph Turner forced John Wallace into bankruptcy, he incurred the wrath of the entire trading body, for Wallace's difficulties were purely the result of Indian marauding on the frontier that had ruined many of his customers. Sometimes creditors were disposed to allow the bankrupt to continue about his business, albeit under close supervision, until as much money as possible had been collected and distributed to them through a series of dividends. They were not, in other words, disposed to grab for quick payment if more could be obtained with patience. Neither were they intent upon ruining a man, unless he deserved it. Any one of the creditors could be next, after all, and an honorable bankrupt had to be honorably dealt with.[15]

15. Girard to Girard and Hourquebie, July 8, 1784, Girard Papers, 2d Ser., Reel 121; Turner to David Barclay and Sons, Sept. 1, 1758, Turner Letterbook, 1753–1774; John Kidd to William Neate, Sept. 5, 1758, John Kidd Letterbook, 1749–1763, HSP. For other

Honorable or not, bankruptcy was not a pleasant condition for the failed trader. His fortune was shattered, his business judgment repudiated, his privacy invaded, and the management of his own business wrested from his hands and placed in the control of a committee of his peers. People with whom he had haggled on an equal footing just days before were now in a position to look at his ledger, give him orders, determine his financial fate. Even if they were generous, he would have to rebuild his business. Not only was his capital gone in many cases, but the disruption of his business operations was likely to shrink his network of customers, as they looked elsewhere for service. The word that merchants reached for to describe their fate was "mortification." "I am reduced," wrote one, "within one Step of a Situation the most mortifying the most distressing that Can fall to the Lot of any one possessed of Sensibility." Another referred to the "Mortification and reproach that must attend a Stop and Surrender to the Creditors." The mortification could be acute indeed, severe enough in two cases, it was said, to lead directly to the death of the hapless merchants involved.[16]

One merchant who survived the trial was John Mitchell, described in 1780 as a "little fat, squat man, fifty years old, a great judge of horses."[17] Starting with a capital of a few thousand pounds, Mitchell went into the business of importing dry goods in a big way in the 1770s and even opened outlets in the hinterland to facilitate inland distribution. Mitchell seemed a bit aggressive and improvident to some of his competitors, but under the restraining hand of his sensible brother Randall he seemed likely to do well enough. This assessment proved to be optimistic, for in 1773, when his finances appeared to be perfectly sound, John Mitchell shocked the city by calling a meeting of his creditors and revealing that he could not pay his obligations on time. He owed nearly £6,513 to the great London firm of Mildred and Roberts and sums of over £1,600 to several other English exporters. Convening

examples, in addition to those cited below, see Girard to Vallee and Duplessis, Oct. 1787, Girard Papers, 2d Ser., Reel 121; Cropley Rose Letterbook, 1779–1781, HSP; Collins to Zachariah Collins, July 12, 19, 1784, Collins Papers, LXI, 43, 45.

16. Thomas Clifford, Jr., to John Clifford, Sept. 28, 1784, Clifford Correspondence, 1778–1785, VII, 125, HSP; Drinker to Frederick Pigou, Jr., July 3, 1784, Henry Drinker Letterbook, 1784–1786, 45, Henry Drinker Papers, HSP; Turner to David Barclay and Sons, Feb. 5, 1759, Turner Letterbook, 1753–1774; William B. Willcox *et al.*, eds., *The Papers of Benjamin Franklin*, XX (New Haven, Conn., 1976), 198 nn. 2, 3.

17. Marquis de Chastellux, *Travels in North America in the Years 1780, 1781, and 1782*, trans. Howard C. Rice, Jr., 2 vols. (Chapel Hill, N.C., 1963), I, 177; Pollard to Bowers, Oct. 28, 1773, William Pollard Letterbook, 1772–1774, 287, HSP; Fuller to Anthony Stocker, Nov. 15, 1773, Fuller Letterbook, 1762–1781.

in secret at Mitchell's house, the creditors examined his books and decided that, even allowing for £600 in bad debts, he would eventually be able to meet his obligations and still have £1,100 left over. The creditors appointed three of their number as "assignees," to whom all the assets of the firm would be assigned. These men in turn appointed two attorneys who were to oversee the collection of Mitchell's debts and the selling of his remaining stock of merchandise. This tedious process was expected to take three years. Since Mitchell had acted even before his firm was suspected of financial weakness, he had displayed exceptionally "honorable and candid conduct" and was rewarded with the "extraordinary" privilege of a salary of £300 per year and the right to keep £200 worth of household furniture. In addition, the two attorneys of the assignees agreed to give Mitchell the salaries they were to receive for aiding the collection of his debts.

Mitchell's bankruptcy was embarrassing and disappointing, but not serious enough to prevent his serving as a wagon contractor for the French and American armies during the Revolution and acquiring enough credit by the end of the war to go broke again.[18] This was a more serious break for Mitchell, and a more obscure one for the historian. In 1785 he was in Charleston, South Carolina, while his family and brother remained in Philadelphia. Mitchell's creditors threatened to attach his estates in New Jersey, and he apparently agreed to a sheriff's sale of his assets, with the proceeds to be distributed among his creditors. This threw the entire family into disarray. The bankruptcy dragged down Mitchell's brother Randall, who had to resettle his family in Alexandria, Virginia, where he hoped to become a shopkeeper. Evidently unable to accept the reversal in her social position and financial circumstances, John's wife Sally became distraught. When she attempted to conceal her distressed condition from the prying eyes of society, a family friend warned, "You are in a Critical situation respecting the opinion of People in General, who will talk freely at times, & if you appear so very much hurt & dissatisfied will be apt to Conclude that it was partly your own Folly & dissipation that brought on the Misfortunes you so sensibly feel & lament." Mitchell himself was also deeply shaken, plaintively soliciting commissions and offering to go anywhere in the world where he could prosper in trade. He must have been jolted by the searing reproof he received from his irascible friend Benjamin Fuller:

> You have spun the thread of deceit so fine, that at last it has crack'd . . . The other day I was ask'd by a Neighbour of mine, what the

18. Fuller to ———, Nov. 24, 1784, to John Mitchell, Dec. 2, 1784, Mar. 7, Apr. 9, 1785, to Mary Mitchell, Feb. 22, 1785, Fuller Letterbook, 1784–1787, 54, 55, 84, 90, 83.

man deserved That had Cheated the Widow, defrauded the Orphan, deceiv'd an Amiable woman and doom'd a Brother (who had a large & helpless Family) to a Jail—I readily answer'd a Rope.

The Response to Adversity

The merchants' response to adversity—to the severe difficulties in which they so frequently became entangled—was neither to accept their lot passively nor to abandon commerce altogether for a less risky profession. Aggressive arrivistes that they were, they conspired and contrived with every means available to switch to some other business opportunity. Despite their lack of capital, they were in a relatively good position to do this, because their role as intermediaries gave them inherent flexibility. What money they had was relatively mobile, convertible into almost any type of asset. Even more important, they were in touch with many markets and many sources of funds, and they were highly experienced at juggling credits, cargoes, remittances, and ships to come up with a profit. This flexibility can be conveyed by examining three distinct cases, among the many that are available: the Guyana venture of Thomas Riche; the fur-trading exploits of Baynton, Wharton, and Morgan; and the iron investments of several merchants.

Thomas Riche was a tough, flamboyant, disorganized, but quite wealthy trader who was particularly active in legal and illegal commerce with the West Indies. During the Seven Years' War he met with heavy losses, which caused him to remark in 1759, "I have had the bad Luck to Miscarrie in 3 sail of Vesels Bown [i.e., bound] your way. which had made a dam Large hole in my Pockit."[19] Riche's luck apparently did not improve in the next few years, for in 1764 he reported that he had lost five thousand pounds during the preceding eighteen months. His reaction to this blow was to try to recoup his fortune by undertaking a highly novel project which, if successful, figured to yield a profit of as much as thirty thousand pounds.

The scheme involved a contract signed with the French government by a New York merchant, John Remsen, in which Remsen agreed to supply the French colony of Guyana, on the northeastern coast of South America, with a variety of provisions produced in North America. Riche in effect subcontracted with Remsen to ship some of these cargoes to Guyana, but he was to be paid directly by the French officials there. The plan was unusual and dangerous in several respects. It involved a long-

19. Riche to Abraham Harris, Dec. 24, 1758, Riche Letterbook, 1748–1764.

term contract, a device rarely adopted by Philadelphia traders in their private business; Riche was highly dependent on Remsen, whom he did not know well; his shipments were subject to seizure by the British navy since they grossly violated the Navigation Acts; and Riche had no experience in dealing with the French government. But Riche was used to large risks, and he badly needed the handsome returns that would accompany success. As he said with reference to a laborsaving crane he wished to use, "Poverty is the mother of invention."[20]

Riche might have added that invention was sometimes the mother of poverty, for from the beginning his Guyana venture was a disaster. Even before the contract was signed, he directed a merchant in New Bern, North Carolina, to ship to Guyana a cargo of foodstuffs and naval stores and to post bond that the destination of the naval stores was Barbados. The evasion somehow failed, however, and the vessel and cargo were seized and confiscated by British officials in North Carolina. Part of a second cargo that did reach Guyana was not accepted by officials there because certain goods had not been specified in the original contract. At this point Riche heard unsettling reports of a change of government in the French colony that raised doubts about the validity of the contract itself. It was too late to back out, so he sent a third cargo worth £1,250 aboard the sloop *Falmouth*. By now Riche believed that the contract was "a very bad one," but his confidence was somewhat revived by the receipt of a substantial bill of exchange from the French colony. Accordingly, he sent out a fourth shipment, this one valued at £1,637. Parts of this cargo also were not accepted in Cayenne, yet this difficulty paled beside a far more serious problem: the bills of exchange drawn on the French treasury by officials in Guyana, which Riche had already received as payment, had not been honored in Paris. The Philadelphian was dumbfounded; if they refused to honor a "solemn contract" that had already been performed, "the French king and all his ministers are dam deceitful—worthless fellows." Justifiably alarmed, Riche engaged his London correspondent to help him recover payment, while also working through Joseph Galloway and Benjamin Franklin (then in London) to secure the same end. At this critical juncture Riche was denied the support of the man who actually signed the contract: John Remsen inconveniently died in 1766.

Throughout the late 1760s and early 1770s Riche exploited every possible means of obtaining payment for his shipments, which totaled

20. James H. Soltow, "Thomas Riche's 'Adventure' in French Guiana, 1764–1766," *Pennsylvania Magazine of History and Biography*, LXXXIII (1959), 409–419 (quotations on 412, 415–416). All discussion of Riche's venture is based on this valuable article, unless otherwise stated.

(excluding the one seized in North Carolina) £5,159. But his position was untenable. How was a British provincial to secure payment from the French court for performance of a contract he had not even signed? Finally, Riche cut his losses: he sold off such trappings of wealth as his country seat and town house and retired to the Jersey countryside to become a sheep farmer. He tried to be philosophical about his losses, but bitterness could not be suppressed. To one creditor he confessed, "Nothing but misfortune has happen^{d} in my Trade for ten years past. which has Really mad[e] me neglect all Business. . . . Damn Pen Ink and Paper I would rather take a small Floging than make ten Entreys or write this Letter."[21]

The fur trade with western Indians was another commercial activity into which certain Philadelphia traders poured capital during the eighteenth century. Involving the exchange of British-made cloth, ironware, trinkets, and liquor for skins and furs that were exported to England, the trade had a value of forty thousand pounds in 1754. It was a dangerous and demanding business requiring long pack trips through the wild forests of western Pennsylvania, shrewd and patient bartering with sometimes hostile Indians, and—as trade approached the Ohio Valley and Great Lakes—increasingly violent competition from tough French traders. Markups and gross profits could be extremely high, but so were the costs of doing business and the threat of serious wartime losses. This was no trade for casual interlopers who had a multiplicity of other interests, and relatively few Philadelphia merchants were involved in it. Although its exact commercial organization demands further study, it appears that the main participants were rugged backcountry traders. A handful of important eastern firms, notably Shippen and Lawrence, and Levy, Franks, and Simon, also specialized in this business and stationed partners in Philadelphia and Lancaster to facilitate transactions. A few other Philadelphia merchants, such as Jeremiah Warder and William West, were engaged in the trade as a sideline.[22]

Two men who used neither of these strategies were John Baynton and Samuel Wharton.[23] Between 1757 and 1763 this partnership engaged extensively in provision trading but also participated in the Indian trade in a major way, sending out "adventures" to such places as Quebec,

21. Riche to Abraham Harris, June 17, 1770, Riche Letterbook, 1764–1771.

22. Albert T. Volwiler, *George Croghan and the Westward Movement, 1741–1782* (Cleveland, Ohio, 1926), 17–54; Edwin Wolf 2d and Maxwell Whiteman, *The History of the Jews of Philadelphia from Colonial Times to the Age of Jackson*, 2d ed. (Philadelphia, 1975), 23–75.

23. This account is based on Savelle, *George Morgan*, 18–75.

Detroit, and Fort Pitt. The business was more remarkable for its scale than for its profitability, and by 1763 Baynton and Wharton were in financial trouble. If liquidated at that time, their firm would not have been able to pay its creditors ten shillings on the pound. Fortunately, the firm was able to secure an infusion of capital by admitting to the partnership its clerk, George Morgan, who possessed an inheritance. The trio used this aid to good effect and reportedly earned a profit of sixty-five hundred pounds between the fall of 1763 and the end of 1764.

Despite this success, Baynton, Wharton, and Morgan was not content to rebuild its fortune in the treacherous arena of overseas commerce. It resolved instead to achieve this goal through one bold, illegal stab into the farthest reaches of the fur-trading region: the Illinois country of the upper Mississippi, which had been ceded to the British Empire by France at the close of the Seven Years' War. In secret partnership with George Croghan, Pennsylvania's leading expert on the western territory, Baynton, Wharton, and Morgan decided to send westward a large shipment of merchandise that would be sold to four groups of customers: the Indians of the upper Mississippi, the French inhabitants of the area, the British garrison stationed there, and the Department of Indian Affairs, which needed a constant supply of goods with which to buy friendship from the Indians.

The first shipment of merchandise, totaling nearly twenty thousand pounds in value, went westward in 1765. Since the Illinois country was legally closed to trade at this time, the goods accompanied a convoy of wagons and packhorses sent to George Croghan, who was already in the country on official business. Legal or not, the shipment was not viewed with equanimity by the Scotch-Irish settlers of Cumberland County, who did not care to see sanctimonious Philadelphia Quakers sell guns and tomahawks to western Indians just two years after Pontiac's Rebellion. Disguised as Indians, a group of frontiersmen attacked the packtrain and destroyed most of the firm's shipment.

Far from being discouraged by this setback, the firm expanded its efforts in 1766. It contracted with wagoners to haul no fewer than sixty wagonloads of goods to Fort Pitt (Pittsburgh), with six hundred packhorses assisting in their transportation over the Allegheny Mountains. At Fort Pitt the goods were transferred to long riverboats of shallow draft that floated down the Ohio River and up the Mississippi to Kaskaskia, about fifty miles south of the present city of Saint Louis. There was nothing modest about this inland navy; in the fall of 1766 alone, sixty-five boats manned by more than three hundred men made the trip. While muscular boatmen sweated and strained to fight the swift current of the Mississippi, George Morgan lay back in his oilcloth shelter with "Gun, Pistols, Sword, Spy Glass, Speaking Trumpet, Pipe, Tea Chest, Compass,

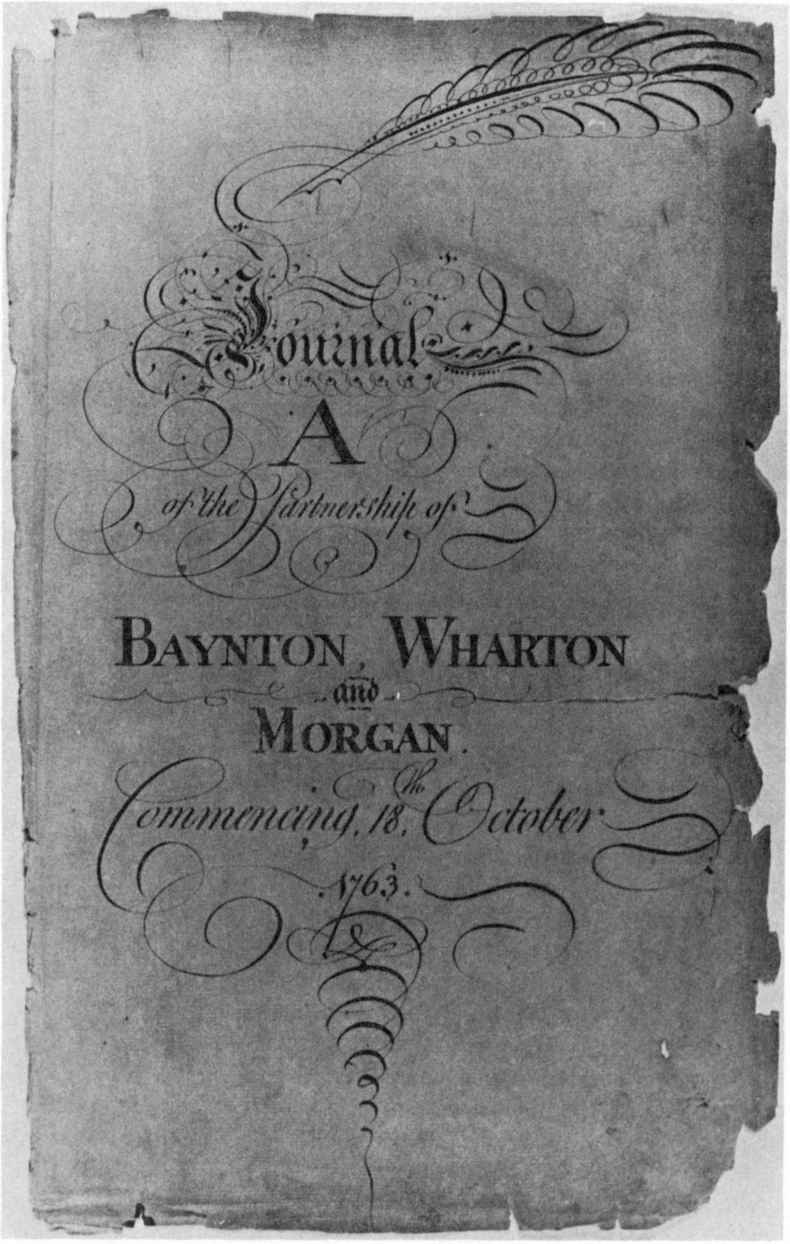

PLATE 18. Journal of Baynton, Wharton, and Morgan. *Courtesy of the Pennsylvania Historical and Museum Commission*

Pen & Ind & Chest of Drawers."[24] Despite his relative comfort, Morgan had much to worry about, for by the end of the year his firm had invested in the project over seventy-five thousand pounds, much of it borrowed from the London merchant William Neate.

Transporting tons of merchandise by wagon, packhorse, and riverboat from Philadelphia to the heart of the Midwest turned out to be the easy part of the firm's project, for the goods commanded disappointing sales in the newly opened territory. The fur trade with the Indians was less extensive than had been imagined and in any case was dominated by experienced, well-established French traders. Not surprisingly, the Frenchmen of the area preferred to trade with one another, rather than with their recent conquerors; and potential British customers were no more openhanded. Morgan could secure long-term contracts with neither the Indian department nor the local British garrison. An undertaking with such high initial costs that was financed with credit required handsome revenues to keep it afloat. When these failed to materialize, the firm promptly called a meeting of its creditors, who determined that its assets were worth at least £120,000, £40,000 more than its liabilities. Since this was an eminently respectable bankruptcy, and because the creditors figured to recover their entire debt in due time, the firm was granted a letter of license to continue in business for three years more, under the supervision of eight of the creditors. Though it appeared that Baynton, Wharton, and Morgan might be able to escape the debacle with reputation intact, the bankruptcy dragged on year after year, scarring the lives of the three adventurers. A rancorous feud broke out between Morgan and Wharton, and John Baynton, who reportedly died from the ordeal of the failure, set down this diary entry in 1770: "Mr. Morgan setts off to Day or to Morrow for that shocking Country the Illinois—My Familys Distress on this grevious Occasion beggars Description."[25] Perhaps this distress was just reward for the firm's avaricious optimism. Nevertheless, its venture was historically important, for it led to the attempt by Samuel Wharton and other Philadelphians to obtain a grant from the British ministry to set up a fourteenth colony in the Ohio Valley. Though this project was also unsuccessful, it was an important precursor to post-Revolutionary attempts by Philadelphia capitalists to open up the West.

The exploits of Thomas Riche, and Baynton, Wharton, and Morgan involved single firms. Iron manufacturing, on the other hand, involved over two dozen Philadelphia merchants, many of whom were

24. *Ibid.*, 28.
25. Quoted in Volwiler, *George Croghan*, 203.

exceptionally wealthy. Since several prominent planters in Maryland and Virginia were also concerned in ironworks, one might conclude that this kind of investment is not a particularly notable example of the northern merchants' penchant for diversification. Such a conclusion would be unwarranted, however. For the southern planter, ironmaking was a natural extension of agricultural activities; for the northern merchant, it constituted a great departure from normal operations. As we have seen, traders owned relatively few fixed assets, and aside from a handful of clerks and captains, they had no full-time employees. Although many traders held land, it was seldom used in close relation to their commercial operations. In contrast to the typical mercantile operation, iron production required the management of thousands of acres and the employment of from fifty to one hundred people, or, in short, a fixed investment of roughly six times the price of a large new vessel.

We must wonder, then, why merchants were attracted to this novel and expensive investment. Their motivation was in part the same ascribed by Robert F. Dalzell, Jr., to the early cotton manufacturers of New England. An ironworks was a good place for a wealthy older merchant to invest a substantial portion of his fortune, for if it was well managed, he could receive a good rate of return without having to juggle the multiplicity of details and decisions that overseas trading entailed. Joseph Turner, William Allen, Henry Drinker, and Abel James all depended on ironworks for a substantial portion of their income in their later years, after they had abandoned day-to-day trading.

A second reason for merchants' interest in ironworks exemplifies well their special ability—indeed, the powerful inducements upon them—to diversify. We have seen that a primary problem of the Pennsylvania economy was its inability to produce anything to exchange for the huge volume of dry goods imported from England. For shipping merchants whose vessels shuttled between Philadelphia and England, this imbalance created a particular difficulty, for they had little with which to fill their vessels on the eastward leg of the circuit. The commodities most commonly used for this purpose were lumber and iron, but high-grade iron was occasionally unavailable, first, because of the limited number of works in the Philadelphia area and, second, because of adverse weather conditions that sometimes put them out of blast for considerable periods. In addition, the quality of the local output was quite variable, dependent as it was on the specific ores used. The shippers' constant need for this scarce commodity gave them a strong motive for financing and supplying an iron plantation in return for a steady supply of its output. James and Drinker, who stated that their ship *Chalkley* virtually had to have some iron in its hold to sail smoothly, served as agents of the

PLATE 19. The Hopewell Furnace. *National Park Service photo by Richard Frear. Courtesy of the National Park Service, United States Department of the Interior*

Durham Iron Works for some time, and they strongly implied that the difficulty of obtaining the metal was a major reason that led them to buy into the Atsion Iron Works in south Jersey. Joshua Fisher and Sons, another wealthy Quaker firm that kept a vessel in the English trade, also found it expedient to become financially involved in iron manufacturing. The firm's ledger shows that between 1769 and 1772 it provided credits of £4,288 to the prominent Jersey ironmaker Charles Read, while receiving payment in iron of £3,370. Although the Fishers never accepted the risks involved in actually owning an ironworks, this generous supply of short-term credit was dangerous enough: Read went bankrupt in 1773 and absconded to the West Indies.[26]

Still another Quaker shipping merchant who traded with England and provided financing for iron production was Thomas Clifford. During the 1760s Clifford's shipments to a New England anchor maker and other customers included significant shipments of bar iron, but he found that iron supplies were extremely unreliable. After 1768, when he acquired

26. James and Drinker to Lancelot Cowper, Aug. 4, 1772, May 15, 1773, James and Drinker Foreign Letterbook, 1772–1785, 8, 106, Henry Drinker Papers, HSP; Joshua Fisher and Sons Ledger, 1769–1773, 77, 131, 151, 202, HSP.

two vessels which he hoped to maintain in a shuttle pattern with England, his need for the metal increased. Clifford's method of securing a steady supply was to provide financing for the Pine Grove Iron Works in Maryland. The principal owner of the works was Walter Franklin, a wealthy New York merchant, but the active partners were Thomas and William Lightfoot, who had been unimportant Philadelphia merchants before moving down to Maryland. For several years Clifford provided the works with a miscellany of services. He shipped to it a variety of provisions. He extended it working capital, sometimes in amounts as high as five hundred pounds. He operated a schooner that shuttled between the works and Philadelphia. He offered advice concerning marketing and management. In return for these services Clifford was rewarded with a torrent of abuse from the querulous Franklin in New York, abuse that was naturally intensified by the eventual bankruptcy of the works. But more than counterbalancing the tedium and rancor connected with Pine Grove was a steady supply of iron to stow in the holds of the *Sally* and the *Betsey*. Here is an excellent example of how the imbalances of Philadelphia's economy impelled its entrepreneurs to extend their reach.[27]

Ironmaking in early America would seem to have been a lucrative investment opportunity that substantiates the people-of-plenty view of American economic development. The high-grade iron ore needed for this industry so dependent on natural resources was readily available to Philadelphia capitalists in both the hills of Pennsylvania and the bogs of south Jersey. The limestone required as a flux for the furnace and the waterpower to activate the bellows and the forge hammer were also locally available. Finally, the enormous amounts of timber—thousands of acres of it—needed to make the charcoal that was continually dumped into the top of the blast furnace were easily obtained. Here especially Pennsylvania had an obvious advantage over western Europe, where the woodlands were severely depleted. And if the supply side of the industry was positive, the demand side was no less so. Pig and bar iron, as well as finished goods such as pots, firebacks, and nails, commanded a large local market. What could not be sold locally found a market in England, in the form of bar iron or pig iron. These advantages were substantial enough to make America's iron industry of worldwide importance. By 1775 a seventh of the globe's production was supplied by the thirteen colonies.[28]

27. Grace Hutchison Larsen, "Profile of a Colonial Merchant: Thomas Clifford of Pre-Revolutionary Philadelphia" (Ph.D. diss., Columbia University, 1955), 122–177.

28. Robert L. Heilbroner, *The Economic Transformation of America* (New York, 1977), 11.

Yet despite this growth, the advantages available to the American ironmaker were partly illusory. It is very clear, in any case, that iron production proved to be no bonanza for many of the entrepreneurs involved. We have already seen that the ironworks with which Thomas Clifford and Joshua Fisher and Sons were associated went bankrupt, and the historian of Hopewell Furnace has concluded: "The first half century of the history of Hopewell Furnace was replete with crises—financial, legal and physical. It was shut down and reopened. The stack was rebuilt and extensively repaired. The sheriff was a frequent visitor. There were disputes over land ownership. Partnerships were formed and dissolved. Water was too abundant or in too short supply." The same could be said of Hibernia Furnace in northern New Jersey, which for a time was owned by an important New York mercantile firm. Other examples could easily be provided, enough to explain why one historian of ironmaking concluded about the industry, "In going over the records one finds, in many cases, that a few years sufficed to bring the undertaking either to permanent grief or a new owner."[29]

In view of the advantages offered by the North American continent, what handicaps could have been severe enough to produce so many failures? Capital shortage was one; an ironworks was an expensive enterprise, requiring at least £10,000 in capital. James and Drinker's ironworks had a total value of £16,800, one of the works owned by Allen and Turner was capitalized at £21,873, and a major iron plantation in Maryland was worth £64,950. Such capital was hard to obtain in America, and it could not be imported from England in the form of commercial credits because a single large block of start-up money was needed to buy the land and build the furnace, forges, and outbuildings. As a result, many ironworks failed for simple lack of funds to sustain them in their early stages of development.[30]

Even if he did scrape together the requisite capital for an ironworks, the American merchant who had spent his life near the waterfront knew little about the myriad technical problems that had to be solved. As David Landes has said, early ironmaking was akin to expert cooking. One had to bake the proper mix of ingredients—limestone, charcoal,

29. Joseph E. Walker, *Hopewell Village: A Social and Economic Study of an Iron-Making Community* (Philadelphia, 1966), 19; Thomas M. Doerflinger, "Hibernia Furnace during the Revolution," *New Jersey History*, XC (1971–1972), 97–114; Arthur Cecil Bining, *Pennsylvania Iron Manufacture in the Eighteenth Century*, 2d ed. (Harrisburg, Pa., 1973), 126. See also National Society of the Colonial Dames of America, *Forges and Furnaces in the Province of Pennsylvania* (Philadelphia, 1914), 1.

30. Henry Drinker Journal, 1776–1791, 219, Drinker Papers, HSP; Turner to Lynford Lardner, Feb. 13, 1764, Turner Letterbook, 1753–1774.

and iron ore—in a blast furnace until pig iron flowed out the bottom. The key ingredient was the ore, for if it was of poor quality, the output of the works would become infamous among blacksmiths on both sides of the Atlantic as being brittle and hard to work. Judging ore was a delicate matter. Henry Drinker sounded more like an alchemist than a capitalist as he inquired of the ore available at a projected works: "Is it poor or rich? does it flux kindly with the aid of Limestone? Some Ore tho' rather poor, produces more Iron in the same time & with the same flux & fuel than a richer kind that is often obstinate & hard to manage—is it very hard or is it maleable? does it incline in any degree to the cold sheen [?] or red sheen [?]?" Good ore, of course, was only a start; the works had to be reasonably close to major markets and served by decent transport routes on which ore, charcoal, supplies, and iron could be moved. It also needed a watercourse that would not run dry in the late summer or flood unduly in the spring. To select a site combining all of these advantages was a difficult undertaking requiring more expertise than most merchants possessed, and because of their distance from Europe, expert advice on the subject was not easily available. A similar difficulty bedeviled some overenthusiastic investors in a copper mine, who had to send samples of their ore to London to have it assayed. The long time lag that resulted greatly increased their losses.[31]

A special aspect of this paucity of techical expertise was a severe lack of skilled labor. The efficiency and profitability of an ironworks depended greatly on the effectiveness of a few key workers. Most critical was a "capable vigilant" ironmaster who lived at the works and was responsible for day-to-day management, keeping the books, and overseeing the labor force. Also important were a founder who operated the blast furnace to produce as much good pig iron as possible and forgemen who were responsible for refining this material into bar iron. Such personnel could be extremely difficult to obtain, as the tribulations of Allen and Turner show. In the mid-eighteenth century this firm established a slitting mill, which flattened bar iron in rollers, creating sheets of metal that were "slit" into spikes and nails. The man who set up and operated the mill for them had the character of a mad scientist. He was not merely competent but "ingenious" while he was on the job, but he was also a "little disordered in the head" and thus had the unfortunate habit of quitting work whenever he pleased, even when there were valuable orders waiting to be filled. "We are Unlucky," reported Joseph Turner,

31. Drinker to Richard Blackledge, Oct. 4, 1786, Henry Drinker Letterbook, 1786–1790, 80; Turner to David Barclay and Sons, Sept. 20, Oct. 24, 1755, Feb. 27, Oct. 26, Dec. 20, 1756, Aug. 21, Nov. 11, 1758, and to John Perks, Dec. 20, 1756, Turner Letterbook, 1753–1774.

"with a man who we believe understands the business well but from Laziness or bad Temper or Some thing else wee can get but Little Done." After suffering much irritation and "monstrous expense" at the hands of this man, Allen and Turner in 1756 asked their Bristol correspondent to find a "sober character well suited to the business." When this firm failed to recruit a replacement, Joseph Turner asked his London correspondent, David Barclay, one of the richest and most influential traders in the city, to find one. Eventually a prospect was found, who corresponded with Turner about the job and even had the audacity to borrow some cash from Barclay. But these negotiations fell through after all, and in 1763—fully seven years after starting a search—the original demented miller was still on the job, leaving work whenever he pleased.

Nor was his case unique. When Allen and Turner built a second ironworks in 1760, they tried to procure an ironmaster and seven or eight forgemen for it, but three years later, after searches in England, Germany, and Sweden, the new works was still limping along without these workers. Primarily for this reason—but also because of drought, depressed iron prices, and an epidemic at the works—Joseph Turner wondered whether it would ever be placed on a solid footing. It was still the case that ironworks "require much attendance & Care . . . its very Difficult to keep them from bringing us in Debt."[32]

The Dynamics of Enterprise: An Overview

When we strip away the welter of details about market structure, capital requirements, shipping patterns, and career paths, the essential dynamics of enterprise in Philadelphia's merchant community may be reduced to four elements: commercial credit, social mobility, risk, and innovation. One could become a merchant in Philadelphia by combining a small amount of capital with a loan from England; and since commercial credit was widely available, the influx of new talent into the merchant community was great. But one man's opportunity was another man's brutal competition: this very ease of entry made trade extremely hazardous for the established wholesaler. Many other factors, as we have seen, compounded the risk of failure in the relatively primitive economy of the Delaware Valley. The high cost of labor and capital, the distant and easily glutted nature of export markets, the volatility of foreign exchange markets, the scarcity of specie for domestic exchange, the fre-

32. Turner to John Perks, Dec. 20, 1756, Aug. 2, 1757, Nov. 23, 1758, July 25, Sept. 26, 1760, to John Griffits, May 24, 1758, to David Barclay and Sons, Oct. 7, 1760, to William Allen, July 13, 1763, Turner Letterbook, 1753–1774.

quency of wars, and the small size of many merchants' estates—all gave rise to a high rate of bankruptcy. These frequent failures, together with the continual expansion of the merchant community, always generated new openings for would-be entrepreneurs. Thus risk and opportunity fed on each other in a symbiotic relationship that may be described, accurately but imprecisely, as "social fluidity."

Because risk was so deeply embedded in their everyday operations, merchants were favorably disposed toward innovation. Subjected to uncertainty day after day, they were emotionally and psychologically prepared to face the stress associated with setting forth in an unfamiliar market or novel enterprise. At a more coldly calculating level, the probability of going bankrupt in such a venture was not inordinately higher than the odds of having to call a meeting of creditors after a run of bad luck in the West Indies or the dry goods market. Moreover, the winds of adversity in these familiar trades frequently blew the merchants off course and into uncharted seas whether or not they desired to be innovative. As the examples of Thomas Riche and of Baynton, Wharton, and Morgan show, merchants in trouble were strongly tempted to try to bail themselves out through innovation. And these men had not only the motive to innovate but the means. They were always in touch with foreign products, technologies, and markets, and their access to European credit, together with the relative flexibility of their own estates, permitted them to seize new opportunities quickly.

These patterns were hardly unique to eighteenth-century Philadelphia; indeed, they were present in many other commercial communities of the precorporate age, ranging from nineteenth-century San Francisco to fifteenth-century Florence.[33] However, adversity and opportunity were clearly more prevalent in the expanding but primitive periphery of the Atlantic trading world than in its more stable, mature core.

In Great Britain, for example, the stratification of the commercial system was so much greater than in Philadelphia as to make the character of the business community fundamentally different. The premier traders of England during the third quarter of the eighteenth century were worth between two hundred thousand pounds and eight hundred thousand pounds Pennsylvania currency; comparable Philadelphia merchants were worth twenty-five thousand pounds to fifty thousand pounds. Moderately wealthy English merchants had estates of about seventy-five thousand pounds, perhaps seven times the fortunes of their

33. On San Francisco, see Peter R. Decker, *Fortunes and Failures: White-Collar Mobility in Nineteenth-Century San Francisco* (Cambridge, Mass., 1978). On Florence, see Richard A. Goldthwaite, *The Building of Renaissance Florence: An Economic and Social History* (Baltimore, Md., 1980), 46–47, 60–65.

American counterparts, and even the poorest English traders were worth far more than lowly Philadelphia traders.[34] As in America, mobility up and down the steeply graded sides of the English commercial pyramid was considerable. Many merchants were recruited from the middle class, and the wealthiest English traders tended to retire from trade, creating openings for new talent.[35] Nevertheless, opportunity for advancement was more limited than in America, and the commercial environment had a more stable, patrician tone. The pinnacle of the British commercial system was generally too lofty to be scaled in a single generation. The wealthiest merchants began their careers with substantial estates, and the swollen capital of these great traders allowed them, and them alone, to dominate such capital-intensive fields as the Levant trade, the East India trade, and the tobacco trade.[36] Since competition was limited and their own personal fortunes were gigantic, the risk of financial failure was moderate for these great men. It was said, for example, that bankruptcy was unheard of among the wealthy woolens exporters of Leeds, and it was possible to conduct the exclusive Levant trade "by rote"—one merchant left his affairs in the hands of an assistant during a pleasure trip to

34. Discussion of the wealth of merchants must distinguish between the trading capital of firms (which compose part of the wealth of one or more individuals), the total estates of individuals, and the wealth of entire families. See R. G. Wilson, *Gentlemen Merchants: The Merchant Community in Leeds, 1700–1830* (New York, 1971), 66–69, 85–87; Ralph Davis, *Aleppo and Devonshire Square: English Traders in the Levant in the Eighteenth Century* (London, 1967), 60–72, esp. 70; Lucy Stuart Sutherland, *A London Merchant, 1695–1774* (London, 1933), 4; Richard Pares, "A London West-India Merchant House, 1740–1769," in Pares and A.J.P. Taylor, eds., *Essays Presented to Sir Lewis Namier* (London, 1956), 107; Devine, *Tobacco Lords*, 10, 23–24, 27.

On the capitalization of wealthy French slave traders (reaching a maximum of 5,000,000 livres tournois, or £364,000 Pennsylvania currency), see Robert Louis Stein, *The French Slave Trade in the Eighteenth Century: An Old Regime Business* (Madison, Wis., 1971), 183–186. La Rochelle slave traders in the mid-eighteenth century had estates in the range of 500,000–800,000 livres tournois (£36,400–£58,240 Pennsylvania currency). See Robert Forster, *Merchants, Landlords, Magistrates: The Depont Family in Eighteenth-Century France* (Baltimore, Md., 1980), 61. John Warder to Jeremiah Warder, July 30, 1776, John Warder Letterbooks, HSP, refers to a French merchant who received a legacy of £50,000 sterling.

35. Walter E. Minchinton, "The Merchants in England in the Eighteenth Century," *Explorations in Entrepreneurial History*, 1st Ser., X (1957–1958), 62–71 *passim*, esp. 64, 67, 68; Davis, *Aleppo and Devonshire Square*, 72.

36. Minchinton, "Merchants in England," *Explorations in Entrepreneurial History*, 1st Ser., X (1957–1958), 67, emphasizes the vast social distance between the elite and the middle rungs of the merchant group. See also Jacob M. Price, ed., *Joshua Johnson's Letterbook, 1771–1774: Letters from a Merchant in London to His Partners in Maryland*, London Record Society (London, 1979), xi, xii, which refers to Quaker grandees in the London tobacco trade that were "second generation firms" and "Old English firms" with antecedents in the trade going back to the 17th century.

the Continent that lasted two years![37] We find references, as well, to "rich respectable W[est] India merch^{ts} who do not go out of their usual line of business & [are] averse to Speculation."[38] Although the aggressiveness of certain wealthy English firms is evident in the huge credits extended to the American colonies, it is clear that, as a group, England's great men were less scrappy and innovative than such American arrivistes as Stephen Girard, Thomas Hancock, John Nicholson, and John Jacob Astor.

Even merchants in the upper-middle segment of the English merchant community, who were worth fifty thousand pounds to one hundred thousand pounds Pennsylvania currency, had large, diversified estates that provided considerable protection against adversity.[39] Moreover, the base of the English trading network was higher than Philadelphia's. Whereas one needed only four hundred pounds to enter trade in Philadelphia, three thousand pounds was a more realistic figure in England. For this reason, young Britishers who lacked the resources to become wholesalers at home migrated to the colonies or the European continent.[40] The ground floor of the American mercantile structure was, in effect, the basement of the English commercial edifice, composed of merchants too poor to get started in England. Many Englishmen of means also migrated to America, though few of the wealthiest British merchants did so. In sum, Philadelphia experienced a steady influx of geographically and socially mobile English merchants but lacked the secure, extremely rich elite that dominated commercial life in England. Consequently, risk and mobility were more pervasive in the Delaware Valley.

To these social differences must be added the economic ones, for the Philadelphians operated in a more primitive and unsettled business environment. The monetary system and foreign exchange market were underdeveloped, the financial institutions inadequate, and the assaults of

37. Wilson, *Gentlemen Merchants*, 79, 80; Davis, *Aleppo and Devonshire Square*, 71, 72.

38. ——— to Cramond, Phillips, and Co., Apr. 7, 1790, Cramond, Phillips, and Co. Letters, Gratz Collection, HSP.

39. William Braund, a successful but not opulent London merchant, was worth about £45,000 sterling (£75,000 Pennsylvania currency) when he died in 1774. Sutherland, *A London Merchant*, 4.

40. Wilson, *Gentlemen Merchants*, 66; Minchinton, "Merchants in England," *Explorations in Entrepreneurial History*, 1st Ser., X (1957–1958), 63, 64. On the migration of firms to Philadelphia, see above, chap. 2. Price, ed., *Joshua Johnson's Letterbook*, vii–xxvii, describes the affairs of a Maryland firm that established a London branch with a working capital of £3,000 sterling (£5,000 Pennsylvania currency). Although this was a large capital by American standards, the firm was a small operator by London standards, shipping goods worth only £10,000–£20,000 sterling to America.

war more violent. In addition, the commercial operations of Philadelphians were less specialized, and this fact alone probably helped make them more flexible than English merchants who had followed their fathers into the predictable routine of a particular business, such as the Levant trade or Portugal trade.[41] Finally, the role of merchants in spearheading economic development was far greater in America because its economy lacked wealthy bankers, manufacturers, and improvement-minded aristocrats.[42]

Naturally, Philadelphia merchants did not react uniformly to the risks of trade in the Delaware Valley. Human beings bring individuality to all of their endeavors. But the range of responses can be conveyed by sketching two ideal entrepreneurial types, the "ascetic accumulator" and the "opulent adventurer."[43] These types represent both the differences between merchants and the conflicting tendencies that might be found within the character of individual traders. The ideal ascetic accumulator was a Quaker who lived by the capitalistic trinity of industry, frugality, and economy. Both the dogma of his faith and the powerful logic of compound interest drove him to lead a simple, inexpensive, orderly life. Not inordinately elitist, even if wealthy, he looked favorably upon young tradesmen in his monthly meeting, whose slender estates and growing families forced them to lead a frugal existence. Such a merchant was likely to be most comfortable in the dry goods trade. If profits were rather circumscribed in this well-worn field of enterprise, so were the risks. In comparison to the provision merchant, who routinely entrusted a quarter of his net worth to a strange agent in a distant market, the dry goods merchant had relatively firm control of his assets. Success came not by speculating boldly in overseas areas, but, rather, by assiduously building a base of local customers and conscientiously collecting debts as they fell due. His ledgers and journals were a model of methodical book-

41. Davis, *Aleppo*; Pares, "West-India Merchant House," in Pares and Taylor, eds., *Essays*; Price, *Joshua Johnson's Letterbook*, xi–xii; and Wilson, *Gentlemen Merchants*, all convey the impression that successful English merchants were entrenched in a particular trade.

42. See Charles P. Kindleberger, *Economic Response: Comparative Studies in Trade, Finance, and Growth* (Cambridge, Mass., 1978), chap. 5, for a discussion of the role of merchants in industrializing European countries. Except perhaps in England, he sees their role as of secondary importance, because they channeled little capital and effort into industry, but their significance was clearly greater in America, which had no traditional industrial business elite. See chaps. 5, 7.

43. For a parallel discussion, see Adam Smith, *An Inquiry into the Nature and Causes of the Wealth of Nations*, ed. Edwin Cannan (New York, 1937), 113–114, which distinguishes between the trader specializing in a "regular, established and well known branch of business [requiring] a long life of industry, frugality, and attention" to build a fortune, and the "speculative merchant," who shifted from trade to trade.

keeping, providing at a glance a complete view of the cash in his strongbox, the goods in his warehouse, and the debts outstanding. Routine though it was, such a business appealed to the man obsessed with order, discipline, and control of detail, content to accumulate a fortune through a lifetime of concentrated effort.

This ascetic accumulator bears a strong resemblance to the early modern capitalist sketched by Max Weber in *The Protestant Ethic and the Spirit of Capitalism*. In a brilliant formulation, Weber contrasted the traditional, hedonistic "adventurer" with the ascetic, rational capitalist. While Weber admitted that the modern entrepreneur had to be "calculating and daring at the same time," he strongly emphasized the "calculating" dimension.[44] Driven by a desire to pursue his God-given "calling," Weber's capitalist "seeks profit rationally and systematically." He is "above all temperate and reliable, shrewd and completely devoted to [his] business"; and his operations are "rationalized on the basis of rigorous calculation."[45] Because he pursues business out of a sense of duty rather than from a lust for possessions, he "avoids ostentation and unnecessary expenditure, as well as conscious enjoyment of his power," and he devotes his entire lifetime to trade, instead of retiring to enjoy his fortune. In all of these respects, Weber suggests, the capitalist differed from the "dare-devil and unscrupulous speculators" of ages past.[46] "Adventurers' capitalism, oriented to the exploitation of political opportunities and irrational speculation," was not to be confused with the steady, disciplined behavior of the modern businessman.[47] Whereas the traditional adventurer was a transient mercenary in the war for economic advancement, the modern capitalist was a hardened professional, serving for life and committed to his calling.

How are we to reconcile Weber's portrait of the ascetic, calculating, disciplined capitalist with the flamboyant behavior of such men as Thomas Riche, or of John Baynton, Samuel Wharton, and George Morgan? These men were precisely the sort of adventurers whom Weber relegated to the premodern era. Mired in financial difficulty, they concocted grandiose projects in order to stay afloat, and when their calculations proved mistaken, they drowned. Such behavior was not unusual, for the small merchant operating in a primitive economy had to combine the worldly asceticism of Weber with the animal spirits of the commer-

44. Max Weber, *The Protestant Ethic and the Spirit of Capitalism*, trans. Talcott Parsons (New York, 1958), 69.

45. *Ibid.*, 64, 69, 76.

46. *Ibid.*, 71, 69; see also 51, 70, 76.

47. *Ibid.*, 76.

cial gambler. When such gamblers, through political corruption and financial manipulation, were able to secure huge amounts of capital, they were tempted to combine speculations in commerce, banking, transportation, manufacturing, and real estate into mammoth business empires. Such was the aim of both John Nicholson and Robert Morris, two of the most influential capitalists of Revolutionary Philadelphia.[48]

The archetype of this speculative capitalist, as manifested in eighteenth-century Philadelphia, is the opulent adventurer.[49] Convivial and polished, equally at home in the countinghouse and the ballroom, his taste for spending money more than matched his ability to make it. If not born with a "plentiful fortune," he envied those who were, and he hoped one day to become an independent gentleman who could mingle pastoral pursuits with political power. Since religion to him was as much a social statement as a personal conviction, he gravitated toward Anglicanism, the religion of gentlemen. Rather than painstakingly accumulating a fortune in the dry goods trade, the opulent adventurer preferred the more elevated plane of international speculation. He was particularly drawn to bold ventures in the provision trade that might generate a fortune in a few years, whether by shipping flour to the West Indies during a war or dispatching valuable cargoes of wheat to Lisbon and Cádiz. These deals were appropriately termed "adventures" in the merchants' ledgers and journals, for that is what they were—risky deals heavily dependent upon chance. Gambling was in the blood of these men, and when luck ran against them, they were tempted to play double-or-nothing in order to mend their fortunes with a single spectacular deal. Whether successful or not, the speculations of the opulent adventurer were frankly made for the sake of this world, not the next. Many businessmen of this ilk retired in their middle years in order to enjoy their material success, and they were eager to display and consume their winnings in public view in order to consolidate their social position. The opulent town houses and country seats of a William Bingham or a Robert Morris had the same social function as the "power houses" built by Elizabethan magnates two centuries before.[50]

Naturally, the most effective merchants combined the virtues of the ascetic accumulator and the opulent adventurer, on the one hand paring costs wherever possible, keeping strict control of assets, and reinvesting

48. On the careers of Morris and Nicholson, see below, chaps. 5, 7.

49. Examples include Robert Morris, William Bingham, John Nicholson, John Ross, William Duer of New York, and Tench Coxe.

50. Mark Girouard, *Life in the English Country House: A Social and Architectural History* (New Haven, Conn., 1978), 1–12.

profits instead of consuming them, and on the other hand making imaginative speculations that yielded vast profits.[51] The central fact to be emphasized, however, is that an aggressive, atavistic, speculative streak ran through early American capitalism that bears little resemblance to the icy worldly asceticism of Weber. And this trait, unseemly though it was, made a critical contribution to the process of economic development. Whether wisely or foolishly, merchants took risks, and it was this fact, rather than their prudence and precision, that most decisively set them apart from eighteenth-century landowners. Indeed, many contemporary estate managers, whether in tidewater Virginia or rural France, were rational, systematic, parsimonious managers, displaying the Weberian virtues in abundance.[52] But they typically lacked the adventurous willingness to gamble that was expressed in the merchants' spirit of enterprise.

51. Stephen Girard, Robert Oliver of Baltimore, James and Drinker, Joshua Fisher and Sons, and Jeremiah Warder fit this description.

52. See Forster, *Merchants, Landlords, Magistrates*, chap. 3. This study treats the Depont Family, La Rochelle nobles who shifted from the high-risk world of slave trading to estate management and office-mongering. Forster observes, 74, that in their new role the Deponts displayed an abundance of "worldly asceticism" by paying scrupulous attention to costs and vigilantly collecting the thousands of fees and rents owed them. Such efforts typified the behavior of French landlords during the feudal revival that occurred during the last few decades of the ancien régime. See, for example, Robert Forster, *House of Saulx-Tavanes: Versailles and Burgundy, 1700–1830* (Baltimore, Md., 1971), 55–108. Far from being parsimonious and ascetic, French merchants lavished large sums on the opera houses and other public buildings of the major ports. See Arthur Young, *Travels in France and Italy during the Years 1787, 1788, and 1789* (London, 1927), 55–58, 108. Across the channel, the situation was similar; Samuel Johnson remarked "with what munificence a great merchant will spend his money . . . whereas you will hardly find a country gentleman who is not a great deal disconcerted at an unexpected occasion to lay out ten pounds" (quoted in Minchinton, "Merchants in England," *Explorations in Entrepreneurial History*, 1st Ser., X [1957–1958], 69).

Part II
The Revolution

4

Reluctant Revolutionaries

In December 1769 the wealthy Philadelphia merchant Henry Drinker relayed the latest political news to his partner, Abel James, who was visiting England. The American boycott of British manufactures, undertaken earlier in the year to protest the Townshend duties, was still in effect, Drinker reported, but its demise was imminent. The boycott was cutting into mercantile profits, and Drinker knew that "Interest, all powerful Interest will bear down Patriotism." Echoing the familiar republican rhetoric of the day, the merchant lamented that "Romans we are not as they were formerly, when they despised Riches and Grandeur, abode in extreme poverty and sacrificed every pleasant enjoyment for the love and service of their Country."[1]

Four years later it was Drinker who seemed to be sacrificing his country to "all powerful Interest." In 1773 the firm of James and Drinker secured a lucrative appointment as one of four Philadelphia consignees for the tea that the British East India Company planned to sell in the American market. The partners expected to earn a handsome commission by auctioning off hundreds of chests of tea that still bore the hated Townshend duties. Only the vociferous protest of Philadelphia radicals and ungracious hints from the "Committee For Tarring and Feathering" persuaded them, after two months of stalling, to resign the commission.[2]

The behavior of Henry Drinker encapsulates an essential paradox in the political motivations of Philadelphia merchants before the Revolution. They genuinely feared British encroachments on American rights and were in fact willing to make real financial sacrifices to oppose them. Yet their opposition to Britain was qualified and inconsistent, their attitudes complex and conflicting; they never offered sustained, united support for the resistance and Revolutionary movements. They neither strenuously lobbied against the Sugar Act, led the opposition to the Stamp Act, initiated the boycott of 1769–1770, nor supported strongly the convening of the Continental Congress. If it had been up to the city's merchants, the Revolutionary movement would have been more circumspect and cautious, more judicious and tem-

1. Henry Drinker, "Effects of the 'Non-Importation Agreement' in Philadelphia, 1769–1770," *Pennsylvania Magazine of History and Biography*, XIV (1890), 41.

2. Benjamin Woods Labaree, *The Boston Tea Party* (New York, 1964), 97–102.

perate, less eager to make the final break with Britain. In short, it would not have been a revolutionary movement at all.

One reason for this ambivalence was that Philadelphia's economy was not especially disordered or depressed between 1760 and 1775, as some neo-Progressive historians have suggested; indeed, the period offered notable entrepreneurial opportunities. The merchants thus had no compelling financial reason to break with England. Quite to the contrary, they were restrained by a variety of countervailing factors. They had close commercial and personal ties with England, they wished to avoid disruption of their trade by boycotts and protests, and the Quakers among them not only discountenanced tumultuous extralegal protests but also feared that the Revolutionary movement would sweep Pennsylvania's turbulent Presbyterian faction into power.[3]

The merchants' growing suspicion of the Revolutionary movement was well placed. The war shattered the economy of the Delaware Valley and injured many traders, and wartime tribulations were compounded by a severe economic downturn in the 1780s.[4] Independence brought cataclysmic political change to Pennsylvania when a faction of radical Presbyterians of middling social origins seized control from the Quaker and Anglican grandees who had traditionally governed the province. Favoring price controls, currency inflation, and political democracy, these radicals threatened the vital interests of wealthy, conservative merchants, who responded to the challenge by leading a counterrevolution at both the state and national levels during the decade after 1777.

The Economic Outlook, 1760–1775

Some modern historians have pointed to Philadelphia's dry goods trade with England as the source of a pre-Revolutionary economic crisis. It has been suggested that "English capital and English decisions increasingly dominated the colonial economy." Aggressive English firms

3. Among the many studies that discuss this subject are Marc Egnal and Joseph A. Ernst, "An Economic Interpretation of the American Revolution," *William and Mary Quarterly*, 3d Ser., XXIX (1972), 3–30; Joseph Albert Ernst, *Money and Politics in America, 1755–1775: A Study in the Currency Act of 1764 and the Political Economy of Revolution* (Chapel Hill, N.C., 1973); Gary B. Nash, *The Urban Crucible: Social Change, Political Consciousness, and the Origins of the American Revolution* (Cambridge, Mass., 1979); Richard Alan Ryerson, *The Revolution Is Now Begun: The Radical Committees of Philadelphia, 1765–1776* (Philadelphia, 1978), 29; Arthur M. Schlesinger, *The Colonial Merchants and the American Revolution, 1773–1776*, Columbia University Studies in History, Economics, and Public Law, LXXVIII, No. 182 (New York, 1918).

4. I discuss the war years in chap. 5, below.

sold huge quantities of merchandise on credit, bypassing and undercutting American firms by selling directly to American shopkeepers and auction houses in the colonies.[5]

The weight of evidence suggests that the dry goods trade was indeed overstocked between 1760 and 1775, following a profitable boom during the Seven Years' War. The constant cry in this period was that Philadelphia was swamped with dry goods, that cloth was cheaper in Philadelphia than in Manchester, and that dozens of importers were about to go broke. It is significant, however, that such complaints were not confined to those years; they were just as common between 1749 and 1758, and 1784 and 1788.[6] It seems doubtful, therefore, that the pre-Revolutionary glut was caused by a general restructuring of the dry goods trade after 1760, as has been suggested. Nonetheless, to analyze this problem effectively, we must dissect the arteries and capillaries of the transatlantic distribution system to discover exactly how a bale of cloth or a crate of hardware could make its way from a warehouse in London to a retail shop in Philadelphia, Lancaster, or Trenton. The historical possibilities are these:

1. The English merchant sold the goods to a Philadelphia merchant on twelve months' credit, while charging a 2.5 percent commission.[7] The Philadelphia wholesaler then sold the goods to shopkeepers on several months' credit.
2. The English merchant sold the goods directly to a Pennsylvania shopkeeper on twelve months' credit and received a 2.5 percent commission.
3. The English merchant adventured goods to Philadelphia on his own account, paying a Philadelphia merchant a commission for selling the goods to retailers.
4. The English merchant shipped the goods to a Philadelphia auctioneer and paid him a commission for selling the goods, typically for cash or short credit. Alternatively, the auctioneer might import the goods on his own account.
5. The English merchant sent a partner of his firm to America to sell goods directly to shopkeepers. The Englishman behaved just like any

5. Egnal and Ernst, "Economic Interpretation," *WMQ*, 3d Ser., XXIX (1972), 3; Nash, *Urban Crucible*, 316–317; Eric Foner, *Tom Paine and Revolutionary America* (New York, 1976), 25.

6. Arthur L. Jensen, *The Maritime Commerce of Colonial Philadelphia* (Madison, Wis., 1963), 114–118; see discussion in chaps. 3, 5, 6.

7. *Ibid.*, 87–106; Thomas M. Doerflinger, "Enterprise on the Delaware: Merchants and Economic Development in Philadelphia, 1750–1791" (Ph.D. diss., Harvard University, 1980), 113–126. See also Philip L. White, *The Beekmans of New York in Politics and Commerce, 1647–1877* (New York, 1956), 361–440.

other Philadelphia merchant, except that he was a transient who repatriated his profits to England.

The documentary record concerning Philadelphia's dry goods trade is massive, and any radical shifts in these modes of distribution should be easily observable. This is the case, for example, with regard to method 5, for its great prominence as a mode of distribution between 1783 and 1785 can be thoroughly documented from a variety of sources.[8] For the period before the Revolution what stands out most clearly is the overwhelming predominance of method 1. We know with certainty that at least thirty-eight merchants used this procedure, and there is considerable evidence that at least ninety-four other Philadelphians did so as well.[9] The pre-Revolutionary dry goods glut did not result from a shift away from this well-established pattern of exchange. English exporters overstocked the market, it seems, simply by filling the orders of the many optimistic merchants eager to speculate with borrowed funds.

As for method 2, direct sales by English houses to Philadelphia retailers were indeed fairly common.[10] But the orders of these minor shopkeeper traders were dwarfed by the imports of the major wholesale firms. In the mid-1780s, a period for which we have informative customs records, the top 12 percent of Philadelphia importers, virtually all of whom were merchants, handled 62 percent of all imports from Britain.[11] In fact, it would have been almost impossible for English exporters to bypass Philadelphia's merchants on a large scale, because most of the retailers whom the Philadelphians served lived in the city's vast rural hinterland and were not accessible to English houses.

One finds relatively little evidence, either in the primary or secondary sources, that method 3 became notably more common as the Revolution

8. See below, chap. 5.

9. See the Bibliography for a list of manuscripts consulted. The William Pollard Letterbook, 1772–1774, and the Joseph Turner Letterbook, 1753–1774, describe the activities of Philadelphia agents for English firms and list many customers of British firms. See also Mildred and Roberts Accounts Current, 1775–1789, and James and Drinker to William Neate, June 1, 1761, James and Drinker Letterbook, 1759–1762, Henry Drinker Papers. All of those manuscripts are in the Historical Society of Pennsylvania (hereafter cited as HSP).

10. Marc Matthew Egnal, "The Pennsylvania Economy, 1748–1762: An Analysis of Short-Run Fluctuations in the Context of Long-Run Changes in the Atlantic Trading Community" (Ph.D. diss., University of Wisconsin, 1974), 124–126, 241–242; Harry D. Berg, "The Organization of Business in Colonial Philadelphia," *Pennsylvania History*, X (1943), 155–177; Doerflinger, "Enterprise," 66–69.

11. Registers of Duties Paid on Imported Goods, 1781–1787, 6 vols., Record Group 4, Pennsylvania Historical and Museum Commission (hereafter cited as PHMC). The figures cited apply to the period May 1785–Dec. 1787.

drew near.[12] Yet it is surprising, in view of the fabled unprofitability of dry goods sales, that more Philadelphia merchants did not insist on selling manufactures on commission. As for method 4, it seems unlikely that auctions were of great importance in overstocking the Philadelphia market. These vendue houses, as they were called, were the discount stores of early Philadelphia. Merchants used them to sell for cash—but often at a loss—goods that were damaged or selling too slowly.[13] Although some vendue masters clearly did receive goods from overseas, there are several good reasons for doubting that auctions held a large share of the market. For one thing, there were hundreds of merchants in Philadelphia and only a few auction houses.[14] None of the city's auctioneers was as wealthy as its premier dry goods importers, and only one owned a four-wheel carriage in 1772, as compared to forty-four merchant owners.[15] If the auctioneers' prices were so low, one may ask, why were they not more successful? One explanation is that they dealt strictly for cash and short credit in an economy that was chronically short of money and capital. Shopkeepers who needed credit had no alternative but to deal with established wholesalers. Moreover, rural shopkeepers probably preferred to deal with wholesalers that could offer reasonably complete lines of merchandise. Finally, the case of Benjamin Fuller's auction house shows that the absence of transatlantic credit also limited the sales volume of vendue masters. Fuller's problem was a shortage of capital. Although textiles bought for cash in England could be profitably sold at his auction house, Fuller had little ready cash to send to England. "I would not dispear of vending Eight or Ten thousand Stl. P Annum," he wrote. "But I am not possessed of a Capital sufficient to go that length." As a result, only "a few particular Articles" were obtained from England.[16]

That Philadelphia's dry goods market was almost chronically overstocked between 1760 and 1775 seems undeniable, but there is good reason to challenge the neo-Progressive argument that direct sales to shopkeepers

12. See, however, Egnal, "Pennsylvania Economy," 176, 178.

13. On vendues, see *ibid.*, 72–73; Jensen, *Maritime Commerce*, 123–124.

14. Jacob M. Price, "Economic Function and the Growth of American Port Towns in the Eighteenth Century," *Perspectives in American History*, VIII (1974), 178, 183, indicates that in 1774 there were 329 merchants in Philadelphia and 7 auctioneers and vendue criers.

15. Robert F. Oaks, "Big Wheels in Philadelphia: Du Simitière's List of Carriage Owners," *PMHB*, XCV (1971), 359–362.

16. Benjamin Fuller to Thomas Parry, Nov. 27, 1769, and to John Scott, Aug. 26, 1768, Benjamin Fuller Letterbook, 1762–1781, Benjamin Fuller Papers, 1762–1799, HSP. See also Fuller and Sinnickson Ledger, 1766–1782, HSP; and Doerflinger, "Enterprise," 222. William S. Sachs, "The Business Outlook in the Northern Colonies, 1750–1775" (Ph.D. diss., Columbia University, 1957), 253, calls vendue sales a "peripheral problem" of the merchants.

and auction houses were the primary cause of this development. Most of the goods entering the port continued to be sold on the traditional twelve months' credit to Philadelphia wholesalers, as we have seen. The main beneficiaries of British largesse were relatively new or small firms that could order large quantities of goods on credit. Those clearly injured by the pattern were wealthy, well-connected Philadelphia firms that would have faced much less competition if British merchants had chosen their customers more selectively. Thus in 1777 one prominent trader anticipated that the huge losses of British traders during the Revolution would tighten the flow of exports and credit after the war, so that "again it will be worth the attention of Money'd Men to enter into the dry goods Business."[17]

If economic self-interest and political action were in fact linked, as neo-Progressive historians have argued, we might expect these wealthy merchants to have led the opposition to England. But it is here that the argument falters, for it was precisely these firms that were most conservative. They refused to enter the nonimportation agreement in 1768, waiting instead until a final attempt at petitioning for repeal of the Townshend Act had failed, and they led the movement to end the boycott in the summer of 1770.[18]

The alarmist view of capital flows held by some historians is also discredited by broad economic considerations. It takes two to make a loan. Why were Philadelphia merchants and shopkeepers so eager to borrow from England if the impact of British credit was so devastating? We saw the answer in Chapter 1: credit was critical to the inception and success of the careers of many of them. The great majority of Philadelphia wholesalers were not merchant princes, but members of the city's middle class, and not a few wholesalers had begun their careers as retailers, artisans, or impecunious immigrants. To these aspiring entrepreneurs English credit offered a ladder of economic advancement. It was, to be sure, a treacherous ladder, from which many traders slipped into bankruptcy, but prudent wholesalers could expand their business rapidly by importing goods on credit.[19] As Arthur M. Schlesinger, Sr., noted, the liberal credits that English merchants extended to colonial merchants were "of great importance" precisely because "the Americans could not have secured such favorable terms from foreign houses; and without such indulgence they would have found diffi-

17. John Warder to Jeremiah Warder, May 21, 1777, John Warder Letterbooks, 1776–1778, HSP.

18. Jensen, *Maritime Commerce*, 174, quotes a report that "eight or ten" "principal" merchants opposed the boycott in the summer of 1768. On the breakup of the boycott, see below.

19. See chap. 1, above.

culty in financing their undertakings."[20] The truth of this observation is demonstrated by developments in the 1780s. Liberated from the British Empire, American traders had the option of shifting their business to the tightfisted merchants of France and Holland, but instead they continued to trade with English houses. A second, often overlooked beneficiary of the aggressiveness of the British firms was the American consumer, who could buy cheap manufactures at shops throughout the Delaware Valley. A more restrictive credit policy would have protected the well-established merchants from competition, but the new, smaller merchants and their thousands of customers would have been injured.

In addition to emphasizing the severity of the pre-Revolutionary dry goods glut, historians have pointed to the commercial downturn of the 1760s as evidence of serious structural problems in Philadelphia's economy. The city's business cycle was complicated because it involved trade not only with England but also with such distinct export markets as New England, Ireland, the West Indies, and southern Europe. Nevertheless, the main outlines of the business cycle can be discerned by analyzing five key economic variables: the volume of imports from England and Scotland, the sterling exchange rate, the price of flour (Philadelphia's major export), the amount of shipping clearing the port for the West Indies and southern Europe (Philadelphia's chief export markets), and the amount of shipping registered by Philadelphia merchants. Analysis of these series and related data suggests that the sixteen years before the Revolution may be roughly divided into three periods: 1760–1763, 1764–1768, and 1769–1775. Only during the second of these three periods were both the dry goods trade and the provision trade stagnant (see figs. 1–4 and table 13). These years were a period of great stress for the merchant community, but since business cycles were a natural part of trade, the downturn of the mid-1760s is hardly evidence of long-term structural crisis.

It has been said that the collapse of the dry goods trade at the end of 1760 "stunned" Philadelphia's economy and "heralded the beginning of a prolonged economic depression."[21] Yet flour prices were higher in 1760, 1761, 1762, and 1763 than during any year of the 1750s. How can an inflated price for Philadelphia's major export be reconciled with economic depression? The depression was obviously restricted to the dry goods trade during the early 1760s, while at the same time Philadelphia mer-

20. Schlesinger, *Colonial Merchants*, 30; Marc Egnal, "The Economic Development of the Thirteen Continental Colonies, 1720 to 1775," *WMQ*, 3d Ser., XXXII (1975), 214–216.

21. Nash, *Urban Crucible*, 247. See also Egnal and Ernst, "Economic Interpretation," *WMQ*, 3d Ser., XXIX (1972), 17.

TABLE 13. *Shipping Registered in Philadelphia by Merchants, 1751–1775*

Period	Registered Tons	% Change from Previous Period
1751–1755	7,092	
1756–1760	8,991	+26.8
1761–1765	13,828	+53.8
1766–1770	11,350	−17.9
1771–1775	16,809	+48.1

Sources: Ship Register of Pennsylvania, 1726–1776, Historical Society of Pennsylvania; Declarations of British Registry, 1727–1776, 12 vols., Record Group 41, Pennsylvania Historical and Museum Commission.

Note: Table covers all individuals identified as merchant on any Philadelphia tax list, 1756–1775.

chants enjoyed strong demand for foodstuffs in the West Indies. Since the provision trade employed most of the port's vessels, the demand for shipping was correspondingly high. James and Drinker gloated in 1762 that "an uncommon demand for all kinds of provisions . . . must continue while there are such fleets and armies in the West Indies who depend on America for supplies and but short crops elsewhere in the colonies."[22] They also reported that "ships have sold very well here and freights have been very brisk for the last six or eight months."[23] In June 1762 the merchants of another firm observed that "the Prospect before us of a good Markett is very great."[24] Five months later they added, "We never have known so great a demand for provisions of all most every kind, flour now sells @ 20/ & so many persons wanting, that they go Eight or Tenn miles down the [Delaware] River to meet the Shallops comeing up" to unload at Philadelphia wharves.[25] Statistical evidence supports these unusually enthusiastic assessments. In 1762 clearances to the West Indies and southern Europe reached a new peak of 17,200 tons, 17 percent above the previous high, set in 1759 (see fig. 1).[26] And the great strength of the shipping industry in

22. Quoted in Egnal, "Pennsylvania Economy," 247; see 227–247 for a fine discussion of Philadelphia's economy between July 1760 and Dec. 1762.

23. Quoted *ibid.*, 248.

24. Samuel and Israel Morris, Jr., to ———, June 9, 1762, Samuel and Israel Morris, Jr., Letterbook, 1757–1763, Morris Family Papers, Eleutherian Mills Historical Library.

25. Samuel and Israel Morris, Jr., to J. Franklin, Nov. 1, 1762, *ibid.*

26. Egnal, "Pennsylvania Economy," 329.

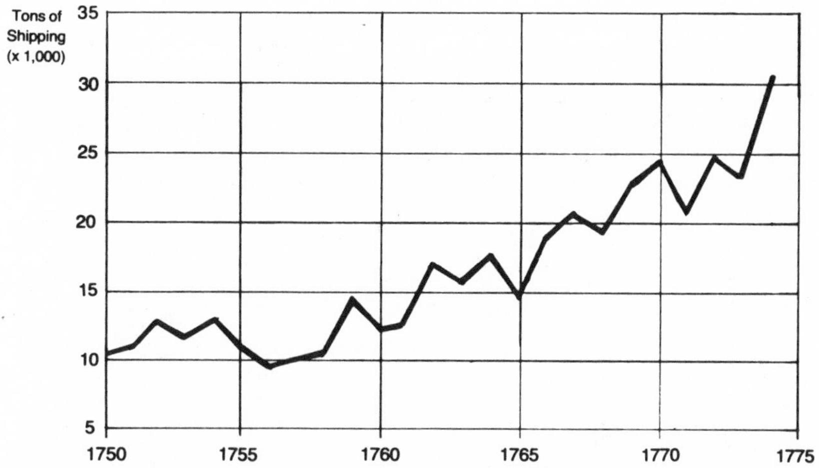

FIGURE 1. Shipping Clearing Philadelphia for the West Indies and Southern Europe, 1750–1774. *Data from Marc Matthew Egnal, "The Pennsylvania Economy, 1748–1762: An Analysis of Short-Run Fluctuations in the Context of Long-Run Changes in the Atlantic Trading Community" (Ph.D. diss., University of Wisconsin, 1974), 328, 329*

these years is demonstrated by a document that was thought lost: the section of the Pennsylvania Ship Register covering the years 1762–1764. We learn from this source that the amount of shipping registered by merchants between 1761 and 1765 was nearly 54 percent higher than in the previous five-year period (see table 13).[27]

Although the relevant data are not fully consistent, it does appear that the years 1764–1768 were marked by severe commercial stagnation. Dry goods imports drifted in these years (see fig. 2); the West Indies trade was unprofitable.[28] The volume of shipping activity in the port was low.[29] In addition,

27. Ship Register of Pennsylvania, 1726–1776, Historical Society of Pennsylvania, constitutes the main portion of the Register, but it is supplemented for the early 1760s by Declarations of British Registry, 1727–1776, 12 vols., Record Group 41, PHMC (hereafter cited as Pennsylvania Ship Register). For discussion of these documents, see Bibliography.

28. Marc Egnal, "The Changing Structure of Philadelphia's Trade with the British West Indies, 1750–1775," *PMHB*, XCIX (1975), 163–166; Sachs, "Business Outlook," 195–199.

29. Tonnage Duties on Incoming Vessels, Nov. 1, 1765–Aug. 30, 1775, 3 vols., Cadwalader Collection, Thomas Cadwalader Section, HSP (hereafter cited as Tonnage Duty Book), gives a more negative impression of shipping volume than the clearances shown in fig. 1. The Tonnage Duty Book shows that the amount of tonnage entering the port was 59,728 tons in 1766, 54,806 tons in 1767, 51,399 tons in 1768, and 58,927 tons in 1769. Thus tonnage entering the port was quite low in 1767 and 1768. See Doerflinger, "Enterprise,"

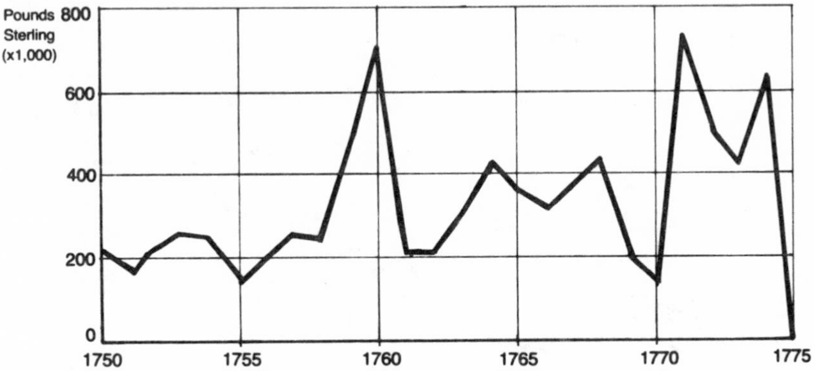

FIGURE 2. Imports into Pennsylvania from England and Scotland, 1750–1775. *Data from Jacob M. Price, "New Time Series for Scotland's and Britain's Trade with the Thirteen Colonies and States, 1740 to 1791,"* William and Mary Quarterly, *3d Ser., XXXII (1975), 324–325*

merchants were frustrated by a serious "shortage of cash" caused by the withdrawal of provincial paper money from circulation and the movement of specie to England to finance the heavy wartime imports.[30] As a result of these problems, the amount of shipping tonnage registered by merchants plunged in the second half of the 1760s (see table 13), and the number of bankruptcies in Philadelphia peaked in 1767.[31]

This downturn ended decisively in 1769, however, when flour and bread exports to the West Indies and southern Europe surged 128 percent above their 1768 levels.[32] Philadelphia's provision trade continued to prosper until 1776. Increased demand for foodstuffs in the West Indies and New England contributed to this buoyancy,[33] but the major new market opportunity for Philadelphians lay in southern Europe. After 1764, shipments to this area increased greatly because poor harvests and rising population in England prevented English merchants from supplying it as they had in the past.[34] Strong demand in the West Indies, southern Europe, and New En-

145. The provision trade was probably more depressed than these shipping figures indicate, because merchants would run their vessels at a loss or minimal profit rather than sell them at a loss. For a casualty of this depressed trade see Orr, Dunlope, and Glenholme Letterbook, 1767–1769, HSP.

30. Sachs, "Business Outlook," 199–202. Sachs notes, 202, that a high volume of economic activity was one reason for this monetary stringency.

31. Egnal, "Pennsylvania Economy," 312; Sachs, "Business Outlook," 132, 133.

32. Jensen, *Maritime Commerce*, 292, table IV.

33. Egnal, "Pennsylvania Economy," 329; Sachs, "Business Outlook," 175, 176.

34. Sachs, "Business Outlook," 172–174.

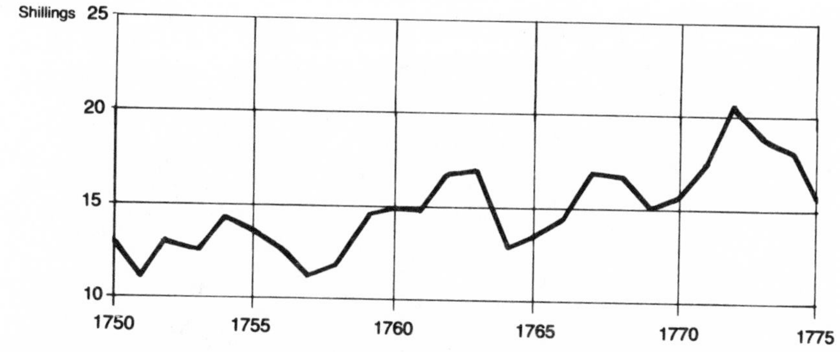

FIGURE 3. The Price of Flour in Pennsylvania, 1750–1775. Prices are wholesale, Pennsylvania currency. *Data from Anne Bezanson* et al., Prices in Colonial Pennsylvania, *Industrial Research Department, Wharton School of Finance and Commerce, University of Pennsylvania, Research Studies, XXVI (Philadelphia, 1935),* 422

gland raised the price of flour to a record high in 1772, and the mean price for the years 1771–1775 was well above the average for the two previous five-year periods (see fig. 3). Tonnage entering the port was 31.6 percent higher in 1773 and 1774 than in 1766 and 1767,[35] and tonnage clearing for the West Indies and southern Europe between 1771 and 1774 averaged 16 percent greater than the 1766–1770 level (see fig. 1). This prosperity is reflected in other shipping data as well: the volume of tonnage registered by merchants in the period 1771–1775 was 48.1 percent higher than in the previous five-year period (see table 13).[36] The buoyancy of the provision trade also enriched Philadelphia's hinterland and made willing consumers of its farmers, artisans, and housewives, who purchased a large volume of dry goods between 1771 and 1775 (fig. 2).[37] Because foreign exchange

35. Tonnage Duty Book. See Doerflinger, "Enterprise," 145. William S. Sachs, "Agricultural Conditions in the Northern Colonies before the Revolution," *Journal of Economic History*, XIII (1953), 285, states that "the strong demand for American foodstuffs is especially noticeable in the tonnage statistics of Philadelphia." The merchants also organized many shipments of wheat to Iberia directly from the Chesapeake region. See William Pollard to Peter Hoare, July 20, 1772, Pollard Letterbook, 1772–1774, 53.

36. This interpretation of the Ship Register agrees with John J. McCusker, "Sources of Investment Capital in the Colonial Philadelphia Shipping Industry," *Jour. Econ. Hist.*, XXXII (1972), 146–157.

37. Sachs, "Agricultural Conditions," *Jour. Econ. Hist.*, XIII (1953), 286–290, provides some evidence of the prosperity of the countryside in the six years before Independence. The credit crisis of 1772 is said to have caused "one of the worst depressions ever experienced in the new world" (Sachs, "Business Outlook," 218; see also Nash, *Urban Crucible*, 317–318). Although this panic may have caused many bankruptcies in London (where it started) and intensified pressure on merchants in northern ports to pay their sterling debts,

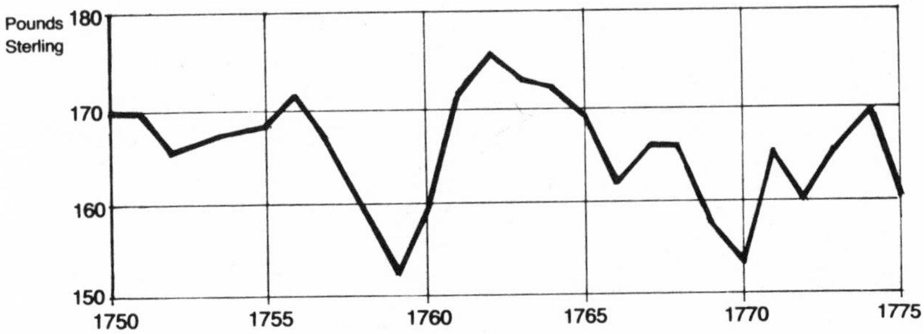

FIGURE 4. The Sterling Exchange Rate in Pennsylvania, 1750–1775. Pounds, Pennsylvania currency, needed to purchase one hundred pounds sterling. *Data from John J. McCusker,* Money and Exchange in Europe and America, 1660–1775: A Handbook *(Chapel Hill, N.C., 1978), 185–186*

earnings were so high in these years, importers were able to pay their heavy sterling debts at modest exchange rates (see fig. 4).

Merchants who failed to profit from these commercial opportunities could take advantage of the strong real estate market in the city, where population grew by 38 percent during the eight years after 1767 and the number of dwellings rose by 80 percent between 1760 and 1774.[38] According to Carl Bridenbaugh, "the unprecedented demand for housing forced real-estate values to dizzy heights, enriching those fortunate enough to own lots and encouraging speculative enterprises."[39] Since a majority of merchants owned land in the Philadelphia area, as a group they stood to benefit greatly.[40]

What we have, then, is a mixed picture: a dry goods market that was glutted as usual, but a strong housing market and a generally buoyant

---

there is little evidence that it caused a wave of bankruptcies in Philadelphia. Egnal, "Pennsylvania Economy," 312, lists the following number of forced sales advertised in the *Pennsylvania Gazette*: 1770, 156; 1771, 91; 1772, 105; 1773, 113; 1774, 130.

38. Gary B. Nash and Billy G. Smith, "The Population of Eighteenth-Century Philadelphia," *PMHB*, XCIX (1975), 366; John K. Alexander, "The Philadelphia Numbers Game: An Analysis of Philadelphia's Eighteenth-Century Population," *PMHB*, XCVIII (1974), 324.

39. Carl Bridenbaugh, *Cities in Revolt: Urban Life in America, 1743–1776* (New York, 1955), 225. See also Nash, *Urban Crucible*, 314, which shows that Philadelphia artisans in the building trades had much larger estates than their Boston counterparts.

40. About 58% of the merchants owned land in Philadelphia City and County in 1774. See Transcript of the Assessment for the 1774 Provincial Tax for the City and County of Philadelphia, PHMC (microfilm copy HSP). This is supplemented by County Tax Duplicates, 1773–1775, for Philadelphia City and County, Philadelphia City Archives.

provision trade. The commercial downturn of the mid-1760s was followed by impressive expansion after 1768. This hardly adds up to a structural economic crisis that would have turned conservative businessmen into revolutionaries. The merchants, in fact, fared relatively well in this period. The number of carriage owners in Philadelphia increased from 29 in 1761 to 84 in 1772, and in the latter year 44 of them were merchants.[41] Shipping records tell a similar story. Because traders had ample capital to invest, the share of shipping entering the port that was owned by the consignee—usually a local firm—increased from 46 percent in 1766 to 75 percent in 1775.[42] It is significant, too, that Philadelphia's merchants could afford to buy increasingly larger shares of vessels. After dropping from 31.1 registered tons in the period 1751–1755 to 24.9 tons in the next five-year period, the mean size of a merchant's investment grew to 38.6 tons by the years 1771–1775.[43]

The records of five individual firms also demonstrate the possibilities for commercial success in this period. Between 1760 and 1763 the commodity trading activities of Mifflin and Massey, which composed the major share of the firm's business, were both extensive and profitable, yielding a gross return of 12 percent on sales of £35,154.[44] Even more significant is the success of two major firms that were active in dry goods distribution. Between 1761 and 1775 the earnings of James and Drinker averaged £2,742 per year. This was 45 percent more than the firm's annual earnings in the prosperous wartime period 1756–1760, though the rate of return on invested capital was not necessarily higher.[45] In 1769 and 1770 Joshua Fisher and Sons earned a 10 percent rate of return on its capital, and during the depression period July 1763–October 1768 Richard Waln's dry goods trade was consistently remunerative, yielding a gross profit of £1,541.[46] More impressive still was the success of a sugar refinery established in 1772 by Samuel Morris, Jr., and Peter Miercken, which was capitalized at £6,771. Within just two years, annual sales volume and profits had reached £17,836 and £2,488, respectively, and the partners were earning an annual rate of return of 37 percent. It is indicative of the favorable economic climate of the prewar years that, after suspension of operations during the Revolution, the

41. Oaks, "Big Wheels," *PMHB*, XCV (1971), 354, 359–362.

42. Tonnage Duty Book. See Doerflinger, "Enterprise," 145.

43. Based on the Pennsylvania Ship Register.

44. Mifflin and Massey Ledger, 1760–1763, HSP.

45. Henry Drinker Journal, 1776–1791, 2, Drinker Papers.

46. Joshua Fisher and Sons Ledger, 1769–1773, 104, 105, 149, 166, HSP; Richard Waln Ledger, 1761–1768, 42, 232, Waln Collection, HSP. Of 38 shipments of dry goods, at least 32 were profitable.

refinery was unable to generate annual sales of more than £14,499 between 1783 and 1790.[47]

Few firms matched the earnings of Morris and Miercken, of course, and bankruptcies continued to be commonplace during the sixteen years before the Revolution. But the early 1760s offered excellent markets in the West Indies, and rising European demand for foodstuffs made the years after 1768 quite prosperous, as we have noted. Thus, despite the downturn of the mid-1760s, the pre-Revolutionary period offered good opportunities for the shrewd trader. This assessment does not imply that Philadelphia society was free from inequality and social strain in the decade and a half before Independence. It is, in fact, consistent with the argument, also insisted upon by neo-Progressive historians, that the distribution of wealth became increasingly unequal during the later colonial period. But how else than through an expansion of commercial profits could merchants have financed the "urban mansions built during the 1760s" and purchased the "four-wheeled coaches and carriages imported from London"?[48]

The Logic of Moderation

It seems clear that Philadelphia merchants were not driven toward revolution by unprecedented economic difficulties. Moreover, their political orientation generally did not predispose them toward radical measures. Although they viewed encroachments of British power with as much dismay as other Philadelphians, politics was not the major concern of most traders. The merchants tended to fear that radical initiatives might sever their close and valuable ties with England and the empire.

There is a plethora of evidence, both private and public, that Philadelphia's merchants sincerely believed that parliamentary taxation of Americans was unconstitutional. In 1768 a committee of Philadelphia traders wrote to a group of leading English merchants that "the Statutes imposing Duties on Paper, Glass, Tea, &c. being a Tax on the Americans, without their Consent, we look upon, [as] Unconstitutional and destructive of our Rights, as your Brethren and Subjects."[49] When the English

47. Morris and Miercken Papers, Hollingsworth Collection, HSP (see typescript guide to this enormous collection at HSP). On sales volume, 1772–1793, see CDXXI, 32–40; CDXXIII, CDXXIV, CDXXV. On profits, see CDXXI, 1; CDXXII, 105; CDXXXV, 136. On the firm's capitalization, see CDXXII, 1.

48. Nash, *Urban Crucible*, 257.

49. "From the Merchants and Traders of Philadelphia in the Province of Pennsylvania to the Merchants and Manufacturers of Great Britain, August 11, 1768," Manuscripts Relat-

merchants admitted that the Townshend duties might be "inexpedient," the Philadelphians pointedly insisted that they were unconstitutional as well.[50] This belief was repeated again and again in the private correspondence not only of leading whig traders but of merchants who were loyalist or neutral during the Revolution. The Quaker John Reynell insisted that "the point in dispute is a very Important one, if the Americans are to be taxed by a Parliament where they are not nor can be Represented, they are no longer Englishmen but Slaves." Another Friend agreed, observing that "those Dangerous Innovasions throw the Continent of America into the utmost Confusion, and if they are submitted to, leave us neither Liberty nor Property of our own." A wealthy Anglican who stayed in Philadelphia during the British occupation of 1777–1778 exclaimed, "I honor and glory in the mother country, as I love my own, whose liberties and interest are most cruelly and unjustly attacked." And Thomas Wharton, whose business interests brought him into close touch with leading British politicians, admitted, "I very ardently wish our superiors would take it into their serious consideration . . . how inconsistent it is with the spirit of our constitution for the property of an Englishman to be taken from him without his consent."[51]

Grounded in the merchants' conceptions of their rights as Englishmen, these constitutional fears were sharpened by their problems as businessmen. The tightening of the customs administration after 1763 greatly complicated life for Philadelphia's smugglers,[52] and both the Sugar Act and the Stamp Act required payment of taxes in specie at just the moment when the Currency Act of 1764 forbade colonial legislatures from issuing legal tender paper money. All three of these acts coincided with the commercial downturn of the mid-1760s, when exchange rates were high and large amounts of specie were shipped to England to extinguish sterling debts. The result was a severe shortage of money. In May 1766

ing to Non-Importation Resolutions, Philadelphia, 1766–1775, American Philosophical Society (hereafter cited as APS).

50. "A genuine Copy of a *Letter* from a Committee of *Merchants* in *Philadelphia* to the Committee of *Merchants* in London," Apr. 8, 1769, in *Pennsylvania Gazette* (Philadelphia), Aug. 31, 1769.

51. The four quotations are, respectively, from Carl Leroy Romanek, "John Reynell, Quaker Merchant of Colonial Philadelphia" (Ph.D. diss., Pennsylvania State University, 1969), 154–155; Grace Hutchison Larsen, "Profile of a Colonial Merchant: Thomas Clifford of Pre-Revolutionary Philadelphia" (Ph.D. diss., Columbia University, 1955), 399; Eugene R. Slaski, "Thomas Willing: Moderation during the American Revolution" (Ph.D. diss., Florida State University, 1971), 299; Thomas Wharton to Anthony Todd, Apr. 5, 1774, Thomas Wharton Letterbook, 1773–1784, Wharton Papers, HSP.

52. Jensen, *Maritime Commerce*, 135–136, 145–152.

John Reynell complained, "Unless we can get some more [paper currency] made, [I] know not what will become of us, nor how we shall be able to pay our debts."[53]

Even in the absence of an economic crisis, one might have expected constitutional grievances to have aligned the merchants unambiguously behind the radical cause. A major task facing the historian, then, is to discern the factors that tended to moderate the merchants' political stance. One factor, certainly, was the speed with which some of the merchants' major complaints were defused. The Stamp Act was never enforced, the Sugar Act was greatly revised in 1766, and the Currency Act did not, in the end, wreck Pennsylvania's paper currency. The act allowed the Pennsylvania legislature to keep outstanding paper in circulation until its regular expiration date, and the colony was able to issue £102,000 of new money that was not legal tender. This was enough to fill most of the colony's monetary needs.[54]

A second explanation for the merchants' caution is that, as a group, they were largely apolitical. To be sure, such traders as Charles Thomson, Thomas Mifflin, George Clymer, Thomas Wharton, and George Bryan were political activists, and many others had clear political affiliations. But despite the political overtones implicit in the concept of a merchant aristocracy, before the Revolution merchants did not dominate political life. The men who articulated the colonists' constitutional position in pamphlets, broadsides, and newspaper articles were not active merchants, for the most part, and Pennsylvania's party chieftains were generally wealthy lawyers, clerics, and landed gentlemen, rather than traders.[55] This was particularly true of the inner circle of the propri-

53. Romanek, "John Reynell," 148.

54. Jack P. Greene and Richard M. Jellison, "The Currency Act of 1764 in Imperial-Colonial Relations, 1764–1776," *WMQ*, 3d Ser., XVIII (1961), 489, 506–508.

55. Of the 32 pamphleteers represented in Bernard Bailyn's collection of Revolutionary pamphlets whose occupations could be determined, only 6 were merchants. Bernard Bailyn, ed., *Pamphlets of the American Revolution, 1750–1776*, I, *1750–1765* (Cambridge, Mass., 1965), xv, xvi, 749–752. Four of these 6—Philip Livingston, Thomas Hutchinson, John Hancock, and James Bowdoin—were gentlemen who inherited substantial fortunes and thus did not have the outlook of the typical merchant. On this matter, see Doerflinger, "Enterprise," 50–55.

On the proprietary side, William Allen was a gentleman and retired merchant, Benjamin Chew and John Dickinson were lawyers, William Smith and Richard Peters were clerics, and James Hamilton, Thomas Penn, and John Penn were gentlemen. As for the Quaker party, Benjamin Franklin was a retired printer, Joseph Galloway was an aristocratic lawyer, Isaac Norris and William Logan were merchant gentlemen whose fortunes rested on the exertions of their influential fathers, and Israel Pemberton was a retired merchant. Of these 13 men, only Allen and Pemberton were really successful traders, and both had largely retired by 1760.

etary party, from which even so capable a leader as Robert Morris was excluded.[56]

Perhaps this detachment from political activity is not surprising. Merchants who had been juggling credits and debits in a countinghouse since their early teens had less exposure to legal and political theory than did genteel graduates of the College of Philadelphia and the Inns of Court. They were fully preoccupied with the risks and rewards of commerce. Henry Drinker confided that he preferred "to be drawn out into publick life as little as may be," and Thomas Clifford has been described as "apolitical": "He held no political office, except for a brief appointment as overseer of the poor in Philadelphia, wrote no pamphlets, led no faction nor joined any, served on none of the political committees formed in the midst of the imperial struggle, and attended no congresses." A substantial proportion of Philadelphia's merchants probably shared Clifford's political indifference. It was said that "Mr. John Ross, who loved ease and Madeira much better than liberty and strife, declared for neutrality, saying, that, *let who would be king, he well knew that he should be subject.*" Certainly it cannot be assumed that the average trader viewed affairs from the same perspective as a learned, well-connected, financially secure gentleman like John Dickinson. Even the most politically active merchant might view public life with ambivalence. Charles Pettit doubted whether politics was worth the time and trouble it required, "unless it should eventually throw business into my hands by which I may obtain a profit." Robert Morris mixed politics and business successfully and "evinced little interest in the problems of political theory that agitated many of his colleagues."[57]

It is clear, furthermore, that many merchants, whether or not politically oriented, identified closely with the British Empire, which was, after all, in part a commercial construct. Merchants were the engineers of commerce who took risks to move goods across the Atlantic; without

56. Stephen Brobeck, "Revolutionary Change in Colonial Philadelphia: The Brief Life of the Proprietary Gentry," *WMQ*, 3d Ser., XXXIII (1976), 431, and table I, 416–417, which lists 22 proprietary party members, of whom about 4 (William Coxe, Thomas Lawrence, John Wilcocks, Jr., and Thomas Willing) were active merchants in the 1770s.

57. Drinker, "Effects of 'Non-Importation,'" *PMHB*, XIV (1890), 44; Larsen, "Thomas Clifford," 322. Alexander Graydon, *Memoirs of a Life, Chiefly Passed in Pennsylvania, within the Last Sixty Years* (Harrisburg, Pa., 1811), 105; Charles Pettit to Joseph Reed, Apr. 18, 1784, Joseph Reed Papers, New York Historical Society; Jack N. Rakove, *The Beginnings of National Politics: An Interpretive History of the Continental Congress* (New York, 1979), 299. The situation was similar in New York City, where "most of the great merchants were never active in public life." See Edward Countryman, *A People in Revolution: The American Revolution and Political Society in New York, 1760–1790* (Baltimore, Md., 1981), 113.

them, the empire was primarily a bureaucratic entity. As the Philadelphia traders wrote to their English colleagues: "We consider the Merchants here and in England as the Links of the Chain that binds both Countries together. They are deeply concerned in preserving the Union and Connection."[58] A variety of contacts combined to form this chain. Dry goods traders in the Delaware Valley were always in touch with some of the most powerful merchants in London and Bristol. On the eve of the Revolution, Pennsylvania land speculators, including some prominent merchants, were angling for a royal grant of a fourteenth colony to be established in the Ohio Valley, and they well understood that British-American friction would injure their prospects.[59] The merchants also remembered that in more than one war their property on land and sea had been protected by His Majesty's army and fleet and that many traders had profited handsomely by servicing these forces. Not a few of the merchants were born in Britain or had relatives there, and prominent Quaker merchants were in close touch with the leaders of the Society of Friends in England.

This identification with the empire was challenged by a key instrument of the Revolutionary movement, the boycotts of 1765–1766, 1768–1770, and 1774–1776. Although the stated aim of the nonimportation agreements was to exert pressure for the repeal of particular measures, their actual reach was far wider. Nonimportation was in fact a tentative declaration of American economic independence, and the enforcement of these agreements by local committees gave rise to some of the earliest extralegal Revolutionary governments in the colonies. The boycotts played an important ideological role as well, for by rejecting the debilitating vices and luxuries of the Old World they translated into action the moral component of a republican ideology. Nonimportation thus provided a means of atoning for the sins of avarice and materialism in an increasingly secular age.[60]

Philadelphia dry goods merchants, particularly the Quakers, did not necessarily reject these radical attitudes in toto. In 1769 John Reynell donned a leather jacket and set his wife to turning out homespun, while Thomas Clifford exclaimed: "Where will profusion and Extravagance lead us to? . . . [M]ake our Wants fewer. Let our living and expenses be

58. Quoted in Schlesinger, *Colonial Merchants*, 31.

59. John Baynton, George Morgan, and Samuel, Thomas, and Charles Wharton were associated with Benjamin Franklin, Joseph Galloway, and others in two companies that sought grants of land in the West. See Thomas Perkins Abernethy, *Western Lands and the American Revolution* (New York, 1959), chaps. 2, 3.

60. Edmund S. Morgan, "The Puritan Ethic and the American Revolution," *WMQ*, 3d Ser., XXIV (1967), 3–43.

less than our Income. Then we may discharge our contracts with honour, and set a good Example to the succeeding generation."[61] But the merchants could hardly overlook the fact that they were the conduit by which pernicious luxuries poured into the Delaware Valley and that not a few of the choicest extravagances ended up in their own parlors and pantries. If fully executed, nonimportation entailed nothing less than repudiation of their profession and destruction of the elaborate trading networks they had laboriously constructed.[62] In this respect the merchants viewed the imperial connection quite differently from Virginia planters, who found that they were increasingly financing their expensive tastes with debt rather than tobacco shipments.

Religion and Politics

The merchants' moderate outlook was also fostered by the interrelated issues of religion and social control, for the Revolutionary movement in Pennsylvania was shaped at every step by bitter antagonism between religious groups, especially between Quakers and Presbyterians. Anglicans and Quakers each constituted over a third of the merchant community, and they dominated its upper stratum even more, making up 94 percent of merchant carriage owners in 1772.[63] Presbyterians, on the other hand, accounted for less than a fifth of the merchants and few traders of the first rank. Thus, the economic muscle of the merchant group, the power to make or break a boycott, rested with the conservative congregations of the Friends' Meeting House and of Christ and Saint Peter's churches.

The principles of the Society of Friends were ill suited to governing during an era of war and revolution, however, for the Quaker peace testimony not only forbade military activity but discouraged riots, rallies, boycotts, and smuggling.[64] The Friends' heritage of persecution in

61. Jensen, *Maritime Commerce*, 180; Larsen, "Thomas Clifford," 366.

62. Morgan, "The Puritan Ethic," *WMQ*, 3d Ser., XXIV (1967), 10–11.

63. These figures, which are very inexact, are based on Robert Francis Oaks, "Philadelphia Merchants and the American Revolution, 1765–1776" (Ph.D. diss., University of Southern California, 1970), 216–236, which lists members of Revolutionary committees and signers of boycotts. The religious affiliations of 173 merchants are listed: 73 Anglicans, 72 Quakers, 13 Presbyterians, and 15 others. However, Anglicans and Quakers may have been overrepresented in these proportions because they included most of the prominent traders. On carriage ownership, see Oaks, "Big Wheels," *PMHB*, XCV (1971), 359–362.

64. Frederick B. Tolles, *Meeting House and Counting House: The Quaker Merchants of Colonial Philadelphia, 1682–1763* (Chapel Hill, N.C., 1948), 4–28, 230–243; Richard Bauman, *For the Reputation of Truth: Politics, Religion, and Conflict among the Pennsyl-*

the Puritan commonwealths of old England and New England made them highly distrustful of all Presbyterians, whether in Massachusetts or in the Scotch-Irish settlements of Pennsylvania's backcountry. In addition, many years of control of Pennsylvania's government, together with their commercial prominence and civic leadership, had imbued the Friends with a conservative, rather complacent outlook. In this respect they resembled many Anglican merchants, who favored the status quo because they had close political and family ties with the colony's proprietors, British descendants of William Penn. The Anglicans' connections with England were also strong because the ministers of the church were ordained in London and because the church in America depended upon financial support from England.[65]

The colony's Presbyterians, on the other hand, were of Scottish descent and had long resisted English domination. They traced their political lineage back to the civil wars which had overthrown both bishop and king, and they felt little love for either. Indeed, Presbyterian ministers, especially those of a New Light persuasion, preached a distinctly republican message, emphasizing "the idea of a fundamental constitution based on law, of inalienable rights which were God-given and therefore natural, of government as a binding contract made between rulers and peoples, of the right of people to hold their rulers to account and to defend their rights against all oppression."[66] The concentration of Presbyterians in Pennsylvania's underrepresented frontier counties minimized their influence in the assembly, but they hoped that their political power would grow as their share of the colony's population increased.[67]

After 1750 a combination of factors poisoned relations between these three major religious groups and brought the colony to the edge of civil

---

vania Quakers, 1750–1800 (Baltimore, Md., 1971). On smuggling, see Hugh Roberts to Benjamin Franklin, May 20, 1765, in Leonard W. Labaree *et al.*, eds., *The Papers of Benjamin Franklin*, XII (New Haven, Conn., 1968), 136; Jensen, *Maritime Commerce*, 143–144; Larsen, "Thomas Clifford," 326–327; and Theodore Thayer, *Israel Pemberton, King of the Quakers* (Philadelphia, 1943), 14–16.

65. Leonard Woods Labaree, *Conservatism in Early American History* (New York, 1948), chap. 3. See Jacob E. Cooke, *Tench Coxe and the Early Republic* (Chapel Hill, N.C., 1978), chap. 1.

66. Alice M. Baldwin, "Sowers of Sedition: The Political Theories of Some of the New Light Presbyterian Clergy of Virginia and North Carolina," *WMQ*, 3d Ser., V (1948), 76. Many of the ministers discussed by Baldwin were educated in New Jersey and Pennsylvania.

67. James H. Hutson, *Pennsylvania Politics, 1746–1770: The Movement for Royal Government and Its Consequences* (Princeton, N.J., 1972), 207–210. On apportionment of seats in the assembly, see Labaree *et al.*, eds., *Papers of Franklin*, XI, 123n–124n.

war. Religious antagonisms would continue to condition the attitudes of merchants until the Revolution. Once the proprietorship of the colony passed to Thomas Penn in 1746, concerted attempts were made to increase the income derived from the holding.[68] Toward this end, Penn shrewdly used the military crisis of the Seven Years' War to push favorable tax legislation through the assembly. Pacifist in any event, the Quaker lawmakers were reluctant to enact a tax bill that would finance the war and grant Penn concessions, and they were also loath to assist the turbulent Scotch-Irish frontiersmen who seemed to be partly responsible for the deterioration of Indian relations. The deadlock was broken only by the resignation of ten Quaker assemblymen, a grudging compromise by the proprietor, and a march on Philadelphia by seven hundred incensed westerners.[69] This crisis occurred again in 1764 when, in the aftermath of Pontiac's Rebellion, a group of Scotch-Irish frontiersmen known as the Paxton Boys marched on Philadelphia in order to deal with some Christianized Indians harbored by the Quakers.[70]

The march of the Paxton Boys triggered a vicious political battle in Pennsylvania. To many Quakers, William Penn's once peaceful province seemed to be lurching toward anarchy, with unruly Presbyterians overrunning the colony. These fears were heightened in 1765 when a band of Scotch-Irishmen in Cumberland County seized and destroyed a large shipment of goods that Baynton, Wharton, and Morgan had en route to Pittsburgh.[71] Fundamental political change, namely, elimination of proprietary control of the colony, seemed to offer the only real solution to the crisis. In pursuit of this goal, the assembly in 1765 dispatched Benjamin Franklin to London to persuade the British ministry that order could be maintained in Pennsylvania only by making it a royal colony. Although some Quakers questioned the wisdom of forfeiting William Penn's prized Charter of Liberties, most Friends agreed that this stratagem offered the only hope for peace. As Thomas Wharton wrote Frank-

68. Hutson, *Pennsylvania Politics*, 6–40; William S. Hanna, *Benjamin Franklin and Pennsylvania Politics* (Stanford, Calif., 1964), 1–53.

69. Bauman, *For the Reputation of Truth*, chap. 2; Daniel J. Boorstin, *The Americans: The Colonial Experience* (New York, 1958), 33–69; Hutson, *Pennsylvania Politics*, 23–40; Ralph L. Ketcham, "Conscience, War, and Politics in Pennsylvania, 1755–1757," *WMQ*, 3d Ser., XX (1963), 416–439.

70. Thayer, *Israel Pemberton*, 97–112, 123–170; Brooke Hindle, "The March of the Paxton Boys," *WMQ*, 3d Ser., III (1946), 461–486; Labaree *et al.*, eds., *Papers of Franklin*, XI, 69–75.

71. Eleanor M. Webster, "Insurrection at Fort Loudon in 1765: Rebellion or Preservation of Peace?" *Western Pennsylvania Historical Magazine*, XLVII (1964), 125–139.

lin, "We are, in a shatter'd and distract'd State, and unless thou art so happy as to releive us; Miserable will be our Fate."[72]

This resonant fear of Presbyterian hegemony was a major factor in the Quaker merchants' view of the Revolutionary movement. They perceived an inexorable logic to the Revolutionary process that had nothing to do with commercial problems, parliamentary taxation, or ministerial tyranny. Like their forefathers of the seventeenth century, the Presbyterians were evidently using discontent over constitutional issues to seize power for themselves and deny their fellow Christians freedom of conscience.

Moderation Applied

The prosperity of most merchants, a habitual detachment from political affairs, close ties with England, and fear of a rising Presbyterian faction all combined to moderate the political stance of the merchants between 1764 and 1776. Although they clearly disliked the Sugar Act, their response to it was very restrained, perhaps in part because they were absorbed by the local political tumults of 1764.[73] The Stamp Act crisis of the following year was powerfully shaped by the contingencies of provincial politics, because the new tax endangered Benjamin Franklin's scheme to make Pennsylvania a royal colony.[74] Franklin was pushing Pennsylvania to embrace royal authority just as imperial pressure was becoming most obnoxious, and it is a tribute to his nimbleness that this error did not shatter his political career. While in England in 1764, Franklin had argued against the proposed Stamp Act, but once it was law, he made the best of the situation by nominating a political crony, John Hughes, as stamp agent for Pennsylvania. Resistance to the Stamp Act was widespread in Pennsylvania, spearheaded by proprietary supporters and Presbyterian leaders who wished to discredit the royal government that Franklin was trying to impose upon the colony. On two occasions they tried to rally mobs to "pull down" the houses of Quaker

72. Hutson, *Pennsylvania Politics*, 41–177; Bauman, *Reputation of Truth*, 117; Thomas Wharton to Benjamin Franklin, July 16, 1765, in Labaree *et al.*, eds., *Papers of Franklin*, XII, 215.

73. Jensen, *Maritime Commerce*, 154–156.

74. Hutson, *Pennsylvania Politics*, 192–203; James H. Hutson, "An Investigation of the Inarticulate: Philadelphia's White Oaks," *WMQ*, 3d Ser., XXVIII (1971), 3–25; Edmund S. Morgan and Helen M. Morgan, *The Stamp Act Crisis: Prologue to Revolution* (Chapel Hill, N.C., 1953), chap. 14; Nash, *Urban Crucible*, 305–309.

party leaders, and the committee that asked John Hughes to resign his post as stamp agent was dominated by merchants from the proprietary faction. Skillfully countering these moves was Franklin's protégé, Joseph Galloway, who was aided by other members of the Quaker faction, including a number of merchants.

Since the attacks on stamp agents constituted the chief form of resistance to the tax, it cannot be said that merchants as a group led the opposition to parliamentary taxation in 1765, as has been suggested.[75] In reality, the trading community was split: Quaker merchants generally did not oppose the Stamp Act, while Anglican and Presbyterian merchants of the proprietary faction did. The one instance in which merchants united to oppose the act was the boycott of British imports, organized in November 1765. Even here, there is evidence that some merchants joined the boycott under duress. Charles Thomson observed, "So exasperated are the People, that to appease them and indeed for their own Safety the merchants are obliged to pawn their word and honour and give from under their hands that they will not import any more Goods." John Reynell feared that his house would be destroyed if he used stamp papers.[76]

Despite their divisions in 1765, the merchants could have played a major role in opposing the Townshend Acts of 1767. By 1768 the animosities between Quaker and Anglican merchants had cooled as the royal government project drifted, and primary opposition to the duties took the form, this time, not of riots, but of a major commercial boycott from March 1769 to September 1770, in which the traders actively participated. According to some analysts, the merchants' causal role was indeed central. Some historians have argued that "nonimportation was only incidentally designed to compel Parliament to repeal obnoxious legislation."[77] Instead, the merchants initiated the boycott primarily to gain an eighteen-month respite from the relentless cascade of British capital and goods, during which they could sell off inventories, pay debts to English suppliers at favorable exchange rates, and build up a cash reserve.[78] This ascription of motives is plausible, and there is enough evidence to demonstrate that the material benefits of the boycott were on

75. Schlesinger, *Colonial Merchants*, 50–90, 305–307.

76. Jensen, 160–161. Thomas Wharton to Benjamin Franklin, Nov. 7, 1765, in Labaree *et al.*, eds., *Papers of Franklin*, XII, 356–360, suggests that the merchants were united behind the boycott. James and Drinker to David Barclay and Sons, Oct. 14, 1765, James and Drinker Letterbook, 1764–1766, states that Friends were not involved in the political disturbances in Philadelphia in 1765.

77. Egnal and Ernst, "Economic Interpretation," *WMQ*, 3d Ser., XXIX (1972), 21.

78. *Ibid.*, 22–24; Ernst, *Money and Politics*, 209–210.

the minds of some traders. Yet it still remains to be asked: Did these mercantile concerns determine the pace and pattern of events?

The answer to this question is an unequivocal no. Neo-Progressives have overlooked an important detail. Far from leading the nonimportation movement in Philadelphia, dry goods merchants stubbornly opposed it throughout 1768, steadfastly ignoring the increasingly vituperative demands of radicals that they place the public welfare above private interest.[79] Pressure steadily mounted on importers to join the boycott, which Boston and New York had already agreed to start. In pamphlets, speeches, and newspaper articles the Philadelphia radicals, led by John Dickinson, showered the merchants with abuse. They even tried to force the issue by enlisting individual merchants, but the intransigence of "eight or ten" wealthy importers scotched the effort.[80] Although they joined in questioning the constitutionality of the Townshend Acts, conservative merchants evidently opposed precipitate action that would violate the Quaker peace testimony and offend valuable correspondents in England.

On the other hand, overt loyalism of the kind shown by the royalist faction in Boston was not part of the merchants' caution. Once the boycott began in March 1769, its legitimacy was generally accepted, and enforcement problems were few.[81] As Henry Drinker exclaimed, "I could not think of deserting a measure we had deliberately gone into for the securing and supporting our Liberties and valuable Rights, drawing on ourselves at once the contempt and indignation of the other Colonies, not to say the exultation and derision of the Mother Country."[82] Drinker was far from alone; when three vessels from "the little dirty Colony of Rhode Island" (the first defector from the boycott) sailed into Delaware Bay, they were barred by the merchants from unloading their wares.[83]

This stance demonstrates a willingness to sacrifice for the patriot cause, because by the spring of 1770 the stoppage of trade was a real burden to the importers, whose stocks were depleted. As early as March, Clement Biddle complained that his inventory was "unsorted." John Reynell also became eager to import more goods, and Henry Drinker was distressed by the fact that many small importers were close to ruin.[84] The extensive dry goods business of Joshua Fisher and Sons was certainly

79. Jensen, *Maritime Commerce*, 172–179; Schlesinger, *Colonial Merchants*, 116–120, 125–131.

80. Jensen, *Maritime Commerce*, 174.

81. *Ibid.*, 181–184.

82. Drinker, "Effects of 'Non-Importation,'" *PMHB*, XIV (1890), 43, 44.

83. *Ibid.*, 44; Biddle to Thomas Robinson, May 25, June 2, 1770, Clement Biddle and Co. Letterbook, 1769–1770, Clement Biddle Papers, HSP.

84. Biddle to Thomas Richardson, Mar. 4, 1770, *ibid.*; Romanek, "John Reynell," 160–161; Drinker, "Effects of 'Non-Importation,'" *PMHB*, XIV (1890), 42, 43.

injured by the extension of the boycott into 1770. As the supply of goods in the Philadelphia market shrank, the firm's profit margins rose substantially in 1770, but this increase was more than canceled by a plunge in the volume of sales, caused by a depletion of inventory. Consequently, the Fishers' profits dropped from £968 in 1769 to £844 in 1770.[85]

Although merchants were willing to accept the financial burdens of nonimportation, the drift of events made the sacrifice seem ever more pointless.[86] In May 1770 most of the duties were repealed, and shortly thereafter Rhode Island defected from the agreement, as did New York in July. The agreements of Maryland, Massachusetts, and New York were less restrictive than Pennsylvania's, and well-documented reports circulated that Bostonians were freely importing large quantities of tea. Worse still, the boycott seemed to be having little impact on the English economy. For all these reasons, many merchants by May 1770 wanted to end the boycott. Nevertheless, it dragged on until September—after it was too late to import many goods until the following spring.

The cause of this delay was a split in the merchants' ranks. During the winter of 1769–1770, for reasons that are unclear, five prominent Quaker and three leading Anglican importers withdrew from the twenty-man merchant committee supervising the boycott. The five Presbyterians on the committee retained their seats, and control of the body passed to Presbyterian Charles Thomson, a minor figure in the city's business community but a shrewd radical politician. In this way, the wealthy importers forfeited control to the radicals.[87] Throughout the spring and summer of 1770 the radicals extended nonimportation by cooperating with a critical new force in Philadelphia politics, the mechanics, who had their

85. Joshua Fisher and Sons Ledger, 1769–1773, 110. The data are as follows:

Year	*Sales*	*Profits*	*Profits / Sales*	*Dry Goods Inventory at Beginning of Year*
1769	£ 10,753	£ 968	9.0%	£ 6,561
1770	6,020	844	14.0	3,379
1771	14,681			2,084

86. Jensen, *Maritime Commerce*, 187–195.

87. There is conflicting evidence about the details of this important process. In a letter to the Boston Committee of Merchants, dated Sept. 25, 1770 (see *Pennsylvania Chronicle and Universal Advertiser* [Philadelphia], Oct. 1, 1770), the Philadelphia Committee of Merchants gave the following account. The original committee had 20 members, of whom 7 "withdrew." Of these 7, 4 "personally resigned." Since an additional committee member (Abel James) was in England, the committee reported that its effective strength was 12. Ryerson, *The Revolution Is Now Begun*, 78, lists 19 "committee men chosen in 1769," of whom 8 (5 Quakers and 3 Anglicans) "opposed the boycott in 1770." These 8 were among 17 merchants, in 14 firms, who signed a letter to the committee dated Sept. 12, 1770, asking for a revision of the agreement (see *Pennsylvania Gazette*, Sept. 20, 1770). Ryerson states (29–30) that "the merchants chose a single committee of twenty-one members," that "in November 1769, if not earlier, chairman John Reynell and several members had re-

own economic reasons for wanting to bar cheap English manufactures.[88] In June, Thomson packed a merchant meeting with mechanics to carry it in favor of continuing the boycott, and the artisans also rallied on their own in its support. Outnumbered but not outwitted, conservative merchants first petitioned the committee to poll the subscribers to the agreement through a house-by-house canvass, a method that would prevent outsiders from exerting influence.[89] When Thomson's committee vetoed this method, conservative merchants finally ended the boycott on September 20 by holding a meeting of subscribers in a tavern too small to accommodate mechanics and other outsiders.[90]

The politics of nonimportation show clearly how patriotism was shaded by self-interest and by the circumspection of the mercantile mind. Anxious not to offend their correspondents in England, the merchants took their time in entering the boycott. Once the initiative was under way, however, they supported it to the point of forgoing profits as their inventories dwindled during 1770. But sacrifice had its limits. When other colonies abandoned the boycott and some of the Townshend duties were repealed, the merchants became eager to get on with trade. Of course the radicals in Philadelphia accused the moderates of being motivated by crass self-interest. To this charge the moderates replied, with some justice, that wet goods merchants were pressing for extension of a boycott that did not affect their own business even as they paid into the royal treasury duties on wine and rum.[91] Furthermore, the radicals' ma-

---

signed from the committee or ceased attending meetings," and that the people "who had probably withdrawn from the committee" by Nov. 25, 1769, included John Reynell, "three other Quakers," and the Anglican Tench Francis. Jensen, *Maritime Commerce*, 183, agrees that the conservative merchants "withdrew" during the winter of 1769–1770 and that the remaining members were not "dry goods merchants of any consequence." But on Apr. 29, 1770, Henry Drinker wrote that a group of wealthy merchants, who were dissatisfied with the agreement, "made it a point to get all the Committee together, tho. J. Reynell, Tench Francis, J. Warder, myself and some others had not attended for some months. We met and were applied to by a number of the importers" ("Effects of 'Non-Importation,'" *PMHB*, XIV [1890], 43). From this conflicting evidence we may infer that the original committee numbered 19, 20, or 21 members, 7 or 8 of whom eventually "withdrew" from the committee, and that 8 members (mostly men who had withdrawn) were among the 17 who opposed the agreement in Sept. 1770. Drinker's remarks show, however, that "resigning" and "withdrawing" were highly informal procedures, since those who had withdrawn in Nov. 1769 met with other committee members the following Apr.

88. Jensen, *Maritime Commerce*, 188–192; Hutson, *Pennsylvania Politics*, 232–236.

89. See the exchange of letters, dated Sept. 12, 14, in *Pennsylvania Gazette*, Sept. 20, 1770.

90. Jensen, *Maritime Commerce*, 194.

91. Drinker, "Effects of 'Non-Importation,'" *PMHB*, XIV (1890), 42; Jensen, *Maritime Commerce*, 190, 191. The degree of commercial specialization of Philadelphia firms was directly related to their size. Smaller companies typically concentrated on one or two

jor allies in Philadelphia, the mechanics, benefited tremendously from the suspension of trade with England.[92] The mechanics, too, could be accused of dubious motives. Republican ideology was thus tempered and twisted by the realities of the marketplace.

Merchants approached with similar ambivalence the British East India Company's plan to unload its huge supply of tea in America. Many undoubtedly viewed the plan as a trick to seduce Americans into importing a dutied commodity,[93] but it is apparent that some merchants had financial reasons for attacking the tea scheme. In addition to injuring directly those relatively few traders who smuggled Dutch tea into Philadelphia, the company's plan concentrated power in the hands of a few prominent traders who had good connections in England. The tea was consigned to only four major firms, who would earn commissions of roughly six hundred pounds by auctioning off the tea.[94] This arrange-

markets at a time, while larger firms were less specialized. Therefore, as Drinker noted, small firms specializing in the dry goods trade were badly hurt by the boycott, but a fairly important West Indies merchant like the radical Daniel Roberdeau could continue his trade unimpeded. On the other hand, many of the leading firms of the city, including the wealthy Quaker "dry goods merchants" who figured so largely in the boycott (such as James and Drinker, Jeremiah Warder and Sons, Joshua Fisher and Sons, and William Fisher) traded not only to England but also to the West Indies, southern Europe, and Ireland. Other wealthy merchants tended to concentrate on shipping provisions to the West Indies and southern Europe. Since major and minor firms were active in every important market of the port, there was no structural imperative in the nonimportation controversy pitting wealthy dry goods importers against poorer West Indies traders. See Drinker, "Effects of 'Non-Importation,'" *PMHB*, XIV (1890), 42; Daniel Roberdeau Letterbook, 1764–1771, esp. Roberdeau to John Boyd, Jan. 17, 1766, 89, HSP. The best way to determine the shipping activities of firms between 1765 and 1776 is through the Tonnage Duty Book, although the provenance of ships is not always stated in 1769 and 1770. See also Joshua Fisher and Sons Ledger, 1769–1773, 40, 106, 153, 193, 231, 246, and James and Drinker Letterbook, 1769–1772. For an analysis of the pattern of mercantile specialization, see Thomas M. Doerflinger, "Commercial Specialization in Philadelphia's Merchant Community, 1750–1791," *Business History Review*, LVII (1983), 20–49.

92. See Ryerson, *The Revolution Is Now Begun*, 77, 79, for a description of a new committee formed in Sept. 1770 to persuade merchants not to resume importation. By my reckoning, four of the nine people on this committee (George Clymer, John Shee, Daniel Roberdeau, and Peter Chevalier) were merchants.

93. This view was even held by tea agent Thomas Wharton. See Wharton to Thomas Walpole, Dec. 27, 1773, May 2, Aug. 2, 1774, and Wharton to Samuel Wharton, Jan. 1, 1773 (actually 1774), Thomas Wharton Letterbook, 1773–1784. See also Labaree, *Boston Tea Party*, 102.

94. Jensen, *Maritime Commerce*, 199, states that the four were to divide equally a 6% commission on the sale of the tea. The invoice value of the tea shipped to Philadelphia was £21,676 sterling, which would have provided a commission for each firm of £597 Pennsylvania currency, if the markup over the invoice cost were 10% and the exchange rate were 167%. For a reproduction of the East India Company's invoice, see APS, HSP, and Library

ment was the antithesis of the open, freely competitive environment that characterized Philadelphia's business world, and local newspapers warned that other oriental goods would soon be distributed in a similarly monopolistic fashion. There is some evidence that in Philadelphia, as in New York, smugglers led the opposition to the tax.[95] As they awaited arrival of the tea shipment in November 1773, James and Drinker foresaw hostility to its landing from Philadelphia smugglers, who were expecting a large tea shipment of their own from the Dutch island of Saint Eustatius.[96]

When news of the Coercive Acts reached Philadelphia in May 1774, wealthy Anglican and Quaker merchants attempted, as one said, "to keep the transactions of our City within the limits of Moderation and not Indecent or offensive to our parent State."[97] They insisted that Boston should pay for the tea ruined at the Tea Party, and they strongly opposed resumption of nonimportation, knowing by now that a boycott was far easier to start than to stop.[98] The convening of the Continental Congress in September 1774, however, deprived them of the power to shape events that they had in the past. In particular, they could not delay the third boycott of the Revolutionary movement, the Association established by Congress, which banned imports after December 1, 1774, and exports after September 10, 1775.

Some traders—Charles Thomson, Thomas Mifflin, and George Clymer, for instance—enthusiastically promoted the Revolutionary cause as it moved forward in 1774 and 1775. Yet many wealthy merchants looked on with dismay as a declaration of independence became more of a likelihood and the familiar social and political landscape was transformed. For Thomas Willing, one historian has noted, "Independence . . . was an economic consideration, not a political one; and the advan-

---

Company of Philadelphia, *A Rising People: The Founding of the United States, 1765 to 1789: A Celebration from the Collections of the American Philosophical Society* (Philadelphia, 1976), 20.

95. On the opposition of New York smugglers, see Pigou and Booth to James and Drinker, Oct. 4, 27, 1773, typescript copies in Drinker Papers; Nash, *Urban Crucible*, 317; John Vanderbilt to Charles Wharton, Nov. 6, 1773, Edward Wanton Smith Collection, HSP.

96. James and Drinker to Pigou and Booth, Nov. 20, 1773, typescript copy in Drinker Papers.

97. Thomas Wharton to Samuel Wharton, July 5, 1774, Thomas Wharton Letterbook, 1773–1784; see also Thomas Wharton to Samuel Wharton, May 31, 1774; and Robert F. Oaks, "Philadelphia Merchants and the First Continental Congress," *Pennsylvania History*, XL (1973), 149–166.

98. Ryerson, *The Revolution Is Now Begun*, 56; Robert F. Oaks, "Philadelphia Merchants and the Origins of American Independence," APS, *Proceedings*, CXXI (1977), 425.

tages of security and stability seemed to lie with America remaining in the empire."[99] Thomas Clifford believed that "the present Contest is very unnatural, and will assuredly prove unprofitable."[100] Pacifism and elitism shaped the reaction of James and Drinker to the impending conflict. They thought that "distress and Ruin" were imminent, and Drinker lamented that "the lower Class of People . . . were generally muster'd by the Presbyterian party," while "Citizens of weight and Fortune" did not even vote in assembly elections.[101] Religious antagonisms continued to be a potent concern, especially for Quakers. James and Drinker discerned a common Presbyterian wellspring behind events in Philadelphia and Boston in 1773: had not the "hasty and violent resolves" of Charles Thomson and other local Presbyterians inspired the intransigence of the Bostonians that led to the destruction of the tea?[102] If Presbyterians finally managed to seize control of Pennsylvania, Quakers imagined that the freedom of conscience that had long graced the colony's constitution would disappear. As Thomas Wharton asked: "What is to be the Next step if England should be Overcome? . . . What redress is to be Expected, what Civil or religious Liberty Enjoyd, should others gain the Ascendency?"[103] In the past, Quakers had battled in the political arena to hold back the Presbyterian tide, but by 1775 the forces of change were too strong, and the Friends defiantly retired from politics.[104] Thus, for these various reasons—economic, social, religious, and political—a substantial proportion of the Philadelphia merchant community refused to enlist in the patriot cause.

The political commitments of Philadelphia's merchants were tempered continually by social and economic self-interest. In the 1760s and 1770s the merchants did not face economic problems that were any more acute than usual and were not propelled by economic conditions into political actions. Despite the nearly chronic glut of the dry goods market and the stagnation of the provision trade between 1764 and 1768, the merchants were reasonably prosperous in the fifteen years before the Revolution, thanks to the strong European demand for provisions. On the other hand, they resented and feared English efforts to tax Americans and were

99. Slaski, "Thomas Willing," 165.

100. Larsen, "Thomas Clifford," 420.

101. Quoted in Oaks, "Origins of American Independence," APS, *Proceedings*, CXXI (1977), 427.

102. James and Drinker to Benjamin Booth, July 7, 1774, typescript copy, Drinker Papers.

103. Thomas Wharton to Samuel Wharton, Jan. 31, 1775, Thomas Wharton Letterbook, 1773–1784. See also Anna Wharton Morris, ed., "Journal of Samuel Rowland Fisher, of Philadelphia, 1779–1781," *PMHB*, XLI (1917), 178.

104. Bauman, *For the Reputation of Truth*, chap. 9, esp. 147–148.

willing to make sacrifices to defend their liberties. Such sentiments did not turn them into revolutionaries, however, because other factors intervened. The contingencies of local politics, close personal and commercial ties with England, fear of Presbyterian hegemony, and economic self-interest all conspired to moderate their stance. These same factors continued to operate after 1776. The same pragmatism, elitism, and materialism that had hitherto made the merchants reluctant revolutionaries predisposed some of them to gain command of the Revolution in its later, more conservative, phase. The crisis of Independence swept into power in Pennsylvania a radical political faction that was attacked and eventually defeated by wealthy merchants and their associates, who were mobilized for the first time into a well-organized interest group.

5 The Shock of War

When the war that they had stubbornly resisted finally arrived, Philadelphia merchants found that their darkest fears were confirmed. Many merchants suffered from harsh persecution during the conflict, and all were financially imperiled by the shock of war. The years of conflict were confused and chaotic, and no less traumatic were the brief boom and subsequent depression of the 1780s. Not until 1789 did Philadelphia's economy return to the solid commercial prosperity enjoyed between 1769 and 1775. The Revolutionary period was a time to retrench and improvise, to scramble for survival in a world at war. But even here many merchants displayed their penchant for speculative innovation. They migrated overseas to find new markets, gambled in the legalized piracy known as privateering, experimented with novel forms of business financing, and avidly speculated in war-torn commodity markets. The war thus highlighted the capacity of the merchants to find opportunity in adversity, to capitalize on risk instead of seeking security. The ultimate effect of their wartime innovations, as developed and elaborated in the postwar decade, was to reshape the economy of the Philadelphia area and increase its efficiency. Commercial banking, securities markets, commerce with continental Europe, the tobacco trade, and heightened land speculation—all originated between 1776 and 1782. Thus the shattering experience of war, rather than retarding the process of economic development in the Delaware Valley, actually accelerated it.

These innovations of the Revolutionary period, in combination with widespread contemporary charges against the merchants for remorseless profiteering, have led some writers to view the Revolution as a capitalistic bonanza, a time of "golden opportunity for the merchant, the contractor, and their ally the lawyer."[1] The Revolution, it is said, was "a powerful stimulant to economic progress. Wartime prosperity resulted in

1. John Richard Alden, *The American Revolution, 1775–1783* (New York, 1954), 217.

an accumulation of native capital," which flowed into "commerce and land speculation on a scale unknown in colonial times."[2] Such a formulation faithfully describes the experience of Robert Morris, William Bingham, Jeremiah Wadsworth, and a few other magnates who amassed great fortunes and invested heavily in imaginative new enterprises. But as a general description of the war years, this view is misleading.

To understand the dynamics of economic development in the Revolutionary era, it is useful to distinguish three separate phenomena: the entrepreneurial exertions of Revolutionary businessmen, the process of economic diversification and development, and generalized wartime prosperity (accelerated rate of capital formation generated by swollen profits). During the period 1776–1782, the first and second phenomena were in evidence, but the third was not.[3] The merchants were indeed highly enterprising, and their innovations ultimately did enhance the efficiency and increase the diversity of the economy. But the mainspring of this spirit of enterprise, and of the economic development that enterprise created, was not general prosperity. Despite the rise of a few great fortunes, the capitals of many merchants shrank or stagnated in this period. The rate of growth of mercantile wealth, measured on a per capita basis, was undoubtedly lower in the years between 1776 and 1789 than in the

2. E. James Ferguson, *The American Revolution: A General History, 1763–1790* (Homewood, Ill., 1974), 173. Other works emphasizing the prosperity of the period include John C. Miller, *Triumph of Freedom, 1775–1783* (Boston, 1948), 439–440; Charles Royster, *A Revolutionary People at War: The Continental Army and American Character, 1775–1783* (Chapel Hill, N.C., 1979), 270–272; E. Wayne Carp, "Supplying the Revolution: Continental Army Administration and American Political Culture, 1775–1783" (Ph.D. diss., University of California, Berkeley, 1981), 259–260; Curtis P. Nettels, *The Emergence of a National Economy, 1775–1815* (New York, 1962), chap. 1, esp. 22. E. James Ferguson, *The Power of the Purse: A History of American Public Finance, 1776–1790* (Chapel Hill, N.C., 1961), chap. 5, stresses the great opportunity available to merchants in the public service, a subject discussed later in this chapter. William Allen Davis, "William Constable: New York Merchant and Land Speculator, 1772–1803" (Ph.D. diss., Harvard University, 1955) (only chaps. 1–4 available), emphasizes the great wartime prosperity of Constable, although the manuscript evidence does not seem to warrant such an optimistic view.

3. Robert A. East, *Business Enterprise in the American Revolutionary Era*, Columbia University Studies in History, Economics, and Public Law, No. 439 (New York, 1938), emphasizes the aggressive entrepreneurial activity of Revolutionary businessmen and the important economic innovations of the period. In making this case, he tends to minimize the disruptive impact of the Revolution, choosing to stress instead that business activity continued during the war. However, East does conclude (217) that "successful wartime merchants [were] a minority." My own empirical findings are not so different from East's, but I am less inclined to overlook the serious distress that a majority of the merchants experienced. Jerome H. Wood, Jr., *Conestoga Crossroads: Lancaster, Pennsylvania, 1730–1790* (Harrisburg, Pa., 1979), 144, writes of Lancaster, Pennsylvania, "Most of the businessmen in the borough experienced a slowdown in their trade" during the war.

twenty years before the Revolution. Wartime enterprise and the economic development that it promoted were the fruit of adversity, not prosperity. The merchants themselves were well aware of this fact. In a petition to the Continental Congress written in 1782, a large group of Philadelphia traders boasted, "The inhabitants of the trading towns of America, possessed of a vigorous spirit of enterprize, that has hitherto surmounted a variety of difficulties & disadvantages, have notwithstanding carried its Commerce to so flourishing an extent, that our enemies have been astonished at its progress, whilst every State in the Union has most sensibly experienced its beneficial effects."[4]

The Economics of Civil War

As an economic event, the Revolutionary War was nearly unique in American history. Typically, during a war, government spending increases and stretches the productive resources of the economy—factories, labor force, capital supplies, technical and managerial talent—to the limit. The volume of business activity increases, and price inflation occurs as demand outstrips supply. In such an environment, a businessman is able to sell at high prices everything he can make, and even though his costs are high and shortage of materials may impede his operations, he stands to make substantial profits. The money income earned in this expansive, inflationary period ultimately retains its value after the war because a postwar recession deflates the level of prices and restores the value of a unit of currency. This general pattern characterized the Seven Years' War, the War of 1812, the American Civil War, and World War I; in each case there was an inflationary boom during the war, followed by deflation.[5]

The Revolutionary War departed from this pattern in two ways. In the first place, the United States was occupied by a hostile power and suffered not only widespread destruction of property but, far more important, a derangement of basic mechanisms of transport and commercial exchange. As a result, the very ability of businessmen to function—to

4. Petition of Philadelphia Merchants to the Continental Congress, Apr. 29, 1782, Papers of the Continental Congress, Vol. VI, item 41, p. 283, Roll 51, National Archives.

5. On changes in price levels during the periods of these wars, see United States Bureau of the Census, *Historical Statistics of the United States: Colonial Times to 1970*, 2 vols. (Washington, D.C., 1975), I, 199, 201, 202, 205, 206. The movement of the price levels was as follows: 1758–1763 up 24%, 1763–1764 down 12% (see 206); 1811–1814 up 40%, 1814–1817 down 30% (205); 1861–1864 up 117%, 1864–1870 down 30% (201); 1915–1920 up 122%, 1920–1921 down 37% (199).

trade and produce—was curtailed, and their profits necessarily shrank.[6] Equally unusual, however, was the method by which the Revolution was financed. American wars have typically been funded mainly with taxes on the current generation and with long-term government bonds paid off through taxes on the income of future generations. If prices climb more rapidly than wages, as occurred during the Civil War, the conflict may also be partly financed by a reduction in the real wages of workers.[7] The Revolution, by contrast, was in large measure financed by paper money that was not backed by taxes and that in short order became worthless. Because Continental dollars issued by Congress were not withdrawn from circulation by a vigorous tax program, the number of dollars available to buy a limited quantity of goods expanded enormously, and the value of each dollar sank. The amount of flour that one hundred pounds in paper currency could buy dropped from 143.3 hundredweight in 1776 to 83.8 in 1777, 63.2 in 1778, 6.67 in 1779, 1.15 in 1780, and .71 in 1781.[8] Since the Revolutionary War was not financed with dollars of real and continuing value, the transfer of real wealth from taxpayers to army suppliers was relatively limited.

But what of the claim, common enough in history books and in contemporary commentary, that during the Revolution "everything was going up." "It required no special business acumen to wax rich in such a market; all that was required was a readiness to gamble in commodities, staking one's fortune on the chance—virtually a certainty—that prices would continue to rise."[9] This analysis overlooks the central paradox of inflation: when everything is "going up," nothing is going up in real terms. The value of paper money is simply declining. If the rum in a merchant's warehouse appreciated by 40 percent during the two months that he owned it, but the cost of firewood needed to heat his town house rose just as rapidly, the merchant's economic position did not improve with respect to his ability to buy fuel (and, by extension, other necessities). What mattered, in other words, was *relative* prices. The speculator did not benefit from an across-the-board rise in prices, but only from a

6. The War of 1812 similarly damaged the economy of the nation, particularly the maritime activities of northern states; and during the Civil War the Confederacy was prostrated by the depredations of the Union Army.

7. See Bureau of the Census, *Historical Statistics of the United States*, I, 165, showing a drop in real wages of 30% between 1860 and 1866.

8. Anne Bezanson *et al.*, *Prices and Inflation during the American Revolution: Pennsylvania, 1770–1790*, Industrial Research Department, Wharton School of Finance and Commerce, University of Pennsylvania, Research Studies, XXXV (Philadelphia, 1951), 321. Prices are for Apr. of each year.

9. Miller, *Triumph of Freedom*, 440. See also Merrill Jensen, *The New Nation: A History of the United States during the Confederation, 1781–1789* (New York, 1950), 182.

particularly sharp rise in the price of the commodity that he owned. Dramatic, lucrative shifts in relative prices were not unknown.[10] But in the long run, price inflation pervaded the economy.

Inflation actually injured businessmen by transferring wealth from debtors to creditors and convulsing the world of commerce. The typical dry goods merchant owed sterling debts to a handful of major suppliers in England, and these obligations could not be liquidated with depreciated currency. On the other hand, he was owed money by dozens of customers who could pay off their debts with depreciated currency. In subtle and insidious ways, hyperinflation poisoned the commercial process itself. To the extent that trade is facilitated by the use of a stable currency, which serves as a store of value and a unit of account, inflation hindered business activity. With prices changing so fast, it was difficult to read markets and plan transactions, that is, to distinguish a real profit from an illusory one. Moreover, merchants became averse to accumulating paper money, since it constantly shrank in value. To avoid loss, they immediately converted their cash into a commodity, thereby losing the essential element of flexibility in mercantile strategy: instead of purchasing commodities at a propitious time for making a profit, they bought immediately to avoid losing money. No longer was money the handmaiden of commerce; now the roles were reversed as commerce became a tool for preserving the value of money.[11]

Apart from the destructive effects of inflation on the monetary system, the war severely disrupted the economy of the middle states in other ways. Property damage was quite widespread. When Philadelphia was occupied in September 1777, British and Hessian troops stripped the city's suburbs of food and fuel.[12] Some Philadelphians lost ships and goods when the British captured Saint Eustatius, a major Caribbean entrepôt, and Philadelphia traders were injured by British depredations

10. In the two years after Apr. 1775, for example, the price of molasses rose by 747% and of rum by 868%, while common flour appreciated by just 59%. Merchants who held large stocks of Caribbean goods or who managed to slip them through the British naval blockade were able to make great profits. But such episodes were not common, especially after general hyperinflation commenced in 1777. See Bezanson *et al.*, *Prices and Inflation*, 322.

11. See Nettels, *National Economy*, 26.

12. Timothy Pickering to John Pickering, Dec. 11, 1777, July 6, 1778, Timothy Pickering Papers, Massachusetts Historical Society, Reel 5; "The Diary of Robert Morton, Kept in Philadelphia While That City Was Occupied by the British Army in 1777," *Pennsylvania Magazine of History and Biography*, I (1877), 7–12, 20–24, 30; "Journal of Captain John Montrésor, July 1, 1777, to July 1, 1778," *PMHB*, V (1881), 412, VI (1882), 38, 39; "Extracts from the Journal of Mrs. Henry Drinker, of Philadelphia, from September 25, 1777, to July 4, 1778," *PMHB*, XIII (1889), 303.

in the Chesapeake region in 1780 and 1781.[13] Philadelphia merchants were also injured by the British assault on the New Jersey coast, a staging ground for privateers.[14] A more silent but equally devastating blow to commerce was the disruption of the flow of commercial credit from England to Philadelphia. French and Dutch merchants were relatively cautious in extending credit to correspondents, and minor traders in the Delaware Valley had little opportunity to form connections with these continental merchants. This may explain, in part, why the city's dry goods trade was controlled by a restricted group of large importers in 1781 and 1782.[15]

Just as scarce as commercial credit during the war was labor, a problem that made it difficult to keep such facilities as ironworks and sugarhouses in operation. One expedient used to overcome this difficulty was the employment of Hessian prisoners.[16] Maritime labor was also difficult to recruit, and merchants complained that "the insolence and difficulty of seamen is beyond bearing."[17] Problems arising from the scarcity of sailors were exacerbated by the shortage of rigging, tackle, and ships

13. Philip Lawrence to Budden, Lawrence, and Co., June 18, 1781, Reed and Forde Papers, box 5, Historical Society of Pennsylvania (hereafter cited as HSP); David MacPherson, *Annals of Commerce, Manufactures, Fisheries, and Navigation . . .*, 4 vols. (New York, 1972 [orig. publ. London, 1805]), III, 677–678; Levi Hollingsworth to Bristol Brown, Mar. 16, 1781, Levi Hollingsworth to Samuel Harrison, Feb. 6, 1781, Levi Hollingsworth Letterbook, 1780–1782, Hollingsworth Papers, HSP.

14. Miller, *Triumph of Freedom*, 453.

15. See below, this chapter.

16. The successful sugar refining house run by Morris and Miercken was closed down during the war. See Morris and Miercken Papers, Hollingsworth Collection, HSP; and Samuel Morris, Jr., to Effingham Lawrence, Dec. 1, 1783, Samuel Morris Letterbook, 1780–1786, Morris Family Papers, Eleutherian Mills Historical Library. The general situation of the iron industry during the war merits further study, but labor shortages were definitely a problem. See Bezanson *et al.*, *Prices and Inflation*, 168; Thomas M. Doerflinger, "Hibernia Furnace during the Revolution," *New Jersey History*, XC (1971–1972), 108–114. Michael Hillegas to Matthias Slough, May 9, 1780, Michael Hillegas Letterbook, 1777–1782, HSP. On damage to ironworks in the Valley Forge area, see Linda McCurdy, "The Potts Family Iron Industry In the Schuylkill Valley" (Ph.D. diss., Pennsylvania State University, 1974), 164. On the disappointing results at Batsto Ironworks in south Jersey, see Theodore Thayer, *Nathanael Greene: Strategist of the American Revolution* (New York, 1960), 236–238. The most thorough general survey of the subject, Lester J. Cappon *et al.*, eds., *Atlas of Early American History: The Revolutionary Era, 1760–1790* (Princeton, N.J., 1976), 105, concludes that the war was "more disruptive than stimulating to the iron industry."

17. Bezanson *et al.*, *Prices and Inflation*, 209. For an example, see Stephen Collins to Potts and Davies, Aug. 12, 1782, Stephen Collins Papers, LX-A, Library of Congress (hereafter cited as LC).

themselves, with the result that the cost of operating a vessel rose dramatically. Robert Morris's complaint touched on the identical problem: "When ship that in common times sold for £1000 by a sudden demand are raised in Value to £4000 & seamens wages jum[p] from £4 to £14 per M°. & every article relative to ship rises in the same proportion what must the freights be to make an equivalent[?]"[18] The difficulty of outfitting ships, when combined with the devastating British blockade of the Delaware Bay, meant that the flow of shipping into the port declined precipitately. Merchants who were accustomed to having a wide range of vessels on which to ship their goods suddenly found that they could not obtain freight space without consigning their shipment to the master of the vessel or a friend of the owners.[19]

Still more serious was the problem of what to export on these vessels, for warfare reduced the agricultural output of the middle states at the very time when consumption was swelled by the presence of two armies. As early as February 1777, Robert Morris wrote that wheat "will be very scarce in America. our last Crop of wheat was the worst ever known and the Consumption [of wheat] of our Army with the destruction [of crops] made by both Armies is immense."[20] By the fall of 1777 the American army had to rely on New England to keep it supplied with beef, despite the fact that the middle colonies had formerly been heavy beef exporters. A year later, purchasers for the Continental army realized that wheat was so scarce in the middle states that they would have to rely on Virginia and Maryland.[21] The commissary's dependence on the Chesapeake region continued through 1780, despite the official embargo on the exportation of grain imposed by state and national governments.[22] Because

18. Willing, Morris, and Co. to William Bingham, Dec. 6, 1776, William Bingham Collection, 1776–1801, LC. On scarcity of rigging, see Woolsey and Salmon to John Pringle, Apr. 5, 1777, Woolsey and Salmon Letterbook, 1774–1785, 247, LC.

19. Willing, Morris, and Co. to William Bingham, Sept. 14, 1776, Kuhn and Kuhn to Garret Cottringer, Aug. 4, 1781, Kuhn and Kuhn Letterbook, 1779–1785, Kuhn and Risberg Papers, Bucks County Historical Society.

20. Robert Morris to William Bingham, Feb. 16, 1777, Bingham Collection.

21. Wayne K. Bodle and Jacqueline Thibaut, "Valley Forge Historical Research Report," 3 vols., MS (Valley Forge, Pa., 1980) (copy in HSP), II, "This Fatal Crisis: Logistics, Supply, and the Continental Army at Valley Forge, 1777–1778," 25; Ephraim Blaine to Peter Colt, Nov. 18, 1777, Feb. 7, 1778, Ephraim Blaine Collection, LC; Chaloner and White to Ephraim Blaine, Nov. 24, 1778, Chaloner and White Letterbook, 1778–1779, esp. 77, Chaloner and White Collection, HSP, showing that supply efforts focused on the area south of Pennsylvania.

22. Clement Biddle to Nathanael Greene, May 27, 1779, Nathanael Greene Papers, American Philosophical Society (hereafter cited as APS).

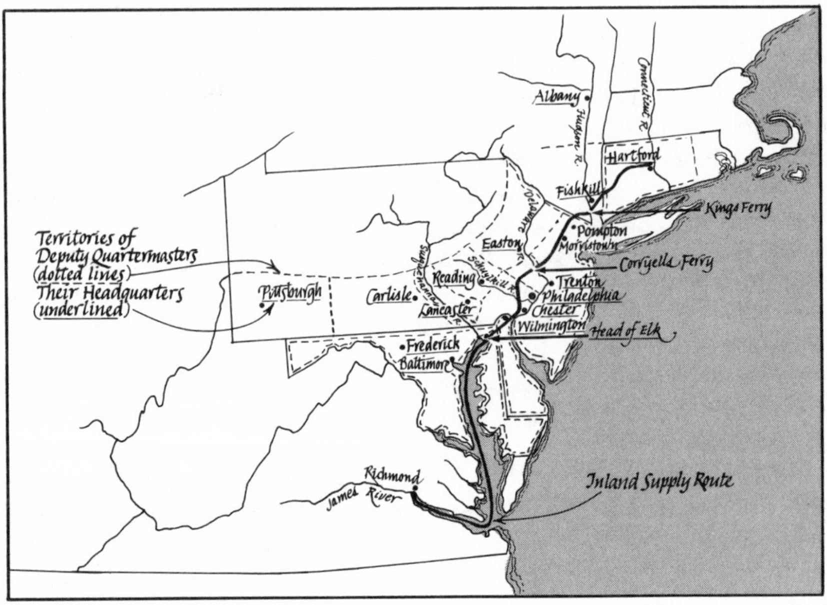

MAP 6. The Continental Army in the Middle Atlantic States.
Drawn by Richard Stinely

Pennsylvania's traditional provision trade with New England was so seriously disrupted by the war, the state of Massachusetts appropriated sixty thousand pounds to purchase foodstuffs from Maryland.[23]

Nothing was more damaging to the economy than the wrenching shift of the interstate transport system from coastwise maritime trade to inland carriage. Before the war, goods were generally transported by roads, rivers, and bays to major ports, from which they could be shipped by sloop or schooner to another city. After 1775 the British blockade often made this impossible: the number of coastwise vessels entering Philadelphia dropped from 294 in 1773 to an average of 11 in 1781 and 1782.[24] In lieu of coastwise trade, goods had to be hauled from place to place by wagon or riverboat, a far less convenient method. Rivers were actually a

23. Lewis Cecil Gray, *History of Agriculture in the Southern United States to 1860*, 2 vols., Carnegie Institution of Washington Publication, No. 430 (Gloucester, Mass., 1958 [orig. publ. Washington, D.C., 1933]), II, 582.

24. Tonnage Duties on Incoming Vessels, Nov. 1, 1765–Aug. 30, 1775, Cadwalader Collection, Thomas Cadwalader Section, HSP (hereafter cited as Tonnage Duty Book); Registers of Duties Paid on Imported Goods, 1781–1787, 6 vols., Record Group 4, Pennsylvania Historical and Museum Commission (hereafter cited as PHMC).

barrier because they ran the wrong way—to the sea, rather than from one major coastal city to another.[25] The heavily traveled route from eastern Connecticut to western Pennsylvania, for example, required the crossing by ferry of no fewer than five major rivers—the Connecticut, Hudson, Delaware, Schuylkill, and Susquehanna—and such crossings could be difficult or impossible when the rivers were flooded or blocked with ice.[26] American roads were rough, muddy, and narrow, and wagon carriage bore hidden costs, beyond its intrinsic inefficiency. The heavy employment of wagoners, who were generally farmers or country laborers, reduced the rural labor supply and thus cut into agricultural output.[27] And because the use of wagons involved a shift from windpower to horsepower, the agricultural economy was drained of thousands of tons of hay and feed grains. In the middle states, shortage of forage was acute by 1778 and constituted a fundamental bottleneck in the wartime economy.

Under these multitudinous pressures the configuration of commerce in Philadelphia changed radically. Key sectors of late colonial trade—particularly coastwise commerce, the dry goods trade with England, the flaxseed trade with Ireland, and the provision export trade with southern Europe—collapsed, while new routes opened up. After the British attack on New York City in 1776 and the attendant shift of fighting to the middle states, Boston became a major port of entry for European goods, some of which were shipped overland to Philadelphia.[28] Since foodstuffs were so scarce, Delaware Valley traders gravitated to tobacco as a new

25. Richard K. Showman *et al.*, eds. *The Papers of General Nathanael Greene*, II (Chapel Hill, N.C., 1980), 321. For two instances when merchants had great difficulty transporting goods, see Woolsey and Salmon to John Pringle, Sept. 5, 1777, Woolsey and Salmon Letterbook, 262; Kuhn and Kuhn to Daniel Clymer, Apr. 11, 1779, and Peter Kuhn to Jacob Kuhn, May 29, 1779, Kuhn and Kuhn Letterbook, 1779–1785.

26. See Henrietta C. Ellery, comp., "Diary of the Hon. William Ellery, of Rhode Island, October 20 to November 15, 1777," *PMHB*, XI (1887), 318–332.

27. See the excellent discussion of transportation problems in Showman *et al.*, eds., *Papers of Nathanael Greene*, II, 319–321. Although the transfer of labor from maritime to landed transport was theoretically possible, it evidently did not happen. There was little pressure on seamen to work on land during the war, since maritime wages remained high. Many wagoners were also farmers, who had the option of choosing either job, depending upon the relative economic benefits. See Joseph Brady to John Davis, Mar. 18, 1779, John Davis Collection, 1755–1783, IV, LC; Henry Hollingsworth to Nathanael Greene, Feb. 4, 1779, Greene Papers.

28. Matthew McConnell to John Davis, Mar. 10, 1779, Davis Collection, III; John De Neufville and Co. to Bache and Shee, Sept. 30, 1782, John De Neufville Papers, New York Historical Society; Thomas Bond, Jr., to John Reed, Apr. 29, 1778; Thomas Lawrence to John Reed, May 13, 1778, Reed and Forde Papers, box 5; East, *Business Enterprise*, 152, concerning an overland venture made in 1781.

export staple, and large quantities were imported from Virginia and Maryland by way of the Chesapeake and Delaware bays.[29] Although a direct trade with Europe, primarily France, developed in the later years of the war, much of Philadelphia's transatlantic trade went by way of the West Indies. Tobacco, lumber, and naval supplies were shipped to the Caribbean, where they were consumed locally or sent on to Europe, and American vessels returned from the West Indies laden with European manufactures and wines as well as tropical groceries. In sum, the effect of the war on commercial activity was severe. The coastal trade was decimated, transatlantic trade was greatly reduced, and trade with the West Indies became proportionally more important. Inland trade with the Chesapeake states and New England increased in significance, and tobacco partly replaced breadstuffs as a major export staple.

Customs documents for 1781 and 1782 provide a rare quantitative glimpse of Revolutionary economic activity and indicate that commercial disruption was extensive indeed, even though these years were not the most confused of the war. Compared to the overseas shipping traffic of the port in 1773, for example, the decline in the number of incoming vessels in 1781 and 1782 was dramatic for every commercial sector (see table 14). On the other hand, this decline was compensated for somewhat by shipment of goods that entered Philadelphia by shallop. The major local shipping points were Hamburg, Pennsylvania, an inland town situated north of Reading on the Schuylkill River; Wilmington, Delaware, located south of Philadelphia on the Delaware River; and various towns in New Jersey (see table 15). It is not entirely clear why the use of these local shipping points suddenly became so important. Evidently vessels entering the Delaware Bay preferred to deposit their cargoes near its mouth, instead of venturing further upriver, where they would be easy prey for British frigates. Goods reaching Philadelphia from Hamburg may have been shipped overland from New England by way of a route that crossed the Hudson River, northern New Jersey, and the Delaware River.

A surprisingly large quantity of merchandise reached Philadelphia through these restricted, circuitous routes. The quantity of sugar imported in other years exceeded prewar levels, and the amount of rum was about a quarter of prewar quantities. On the other hand, only trivial amounts of molasses entered Philadelphia, probably because it was so difficult during the war to distill it into sugar or rum (see table 16). The few ships that reached Philadelphia from Europe managed to bring enor-

29. The tobacco trade is discussed in detail below, chap. 7. See particularly the Hollingsworth Papers, esp. Levi Hollingsworth Ledger, 1780–1782, and Levi Hollingsworth Invoices, 1764–1789, 3 boxes, for the years 1779–1782; Charles Wharton Daybook, 1775–1785, Wharton Papers, HSP; John Pringle Invoice and Sales Book, 1775–1785, LC.

TABLE 14. *Vessels Entering Philadelphia, 1773, 1781, 1782*

	Vessels Entering		
Origin	1773	1781	1782
Coastwise	293	13	9
West Indies	286	106	36
Europe and the wine islands	172	21	9
Total	751	140	54

Sources: 1773: Tonnage Duties on Incoming Vessels, November 1, 1765–August 30, 1775, 3 vols., Cadwalader Collection, Thomas Caldwalader Section, Historical Society of Pennsylvania. This document indicates the provenance of 664 of the 751 vessels entering the port in 1773. Using the sectoral proportions of those 664 vessels, the estimated total number of arrivals from each sector was computed. 1781, 1782: Registers of Duties Paid on Imported Goods, 1781–1787, 6 vols., Record Group 4, Pennsylvania Historical and Museum Commission.

mous amounts of dry goods, so that the city was relatively well stocked with cloth. Substantial quantities of tea and wine also reached the Delaware Valley. Estimates of the total monetary value of imports in the war years, which must be inexact because reliable prices for every commodity are not available, suggest that it amounted to roughly 80 percent of import levels in the depressed period 1785–1787.[30] Although the British fleet managed to shatter normal routes of trade, Philadelphia merchants and captains successfully met the challenge and brought large quantities of goods to market.

The Four Phases of Commercial Disruption

Trade fluctuated violently during the war, moving through four fairly distinct stages. The first of these periods, lasting from the

30. The value of "merchandise" is listed in the customs documents for 1781 and 1782. The prices of madeira wine, sugar, loaf sugar, coffee, cocoa, rum, molasses, and bohea tea were taken from Bezanson *et al.*, *Prices and Inflation*, 337, 338. For brandy, teneriffe wine, and fayal wine, prices in the customs books for 1785–1787 were used, and the price of green (or hyson) tea was taken to be 2.5 times that of bohea tea, a ratio suggested in Benjamin Woods Labaree, *The Boston Tea Party* (New York, 1964), 335. By far the most important components of imports were merchandise, whose value is stated in the customs books, and Caribbean groceries, for which the price data are reliable.

TABLE 15. *Vessels Entering Philadelphia, 1781, 1782*

	Vessels Entering	
Origin	1781	1782
Coastwise		
North	11	9
South	2	0
Total	13	9
West Indies		
St. Domingue	31	6
Havana	43	18
Other islands	32	12
Total	106	36
Europe		
France	11	6
Other nations	10	3
Total	21	9
Local		
New Jersey	6	36
Hamburg, Pa.	0	50
Wilmington, Del.	46	166
Total	52	252
Other, unknown	0	2
Grand Total	192	308

Source: Registers of Duties Paid on Imported Goods, 1781–1787, 6 vols., Record Group 4, Pennsylvania Historical and Museum Commission.

spring of 1776 to the fall of 1777, was undoubtedly the most lucrative for the merchants of Philadelphia. The embargo on imports imposed by the Continental Congress in December 1774, which was reinforced and extended by the naval blockade of Admiral Lord Howe, dramatically increased the price of West Indies goods and dry goods in the ensuing months. Small, fast sloops and schooners that could slip through the British blockade were able to bring lucrative cargoes into the city. For

TABLE 16. *Importation of Selected Products into Philadelphia, 1768–1783*

	Average Annual Imports			
Period	Sugar (Cwt.)	Rum (Gals.)	Molasses (Gals.)	Merchandise (Pennsylvania Currency)
1768, 1769 1770, 1772	23,965	899,580	604,517	£ 780,189[a]
1781, 1782	37,786	249,675	14,775	541,480
1783	53,707	612,440	283,995	1,710,711

Sources: 1768–1772: Arthur L. Jensen, *The Maritime Commerce of Colonial Pennsylvania* (Madison, Wis., 1963), 294, 295, 297. 1781, 1782: Registers of Duties Paid on Imported Goods, 1781–1787, 6 vols., Record Group 4, Pennsylvania Historical and Museum Commission.

[a]Mean of total imports from Great Britain in 1772 and 1773.

merchants who normally struggled to squeeze a small profit out of the West Indies trade, blockade-running was an attractive prospect indeed. Robert Morris enthusiastically informed a correspondent in 1776, "You ask what articles are most in demand here or what are likely to be most so, to which we may safely reply that every thing is wanted, it is hardly possible to go amiss."[31] Philadelphia's merchants swung into action, eagerly seizing this unusual speculative opportunity. "The Spirit of Enterprize has seized most people & they are making or trying to make Fortunes," wrote Morris. "Their Attempt will probably have the happy Effect of procuring us many Supplies that we stand in need off."[32]

Among the firms seized by the "Spirit of Enterprize" was the partnership of John and Peter Chevalier, a well-established shipping firm.[33] In 1776 the Chevaliers purchased major interests in no fewer than six vessels—five schooners and one sloop—and sent them down to the West Indies. One vessel was sold for a profit after a year, leaving no indication of how many voyages it ran; two vessels made at least one successful trip to the Caribbean and back; and three ships ran at least two successful voyages. On the eight recorded voyages, the ships returned to Philadel-

31. Willing, Morris, and Co. to William Bingham, Sept. 14, 1776, Bingham Collection.
32. Willing, Morris, and Co. to William Bingham, Oct. 20, 1776, *ibid.*
33. John and Peter Chevalier Ledger, 1770–1781 (microfilm), PHMC.

phia with cargoes that sold for an average of £4,569, as compared with a normal peacetime level of £800–£1,200. Though profits were reduced by the "monstrous expense" of buying and operating vessels at this time, there is little doubt that the Chevaliers came out well ahead in 1776 and 1777. So, too, did their fellow trader Thomas Mifflin, the first quartermaster general of the Continental army. When he entered public service in 1776, Mifflin's friends interested him in four vessels, to a total amount of £2,401.[34] A small schooner was lost immediately, but the other three were successful on their first voyage. One particularly fortunate brig returned from Saint Eustatius in 1776 and yielded the staggering profit of £27,664, or nearly £4,000 for each of its seven owners.[35] Combined with the more moderate success of the other two vessels, Mifflin earned, by the close of 1777, a total profit of £6,106. Adjusted for overall price inflation, Mifflin received an annual rate of return, over a fifteen-month period, of about 50 percent.

These opportunities came to an end with the occupation of Philadelphia by the British army in September 1777. In the second phase of the wartime economy, patriot merchants scattered to such inland towns as York, Reading, and Lancaster, from which it was difficult, though not impossible, to orchestrate voyages. Many of the merchants who remained in Philadelphia did not do much better. They faced stiff competition from about 120 Scottish and foreign merchants who swept into Philadelphia in the wake of Howe's army, and they learned that one needed the cooperation of the British army and loyalist authorities to conduct much business.[36] Although well-connected merchants could import large quantities of goods and sell them at a profit, opportunities for most wholesalers seem to have been limited.[37] With living expenses high and destruction by two armies considerable, the period of occupation was difficult for both patriots and loyalists.

In the Delaware Valley, the third phase of the wartime economy, lasting from the middle of 1778 to the end of 1780, was the economic nadir of the Revolution, because the continuing presence of the British and American armies drained the region of its economic lifeblood, grain.

34. Thomas Mifflin to the Citizens of Philadelphia, *Pennsylvania Packet or the General Advertiser* (Philadelphia), Feb. 7, 1782.

35. The accounts of the brig *Delaware* appear in the Matthew Irwin Journal, 1769–1784, 172, 181, 182, LC.

36. Willard O. Mishoff, "Business in Philadelphia during the British Occupation, 1777–1778," *PMHB*, LXI (1937), 166–167; Morton, "The Diary of Robert Morton," *PMHB*, I (1877), 33n.

37. Jacob E. Cooke, "Tench Coxe, Tory Merchant," *PMHB*, XCVI (1972), 48–88; Charles Wharton Daybook, 1775–1784.

John Jay observed in December 1778: "The middle and eastern states cannot supply more wheat this year than the inhabitants and army will consume. New York, New Jersey, and Pennsylvania have been so much embarrassed and injured by military operations, as to afford at present but a small proportion of their usual supplies."[38] Jay observed that the next year would be better, but his optimism was ill founded, however, for diminished grain production, competitive purchasing by agents for the French and American forces, and general price inflation increased the price of foodstuffs eightfold in 1779.[39] This inflation led in turn to price controls and scattered disorders by workers and radical militiamen in Philadelphia.[40]

The maritime economy was equally deranged in this period. In May 1779 it appeared "infinitely hazardous to keep any Concern in shipping just at this time," and in fact the British blockade held the shipping tonnage leaving the port to 3,622 tons in the year ending in July 1779, as compared with the 62,143 tons entering the city in 1773.[41] Dry goods were so scarce in the Philadelphia market that there was spirited competition among buyers for the few arriving cargoes, and manufactures landed at Baltimore were occasionally advertised in the Philadelphia press.[42] With the currency collapsing, the survival of the Continental army open to question, and the streets of Philadelphia controlled by radical militiamen, these were evil times for most businessmen.

By 1781, however, if not a bit earlier, conditions had improved, and one may perceive a fourth phase of activity. The center of fighting had moved further south, the currency was stabilized, and the supply of grain was ample enough for Robert Morris to report, "All our ships have been and continue to be constantly employed in carrying flour to the French and Spanish Islands, our port is filled in return with West India produce,

38. Quoted in Bezanson *et al.*, *Prices and Inflation*, 87–88.

39. *Ibid.*, 336.

40. Eric Foner, *Tom Paine and Revolutionary America* (New York, 1976), chap. 5; Robert L. Brunhouse, *The Counter-Revolution in Pennsylvania, 1776–1790* (Harrisburg, Pa., 1942), 68–76.

41. Jacob E. Cooke, *Tench Coxe and the Early Republic* (Chapel Hill, N.C., 1978), 47. East, *Business Enterprise*, 151; Tonnage Duty Book. East, quoting Chaloner and White, writes that "121 ships of 3632 tons burden" had sailed from Philadelphia, indicating an average tonnage per vessel of just 30, as compared with a mean tonnage of about 82 in the prewar decade. Some of the vessels in Chaloner and White's total must have been small river craft.

42. See Hubertis Cummings, "Robert Morris and the Episode of the Polacre 'Victorious,'" *PMHB*, LXX (1946), 239–257; and Charles Pettit to Nathanael Greene, May 13, 1779, Greene Papers; *Pennsylvania Journal and Weekly Advertiser* (Philadelphia), Sept. 15, 1779, advertisement of Samuel and Robert Purviance.

some European goods and many Spanish dollars, and flour remains so plenty that there has not been a day in which I could not buy 5,000 to 10,000 barrels in this city and the price has fallen from 28 and 30 shillings which was asked and given at first to 17 shillings which is now asked, but I think 15 shillings or two hard dollars will buy 112 pounds very soon."[43] Although the British navy remained a serious menace, significant quantities of merchandise reached Philadelphia wharves in 1781 and 1782, as we have seen. General trade statistics indicate that French exports to America increased decisively between 1780 and 1781, and by 1782 nearly equaled peacetime levels (see fig. 5).

Since New York City and the Lower South were controlled by the British while Boston harbor had been open to traffic earlier in the war, we may deduce that Philadelphia was a prime beneficiary of this expanded flow of French exports. This view is confirmed by the fact that certain Philadelphia firms established a successful trade with Nantes and Lorient in 1781 and 1782.[44] The trials of Philadelphia traders were far from over with the return of peace, however, for they were tormented by the inflationary boom of 1783–1784 and the depression that followed.

The Wartime Experience of the Merchants

Many traders plunged fearlessly into the churning river of war, attempting to pluck profits from the wreckage that swirled around them. Not virtue and patriotism, but getting and spending, seemed to be the twin passions of the day. "There is such a thirst for gain," remarked Washington in 1778, "and such infamous advantages taken to forestall, and engross those Articles which the army cannot do without, therby enhancing the cost of them to the public fifty or a hundred percent, that it is enough to make one curst their own Species."[45] The acquisitive spirit of wartime Philadelphia was embodied in the commanding figure of Robert Morris—rotund, hearty, and convivial, but also shrewd, grasp-

43. Quoted in Bezanson *et al.*, *Prices and Inflation*, 95.

44. Tench Coxe traded successfully with Jonathan Nesbitt and Co. of Lorient, France, in 1781 and 1782. Cooke, *Tench Coxe*, 52–54, 56–57. Nesbitt was obviously very successful, for he wrote in Jan. 1783, "The Prospect of Peace is another source of uneasiness to me, for Heaven knows it is the thing . . . I desire least for twelve months to come." Joseph A. Goldenberg, "The *William* and the *Favorite*: The Post-Revolutionary Voyages of Two Philadelphia Ships," *PMHB*, XCVIII (1974), 328. Philadelphia newspaper advertisements increased in number between 1779 and 1782, an indication that the volume of commerce was growing.

45. Quoted in Miller, *Triumph of Freedom*, 454.

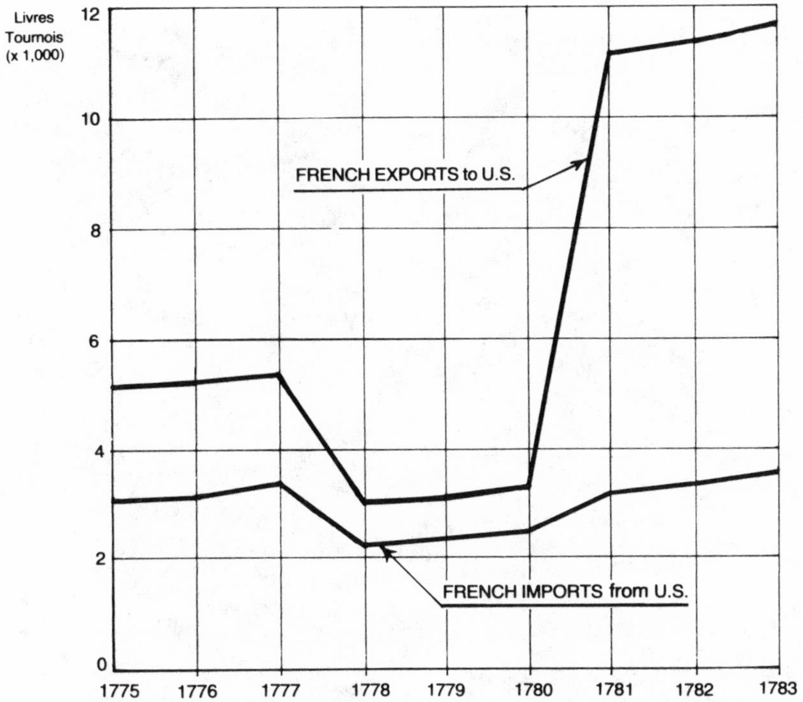

FIGURE 5. French Trade with the United States, 1775–1783. *Data from Edmund Buron, "Statistics on Franco-American Trade, 1778–1806,"* Journal of Economic and Business History, *IV (1931–1932), 571–580*

ing, and indomitable—who was somehow able to manipulate the fiscal reins of government with one hand while multiplying his fortune with the other.

Morris symbolizes the spirit of the merchant community, but he does not personify the reality. Ruthless gamblers the wartime merchants may have been, yet few left the Revolutionary poker table with large winnings, if any. A few traders nearly equaled Morris's astounding success, to be sure, and a number of others advanced their fortunes by trading commodities, investing in privateers, and serving in the supply departments of the Continental army. For many more, however, the war was a wrenching, disorienting period that heightened risks without raising profits. Even successful merchants were tormented by the "Difficulties & Distress of the Times which occasion much unexpected Strokes of Adverse Fortune, against which the most consummate Prudence can-

PLATE 20. Robert Morris. By Charles Willson Peale. *Courtesy of Independence National Historical Park Collection, Philadelphia*

not provide."[46] The economy of the Delaware Valley was "stript and drained" by seven years of war, and Gouverneur Morris was not far wrong when he claimed that the Revolution left American merchants "poorer by millions."[47] As one merchant wrote in 1783: "The Face of

46. William Bingham to Willing, Morris, and Co., Aug. 10, 1777, Bingham Collection.
47. Henry Drinker to Hoare and Potts, Oct. 28, 1786, Henry Drinker Letterbook, 1786–1790, 107, Henry Drinker Papers, HSP; East, *Business Enterprise*, 217.

trade has greatly altered here in the Course of the war, many people are ruined & others next door to it."[48]

A significant number of merchants, particularly loyalist Quakers, suspended commercial operations entirely during the Revolution, and others were forced to reduce their commercial activities far below peacetime levels. The ledgers and letterbooks of the Revolutionary period contain long gaps, lasting several years, in which few or no transactions were recorded.[49] As late as 1781 and 1782, when the worst confusion of the war had subsided, only 202 Philadelphia firms imported goods worth five hundred pounds or more, whereas 522 firms did so during a 31-month period in the mid-1780s, when trade was depressed.[50] Although exact measurement is impossible, it appears that there may have been about 200 active merchants in the later years of the war, as compared with about 320 in 1774 and 500 in 1785.[51]

Amidst the vagaries of war, most of these merchants had disjointed careers. The British occupation of Philadelphia and New York, the rapid decline of the Continental dollar, the postwar boom and ensuing depression, the fickle policies of the Continental Congress, the blockades of the British fleet—all of these factors constantly conspired to frustrate the merchants' ambitions. High profits earned in one phase of the war were frequently offset by staggering losses in another. As a result, the merchants' careers had a peculiarly segmented quality; it was seldom possi-

48. Stephen Collins to Harrison and Ansley, June 17, 1783, Collins Papers, LX-A.

49. Bezanson *et al.*, *Prices and Inflation*, 1, 25. Examples include Morris and Miercken in the Morris section of the Hollingsworth Papers; Richard Waln in the Waln Collection, HSP; Benjamin Fuller in the Benjamin Fuller Papers, 1762–1799, HSP; Charles Wharton Daybook, 1775–1784; Thomas Wharton Papers in the Wharton Papers and the Leonard T. Beale Collection, HSP; Henry Drinker in the Drinker Papers; Clement Biddle Journal, 1781–1784, Thomas A. Biddle Collection, HSP; Thomas Clifford, Sr., in the Clifford Correspondence, 1778–1785, HSP; Stephen Collins in the Collins Papers; Thomas Canby, in Philadelphia Merchant Daybook, 1770–1788, HSP.

50. Based on Registers of Duties Paid.

51. This conclusion is based on an analysis of names appearing in customs records for 1781 and 1782, newspaper advertisements for the period 1779–1782, a petition to the Continental Congress written in 1781, letters of marque and reprisal for the entire war, and subscribers to the Bank of Pennsylvania. See *ibid.*; *Pennsylvania Gazette*; *Pennsylvania Journal and Weekly Advertiser*; *Pennsylvania Packet*; *Papers of the Continental Congress*, Roll 51, item 41, VI, 269; Library of Congress, *Naval Records of the American Revolution, 1775–1788*, comp. Charles Henry Lincoln (Washington, D.C., 1908), 217–549; Lawrence Lewis, Jr., *A History of the Bank of North America: The First Bank Chartered in the United States* (Philadelphia, 1882), 19–20. There were 174 firms that appeared on two or more of these documents (including only firms appearing in the customs records that imported more than £1,000 in 1781 and 1782 combined) or invested in three or more privateers, or imported over £10,000. Of these 174, 53 were very active traders.

ble, as it had been during the Seven Years' War, to stake out a lucrative niche that yielded ample returns for several years in a row.

In the summer of 1775, for example, Benjamin Fuller moved twenty-five miles outside of Philadelphia to avoid the impending warfare, and upon returning in the summer of 1778 found that he had lost "the greatest part" of his fortune. After surviving a serious illness that lasted until March 1780, Fuller managed to rebuild his fortune by vending a product that was much in demand in the last years of the war, maritime insurance.[52] He then shrewdly purchased a block of stock in the newly created Bank of North America, whose monopoly on local banking activity made it a very profitable investment.[53] Equally fragmented was the wartime career of Tench Coxe, which ran through four distinct phases, two of them prosperous and two of them not. And John Reed, in addition to serving in the army for a while, led a wagon train on a trading venture to Boston, spent some time in the West Indies, and made an abortive attempt to operate a store in Wilmington, Delaware.[54] Anthony Butler eventually lost most of the capital that he had amassed in the early stages of the war, and John Mitchell, as we have seen, went bankrupt after holding the important position of deputy quartermaster general for Philadelphia.[55] Mitchell's brother, Randall, purchased a farm near Trenton at the start of the war, and in 1777 he hoped to buy additional acreage either in the backcountry of Pennsylvania and Maryland or on the Jersey shore. But even land was a vulnerable asset during this civil war. British and Hessian troops threatened to seize Mitchell's wheat crop and herd of cattle, and to save his property he had to swear his loyalty at various times to both General Howe and General Washington. Asked Mitchell with resignation, "Are we not obliged to submit to whoever are our masters for the day[?]"[56]

Stephen Girard formed a succession of ephemeral, disappointing partnerships during the war; although high prices in America seemed to promise handsome trading gains, solid profits proved to be elusive. The British seized one of his vessels when they occupied Philadelphia, and his investments in privateering were unsuccessful. At one point Girard had

52. Benjamin Fuller to Judith Sober, Apr. 8, 1788, Fuller Letterbook, 1787–1791, 89, Fuller Papers.

53. Benjamin Fuller Journal, 1782–1789, 360–364, William West Account Books, 1769–1804, HSP.

54. Reed's career may be followed in the Reed and Forde Papers.

55. Collins to Harrison Ansley and Co., Apr. 23, 1784, Collins Papers, LXI, 1. Mitchell's career may be followed in the Greene Papers; *Papers of the Continental Congress*; the Fuller Letterbook, 1784–1787; and the John Mitchell Sequestered Papers, PHMC.

56. Randle Mitchell to John Mitchell, Feb. 9, 1777, Mitchell Papers, box 4.

"nothing to sell in the store except 20 hogs heads of cider and 2/3 of a barrell of whiskey," and near the end of the conflict his capital amounted to less than twenty-five hundred pounds.[57] Nor was the war a boon to Samuel Morris, Jr., who had to close down his highly profitable sugar refinery for seven years.[58] Joseph Irwin, a young Irish merchant, undertook a dizzying succession of wartime ventures, including two trips to France and one to Martinique. Irwin's luck was remarkably good until, during an engagement with a British frigate, he was shot through the shoulder and lost the use of his right arm.[59]

Because the center of a civil war was a poor place to make money, Philadelphia traders scattered to the distant corners of the Atlantic world in search of profits. Conservative Quakers returned home to England to continue their commercial activity, and agents of the Continental Congress took up residence in major ports of Europe and the West Indies. Partners of several Philadelphia shipping firms established branches in Nantes and Lorient, where they could receive tobacco shipments from America and send manufactures back across the Atlantic. To facilitate the flow of tobacco to the Delaware Valley, some Philadelphia merchants traveled frequently in the Chesapeake region, despite the rigors of overland trade. Upon returning from Richmond, one trader proudly lamented, "I rode the 300 miles up in 5 Days notwithstanding the heat of the Weather—be assurd it has not benefited my Health."[60] Still other traders traveled as far north as Boston and as far south as Charleston to seize commercial opportunities not available in Philadelphia.[61] Delaware Valley businessmen were also attracted to the West Indies, particularly the tiny Dutch Island of Saint Eustatius, which became a sort of international bazaar where the produce of all nations could be bought and sold. One harried visitor to the island wrote, "I have never found anything which approaches it." "There is here a swarm of men from all parts of the world only occupied in settling their affairs quickly to get away as

57. Girard to ——— Baldesqui, n.d., Stephen Girard Papers, 2d Ser., Reel 13, p. 17; Stephen Girard Ledger, 1780–1783, 62, 63, Girard Papers, 3d Ser., Reel 48 (all references to the Girard Papers are to the microfilm collection in APS); John Bach McMaster, *The Life and Times of Stephen Girard, Mariner and Merchant*, 2 vols. (Philadelphia, 1918), I, 10–37.

58. Samuel Morris, Jr., to Effingham Lawrence, Dec. 1, 1783, Samuel Morris Letterbook, 1780–1786, Morris Family Papers; Morris and Miercken Papers.

59. "A Philadelphia Merchant in 1768–1791," *PMHB*, XIX (1895), 397–402.

60. William Constable to James Seagrove, June 11, 1782, William Constable Letterbook, 1782–1790, 8.

61. Clarence L. Ver Steeg, "Stacey Hepburn and Company: Enterprisers in the American Revolution," *South Carolina Historical Magazine*, LV (1954), 1–5. On travel by merchants in Europe, see East, *Business Enterprise*, 133–134.

soon as possible from the inconveniences of the island. The heat is insupportable. The price of living very high; after having searched and researched for three days I have finally found a lodging in a little corner which shuts in a miserable little bed."[62] In February 1781 Adm. George Rodney of the British navy put an end to the merchants' lucrative misery by invading the island and seizing 173 vessels and the mass of merchandise that filled the warehouses of Saint Eustatius and covered its beaches.[63]

The Loyalists

The political allegiance of individual traders, as well as general economic trends, affected the wartime fortunes of firms. The result was extreme diversity of experience in a business community never notable for its cohesion. Some merchants ignored politics, others strongly supported the patriot cause, and still others were loyalists. Each of these political stances could be profitable or ruinous, depending upon the merchant.[64] Tench Coxe, a well-connected young tory, remained lucratively ensconced in Philadelphia during the British occupation and never suffered significantly for choosing the wrong side. He was pardoned for his transgression by Chief Justice Thomas McKean, a friend of his father's.[65]

In contrast to Coxe's opportunism, the leaders of Philadelphia's Quaker community tenaciously adhered to pacifist principles during the war and claimed to be completely neutral.[66] Their stance infuriated Revolutionary authorities, who were struggling for legitimacy at a time of political and military crisis. Pennsylvania radicals demanded explicit recognition of their own authority, as signified by oaths of allegiance and the acceptance of paper money.[67] Some Friends actively supported the patriot side, and a number of others quietly made their peace with the

62. Stephen Girard to Joseph Baldesqui, Apr. 14, 1780, Girard Papers, 2d Ser., Reel 1.

63. MacPherson, *Annals of Commerce*, III, 678.

64. A survey of 287 people who were merchants in 1774 indicated that 60 were tories, 84 were whigs, and 143 were of undetermined affiliation. Most of these loyalists were people who remained in Philadelphia during the British occupation and signed a petition appearing in J. Thomas Scharf and Thompson Westcott, *History of Philadelphia, 1609–1884*, 3 vols. (Philadelphia, 1884), I, 365, 366. See also Stephen Brobeck, "Revolutionary Change in Colonial Philadelphia: The Brief Life of the Proprietary Gentry," *William and Mary Quarterly*, 3d Ser., XXXIII (1976), 431–433.

65. This account is based on Cooke, *Tench Coxe*, chaps. 2, 3.

66. See Brunhouse, *Counter-Revolution*, 24.

67. Owen Stephen Ireland, "The Ratification of the Federal Constitution in Pennsylvania" (Ph.D. diss., University of Pittsburgh, 1966), 74–83.

Revolutionary authorities. But the redoubtable leaders of the Philadelphia Yearly Meeting, abhorring war, tumult, and Presbyterians—and secretly hoping for a British victory that would restore the charter of William Penn—stood their ground and invited tough persecution.

They were not disappointed. Leading Philadelphia Quakers lived in constant fear that their mail would be intercepted and their houses vandalized. When the British army approached in October 1777, twenty prominent Friends were seized without trial and carted off to Winchester, Virginia, where they spent the winter under house arrest.[68] The stores of Joshua Fisher and Sons were boarded up in 1776, and the firm's books were examined; two years later Benedict Arnold stole from the firm goods valued at two thousand pounds.[69] Persecution of the Quaker community reached a climax during the celebration of the victory at Yorktown in 1781.[70] On the night of October 24 carousing revolutionaries patrolled Philadelphia, demanding that every householder place candles in his windows in order to illuminate the streets in a blaze of candlelight. With characteristic intransigence, many Friends scorned this request. But the mob responded by pelting their houses with rocks, smashing windows, shutters, and doors. Several houses were entered, and their furniture was destroyed. John Drinker was beat up, and half of the goods were stolen from his store; the "Walns' pickles were thrown about the streets and barrels of sugar stolen."[71]

Few conservative Quaker merchants suffered more than Samuel Rowland Fisher, who was arrested in 1779 for sending letters to his brother in New York City that mentioned the scarcity of flour and quoted prices in hard money rather than Continental.[72] For this action Fisher was tried as a spy by the state of Pennsylvania, but his real crime was refusal to acknowledge the legitimacy of the Revolutionary government. After a raucous trial in which the judge chastised the jurors for finding a verdict of not guilty and sent them out of the courtroom to arrive at the correct determination, Fisher was thrown in jail in September 1779.[73] During a two-year confinement at Third and Market streets, he had the opportu-

68. Robert F. Oaks, "Philadelphians in Exile: The Problem of Loyalty during the American Revolution," *PMHB*, XCVI (1972), 298–325.

69. Joshua Fisher and Sons Journal, 1776–1796; Anna Wharton Morris, ed., "Journal of Samuel Rowland Fisher, of Philadelphia, 1779–1781," *PMHB*, XLI (1917), 422.

70. "A Loyalist's Account of Certain Occurrences in Philadelphia after Cornwallis's Surrender at Yorktown," *PMHB*, XVI (1892), 104–106. For other examples of the harassment of Friends, see Morris, ed., "Journal of Samuel Rowland Fisher," *PMHB*, XLI (1917), 169–171.

71. "A Loyalist's Account," *PMHB*, XVI (1892), 106.

72. Morris, ed., "Journal of Samuel Rowland Fisher," *PMHB*, XLI (1917), 156–158.

73. On the trial, see *ibid.*, 155–166.

nity, rare for a wealthy man, to sit in the eye of the Revolutionary hurricane, to be in the specific place where radicalism reached its zenith in America as inflation ravaged the economy and enraged the populace.

Life in prison was difficult but not intolerable. Fisher had the best room in the house, ate fairly good food, received a regular stream of visitors, and even enjoyed the use of a telescope. He led an orderly existence of writing, reading, praying, and carving hickory canes for relatives and friends.[74] There were indignities, to be sure. Fisher had to endure the sermons of Presbyterian ministers and the musings of "Cadwalader Dickenson, a Shoemaker & a very active Statesman of the present times." Though he generally steered clear of his fellow prisoners—"a most dissolutely wicked Company of Men & Women I ever saw"—Fisher could not escape steady abuse and occasional beatings from an alcoholic roommate.[75] On one occasion he was alarmed by reports that "the Militia were about to take up all the Tories & Quakers & would certainly create a most dreadful scene in the City." But he took silent comfort in the providential news of British victories.[76]

In this unnerving setting Fisher was perfectly situated to calculate how William Penn's beneficent province could have skidded off the track of peaceful toleration into a morass of delusion and violence. The underlying cause was clearly a conspiracy by Presbyterians, "who have long secretly been meditating their favorite plan of establishing their religion & Politicks without being subject to any kind of restraint from any King or Kingly Government." It was obvious that Presbyterian misrule was already rotting the vitals of American society. The recent rash of robberies in Philadelphia was hardly surprising when the rulers "have been the means of debasing the minds of the Inhabitants & overspreading the Land with deceit, Hypocrisy, & almost all manner of vice, so that none of them are a Terror to Evil Doers." The alliance with "such a restless, deceitful, persecuting Power as France" would probably lead to the repeal of the Reformation itself.[77] And the principles of integrity and fairness, the very basis of civil society, had been expunged by the Continental dollar, a sham currency of more service in the outhouse than the countinghouse.[78]

The Presbyterians had seized the province because thousands of well-meaning citizens had compromised with them on small matters, thereby allowing the mob to sweep into power.[79] Fisher was careful not to make

74. *Ibid.*, 167, 186, 276, 405, 423, 450.
75. *Ibid.*, 166, 169, 450.
76. *Ibid.*, 168–169, 177, 282.
77. *Ibid.*, 178, 455.
78. *Ibid.*, 333.
79. *Ibid.*, 286; see also 295.

this error. In his every word and action he announced his disdain for the Revolutionary government by consistently referring to "the so-called Council," "the president so-called," and "what is called the city court." It was because of these convictions that he refused to use Continental currency and declined to ask President Joseph Reed for a pardon. In Fisher's opinion it was Reed who needed the pardon. In thus standing by principle and paying strict attention to form as well as substance, Fisher knew that he was following in the path of the great Quaker martyrs of the previous century. But he was haunted by doubt nevertheless. Was he being courageous or merely obstinate? Was he bringing opprobrium and further persecution upon the entire Quaker community by taking his opposition to excessive length? These were the troubling questions that delegations of Friends put to him month after month, intimating that disownment might be necessary if he did not relent.[80] The isolation and pressure of solitary martyrdom, the suffering for a cause that even his compatriots did not understand, wore on Fisher and drove him to despondency and depression. He became increasingly distracted and irritable, unable even to stay in a room when two unsympathetic Friends came to visit. When finally pardoned by Reed, Fisher feared that acceptance of the reprieve would compromise his principles, but he concluded that it would simply constitute the last act of his program of counterrevolution through passive submission.[81]

Amidst such persistent harassment most prominent Friends abandoned overseas commerce during the war and concentrated on preserving their estates.[82] Henry Drinker's survival strategy, probably used by others as well, was to curtail commercial operations in 1775, collect the book debts of customers before currency depreciation became serious, and invest the proceeds in farms and rental properties.[83] Money left in the hands of English merchants or reliable firms in the West Indies and southern Europe was relatively safe, and physical property such as vessels and store goods generally increased in value during the war.[84] Far

80. *Ibid.*, 168, 183, 184, 187, 430, 431.

81. *Ibid.*, 408, 412, 413, 417, 425, 451.

82. No prominent neutral Quaker was a partner of one of the 64 firms that received goods worth over £4,000 in 1781 and 1782, combined. A survey of newspaper advertisements for the years 1779–1782 likewise indicates limited commercial activity by wealthy Friends. See above, n. 51.

83. Drinker wound up his partnership with Abel James in 1776 and bought two farms, Retreat Plantation and Mount Carmel, as well as timberlands. See Henry Drinker Ledger A, 1776–1792, 20, 21, 24, and Henry Drinker Journal, 1776–1791, 4, 9, Drinker Papers. Drinker had much other real estate as well.

84. On the high cost of vessels, see Willing, Morris, and Co. to William Bingham, Dec. 6, 1776, Bingham Collection; Woolsey, Salmon, and Co. to John Pringle, Jan. 20, 1777, Woolsey and Salmon Letterbook, 232.

more vulnerable were book debts scattered about the countryside. Henry Drinker complained of losing thousands of pounds through nonpayment of debts or payment in worthless currency, and other merchants undoubtedly faced the same problem.[85] Since construction activity was minimal during the war, urban rental income was healthy, and suburban farms provided essential foodstuffs.[86] Unfortunately, in 1777 and 1778 these farms were devastated by the American and British armies, which systematically stripped them of crops, livestock, and fences.[87] The cost of imported necessities rose greatly during the war, and foodstuffs were very scarce during the British occupation.[88] With expenses high, income sharply reduced, and the value of paper assets undermined by inflation, the war at best was a financial shock to wealthy Friends.

An attractive alternative to martyrdom in Philadelphia was emigration home to England.[89] So many Friends followed this course that an expatriate Quaker community, composed of Philadelphia merchants, their major suppliers, and their British relatives, took shape in England. Among the Philadelphia Quaker merchants who became part of this group were John Warder, Jabez Fisher, Thomas Clifford, Jr., Richard Vaux, John Pemberton, Matthias Aspden, Thomas York, and Samuel Shoemaker. Only the last two of these men were attainted for treason and stripped of their estates; the others generally were allowed to leave in peace to pursue their business careers. Thomas Clifford, Jr., lived in Bristol and formed, with his brother-in-law, a marginally profitable partnership that dealt in ironware. After the war Clifford acted as an English commission merchant, sending dry goods to his old friends in Philadelphia, where he was represented by his brother. Upon leaving Philadelphia in 1776, Richard Vaux apparently spent almost as much time at sea

85. James and Drinker to Hoare and Potts, June 30, 1785, James and Drinker Foreign Letterbook, 1772–1785, 374, Drinker Papers; Morris, ed., "Journal of Samuel Rowland Fisher," *PMHB*, XLI (1917), 450; Warder to John Lemprier and Co., June 19, 1777, John Warder Letterbooks, 1776–1778, HSP; Benjamin Fuller to Jeremiah Williamson and Co., Dec. 9, 1784, Fuller Letterbook, 1784–1787.

86. East, *Business Enterprise*, 152, writes that urban rents were 50%–75% above prewar levels by 1780.

87. Timothy Pickering to John Pickering, Dec. 11, 1777, July 6, 1778, Pickering Papers, Reel 5; "Diary of Robert Morton," *PMHB*, I (1877), 7–12, 20–24, 30; "Journal of Captain John Montrésor," *PMHB*, V (1881), 412, VI (1882), 38, 39; "Extracts from the Journal of Mrs. Henry Drinker," *PMHB*, XIII (1889), 303.

88. "Letter of Friends in Philadelphia to Friends in Ireland, Soliciting Aid during the Occupation of Philadelphia by the British," *PMHB*, XX (1896), 125–127; Mishoff, "Business in Philadelphia," *PMHB*, LXI (1937), 166–171; Bezanson *et al.*, *Prices and Inflation*, 84, 293–294.

89. See John Warder Letterbooks, 1776–1778, HSP; Richard Vaux Diaries, 1779–1782, HSP; Clifford Correspondence, VI, VII.

as on land. His laconic diary shows that between 1779 and 1781 he traveled to the following places in succession: England, Antigua, Saint Eustatius, Antigua, Holland, England, Saint Eustatius, England, France, and back to the West Indies.

John Warder, by contrast, was content to stay in England and make money.[90] A junior partner in one of Philadelphia's most successful firms, Warder went to London in 1775 to consolidate the company's affairs, a task expected to take several months. When he first arrived in England, Warder sensed opportunity all around him; at one point he was concocting a scheme to send to America a fleet of nine vessels laden with salt. But such opportunities proved to be illusory, for Warder was handicapped by the high cost of vessels and by his own misjudgment of events. At various times Warder believed that the war would end early in 1777, that British troops had occupied Philadelphia late in 1776, that France would not enter the war, and that Philadelphia radicals had imprisoned ten thousand Quakers and tories. But ample capital partly compensated for poor intelligence, and Warder was able to undertake a variety of ventures, including commodity speculation, whaling, commerce with New York City, and voyages to the West Indies.

The Staff Officers

While conservative Friends sullenly waited for the Revolution to collapse under the dead weight of its own wickedness, many other merchants energetically supported the war effort. Over twenty-five Philadelphia merchants served in the staff departments of the Continental army, primarily the commissary and quartermaster departments. These bureaucracies played a central role in the American war plan, because after the disastrous engagements in the New York City area in 1776, Washington's strategy emphasized survival rather than decisive victory. As long as the army survived, the Revolution itself was alive. With French support, the United States could wait for the British to grow tired of the war. But even this cautious approach was nearly subverted by the inner logic of the Revolution, for Americans were not inclined to substitute taxation and bureaucratic coercion by the Continental Congress for that imposed by Parliament.

Staff officers therefore struggled on two fronts in order to keep the army functioning. It was difficult enough to battle the economic disruptions caused by the war, but no less vexing was the libertarian spirit

90. Warder Letterbooks.

of the Revolution, which greatly impeded effective mobilization of resources. American radicals distrusted oppressive government in all its manifestations—not only excessive taxation but also standing armies, stockjobbers, government contractors, and bureaucrats. They expected the young American republic to start afresh, free of the rapacious materialism of England, cleansed of venal office-mongering and sordid peculation. To American radicals, staff officers were therefore suspect on several counts, for they were at once merchants, bureaucrats, and military men.[91]

From the first the Continental Congress hesitated to give these officers much operational autonomy, and the decline of the Continental dollar in 1778 and 1779 seemed to confirm their worst suspicions. The ravenous leeches of the commissary and quartermaster departments were evidently driving up the price of the goods they purchased in order to inflate their own commissions. Whether accurate or not, this analysis was appealing to Americans who preferred to believe that inflation could be contained by curbing corruption instead of sharply raising taxes.

Staff officers, of course, took a different view. They considered themselves skilled businessmen whose services were vital to the army's survival. Their labors were intense and their working conditions poor, and when necessary they bought goods on personal credit for the use of the public. It was only reasonable that such work be fairly compensated with adequate salaries and commissions.[92] Congressmen ensconced in Philadelphia underestimated what was required to keep a nomadic city of twenty thousand people clothed, housed, nourished, and armed.[93] The

91. Henry Laurens, "Notes of Proceedings, (May 17, 1779)," in Edmund C. Burnett, ed., *Letters of Members of the Continental Congress*, IV (Washington, D.C., 1928), 215; Daniel of St. Jenifer to ———, May 26, 1779, *ibid.*, 235; William Shippen to Richard Henry Lee, June 22, 1779, *ibid.*, 282; Carp, "Supplying the Revolution," chap. 5.

92. Joseph Trumbull resigned as commissary general in large part because he was not paid a commission. On the demand of Charles Pettit and John Cox for commissions, see Showman *et al.*, eds., *Papers of Nathanael Greene*, II, 310. Though commissions might appear to be an invitation to raise the prices of purchased goods, businessmen viewed them as a standard commercial tool. Commissions were particularly favored as a type of compensation because they were relatively immune to inflation. These attitudes revealed the same pragmatic, materialistic mentality that had shaped the merchants' attitude toward the revolutionary movement of the 1760s and 1770s. The staff officers were patriots but not political enthusiasts. As men of affairs, they understood the inner workings of the economy and the army too intimately to reduce the complexities of logistics to such sweeping abstractions as vice and corruption.

93. On the impatience of staff officers with Congress, see the correspondence between Charles Pettit and Nathanael Greene: Pettit to Greene, Dec. 28, 1779, Jan. 18, 1780, Greene Papers; Pettit to Greene, Jan. 12, 1780, *Papers of the Continental Congress*, Roll 193, V, 249.

staff officers of the army were willing to take on this formidable assignment, but not for free.

These tensions between Congress and the staff departments consistently subverted supply operations. Congressmen had little firsthand knowledge of logistical problems and in any case were busy with heavy responsibilities in many other areas.[94] Overworked and poorly informed, they were not in a position to make rapid, intelligent decisions on logistical matters. Yet they were too suspicious of staff officers to leave these decisions to the quartermaster general and commissary general and constantly meddled in administrative details in a slow, clumsy way.

Bureaucratic clashes aside, there was no way to supply the army adequately without raising taxes. Consequently, the staff departments lurched from crisis to crisis and from reform to reform.[95] Early ad hoc experiments in 1775 and 1776 gave way to ill-conceived reforms in 1777, followed by a more decentralized system in 1778, which was subverted by inflation in 1779. A system of requisitioning the states for supplies was introduced in 1780, which was replaced finally by Robert Morris's approach of making supply partnerships with private firms. This process of trial and failure over an eight-year period made the wartime careers of staff officers a harrowing series of logistical crises and bureaucratic confrontations. Top staff officers found that the only way to escape this Hobbesian existence was to quit their posts. No fewer than four commissaries general and three quartermasters general served the army in succession during the war, often departing amid bitter recriminations.[96]

After two turbulent years of development, the supply bureaucracy of the Continental army had, by the spring of 1778, assumed a definite, if confusing, shape. Certain important but secondary functions were handled by smaller independent departments, such as the medical

94. Lynn Montross, *The Reluctant Rebels: The Story of the Continental Congress, 1774–1789* (New York, 1950), 8, 9; Jack N. Rakove, *The Beginnings of National Politics: An Interpretive History of the Continental Congress* (New York, 1979), 198–205.

95. The single best work on this subject is Carp, "Supplying the Revolution," a study to which I am deeply indebted. See also Erna Risch, *Quartermaster Support of the Army: A History of the Corps, 1775–1793* (Washington, D.C., 1962); Bodle and Thibaut, "Valley Forge."

96. Thomas Mifflin, Nathanael Greene, and Timothy Pickering successively served as quartermasters general; Joseph Trumbull, William Buchanan, Jeremiah Wadsworth, and Ephraim Blaine acted as commissaries general. Mifflin, Greene, Trumbull, Buchanan, and Wadsworth left the service amidst crisis and controversy. It is my impression, however, that the turnover rate for assistant and deputy commissaries and deputy quartermasters was lower.

department, the clothier department, and the military stores department, which produced equipment at a depot in Carlisle, Pennsylvania.[97] Far more important were the quartermaster and commissary departments, which consumed over 89 percent of the money spent on logistics between 1777 and 1779.[98] The commissary department purchased and distributed to the army various types of food, particularly meat, flour, and salt, while the quartermaster department was responsible for buying or manufacturing many kinds of equipment for transportation and encampment. Saddles, wagons, horses, riverboats, tents, knapsacks, carpenter's tools, and entrenching implements were all to be found in the supply depots of the quartermaster department.[99] Although theoretically separate, the spheres of the two departments overlapped, because the commissary department needed wagons and horses to transport provisions, and the quartermaster department purchased forage which commissary officers also sought.

Because of the destruction of the coastwise trade, staff officers had to rely on rivers and roads. One route joined the Chesapeake area with Philadelphia and consisted of water transportation northward to Head of Elk (a town at the northern tip of Chesapeake Bay), overland transport to the Delaware River, and travel up the Delaware to Philadelphia by shallop. Heavily used before the war, this route gained in importance once coastwise trade between Virginia and Philadelphia became impossible. To be sure, it was not immune to disruption by British cruisers on either the Delaware River or Chesapeake Bay or by the occupation of Philadelphia in the winter of 1777–1778.[100] Nevertheless, the corridor was used frequently enough for Deputy Quartermaster Henry Hollingsworth to build a store and wharf at Head of Elk to facilitate government operations at the town.[101] This route became increasingly important to the quartermaster and commissary departments as the middle states

97. On the medical department, see Carp, "Supplying the Revolution," 14–19; on the clothing department, see Risch, *Quartermaster Support*, 23, 24, 29, 49–52; and Bodle and Thibaut, "Valley Forge," II, 246–349; on the military stores department, see Bodle and Thibaut, "Valley Forge," II, 351–435.

98. Calculated from Carp, "Supplying the Revolution," 122.

99. See, for example, "A return of stores in the Quarter Master General's Dept. . . . at Philadelphia, Aug., 1779," in Continental Army Returns, Container 54, LC.

100. Ephraim Blaine to Peter Colt, Feb. 7, 1778, Blaine Letterbook; Levi Hollingsworth to Marsden and Smith, Oct. 10, 1780, Sept. 8, 1781; Levi Hollingsworth to George Anderson, Oct. 31, 1780, to Henry Armistead and Co., May 8, 1781, Levi Hollingsworth Letterbook, 1780–1782 (Vol. CDLXXII), Hollingsworth Papers; Clement Biddle to Nathanael Greene, Feb. 20, 1779, Greene Papers.

101. Henry Hollingsworth to Nath. Greene, Oct. 13, 1779, Jan. 5, 1780, Charles Pettit to Nathanael Greene, May 5, 1779, Greene Papers.

were stripped of foodstuffs and southern grain was needed to feed the army.[102] To purchase forage and other supplies in the area, four quartermasters were stationed nearby: Henry Hollingsworth, at Head of Elk, was active on Maryland's eastern shore; Francis Wade operated in the state of Delaware; James Calhoun (stationed at Baltimore) worked the western shore of Maryland; and Cornelius Sheriff was responsible for Chester County, Pennsylvania.

A second important corridor, which was essentially a wartime innovation, connected Pennsylvania with New England. Because it was relatively free of wartime destruction, New England provided large amounts of beef and European manufactures for the American war effort.[103] These goods could not be shipped safely by coastwise vessels, nor could they be hauled overland via New York City and New Brunswick to Philadelphia once New York City was occupied by the British in August 1776. Therefore, a new wartime route was devised, which crossed the Hudson at Kings Ferry (thirty-two miles north of Manhattan), ran southwest through Morristown, New Jersey, and then crossed the Delaware at Corryells Ferry or at Trenton. From here goods could be sent downriver by boat to Philadelphia or hauled by wagon into the interior of Pennsylvania.[104] Several inland towns connected with this route became important supply depots during the war. In the Hudson River valley, New Windsor was an important supply post, as was Fishkill, the headquarters of Deputy Quartermaster Udney Hay. Morristown, New Jersey, was an important logistical center, while Deputy Quartermaster Moore Furman operated out of Trenton and Robert Lettis Hooper, Generalissimo of the upper Delaware, was based in Easton, Pennsylvania.

After the British evacuated the city in May 1778, Philadelphia became an important center of quartermaster activity, under the direction of John Mitchell. Deputy quartermasters were also stationed in a number of inland towns. Situated in the heart of Pennsylvania's iron country, Reading and Lebanon became important centers of manufacture, and Lancaster was likewise a key base for logistical operations, especially the collection and processing of food.[105] The deputy quartermaster sta-

102. James Calhoun to John Davis, Sept. 15, 1778, Davis Collection, II; Chaloner and White to Ephraim Blaine, Nov. 24, 1778, Chaloner and White Letterbook, 1778–1779.

103. Bodle and Thibaut, "Valley Forge," II, 345, 347; Ephraim Blaine to Peter Colt, Feb. 7, 1778, Nov. 18, 1777, Blaine Letterbook; John De Neufville to Bache and Shee, Sept. 30, 1782, John De Neufville Papers.

104. See William Buchanan to John Davis, Oct. 1, 1777, Davis Collection, I; Robert Lettis Hooper to Clement Biddle, Jan. 28, 1779 (extract), in Greene Papers.

105. On Reading and Lebanon, see James Abeel Letterbook, 1778, LC. On activities in Lancaster, see Ephraim Blaine to John Patton, Sept. 13, 1777, John Chaloner to William Buchanan, Oct. 11, 1778, Blaine Letterbook.

tioned at Carlisle obtained large numbers of horses and wagons in York and Cumberland counties and facilitated the movement of forces westward toward Pittsburgh, where still another deputy quartermaster was stationed.[106] In addition, supplies were procured in Maryland's prosperous backcountry by a deputy quartermaster stationed at Frederick.

Although their specific activities varied with the time and place of command, deputy quartermasters carried on multifarious business on a scale far beyond that of most private businessmen. Purchases of one hundred cattle or fifty wagons were routine, and over a thousand army horses were sometimes quartered in a single district.[107] Quartermasters were likely to operate a warehouse, superintend a sizable force of artisans, direct a group of assistants who ranged across the countryside purchasing forage and horses, and manage a large group of wagoners. John Mitchell, deputy quartermaster for Philadelphia, was responsible for stores, a magazine, a woodyard, several stables, and over three hundred workers that reported to him. Such an establishment was three times the size of many contemporary ironworks, which were among the largest business establishments in the nation.[108]

Purchasing supplies was the most important task of a staff officer, and also one of the most difficult. As the biggest buyer in a market, an officer could not easily get bargains, because potential sellers knew that he needed to make large purchases. Patience and vigilance were necessary. After the British left Philadelphia in 1778, John Chaloner and James White entered the city to buy up rum, salt, and other supplies, but soon found themselves locked in a battle with "those monsters in human shape," the speculators, who were charging exorbitant prices for goods. Less-skilled market operators might have been tempted to pay these high prices before they moved still higher, but Chaloner and White waited for new supplies to enter the port and were able to make purchases at lower prices.[109]

When buying wagons and horses for an upcoming campaign or food for the approaching winter, purchasers did not have the luxury of wait-

106. See John Davis Papers, esp. Nathanael Greene to John Davis, Mar. 23, 1778, Davis Collection, I; Davis to Charles Pettit, Apr. 30, 1779, Davis Collection, IV.

107. See Blaine to Peter Colt, Nov. 18, 1777, Blaine Letterbook; Joseph Brady to John Davis, Apr. 18, 1779, John Davis to Charles Pettit, Apr. 30, 1779, John Davis Collection, LC. Robert Lettis Hooper to Nathanael Greene, May 27, 1779, Greene Papers. See also Archibald Steel to Charles Pettit, July 28, 1779, Greene Papers.

108. "A Return of Persons in the Quarter Master General's Department, under the inspection of John Mitchell, D Q M G in Philadelphia, Dec. 1, 1779," *Papers of the Continental Congress*, Roll 46, III, 381.

109. Chaloner and White to Ephraim Blaine, Nov. 1, 1778, Chaloner and White Letterbook, 1778–1779, 66.

ing several weeks for prices to fall: they had to scramble to buy whatever was available. In such situations speculators could move in, sometimes posing as staff officers, and buy goods in order to resell them to the army.[110] But there is no reason to assume that speculators were any more savvy and shrewd than the farmers themselves. Nathanael Greene sounded like a classical economist as he discussed how to hire farmers as wagoners: "Interest is the Governing principle with the farmers as well as almost that of every other order of men. if you propose any terms to the farmers short of those [as] advantagious [as those] which they can make in any other Employ they will leave your service."[111] In 1778 an exasperated staff officer observed, "Unless some Law to enable us to procure grain takes place, I am pretty certain we must go without—The Farmer has the Ball at his own Foot and kicks it when he pleases." Later he said, "The Farmers are determined to keep a Head of us, let us do as we will; for Example, when 15/ was *our* price for corn *they* demanded 18/9, when we offer'd *that*, they asked 20/; now we offer 20/, and their price is between three and four Dollars."[112]

In Philadelphia and several inland towns, quartermasters supervised the production of such diverse articles as shoes, tents, nails, and boats. Using hides provided by the commissary department, factories in Newark, Delaware, in Allentown, Pennsylvania, and in other towns were turning out several thousand shoes per year.[113] James Abeel produced two hundred tents per week in Reading, Pennsylvania, and in 1779 about twenty-eight hundred packsaddles were made for one campaign.[114] John Davis received orders to buy a plantation near Carlisle and establish a nail factory employing twenty men. In Philadelphia a large number of riverboats were built under army supervision.[115] These efforts were impeded by a shortage of materials, especially imported goods such as cloth. When a French vessel carrying a shipment of manufactures entered

110. Henry Hollingsworth to Nathanael Greene, Feb. 10, 1779, Greene Papers.

111. Nathanael Greene to Henry Hollingsworth, Feb. 14, 1779, *Papers of the Continental Congress*, Roll 193, IV, 115.

112. James Burnside to Moore Furman, Nov. 13, 1778, James Burnside Letterbook, 1778–1779, HSP.

113. Timothy Pickering to George Washington, Apr. 9, 25, May 24, 1779, Pickering Papers, Roll 33, 228, 230, 243. The latter, rather confused, letter seems to suggest that about 6,600 shoes were on hand at that time. On manufacturing activity during the war, see Wood, *Conestoga Crossroads*, 144–149; Charles H. Kessler, *Lancaster in the Revolution* (Lititz, Pa., 1975), 104.

114. James Abeel to Charles Pettit, May 27, 1778, James Abeel Letterbook, 1778, LC; Nathanael Greene to John Jay, Sept. 19, 1779, *Papers of the Continental Congress*, Roll 175, I, 171.

115. Matthew Irwin and Isaac Melchior to John Davis, Dec. 27, 1777, Davis Collection, I; Benjamin G. Eyre to Nathanael Greene, July 1, 1779, Greene Papers.

Philadelphia, Clothier General James Mease and Deputy Quartermaster John Mitchell pounced upon materials that they wanted and quarreled violently over a parcel of linen, which Mease needed for making hunting shirts and Mitchell wanted for producing tents.[116] The Board of War moderated the dispute and reproved Mitchell for displaying excessive ardor in the cause, because it was likely to raise prices. Staff officers found that labor was nearly as scarce as cloth. Carpenters were difficult to come by in Philadelphia, and Henry Hollingsworth, while building the wharf at Head of Elk, lamented: "The difficulty of procuring Hands has been such (unless I would have given the most enormous Prices) that it was impossible to hasten on the Work . . . at Harvest for near six Weeks [I] was oblig'd to lay by or give twenty Dollars P Day to Labourers."[117]

Transportation also absorbed the attention of staff officers. Overland transportation in Revolutionary America was exceedingly slow and tedious: roads were bad, wagons broke down, horses went lame, ferries were unreliable, and forage was scarce. A day on the road could amount to thirteen exhausting hours of frustration, as the diary of Joseph Joslin shows:

> It is Exceeding Stormy Snow North wind and very hard & we heard they ware a Suffering for hay at Danbury & So we must go we set out about 10 o'clock and got a Little way and my Cart one wheel Sunk So far down in a hole that it Over Set the load the Snow was full of warter & the wheels would Sink into the [mud] and very heavy Carting indeed and we must waid about knee Deep the Chief of the way. With 10 cattel [oxen] we got to Danbury just Dark 7 miles and then I went to Capt hoyt's & laid in bed. It has bin a very tedious day.[118]

The wagoners who struggled with the rigors of the road were not always as dependable as Joslin appears to have been. Like other unskilled preindustrial workers, they had an imprecise sense of time and distance, and after fighting snow, mud, and boredom for endless hours, they often succumbed to the various temptations of the road, especially taverns where one could escape the cold, have a drink, and maybe do some gambling. Unlike factory workers and seamen, wagoners did not face the

116. Charles Pettit to Nathanael Greene, May 13, 1779, Greene Papers.

117. Benjamin G. Eyre to Nathanael Greene, July 1, 1779, Henry Hollingsworth to Nathanael Greene, Nov. 23, 1779, *ibid.*

118. Lynn Montross, *Rag, Tag, and Bobtail: The Story of the Continental Army, 1775–1783* (New York, 1952), 272.

unyielding discipline of a boss.[119] Staff officers complained that wagoners traveled only ten miles per day—half as far as they were supposed to. If they failed to load their wagons and draw forage the night before, wagoners got a slow start the next day and might travel only three or four miles.[120] When traveling was especially difficult, wagoners sometimes abandoned their wagons or lightened their load by throwing part of it onto the side of the road.[121] Staff officers could do little about such "indolence," "negligence," and "impertinence": since labor was scarce and the army offered lower wages than the private sector, errant wagoners could not be easily replaced.[122]

Like any bureaucracy, the staff departments were held together by yard upon yard of red tape. Fearing corruption and desiring a precise knowledge of available supplies, Congress inundated staff officers with demands for accounts of expenditures, returns of employees in service, and inventories of supplies. As Charles Pettit caustically observed, "They are calling for estimates & returns &c, scarcely themselves knowing what they ask for, nor what to do with the answers when they have got them."[123] The volume of paperwork was further increased by the frequent reorganizations of the staff departments.

Between buying provisions, supervising workers, managing inland transport systems, and keeping voluminous accounts, staff officers faced a grueling work schedule. But far more disheartening than the crushing volume of labor was the attendant multitude of frustrations and indignities. Whereas battlefield commanders received glory and praise, staff officers endured the meddling of Congress, the hostility of state governments, and the vilification of the general public. While struggling to keep the army alive, they were portrayed as magnates enriched by corruption. Because they received commissions that grew with the volume of their purchases, they were even held responsible for their own greatest problem: the decline of the Continental dollar. As Nathanael Greene observed, the evil effects of inflation were pervasive: "The principal source of all our difficulties, is the state of our Money: the depreciation of which locks up almost every specie of supplies, deprives us of the oppor-

119. See the excellent discussion in Carp, "Supplying the Revolution," 108–113; Peter Kuhn to Jacob Kuhn, May 29, 1779, Kuhn and Kuhn Letterbook, 1779–1785, Kuhn and Risberg Papers.

120. James Abeel to Nathanael Greene, June 7, 1778, Abeel Letterbook, 1778.

121. Risch, *Quartermaster Support*, 35; Alexander Patterson to Robert Lettis Hooper, May 17, 1779, Greene Papers.

122. John Davis to Charles Pettit, Apr. 30, 1779, Charles Lukens to John Davis, May 25, 1779, Davis Papers, IV.

123. Charles Pettit to Nathanael Greene, Dec. 28, 1779, Greene Papers.

tunities of making contracts, or of gaining credit, and obliges us to employ innumerable Agents to collect from the People, what they would be glad to furnish, was the representative of property upon a more stable footing."[124]

The pressures of the job were intensified by the magnitude of the stakes: staff officers knew that a potential supply crisis always lay beyond the next harvest. They were tortured by the image of starving soldiers turning to desertion and trudging home through the snow, at once ending their own misery and the Revolution itself. When such a calamity seemed imminent in the fall of 1777, an anguished Ephraim Blaine ticked off the reasons why he wished to resign: "Numbers of those persons, I have under my Directions, [are] not equal to my expectation, Disappointments, and losses daily, complaints hourly, . . . my Character lost, any money spent, the very unreasonable and exorbitant prices of every necessary wanted for the army."[125] These words of desperation were echoed by Charles Pettit two years later: "We are growing from day to day more wretched & distressed; our horses unable to perform service for want of Forage; daily losing flesh & becoming weaker; the hired Teams quitting the service for want of Forage as well as lack of pay; the Roads becoming bad & the rivers impassable by means of the Thaw & the navigation still impeded. Our supplies of money not equal to a third of the requisite sum for current expences exclusive of paying former debts . . . I find myself growing impatient, fretful & angry, . . . What is to become of us?"[126]

There can be no doubt that patriotism, devotion to the army, and regard for personal reputation were the primary motivation of the staff officers in the Revolutionary war.[127] The widespread belief at the time that these men were becoming wealthy in office was largely untrue. Contemporaries unfortunately seldom acknowledged the enormous stamina, grit, and devotion to the cause of the supply officers. But observers were not entirely incorrect when they alluded to the upwardly mobile staff officer who had been "a two penny Jack who never in his life was capable, by any business he had been engaged in, of making a Shilling more than maintained his family and that but in a very so so

124. Nathanael Greene to Samuel Huntington, Dec. 12, 1779, *Papers of the Continental Congress*, Roll 175.

125. Ephraim Blaine to William Buchanan, Oct. 28, 1777, Blaine Letterbook.

126. Charles Pettit to Nathanael Greene, Feb. 26, 1780, Greene Papers.

127. I am following here the convincing argument presented by Carp, "Supplying the Revolution," chap. 6.

manner."[128] Many staff officers were indeed opportunistic as well as altruistic. No fewer than ten staff officers entered the Philadelphia merchant community after the war, and three minor merchants of pre-Revolutionary years became much wealthier after stints in the staff departments. Two other Philadelphia businessmen who were closely associated with the merchant community also benefited materially from their support for the war effort.[129]

Although the personal financial careers of staff officers are not well documented, the main causes of their success can be discerned. The most obvious benefit of their positions was the pay, particularly commissions of .5–1.5 percent on goods purchased.[130] Although there is little direct evidence on how much income such commissions generated, the large scale of operations of deputy quartermasters and assistant commissaries leaves no doubt that the earnings were significant. Moreover, official duties enhanced the officers' capacity to transact business.

At a time when many businessmen were immobilized by political persecution, the occupation of cities, the paralysis of transportation networks, and lack of credit, assistant quartermasters and commissaries managed massive purchasing networks. They were in continual touch with markets—monitoring prices, maintaining contacts with buyers and sellers, managing a cadre of clerks and assistants. Moreover, they were experts in the intricacies of doing business in a nation at war. They were familiar with the government bureaucracies, the market in French bills of exchange, the inland wagon routes. Thus, quite apart from the prestige that it conferred, the war experience of these men qualified them to handle private business as well. It was probably a simple matter, for example, for John Davis to buy twenty or thirty head of cattle for William Pollard, in addition to the hundreds that he purchased for the Con-

128. William Shippen to Richard Henry Lee, June 22, 1779, in Burnett, ed., *Letters of Members of the Continental Congress*, IV, 282.

129. The ten new merchants were John Reed, Standish Forde, Gustavus Risberg, Robert Towers, John Patton, Francis Wade, George A. Baker, John Moyland, Timothy Pickering, and Samuel Hodgdon. The three upwardly mobile merchants were John Chaloner, Clement Biddle, and Levi Hollingsworth. The two near-merchants were Haym Salomon, who was a bill broker, and Samuel Wetherill, a paint and drug seller after the war. Hollingsworth may not have had an official staff position, but he was retained by Robert Morris to sell flour for the public in 1782. See Levi Hollingsworth to Henry Hollingsworth, Feb. 26, 1782, in Hollingsworth Letterbook, 1780–1782. Wetherill was not a staff officer, but he helped to manage the United Company for Promoting Manufactures. See Miriam Hussey, *From Merchants to "Colour Men": Five Generations of Samuel Wetherill's White Lead Business* (Philadelphia, 1956), 1–5.

130. Carp, "Supplying the Revolution," 73–74.

tinental army.[131] Who could more effectively purchase a bill of exchange on France at advantageous rates than "Haym Salomon, Broker to the Office of Finance, to the Consul General of France, and to the Treasury of the French Army"?[132]

Staff officers had certain less legitimate advantages as well. Although the indiscriminate indictment of staff officers as corrupt was unfounded, they were not above using public property for private gain. A primary area of abuse involved public wagons. In a period when transportation systems were partly paralyzed, access to wagons meant access to profits. In 1779 a Philadelphia trader reported that the demand for wine was enormous, that "Numbers are waiting for the Arrival of it, with whom we can make our own Price."[133] Such opportunities created great temptations to employ public vehicles for private ventures, temptations to which staff officers often succumbed. An investigation by Congress concluded that in the winter of 1777–1778 Robert Lettis Hooper sent a brigade of public wagons "to New Windsor, Newburgh, Hartford, and Boston with flour and Iron on private forage along the route."[134] In 1778 a young trader named John Reed, who served in the medical department during part of the war, took a sum of money and several wagonloads of goods to Boston, where they were to be exchanged for knives, forks, pewter, saddlery, medicines, and other goods.[135] One of Reed's partners in this venture was Thomas Bond, Jr., an official in the medical department, who advised Reed to use Bond's influence with commissaries and quartermasters to secure goods and additional wagons in Boston. To smooth his path Reed was also directed to distribute "presents" as necessary, and on the return leg he was instructed to secure the assistance of the chief barrack master at Fishkill.

Corruption took many other forms as well. A clerk in the commissary department purchased on his private account forty hogsheads of rum, which he intended to sell to the public at a profit, and there were well-founded reports of irregularities in the quartermaster department in

131. William Pollard to John Davis, June 1, 1779, Davis Collection, V.

132. Edwin Wolf 2d and Maxwell Whiteman, *The History of the Jews of Philadelphia from the Colonial Times to the Age of Jackson*, 2d ed. (Philadelphia, 1975), 107.

133. ——— to Col. Daniel Clymer, Apr. 11, 1779, Kuhn and Kuhn Letterbook, 1779–1785, Kuhn and Risberg Papers.

134. Worthington Chauncey Ford, ed., *Journals of the Continental Congress, 1774–1789*, XII (1778) (Washington, D.C., 1908), 1245.

135. Thomas Bond, Jr., to John Reed, Apr. 29, 1778, Thomas Lawrence to John Reed, May 5, 1778, Thomas Lawrence to John Reed, May 13, 1778, Anthony Butler to John Reed, May 26, 1778, Thomas Bond, Jr., to John Reed, June 6, 1778, Reed and Forde Papers, box 1. See also "Adventure to Boston on Account of Messrs. T. Bond, Col. J. Melchor, and T. Lawrence, August 1778," in box 15.

western Pennsylvania.[136] Particularly scandalous was the case of Cornelius Sweers, an inconsequential Philadelphia merchant who took control of the department of military stores when its chief became ill. Sweers defrauded the department of thousands of pounds, raised the suspicion of his peers by spending his treasure as fast as he stole it, and eventually found himself in the Walnut Street jail.[137]

These economic advantages of staff officers were not sufficiently large to allow them to build up solid blocks of capital or to organize consistently profitable businesses. But because they remained in business, made valuable contacts, and enjoyed preferred access to public resources, staff officers had the opportunity to improve their economic position, relative to other merchants. They were then well placed to benefit from a second key source of social mobility in the Revolutionary period: the huge quantity of commercial credit extended to American merchants by Europeans in the boom years 1783 and 1784. To be sure, career advances based on these forces were tenuous and fragile, but one can point to certain clear beneficiaries of service in the supply departments.

One example is John Chaloner, a recent immigrant from England who served as an assistant deputy commissary of the Continental army.[138] Based in Philadelphia, he purchased goods within the city, dispensed money to regional purchasing agents, and became in effect an assistant manager of the middle department, under Deputy Commissary Ephraim Blaine. Chaloner also communicated regularly with Blaine's superior, Jeremiah Wadsworth, commissary general of purchases. When Wadsworth left the Continental service in December 1779 and obtained the lucrative job of commissary for the French troops in America, he employed Chaloner as his Philadelphia agent. As Wadsworth's fortune grew, so did Chaloner's. The young merchant helped his patron to speculate in bank stock, underwrite marine insurance, sell dry goods, and negotiate bills of exchange. Chaloner's compensation for these services was large

136. Chaloner and White to Ephraim Blaine, Oct. 23, 1778, Chaloner and White Letterbook, 1778–1779, 60; Charles Pettit to John Davis, Sept. 3, 1779, Davis Papers, VI.

137. Bodle and Thibaut, "Valley Forge," II, 391–392, 410–411, 432–435; Timothy Pickering to President of Congress, Aug. 4, 1778, Pickering Papers, Reel 50.

138. John Chaloner's career may be followed in the Chaloner and White Collection. See Henry Thompson to Chaloner, July 27, 1771, Nathan Norton to Chaloner, Oct. 28, 1772, box 5; Chaloner and White Letterbooks, 1778–1779, 1779 (2 vols.), concerning his work in the commissary department; John Chaloner Letterbook, 1782–1784, showing his relationship with Jeremiah Wadsworth and entry into the dry goods business; and, on his financial problems in the 1780s, John Barker Church to John Chaloner, July 20, 25, 1785, Jeremiah Wadsworth to John Chaloner, Feb. 2, 1790. On Chaloner's saltworks, see Chaloner to Richard Wade, Aug. 9, 1783, Chaloner Letterbook, 1782–1784, 168.

enough to allow him to invest heavily in an ill-fated saltworks and to enter the dry goods trade in a major way in 1784.

The Fortune Builders

By disrupting markets and distorting normal patterns of competition, the Revolution provided phenomenal opportunities for a handful of well-situated traders. In Philadelphia it was Robert Morris who most dramatically capitalized on the opportunities at hand. The junior partner in one of Philadelphia's wealthiest and most aggressive firms, Morris was elected to the Continental Congress in 1775 and became a member of the Secret Committee of Correspondence, the Secret Committee of Trade, and the Marine Committee.[139] Since relatively few congressmen were merchants conversant with the complexities of exchange rates, cargo selection, vessel management, and market timing, they were content to grant Morris great discretion in commercial matters. This arrangement was particularly convenient because it allowed shipments of arms and supplies on the account of Congress to be disguised as private shipments of Willing and Morris. Morris's position was further strengthened by the alarming military situation of the country in 1776, following the defeat of Washington at Brooklyn Heights in August 1776 and his subsequent retreat across New Jersey. Supplies of all kinds were needed immediately—muskets and powder, blankets and bullets, medicines, rum, and salt. But such goods were scarce by 1776, because of the cessation of trade with England, the British blockade of the American coast, and the ban on imports imposed by Congress itself at the end of 1774.

At this critical juncture Robert Morris took charge. Gaining ascendancy over the Secret Committee of Trade, he stayed in Philadelphia in the last months of 1776 after Congress, expecting an invasion of the city by Howe's army, had fled to Baltimore. Morris worked tirelessly to dispatch ships to the West Indies before the British arrived or the Delaware froze up, and he urged his foreign agents to forward the many supplies needed by the army. To Washington he wrote: "I am up very early this morning to dispatch a supply of $50,000 . . . but it will not be got away

139. This account of Morris's wartime activities relies primarily on Clarence L. Ver Steeg, *Robert Morris: Revolutionary Financier, With an Analysis of His Earlier Career* (Philadelphia, 1954), 6–27; Ferguson, *Power of the Purse*, 70–105; East, *Business Enterprise*, 126–148; Margaret L. Brown, "William Bingham, Agent of the Continental Congress in Martinique," *PMHB*, LXI (1937), 54–87.

so early as I could wish, for none concerned in this movement, except myself, are up. I shall rouse them immediately."[140]

During 1776 and 1777 Morris conducted commerce through a loose network of traders situated at key points around the Atlantic basin. In Paris was the Yankee Silas Deane, a former member of the Secret Committee of Trade. The young Philadelphia merchant William Bingham was stationed in Martinique. John Ross, also a Philadelphia merchant, was circulating in France as an agent for Willing and Morris. Within America itself, Morris had important correspondents in Alexandria, Williamsburg, Edenton, and Charleston. Certain prominent French and Dutch firms also became involved in the network, as did such leading Philadelphia traders as J. M. Nesbitt, George Meade, and John Wilcocks. If the specific operations of this far-flung network were often complicated and obscure, its basic aims were simple enough. On the one hand, it imported European manufactures (often of British origin) into America from such ports as Hamburg, Amsterdam, and Nantes. In addition, salt, molasses, and rum were shipped into America from the West Indies. To pay for these imports the American staples—grains, rice, indigo, and tobacco—were shipped back to Europe. But because the main source of supply, France, was officially neutral until February 1778, most of these goods were routed through the French island of Martinique, which became the hub of the network. To supplement this commodity trading, Morris's group made investments in shipping and privateers and speculated in currencies, American bonds, and British stocks.

Although Morris, Deane, and Bingham were official employees of the United States, all of the members of the group were eagerly trying to build their fortunes. Morris excitedly urged Bingham in 1776 to trade aggressively, for "where cargoes arrive either one way or the other, the profits are now so great it is well worth risquing largely." This assessment was correct. Bingham founded his enormous fortune on profits garnered in 1776 and 1777, while Morris announced early in 1778, "I am as well provided with funds to carry on business as any occassion I can have will require." He was able to purchase bills of exchange worth twenty thousand pounds without touching large stocks of funds lodged with his factors in Virginia and Charleston.[141]

As we have seen, the source of this success was not the *general* stimulation of Philadelphia's economy by war, but, rather, the opposite.[142] The success of Morris and his associates was based not on the general pros-

140. Quoted in Ver Steeg, *Robert Morris*, 9.
141. *Ibid.*, 16, 17, 29.
142. East, *Business Enterprise*, 36.

perity of the period, but rather on their special competitive advantage over other American traders. There were exceptional commercial opportunities in 1776 and 1777 because of the huge differences in commodity prices in various parts of the Atlantic world. Tobacco, for example, was far more dear in Paris than in Virginia, while the reverse was true of textiles and hardware. These differentials arose from the formidable barriers to trade, which inhibited the normal process of price adjustment through commerce. The members of the Morris group possessed extraordinary advantages in breaking through these barriers. They had access to inside information at a time when many traders expected the war to end quickly. Although shipping was difficult to obtain, they could employ fast, well-armed vessels to carry their private cargoes. While the freezing of trade with Europe denied most firms the advantage of European credit, the Morris group used public funds to establish financial relationships with firms in France and Martinique. And, as if these advantages in private trade were not enough, Morris and his friends were able to make huge sales, amounting to over £230,000 between 1775 and 1777, directly to the Continental Congress. These deals could hardly fail to be profitable, for the contracts were made with the head of the Secret Committee of Trade, who happened to be Robert Morris.[143]

But Morris was never satisfied. Instead of prudently investing his winnings in tangible assets that could withstand the vagaries of war, he resigned from Congress in 1778, departed from the firm of Willing and Morris, and participated in at least nine new ventures in 1778, 1779, and 1780.[144] The usual pattern in these companies was for Morris to contribute part of the capital as well as his prestige and contacts, but to leave day-to-day management to other partners in the concern. The result was a sort of controlled chaos; Morris was a one-man conglomerate, simultaneously overseeing (or not overseeing) investments in tobacco shipments, military contracting, dry goods importations, and land speculations.

These diverse operations, predictably, were not uniformly successful. "Miss Fortune is fickle and coy," Morris wrote in the spring of 1781. "She has played the Devil with me last summer, fall, and winter, but still I hope to put her in better humour this Spring and a few of her smiles may make amends for all the frowns her ill temper cast on me."[145] Yet despite these setbacks, Morris was far richer than any other merchant in Philadelphia. No longer merely a merchant prince, he reigned as the

143. Ferguson, *Power of the Purse*, 77. I have assumed a depreciation rate for the Continental dollar of .9.

144. This is based on Ver Steeg, *Robert Morris*, 28–36.

145. *Ibid.*, 36.

acknowledged commercial king of Philadelphia amidst a throng of lesser gentry. The marquis de Chastellux wrote admiringly, if with some exaggeration, "It will scarcely be believed that amid the disasters of America, Mr. Morris, the inhabitant of a town barely freed from the hands of the English, should possess a fortune of eight million *livres* [£300,000–£400,000 sterling]. It is, however, in the most critical times that great fortunes are acquired and increased."[146]

Such wealth was bound to draw criticisms. While well-placed merchants were building estates of unprecedented proportions, half-naked privates shivered and starved at Morristown and Valley Forge, and dozens of congressmen managed to serve their country without becoming wealthy. Bitter castigation of Morris was the inevitable result. The little people of Philadelphia, driven to near-destitution by the sharp increase in the price of foodstuffs between 1778 and 1780, considered wealthy merchants to be the source of their problems. Businessmen were charged with "basking in the sunshine of monopoly, forestalling and extortion and withal pampering their vile natures in ease, superfluities and luxury."[147] Armed and angry, the working classes demanded price controls and restrictions on the exportation of foodstuffs. Civil disorder was rampant in 1778 and 1779. Meanwhile, radicals in Congress were excoriating Morris for sacrificing the public good to his financial ambitions. Congress conducted several investigations of charges against both Morris and his associate Silas Deane, and Morris was probably relieved to retire from public service in 1778. But neither these probes nor scrutiny by modern historians has uncovered more than a handful of cases of outright malfeasance. Undoubtedly, the record would be more damaging to Morris if it had not been written by the defendant himself. But the paucity of proven charges also suggests that Morris's fortune was based not on actual theft, but, rather, on systematic exploitation of privileged access to government contracts, funds, vessels, and intelligence.

As for Morris himself, he protested his innocence, while insisting that the quest for profits went "hand in hand" with the public welfare. Displaying the disdain for radical republican values that had consistently informed the approach of rich merchants to the Revolution, Morris insisted that restraints on trade were self-defeating because commerce must be "as free as air to place it in the most advantageous state to mankind."[148] These sentiments were not merely for public consumption; Morris confided to Silas Deane that although some might think "private

146. Marquis de Chastellux, *Travels in North America in the Years 1780, 1781, and 1782*, trans. Howard C. Rice, Jr. (Chapel Hill, N.C., 1963), I, 135–136.

147. Foner, *Tom Paine*, 156.

148. Ver Steeg, *Robert Morris*, 38.

gain is more our pursuit than Public Good . . . I shall continue to discharge my duty faithfully to the Public and pursue my Private Fortune by all such honorable and fair means as the times will admit of, and I dare say you will do the same."[149]

Such defenses probably sounded hollow to the patriot who saw Morris's magnificent coach rumble down Market Street, but the great merchant acquitted himself well in the arena of action. Many members of Congress were rather more adept at bickering with each other than at prosecuting the war with England. With the Continental dollar worthless by 1780, it was said that "nothing can be more wretched and distressing than the condition of the troops, starving with cold and hunger, without tents and camp equipment." As the Pennsylvania line mutinied and Clinton's army swept through the South, defeat seemed imminent. Morris was the man to turn this crisis around. If congressional radicals found it difficult to brook the complacent rapaciousness of this corrupt Mandeville (as he was called), they found it even harder to do without him. So in the spring of 1781, with the army demoralized and national finances in disarray, the fox was brought back into the chicken coop. The commercial czar of 1776–1777 became the financial dictator of 1781–1784. His task was nothing less than to restore the solvency of the national government. True to his principles, Morris accepted the post only on the condition that he be allowed to continue to expand his personal fortune.[150]

Morris was unique but not alone: how many other fortune builders were there in Revolutionary Philadelphia? An analysis of privateering records, tax lists, and customs documents suggests that roughly sixteen other traders fall into this category.[151] Six of the sixteen were, like Morris, wealthy Philadelphians before 1776 who expanded their fortunes during the war; six were not extremely rich before achieving their wartime success; and four migrated to Philadelphia during the war with substantial estates, which they continued to enlarge.[152] Significantly, seven of these sixteen fortune builders were Irishmen who generally sup-

149. Ferguson, *Power of the Purse*, 74.

150. Ver Steeg, *Robert Morris*, 48, 59.

151. The most important documents used were the Registers of Duties Paid, which have been broken down firm by firm for the years 1781–1782, May 1785–Dec. 1787, and County Tax Assessment Ledgers, City and County of Philadelphia, 1789, Philadelphia City Archives.

152. The three groups are John Ross, Andrew Caldwell, John Nixon, John M. Nesbitt, John Wilcocks, Thomas Fitzsimons; William Bingham, Isaac Hazelhurst, John Pringle, Blair McClenachan, Mordech Lewis, John Field; Peter Whitesides, John Donnaldson, George Haines, Samuel Inglis. This list is, of course, very imprecise. Other candidates include Joseph Ball, Charles Pettit, and William Turnbull.

ported the war effort and expanded their influence at the expense of conservative Quakers.[153]

Although we cannot discern exactly why these fortune builders, rather than many other aspirants, succeeded, generally it may be said that the disruptions of war conferred advantages upon them that their competitors lacked. Not the least of these advantages was close business ties with Robert Morris himself, a distinction that eleven of the sixteen fortune builders could claim.[154] In many cases, this advantage was related in turn to the fact that they already had a solid capital with which to finance wartime trade. Because they did not rely solely on commercial credit, which was often unavailable during the war, wealthy merchants could continue to seize such commercial opportunities as appeared after 1776, and not infrequently these attractive deals involved the ubiquitous Morris. Similarly, outsiders who came to Philadelphia with large shipments of goods probably had sources of supply that local traders, long dependent on ties with London and Bristol houses, could not match.

This reorientation of competitive patterns is clearly reflected in customs data for 1781 and 1782.[155] As we have seen, the confused economic conditions of those years permitted just 202 people to handle over £500 worth of goods, as compared to 522 traders in the years 1785–1787. The total value of imports in 1781 and 1782 was roughly 80 percent of the level of the mid-1780s. But despite this fact, the largest importers received *far more* goods in 1781 and 1782 than they generally did during peacetime. In the mid-1780s the top eleven firms received goods worth an average of £21,003 per year, whereas in 1781 and 1782 the top nine firms imported an average of £46,085, or over twice as much. These nine magnates received nearly half of all the goods that entered Philadelphia in 1781 and 1782, as compared with a share of about 20 percent for the top eleven importers of the mid-1780s. Significantly, many of the city's major importers—nine of the top eighteen, and seven of the top nine—were newcomers to Philadelphia. Some of these interlopers were transients who soon disappeared, but others settled in the Delaware Valley and became leading figures in the postwar business community.

The reasons for the pronounced inequality of the war years are not completely clear but seem to involve the scarcity of shipping. Before the

153. Caldwell, Nesbitt, Fitzsimons, Pringle, McClenachan, Donnaldson. Other Irish merchants who were staunch patriots included Walter Stewart, Stephen Moylan, John Mitchell. Benjamin Fuller to John Donnaldson, Nov. 17, 1784, Fuller Letterbook, 1784–1787, 47.

154. The five exceptions are Pringle, McClenachan, Field, Donnaldson, and Haines.

155. Registers of Duties Paid.

war, when cargo space was abundant, thirty or forty merchants would typically receive shipments of dry goods that came as freight on a single large ship, entering from London. The vessel itself was owned by only two or three firms. During the war, by contrast, the entire cargo of dry goods on a vessel entering from Europe was typically consigned to just one or two firms, which probably owned the vessel as well. Over 40 percent of Philadelphia's total imports in 1781 and 1782 arrived on just thirteen ships, eleven of them from Lorient. The dry goods cargoes of these vessels averaged fifty-eight thousand pounds and were usually consigned to a single firm of one to six people. Just one such cargo could exceed in value the total imports received by a major firm during three years of peace. Evidently, rich and well-connected merchants, able to operate a large brig during the war and to finance a major shipment of goods, had the field to themselves. They were not inclined to rent freight space to minor firms when they could fill their vessels with their own lucrative shipments. The bane of pre-Revolutionary dry goods importers—intense competition from dozens of minor firms operating on credit—was absent during the Revolution.

The Immigrants

It may be argued that Philadelphia's merchant community was jolted no more violently by the Revolutionary war than by the peace that followed, for in 1783 and 1784 a huge wave of European manufactures rolled into the port, twisting the careers of local merchants and sweeping dozens of European traders into the Delaware Valley. Many of these foreigners quickly drifted back to Europe, but enough of them stayed in Philadelphia to alter the character of the merchant community.

In 1783 the merchants and manufacturers of England were entering the heroic age of commercial conquest and technological innovation known as the Industrial Revolution. Having expanded their exports rapidly, if unevenly, since the middle of the eighteenth century, they enjoyed particular prosperity during the 1770s. The American boycotts of 1769–1770 and 1774–1776 had barely injured them. It was said in 1777 that the cloth producers around Manchester were so swamped with orders that they could easily have employed twenty-five thousand more people.[156] Such prosperity generated substantial profits, and the enterprising British businessmen were impatient to reestablish their commercial position in America. But the Britishers faced competition from many conti-

156. Warder to [Mr. and Mrs. Jeremiah Warder], May 21, 1777, Warder Letterbooks.

nental merchants, who were likewise eager to penetrate the markets of the robust young republic. Their desire for conquest had been sharpened by flirtations during the war, for many continental traders had sailed to America to supply the military forces there, while others had dealt with Americans on various missions in Europe.[157]

A few merchants, English as well as French, were drawn to America by its reputation for republican virtue, as epitomized by the urbane but simple Franklin captivating the French court in his beaver hat. A primary ambition of the English gentleman Samuel Vaughan in the New World was to "visit all the battlefields of the Revolution that had any connection with General George Washington."[158] Vaughan's son John, who probably met John Ross in France during the war and who later became his partner, preceded his father to America and warned him that republican simplicity was hard to find in the Quaker City, which was "Gay and extravagant rather beyond our capacity." "Americans," he was forced to conclude, "were men, not angels."[159] Several years later Brissot de Warville was sent to America by a business group to explore the possibility of speculating in American securities and, perhaps, of buying up a piece of land that could be "prepared in all circumstances for a republic, in the same manner as you prepare a house for your friends."[160]

In combination with the usual aggressiveness of Philadelphia importers, the optimism of the Europeans ignited explosive growth in Philadelphia's dry goods trade. Stephen Collins remarked in 1783 that "the arrival of Vessels & Good here for two months past is beyond Credibility," while another trader wrote to England, "the Extencive C^r. [credit] given this City on your side of the Water, is far beyond what the moast Sanguan could have expected." Observers in England agreed. One wrote in March 1784, "You will scarce Credit the Circumstance but it is Strictly Fact—that there are orders still in hand at Manchester that will not be ready until Midsummer next tho' actually given out in Oct^r. & Novr. last—such is & has been the demand for goods of that Manufacture particularly."[161]

157. On American merchants in France, see East, *Business Enterprise*, 38–39.

158. Sarah P. Stetson, "The Philadelphia Sojourn of Samuel Vaughan," *PMHB*, LXXIII (1949), 463.

159. *Ibid.*, 460–461.

160. Joseph Stancliffe Davis, *Essays in the Earlier History of American Corporations*, 2 vols., Harvard Economic Studies, XVI (Cambridge, Mass., 1917), I, 153–155.

161. Collins to Harrison and Ansley, June 17, 1783, Collins Papers, LX-A; Armat to Fisher and Bragg, May 10, 1784, Thomas Armat Letterbook, 1781–1794, and Champion and Dickason to Armat, Mar. 28, 1784, box 1, Thomas Armat Papers, in Loudoun Papers, HSP.

Precise measurements of the reality behind these excited impressions are difficult to make, for the relevant commercial figures are surprisingly incomplete. Nevertheless, it is clear that the postwar influx of goods far exceeded any pre-Revolutionary boom. John Chaloner reported that dry goods worth £1,900,000 entered the port in 1783, and one historian has put dry goods imports for 1784 at £2,899,954.[162] Shipping data and official British trade figures confirm the fact that imports in 1784 exceeded those of 1783. If these figures are correct, the total influx of dry goods in 1783 and 1784 was roughly twice as great as the largest importations for two consecutive years before the Revolution (1771 and 1772).[163] Clearly a key reason for this extraordinary surge was that non-British firms were entering the Philadelphia market in a major way. In 1783, for instance, imports from the Continent, chiefly Holland and France, were 78 percent as great as the imports from Great Britain.[164]

Dozens of European merchants were carried into Philadelphia by this rise in imports. By 1785 there were 514 merchants in the city—60 percent more than in 1774. "We have a great number of Emegerants from most parts of Europe," wrote one merchant, "& the trade on these account[s] is more precarious, & some of the oldest Merchants here are frequently disapointed in their Expectations by the unexpected Influx of Foreigners & Merchandize."[165] The great majority of these newcomers were from England, Holland, France, and Germany, but Denmark and Italy were also represented. While their precise number cannot be determined, we can identify about eighty-four immigrants, and it is probable that well over one hundred entered the city after the war. Not a few of them were men of means. Customs records show that many Europeans

162. Chaloner to Wadsworth and Carter, Apr. 3, 1784, Chaloner Letterbook, 1782–1784, 274; Gordon Carl Bjork, "Stagnation and Growth in the American Economy, 1784–1792" (Ph.D. diss., University of Washington, 1963), 97. The figure cited by Chaloner is 30% higher than the total value of "merchandize" imported from Europe and New York, listed in Registers of Duties Paid.

163. Rezin Fenton Duvall, "Philadelphia's Maritime Commerce with the British Empire, 1783–1789" (Ph.D. diss., University of Pennsylvania, 1960), 354, states that vessel entries from England in 1783 and 1784 were 60 and 90, respectively. According to British customs records, exports to America in 1783 and 1784 were £245,258 sterling and £689,491 sterling, respectively. The 1783 customs figure seems seriously in error, since it suggests a considerably lower volume of trade in this boom year than in 1764, 1765, 1766, and 1767, when trade was at a low ebb and the Delaware Valley market was much smaller. See Jacob M. Price, "New Time Series for Scotland's and Britain's Trade with the Thirteen Colonies and States, 1740 to 1791," *WMQ*, 3d Ser., XXII (1975), 324, 325; John J. McCusker, "The Current Value of English Exports, 1697 to 1800," *WMQ*, 3d Ser., XXVIII (1971), 607–628.

164. Registers of Duties Paid.

165. Armat to Fisher and Bragg, May 10, 1784, Armat Letterbook, 1781–1794.

received large quantities of goods, and two foreign firms managed to amass debts of £70,000 and £130,000 before going bankrupt.[166]

In addition to drawing Philadelphia closer to continental commercial centers, the postwar boom had the paradoxical effect of making the port's ties with England even stronger than they had been before the war. There was, in fact, a temporary interpenetration of the British and American commercial communities. Quaker merchants who moved from Philadelphia to England during the war became dry goods merchants during the 1780s and shipped off wares to their friends in Philadelphia. At the same time, new English firms entered the American trade after the war and experimented with novel marketing strategies. Instead of allowing their American correspondents to take title to all of the goods they exported, many firms shipped off large cargoes on their own account. To make sure that they were properly sold, as well as to drum up additional commission business, these firms often dispatched young partners to the New World. Furthermore, a number of English adventurers simply purchased goods on credit, took them to Philadelphia, rented a store, and sold them on their own account. The effect of all this innovation was to blur the distinction between English and American merchants. The Philadelphian Thomas Clifford, Jr., was now a Bristol dry goods merchant, while the Manchester tradesman Andrew Clow took a cargo of goods to Philadelphia and promptly went broke, then returned to England to right his affairs, but finally settled down in Philadelphia. Meanwhile, the young Philadelphian James C. Fisher joined a shipping syndicate that included several Bristol merchants, and in addition Fisher sold manufactures on commission for two British merchants who were themselves residing in America.[167]

The headlong rush of merchants, merchandise, and money into Philadelphia briefly created a frenetic speculative atmosphere in which fortunes were won and lost in a few months. Ships, for example, nearly doubled in price: two substantial vessels that were built after the war cost five thousand pounds and sixty-four hundred pounds, respectively. Stores were difficult to rent for any sum in these years, and the

166. Chaloner to Wadsworth and Church, July 3, 1784, Chaloner Letterbook, 1782–1784, 325.

167. Clifford Correspondence, VII; Papers of Andrew Clow and David Cay, in Claude W. Unger Collection, Franklin and Marshall Collection, and Gratz Collection, HSP; James C. Fisher Journal, 1783–1787, Leonard T. Beale Collection, HSP. For other evidence of this phenomenon, see Armat to Fisher and Bragg, May 10, 1784, Armat Letterbook, 1781–1794. See Collins Papers, LX-A, CVII, concerning Stephen Collins's relationship with Harrison, Ansley, and Co., and with Knox and Cowan, which had a partner in New York.

cost of town houses soared.[168] When Henry Drinker computed his net worth in 1784, he estimated the value of his fine dwelling at four thousand pounds—33 percent higher than its 1775 value—but the houses of some of his neighbors sold for as much as seventy-five hundred pounds or eight thousand pounds.[169]

Like most speculative booms, however, this one was founded on illusion, not reality. The illusion was that Americans had been unable to buy manufactures at a reasonable price for eight years and were therefore willing to snatch up almost any quantity of goods that came to market. The reality was that substantial shipments of manufactures had in fact reached Philadelphia in the later phases of the war, while additional quantities were brought in from New York at the end of the conflict. Certainly, many of the goods that entered Philadelphia in 1783 did yield substantial profits, but later consignments of goods were simply superfluous. Already by 1784 Philadelphia traders were scrambling to sell off their inventories in New York and Charleston. Payments to Europe soon became as difficult to make as profitable sales were, for the city's supply of gold and silver was shipped abroad, while the price of bills of exchange rose, by March 1786, to 7.8 percent above par.[170] Once these facts became known in Europe—once it was understood that Philadelphia was a better place to lose money than to make it—the flood of imports ceased suddenly. The city's imports from areas other than the West Indies fell by 75 percent between 1784 and 1786–1787. In the latter period one merchant remarked, "Business Can hardly be said to be dull here, unless a thing Can be said to move sloley that stand[s] stock still."[171]

Careers as well as commerce collapsed in this speculative maelstrom; Philadelphia firms went bankrupt at the rate of over one per month during the year ending in June 1785. The lengthening list of casualties was scornfully detailed by Stephen Collins in a series of letters to his son. Among the first to fall was a man named Sluyter, and he was soon followed by the reckless French firm of Basse and Soyer. "Soyer would not go to goal [gaol] without ordering up his coatch to ride" there, Collins reported, "so that he went at least in taste, & if there is any pleasure to going to goal in that way I do not begrudge him it." Next to fall were Vanuleck and Barton, who were followed by "a poor Pettyfog-

168. James C. Fisher Journal, 1783–1787, 269–272; Clifford Papers, VII, 37.

169. Henry Drinker Journal, 1776–1791, 1, 18, Drinker Papers; Chaloner to [Wadsworth and Carter], Sept. 26, 1783, Chaloner Letterbook, 1782–1784, 180.

170. Bezanson *et al.*, *Prices and Inflation*, 346.

171. Bjork, "Stagnation and Growth," 60; Collins to Pearsall and Glover, June 7, 1785, Collins Papers, LXII-A, 24.

ing Dutch Shopkeeper in Market Street" and a French merchant who "Loaded two Ships for the West Indies which he sent away & very cunningly concluding that it would make all the Difference to him whether he paid for it or not, so he took the modest Resolution to save the whole & was Journeying down the River when he was overtaken at Chester & without any Ceremony was put into the goal." Far more disquieting to Collins was the ignominious collapse of Abel James, a venerable Philadelphia Friend whose name had been synonymous with prudence and propriety for over four decades. Tormented by illness and apparently befuddled by his medication, James speculated wildly in urban real estate in 1783 and 1784, paying exalted prices for properties to which, in some cases, he did not even gain clear title. When he finally called in his creditors, his debts amounted to seventy-five thousand pounds, but he still hoped to meet his obligations in full.[172]

The parade of bankruptcies continued into 1785, and no fewer than sixty-eight traders called in their creditors between 1784 and 1790.[173] Many other merchants disappointed in trade transferred to new occupations or quietly left the city, and the merchant community shrank by 14 percent between 1785 and 1791. Particularly susceptible to failure were the immigrants and upwardly mobile traders, for their fortunes were closely tied to the flood of imports, and they generally lacked the skill and resources needed to weather the ensuing downturn. Of fifteen upwardly mobile staff officers, three went bankrupt, two fell deeply into debt to English merchants, two became auctioneers (at least one because of financial difficulties), one abandoned trade and moved west to become a land speculator, one left a small and involved estate when he died in 1785, and one left the city between 1785 and 1790.[174] Of the fifteen, just one had entered the mercantile elite by the end of the decade, while four others were modestly successful traders.[175]

Many immigrants fared no better, for they arrived in Philadelphia with a dim understanding of the state of the market, the tastes of American

172. Collins to Zachariah Collins, July 5, 12, 19, 26, 1784, Collins to James Cumming, July 12, 1784, Mar. 8, 1785, and Collins to David Knox, Mar. 8, 1785, Collins Papers, LXI, 39, 43, 44, 45, 51, 158, 161. On the bankruptcy of Abel James, see Henry Drinker to Frederick Pigou, Jr., July 3, 29, 1784, to George Bowne, Aug. 17, 1785, to Andrew Elliot, Nov. 10, 1785, Henry Drinker Letterbook, 45, 55, 185, 207.

173. See above, chap. 3.

174. These merchants are, in order, Clement Biddle, George A. Baker, and Francis Wade; John Reed and Standish Forde; John Chaloner and John Patton; Timothy Pickering; Haym Salomon; John Moyland.

175. Levi Hollingsworth had entered the merchant elite by 1790; Robert Towers and Samuel Wetherill were drug and paint merchants; Samuel Hodgdon and Gustavus Risberg were wholesalers who operated on a moderate scale.

consumers, and the creditworthiness of local businessmen. It was said in 1783, "The Europeans who arrived here in the Summer are many of them returning and are very sick of their Adventures from the great Quantities of goods brot by them unsiutable for this market. Many must have suffered very Considerably."[176] Of the twenty-two firms that are known to have failed in 1784 and 1785, and for which there is detailed information, half were foreign. A British chronicler later wrote, "Many of those adventurers immediately upon their arrival in America converted their goods into ready money at any prices, and then shipped themselves off for the Continent of Europe, or hid themselves in the boundless back countries of America under the new-assumed character of land-jobbers."[177]

But of course not all of the climbers and immigrants failed after the war, and some of those who survived became extremely prominent traders. John Vaughan, Peter LeMaigre, John Fry, Hugh Holmes, William Cramond, Michael Morgan O'Brian, and Philip Nicklin were all post-Revolutionary immigrants who cut large figures in the merchant community of the 1780s and 1790s. The correspondence of William Cramond reveals just how substantial their resources could be. Cramond was a young partner in a sprawling British firm which boasted many wealthy partners and strong backing from English bankers. Believing that "in such an infant Country new objects of speculation must frequently present themselves," the firm sent Cramond to America to find customers in the dry goods and provision trades and to speculate in land and securities. To prosecute these schemes Cramond did not employ the usual £2,000 or £3,000 of the hopeful young trader, or even the £20,000 of the substantial operator, but a line of credit of £167,000. This was a capital sum that pre-Revolutionary Philadelphia merchants had merely read about in the *Gentleman's Magazine*.[178]

The influx of such wealthy foreigners as Cramond, combined with the heightened mobility of local traders, altered the composition of Philadelphia's mercantile elite with unusual rapidity in the fourteen years after 1774. Of the elite merchants of 1791, 61 percent had not been in the city in 1774. For comparison it may be noted that only 42 percent of the elite group of 1774 had not been in Philadelphia in 1756. A prospective analysis tells the same story: 28 percent of the 1756 mercantile leaders

176. Chaloner to Wadsworth and Carter, Nov. 1, 1783, Chaloner Letterbook, 1782–1784, 197.

177. Quoted in Duvall, "Philadelphia's Maritime Commerce," 378.

178. Cramond and Phillips Papers, Gratz Collection, HSP, esp. George Phillips to William Cramond, Feb. 11, 1790, John Phillips, Jr., to William Cramond, Dec. 31, 1791.

TABLE 17. *Career Patterns of Elite Merchants in Philadelphia, 1756–1791*

	Base Year as Elite Merchant			
	1756 (N=36)	1774 (N=65)	1774 (N=65)	1791 (N=82)
Earlier / Later Occupational Status	Retrospective / Prospective Year			
	1774	1756	1791	1774
Elite merchant	28%	15%	14%	11%
Nonelite merchant	14	26	12	18
Nonmerchant in Philadelphia	19	17	28	10
Nonresident of Philadelphia	39	42	26	61

Sources: Tax lists for 1756, 1772, 1773, 1774, 1775; Francis White, *The Philadelphia Directory* (Philadelphia, 1785); Clement Biddle, ed., *The Philadelphia Directory* (Philadelphia, 1791).

were still in the elite in 1774, while only 14 percent of the 1774 elite were also in the 1791 elite (see table 17).

In addition to restructuring the mercantile elite, the convulsions of the 1780s transformed the general character of the merchant community by making it far more unstable and anonymous. There were at least 50 percent more merchants in the city after the war than before, and they came and went far more freely. Only about 50 percent of the merchants present in 1785 had been in Philadelphia three years earlier, and about 30 percent of them had left the city by 1791. Of those staying in the city, roughly 33 percent were no longer merchants. Comparable mobility rates for the prewar period were much lower: fully 74 percent of the merchants present in 1774, for example, had been in the city seven years earlier, and 69 percent of the merchants of 1756 were still in the city eleven years later. The combination of larger numbers present at a given time and higher mobility rates meant that the number of merchants who *passed through* the city grew enormously. Inspection of many tax lists covering the period 1756–1775 turned up 503 merchants who were in the city at some time before the war, while 834 merchants appeared in two city directories spanning the period 1785–1791.

Viewed as a whole, it can be said only that the experiences of Philadelphia traders during the war were extremely diverse. On the one hand, the particular political positions of traders greatly affected their business success. Such insiders as Robert Morris and his friends profited spectacularly from their favored position, strict Quakers strived simply to survive in the face of vindictive persecution, and the mass of merchants had to cope with the chaos of war without the benefit of any particular advantages. In addition, there was tremendous diversity *within* the Revolutionary career of each merchant. Almost none of the traders described in this chapter were able to pursue a stable, constant business strategy throughout the war. The British occupation of Philadelphia and New York, the rapid shifts in the relative prices of commodities, the postwar boom and ensuing depression, the selective blockade of the British fleet—all these factors relentlessly changed the business climate, compelling merchants to scramble and improvise from one year to another. It was not at all unusual for a merchant to lose his capital in one phase of the war and get it back in the next.

This pronounced diversity of experience accentuated the central structural features of the merchant community. Already large in 1774, it grew by over 50 percent in the next decade, and the turnover rate also increased rapidly in this period. The heterogeneity of the community, with the addition of French, German, and Dutch traders, similarly increased. The large fortunes of some of these newcomers, combined with the successes of the fortune builders, appreciably increased the degree of stratification in the community. While the base of the merchant community was broadened by the entry of many newcomers, the peak thrust higher and higher. An enhanced spirit of emulation and material display was one consequence of greater stratification, for the newly rich attempted to consolidate in the social sphere their recent financial gains. This trend was strengthened by the relative decline in the social and economic position of the distinctly unostentatious Quaker merchants.

Not only the structural but the behavioral characteristics of the community were reinforced by the Revolution, for the relationship between enterprise and adversity was strengthened. There can be no doubt that more merchants went bankrupt during the decade after 1775 than in any other ten-year period encompassed by this study. With the business world in a state of chaos, no merchant could be certain that he would not be the next to fail. Even certain associates of Robert Morris struggled through anxious weeks of doubting whether they would be able to meet their obligations. Clearly, the nerve-racking adversity that constantly dogged eighteenth-century merchants was particularly severe in these years. However, the merchants reacted to the rigors and dangers of the wartime economy by undertaking bold and innovative ventures.

6 The Federalist Reaction

By rupturing the economic and governmental framework of colonial Pennsylvania, the Revolution transformed the political apathy of the merchant community, turning it for the first time into an articulate interest group. Only a handful of merchants became active politicians, but these leaders pursued goals supported by the trading body as a whole. At the state level, they battled the radical Presbyterian faction that had seized power in 1776, and in national affairs they attempted to expand the power of the central government, particularly its power to tax. Toughened and tutored by a decade of bitter controversy and strategically situated in the capital of the nation, the merchants were well positioned to spearhead the drive for a Federal Constitution. Indeed, it is doubtful whether any other local occupational group in the nation did more to advance the Federalist cause.

This activism was a dramatic departure from the pre-Revolutionary political behavior of the merchants. During the colonial period, it will be recalled, Philadelphia traders tended to leave politics to wealthy gentlemen and professionals who had higher social status, better education, and more free time to devote to public life. Moreover, in the period 1750–1770 the merchant group was divided almost evenly between Anglican supporters of the proprietor and Quaker adherents to the assembly faction. Lacking unity or effective leadership, the merchants were unable to control the flow of events between 1764 and 1776, and they were, in any case, ambivalent about the Revolutionary movement. The merchants' opposition to British encroachments on American liberties, though sincere enough, was tempered by compelling countervailing considerations, including their transatlantic connections and attachment to the empire, their deep suspicion of Presbyterian influence on the Revolutionary movement, and the benefits they were deriving from the general economic prosperity of the prewar period. For all these reasons, the merchants had ultimately been more obstructionist than supportive of the Revolution; they were too pragmatic, materialistic, and elitist to lead the drive toward Independence. But these very qualities made them particularly well suited to shape events after 1776. Once Independence was an established fact, Americans were suddenly confronted with the problem of how to transform the nation from a Revolutionary idea into a functioning state. There was much work to be done. The practical shortcomings of the Confederation rapidly became clear, and merchants, as energetic managers well versed in commerce and finance, took the lead in building a more efficient governmental framework.

This process went forward in two distinct stages. Between 1781 and 1784 a small but powerful band of Nationalists in Congress and the army, led by Robert Morris, tried to centralize fiscal and administrative activities. Despite some success, the rationale for their unpopular initiatives was undercut by the return of peace. But as the nation drifted and floundered in the 1780s, a far wider segment of the Philadelphia commercial community became mobilized behind the cause of constitutional reform. Stung by commercial depression and alarmed by the attack on the Bank of North America and the return of paper money, the merchants were disgusted by the inability of Congress to regulate commerce, pay its foreign debts, and maintain order. No doubt they exaggerated the objective severity of these problems. But after their harrowing wartime experience of monetary collapse and popular tyranny, Philadelphia traders were not inclined to take chances.

The Pennsylvania Revolution

Paradoxically enough, the very moderation of Pennsylvania, so evident in the decade before 1776, gave rise to an extremely radical state government once the separation from England was finally effected.[1] Stubbornly refusing to declare Independence in June 1776, the colony's assembly became politically irrelevant and was superseded by the network of Revolutionary committees that had emerged in Philadelphia to coordinate the war effort and to discipline tories. The leaders of this shadow government were primarily artisans, shopkeepers, tradesmen, and middle-class professionals who wished to eradicate the aristocratic character of the provincial government by drafting a truly democratic constitution for the new state. Pennsylvania's constitution of 1776 permitted all taxpayers to vote, and legislative authority was concentrated in a unicameral legislature that was elected annually. The executive func-

1. The course of Pennsylvania politics between 1775 and 1787 may be followed in Richard Alan Ryerson, *The Revolution Is Now Begun: The Radical Committees of Philadelphia, 1765–1776* (Philadelphia, 1978); Robert L. Brunhouse, *The Counter-Revolution in Pennsylvania, 1776–1790* (Harrisburg, Pa., 1942); and Owen Stephen Ireland, "The Ratification of the Federal Constitution in Pennsylvania" (Ph.D. diss., University of Pittsburgh, 1966).

tion was lodged in the Supreme Executive Council, composed of one popularly elected representative from each county. Together with the assembly, this council elected a president, who was largely a figurehead. Appointed by the council for only a seven-year term, and dependent on the assembly for its salary, the Supreme Court was no more capable of independent action than the executive, particularly since judicial salaries were set by the assembly. And lest the assembly itself somehow manage to thwart the will of the people, the constitution ingeniously provided for the election, every seven years, of a Council of Censors to review recent legislation and to ensure that it was consistent with the spirit of the constitution.

Although largely the work of coffeehouse radicals from Philadelphia, the Pennsylvania constitution was nurtured and protected primarily by Scotch-Irish Presbyterians from the western counties, who formed the core of the Constitutionalist party. Westerners had been excluded from politics in provincial days, when the frontier counties were underrepresented in the assembly, but after 1776 they gained political leverage for two reasons. The new state constitution, by allotting an equal number of seats to each county until 1779, gave the sparsely settled western counties disproportionate power in the assembly. Second, even in the eastern counties the Constitutionalists wielded great strength as a result of the test acts they introduced requiring all citizens to swear their allegiance to the independent state of Pennsylvania before they could vote. Until its repeal in 1787, this requirement effectively disenfranchised Quakers, German Pietists, and many other loyalists, who constituted a large bloc of the electorate that strongly disapproved of the Constitutionalists' regime.[2]

Historians have disagreed about whether the Constitutionalists are best described as an economic, a geographical, or a religious faction, but whatever the case, there can be no doubt that the three variables were highly correlated. Constitutionalists tended to be Scotch-Irish Presbyterians; they were typically of moderate economic status; and they generally lived in the northern and western portion of the state, beyond a line, as Jackson Turner Main observed, that ran from Hagerstown in western Maryland, to Harrisburg on the Susquehanna, to Easton on the upper Delaware.[3] Religion was, however, an important independent variable,

2. Ireland, "Ratification," 198, estimates that 25%–75% of the electorate were disenfranchised by the tests.

3. Jackson Turner Main, *The Anti-Federalists: Critics of the Constitution, 1781–1788* (Chapel Hill, N.C., 1961), 41. See also the electoral map concerning the vote for the Pennsylvania Ratifying Convention of 1787 in Lester J. Cappon *et al.*, eds., *Atlas of Early American History: The Revolutionary Era, 1760–1790* (Princeton, N.J., 1976), 63.

and there was a strong tendency for eastern Presbyterians to support the Constitutionalists. This support lent badly needed depth to the party's leadership, for a handful of wealthy eastern Presbyterians, including Thomas McKean, Charles Pettit, Joseph Reed, John Bayard, and William Moore, backed the radical cause with a genteel forcefulness that few backcountry farmers could muster.[4]

Initially the Constitutionalists faced little organized opposition. State leaders were temporarily absorbed by the threatened invasion of the British army in the fall of 1776 and by their successful occupation of Philadelphia a year later. However, in March 1779 eighty-two people met in Philadelphia to form the Republican Society, whose stated purpose was to secure repeal of the new constitution, on the grounds that its "general tendency and operation will be to join the qualities of the different extremes of bad government. It will produce general weakness, inactivity and confusion; intermixed with sudden and violent fits of despotism, injustice and cruelty." Although it claimed to represent no particular interest or faction, the Republican Society was dominated by conservative Anglican whigs from the eastern counties.[5] More important for our purposes, at least ten of the eighty-two were staff officers, and thirty-five were merchants.

On a superficial view, the Republican Society may appear to be a revival of the aristocratic elite that had lost power in the upheaval of 1776. In fact, however, the onset of Independence had shattered colonial Pennsylvania's conservative political elite, thereby magnifying the role of merchants in public life. Most obviously, the powerful Quaker faction, led by such gentlemen as Joseph Galloway, Benjamin Franklin, Israel Pemberton, William Logan, and Isaac Norris, was destroyed by Independence. Although few wealthy Quakers were permanently expelled from the colony, they were discredited by their neutrality and were no longer a major factor in politics. As a result, the conservative side of the political spectrum was in the hands of Anglicans, and these Anglican conservatives were, for the first time, primarily merchants.

Thanks to the careful analysis of Philadelphia's social elite by Stephen Brobeck, we can trace precisely the ascent of the Anglican merchants to the pinnacle of political and social life. Brobeck has found that of the forty-six people who composed the pre-Revolutionary Anglican elite in Philadelphia, eleven formed a particularly prominent and cohesive core group, which was dominated by the Penn family and the family of Chief

4. Roland Milton Baumann, "The Democratic-Republicans of Philadelphia: The Origins, 1776–1797" (Ph.D. diss., Pennsylvania State University, 1970), 14–65, is a well-informed discussion of the Philadelphia Constitutionalists.

5. *Pennsylvania Gazette* (Philadelphia), Mar. 24, 1779.

Justice William Allen. Nine of the eleven elite leaders in this prewar period were officeholders or professionals, and only two were active merchants. Holding positions in the provincial Council, the Philadelphia City Corporation, and the proprietary government, these were the well-connected gentlemen who had traditionally dominated political affairs in the colony. The Revolution did not treat such men kindly. The Penns and Allens, along with such allied families as the Chews, Hamiltons, and Shippens, generally were loyalist. Some family members were attainted for treason, others had property confiscated or lost lucrative proprietary offices, and still others fled Philadelphia to live in Europe or in other parts of America.[6]

Coinciding with the voluntary withdrawal of Quaker grandees from politics, the destruction of the proprietary leadership created a power vacuum in Pennsylvania's upper class at precisely the time when agrarian radicalism was on the rise. Into this vacuum stepped wealthy Philadelphia businessmen who had been relatively inferior members of the Anglican elite on the eve of the Revolution: Robert Morris, Thomas Willing, Thomas Fitzsimons, J. M. Nesbitt, John Nixon, George Clymer, Samuel Meredith, Henry Hill, and the brilliant lawyer James Wilson, who was a newcomer to the Anglican elite.[7] Wilson was a reckless land speculator who eventually went to debtors' prison, and his eight colleagues were active merchants who were still building their fortune. These people were the workhorses of the Republican faction. They wrote pamphlets, ran for office, addressed caucuses, circulated petitions, and plotted strategy. In addition to membership in the Republican Society, nearly all of them were leaders of the Bank of North America founded in 1781, and four of them were delegates to the Constitutional Convention in 1787.

The fissure between the Constitutionalists and Republicans was deepened by the strains and stress of controversy—bitter, even vicious, political warfare that deeply divided the state until 1788.[8] At the center of the

6. Steven James Brobeck, "Changes in the Composition and Structure of Philadelphia Elite Groups, 1756–1790" (Ph.D. diss., University of Pennsylvania, 1972), 145–166, 194–242. For the membership of the non-Quaker elite group in 1775 and 1789, see 325–326, 353–354.

7. Brobeck, "Philadelphia Elite Groups," 220–226, contains a fine discussion of the social climbing of these people during the Revolution. Ireland, "Ratification," 242, analyzes the interrelationships within the Republican Society core group. See also Jerry Grundfest, "George Clymer, Philadelphia Revolutionary, 1739–1813" (Ph.D. diss., Columbia University, 1973), 227–324, which describes the close ties between Clymer, Hill, and Meredith, who were business partners.

8. See Ireland, "Ratification," 66–117. The Republicans discussed here, who constituted the nationalistic, conservative faction in Pennsylvania state politics, are not to be confused with the Jeffersonian Republicans who emerged as a liberal faction in national politics during the 1790s.

struggle was the state constitution itself. In 1779 and again in 1783 Republicans had opportunities to rewrite the document, but on both occasions the Constitutionalists turned back the threat. Not until 1790 did Pennsylvania receive a more moderate frame of government. The Republicans also tried to moderate or eliminate the test acts requiring an oath of allegiance to the independent state of Pennsylvania. Hatred of tories, particularly wealthy Quaker and Anglican tories, was too profound to permit such moderation while the war was in progress, and the test acts themselves continued to be a source of division until 1787. A third controversy that laid bare the religious dimension in political strife was an assault by Presbyterian politicians on a stronghold of unregenerate Anglican loyalism, the College of Philadelphia. Charging that the college discriminated against Presbyterians and had not foresworn allegiance to the king of England, the Pennsylvania Assembly in 1779 converted it into a Presbyterian institution with an entirely new board of trustees and a new name, the University of Pennsylvania.

Because the majority of Philadelphia's merchants were conservative Anglicans and whigs, they naturally supported the Republican faction in its endless fight with the political heirs of Oliver Cromwell. But there was another issue that bound traders together even more strongly, because it struck at the heart of their livelihood: the problem of inflation and price controls. As prices rose from month to month during the war, social antagonism increased proportionally. By 1779, when prices were rising at a compound rate of 17 percent a month, the issue had spilled out of the statehouse and into the streets. Perplexed by the paradox of unaffordable provisions in a region of agricultural abundance, the little people of Pennsylvania, some of whom were mobilized in well-organized militia units, blamed inflation on wealthy tories who were allegedly manipulating commodity markets and refusing to accept Continental money.

Tensions rose sharply through the first nine months of 1779.[9] Early in the year the flour merchant Levi Hollingsworth was seized and briefly held by a crowd, and an elaborate, acrimonious investigation was launched when a vessel loaded with grain entered the port, consigned to Robert Morris. Because he did not immediately sell the flour, which was

9. On civil unrest in Philadelphia in 1779, see Brunhouse, *Counter-Revolution*, 60–75; Hubertis Cummings, "Robert Morris and the Episode of the Polacre 'Victorious,'" *Pennsylvania Magazine of History and Biography*, LXX (1946), 239–257; John K. Alexander, "The Fort Wilson Incident of 1779: A Case Study of the Revolutionary Crowd," *William and Mary Quarterly*, 3d Ser., XXXI (1974), 589–612; Anne Bezanson, "Inflation and Controls, Pennsylvania, 1774–1779," *Journal of Economic History*, VIII (1948), supplement, 1–20.

imported for the use of the French army, Morris was suspected of "forestalling" in order to raise prices. The month of May brought a mass meeting in Philadelphia which created two committees whose mission it was to curb inflation by rolling back prices to their level of January 1, 1779. In July a group of one hundred militiamen, armed with clubs, prevented the Republican John Cadwalader from delivering a speech against price controls. By this time it appeared to some that public order was nearly at an end, "for every man who takes a club in his hand to town meetings (which, by-the-by, have been very frequent of late) undertakes to be governor."[10] But the wave of disorder had not yet peaked. On October 4, handbills appeared in the streets of the city urging militiamen to "fall on a plan, to drive from the city, all disaffected persons, and those who supported them."[11] After meeting at Burn's Tavern, soldiers rounded up four reputed tories and then marched on the large town house of James Wilson, in which twenty to forty Republicans were barricaded. Insults were exchanged, shots were fired, the militiamen stormed the house, and five or six soldiers were killed. Under the twin pressures of hyperinflation and politicization Philadelphia's social equilibrium finally seemed to have shattered. "We are at this moment on a precipice," exclaimed one Continental congressman, "and what I have long dreaded and often intimated to my friends, seems to be breaking forth—a convulsion among the people."[12]

Thanks to the effective guidance of Constitutionalist leaders, the city pulled back from this precipice, but the related problems of hyperinflation and public tumult were not quickly forgotten by Philadelphia traders. As we have seen, the merchants were tormented by inflation throughout the war. They lost thousands of pounds in book debts that were paid off in depreciated currency, and their commercial operations were deranged by violent fluctuations in the price level. Yet, ironically, the merchants themselves were blamed for the currency collapse; and in addition to all of the inevitable military barriers to wartime trade, they had to grapple with mobs, regulations, committees, investigations, and price-fixing. In a memorandum to the Philadelphia Price Committee, eighty leading merchants defended the free market with reckless candor, even going so far as to liken engrossers (who purchased commodities in expectation of a price rise) to a wise and provident ship captain who puts his crew on short rations before provisions become truly scarce. As for the solution to inflation, the merchants insisted that it could not be

10. Quoted in Brunhouse, *Counter-Revolution*, 71.

11. Quoted in Alexander, "Fort Wilson Incident," *WMQ*, 3d Ser., XXXI (1974), 601.

12. Quoted *ibid.*, 589.

ended simply by making it illegal. "If you wish to remove an effect you must begin by removing the causes, and not hope to wither the causes by lopping off the consequences." The cause of inflation, the merchants insisted, was not the perfidy of engrossers and monopolizers, but the "quantity of money . . . the winds, the seasons, the ravages of war, the calls for militia, for carters, for batteau men, horses and a thousand other contingencies," as well as the high prices of vessels and of maritime insurance.[13] Here was an issue that nearly every merchant—Quaker or Anglican, rich or middling, tory or whig—could understand, and it was an issue that continued to unite the trading body until 1788. Currency, the merchants knew, was the "grand instrument of commerce"; without it, trade itself could not go on.[14] The monetary chaos of the war years and the searing experience with mob rule in 1779 taught them to take nothing for granted in protecting the integrity of the currency.

The Counterrevolution in Congress

The disorders that rocked Philadelphia in 1779 were part of a larger national crisis that nearly paralyzed the Revolutionary effort. Although Congress stopped issuing paper money in the fall of 1779, it was too late to stave off the total collapse of the Continental dollar, which in turn destroyed the system of staff departments managed by Jeremiah Wadsworth and Nathanael Greene. Henceforth, the army would have to live off clumsy and uncertain requisitions from the states or simply take what it needed from local farmers. The final collapse of the logistical system coincided with the most severe winter on record. Washington's troops were pushed toward starvation and mutiny as they huddled in the deep snow near Morristown, New Jersey. The spring of 1780 brought fresh disasters. After capturing Charleston in May, the British army sliced northward into North Carolina and, before the American victory at Kings Mountain in October, seemed to be gaining firm control of the entire lower South. The treason of Benedict Arnold in 1780 and the mutiny of the Pennsylvania line in 1781 further battered American morale.

This confluence of crises discredited the makeshift attempt by Congress to wage war with a profusion of paper money and the committee system. Fresh methods and new leadership were needed, and both were supplied by businessmen from the middle states, including several mem-

13. *Pennsylvania Packet or the General Advertiser* (Philadelphia), Sept. 10, 1779.
14. *Pennsylvania Gazette*, Mar. 2, 1785.

bers of Pennsylvania's Republican faction. In the spring of 1780 Philadelphia's merchants lent assistance to the Continental army by forming the Bank of Pennsylvania, which was not a bank at all, but, rather, a collective loan by private citizens to a nearly bankrupt nation. The bank's managers scoured Pennsylvania for flour and made some timely deliveries to the destitute army.[15] In the spring of 1781 the involvement of Philadelphia's traders in the rescue of the Independence movement proceeded a step further as Robert Morris was appointed superintendent of finance and vested with broad powers to reform the nation's fiscal and administrative affairs. Efficient and elitist, Morris gathered around himself a group of like-minded supporters who intended to curb democratic localism by strengthening the hand of Congress.[16] Such men as Jeremiah Wadsworth, Timothy Pickering, Silas Deane, and Morris himself discovered the need for centralization while serving as suppliers to the army; others—James Madison, Gouverneur Morris, James Wilson, Alexander Hamilton, and George Washington among them—had done so while serving in Congress or the army. These Nationalists, as they are called by historians, were supported by many congressmen from the South, where Independence hung by a thread, but the core of the faction's support came from the middle states.[17] Although some of them were men of distinguished social background, these Nationalists tended to be a materialistic, hard-driving, upwardly mobile lot, not averse to fusing public and private affairs in order to enhance their estates. The spirit of 1776 was not what drove them. Centralized power disturbed them far less than the licentiousness of the people and the shortsighted localism of state legislatures. These acquisitive men of affairs hoped that a vigorous government and an enterprising citizenry would turn the United States into a state of "power, consequence, and grandeur."[18]

It was no coincidence that the Nationalists drew their primary support from the middle states—precisely the area that had approached Independence with the greatest caution. Both phenomena—fear of the break with England and support for a stronger Revolutionary government—were inspired by the intrinsic conservatism of the region's leaders. Angli-

15. On this bank, see Lawrence Lewis, Jr., *A History of the Bank of North America: The First Bank Chartered in the United States* (Philadelphia, 1882), 17–23.

16. E. James Ferguson, *The Power of the Purse: A History of American Public Finance, 1776–1790* (Chapel Hill, N.C., 1961), 109–178. For an opposing view, see Jack N. Rakove, *The Beginnings of National Politics: An Interpretive History of the Continental Congress* (New York, 1979), 297–330.

17. H. James Henderson, *Party Politics in the Continental Congress* (New York, 1974), 281–317, analyzes state alignments in Congress.

18. Ferguson, *Power of the Purse*, 120.

can businessmen and gentlemen from Pennsylvania and New York were far less suspicious of the centralized power and unbridled materialism embodied in the Nationalist program than were most Virginia planters and New England congregationalists. Indeed, many whigs viewed with alarm the spreading power of the Colossus from Philadelphia, the Great Man who embodied at once the most dangerous qualities of a prime minister, a financial manipulator, and a merchant prince. But there was a war to be won, and perhaps Morris could succeed where the radicals had nearly failed. The result was a fine symmetry in the regional dynamics of the American Revolution. Men of action interceded to complete what the visionaries had started. But the Nationalists' task was completed not in 1783, but in 1788, when the problems associated with peace, as well as those stemming from war, had been solved.

Expertly described by E. James Ferguson in *The Power of the Purse*, the specific elements of the Nationalists' program between 1781 and 1783 need only a brief description here.[19] Using Great Britain as a model, Morris attempted to strengthen the Federal government by restoring its credit and uniting its interests with those of the propertied classes. He shored up the public credit with his private wealth and created the Bank of North America, which, though controlled by private investors, provided financial assistance to the government. Morris also attempted to consolidate and enlarge the federal debt and consistently opposed the efforts of certain state legislatures—including Pennsylvania's—to assume responsibility for portions of the nation's financial obligations. So long as the central government had debts, it had a reason to tax, and the centerpiece of Morris's program was a 5 percent customs duty on imports, which he hoped would be only the first plank in a solid fiscal foundation for the government. In the future he intended to add taxes on polls, property, and commodities. By paying the interest on the Federal debt, these revenues would not only secure the loyalty of bondholders to the national government but would also transfer capital to moneyed men who would use it to build up the economy. In the realm of administrative reform Morris achieved major economies by abolishing many superfluous departments and employing private contractors to supply the army.

In the three years that he was in office, Morris achieved extraordinary success in rationalizing the operations of the Revolutionary government. Indeed, he was too successful: after the reduction of the British threat in the Battle of Yorktown, the impulse to strengthen the central government subsided. Morris did his best to keep the pressure on Congress by pursu-

19. *Ibid.*, 125–145.

ing fiscal policies that made both the Federal bondholders and the Continental soldiers dependent on Federal revenues. But the basis of the Nationalists' support was too narrow, both geographically and ideologically, for them to prevail in peacetime. Even the impost, which had wide backing in Congress, was never adopted by all thirteen states. By January 1784 an opponent of the Nationalists could gloat, "Their schemes are now entirely defeated; their web is broken, which they have with so much art and industry been for several years spinning."[20]

The Commercial Context of Constitutional Reform

The eclipse of the Nationalist drive was mirrored by events in Pennsylvania, where the Constitutionalists seized control of the assembly in 1784 and held it for two years. Despite this setback, Philadelphia's trading community remained politically powerful, because the Republican faction continued to be led by an energetic band of traders—Robert Morris, Thomas Mifflin, George Clymer, John Nixon, J. M. Nesbitt, Thomas Willing, Samuel Meredith, and Thomas Fitzsimons. The power of these Republican merchants was enhanced by their control of the Bank of North America, an institution whose influence extended well beyond finance. In 1784, nevertheless, this group was still a clique; dozens of important merchants who had been neutral or loyalist during the war remained politically inert. During the next four years, however, the situation changed as a complex of pressing issues—paper money, the survival of the Bank of North America, trade regulation, and the debility of the Continental Congress—attracted many new traders to the Republican fold. By 1787 the merchant community was broadly mobilized in favor of the Federal Constitution and was able to make a major contribution toward ratification.

The political outlook of merchants was shaped by business conditions during the 1780s, a subject that has provoked sharp historical debate. Many historians have claimed that there was a serious depression during the 1780s, but others have insisted that the period was prosperous. Merrill Jensen argued: "The period was one of extraordinary economic growth. Merchants owned more ships at the end of the 1780s than they had at the beginning of the Revolution, and they carried a greater share of American produce. By 1790 the export of agricultural produce was

20. *Ibid.*, 175.

double what it had been before the war."[21] Gordon Wood concurs, writing: "On the surface at least the American states appeared stable and prosperous. . . . Despite a temporary depression in the middle eighties the commercial outlook was not bleak. As historians have emphasized, the period was marked by extraordinary economic growth."[22] On the basis of customs data that are not displayed, Forrest McDonald concluded: "The fall exporting season of 1787 broke all previous records for Philadelphia shipping. Thus in the year the Constitution was formulated and at the moment the Pennsylvania ratifying convention was sitting, commercial prosperity in the state was near an all-time peak."[23]

Any attempt to assess these claims must distinguish two separate problems: the character of the business cycle between 1783 and 1790, and the larger economic context in which that cycle occurred. The contours of the business cycle itself are fairly well documented (five of the essential statistical series are displayed in figs. 6–10). As described in the previous chapter, a huge quantity of dry goods, amounting to twice the peak import levels of the colonial period, entered Philadelphia from Europe in 1783 and 1784. Just as happened in 1760, the importers overshot the market by a wide margin; there simply was not enough real buying power in the economy to pay for all these goods. Consequently, they piled up throughout the distribution system, purchased but unpaid for, in the warehouses of London exporters and Philadelphia importers, in the shops of rural retailers, in the houses of individual consumers who had purchased on credit. These delinquent purchasers simply could not secure the commodities, specie, or bills of exchange needed to pay for the goods they had purchased.

The inevitable result of this miscalculation, as we have seen, was a rash of bankruptcies in 1785 and 1786. We have direct evidence on the failure of 68 firms during the eighties, and many others undoubtedly went out of business.[24] This violent shakeout is also documented in the city directories for 1785 and 1791, which show a reduction in the number of firms from 514 to 440. Many of these failed firms were extremely marginal operators, and a disproportionate number were recent arrivals from Europe who were particularly prone to failure because of their ignorance of the American market. But the dry goods bubble

21. Merrill Jensen, *The New Nation: A History of the United States during the Confederation, 1781–1789* (New York, 1950), 423–424.

22. Gordon S. Wood, *The Creation of the American Republic, 1776–1787* (Chapel Hill, N.C., 1969), 394.

23. Forrest McDonald, *We the People: The Economic Origins of the Constitution* (Chicago, 1958), 167–168.

24. See chaps. 3, 5.

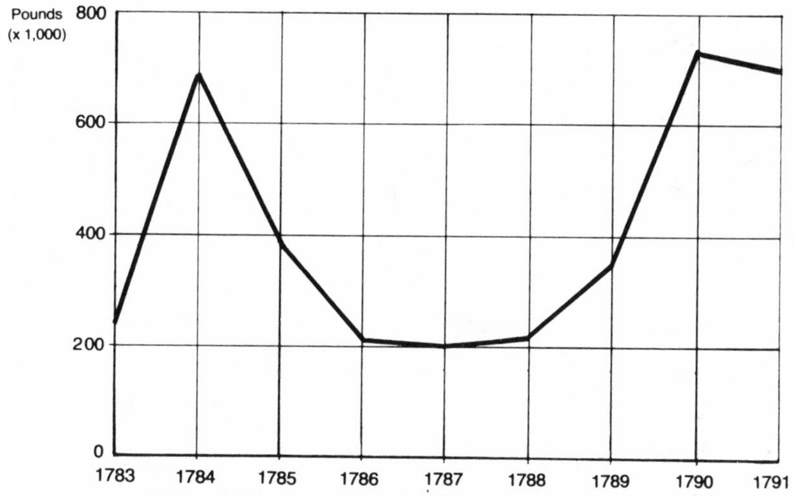

FIGURE 6. Imports from England, Scotland, and Wales into Pennsylvania, 1783–1791. Official sterling values. *Data from Jacob M. Price, "New Time Series for Scotland's and Britain's Trade with the Thirteen Colonies and States, 1740 to 1791,"* William and Mary Quarterly, *3d Ser., XXXII (1975), 325*

of 1784 also leveled some of the great mercantile names in the city, including Abel James, George Meade, and Clement Biddle. Chastened by the financial carnage, dry goods importers nursed their wounds and attempted to call in their debts between 1785 and 1789, while paying their own debts in Europe. These efforts were hampered by the high rate of exchange: with so many traders attempting to buy bills at the same time and with the supply of bills restricted by the modest level of exports during the eighties, the exchange rate averaged 5 percent above par between 1784 and 1789 (fig. 7).

The collapse of the dry goods trade was accompanied by a contraction of credit during the 1780s and a consequent reduction of activity in other economic sectors. The price level of fifteen commodities declined from 129 in 1784 to 90 in 1788 and 92 in 1789, before shooting up to 110 in 1790 (fig. 8). The value of exports dropped as well, from $3,724,527 in 1784 to only $2,058,601 in 1786 (fig. 9). In these years exports to the West Indies were stable but not particularly high, while markets for foodstuffs in Europe were quiescent.[25] Stagnation in the provision trades in turn decimated a major subsidiary activity in the city,

25. Gordon Carl Bjork, "Stagnation and Growth in the American Economy, 1784–1792" (Ph.D. diss., University of Washington, 1963), 60.

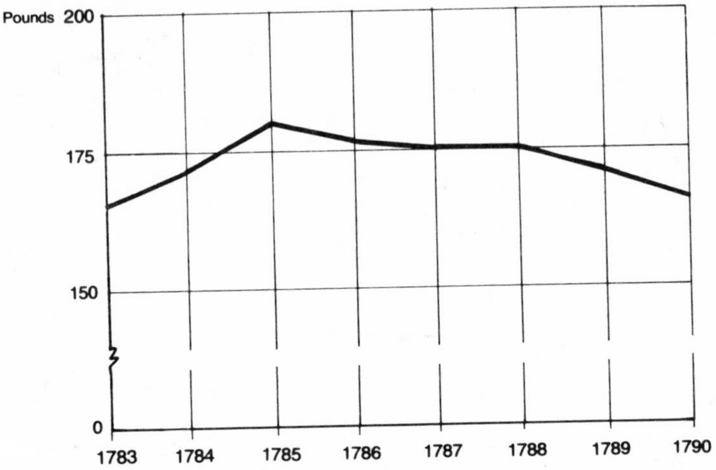

FIGURE 7. Sterling Exchange Rate in Pennsylvania, 1783–1790. Pounds, Pennsylvania currency, needed to purchase one-hundred-pound-sterling bill of exchange (June of each year). *Data from Anne Bezanson* et al., Prices and Inflation during the American Revolution: Pennsylvania, 1770–1790, *Industrial Research Department, Wharton School of Finance and Commerce, University of Pennsylvania, Research Studies, XXXV (Philadelphia, 1951), 346*

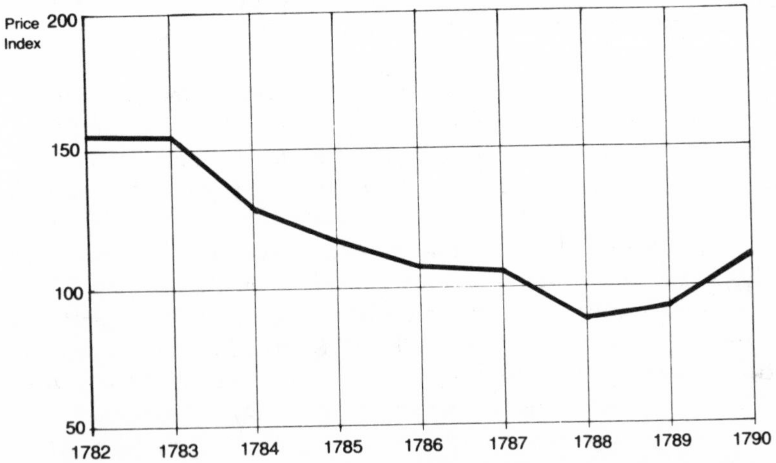

FIGURE 8. Commodity Price Levels in Philadelphia, 1782–1790. Weighted averages of fifteen commodities (January of each year). *Data from Anne Bezanson* et al., Prices and Inflation during the American Revolution: Pennsylvania, 1770–1790, *Industrial Research Department, Wharton School of Finance and Commerce, University of Pennsylvania, Research Studies, XXXV (Philadelphia, 1951), 344*

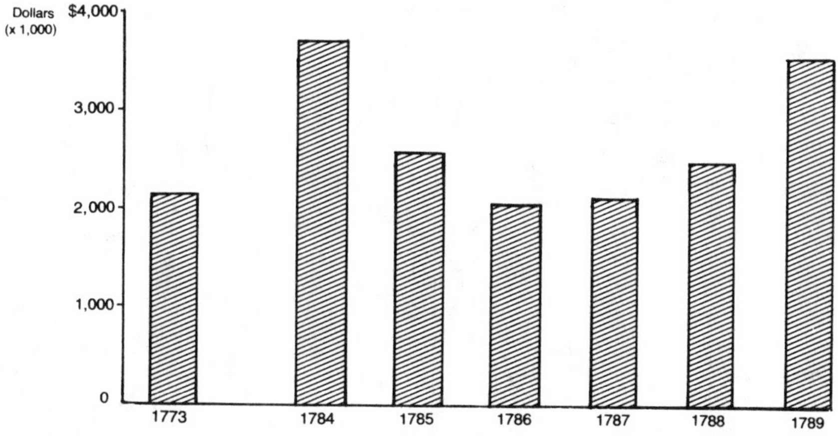

FIGURE 9. Phildelphia Exports, 1773, 1784–1789. *Data from Gordon Carl Bjork, "Stagnation and Growth in the American Economy, 1784–1792" (Ph.D. diss., University of Washington, 1963), 54, 55*

shipbuilding (fig. 10). During the inflationary boom of 1783 and 1784, an annual average of forty-two vessels, with a mean tonnage of 4,890 tons, slid off the stocks and into the Delaware. But in 1786 only thirteen ships, with a total tonnage of 905 tons, were produced—the lowest level since 1745.[26]

Although the worst of the depression may have been over by 1787, a clear rebound did not occur until 1789 or 1790. In 1788 the price level was still low, the exchange rate was well above par, and both total exports and dry goods imports were weak. Exports picked up decisively in 1789, as shipping merchants rushed to feed the starving peasants of Europe, and by 1790 the business outlook had changed dramatically. Thanks to healthy demand for foodstuffs in Europe and the West Indies, the exchange rate declined in 1790, the price level moved up sharply, and imports from Great Britain climbed to an all-time high. By this time dry goods importers had regained their financial liquidity and worked off their old inventories, while the ample exports to Europe increased the income of farmers and raised the supply of foreign exchange. These developments encouraged Philadelphia's merchants to forget the havoc of 1784 and place large orders in London and Liverpool. In short, after the boom of 1783 and 1784 and the depression of 1785–1788, 1789 was a year of transition, and 1790 and 1791 were years of great prosperity.

26. Charles Lyon Chandler, *Early Shipbuilding in Pennsylvania, 1683–1812* (Philadelphia, 1932), 29; Simeon J. Crowther, "The Shipbuilding Output of the Delaware Valley, 1722–1776," American Philosophical Society, *Proceedings*, CXVII (1973), 93.

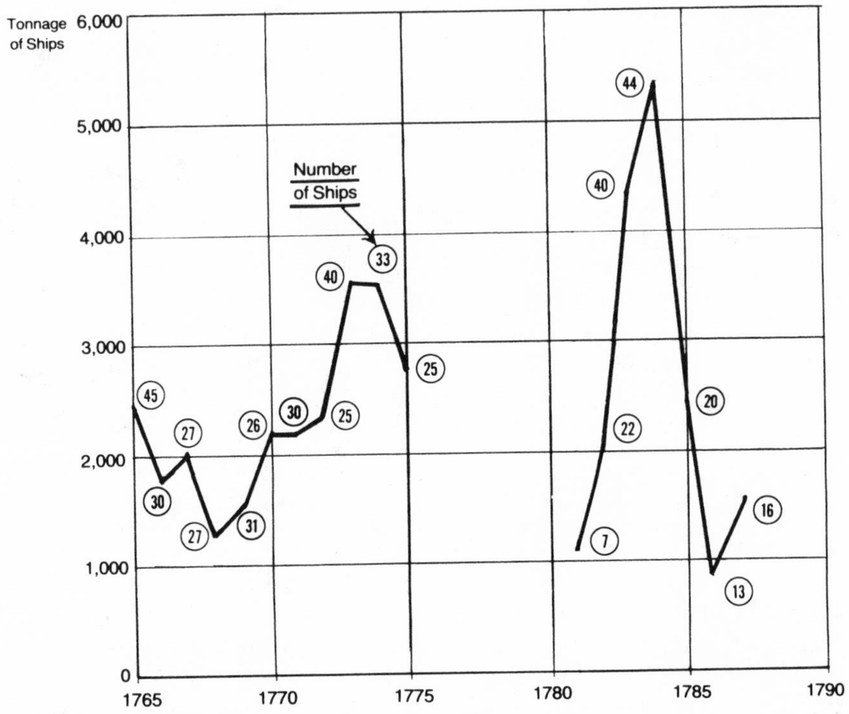

FIGURE 10. Ships Constructed in Philadelphia, 1765–1775, 1781–1787. Number of ships constructed and registered tonnage. *Data from Simeon J. Crowther, "The Shipbuilding Output of the Delaware Valley, 1722–1776," American Philosophical Society,* Proceedings, *CXVII (1973), 93; and Charles Lyon Chandler,* Early Shipbuilding in Pennsylvania, 1683–1812 *(Philadelphia, 1932), 29*

In essence, the depression of the 1780s resembled that of the 1760s: merchants imported too many dry goods on credit, many of them went broke, and a widespread contraction of economic activity followed. But the depression of the eighties was considerably more distressing for several reasons. Whereas the collapse of the dry goods trade in 1760 had been cushioned by continued prosperity in the provision trade between 1760 and 1763, in the mid-eighties both the dry goods and shipping trades were depressed. Moreover, the contraction of the sixties followed years of great prosperity during the Seven Years' War, whereas merchants had to endure the downturn of 1784–1788 after living through eight years of economic chaos during the Revolution. By 1788, commercial stagnation seemed to have replaced the commercial expansion of colonial days. The value of Philadelphia exports in 1787 was only 20 percent higher than in 1773, while the merchant community had grown by about 50 percent and Pennsylvania's population had risen by about 40 percent. A merchant in 1787 could look back on only one or two good years in the preceding decade, as against six or seven years of economic confusion. The basis of the economy had no less promise in 1787 than it had in 1760 or 1775: Pennsylvania was needed as a primary source of food for the slaves, peasants, and workers of the Atlantic world. But for over a decade the shock of war and the contingencies of the business cycle had curtailed the merchants' ability to serve these markets. Only when famine stalked Europe in 1789 did foodstuff exports finally explode, but it must be emphasized that there was no gradual and steady growth in the economy from 1783 to 1789. To use export data for the latter year to demonstrate prosperity during the mid-eighties is simply untenable. Furthermore, one reason for the boom of the 1790s, widely recognized at the time, was that the adoption of the Constitution and the introduction of Hamilton's financial program markedly increased the confidence of businessmen—both foreign and domestic—in the American economy.

The Shaping of a Federalist Consensus

Thus there can be little doubt that the merchants approached the political issues of the 1780s from a position of extreme financial weakness. Their economic difficulties were not directly caused by the debility of national government under the Articles of Confederation, but the merchants had logical reasons for fearing that government policies or government weakness would seriously *compound* their financial problems instead of alleviating them. The chief danger was inflation. Like most market operators, the merchants had short memories; they tended to overlook the success of paper money during the colonial period and to focus instead on the horrors of inflation during the Revolution. And the merchants knew that inflation would be particularly devastating at this stage in the business cycle because they were owed large sums by shopkeepers and artisans, to whom they had sold dry goods on credit in 1783 and 1784. If Pennsylvania issued large amounts of paper money, these debts would be paid off just as they had been during the Revolution—with depreciated paper dollars. In sum, the business cycle, the memory of economic problems during the Revolution, and the leading policy issues of the day meshed precisely in the 1780s to politicize the merchants. Far more than in the 1760s or 1770s, political issues over which the merchants had some control struck at the heart of their business activities.

The paper money issue in Pennsylvania was inextricably bound up with the Bank of North America (whose early history is examined in more detail in the next chapter). Although founded to strengthen the national government, the bank was owned by private shareholders and made short-term commercial loans to merchants and other businessmen. Apart from deposits, its liabilities consisted of notes that could be redeemed at the bank for gold, and these notes circulated in the economy as a form of private currency. The bank was a remarkably successful institution that earned large profits by providing a financial service that was much in demand.

Originally identified with Robert Morris and other Republicans, the bank widened its support in 1784 by shrewdly absorbing an opposing group of merchants who wished to establish a bank of their own. A group of traders, impressed by the high profits of the Bank of North America but unable to buy its stock without paying a premium over par, applied to the Pennsylvania legislature for a charter to start a new bank. Although a few radicals were included for balance, the thirteen-man board of directors of the proposed bank was heavily weighted with rich Quaker and Anglican loyalists whose commercial activities had been hampered by the war. The Bank of North America deftly bought off these challengers by selling stock to them at par, instead of charging a premium. Thereafter the bank's shareholders included merchants of every political stripe, a fact of great importance in ensuring the political unity of the merchant community.

The bank and most traders feared paper money during the 1780s, but cheap money had two influential constituencies. A small but powerful group of securities speculators, led by merchants Charles Pettit and Blair McClenachan, backed it as a way for Pennsylvania to assume its share of the Federal debt and to pay the interest and principle thereon. This anti-Federal proposal was strongly opposed by Robert Morris and other Nationalists who considered the Federal debt a means of fostering the loyalty of moneyed men to the union. Although a few Republican merchants briefly supported assumption in 1782 and 1783 because it would increase the value of their own portfolios, they had backed away from such support by 1785.[27] A second and far more broadly based source of support for paper money was Pennsylvania's agrarian interest. Before the war, the provincial government issued paper money in the form of loans to farmers secured by the farmers' own lands. This land bank, as it were, had worked well, because it simultaneously performed three functions:

27. Baumann, "Democratic-Republicans," 43–55, expertly analyzes the proponents of funding.

Pennsylvania's economy received a circulating medium, the provincial government earned interest on the loans, and the farmers received loans with which to finance property improvements. During the 1780s farmers were understandably eager to revive this successful institution, and paper money would be particularly welcome in the midst of a depression, when hard money was so difficult to obtain. Quite apart from these compelling practical considerations, paper money was favored by many agrarians on ideological grounds as an alternative to the Bank of North America. The paper money bill that was passed by the assembly in March 1785 reflected these disparate sources of support. Of the £150,000 issued, £100,000 was to be used to pay the interest and principal on Pennsylvania's share of the national debt, and £50,000 was to be used to fund a land bank. The paper was not made legal tender but was amply backed by provincial taxes, which would remove it from circulation before it lost value.[28]

Despite the success of paper money in colonial times and the responsible nature of the current issue, the merchants categorically rejected the legislature's scheme. The memory of the Revolution was too recent and their financial condition too precarious for them to do otherwise. In a mass meeting the merchants approved, almost unanimously, a resolution stating: "Money being the grand instrument of commerce, and the measure of value, it is an indispensible condition of it that its own value be determined and known. . . . Gold and Silver alone possess this property, and no substitute for them can safely be relied on as a medium of commerce, which has an intrinsic principle of fluctuation. . . . It plainly appears, from the many abortive and ruinous attempts made since the revolution, that Government has it not always in its power to give to paper money this indispensible property of gold and silver."[29]

The officers and directors of the Bank of North America had special reasons for fearing the assembly's paper issue. The commercial crisis had depleted its reserves of specie because depositors withdrew gold and silver and sent it to Europe to pay debts, and the bank was damaged also by sizable loan losses. These shocks reduced the bank's profits significantly and forced it to stop lending for a time. The bank's managers were understandably cautious and fearful, for they were running the only well-established commercial bank in America and were weathering their first commercial crisis. The confidence of shareholders, noteholders, and depositors had to be retained at all cost. There could not have been a more dangerous time for the bank to have to accept paper money. For if the

28. Ireland, "Ratification," 119–131.

29. *Pennsylvania Gazette*, Mar. 2, 1785.

bank were legally obliged to value the paper at par value even though it was trading at a discount to specie in the private economy, its vaults might quickly become filled with the less valuable paper as customers deposited paper and withdrew specie. Recognizing this danger, Thomas Willing strongly opposed the paper money bill, and when it passed, he offered to accept the paper but to segregate it strictly in the bank's accounting system: a customer who deposited paper could withdraw only paper.

Once it became entangled in the paper money issue, the bank became the target of Presbyterian politicians in the assembly, who repealed its charter in September 1785.[30] Hatred of the bank existed on three related levels. In the technical realm of economic policy, the bank was blamed for the economy's current ills. It allegedly encouraged overtrading and mercantile bankruptcies by enticing traders to borrow too much from the bank. It was accused of reducing the supply of hard money by allowing depositors to withdraw specie and ship it to Europe and by paying specie dividends to foreign shareholders. (The initial investment of specie that these foreigners had made in Pennsylvania's economy was somehow overlooked.) Finally, the monopoly status of the bank was attacked again and again, with good reason, and it was criticized also for failing to provide long-term credit for farmers.

Following directly from this economic indictment was the more general social criticism of the bank that it favored the state's commercial interest—considered an unscrupulous band of ambitious aristocrats—at the expense of farmers and tradesmen.[31] "The commercial interest is already too powerful, and an overbalance to the landed interest," it was said. "They have no need of so energetic an institution to give springs to their action, which is already too great." Impelled by "an amazing desire to accumulate wealth," the merchants would form a dangerous aristocracy that would threaten the liberties of their social inferiors.[32] Just as the great banker Lorenzo de Medici had seized control of Renaissance Florence, so would Pennsylvania become the fiefdom of Robert Morris and his Republican junto.[33] Perhaps, it was sarcastically proposed, the

30. See Eugene R. Slaski, "Thomas Willing: Moderation during the American Revolution" (Ph.D. diss., Florida State University, 1971), 297–317; Lewis, *Bank of North America*, 54–73; Bray Hammond, *Banks and Politics in America from the Revolution to the Civil War* (Princeton, N.J., 1957), 53–54.

31. See Janet Wilson, "The Bank of North America and Pennsylvania Politics: 1781–1787," *PMHB*, LXVI (1942), 3–28; Ireland, "Ratification," 132–140; Slaski, "Thomas Willing," 297–317; Eric Foner, *Tom Paine and Revolutionary America* (New York, 1976), 192–203.

32. *Freeman's Journal: or, the North-American Intelligencer* (Philadelphia), Feb. 7, 1787.

33. *Pennsylvania Packet*, June 28, 1786.

state would be governed like the bank itself, with the voting power of citizens made proportionate to their wealth. If the counties west of the Susquehanna should object to this scheme, they could simply be split off from the state. And should there be objections from "the common mass of inferior traders, mechanics, and others in dependent situations" in the east, "the smiles and frowns of superiors will teach them their duty, or at least prevent them from active opposition."[34] To the supporters of the Pennsylvania constitution, then, the bank was not only an economic blight but a social and political menace as well.

The attack on the bank and passage of the paper money bill underscored the economic weakness and political isolation of the merchant community. By importing excessive amounts of dry goods and selling them on credit, Philadelphia's wholesalers had already put a gun to their heads. Now the radicals in the assembly proposed to pull the trigger by flooding the state with paper money. In addition, the government of New Jersey threatened to compound the problem by issuing a currency of its own. Rural shopkeepers and mechanics would pay their debts, all right—with depreciated paper. Already racked by a decade of financial chaos, the merchants would have to endure another round of expropriation through inflation. Meanwhile, the merchants' own solution to the monetary problems of the war years, the Bank of North America, had been nearly destroyed.

In their private correspondence the merchants described how the assembly's actions had undermined confidence in the economy. "Our Assembly at their last Setting publish'd a Bill for consideration, to take away the Bank Charter & destroy it," wrote Benjamin Fuller. "You cannot conceive the effect it has had on Trade in general, little or no Money sturring for any Article, and produce falling hourly—this with the horrors of an Approaching paper Currency has thrown all kind of business into confusion & each man is fearfull of his Neighbour—All at present is Gloom."[35] Stephen Collins, in the winter of 1785, wrote: "I think I shall not import more than half so many Good in the fall as I have wrote for in the spring. my courage more & more fails me and much more from the appearances of Publick afairs then from Trade being overdon, that will work its own cure. N Jersey are now pushing for a large Sum of Paper mony to be a Tender in Discharge of any Debts within the state. What but the Devel could Induce such a measure."[36] Perversely enough,

34. *Freeman's Journal*, Jan. 3, 1787; see also Aug. 22, 1787.

35. Fuller to Robert Totten, Apr. 21, 1785, Benjamin Fuller Letterbook, 1784–1787, 98, Benjamin Fuller Papers, 1762–1799, Historical Society of Pennsylvania (hereafter cited as HSP).

36. Collins to Pearsall and Glover, Dec. 17, 1785, Stephen Collins Papers, LXII-A, 109, Library of Congress (hereafter cited as LC).

paper money actually seemed to reduce the supply of money in the economy because it encouraged hoarding of gold and silver. Wrote Robert Morris in 1786, "Money is cursedly scarce, all the specie that goes into the hands of People not in trade is locked up and will not see daylight untill the paper Money Game is Up."[37] George Clymer concurred with this analysis, reporting, "I suppose you have heard of the great dearth of gold and silver here, the truth is these honest gentry of intrinsic worth begin to lock themselves up as if afraid of the bad company that is preparing for them in our paper treasury."[38]

The prospect of further financial disarray was only the worst problem facing the merchants in the mid-eighties; they were also concerned about the failure of Congress to protect American commerce. In 1783 Great Britain issued an order banning American ships in the British West Indies, and the merchants formed a committee to encourage an effective response to this commercial discrimination.[39] Yet it was doubted whether a league of separate states could successfully spar with European nations. John Chaloner wrote in 1784: "Our Merchants Grumble much at the Regulations of trade in Europe. I doubt much Congress being furnished with sufficient powers from the several states to Counteract the policy of Great Britain & France. No Individual state will adopt particular measures because it will throw the trade from her to her Neighbour—So I fear we must grin & bear it."[40] This pessimistic assessment was not unjustified. Delaware's refusal to pass a duty comparable to Pennsylvania's encouraged smuggling into the latter state, and New Jersey and Connecticut feuded with New York for placing tonnage duties on small coastal vessels. And this conflict in interstate trade was mirrored by civil disorder within the nation—an issue about which the merchants had become particularly sensitive after the unrest of 1778 and 1779. Glumly reviewing the various theaters of conflict in 1784—land wars arising from confused titles in Pennsylvania's Wyoming Valley, border clashes between New Yorkers and Vermonters, a border dispute between New York and Massachusetts—John Chaloner concluded, "All

37. Robert Morris to Constable, Rucker, and Co., Aug. 20, 1786, Constable, Rucker, and Co. Papers, LC.

38. Quoted in Grundfest, "George Clymer," 177.

39. See Jensen, *New Nation*, 400–407; Irving Brant, *James Madison, the Nationalist, 1780–1787* (Indianapolis, Ind., 1948), 375–387; letter of Charles Pettit, Thomas Fitzsimons, *et al.*, Jan. 3, 1784, Tench Coxe Papers, Reel 45. All references to the Coxe Papers are to the microfilm collection, available in HSP and other libraries, of the original Coxe Papers in HSP.

40. Chaloner to Jeremiah Wadsworth, Dec. 28, 1783, John Chaloner Letterbook, 1782–1784, 235, Chaloner and White Collection, box 4, HSP.

this must bring about a dissolution of the present Confederation or else increase its powers & authorities sufficient to protest all the Subjects of America—at present it is but a Shadow."[41]

If it was to gain substance, instead of remaining a shadow, the Continental Congress needed two things above all else: money and talented leadership. In the mid-1780s it had neither. After six years of begging state legislatures for an impost, Congress was rebuffed by New York in 1786, and the issue seemed settled finally. Lacking an independent source of funds, Congress had to parcel out the public debt to the state governments and finance operations with requisitions from the states, which often had better things to do with the money. The resulting poverty made Congress nearly incapable of energetic administration; it even defaulted on its debt to France. So desperate were its finances that Rufus King confided to Elbridge Gerry, "You may depend on it, that the Treasury now is literally without a penny."[42] Weak and demoralized, Congress attracted second-rate politicians. Remarked one observer of the body, "Had you been present you would have trembled for your country, to have *seen*, and *heard*, and *observed* the men who composed its rulers."[43] And leadership seemed no better in the state governments, which were controlled by men of narrow vision and limited ability who had never traveled widely or considered the problems of the nation as a whole. Inevitably, the manifold deficiencies of the Confederation reduced the standing of the United States. Spanish officials in New Orleans were treating with James Wilkinson to deliver Kentucky into His Majesty's dominion, and British officials could think of no compelling reason for evacuating their forts along the Great Lakes, as stipulated by the Treaty of Paris. Some observers were already wondering whether Pennsylvania would align itself with New England or the South, once the Confederation disintegrated.

Merchants and the Federalist Coup

Though no single problem was fatal in itself, the deficiencies of the Confederation were numerous and alarming. A severe if temporary commercial depression had been exacerbated by the threat of paper

41. Chaloner to Wadsworth and Church, Mar. 1, 1784, *ibid.*, 259.

42. Quoted in Forrest McDonald and Ellen Shapiro McDonald, eds., *Confederation and Constitution, 1781–1789* (Columbia, S.C., 1968), 46.

43. Quoted in Robert C. Alberts, *The Golden Voyage: The Life and Times of William Bingham, 1752–1804* (Boston, 1969), 171.

money, the attack on the bank, and a weak commercial policy, while civil disorder and political disarray called into question the very future of the country. These problems were not likely to be solved—indeed, had in part been created—by an impotent Congress and erratic state legislatures. With uncharacteristic unanimity and fervor the merchants forecast the calamitous fate awaiting the country. "The Affairs of this Country is going fast into Convulsions and I am Opinion Blood will be the Consequence before many Years pass or a great Change of some kind must take Place," wrote Benjamin Fuller.[44] "You ask my political oppinion as to the new Constitution," wrote Levi Hollingsworth in 1788. "I answer that I am for the Unconditional adoption of it—nothing else can save America from general Ruin, in my judgement."[45] Already by December 1785 Stephen Collins believed, "I am perfectly a novis in Publick afairs, if some Political Confusion & Revolution in this cuntry dont arise er long."[46] Collins proved that he was no "novis in Publick afairs" when this prediction was spectacularly fulfilled by Shays's Rebellion. Now the apocalypse seemed to be at hand: "What will be the fate of Massachusetts & will it not spread and set fire to other states[?] we think it looks gloomy & no Dependence on the Honesty of the people."[47] Whether justified or not, the very perception of instability imposed costs of its own on merchants trying to close transatlantic deals. Levi Hollingsworth concluded that he could not sell his western lands to Europeans, because they had "such horrid oppinions of our Governments." "In so bad Credit is America in Europe," he wrote, "that no purchaser can be found."[48] By 1787 these perceptions had created within the merchant community a general consensus for reform. As one strict Quaker later wrote, "The late Congress had become so very low in general estimation, a change with enlarged powers and proper balance seemed to be absolutely necessary."[49]

The bleak prospects of the nation were all the more distressing because a simple change of government offered the prospect of prosperity and greatness for the United States. As William Bingham wrote in the spring of 1787: "[America] wants nothing now but a strong efficient Govern-

44. Fuller to Robert Totten, Mar. 30, 1787, Fuller Letterbook, 1784–1787, 319.

45. Hollingsworth to Dorsey Pentacost, Mar. 12, 1788, Levi Hollingsworth Letterbook, 1786–1791, 205, Hollingsworth Papers, HSP.

46. Collins to Pearsall and Glover, Dec. 17, 1785, Collins Papers, LXII-A, 109.

47. Collins to Pearsall and Glover, Dec. 28, 1786, *ibid.*, LXII-B, 71.

48. Hollingsworth to Dorsey Pentacost, Mar. 12, Apr. 22, 1782, Hollingsworth Letterbook, 1786–1791, 205, 233.

49. James Pemberton to John Pemberton, Sept. 20, 1787, in Merrill E. Jensen, ed., *The Documentary History of the Ratification of the Constitution*, II, *Ratification of the Constitution by the States: Pennsylvania* (Madison, Wis., 1976), 133.

ment, which will command Respect & Confidence abroad, & act with Vigour & Energy at home. . . . I am convinced that all our political Misfortunes flow from the Weakness of our federal Government."[50] Another trader remarked, "I flatter myself that on the foederal Government taking place a new Spring will be given to Trade and agriculture throughout the States."[51] And these hopes found support in foreign ports. Following ratification a firm in Gibraltar wrote, "We some time ago heard with pleasure the establishment of your new Constitution And sincerely hope that it will greatly advance the Interests of Trade to you and render your situation every way more eligible secure & certain all over the Continent."[52] Thus the merchants believed that the nation was at a crossroads. One avenue led to weakness, chaos, and poverty; the other, to order and abundance.

By 1787 the merchant community was in a position to translate this dichotomous assessment of the nation's future into a concrete political program. For it was no longer the apolitical, religiously divided occupational group of 1765 or the war-torn body of 1779. The trials of war and the disappointments of peace had united and mobilized the merchants, preparing them for effective political action in 1787. This process began with the emergence in 1779 of the Republican faction, and the proliferation of economic problems mobilized the merchants still further, forcing them to convene to formulate common political positions on price controls, commercial policy, paper money, and other matters. The Bank of North America also became a major bulwark of mercantile unity, as we have noted. Though controlled by the Morris clique, the bank served hundreds of merchant depositors and borrowers, and the second stock issue of 1784 attracted the funds of dozens of merchants, including Quakers and Anglican tories, who normally distrusted Morris. The emergence of the traders as an interest group was reflected in the effort of Tench Coxe, albeit unsuccessful, to form a chamber of commerce whose express purpose was to "unite the mercantile Body" and to "form a city interest that may create some small counterbalance for the too great weight of the Country interest in this state."[53]

The political mobilization of the merchant community exemplified a general reorientation in America's political structure during the Revolution. Political life in the colonial period reflected the paradigm of mixed

50. Quoted in Alberts, *William Bingham*, 171.

51. Hollingsworth to Mark Pragers, Apr. 21, 1788, Hollingsworth Letterbook, 1786–1791, 228.

52. Peter Ronaldson to Andrew Clow and Co., Mar. 9, 1788, Andrew Clow Papers, Gratz Collection, HSP.

53. "Plan for a Chamber of Commerce," Oct. 21, 1784, Coxe Papers, Reel 46.

government, in which there was a correspondence between political institutions (governor, council, legislature) and social strata (royalty, aristocracy, and commoners). Following this model, merchants had left politics to their social superiors, the independent gentlemen. The destruction of traditional political elites, the upsurge in popular political participation, and the emergence of divisive economic issues during the war had eroded the values of mixed government and converted occupational groups into organized, articulate political factions. In Philadelphia it was the artisans who united first. Originally organized to prolong the profitable commercial boycott of 1769–1770, mechanics used diverse methods to shoulder their way into the city's political structure. They held a number of mass meetings before the war, formed the Patriotic Society in 1772, and played a major role in the Committee of Observation and Inspection that controlled the city between 1775 and 1777. By 1781 the state's western farmers had seized control of a still stronger level of power, the Pennsylvania Assembly, whose leaders self-consciously defended the state's agricultural interests.

Partly in reaction to the mobilization of artisans and farmers, merchants also combined to defend their particular interests. Because traders were deeply divided by the Revolution, this process was not complete until 1786. The recasting of political participation along occupational lines was remarked upon by contemporaries and seemed to be a fundamental trait of modern republics. As James Madison observed in Federalist 10: "The most common and durable source of factions has been the various and unequal distribution of property. . . . A landed interest, a manufacturing interest, a mercantile interest, a moneyed interest, with many lesser interests, grow up of necessity in civilized nations, and divide them into different classes, actuated by different sentiments and views."[54] Such an analysis would have been irrelevant to colonial Pennsylvania, whose political life consisted of "jousting at the top" by wellborn gentlemen.[55] But political deference had fallen prey to the popular mobilization and economic fragmentation of the Revolutionary era.

The merchants used their newfound unity with telling effect in the Federalist revolution of 1787–1788. One Antifederalist pamphleteer remarked at "the infatuation of some of our merchants, who, elated with the imaginary prospect of an improved commerce under the new govern-

54. Alexander Hamilton *et al.*, *The Federalist*, ed. Henry Cabot Lodge (New York, 1888), 54. Similar trends occurred in New York. See Edward Countryman, *A People in Revolution: The American Revolution and Political Society in New York, 1760–1790* (Baltimore, Md., 1981), 294–295.

55. The phrase is from William S. Hanna, *Benjamin Franklin and Pennsylvania Politics* (Stanford, Calif., 1964).

ment, overlook all danger."[56] Pennsylvania's lone delegate to the Annapolis convention was a merchant, Tench Coxe, as were four of the state's eight representatives to the Constitutional Convention: Robert Morris, Thomas Fitzsimons, Thomas Mifflin, and George Clymer. A fifth delegate, James Wilson, was a close associate of Robert Morris, and a sixth, Gouverneur Morris, was also a staunch Nationalist and an occasional business associate of Morris. And traders played a prominent role in the virtual coup d'etat that constituted the state's ratification procedure. Eager to get the tortuous series of state ratifying conventions off to an auspicious start, Federalist merchants in the Pennsylvania Assembly pressured the House in December 1787 into calling a state convention at once—before western opponents of the Constitution could rally their forces. Outnumbered but not outwitted, resourceful Antifederalists paralyzed the House by refusing to enter the chamber, thus depriving it of a quorum. But the Federalists matched cunning with force by allowing a mob to drag two recalcitrant absentees into the statehouse to watch the process of ratification begin.[57]

Such Philadelphia traders as Tench Coxe, Pelatiah Webster, and Timothy Pickering also fought aggressively in the propaganda war of 1788, filling the public prints and their private correspondence with tedious defenses of the new government.[58] Coxe credited himself with nearly thirty separate publications, and he eagerly traced the course of ratification in state after state by soliciting friends on the spot for the latest news.[59] The important position of merchants in the Federalist revolution was revealed no less clearly by the Antifederalist critique of the movement. In the proposed new institutions of a senate and a presidency, writer after writer detected the plot of an opulent aristocracy to trample the liberties of the people. In Pennsylvania this "conspiracy of the well-born" was identified by the influential pamphleteer Centinel (George Bryan) with the Republican clique headed by Robert Morris and James Wilson. These men were portrayed as a band of ambitious plutocrats whose appetite for power and wealth knew no bounds:

> View the monopolizing spirit of the principal of them. See him converting a bank, instituted for common benefit, to his own

56. John Bach McMaster and Frederick D. Stone, eds., *Pennsylvania and the Federal Constitution, 1787–1788* (Philadelphia, 1888), 625.

57. This maneuvering may be followed *ibid.*, 27–82.

58. Jacob E. Cooke, *Tench Coxe and the Early Republic* (Chapel Hill, N.C., 1978), 109–131; Charles W. Upham, *The Life of Timothy Pickering*, 4 vols. (Boston, 1867–1873), II, 350–368.

59. Cooke, *Tench Coxe*, 110.

> and creatures' emoluments, and by the aid thereof, controlling the credit of the state, and dictating the measures of government. . . . Recollect the strenuous and unremitted exertions of these men, for years past, to destroy our admirable Constitution. . . . And then answer whether these apprehensions are chimerical, whether such characters will be less ambitious, less avaricious, more moderate, when the privileges, property, and every concern of the people of the United States shall lie at their mercy, when they shall be in possession of absolute sway?[60]

Bryan's indictment of Pennsylvania's Republicans, who were now leading national Federalists, contained more than a kernel of truth. The Revolution had indeed given rise to a group of fortune builders in Philadelphia, far richer and more powerful than most pre-Revolutionary merchants. As the next chapter will make clear, they moved aggressively into many new fields in the two decades after 1775, and Robert Morris was involved in almost all of them. In the year that Bryan penned his indictment of the Federalists, Robert Morris monopolized the tobacco trade with France, headed a mercantile firm that handled 4 percent of Philadelphia's imports, controlled the port's only bank, dealt largely in public securities, and was about to sell multimillion-acre tracts in western New York to some of the richest men in Europe. A large proportion of the arriviste merchants of Philadelphia were associates of this Colossus, and Alexander Hamilton's generous financial plan would soon make some of them richer still. By the mid-nineties these merchants would lay claim to millions of unsettled acres in states from Maine to Georgia, acreage they intended to sell in lucrative little pieces to individual pioneers. So Bryan's analysis was exaggerated but not totally implausible. He correctly perceived the swollen, multifaceted ambitions—political, social, and financial—of the Federalist leaders in Pennsylvania. This is not to suggest that the merchants were motivated purely by the prospect of private gain. On the contrary, they were farsighted patriots possessed of a fresh, compelling vision of national greatness, and they made great sacrifices to turn this vision into reality. But they were disposed where possible to make the most of these sacrifices, and in 1787 and 1788 public and private interest meshed with uncommon nicety.

It may be said, then, that the Constitution did have economic origins, as Charles Beard claimed years ago. But Beard put a generation of historians on the wrong track, and vitiated his own keen insights, by suggesting that the framers were motivated by crass profiteering schemes. In

60. In McMaster and Stone, eds., *Pennsylvania and the Federal Constitution*, 625–626.

Pennsylvania the Constitution actually clouded the investment outlook for securities speculators because the state had already assumed its share of the Federal debt.[61] But many important Federalists pursued constitutional reform in order to solve tangible political and economic problems that not only endangered the future of the nation but also injured their own businesses. The origins of the Constitution are distorted if these economic problems are minimized and the Federalist movement is interpreted simply as an exercise in constitutional reform driven by the ideals of republicanism.[62] Even James Madison, a far more disinterested Feder-

61. See Matthew M'Connell to William Irvine, Sept. 20, 1787, in Jensen, ed., *Documentary History*, II, 132, for the ambivalent attitude of one speculator toward the Constitution: "This would derange all our funding and land office laws it is true, but perhaps it might be as well for the creditors in the end, provided Congress get stable and permanent funds." Beard's effort to trace the political attitudes of the framers directly to the type of property—"personalty" and "realty"—that they owned was also untenable. However, a broader distinction between "localistic" "agrarian" Antifederalists and "cosmopolitan" "commercial" Federalists works well, as Main, *Anti-Federalists*, and Ferguson, *Power of the Purse*, demonstrate in rather different ways. See the fruitful debate in Stuart Bruchey, "The Forces behind the Constitution: A Critical Review of E. James Ferguson's *The Power of the Purse*, With a Rebuttal by E. James Ferguson," *WMQ*, 3d Ser., XIX (1962), 429–438. Bruchey suggests that " 'independent men,' " "animated by an essentially nonpersonal concern over the viability of the fledgling Republic," played a key role in the Federalist cause (434). This takes us into the ultimately unknowable realm of human motivation; it is impossible to determine whether a merchant supported the Constitution *primarily* out of patriotism or in order to protect his estate. Of course, the merchants themselves made no such distinction, for the two motivations were mutually reinforcing. What is clear is that most merchants were directly affected financially by the debility of the national government, and this fact heightened their desire for a stronger government.

62. Wood, *Creation of the American Republic*, 393–403, seems to put forth this view. Wood writes: "But the complaints were far from imaginary. They were real, intensely real, rooted, however, not in poverty or in real deprivation but rather in prosperity and in the very unintended promises the Revolution seemed to be offering large numbers of Americans. . . . Because the Revolution represented much more than a colonial rebellion, represented in fact a utopian effort to reform the character of American society and to establish truly free governments, men in the 1780's could actually believe that it was failing" (395). This insight is valuable, so long as we recognize the limits of its applicability. Many conservative Federalists—including most Philadelphia merchants—had approached Independence with ambivalence or hostility; it makes little sense to interpret their actions in the 1780s as an attempt to perfect the utopian experiment of the Revolution. Such men were in fact reacting against the radical whig ideology that had prevailed in 1776. The central values of republicanism—a fear of power and corruption, a predilection for social equality, a suspicion of commerce, and so forth—did not shape the outlook of such men as Robert Morris, Thomas Willing, Tench Coxe, and William Bingham. A more useful framework for understanding their mentality is nationalism—a desire to build a nation that was politically and economically powerful. As I have suggested, this ideology was shaped by both a spirit of patriotism and a desire for personal economic advancement: an effective central govern-

alist than the typical merchant, knew that "most of our political evils may be traced up to our commercial ones."[63] The relevance of Madison's remark to the actual work of the convention is demonstrated by the many clauses of the document that addressed specific "commercial evils" prevalent in the 1780s. It was no accident that the Constitution gave the federal government the power to tax, to regulate commerce, to pay the national debt, to coin money, to issue patents for inventions, to grant letters of marque and reprisal, and to suppress insurrections. Federalist merchants, quite simply, had gotten what they wanted: a stable constitutional framework within which they could prosper. This is exactly what they would proceed to accomplish in the heady years of economic expansion between 1789 and 1792.

---

ment would facilitate their private business projects, which in turn would build up the national economy. The bitter divisions of the 1790s stemmed from the success of Alexander Hamilton in pursuing public policies that facilitated this process, for they were abhorrent to statesmen of strong Republican sensibilities.

63. Quoted in Broadus Mitchell, *Alexander Hamilton: Youth to Maturity, 1755–1788* (New York, 1957), 357.

Part III
Merchants and Economic Diversification

7
The Entrepreneurial Efflorescence

The decade and a half after 1776 witnessed an extraordinary efflorescence of mercantile innovation in the Delaware Valley. Banks were established, trade with China and the settlements of the Mississippi Valley was begun, and southern tobacco temporarily became an important export commodity. Extensive speculations in public securities and wilderness lands were undertaken, and a novel transportation project was completed. Traders also plotted to import the revolutionary cotton-spinning technology recently developed in England. And after 1788, Philadelphia's trade with the various parts of the Atlantic basin rapidly grew to an unprecedented volume.

It might seem paradoxical that a business community rocked by a destructive civil war and a severe depression would have been able to muster the self-confidence and capital needed to launch such enterprises. But readers will recognize that the confluence of adversity and enterprise was a natural phenomenon in Philadelphia's merchant community. It was quite rational to consider sending a vessel to Canton if one could not procure a remunerative freight for Bristol.[1] In a port stripped of hard money and bursting with unsalable dry goods, why not try one's luck at investing in western lands that could be bought with paper money and public securities? If imported dry goods could not be sold for a profit in the counties surrounding Philadelphia, why not send them over the Appalachian Mountains to the frontier settlements along the Ohio, Monongahela, and Mississippi rivers?

A number of forces propelled such activities. Freed from the restraints of the Navigation Acts, American merchants could trade directly with China and India. Also, wartime dislocations opened new investment opportunities. The eviction of major British mercantile firms from the Chesapeake region created at least a temporary entrepreneurial vacuum in the tobacco trade, into which northern merchants darted. Moreover, a

1. John Clifford to Thomas Clifford, Jr., Aug. 2, 1785, Clifford Correspondence, 1778–1785, VII, 250, Historical Society of Pennsylvania (hereafter cited as HSP).

war without taxes scrambled the finances of the state and federal governments so severely that only sweeping reforms could restore order. One such innovation was the creation of the Bank of North America, a key element in the financial program formulated by Robert Morris in 1781. Land speculation was similarly encouraged by the financial pressure on the state governments, which were then obliged to call in their outstanding bonds in exchange for millions of acres of wilderness lands. Finally, the war introduced into America a sizable government debt, which became the object of intense, highly lucrative speculation.

The merchants seized these and other opportunities not only to build their estates but also to increase the strength of the nation itself. In pursuing this goal they possessed an inspiring, if formidable, model in their recent foe and chief trading partner, which was entering the Industrial Revolution in these years. Both the Bank of North America and the Bank of the United States were roughly patterned on the Bank of England, and the creation of an American national debt was likewise inspired by the British example. Developments in England also motivated attempts to establish cotton-spinning factories in America. Robert Morris sent the first American vessel to Canton in 1784 in order to encourage American competition with the British East India Company. And in addition to encouraging innovation for competitive reasons, patriotism colored the merchants' assessment of financial opportunities. Their heavy investments in western land, for example, reflected an overoptimistic certitude, a mixture of faith and hope, that the United States would rapidly become a huge, densely settled nation.

The acceleration of social mobility in the merchant community between 1775 and 1789 was another powerful stimulus to economic innovation. Upwardly mobile men, both fortune builders and lesser traders, grew accustomed during the war to improvising boldly amidst great risks. As we have seen, most of these men had participated in the War for Independence, so they were conversant with the complex changes in the American business structure that the conflict had created. They were, therefore, adept at using these innovations, particularly the credit extended by commercial banks, to conduct their speculations in securities, land, and overseas trade. In addition, the Revolution tended to concentrate unprecedented amounts of capital in the hands of a few enterprising traders, a process that greatly facilitated the financing of risky new ventures.

For all these reasons, the economic resurgence of the 1780s and early 1790s was led by a few major fortune builders, notably Robert Morris, William Bingham, Joseph Ball, Charles Pettit, Jeremiah Wadsworth of

Connecticut, and William Duer of New York.[2] With striking consistency the key lieutenants of these entrepreneurs—their supercargoes, salesmen, agents, and aides—were enlisted from the same group of people who had served them during the war: the secondary officials of the Revolutionary armies and governments. This is not to say that neutrals and tories were entirely shut out of postwar innovation; many of them invested in the new enterprises of the day, and at least one, Tench Coxe, was among their most important promoters. But one finds relatively few tories and Quakers establishing the new corporations and making the biggest transactions. This role was reserved for the great merchants who had staked their fortunes on a risky cause and had won. They possessed the wealth, knowledge, and self-confidence to initiate projects and the prestige to enlist European capital in their undertakings.

The complexity and variety of these novel schemes make a complete description of each of them in a single chapter quite impossible; indeed, several of them deserve book-length treatment. But it is important here to convey the essential character of each, suggesting why it succeeded or failed and how it contributed to the process of economic development. And, since a topical treatment obscures the pace and progression of innovation, a chronological preview may be useful. Although the various activities occurred nearly simultaneously, investor interest in them peaked in different years, in roughly the following sequence: banking (Bank of North America founded in 1781, enlarged in 1784); the China trade (begun in 1784); securities speculation (peaked between 1789 and 1791); the launching of the Lancaster Turnpike and the Society for the Encouragement of Useful Manufactures (1791); and the speculative mania for frontier land (1792–1795).

This sequence may in turn be divided into two distinct phases. The years 1776–1788 were a period of creative ferment in which nearly all of the major innovations were begun, but they were relatively sober and restrained, as befitted a time marked by commercial depression and political uncertainty. After 1788, however, economic, political, and financial forces converged to create a reckless, speculative environment in

2. The main new activities of these men were as follows: Robert Morris, banking, China trade, tobacco trade, land speculation; William Bingham, banking, China trade, Lancaster Turnpike, land speculation, securities speculation; Joseph Ball, Mississippi trade, Insurance Company of North America; Charles Pettit, securities speculation; Jeremiah Wadsworth, banking, securities speculation; William Duer, securities speculation, land speculation, Society for the Encouragement of Useful Manufactures. Also important was the Philadelphian John Nicholson, who ascended during the Revolution through government posts relating to public finance and land policy, rather than through commerce.

which anything seemed possible. Poor harvests in Europe brought unprecedented agricultural and commercial prosperity to the Delaware Valley in 1790, at about the time when the United States Constitution was becoming law and the Federalists were establishing political hegemony. Alexander Hamilton wasted no time in winning the confidence of the nation's business community. One of the Washington administration's first official acts was to pour thousands of dollars into the pockets of prescient speculators by funding depreciated American bonds at 100 percent of their face value. The resulting ebullience in the investment markets facilitated the flotation of a series of new companies, including the Bank of the United States, the Society for the Encouragement of Useful Manufactures, and the Lancaster Turnpike. In conjunction with the commercial prosperity and buoyant nationalism of the early 1790s, Hamilton's funding program also helped to generate a speculative boom in western lands by enriching investors, both domestic and foreign, thereby encouraging them to strive for a second killing in America's investment markets.

Commercial Innovation

Although the merchants after the war made wide-ranging efforts to diversify out of commerce, we must not lose sight of the fact that, for the community as a whole, trade remained its primary concern. Following the ill-fated boom of 1783–1784, trade stagnated through the year 1788, when exports were only 18 percent above their level in 1773. But the crisis of subsistence that devastated Europe and toppled the French monarchy also enriched Delaware Valley traders who rushed to fill the food deficit. Between 1788 and 1789 the value of Quaker City exports leaped 45 percent to the level of $3,510,765, and they continued to climb to the extraordinary level of $17,513,866 in 1796. With Americans serving as neutral maritime carriers for the warring nations of Europe, the shipping industry also flourished. The amount of tonnage registered for foreign trade increased by 267 percent between 1789 and 1796.[3]

Although beyond the range of this study, the upsurge in the Federalist period appears to have altered commerce substantially. To be sure, expansion did not imply security. Risks were as acute as ever for traders who now faced the constant threat of war, financial panic, and attacks

3. Gordon Carl Bjork, "Stagnation and Growth in the American Economy, 1784–1792" (Ph.D. diss., University of Washington, 1963), 54; *Register of Pennsylvania*, II (1828), 45.

by English, French, and Algerian cruisers. But what speculators today call the "upside potential" of trade—the probability of making huge profits rapidly—undoubtedly improved decisively in the 1790s. Traders with adequate credit and access to good vessels could now handle huge quantities of foodstuffs to meet the burgeoning European demand. Stephen Girard, for instance, exported goods worth £20,570 to France in just two years, in addition to substantial exports to the West Indies, and during the 1790s the Fisher brothers regularly sent cargoes worth £2,000 or £3,000 to the Iberian Peninsula. A trader who speculated successfully on such a large scale could amass a fortune in a few years, instead of laboriously accumulating one over decades.[4]

But the restless Philadelphians did not wait until the French Revolution to expand and diversify their commercial activities. During the convulsions of the 1780s they experimented successfully in three novel theaters of enterprise: the tobacco trade, the China trade, and commerce with the settlements of the Ohio and Mississippi valleys. All three of these innovations reveal the striking versatility, both technical and psychological, of the Philadelphia traders.

In 1776 the tobacco trade was not wholly unfamiliar to Quaker City traders. Whenever the foreign exchange market became tight and the rate of exchange climbed to unacceptable levels, merchants were tempted to liquidate their debts in England by sailing a ship to the Chesapeake, loading it with tobacco, and sending it to London or Bristol.[5] But this was a temporary expedient. The Philadelphians entertained no thought of mastering the intricate regional grades of tobacco, extending long-term credit to the planters, and challenging the major Scottish and English firms that dominated the trade. It made more sense for Philadelphians to concentrate on the lumber, flour, and wheat that they knew so well.

The Revolution changed this calculus for two reasons. Flour rapidly became an unsuitable export once it was needed to feed local armies, and the disruption of trade with England paralyzed the British firms in the Chesapeake and opened up a business vacuum there. It did not take

4. Stephen Girard Journal, 1786–1790, 122–230, Stephen Girard Papers, 3d Ser., Reel 113. All references to the Girard Papers are to the microfilm collection in the American Philosophical Society (hereafter cited as APS). Samuel and Miers Fisher Journal, 1792–1795, HSP. See also David Cay to Andrew Clow, Mar. 19, July 13, 1789, Franklin and Marshall Collection, HSP.

5. C. Willing and Son to James Campbell, June 15, 1754, to John Perks, Aug. 3, Oct. 15, 1754, Willing and Morris Letterbook, 1754–1761, 1, 12, 31, HSP; Kidd to Neate and Neave, Nov. 20, 1750, John Kidd Letterbook, 1749–1763, HSP.

Philadelphians long to seize the opportunity presented by this vacuum. Beginning in 1776, Philadelphia traders moved into the Chesapeake market in a major way, buying up tobacco for shipment to Europe both directly from Virginia and Maryland and indirectly via Philadelphia. The exact magnitude of this traffic cannot be determined, but there is no question it was of considerable importance when measured against the reduced scale of the Revolutionary years. Robert Morris remarked in 1776, "Great numbers of our people that had Continental Money on hand have gone down to buy tobacco"; and twice in 1779 Charles Wharton observed, "Tobacco has of late been our Staple Commodity."[6] Levi Hollingsworth's sloops regularly transported tobacco to Philadelphia in 1780 and 1781, hauling a total of well over 1,000 hogsheads per year.[7] The existing trade statistics, although fragmentary and conflicting, also suggest that Philadelphia's tobacco trade was quite large. In 1786 Thomas Fitzsimons, himself very active in the tobacco trade, stated, "There have been shipped from this port 14,000 hogsheads of tobacco, in a year, at £3 per hhd. worth £42,000 exclusive of freight." Fitzsimons also stated, "In the year 1784, 12,000 hogsheads tobacco, the produce of Virginia and Maryland, were shipped from this port." A modern historian goes still further, placing tobacco exports in 1784 at 18,563 hogsheads, worth £574,284. Whichever figure is correct, it is evident that Philadelphia directly controlled a respectable share of the nation's tobacco trade, for the Virginia crop during the 1780s amounted to about 57,000 hogsheads per year.[8]

Indirectly, Philadelphia controlled still more of the tobacco trade, for her merchants organized and financed shipments of tobacco directly to Europe from the Chesapeake. In the early years of the Revolution the Morris-Bingham-Deane group did this on a substantial scale by employing major Virginia firms to ship tobacco to France, and for several years

6. Robert W. Coakley, "Virginia Commerce during the American Revolution" (Ph.D. diss., University of Virginia, 1949), 321; Wharton to John Bulkeley and Co., Aug. 18, 1779, to William Carr, Sept. 7, 1779, Charles Wharton Letterbook, 1779–1785, Sarah A. G. Smith Collection, box 2, HSP. See also Charles Wharton Daybook, 1775–1785, Wharton Papers, HSP.

7. Levi Hollingsworth Ledger, 1780–1782 (Vol. CCCLXXXIII); Levi Hollingsworth Invoices (3 boxes), folders for 1780, 1781, 1782, Hollingsworth Papers, HSP. See also Hollingsworth to John Sterrett, July 27, 1781, to Low and Russell, Aug. 13, 1781, Levi Hollingsworth Letterbook, 1780–1782, Hollingsworth Papers; and Edward C. Papenfuse, *In Pursuit of Profit: The Annapolis Merchants in the Era of the American Revolution, 1763–1805*, Maryland Bicentennial Series (Baltimore, Md., 1975), 112–113.

8. Matthew Carey, ed., *Debates and Proceedings of the General Assembly of Pennsylvania, on the Memorials Praying a Repeal or Suspension of the Law Annulling the Charter of the Bank* (Philadelphia, 1786), 101, 102; Bjork, "Stagnation and Growth," 54.

after the war a continuation of shipments was encouraged by a number of forces. Tobacco prices were still high in Europe, while foreign demand for wheat was stagnant, and the heavy importation of dry goods meant that the price of foreign exchange was high. Therefore, shipment of tobacco was attractive both as a commodity speculation and as a vehicle for paying foreign debts. We know of several instances when Philadelphia firms arranged single shipments of tobacco to Europe from the Chesapeake,[9] but what is more important is the emergence of integrated marketing networks to handle this commerce. The Philadelphian Peter Kuhn remarked that the tobacco trade was best carried on directly between Europe and Virginia, "which has induced the principal merchants here to provide themselves there with good agents."[10] A case in point was Thomas Fitzsimons, who teamed up with the Alexandria firm of Hooe and Harrison to buy up large quantities of tobacco that was intended for sale in Philadelphia and Europe. A single major purchase by this firm involved a sum of £22,355. In 1785 Donnaldson and Coxe also organized major shipments of tobacco to England and Holland from various Chesapeake towns and from Philadelphia itself. Although operating on a smaller scale, Kuhn and Risberg set up stores in Fredericksburg and Port Royal after the Revolution and, in 1787, in Staunton.[11]

Philadelphia's involvement in the Chesapeake tobacco trade is well illustrated by the operations of John Wilcocks, Jr., a wealthy Anglican shipping merchant who had strong West Indian connections.[12] In 1782 the Wilcocks family firm teamed up with Nicholas Low, a major New York merchant, to trade tobacco in the James River region. Making an initial investment of eight thousand pounds Virginia currency, which was

9. R. and F. to Henry Cruger, Apr. 14, 1787, Reed and Forde Letterbook, 1787, 10, Reed and Forde Papers, HSP; Andrew Clow to David Cay, Apr. 14, 27, 1788, Gratz Collection, HSP; David Knox to Collins, Oct. 9, 17, 1783, Correspondence, XXII, Stephen Collins Papers, Library of Congress (hereafter cited as LC).

10. Anne Bezanson *et al., Prices and Inflation during the American Revolution: Pennsylvania, 1770–1790*, Industrial Research Department, Wharton School of Finance and Commerce, University of Pennsylvania, Research Studies, XXXV (Philadelphia, 1951), 264. Bezanson *et al.*, chap. 5, endorse Kuhn's assessment.

11. Thomas Fitzsimons Journal, 1781–1785, esp. 206, HSP; Donnaldson and Coxe Journal, 1785–1786, 531, 602, 613, 618, 647, 659, Baker Library, Harvard University Business School; Kuhn and Risberg to James Finlay, Apr. 9, 1785, to William French and Co., July 29, 1787, and other letters to these correspondents in Kuhn and Risberg Letterbook, 1785–1788, Bucks County Historical Society.

12. Nicholas Low Papers, boxes 3, 5, 6, 8, 10, LC. On financial arrangements, see especially Wilcocks to Low, July 16, 1785, Nelson, Heron, and Co. to Wilcocks, Aug. 26, 1785, box 8. On commercial operations, see Wilcocks to Isaac Moses and Co. and Nicholas Low, Feb. 8, 1784, Wilcocks to Low, Feb. 21, Mar. 1, 8, Apr. 3, 7, 14, 17, 21, May 18, 24, 1784; and Wilcocks to Nelson, Heron, and Co., May 25, 1784, all in box 5.

supplemented by sizable credits from European merchants, Wilcocks and Low established a pair of junior partners, Alexander Nelson and John Heron, at stores in Richmond and Norfolk. Nelson, Heron, and Company imported dry goods from Europe for sale to local planters and farmers and shipped dozens of cargoes of tobacco to Philadelphia, New York, and the major ports of Europe. The volume of these shipments cannot be measured precisely, but it was large enough to involve no fewer than eight different vessels in the spring of 1784. The high tobacco prices of the early 1780s made this trade extremely lucrative: by the spring of 1786 the initial investment of eight thousand pounds had grown to approximately thirty-four thousand pounds, of which the northerners' share amounted to over twenty thousand pounds. Several other Philadelphia tobacco firms fared equally well in these years, and John Wilcocks was understandably eager to expand operations by building a store, warehouse, and granary in Norfolk and establishing a store in Petersburg.[13]

Despite its success, the tobacco trade of Low and Wilcocks experienced serious managerial problems which, together with a drop in tobacco prices, brought them eventually to curtail operations. Partly because of the inattention of Nelson and Heron, the capital of the firm was quickly soaked up in long-term credits to farmers, planters, and other buyers of dry goods. Slow collection of these debts meant that the Virginians did not have enough liquid capital to buy tobacco at the best prices and to dispatch vessels as quickly as possible. To the great distress of Wilcocks, who was also attempting to support a trade with the West Indies at this time, Nelson and Heron solved their liquidity problem by drawing on Wilcocks and Low when they needed cash. Even this expedient did not suffice; several tobacco ships were delayed at dockside in the James River for lack of cash, and an excellent opportunity to make a major tobacco purchase had to be passed up. Dissension between Heron and Nelson further hindered operations, and the young Virginians demanded a larger share of the firm's profits, claiming that one of their competitors, who was generously financed by Irish merchants, received far better compensation than they did.[14]

The operations of Wilcocks and Low were impressive enough, but they were dwarfed by the speculations of Robert Morris, who used his wealth and prestige to dominate the French tobacco market in 1785, 1786, and

13. Daniel Tyson and another Philadelphian named Pennock reportedly made large profits in this trade. See Wilcocks to Low, Aug. 28, 1784; Nelson, Heron, and Co. to Wilcocks, June 12, 1784, *ibid.*, box 6.

14. Nelson, Heron, and Co. to Wilcocks, Aug. 12, 1785, *ibid.*, box 8.

1787.[15] The tobacco trade in France was legally monopolized by the Farmers General, which had, before 1775, purchased its supplies from large Glasgow firms. Preferring to deal directly with the American market, rather than through France's perennial foe, the Farmers General contracted with Robert Morris to deliver sixty thousand hogsheads over three years at a fixed price of £1 7s. 11d. Virginia currency per hundredweight. For Morris, this price was the key; it had to be higher than the average price at which he bought the tobacco that he sent to France. If not, he would lose money. Morris was, in effect, in the position of a man who swims through a tunnel and will drown if the water level (the price of tobacco) rises substantially before he reaches the end of the tunnel (the fulfillment of the contract). From an economic standpoint, Morris made a shrewd deal. Early in 1786 the market price of Virginia tobacco dropped to about 29 percent below the contract price, so that he made money on every hogshead he bought. But political pitfalls trapped the great speculator. Morris's monopolistic purchasing contract infuriated jealous rival merchants in France and the Chesapeake region, as well as the indebted planter Thomas Jefferson, at the time America's ambassador to France, who favored spirited competition for his crops. This opposition caused the contract to be altered so that the Farmers General, while retaining their agreement with Morris, bought additional quantities on the open market. This move tended to raise the American price of the weed, which ruined the profitability of the contract for Morris, who probably sustained a loss after spending £1,500,000 on Chesapeake tobacco. As the provision trade regained its attractiveness in the late 1780s, he was probably glad to join his fellow Philadelphia traders in leaving the tobacco trade to the wealthy, experienced British tobacco firms.

On February 22, 1784, a three-hundred-ton vessel called the *Empress of China* departed New York harbor on a thirteen-thousand-mile voyage to Canton.[16] It was sent off with a thirteen-gun salute, symbolic perhaps of the significance of the enterprise: for this voyage was the quintessential business innovation of the 1780s, embodying many of the essential traits of other entrepreneurial experiments of the time. It was a national effort, drawing on the resources of several states. Capital was supplied by firms in Philadelphia and New York, the vessel

15. Jacob M. Price, *France and the Chesapeake: A History of the French Tobacco Monopoly, 1674–1791, and of Its Relationship to the British and American Tobacco Trades*, 2 vols. (Ann Arbor, Mich., 1973), I, 741–743, 745–758, 761–786, 1088–1099.

16. Foster Rhea Dulles, *The Old China Trade* (Boston, 1930), chap. 1.

was built in Baltimore, and the voyage was managed by a young man from Boston, Samuel Shaw, who acted as supercargo. Robert Morris, as usual, was the main promoter of the voyage, and his aims were frankly nationalistic. By audaciously challenging the powerful British East India Company in its own market, Morris hoped not only to earn a profit for himself but to "encourage others in the adventurous pursuit of commerce." And as was so often the case in this period, the venture was closely related to wartime experience; the vessel itself had been a privateer, while Samuel Shaw, a former aide-de-camp to Henry Knox, was highly recommended by Washington himself.

What was less typical of the *Empress of China*'s pioneering voyage was its unqualified success. Returning to New York in March 1785 with a cargo of assorted teas and cotton prints, the vessel earned a 25 percent profit for its owners.[17] Other merchants in Salem, New York, and Philadelphia, disappointed in their conventional routes of trade, responded with alacrity to this new opportunity. The first Philadelphia ship to enter the China market, the *Canton*, left the Delaware Valley in January 1786, earned a "good profit" in a seventeen-month voyage, and promptly returned to China again.[18] Although complete data are unavailable, it is evident that this trade rapidly became a permanent and important part of the city's commerce. Already by the return of the second voyage of the *Canton*, in the spring of 1789, the market for teas had been glutted by the simultaneous arrival of several other China traders, which is some indication of success in establishing of a new trade. One Philadelphia merchant, Benjamin Fuller, was interested in four Pacific ventures in 1789.[19] Philadelphia remained a leader of the China trade during its first two decades, sending out as many as seven ships per year, in addition to ventures to India and North America's Pacific coast.[20]

Seven voyages may seem to be a trivial addition to the commerce of a port that received over seven hundred vessels annually, but this simple numerical proportion is misleading. The true significance of the China trade can be discerned only by viewing it from the perspective of the merchants themselves, that is, as the value of capital over time. To fit out

17. *Ibid.*, 26.

18. Jacob E. Cooke, *Tench Coxe and the Early Republic* (Chapel Hill, N.C., 1978), 74–77.

19. *Ibid.*, 77; Benjamin Fuller Journal, 1782–1789, 360–361, William West Account Books, 1709–1804, HSP.

20. Dulles, *Old China Trade*, 28; Jonathan Goldstein, *Philadelphia and the China Trade, 1682–1846: Commercial, Cultural, and Attitudinal Effects* (University Park, Pa., 1978), 34. No precise conclusions on this subject are possible at present, but it is evident that no other port greatly outstripped Philadelphia in the trade.

a vessel for the China trade and load it with an appropriate cargo required a huge sum of money; four early ventures for which we have data had an average capitalization of £28,513.[21] This capital was tied up not for a few months, but for over a year. Consequently, if Philadelphia received just four vessels from Canton per year, each with an investment of £25,000, then the China trade would have tied up £100,000. Such a sum could theoretically have financed over one hundred voyages per year in the West Indies trade, where vessels and cargoes were smaller and voyages much shorter.

This calculation reveals the crucial bottleneck facing the early China traders. Doing business in Canton was not in itself inordinately difficult. Although the American interlopers had to meet jealous competition from the traders of Europe, the Chinese merchants treated them evenhandedly. As for the dangers of the voyage itself—scurvy, piracy, typhoons, and South Sea Indians—they were the concern of captain and crew. After all, the vessel was insured. But the merchants had to come up with the money. For the outward voyage, financing with credit was out of the question; one could not sell a bill of exchange in Philadelphia drawn on a Chinese merchant in Canton. Instead, the merchants had to invest ready money by pooling their cash in sizable investment syndicates that apparently numbered as many as seventeen firms. Even with this expedient the early voyages were thinly capitalized. The captain and supercargo of one vessel, Thomas Truxton, declared, "The Many great disadvantages I have laboured under in the prosecution of this voyage from the Smallness of Our Capital &c &c &c would fill a Quire of Common post paper to describe." An additional problem was the familiar one of market timing. Most voyages made directly to Canton and back earned their profit on the return cargo of tea, silk, and cotton prints, but it was almost impossible to foresee what the price of these goods would be in twelve or fifteen months. Thus the China trade was an expensive, risky gamble.

During the depression of the 1780s certain merchants looked not to China or Europe for new markets, but to the interior of the continent itself. The most important potential market in the trans-Appalachian West was Kentucky, a rapidly growing frontier community of seventy thousand that stretched along the southern bank of the Ohio River. Kentucky in the postwar period was in a state of extreme flux.

21. Dulles, *Old China Trade*, 26; Cooke, *Tench Coxe*, 75 n. 46, 76 n. 50; Fuller to Warder, Dearman, and Co., Apr. 18, 1788, Benjamin Fuller Letterbook, 1787–1791, 95, Benjamin Fuller Papers, 1762–1799, HSP.

It was in the process of breaking off from Virginia and becoming a separate state, and it was also embroiled in international politics because it needed a port through which to export its tobacco, skins, and flour. The logical choice was New Orleans, but this city had been closed to American trade by the Spanish.

Into this complex situation stepped James Wilkinson in 1783. Neither planter nor merchant, Wilkinson was a brash young war hero on the way to becoming a professional intriguer. Wilkinson quickly recognized the chance to fuse business, politics, and diplomacy in a single venture by taking a cargo of goods down the Mississippi to sell at New Orleans. By opening this valuable outlet for Kentucky farmers he could establish his political popularity in the region while earning a good profit for himself. Wilkinson skillfully used a diplomatic lever to open the port; he held out to the Spanish governor the possibility that Kentucky would split off from the United States and join the Spanish Empire if it were allowed access to the Gulf of Mexico. But if denied this privilege, he warned the gullible Spaniards, Kentucky might ally itself with Great Britain, which still controlled forts along the Great Lakes, or even fight the Spanish by itself. Fortified by generous bribes, these blandishments succeeded, and Wilkinson was able to send four caravans of riverboats down to New Orleans in 1788 and 1789, in addition to one upriver venture.[22]

Although born in Maryland, Wilkinson had close ties with the Philadelphia merchant community. He originally went to Kentucky as an agent for the Philadelphia firm of Barclay, Moylan, and Company, and he was married to the sister of the merchants Clement and John Biddle. Wilkinson also had financial connections with the Philadelphia merchant Joseph Ball, as well as with Oliver Pollock, an occasional resident of Philadelphia who served as Robert Morris's correspondent in New Orleans. Pollock himself may have tried to ship Pennsylvania foodstuffs to New Orleans by the river route. The former Philadelphia merchant Daniel Clark was also involved in this commerce.[23]

The Philadelphia firm that became most heavily involved in the Kentucky-Mississippi trade, however, was Reed and Forde, and its experience is of special interest because it clearly reveals the dynamic interaction of adversity and innovation in Philadelphia's merchant commu-

22. James Ripley Jacobs, *Tarnished Warrior: Major-General James Wilkinson* (New York, 1938), chap. 4.

23. *Ibid.*, 71, 83–89; Biddle to James Wilkinson, Apr. 10, Oct. 7, 1789, to [Rudolph] Tillier, Apr. 24, 1789, to Isaac B. Dunn and Abner W. Dunn, July 22, 1789, Clement Biddle Letterbook, 1789–1792, HSP.

nity.[24] John Reed and Standish Forde were social climbers during the Revolution. Reed secured a commercial foothold by running errands for older merchants, and the pair expanded their operations at the end of the war by importing on credit a considerable quantity of dry goods. At about the same time, they also bought approximately ninety thousand acres of wild lands in western Virginia and Kentucky which, like the dry goods, they hoped to sell for a quick profit.[25]

In fact, neither their land nor their dry goods could be sold profitably once the postwar boom collapsed, yet the firm owed over £11,000 to its British supplier, which was angrily demanding immediate payment.[26] This dilemma holds the key to explaining Reed and Forde's activities between 1785 and 1792. Scrambling to avoid imminent bankruptcy, they took large risks to command the speculative gains needed to pay their debts. As one historian has written, "In the course of these various enterprises, they were constantly taking risks that appalled their more conservative creditors—for, though they lent money, they themselves were deep in debt throughout most of this period, and that fact doubtless goes far to explain their conduct."[27] The specific character of the firm's illiquid assets actually helped to set the course of their speculations. Possessing both lands in the Monongahela Valley and unsalable goods in its Philadelphia warehouse, the firm combined the two in a single westward venture. In 1788 Reed and Forde established a store near Tenmile Creek, West Virginia, where they managed to sell goods worth about £1,035. A logical extension of this strategy was to send dry goods by wagon and riverboat to Kentucky; exchange them for tobacco, furs, and flour; take these commodities by riverboat to the Spanish settlements of the lower Mississippi; and exchange them for specie that could be shipped back to Philadelphia.[28]

This plan was, in effect, an inland version of the triangular trade

24. This account is based upon both the Reed and Forde Papers and Arthur P. Whitaker, "Reed and Forde: Merchant Adventurers of Philadelphia," *Pennsylvania Magazine of History and Biography*, LXI (1937), 237–262, a most valuable article.

25. *Ibid.*, 242 n. 8.

26. Cruger, Lediard, and Mullet, Account Current with Reed and Forde, Reed and Forde Papers, box 2.

27. Whitaker, "Reed and Forde," *PMHB*, LXI (1937), 240.

28. R. and F. to Cruger, Lediard, and Mullet, Nov. 20, 1787, Reed and Forde Letterbook, 1787, 78, to Samuel Hanway, Jan. 25, 1788, to William Forwood, Sept. 24, 1788, to ———, Sept. 24, 1788, to John Lewis, Oct. 10, 1788, Reed and Forde Letterbook, 1788–1790, 101, 177, 184, 194. Sales at the "Monongahela Store" are listed in the Reed and Forde Daybook, 1785–1791, Reed and Forde Papers.

routes that merchants often used in the Atlantic basin, but it was a good deal more rigorous. A small, half-legible diary kept by the leader of one of the trips is a harrowing litany of trials and frustrations to which debtors' prison might have been an attractive alternative. Although Indians were a danger, repeated groundings on sandbars were the major hazard. The highly variable level of the rivers meant that the heavy boats, fully laden with flour, tended to snag on a bar in high water and become completely grounded when the water level later dropped. So serious was a grounding that occurred on December 27, 1790, that the leader of the expedition was forced to travel downriver to hire additional men to drag the boat back into the water. Hampered by ice and lack of provisions, his party was not able to return to the boat until January 6, and it took three more days of grueling effort, part of it spent wading in the swift, frigid water—"The men suffer much," the diarist wrote—before the boat was finally moving again.[29]

Working partly in concert with James Wilkinson, Reed and Forde carried out such ventures in 1788, 1789, and 1790, investing approximately two thousand pounds in each one.[30] In addition, they seem to have conducted a direct maritime trade with New Orleans. Five of nine vessels entering Delaware Bay from the port in 1791 were consigned to them, and they traded heavily with the Louisiana city through the 1790s. Although their affairs continued to be dogged by misfortunes that resulted, in part, from their own carelessness and overconfidence, these tireless adventurers did much to open up trade with Louisiana.

The Bank of North America

The furthest-reaching economic innovation of the 1780s, the Bank of North America, not only yielded a good profit for its shareholders but also spearheaded the financial modernization of Philadelphia.[31]

29. "A Journal of a Trip to New Madrid," 1790, Reed and Forde Papers, box 3.

30. Whitaker, "Reed and Forde," *PMHB*, LXI (1937), 246–251; Reed and Forde Daybook, 1785–1791, 228, 259, 289, 308, 324.

31. In addition to the bank's papers in the HSP, see Lawrence Lewis, Jr., *A History of the Bank of North America: The First Bank Chartered in the United States* (Philadelphia, 1882), 24–80, 133–147; Bray Hammond, *Banks and Politics in America from the Revolution to the Civil War* (Princeton, N.J., 1957), 40–88; Fritz Redlich, *The Molding of American Banking: Men and Ideas*, Pt. I, *1781–1840*, 2d ed. (New York, 1968), 24–42; Slaski, "Thomas Willing," 269–317; George David Rappaport, "The First Description of the Bank of North America," *William and Mary Quarterly*, 3d Ser., XXXIII (1976), 661–667. Of the many pamphlets on the bank, the best is Carey, ed., *Debates and Proceedings*. The best study of one of the first generation of American banks is N.S.B. Gras, *The Massachu-*

The bank was a war measure, a central pillar in Robert Morris's plan to restore the financial integrity of the United States government after the collapse of 1780–1781. Morris believed that the financial standing of the government was too thoroughly discredited to be rebuilt directly. Instead, he decided to erect a parallel scaffolding of independent financial institutions that could, as it were, prop up the credit of the government.[32] One segment of this scaffolding was the private credit of Morris himself; a second part was the Bank of North America. As conceived of by Morris, the bank's stock would be owned by private investors, but it would receive deposits from and make loans to both individuals and the federal government. By issuing banknotes the bank would also furnish the nation with a new paper currency to replace the discredited paper money issued by the government. Because its depositors and shareholders would be the nation's businessmen, the bank would unite the interests of the central government and moneyed men who had been alienated by the recent hyperinflation.

Morris's proposal for the bank passed Congress in May 1781, but successful launching of the enterprise depended upon actually raising the necessary capital, and investor interest was tepid at best. For the one thousand shares worth $400 (£150) each that were offered to the public, only 193 people came forth, with the typical commitment being a purchase of one or two shares. The bank could never have commenced operations without tapping two other sources of capital.[33] One was the government; fully 63 percent of the bank's shares were originally subscribed by the United States, using part of a huge cargo of specie that was shipped to Boston from France. Even this was merely a paper investment, however, because once it commenced operations, the bank promptly lent the money back to the government. A more meaningful source of capital was the strongboxes of four magnates: Robert Morris, William Bingham, Jeremiah Wadsworth, and Wadsworth's partner John Barker Church. Owning roughly one hundred shares each after the United States liquidated its interest in the bank, these four men controlled 40 percent of the shares by 1783. Thus the bank, like the pioneering voyages to Canton, depended heavily on venture capital supplied by the great merchants of the Revolutionary era.

Despite the substantial investments by Wadsworth and Church, the

---

setts First National Bank of Boston, 1784–1934, Harvard Studies in Business History, IV (Cambridge, Mass., 1937).

32. E. James Ferguson, *The Power of the Purse: A History of American Public Finance* (Chapel Hill, N.C., 1961), 121–124.

33. See Lewis, *Bank of North America*, 133–135.

bank was a creature of Robert Morris's throughout the 1780s. In addition to being its founder and one of its leading stockholders, Morris controlled the government's deposits in the bank until he resigned as superintendent of finance in November 1784. The board of directors was dominated by his Philadelphia business associates, and the chief of day-to-day operations was Morris's former partner, Thomas Willing. The cashier, Tench Francis, was also a member of Philadelphia's Anglican mercantile elite. Despite the potential for incestuous lending to insiders, this management team performed well and was not changed even after the bank's stock was enlarged. The officers and directors trusted one another, and the innovative brilliance of Morris was well balanced by the plodding steadiness of his former partner.[34]

By any measure the bank was a bold innovation. Not only was the corporate form of business organization previously unknown in Philadelphia commerce, but short-term lending as conducted by the bank was rare before the war. The bank's technical problems were, in themselves, formidable. In addition to making prudent loans and guarding against bad checks and counterfeit banknotes, Willing and his staff had to maintain the accounts of over five hundred very active depositors. In short, commercial banking was terra incognita to Philadelphia's traders. As Willing wrote to the founders of a Boston bank,

> When the Bank was first Opened here the Business was as much a Novelty to us, who undertook the management of it as it can Possibly be to you—It was a pathless wilderness, ground, but little known to this Side [of the] Atlantick, no Book then spoke of the Interior Arrangements or Rules observ'd in Europe—Accident alone threw in our way, even the form, of an English Bank Bill.[35]

Willing wisely conducted his trek into this "pathless wilderness, ground" with great caution. He restricted loans to maturities of thirty days or fewer and maintained ample reserves of cash to cover the bank's liabilities. Although such caution theoretically reduced the bank's profitability, this mattered little, for the bank dominated the market for a commodity to which aggressive merchants and an impecunious government were utterly addicted—short-term credit. One did not have to take great risks to make money in such a market. "I am so very much engrossed . . . , by the very great increase of business," Willing wrote, "that I have never

34. Redlich, *Molding of American Banking*, 26; Slaski, "Thomas Willing," 276–298.

35. Thomas Willing to William Philips *et al.*, Jan. 6, 1784, Bank of North America Minutebook, 1781–1792, Bank of North America Papers, HSP (hereafter cited as BNA Papers). This famous, informative letter is printed in Gras, *First National Bank of Boston*, 209–212.

spent half an hour out of the bank since you left me."[36] Despite its initially weak financial underpinnings, the bank was able to declare a dividend of 8.74 percent in 1782, and it remained profitable until the end of the century.[37]

Nevertheless, the enterprise faced serious threats during its early years; at times its very survival was in question.[38] Competition within Philadelphia was one source of concern. The impressive early dividends of the bank prompted speculation in the shares already sold to subscribers, which pushed their market price above the original offering price of four hundred dollars per share. Since the company was still poorly capitalized, this seemed to be a propitious time to sell additional stock. It was only fair for new investors to pay the advanced market price for shares, for while the initial subscribers had risked their funds in an untested project, the feasibility of the bank had now been demonstrated. Accordingly, the board of directors decided in 1784 to issue one thousand more shares at the price of five hundred dollars.

Potential purchasers of this stock were far too resourceful, however, pliantly to pay a 25 percent premium for entry into Robert Morris's bank. They decided instead to start a bank of their own, to be called the Bank of Pennsylvania, and asked the Pennsylvania legislature for a charter.[39] It is often assumed that these rival bankers were Quaker merchants, but this assessment is far too simple. In a penetrating letter John Chaloner dissected the background of the president and directors of the proposed bank, and it is evident that, in order to counter the commanding prestige of Robert Morris, Thomas Willing, and William Bingham, a shrewdly balanced directorate was constructed. Only four of the thirteen men were Quakers, and the founders were careful to include a German and an Irishman on the board. As for their political leanings, four were whigs (of whom three supported Pennsylvania's radical constitution), two were tories, five had been "perfect neuters" during the war, and two were of ambiguous persuasion. They were, in general, members of Philadelphia's pre-Revolutionary mercantile elite who had bided their time during the war while the future founders of the Bank of North America were enlarging their fortunes. Though now overshadowed by Morris and Bingham, their estates were intact and their credit sound, and together

36. Quoted in Slaski, "Thomas Willing," 286.

37. For the bank's dividends, see Joseph Stancliffe Davis, *Essays in the Earlier History of American Corporations*, 2 vols., Harvard Economic Studies, XVI (Cambridge, Mass., 1917), II, 104.

38. Chaloner to Jeremiah Wadsworth, Oct. 19, 1784, John Chaloner Letterbook, 1782–1784, 401, Chaloner and White Collection, HSP.

39. Chaloner Letterbook, 1782–1784; Cooke, *Tench Coxe*, 87–92.

they constituted a formidable combination of talent and wealth. It was an astoundingly eclectic coalition to find one year after the close of a civil war. As Chaloner wrote:

> Interest Unites the Violent Constitutionalist, the Neutral Character & the Tory. those who have been persecuted, now persue the same object of their persecutors, and in doing this hail each other as friends. Interest no longer draws them assunder. The high Churchman, the rigid Presbyterian, The plain coat Quakers headed with a Limb of the Law, are here joind together. They have Wisdom & cunning to devise Resolutions to prosecute, and prudence to ad to what they have gaind. Under the Auspices of such Characters I have no doubt but they will equal the other Bank in every assential matter proportionable to their Capital.[40]

Thomas Willing evidently shared this assessment, for he rushed to appease the interlopers by reducing the price of the new stock to four hundred dollars. Simple timidity and a fondness for monopoly partly explain Willing's accommodating posture, but another consideration affected his judgment. Willing doubted whether two rival banks could survive in the same city, because they would continually raid each other's supply of specie.[41] This raiding had, in fact, already occurred. Investors in the Bank of Pennsylvania had bought their shares with Bank of North America banknotes, which officers of the new bank had promptly presented to Willing for redemption in specie. To avoid a possibly ruinous bank war, Willing was happy to reduce the price of the newly issued shares and, in effect, buy off his opponents.

This move was of political significance during the 1780s, for it meant that Robert Morris's bank was now the bank of the merchant community as a whole. Most leading traders in the Quaker City owned at least a few shares in it, and they used it as well to receive loans and transfer funds. However, as we saw in the preceding chapter, this important commercial tool became locked in a death struggle with the Pennsylvania Assembly, whose agrarian leaders, not unlike their Jacksonian successors, considered it a political and economic menace. On September 13, 1785, the bank's state charter was revoked, and it was forced to depend upon its federal charter and a charter granted by the state of Delaware. Not until

40. Chaloner to Wadsworth and Carter, Feb. 14, 1784, Chaloner Letterbook, 1782–1784, 252.

41. Anna Jacobson Schwartz, "The Beginning of Competitive Banking in Philadelphia, 1782–1809," *Journal of Political Economy*, LV (1947), 417–420.

it received a new charter from Pennsylvania in March 1787 was the bank's legitimacy assured.

The bank was also tested by the depression of the 1780s, for the heavy outflow of specie to Europe in payment for dry goods depleted its reserves, while a couple of major debtors went bankrupt. These problems forced the cautious Willing to suspend discounting (lending) for a time. It is a measure of how rapidly the bank had become enmeshed in the port's financial system that this move injured many traders, though it evidently caused no bankruptcies.[42] Suspension of discounting also cut into the earnings of the bank itself, which reduced its dividend to 6 percent in 1785, 1786, and 1787. But with the restoration of commercial prosperity, loan demand soared. The dividend was a remarkable 13.5 percent in 1791 and 12.5 percent in 1792. Significantly enough, the profitability of the bank was not seriously affected by the founding of the Bank of the United States in 1791 and the Bank of Philadelphia in 1793.

The bank's financial structure can be understood by reviewing its basic sources of funds for lending: capital stock, deposits, and the banknotes that it issued. After the second stock issue in 1784 the equity capital of the bank remained in the range of $750,000–$850,000 until the 1790s.[43] The reason the capital base of this successful corporation did not grow was that its "pay-out ratio"—the percentage of profits that were distributed to shareholders as dividends—was very high.[44] Almost no earnings were retained for reinvestment in the company. This financial strategy probably reflected two considerations. For one thing, high dividends in 1783 and 1784 were a wise move because they excited investor interest in the bank, making it relatively easy to sell more stock. Furthermore, the bank's major shareholders were aggressive capitalists who normally had a pressing need for funds to invest in new projects.

42. Chaloner to Wadsworth and Carter, Oct. 18, 1783, May 15, 1784, Chaloner Letterbook, 1782–1784, 193, 296. F. and J. West to Haxall and West, Apr. 12, 1785, Francis and John West Letterbook, 1783–1786, 113, William West Account Books, 1769–1804, HSP.

43. This was well below the $2,000,000 worth of stock actually authorized, and also below its peak level of stock outstanding in the 1780s. After the extension of the second stock issue in Mar. 1784, the outstanding stock amounted to about 2,171 shares, or $868,400. See Lewis, *Bank of North America*, 133–147, and Slaski, "Thomas Willing," 314. But in a letter to Alexander Hamilton of Oct. 1, 1789, Thomas Willing said that the bank's capital was "exactly 728,400 dollars," and in Mar. 1792, it was $743,600 (see Minutebook, 1781–1792, and State of the Bank, 1792–1796, BNA Papers). This shrinkage occurred because some stockholders sold back their shares, perhaps in order to cover loans that they could not pay off during the depression of the 1780s. See Ledger, 1784–1785, 599, 600, BNA Papers.

44. See Profit and Loss Account in Ledger, 1784–1785, 618, BNA Papers.

TABLE 18. *Deposits in the Bank of North America, 1789*

Account Size	No. of Accounts	Proportion of All Accounts
0–$50	185	29%
$51–$100	51	8
$101–$250	126	20
$251–$500	109	17
$501–$1,000	86	13
$1,000+	84	13
Total	641	100

Source: Bank of North America Ledger, 1789–1790, Bank of North America Papers, Historical Society of Pennsylvania.

They probably were not content to reinvest their money in a relatively staid company when speculation in land or securities held out the promise of tripling their capital in a few years.

In the 1780s the bank had roughly six hundred depositors, and in 1792 total deposits on hand amounted to $896,047, or 21 percent more than the capital stock.[45] That the typical balance was not large was probably because no interest was paid on deposits. Not surprisingly, only 13 percent of the deposits in 1789 exceeded $1,000 (£375)(see table 18). Many of these bank accounts were extremely active, for a busy merchant made frequent deposits and might write forty or fifty checks per month.[46] As early as 1784, between 300 and 450 entries were made in the bank's giant ledgers each day.[47] Thus, although not yet the standard mode of payment they would later become, checks were already ubiquitous in Philadelphia commerce.

Compared with deposits, banknotes were a relatively simple liability for the bank to manage; they were printed, issued to borrowers, and pasted into books when they finally wore out. The notes held their value in the financial marketplace because they were convertible into specie at the bank on demand. Despite their efficiency, however, the notes were

45. State of the Bank, 1792–1796, entries for March 1792, *ibid.*

46. See ledgers, *ibid.*; Charles Wharton Daybook, 1775–1785, last 16 pages; Clement Biddle Journal, 1781–1784, 63–68, 70, 72, 76, 81, 86, 90, 117, 120, 128, 130, 157, 161, Thomas A. Biddle Collection, HSP.

47. See above, n. 35.

issued surprisingly sparingly. In March 1792 the bank's outstanding notes were worth $764,250, or 3.5 percent less than deposits and only 2.7 percent more than shareholders' capital. According to Thomas Willing, the value of outstanding notes during the 1780s equaled only about $364,200.[48] Thus, under the cautious guidance of Thomas Willing, the bank did not function as some of its major boosters, including Robert Morris, had anticipated. Pelatiah Webster, an influential pamphleteer, wrote, for example, that the bank would be able to support a note issue equal to 200 or 300 percent of its paid-in capital. Actually, it was closer to 50 percent in the 1780s, a fact of considerable economic significance.[49] This restraint suggests that banknotes played a much smaller role in the Delaware Valley's money supply than either contemporary observers or modern historians have supposed. During the 1780s the bank's outstanding notes were actually worth 54 percent less than the value of paper money in circulation in Pennsylvania in 1766—this despite the great expansion of the economy in the intervening period.[50] Evidently there was a fairly gradual transition from the colonial money supply of specie and paper money issued by provincial governments to the nineteenth-century pattern of specie supplemented by commercial paper and a profusion of private banknotes.

Having accumulated liabilities by selling stock, receiving deposits, and issuing banknotes, the bank earned money with these funds by lending them out for very short terms, as we have observed, normally thirty days or fewer, through an operation called discounting. As will be explained in greater detail below, discounting simply involved buying promissory notes before they matured. It could be a risky operation, particularly in financially turbulent periods like the 1780s, because large sums could be lost by purchasing the notes of firms that were on the verge of bankruptcy. "This is the most Critical part of the Business," wrote Thomas Willing, "& to avoid confusion, it must be very carefully attended to."[51] Accordingly, discounting was performed by the entire board of directors, on Thursdays only, and a single director could veto a decision to buy a note.

The Bank of North America was plainly a bank for businessmen,

48. State of the Bank, 1792–1796, BNA Papers; Thomas Willing to Alexander Hamilton, Oct. 1, 1789, Minutebook, 1781–1792, BNA Papers.

49. Pelatiah Webster, *An Essay on Credit* . . . (Philadelphia, 1786), 12, notes that deposits or capital could support two or three times their value in banknotes.

50. Based on a comparison of the figure of $364,200, cited above, with data in Joseph Albert Ernst, *Money and Politics in America, 1755–1775: A Study in the Currency Act of 1764 and the Political Economy of Revolution* (Chapel Hill, N.C., 1973), 368.

51. See above, n. 35.

TABLE 19. *Occupational Distribution of Account-Holders in the Bank of North America, 1784–1785*

	All Accounts		Very Active Accounts	
Occupational Status	No.	Proportion	No.	Proportion
Merchant	199	47%	86	68%
Retailer	61	14	15	12
Artisan	43	10	3	2
Gentleman	45	11	8	6
Professional	10	2	1	1
Miscellaneous[a]	68	16	13	10
Total	426	100	126	100

Sources: Bank of North America Ledger, 1784–1785, Bank of North America Papers, Historical Society of Pennsylvania; Clement Biddle, ed., *The Philadelphia Directory* (Philadelphia, 1791).

Note: Data are based on 426 of the 832 depositors in bank, and occupational distribution is based on the 1791 Philadelphia city directory. Some of those listed as "gentleman" were probably merchants in 1784 and 1785.

[a]Primarily brokers, government employees, and manufacturers in processing industries.

especially merchants, but its clientele was nevertheless fairly broad. Operating in a city with roughly 7,600 heads of households in 1790, it had accounts with about 830 people or firms in 1784–1785, and it discounted the notes and bills of over 1,200 people in 1790 and 1791 (see occupational distributions in tables 19, 20). While merchants clearly predominated, substantial numbers of artisans and retailers also used the bank. Grocers in particular were prominent customers; the volume of their trade rivaled that of many mercantile firms. By contrast, very few professionals are represented, perhaps because they seldom used the commercial instruments handled by the bank and were loath to deposit money in an institution that paid no interest.

In one of the few appraisals of the economic impact of the early commercial banks, N. S. B. Gras questioned Thomas Willing's assertion that commercial banking was a "pathless wilderness, ground"

TABLE 20. *Occupational Distribution of Discounters in the Bank of North America, 1790–1791*

Occupational Status	All Discounters		Very Active Discounters	
	No.	Proportion	No.	Proportion
Merchant	162	34%	50	57%
Retailer	126	27	28	32
Artisan	96	20	0	0
Gentleman	38	8	2	2
Professional	9	2	0	0
Miscellaneous	44	9	7	8
Total	475	100	87	100

Sources: Bank of North America Discount Book, Bank of North America Papers, Historical Society of Pennsylvania. Clement Biddle, ed., *The Philadelphia Directory* (Philadelphia, 1791).

Note: Data based on borrowers with initials A–L (675) who appear in *Philadelphia Directory* for 1791 (475); estimated total number of discounters is 1,350.

when the Bank of North America opened its doors.[52] Gras suggested that the creation of a banking corporation simply allowed merchants to centralize in a single institution the short-term lending operations they had been carrying on privately for some time. This may have been true of Boston, which Gras has studied in some detail, but it does not describe the situation in Revolutionary Philadelphia. Willing was right. It is no exaggeration to say that the Bank of North America was part of a general restructuring of Philadelphia's financial markets between 1775 and 1790. This reorganization impressively modernized the port's financial system by increasing the liquidity, or flexibility, of businessmen's assets, thereby allowing them to transact more business with the same amount of property. The commercial capital of the port was, in effect, mobilized and extended—a valuable improvement in a capital-short economy.

The basic evidence for this financial reorganization in Phildelphia lies not in the records of the bank itself, but in the ledgers and journals of

52. Gras, *First National Bank of Boston*, 12.

individual merchants. These records demonstrate that in colonial Philadelphia there was almost no commercial paper, whereas after the war it was common. Commercial paper is essentially a promise to pay in the near future—usually one to six months. If Merchant A bought wheat worth one hundred pounds from Merchant B, he could pay for it in several ways:

1. A could give B one hundred pounds in currency.
2. A could tell B that he would pay him in the future. B would keep a receipt to document the transaction and debit A one hundred pounds in his ledger. This entry created an asset for B, called a book debt.
3. A could give B an IOU, or "note," promising to pay B at some specified time in the future, such as thirty days.
4. A could pay B with a draft, or "bill," on C (who owed money to A). Usually C was not expected to pay this draft immediately, but, rather, within thirty or sixty days.

Commercial paper was simply the notes and bills described in methods 3 and 4. The financial reorganization of Philadelphia trade consisted of a partial but highly important shift to these forms of payment from the cash transaction of method 1 and the book debt of method 2. Prewar ledgers and journals make no mention of notes and bills,[53] but both the massive evidence in the bank records and the papers of many firms indicate that payment with commercial paper was very common in the 1780s. A postwar ledger normally included an account of "notes and bills receivable" (IOUs and time drafts which the owner of the ledger could present for payment when they matured) and an account of "notes and bills payable," which had been issued by the owner of the ledger and would have to be paid by him when they fell due. (Table 21 gives a good sense of this system by stating the financial assets and liabilities of three postwar merchants, a few among the many traders who regularly used commercial paper.)[54]

53. See Joshua Fisher and Sons Ledger, 1769–1773, HSP; Mifflin and Massey Ledger, 1760–1763, HSP; Thomas Riche Journal, 1757–1761, Thomas Riche Papers, HSP; John and Peter Chevalier Daybook, 1760–1766, HSP; John Greeves Ledger, 1753–1757, HSP; Samuel Neave Ledger, 1752–1756, HSP; John Baynton Ledger B, 1754–1757, Baynton, Wharton, and Morgan Papers, Reel 7, Pennsylvania Historical and Museum Commission.

54. Charles Wharton Daybook, 1775–1785; Clement Biddle Journal; James and John Cox Ledger, 1788–1802, Thomas A. Biddle Collection, HSP; Samuel and Miers Fisher Journal; Thomas Armat Ledger, 1781–1784, Thomas Armat Papers, in Loudoun Papers, HSP; Coxe and Frazier Journals, 1783–1785, 1785–1787, Tench Coxe Papers, Reel 20 (all references to the Coxe Papers are to the microfilm collection, available in HSP and various other libraries, of the original Coxe Papers in HSP); Fitzsimons Journal.

TABLE 21. *Financial Assets and Liabilities of Three Philadelphia Merchants*

	Stephen Girard 1785	Levi Hollingsworth 1785	Benjamin Fuller 1789
Assets			
Cash	£ 527	£ 99	£ 0
Notes and bills receivable	1,814	0	481
Book debts due	5,115	19,236	6,222
Bank stock	0	300	5,215
Other	338[a]	165[b]	0
Total	7,794	19,800	11,918
Liabilities			
Notes and bills payable	1,481	1,469	142
Book debts due	6,968	13,780	4,953
Bills of exchange	189	0	17
Other	600[c]	0	0
Total	9,238	15,249	5,112

Sources: Stephen Girard Journal, 1783–1786, 90–92, Girard Papers, 3d Ser., Reel 113, American Philosophical Society; Levi Hollingsworth Journal, 1784–1785, 377–398, Hollingsworth Papers; Benjamin Fuller Journal, 1782–1789, 360–363, William West Account Books, Historical Society of Pennsylvania.

[a]Bills of exhange.

[b]Bank deposit plus public securities.

[c]Bond.

This is not to suggest that commercial paper had replaced book debts entirely—only that they supplemented them after the war. The relevant gauge of the importance of these new instruments is their quantity relative not to book debts, which still composed most of the merchants' financial assets, but to their only other liquid asset: cash. Notes and bills receivable might equal or exceed in value the cash holdings of a merchant. The reason for this shift to commercial paper cannot be precisely established, but it seems to be related to the inflation brought on by the Revolutionary war. Since the value of book debts shrank rapidly during the war, creditors probably insisted on receiving short-term debt instruments that matured at a specific time in the near future.

Commercial paper and the bank were like a nut and a bolt: neither made sense without the other, and the thread that engaged them was the process of discounting. A hypothetical example will illustrate the nature of discounting and how it streamlined the commercial process. Let us suppose that Stephen Girard had to load a vessel for the West Indies with flour. The estimated cost of the cargo was £1,000, but he had only £500 in cash in his strongbox. Since he had already sold the inward cargo of rum to a grocer, William Jennings, receiving a sixty-day note worth £1,000 in payment, Girard now had two options. He could keep the vessel in port for sixty days, tying up capital and running up port charges; finally receive the £1,000 from Jennings by presenting the note; and use this cash to buy flour for the outward cargo. Or he could obtain the cash immediately by *selling* the note to the bank for £980. By holding the note until it matured, the bank would earn £20 (£1,000 − £980). Girard had paid 2 percent on his money in just two months, or 12 percent annually, in order to get his ship out of port quickly.

There were, of course, many possible variations on this example. Instead of discounting the note of a customer, Girard could have issued his own note, backed by securities or by goods. Alternatively, he could have written a bill (time draft) on a debtor and discounted that instrument. The key point is that any of these methods would allow Girard to turn into cash an asset—whether a piece of physical property or a debt owed —that might have been illiquid before the war.[55] In 1792, for example, William Wilson and Company of Alexandria, Virginia, was speculating in securities and loading two ships for the West Indies when it found itself short of cash. It instructed its Philadelphia agent, Andrew Clow and Company, to lodge in a Philadelphia bank securities worth nine thousand dollars that belonged to Wilson and Company. Using the securities as collateral, Clow was to discount bills at the bank and send the proceeds down to Alexandria.[56]

The importance of the bank went beyond simply discounting, however, for it also acted as a large and powerful clearing house for commercial paper. One of its major functions was to collect payment on matured notes and bills. If Merchant A gave a thirty-day note to Merchant B, B could deposit it in his account at the bank, which would collect the cash

55. Robert Morris and Thomas Fitzsimons made this point in defending the bank against its agrarian critics in the Pennsylvania Assembly. See Carey, ed., *Debates and Proceedings*, 43, 94, 105.

56. Wilson and Co. to Andrew Clow and Co., Apr. 6, 1792 (extract), Andrew Clow Papers, Baker Library.

from A. If A had a deposit at the bank, the officers would do this by simply deducting the value of the note from this deposit. If A's deposit balance was too small to permit this, the bank, as Philadelphia's largest and most dependable source of short-term credit, had tremendous financial power with which to coerce payment. It was generally understood in commercial circles that the bank demanded greater "punctuality" than private creditors. Thus the bank played a moral as well as a mechanical role in making the commercial paper network operate smoothly in Philadelphia. This ensured that a merchant's funds in the hands of others were reasonably liquid and not tied up for an indeterminate period of time.[57]

The essential elements of Philadelphia's financial reorganization, then, were the concurrent emergence of commercial paper as a means of payment and of a bank that discounted and collected this paper. The economic ramifications of these innovations were wide. By allowing merchants to procure cash when they needed it, the new system fundamentally altered the commercial process itself, speeding the movement of goods in and out of port and reducing the amount of capital tied up in idle inventory. Moreover, the bank was part of a basic restructuring of the money supply of the Delaware Valley. Before the Revolution the main components of the money supply were specie and paper money. In addition, many transactions were conducted through a modified barter system, in which goods were sold on credit, and the resulting debt was eventually paid off either with goods or with cash. One consequence of the war, however, was that government-backed money was discredited as a medium of exchange. In its stead were substituted notes issued by the Bank of North America; deposits in the bank on which checks were constantly written; government bonds, which could be bartered for goods or used to buy public lands at the Pennsylvania land office; and commercial paper. We have seen that banknotes were a less important segment of the money supply than has been supposed. On the other hand, commercial paper was a very significant medium of exchange.[58] Merchants could buy goods with promissory notes, write bills on funds that were in the hands of other traders, or even pass paper to an associate that involved only third and fourth parties. (In the last case, A would pay B with a draft of C on D, which C had originally given to A in

57. On the bank's handling of commercial paper, see Ledgers, 1783–1784, 1784–1785, and items 13, 14, and 15 of the minutes of a board of directors meeting held on Nov. 12, 1782, in Minutebook, 1781–1792, BNA Papers. On the "punctuality" encouraged by the bank, see Hammond, *Banks and Politics*, 86.

58. Thomas Paine, *Dissertations on Government, the Affairs of the Bank, and Paper-Money* (Philadelphia, 1786), 44, notes that commercial paper was no less a form of money than a banknote, because it could be converted into money.

payment for goods.) Already common by 1790, these various uses of commercial paper became nearly universal in nineteenth-century trade.[59]

Securities Speculation

Still another novel activity of post-Revolutionary entrepreneurs, one rendered rather too famous by Charles Beard, was investment in the bonds issued by the federal and state governments during the Revolution. The desirability of these securities varied greatly according to the precise provisions made to retire them and to pay the interest. The best bonds of the federal government were "loan certificates," on which interest was paid with bills of exchange, equivalent to specie, until 1782. But because the supply of such bonds was limited, a more important speculative medium was the "final settlements" paid to officers and soldiers of the Continental army in 1784. State debts likewise varied in quality according to whether interest was paid with paper money, specie, or merely certificates of interest and according to the method used to withdraw them from circulation. Many states paid off their obligations through taxation, while others, including Pennsylvania, New York, and Massachusetts, also exchanged them for frontier lands. Changing with every shift in government policies, these complex factors were reflected in the market price of the securities, which generally ranged from ten cents to forty cents on the dollar before 1785.[60]

Whether it was for the purpose of making a long-term speculation or buying frontier acreage at the Pennsylvania land office, a number of Philadelphia merchants dealt in securities during the first half of the 1780s. Although some firms may simply have bought and held, waiting for financial reforms that would raise security values, others traded actively in the depressed issues. The journal of Reed and Forde, for instance, shows that between January 1785 and December 1788 they bought securities valued at £1,436 while making sales worth £2,577.[61] Whatever their trading strategy, securities speculators were very prudent buyers throughout most of the decade. As late as March 1789 final settlements were selling for 4s. 6d. on the pound, a discount of 77.5 percent from face value. But prices were steadily inflated by ratification of the United States Constitution in 1788, formation of a conservative national government in 1789, and the emergence during 1790 of Alexan-

59. Anthony F. C. Wallace, *Rockdale: The Growth of an American Village in the Early Industrial Revolution* . . . (New York, 1978), 162–163.

60. Ferguson, *Power of the Purse*, 251–255.

61. Reed and Forde Daybook, 1785–1791.

der Hamilton's dual financial plan for "funding" federal debts at 100 percent of their face value and "assumption" of the states' debts by the federal government. By December 11, 1791, a Philadelphia broker reported that the price of final settlements had reached a value of twenty shillings on the pound. Thus, securities presented one of the extraordinary speculative opportunities in American history. Very seldom has an entire class of property quadrupled in price in three years without soon declining in value just as sharply.[62]

In combination with the explosion of wheat exports after 1788, this upsurge in securities prices engendered an increasingly speculative business environment in northern ports. The brokers who had cropped up during the Revolution to peddle bills of exchange, bank stock, and commercial paper avidly hawked depreciated debt in taverns and coffeehouses. Bags of gold and silver were rushed south to buy up inexpensive state bonds from unwary creditors, who did not realize that federal assumption of state debts was just months away. Well-connected merchants traveled to Europe to peddle the American debt to syndicates of wealthy men in London, Paris, and especially Amsterdam. With characteristic aggressiveness Robert Morris concocted a scheme to sell the entire national debt to a group of Frenchmen.[63] Like other speculative activity of the period, stockjobbing was closely related to commercial banking, for securities were often used to secure loans, and bank loans, in turn, partly financed the sophisticated maneuvers of the speculators. In the ebullient market of 1785–1792, securities of increasing value secured loans of increasing size, which provided stockjobbers with the liquid funds used to bid up the price of securities still further.[64]

The hub of this feverish activity was not Philadelphia, but New York. Since bonds held by foreigners had to be registered at the Treasury Department in New York (the nation's capital between 1785 and 1791), most of the American agents of foreign investors were New Yorkers.[65] Still more important, Manhattan was the best place to hear the vital leaks and rumors that might foreshadow the fate of the state and federal debt. Lest he miss such valuable intelligence, at least one dedicated speculator moved into a New York boardinghouse that accommodated sev-

62. The prices of securities may be traced in the Clement Biddle Letterbook and in Davis, *Earlier History*, I, 210, 211, 339–340, 342–345.

63. Whitney K. Bates, "Northern Speculators and Southern State Debts: 1790," *WMQ*, 3d Ser., XIX (1962), 30–48; Davis, *Earlier History*, I, 174–212; Robert C. Alberts, *The Golden Voyage: The Life and Times of William Bingham, 1752–1804* (Boston, 1969), 199–200; Ferguson, *Power of the Purse*, 258–272.

64. See Clow Papers, Baker Library, for an example.

65. Ferguson, *Power of the Purse*, 258; Davis, *Earlier History*, I, 200–201.

eral prominent congressmen.[66] But if prices were set in Manhattan, the market for securities extended to Philadelphia as well. When market conditions were changing rapidly, communication between the two cities was well-nigh continuous. In 1791 a New Brunswick, New Jersey, newspaper reported,

> Not less than twenty expresses have passed through this city within one week, from New York to Philadelphia and back—they travel with uncommon speed, from which it appears something of great importance is carrying on; it is, however, we believe, no more than the ordinary business of the day, namely stock-jobbing.[67]

Intoxicated by the explosive appreciation of government bonds, speculators expanded their portfolios to include any piece of paper that could claim the name "stock." Securities of the Society for the Encouragement of Useful Manufactures, an industrial company sponsored by Alexander Hamilton, sold rapidly in 1791, while the shares of the Lancaster Turnpike were so ravenously consumed that a lottery had to be used to distribute 1,000 shares among investors who had subscribed for a total of 2,276 shares.[68] Wilder still was the scramble for the stock of the Bank of the United States. In only two hours, 25,000 shares were sold for a down payment of $25, for which receipts, or pieces of "script," were issued. This script became the object of frenzied bidding, which in Philadelphia drove the price of a share to $325, or 1,300 percent of par value. Such grotesque speculation was a disheartening spectacle for virtuous republicans, who, after vanquishing British tyranny in a grueling civil war, were rewarded with a replay of the infamous South Sea Bubble of 1720. This catastrophic financial panic had inspired the whigs' ideological heroes, John Trenchard and Thomas Gordon, to pen *Cato's Letters*, which called the bubble "a Conspiracy of Stock-Jobbers, who were, with merciless and unclean Hands, rifling the Publick itself, ingrossing all its Wealth, and destroying, at once, all public and private Faith."[69] The Philadelphia physician Benjamin Rush felt that speculation had "introduced into our country half the miseries and vices of hell itself." "You hear of nothing but *script* and of all the *numbers* between 50 and 300 at every corner. Merchants, grocers, shopkeepers, sea captains, and even prentice boys have embarked in the business." When the bubble burst, Rush reported,

66. Davis, *Earlier History*, I, 189.

67. Quoted *ibid.*, 203.

68. Alberts, *Golden Voyage*, 236; Davis, *Earlier History*, I, 201–203, 373.

69. [John Trenchard and Thomas Gordon], *Cato's Letters: or, Essays on Liberty, Civil and Religious, and Other Important Subjects*, 4 vols. in 2 (New York, 1969 [rpt. of London, 1733 ed.]), I, 22.

one man lost $2,000 and promptly hanged himself. Another Philadelphian wrote: "My office was deserted the whole day by Mr. Davis and my apprentices, they having been infected with the Turnpike Rage. Everything is now turned into Speculation."[70]

Though distinctly less edifying than the China trade or the founding of banks, securities speculation nevertheless contributed to economic development, even as it increased social inequality and poisoned the political atmosphere. Just as Robert Morris, William Bingham, and Alexander Hamilton had hoped, speculative activity concentrated large amounts of wealth in the hands of aggressive entrepreneurs, and in a form that could be used as collateral for bank loans and finance innovative projects. Both the Bank of the United States and the Society for the Encouragement of Useful Manufactures, for example, were financed in part with subscriptions of federal bonds. In addition, the very process of speculation tended to strengthen the communications network that animated the economy of the sprawling republic like a central nervous system. "There are paper speculators dispersed over every part of the United States," wrote one merchant. "They keep up a constant & accurate communication. The information flies from one to another in every direction like an electrical shock."[71] The bonanza in public debt also lured back into the American economy European capitalists who had avoided the nation since the debacle of 1783–1784. Enriched by American securities while the ancien régime collapsed around them, not a few of these firms would return for a second dip in the American investment market—a scalding plunge into wilderness lands.

Despite its undoubted signifiance, when viewed in proper perspective, securities speculation turns out to be far less important to contemporary merchants than Charles Beard and his innumerable critics imagined. It was merely one activity among many, and generally not the most important. While an important clique of New York capitalists did become hopelessly addicted to stockjobbing, businessmen in Philadelphia and other cities were more restrained, their investments more diversified. Of seven Quaker City firms active in the 1780s for which we have information, only two were active securities investors, and even they were involved in many other concerns.

Documents concerning registration of the debt seem to confirm these findings. E. James Ferguson has found that seventy-eight investors in

70. Benjamin Rush to Mrs. Rush, Aug. 12, 1791, in L. H. Butterfield, ed., *Letters of Benjamin Rush*, 2 vols. (Princeton, N.J., 1951), I, 602–603; Charles I. Landis, "History of the Philadelphia and Lancaster Turnpike: The First Turnpike in the United States," *PMHB*, XLII (1918), 133.

71. Quoted in Ferguson, *Power of the Purse*, 254.

Pennsylvania owned securities, issued either by the United States or by the state of Pennsylvania, with a face value of ten thousand dollars or more. This figure does not include investment in the securities of other states, and it covers only about three-quarters of the securities issued by the United States and Pennsylvania that were held by Pennsylvanians. On the other hand, many of these seventy-eight investors were not Philadelphia merchants. And even an investment in securities worth ten thousand dollars represents a fairly modest initial outlay, because this figure refers to the *face value* of the securities, not the amount actually paid for them, which was typically much less. On balance it seems probable that fewer than 40 of Philadelphia's 450 merchants actually invested over three thousand pounds (eight thousand dollars) in securities and that the great majority of traders had little to do with them. Such was the conclusion also of a contemporary article in the *New York Gazette* that claimed that "about forty persons in Philadelphia, forty more in New York, thirty in Boston, ten or a dozen in Baltimore, half a dozen in Charlestown, possessed themselves of the greatest proportion of the public securities."[72] While securities holders may have been a fairly potent lobby favoring certain financial policies, they did not in themselves compose an important economic group. They were by no means equivalent to the merchants or businessmen of the northern ports.

Land Speculation

After the Revolution, a significant number of merchants and other businessmen purchased huge tracts of wilderness land and labored strenuously to make their investments profitable. As in the case of banking and securities speculation, this undertaking was a direct outgrowth of the exigencies of war. Millions of acres of unimproved land were thrown on the market during the 1780s and 1790s because states wished to reduce their indebtedness without increasing taxes. A simple, if unwise, way to do this was simply to exchange unsettled lands for cash or public securities.

A second factor pushing merchants toward land speculation during the 1780s was the familiar one of commercial adversity. As one historian has noted, "With many former markets now closed to them, and lacking specie and bills of exchange to pay balances due, the merchants began to give more thought to lands."[73] At least one Philadelphia trader

72. *Ibid.*, 277–280; Davis, *Earlier History*, I, 191.

73. Norman B. Wilkinson, "Land Policy and Speculation in Pennsylvania, 1779–1800" (Ph.D. diss., University of Pennsylvania, 1958), 84.

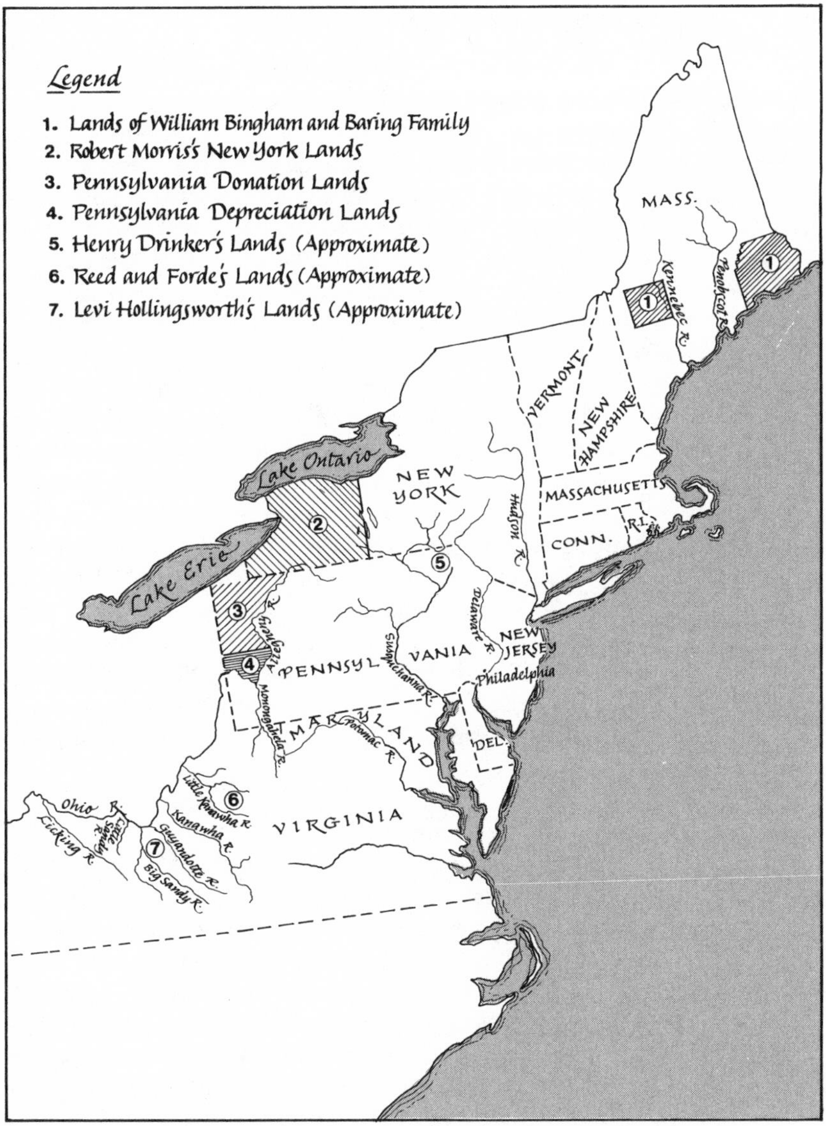

MAP 7. Land Speculation of Philadelphia Merchants, 1775–1796.
Sources: Lester J. Cappon et al., *eds.*, Atlas of Early American History: The Revolutionary Era, 1760–1790 *(Princeton, N.J., 1976); Robert C. Alberts,* The Golden Voyage: The Life and Times of William Bingham, 1752–1804 *(Boston, 1969), 233; Henry Drinker to George Joy, Dec. 20, 1790, Henry Drinker Letterbook, 1790–1793, 114, Henry Drinker Papers; Levi Hollingsworth to Enoch Story, Jan. 2, Oct. 10, 1797, to Mark Pragers, Nov. 12, 1787, Levi Hollingsworth Letterbook, 1786–1791, 12, 148, 158, Hollingsworth Papers; Reed and Forde to Samuel Hanway, Apr. 11, Sept. 10, 1789, Reed and Forde Letterbook, 245, 274, Reed and Forde Papers, all at Historical Society of Pennsylvania. Drawn by Richard Stinely*

turned his attention to western lands because he did not have sufficient "business in Philadelphia to maintain my family."[74] Although the original incentive might have been the rational decision to diversify into a more promising market, the move to land sometimes became an escapist flight from trade, a way to build up a fortune without enduring the drudgery and risks of day-to-day commerce. Many traders agreed with Silas Deane: "If we review the rise and progress of private fortunes in America, we shall find that a very small proportion of them has arisen or been acquired by commerce, compared with those made by prudent purchases and management of land."[75] To attain quick wealth in real estate, many merchants avidly snatched up more land than they could afford to hold, hoping to be able to sell it wholesale, at huge markups, to European investors, or to retail it to an advancing tide of settlers. This was indeed a powerful investment concept. Was it not more promising to control hundreds of square miles of virgin forest in the Ohio Valley or on the Maine coast than to eke out a profit by dealing in such mundane commodities as flour, salt, and wheat? What could be a better investment in a young and rising country than a piece of the country itself? This logic was particularly persuasive to the trader who had suffered commercial setbacks in the 1780s and who now saw a chance to buy land at low prices with public securities that were themselves depreciated.

Land speculation was an intrinsically decentralized activity that varied from state to state, from merchant to merchant, and from decade to decade. There was no integrated land market comparable to the securities market, but, rather, a series of separate deals negotiated in America or Europe. A comprehensive survey of these transactions is impossible, but their essential character may be conveyed by describing several representative examples.

Directly after the Revolution, Levi Hollingsworth and four other Philadelphia businessmen engaged Dorsey Pentacost, an experienced wilderness surveyor and Indian fighter, to buy up choice land in the Ohio Valley from the state of Virginia.[76] The exact acreage purchased for Hollingsworth's account cannot be determined, but he seems to have owned at least five hundred thousand acres in Virginia and Kentucky. One of his major holdings was a strip of land, in the present state of West Virginia, along the banks of the Big Sandy and the Guyandotte rivers, which flow north into the Ohio. Hollingsworth's financial commitment

74. Charles W. Upham, *The Life of Timothy Pickering*, 4 vols. (Boston, 1867–1873), II, 261–262.

75. Quoted in Wilkinson, "Land Policy and Speculation," 86.

76. This account is based on Levi Hollingsworth Letterbook, 1786–1791.

to these lands was not so large as their extensiveness would suggest; his ledger for 1785 indicates a total investment in frontier lands of about £4,249—considerably less than the value of his store on Philadelphia's waterfront.[77]

Nevertheless, these wilderness lands soon became a drag on his business; he could neither use them himself nor rent them out. Why, then, had he bought them? Like his fellow merchants, Hollingsworth was impressed by two factors that, in combination, seemed to offer huge profits free of the unnerving risks and frustrations of trade.[78] One was the land itself. In the comfort of his Philadelphia parlor, Hollingsworth envisioned the "various & almost incredible Productions of this Western world where the Winters are so moderate & Grass with various kinds of Herbage so plenty that the labour of man is scarce necessary to support the domestick animal that dayly administers either to his wants or his Conveniences." Into this Elysian wilderness would descend a flood of settlers, accumulating in the thriving town of Pittsburgh and cascading down the Ohio River like the April ice floes: "The Spirit of Emigration to that Country now rages so violently that it is said not less than thirty thousand Inhabitants have settled in the district of Kentuckee in the course of Two Years past." With Philadelphia entrepreneurs acting as the catalyst, the union of land and man would produce vast profits once settlement started; indeed, lands "have been found to Increase in Value to an almost incredible degree." Profits of 400 percent in only two years were not unknown.

But with the postwar depression cutting into the earnings from his flour wholesaling business, Hollingsworth could not wait a few years to sell his lands. He needed cash immediately. Accordingly, in December 1786 he asked a friend named Enoch Story, then living in Amsterdam, to try to sell 100,000 or 200,000 acres to wealthy Dutch merchants. He described the glories of his property and proposed a scheme that would hasten settlement: let a land company be formed, in which a group of investors would each own part of a tract of roughly 150,000 acres. The owners would hire an agent, who would reside either on the land itself or upriver in Pittsburgh, to excite interest in the land and sell 250-acre lots on easy terms. The early settlers would be required to cultivate their land and build a dwelling on it, but the proprietors would help them prosper

77. See Levi Hollingsworth Journal, 1784–1785, 390, Hollingsworth Papers, HSP. Hollingsworth owned lands worth a total of £16,576 15s. 8½d., including an estate on Water Street (£5,385 8s. 8d.), a house and lot (£1,668 6s. 9d.), and an "Estate on Penny Pack" (£3,127 16s. 8d.).

78. This paragraph is based on "A Plan for the Purchase Settlement & Improvement of Lands on the Waters of Ohio," Hollingsworth Letterbook, 1786–1791, 13.

by building a series of gristmills and sawmills. It was not important to Hollingsworth that these initial land sales be profitable. In the parlance of the day, they were to be subsidized "hothouse settlements" that would demonstrate the desirability of the tract, create a rudimentary community on it, and attract more settlers like a magnet. Then the owners could sell the rest of their land at huge profits.

Despite its plausibility, Enoch Story was not able to sell this scheme to European investors, and neither could four other agents employed by Hollingsworth. In 1789 the Philadelphian wrote that "the Agencies for sales of Lands in Europe have all failed[;] the patents from Ireland & England are all returned Loaded with expence."[79] Perhaps the two French bankrupts whom he dispatched to France in 1791 were able to peddle his land to panic-stricken royalists. In any case, Hollingsworth eventually tried to encourage settlement in a more direct fashion by sending two agents westward, each to lead about twenty-five families onto his lands.

Poor sales were only the beginning of Hollingsworth's problems. Dorsey Pentacost, the agent who surveyed the acreage, proved to be incompetent and untrustworthy. There were recurrent rumors that title to some of the lands was not clear, and in 1789 Hollingsworth heard an authoritative report from a western settler that part of the land that Pentacost had located was "very indifferent being mostly Rocks and mountains."[80] Incredibly enough, not until 1790—seven years after the initial purchase and four years after the enthusiastic launching of his European sales campaign—did Hollingsworth bother to make certain that his lands were indeed cultivable at all. In addition to all this, Pentacost fell deeply into debt to Hollingsworth and was partly responsible for embroiling him in four vexing lawsuits. Moreover, Hollingsworth had to pay fairly onerous taxes on some of his Virginia lands. This combination of problems, exacerbated by the illiquidity of the lands themselves, forced Hollingsworth to conserve his cash very carefully for at least a year. Instead of generating quick profits, his western lands had yielded only taxes, lawsuits, expenses, and disappointment.

Hollingsworth's experience was not exceptional. Reed and Forde, whose flamboyant trading ventures in the Mississippi Valley were chronicled above, had a remarkably similar experience. After the war they purchased about ninety thousand acres in western Virginia and Kentucky, including a thirty-four-thousand-acre tract on the Little Kana-

79. Hollingsworth to Dorsey Pentacost, May 2, 1789, *ibid.*, 355.
80. Hollingsworth to Dorsey Pentacost, July 2, 1789, *ibid.*, 388.

wha River.[81] When excessive importations of dry goods pushed them to the brink of bankruptcy, they scrambled to sell some of their acreage to Europeans or Americans in 1787, but without success. Unlike many Philadelphia land jobbers, Reed and Forde were not armchair adventurers, but energetic, mobile entrepreneurs who frequently traveled to the backwoods of the South and West. Nevertheless, when Reed and Forde finally managed to find settlers who were willing to buy acreage on the Little Kanawha, they were remarkably ignorant about their holdings there. Among the questions about the lands that they addressed to a friend on the frontier were how far they were from Morgantown, whether there were already settlements on the river, and whether the lands could be reached by wagon.[82]

After 1788 American land jobbers began to employ ever more risky investment strategies. Instead of buying lands with the primary intention of selling them to settlers, some traders began to buy enormous tracts in order to resell them to other speculators. A few of these transactions were simply gambles by buyers who barely had enough money to make a down payment on their purchase, let alone buy the entire tract and promote settlement of it. This strategy became feasible when Europeans once again became attracted to the American market. Injured by the dry goods panic of 1784 and disturbed by the political and economic disarray of the mid-1780s, Europeans avoided American investments for several years, as Levi Hollingsworth's experience attests. But after 1789, wealthy capitalists in London, Amsterdam, and Paris found much to admire in the Federalist hegemony. The upsurge in European foodstuff prices had allowed them to make extremely profitable speculations in American grain, and Hamilton's funding program made purchases of the nation's public debt no less lucrative. Since Europe was catching the revolutionary fever from which America had just recovered, it seemed only prudent to transfer some funds to the New World and invest them in a solid, tangible asset like land.[83]

Brash American land jobbers dutifully met this demand by selling large chunks of their country to the highest bidder, and one of their prize properties was the state of New York. To resolve a long-standing bound-

81. Reed and Forde Letterbooks, 1787, 1788–1790.

82. R. and F. to Samuel Hanway, Apr. 11, 1789, *ibid.*, 1788–1790, 245.

83. For a good account of the interaction in England of the American and British elites after the war, see Helen I. Cowan, *Charles Williamson: Genesee Promoter—Friend of Anglo-American Rapprochement*, Rochester Historical Society Publications, XIX (Rochester, N.Y., 1941), 1–33.

ary dispute with Massachusetts, New York had granted to the Bay State ownership, but not political or legal control, of about six million acres in the western half of the state.[84] Eager to relieve its taxpayers in the wake of Shays's Rebellion, the Massachusetts government sold these lands in 1788 to Oliver Phelps and Nathaniel Gorham for three hundred thousand pounds Massachusetts currency. Since this sum was payable in the depreciated debt of Massachusetts, the effective price was much lower. But when the price of securities rose in 1789, Phelps and Gorham could meet only the first of three installments, giving them title to two million acres, while the other four million acres reverted to Massachusetts.

Into this shattered deal stepped Robert Morris and some associates, who bought 1,000,000 acres from Phelps and Gorham for $113,872, as well as the entire 4,000,000-acre tract that had reverted to the Bay State, for which they paid $366,333. Morris and his associates thus paid out $480,205 (£180,077 Pennsylvania currency) for 5,000,000 acres of land. Morris had no more intention of personally promoting settlement on these huge tracts than Phelps and Gorham had had. The 1,000,000-acre tract purchased from the pair was promptly sold to Sir William Pulteney, "the greatest land capitalist in Great Britain," and his associates for $330,000, giving Morris a profit of $216,128, or a 190 percent return on his investment in the space of a year. Of the remaining 4,000,000 acres purchased by Morris, 2,800,000 acres were sold for $834,000 to a powerful Dutch investment group, already enriched by speculations in American debt, that now styled itself the Holland Land Company. If the 1,200,000 acres retained by Morris are valued at their cost to him of $.096 per acre, then the total value of these lands, plus proceeds from his land sales, amounted to $1,279,200, or 166 percent more than he had paid for them. Within the space of two and a half years the Morris group had amassed a profit of $798,995, or £299,623 Pennsylvania currency.

As for Morris's European customers, the Holland Land Company

84. A succinct account of this highly complex transaction is A. M. Sakolski, *The Great American Land Bubble: The Amazing Story of Land-Grabbing, Speculations, and Booms from Colonial Days to the Present Time* (New York, 1932), 54–63. A far more detailed description is Barbara Ann Chernow, "Robert Morris: Land Speculation, 1790–1801" (Ph.D. diss., Columbia University, 1978 [publ. New York, 1978]), 41–67. The exact amount of acreage involved was not known by the parties to the transactions, and the value of the payments cannot be determined because of various discounts, commissions, interest charges, and options. I have used the gross monetary values, which tend to overstate the profits of the Morris group. See also Cowan, *Charles Williamson*, 11–14; Paul Demund Evans, *The Holland Land Company*, Buffalo Historical Society Publications, XXVIII (Buffalo, N.Y., 1924), 25–32; and "The Pulteney Purchase," *Quarterly Journal of the New York State Historical Association*, III (1922), 83–104; Neil Adams McNall, *An Agricultural History of the Genesee Valley, 1790–1860* (Philadelphia, 1952), 12–19.

(which bought an additional million acres in northwestern Pennsylvania to flesh out its holdings) seems to have earned an acceptable rate of return on its investment. But the Pulteney Associates' first manager in America, the irrepressible Charles Williamson, pushed the hothouse theory of land management to the absurd extreme of building not only roads and mills to attract settlers but a tavern, theatre, race track, hotel, and, indeed, an entire town. In less than a decade he ran up a bill of over two hundred thousand pounds sterling, or more than two and a half times the purchase price of the land itself.

In another instance of gigantic speculation, three million acres of wilderness in the district of Maine, which was still part of Massachusetts, passed through a progression of owners nearly parallel to that of western New York.[85] In 1791 and 1792 Secretary of War Henry Knox and the New York speculator William Duer made a down payment on the land but quickly sold out to the Philadelphia magnate William Bingham. Not even Bingham could afford the large payments due to the state of Massachusetts, however, so he ransacked Europe for a well-heeled partner and finally sold a major interest to the House of Baring, England's premier merchant banking firm. Although Bingham and the Barings knew very little about Maine, they were confident that once its virtues as a wheat-growing region were recognized, it would attract many immigrants from the thickly settled parts of New England. But settlers were one essential commodity that speculators could not buy. Yankee farmers knew perfectly well that the backwoods of Maine were rugged, rocky, and cold and no place to grow wheat. The investment was a fiasco.

However large the sums involved, most frontier land speculations were not economically constructive, if only because the promoters did not have the time, energy, and capital needed to promote settlement effectively. To understand what such an undertaking required, it is instructive to review the land operations of an exceptionally assiduous and careful speculator, Henry Drinker. Having retired from commerce in 1775 with a large fortune, Drinker could afford to devote large amounts of time and money to his land operations. During the 1780s and 1790s he derived a steady income from several rental properties, a sawmill in northern Pennsylvania, and a successful ironworks in southern New Jersey.[86] Beginning in 1788 much of the cash flow from these enterprises

85. This account is based on Alberts, *Golden Voyage*, 228–236, 269–277, 284–290; Frederick S. Allis, Jr., ed., *William Bingham's Maine Lands, 1790–1820* (Colonial Society of Massachusetts, *Publications*, XXXVI, XXXVII, *Collections* [Boston, 1954]).

86. On Drinker's estate, see Henry Drinker Journal, 1776–1791, 1, 2, 3, 17, 18, 20, 288, Henry Drinker Papers, HSP. On sales of iron and lumber, which may be incomplete, see

was plowed into the development of the Beech Lands, which Drinker owned outright and carried on his books at a value of seven thousand pounds. This fifty-thousand-acre tract was situated about 140 miles north of Philadelphia, in the northeastern corner of Pennsylvania, just south of the New York border.[87] Drinker was understandably optimistic that the land would rapidly attract settlers. Though somewhat rough and thickly forested, the land was fertile, its location excellent. It lay on the western side of the Delaware River within 20 miles of the river, and it was also near the eastern branch of the Susquehanna River, which drained south-central New York State. Many prominent speculators had purchased land in the region, and further up the Susquehanna lay the prosperous new settlement at Cooperstown.

Drinker imagined that his land would attract settlers because they could easily ship produce down the Delaware to market. Moreover, settlers in the Susquehanna Valley could send produce downriver to a post called Harmony on the Great Bend of the Susquehanna, transport the goods 15 miles overland to the town of Stockport on the Delaware, and send it downriver to Philadelphia. Drinker owned both Harmony and Stockport and hoped that they would become thriving commercial centers.[88] The entire plan had a logical coherence absent from most real estate projects. The missing ingredient was good transportation facilities, and with his usual industry Drinker set about creating them.[89] An influential member of Pennsylvania's internal improvement lobby, he served as a commissioner for two publicly funded roads that totaled 130 miles. Using both public and personal funds, Drinker also cut a portage road between Harmony and Stockport, and he hired two men to clear the upper reaches of the Delaware of rocks, logs, and other obstructions.

Promoting settlement of the Beech Lands involved Drinker in dozens

---

Henry Drinker Ledger A, 1776–1792, fols. 32, 42, 50, 14, 58 (for castings); 30, 46, 59 (for bar iron); 31, 36, 54, 55 (for lumber), Drinker Papers. Reflecting the larger business cycle, Drinker's sales of these commodities dropped from £7,499 in 1786 to £4,703 in 1787 and then rose steadily to £13,016 in 1791. This pickup in economic activity encouraged land speculation by increasing the liquid wealth of speculators and enhancing the prospective rents and sale prices of the lands they purchased.

87. See Henry Drinker Journal A, 1776–1791, 230, and Henry Drinker to George Bowne, Jan. 14, 1789, Henry Drinker Letterbook, 1786–1790, 344, Drinker Papers.

88. Henry Drinker to Samuel Preston, June 8, 1791, Henry Drinker Letterbook, 1790–1793, 181.

89. On transportation improvements, see Wilkinson, "Land Policy and Speculation," 121–127; Henry Drinker to Samuel Preston, June 29, 1791, Henry Drinker Letterbook, 1790–1793, 191, to George Joy, Dec. 20, 1790, 114, to Samuel Preston, Aug. 1, 1791, 199, Dec. 7, 1791, 244.

of disparate tasks.[90] Unlike many speculators, Drinker carefully inspected his acreage and corresponded frequently with the manager and part-owner of the Stockport estate, Samuel Preston, whose disagreeable temper threatened the popularity of the settlement. Preston operated a gristmill and a sawmill at Stockport, helped to build the roads in the area, and by 1792 was beginning to develop the village at Harmony. Three or four times each year Drinker sent by riverboat or wagon substantial loads of supplies, worth about one hundred pounds, to feed and clothe the workmen on his property. In return he received rafts of lumber that floated down the Delaware on the spring freshets, unless they were caught on snags and sandbars. Drinker also attempted to encourage development by settling enterprising men on the property—particularly Quakers from New England, Pennsylvania, and New Jersey whose labor would quickly raise property values throughout the area. A special object of Drinker's concern was maple sugar, which the earnest Friend hoped would supplant the "polluted & wicked" Caribbean cane, once its virtues were appreciated by American consumers and sugar refiners. In cooperation with William Cooper of Cooperstown, he manufactured one thousand fifteen-gallon sugar kettles at his New Jersey ironworks for use in the north country, and he attempted to recruit a skilled sugar boiler to work there. When James Madison and Thomas Jefferson took a trip to northern New York, he encouraged them to study the maple sugar industry, and using Robert Morris as an intermediary, he presented President Washington with a box of maple sugar. In addition to all of these details, Drinker attended to the myriad financial matters involved in selling land to settlers and buying additional tracts. It is doubtful whether the profits justified Drinker's substantial investment in the Beech Lands, but it is clear that he contributed to the economic development of Pennsylvania's northern frontier.

Not immersing themselves in the dull details of land development in the manner of Henry Drinker, most speculators had no understanding of the real value of the property they acquired. Transfixed by the excitement of the land market and out of touch with underlying

90. On this subject, see Henry Drinker Letterbook, 1790–1793, esp. HD to William Cooper, Jan. 15, Feb. 7, Mar. 16, Apr. 14, 1791, 129, 138, 158, 164, to Franklin, Robinson, and Co., June 9, 1790, 29, to Samuel Stanton, June 30, 1792, 350, to Samuel Preston, June 8, 29, Aug. 1, 4, Nov. 15, Dec. 7, 15, 1791, Apr. 8, May 5, 1792, 181, 191, 199, 201, 235, 244, 249, 285, 302. The quotation is from Drinker to William Cooper, Mar. 29, 1792, 279. On shipments of supplies, see Henry Drinker Journal, 1776–1791, 308, 310, 339, 346, 357, 369, 436.

economic reality, they bought land simply because it was expected to go up in price, as indeed it did while speculators were eagerly buying up acreage. By the mid-1790s these land jobbers had been sucked into a sordid whirlpool of land-grabbing that eventually filled the Prune Street debtors' prison with some of the greatest businessmen of the Revolutionary era. Although acreage from New York to Georgia became part of this bubble, the focus of speculative activity was Pennsylvania itself.[91] The lands of the commonwealth were admired for their propinquity to either Philadelphia or the Ohio Valley, their generally high quality, and for the fact that they could be owned outright by foreigners. Unlike Massachusetts, Pennsylvania did not dispose of its acreage in a few huge blocks whose sale could be regulated with carefully formulated, strictly enforced contracts. Instead, they were distributed piecemeal by a land office in Philadelphia through a fairly complicated procedure. A speculator secured at the land office a warrant for a certain amount of land in a specific district; this land was then located by land-office surveyors; and after the speculator paid for the land, he received a patent. Though designed to permit the individual settler to buy land directly from the state, this process became dominated by the rich and well-connected and was pervaded by corruption. Major speculators formed secret partnerships with land-office surveyors in order to secure first claim to the best land; intrigue and bribery were used to avoid taxes and to circumvent provisions in the law requiring rapid settlement of the land.

The bubble was inflated by the familiar vision of a surging population swarming over a finite resource, bidding up its price to unthinkable heights. As one speculator wrote of Washington, D.C., "All other places have risen by slow degrees, this will astonish the world by its rapidity, the people are all ready and only wait for houses to rush in."[92] Accordingly, the speculators themselves rushed in, propelled by the powerful momentum of competition. Certain structural features of the land market gave these gamblers full rein to indulge their delusions. For one thing the reorganization of Philadelphia's financial system (described above) gave influential speculators enormous amounts of credit with which to finance their operations. By 1793 loans could be obtained from three Philadelphia banks, and speculators issued huge quantities of commercial paper backed by the land they claimed to possess. Some of this paper had maturities of several years, instead of the one to four months normally used in commercial transactions.[93]

91. The best account is Wilkinson, "Land Policy and Speculation."

92. Quoted in Robert D. Arbuckle, *Pennsylvania Speculator and Patriot: The Entrepreneurial John Nicholson, 1757–1800* (University Park, Pa., 1975), 115.

93. *Ibid.*, 190–191.

The speculators were also encouraged to plunge ahead by a few highly profitable sales to Europeans, such as Robert Morris's deals with the Holland Land Company and the Pulteney Associates. These successes not only seemed to demonstrate the profitability of land grabbing but also gave some speculators additional capital with which to operate. Moreover, many speculators were drawn deeper and deeper into debt by the possibility of buying land on margin. This could be done by purchasing the warrant for a piece of land, but not the patent. When the stipulated time for buying the patent arrived, the speculator faced the unpleasant choice of forfeiting his initial investment in the warrant and survey fees or borrowing money to buy the lands. The latter option was usually chosen, and the loan was secured with real estate. Through these various mechanisms it was possible for a speculator to hold some sort of claim to millions of acres of land without owning a single square foot outright. Of nearly 10,000,000 acres of land claimed at the Pennsylvania land office between 1792 and 1794, "only something over 700,000 acres had been paid for by the later date."[94]

The transfixing effect of western lands in the 1790s is exemplified by Tench Coxe, whose speculative career has been expertly traced by Jacob Cooke.[95] Although he already owned, through inheritance and purchase, a considerable quantity of undeveloped lands, Coxe bought 30,000 acres in 1792 and, in the following year, an additional 31,000 acres. This brought to about 292,000 acres the amount of property that he "owned, held warrants, or had contracted for." Despite the fact that he had been repeatedly deceived by land brokers and was unable to sell any of this acreage in 1794, Coxe wrote early in 1795, "I have ascertained to a certainty purchases in Virginia, Penns. and New York to the amount of 1,100,000 Acres in the present and last Week."[96] While he may not have exercised all of these claims, Coxe did plunge into Carolina lands in 1795 with an initial purchase of 180,000 acres. This was followed by purchases of 90,000 acres (prudently scaled down from 360,000 acres), 122,240 acres, and 40,000 acres. Like several other projectors of the day, Coxe dreamed of erecting a thriving model city on his vast acreage, even though he was able to make very few profitable sales of the land he had bought. Coxe's affairs became a maze of lawsuits, and only the largesse of his father prevented his frantic schemes from reducing him to bankruptcy.

Of course, the madness could go only so far. Eventually the loans had to be paid off with land sales, not more loans, and by 1795 some specu-

94. Cooke, *Tench Coxe*, 312 n. 2.
95. *Ibid.*, 311–333.
96. *Ibid.*, 315.

lators realized that they would soon drown in a sea of debt unless they managed to sell off some of their holdings to the only potential purchasers who still had liquid assets: the moneyed men of Europe. The greatest land jobbers of the day, Robert Morris and John Nicholson, pooled six million acres of land—only a part of their vast holdings—and tried to sell them in Europe. It did not matter that much of this land was of dubious quality, only partly paid for, and heavily encumbered with debt; publicity and promises would prevail. The partners' sales vehicle was a corporation called the North American Land Company.[97] The company had thirty thousand shares, each representing two hundred acres of land and costing a very generous one hundred dollars, which would be sold to investors. The subscribed capital would be controlled by a board of directors, who would use the funds to develop the land and sell it for vast profits. To show that the risk was minimal, Morris guaranteed a return of at least 6 percent, even though he and Nicholson were stripped of ready money. In his promotional literature, Morris presented himself as a paternalistic monopolist who united the interests of rich and poor: "The honest and industrious labourers of all countries, particularly of America, will seek under its protection an independent livelihood, and the means of providing for their innocent offspring. Moneyed men will see in it the means of augmenting their property." But Morris made it clear that "honest and industrious labourers" had little choice but to settle on the company's lands, because virtually all of the western land had been preempted, with the exception of "the summits of mountains, abrupt precipices, or plains covered with stones."[98]

When European investors wisely avoided this fraudulent scheme, the fate of Morris and Nicholson was sealed. With his enormous new mansion (plate 21) standing half-finished for lack of funds, Morris took refuge from a flock of creditors by locking himself in his country seat, now renamed Castle Defiance. Finally the bland, disingenuous optimism had disappeared. In one of the dozens of anguished notes that he sent to Nicholson, Morris reflected, "I do not wonder that the world abandon us and flees as they would from pestilence for it seems that all who touch us are brought to trouble."[99] When he was finally about to go to prison in February 1798, Morris succinctly summarized his fate: "My money is gone, my furniture is to be sold, I am to go to prison and my family to starve, good night."[100]

97. Arbuckle, *John Nicholson*, chap. 10; Wilkinson, "Land Policy and Speculation," chap. 5. See also Chernow, "Robert Morris," 170–198.

98. Quoted in Wilkinson, "Land Policy and Speculation," 242, 243.

99. Quoted *ibid.*, 299.

100. Arbuckle, *John Nicholson*, 197.

PLATE 21. Robert Morris's Unifinished Mansion. *From W. Birch and Son,* The City of Philadelphia . . . As It Appeared in 1800. *Courtesy of The Historical Society of Pennsylvania*

The often calamitous results of land speculation have led some historians to suppose that it was intrinsically unprofitable, but this view is extreme. If approached with discipline and good sense, investment in wilderness lands could be lucrative. Timothy Pickering's investment in lands in the Wyoming Valley of the Susquehanna River appreciated more than fifteen times in about a decade, while William Cooper, father of the novelist and founder of Cooperstown, New York, made a fortune in land speculation.[101] It is no coincidence that both of these successful speculators settled near the land they owned. Pickering and Cooper were in a position to provide useful social leadership for their pioneer communities, in the manner of Henry Drinker, instead of assuming the largely parasitic role played by most speculators. Furthermore, their intimate knowledge of the area allowed these resident speculators to judge the quality of the thing that most affects the success of any real estate investment: location.

101. Sakolski, *Great American Land Bubble*, 30; Upham, *Timothy Pickering*, II, 177–411.

By contrast, most speculators made the fatal error of substituting a general idea for the shrewd purchase of specific properties. Their minds were gripped by the simple equation: "Land plus population growth equals profits." Amidst the buoyant nationalism and prosperity of the early 1790s and the speculative crush of the land market itself, many merchants somehow convinced themselves that there was a land shortage. Partly for this reason, it seemed unnecessary to pay close attention to exactly what lands were purchased. Busy with mercantile affairs, seized by an acquisitive impulse that assumed that later would be too late, and supposing that all of the West would soon be thick with settlers, normally sober merchants bought huge tracts of land sight unseen. Not infrequently, the general region of the purchase was poorly suited for agriculture, and the specific tracts selected by the speculators' careless, unscrupulous agents had physical defects and clouded titles. Moreover, in their rapacious haste the merchants used borrowed money to buy much more land than they could afford to hold, under the assumption they would be able to sell it very quickly. Since sales to real settlers were slow and tedious, a quick turnover was possible only by selling to other speculators. In effect, the speculators were peddling an investment idea rather than physical properties to be sold to prospective settlers on the basis of their actual merits. In the speculative environment of Philadelphia, New York, London, and Amsterdam, land prices seemed to rise daily. It was easy to lose sight of economic reality, to forget that, ultimately, land was worth no more than settlers could afford to pay for it and—in view of the vast extent of the American wilderness—needed to pay for it.

Although a number of careful regional studies will be necessary before the net economic impact of land-grabbing can be determined, some of its consequences are clear. Of at least modest importance was the transfer of wealth from the speculator to the taxpayer, a partial retribution for the enrichment of securities speculators at public expense. The major alleged contribution of land speculation to economic development—the promotion of western settlement—was not of decisive importance, for settlers were rapidly moving westward of their own accord. A chance to buy from a land jobber rather than the state made wildlands no more attractive to the farmer. Indeed, the scrambling of land titles and the friction between settlers and speculators may have made land-grabbing economically counterproductive.

Perhaps the only unambiguously positive contribution of land speculators to western development was their promotion of transportation projects. The Holland Land Company and Pulteney Associates built a number of roads in western New York, some of which linked up with roads built by Philadelphia speculators in northern Pennsylvania. Led by Robert Morris, Philadelphia land jobbers also established, in 1789, the Pennsylvania Society for Promoting the Improvement of Roads and Inland Navigation. With characteristic overeagerness, this group started an ambitious series of canals, which foundered and were abandoned for lack of capital during the 1790s. If their timing was poor, at least the speculators' geographical instincts were sound, for much of their proposed canal network was eventually built in the nineteenth century. One project that did not have to be postponed was the hugely successful Lancaster Turnpike, a stone-and-gravel toll road between Lancaster and Philadelphia, completed in 1794, that earned at least a 10 percent return for its shareholders for several decades.

Manufacturing

After the Revolution, Philadelphia and New York became the centers of an ambitious effort to introduce into America the new methods of manufacturing that were beginning to revolutionize British industry. In important ways this initiative was merely an extension of pre-Revolutionary efforts to promote manufactures, but now it took the form of the grand projects of a self-important young nation. Continuing a theme that had inspired the building of a workhouse in Philadelphia before the war, advocates of manufacturing observed: "Employment, in manufactures, of such of our poor, as cannot find other honest means of subsistence, is of *the utmost consequence.* A man oppressed by extreme want is prepared for all evil, and the idler is ever prone to wickedness; while the habits of industry . . . do not leave leisure for meditating or executing mischief." Still more potent prods to industrial innovation were straightforward nationalism and the economic dislocation of the war. By 1787 the new United States had suffered the double indignity of extreme deprivation of manufactured goods during the war, when soldiers sometimes had to endure winter months without shoes or blankets, and then a commercial depression caused by excessive importation of manufactures. Thus in war and in peace the new nation remained a slave to her former master because manufactured articles were not produced in the New World. Nothing less than "NATIONAL SALVATION" seemed to depend upon the development of a domestic industrial base.[102]

102. Tench Coxe, *A View of the United States of America, in a Series of Papers, Written at Various Times, between the Years 1787 and 1794* (Philadelphia, 1794; rpt. New York, 1965), chap. 3, esp. 49, 56. On manufacturing schemes in prewar Philadelphia, see Gary B. Nash, *The Urban Crucible: Social Change, Political Consciousness, and the Origins of the American Revolution* (Cambridge, Mass., 1979), 327–331.

These were traditional themes, merely intensified by the Revolutionary experience. But an original and prophetic addition to the argument for manufactures was made by the Philadelphia merchant Tench Coxe, who has been called "the Defoe of America."[103] In a long series of detailed pamphlets and speeches, Coxe confronted the fundamental impediment to manufacturing in America: the scarcity and high cost of labor. Coxe argued that this difficulty could be overcome by using the laborsaving devices recently invented in England. He described with a sense of wonderment how "factories which can be carried on by water-mills, wind-mills, fire, horses and machines ingeniously contrived, are not burdened with any heavy expense of boarding, lodging, clothing and paying workmen, and they supply the force of hands to a great extent without taking our people from agriculture." In effect Coxe introduced the Industrial Revolution into the American imagination, for he recognized the potentially transforming effect of these "machines ingeniously contrived": "[The manufactures] of England have been more improved within the last twelve years, than in the preceeding fifty."[104]

Post-Revolutionary businessmen were not in the habit of allowing a promising idea to lie fallow for long, and the prospects of manufacturing were no exception. In 1787 merchants in Philadelphia set up the Pennsylvania Society for the Encouragement of Manufactures and the Useful Arts, which began by establishing a cotton factory. The enterprise was poorly conceived, however, and foundered financially before burning to the ground in 1790. At about the same time, Tench Coxe contracted with one Andrew Mitchell of western Pennsylvania to go to England and smuggle out of the country models of the new cotton-spinning machinery. Although this attempt failed, Coxe and his colleagues were ultimately quite successful at stealing Britain's technology. The basis of their success was a shift in their efforts from smuggling out abstract information, such as models and plans, to attracting skilled English artisans conversant with the new technology. The most famous of these immigrant artisans was the founder of the Rhode Island cotton-spinning industry, Samuel Slater, who came to America in response to the bounties available in Philadelphia "for a machine to make cotton rollers, &c." Although Slater established himself in New England, a number of other inventors stayed in the Philadelphia area.[105]

103. Leo Marx, *The Machine in the Garden: Technology and the Pastoral Ideal in America* (New York, 1964), 151, quoting Joseph Dorfman.

104. Coxe, *View of the United States*, 38–40, 42. See Cooke, *Tench Coxe*, chap. 5.

105. George S. White, *Memoir of Samuel Slater, The Father of American Manufactures . . .* (Philadelphia, 1836), 37. Cooke, *Tench Coxe*, 106–108. See also David J. Jeremy, "British Textile Technology Transmission to the United States: The Philadelphia Region

These efforts presaged the major Federalist project in high-technology manufacturing, the Society for the Encouragement of Useful Manufactures (the SEUM).[106] Founded in 1791, the society was simply a joint-stock company that built a manufacturing town at the falls of the Passaic River, near Newark, New Jersey. Initially conceived of by Tench Coxe, the SEUM was energetically promoted by Coxe's superior in the Treasury Department, Alexander Hamilton. But even the brilliance of Hamilton could not save the society from a brief and unhappy life. Probably its greatest flaw was managerial, for instead of being led by an energetic president and close-knit board of directors (as was, for example, the Bank of North America), the society was run by a loose absentee committee of New York and New Jersey businessmen. Worse still, many of these men were stock market plungers who had little time to devote to the company. Indeed, the society almost sank before it was launched when four directors, including President William Duer, went bankrupt in the panic of 1792. Stripped of part of its capital and much of its initial leadership, the SEUM quickly became a ludicrous failure. Its management continued to be ineffectual, while the New Jersey site (a politic compromise between New York and Philadelphia) possessed inadequate supplies of labor and industrial materials. Its grandiose plans were too costly to execute as originally conceived, and its designer, Major Pierre L'Enfant, did not keenly apply himself to the demanding engineering problems at hand, because he fancied himself an architect, not an engineer. This French gentleman did not get on well with the artisans who had been recruited from England to build the machinery, and the artisans were themselves unsatisfactory. A project plagued by such problems had little chance of challenging an industrial giant like England that possessed a far cheaper labor supply, and the SEUM collapsed in a few years.

In 1794 the machinery of the SEUM was sold to John Nicholson, who was building an elaborate manufacturing complex at the falls of the Schuylkill River, not far from Philadelphia. Nicholson, however, was nearly bankrupt from his land speculations and never found the funds—more accurately, the credit—to complete this project. But he did become a patron to some talented technical innovators,[107] including William Pollard, a capable Philadelphia merchant, originally raised in the English

Experience, 1770–1820," *Business History Review*, XLVII (1973), 24–52; and *Transatlantic Industrial Revolution: The Diffusion of Textile Technologies between Britain and America, 1790–1830s* (Cambridge, Mass., 1981), 74–92.

106. The standard account is Davis, *Earlier History*, I, 349–518.

107. Arbuckle, *John Nicholson*, 139–164; Anthony F. C. Wallace and David J. Jeremy, "William Pollard and the Arkwright Patents," *WMQ*, 3d Ser., XXXIV (1977), 404–425.

textile trades, who was driven into manufacturing by repeated financial reverses. A few years before the liquidation of the SEUM, in 1788 or 1789, Pollard had bought a model of a machine for roving and spinning cotton from a man who had already tried to sell it to Tench Coxe. After improving the model considerably, Pollard received a United States patent for it in 1791 and eventually turned to John Nicholson for financial assistance in building the machinery and establishing a factory. With the help of specialized craftsmen from Philadelphia and New York, Pollard was able to build some of the most sophisticated manufacturing equipment yet seen in America, but both he and his beloved machines became victims of Nicholson's financial machinations.

The experiences of the Pennsylvania Society for the Encouragement of Manufacturing and the Useful Arts, of the SEUM, and of William Pollard are a record of unrelieved financial failure. Yet out of the wreckage of these early experiments emerged two solid achievements. On an ideological level, it was established by the 1790s that even an overwhelmingly agricultural country like the United States might aspire to industrialization, because machines could supplement one of America's scarcest productive factors, labor. Furthermore, the early industrialists were impressively successful at stealing, and converting into functioning machinery, the closely guarded technical secrets of England. Though textile production had yet to produce a profit in the Delaware Valley, the groundwork had been laid. Once the labor supply of the region expanded and textile manufacturing was undertaken by careful entrepreneurs rather than optimistic speculators, textile production would become an important industry in the Philadelphia region. As was so often true in American economic history, success was preceded by failure.

This sequence of innovation deserves careful scrutiny because it belies the view of certain economists that the simple interaction of macroeconomic forces caused industrialization in America. Philadelphia in the 1790s had a small market, scarce capital, and costly labor, and it lacked the technological head start of Great Britain. It was eminently rational, from the standpoint of maximum profits, for entrepreneurs to steer clear of textile manufacturing. But stung by commercial setbacks and driven by nationalistic zeal and a speculative impulse, northern entrepreneurs gambled creatively in this field, laying the basis for future success. Undoubtedly the greatest advantage that northern merchants had over southern planters in pursuing this endeavor was not economic, but social or cultural. In the rapidly changing textile industry of the eighteenth century, technological secrets were stored in brains, not books. Expanding, heterogeneous cities like Philadelphia and New York were far more attractive to foreign artisans and businessmen than a rural culture dominated by slaves and planters. Moreover, the division of labor possible in a large city greatly facilitated the building of complicated machines, as did the concentration of ideas, information, and capital.

Even while squandering sizable sums in speculative folly, the merchants of Philadelphia took giant steps down the road of economic development in the sixteen years after 1775. They expanded their commercial operations impressively, not only by establishing ties with many new ports in the Atlantic basin but also by carving out a profitable niche in the China trade. Moreover, Philadelphia's involvement in the tobacco trade foreshadowed northern domination of the American cotton trade in the nineteenth century. But the city's merchants did not permit these maritime opportunities to obscure the huge potential of the North American continent itself. The Revolutionary years witnessed several significant, if still tentative, inland initiatives, involving road building, industrial innovation, and trade with the Ohio and Mississippi valleys. One reason for this progress was the merchants' success in circumventing one of the critical bottlenecks to economic development in North America, the lack of capital. Rich new sources of financing in Holland, England, and France were discovered in these years; no longer were American merchants dependent on the largesse of a handful of London and Bristol dry goods firms. Even more important, the available capital of the Delaware Valley was mobilized and extended through the establishment of a banking system and securities markets and through the widespread use of commercial paper. William Bingham was so enthralled by the possibilities these financial innovations offered for enriching himself and the nation that he considered America's traditional reliance on English credit a thing of the past. "Our monied capital has So much increased from the Introduction of Banks, & the Circulation of the Funds," he explained, "that the Necessity of Soliciting Credits [from England] will no longer exist, & the Means will be provided for putting in Motion every Species of Industry."[108] Although Bingham's prediction of independence from British capital was premature by more than a century and failed to take account of the wrenching financial panics that inevitably followed rapid credit expansions, his enthusiasm was not misplaced.

The various achievements of the Revolutionary merchants meant that the Philadelphia of 1791 was substantially changed from the Quaker City of midcentury. Yet the difference was subtle. It would not have been

108. William Bingham to ———, Oct. 22, 1791, William Bingham Letterbook, 1791–1793, HSP.

evident to an observer after a casual stroll down Market Street, nor does it impress the historian who peruses the aggregate data of Phildelphia's economy. Philadelphia in 1791, as in 1751, remained a preindustrial port, a city of shops, docks, and countinghouses, with not even one massive factory to augur the coming of a new age. As for the quantitative test of economic growth, the gross national product per capita may have been rising in these years, but not particularly rapidly, for Philadelphia's population was growing as fast as its economy.

To appreciate the critical changes in Philadelphia's economy, one must look beyond the social symbols and superficial data to the minute details of commercial life. One must enter the countinghouse, open the ledger, and scrutinize individual accounts. Then it can be seen that merchants were turning to investments in securities and land, trading to unfamiliar ports, paying their debts with commercial paper rather than cash, buying shares of banks and turnpikes, specializing in narrower commercial lines, and rapidly building up their capital stocks. These were the bases of preindustrial economic development, the qualitative preparation for the quantitative ascent.

8 American Economic Development and the Case of Philadelphia

Philadelphia and Her Competitors, 1780–1840

Although Philadelphia was exceptionally prosperous during the second half of the eighteenth century, the entrepreneurial character of the city was fundamentally the same as that of other major ports. The similarities between New York and Philadelphia are especially clear. The economic function of the two ports was similar, and they both possessed expanding, heterogeneous trading communities.[1] By the 1750s, these communities included a number of influential Irish merchants as well as important Jewish and Quaker traders. Since the pre-Revolutionary English suppliers of dry goods to New York included the same great export firms that served Philadelphia, both cities were inundated with commercial credit and manufactures that distressed established importers but aided aspiring shopkeepers and minor traders.[2] Finally, after the Revolu-

1. Virginia D. Harrington, *The New York Merchant on the Eve of the Revolution* (New York, 1935), 11–205, shows that New York's merchant group generally resembled that of Philadelphia. Jacob M. Price, "Economic Function and the Growth of American Port Towns in the Eighteenth Century," *Perspectives in American History*, VIII (1974), 157, writes that although "at first glance, New York was very similar to Philadelphia in its commerce and population structure," it also resembled Boston. New York's provision trade with the West Indies and southern Europe was much smaller than Philadelphia's (as was shipbuilding), but it managed to achieve a positive balance of trade with Great Britain, thanks to flaxseed, fur, iron, Caribbean groceries, and other exports.

2. Philip L. White, *The Beekmans of New York in Politics and Commerce, 1647–1877* (New York, 1956), 408–530, shows that James Beekman had some of the same suppliers, including Samuel and Thomas Fludyer, Robert and Nathan Hyde, and Peach and Pierce, who served Philadelphia. See also William Pollard to Benjamin and John Bowers, Dec. 21, 1772, May 13, 1773, William Pollard Letterbook, 1772–1774, 129, 217, Historical Society of Pennsylvania (hereafter cited as HSP), showing that Pollard represented this Manchester

tion New York attracted many new European merchants, just as Philadelphia did. There are striking similarities, for example, between the careers of Stephen Girard and John Jacob Astor—aggressive continental traders, of more perseverance than polish, who piled up huge fortunes while remaining outside the social elites of their cities.[3]

In addition to all of the foregoing, the business affairs of New York and Philadelphia intersected at many points. Several New Yorkers were in partnership with prominent Philadelphians, and the two cities pursued many of the same economic innovations after the Revolution.[4] Banking came to Manhattan just two years after it reached Philadelphia, and the two ports entered the China trade virtually simultaneously. As the national capital during the 1780s, New York became the center of securities speculation, but there was virtually a shadow stock market in Philadelphia. Rumors and price fluctuations in Manhattan coffeehouses were quickly transmitted across New Jersey to Philadelphia, as though the New Brunswick Road were a giant nerve connecting two ganglia.[5] If New York led in the securities market, Philadelphia was the nation's premier center for land jobbing in the eighties and nineties, but many important New Yorkers also proceeded into the minefield of frontier land speculation. It cannot be said, however, that the business communities of the two cities were identical. Philadelphia possessed many more Quaker merchants than New York and lacked its old-line Dutch element, and New York eventually attracted a swarm of extremely able Yankee merchants from Connecticut and other New England states.[6]

---

firm in New York as well as Philadelphia. Historians have assumed that the dry goods glut was common to all of the northern ports. See Marc Egnal and Joseph A. Ernst, "An Economic Interpretation of the American Revolution," *William and Mary Quarterly*, 3d Ser., XXIX (1972), 3–32; William S. Sachs, "The Business Outlook in the Northern Colonies, 1750–1775" (Ph.D. diss., Columbia University, 1957), 127–137, 203–208.

3. Kenneth Wiggins Porter, *John Jacob Astor: Business Man*, 2 vols., Harvard Studies in Business History, I (Cambridge, Mass., 1931); John Bach McMaster, *The Life and Times of Stephen Girard, Mariner and Merchant*, 2 vols. (Philadelphia, 1918).

4. William Constable and Gouverneur Morris were occasional partners of Robert Morris; Tench Coxe was a partner of Edward Goold during the Revolution; and John Wilcocks was a partner of Nicholas Low. See William Allen Davis, "William Constable, New York Merchant and Land Speculator, 1772–1803" (Ph.D. diss., Harvard University, 1957), 77–102; Joseph Stancliffe Davis, *Essays in the Earlier History of American Corporations*, 2 vols., Harvard Economic Studies, XVI (Cambridge, Mass., 1917), I, 151–212; Jacob E. Cooke, "Tench Coxe, Tory Merchant," *Pennsylvania Magazine of History and Biography*, XCVI (1972), 48–88; Nicholas Low Papers, boxes 5, 6, 8, Library of Congress (hereafter cited as LC).

5. See Davis, *Earlier History*, I, 174–212, esp.203; Foster Rhea Dulles, *The Old China Trade* (Boston, 1930), 1–12, 26, 27.

6. Robert Greenhalgh Albion, *Rise of New York Port [1815–1860]* (New York, 1939), 241–252.

The links between Philadelphia and Baltimore were also strong. During its early years of explosive growth, Baltimore drew much of its business talent from its northern rival, and during the 1780s the city benefited from serving as a headquarters for Robert Morris's massive tobacco purchase.[7] Two of Baltimore's leading post-Revolutionary merchants, Robert Gilmore and Robert Oliver, were in partnership with Philadelphia traders.[8] Compared to New York and Philadelphia, Baltimore may have recruited fewer businessmen from its planter-dominated hinterland, but like its larger competitors, it attracted many foreign traders, notably Irishmen, Scots, and Germans.[9] Like the New Yorkers and Philadelphians, these traders concentrated on shipping wheat to the West Indies, southern Europe, and other overseas markets.[10] As Baltimore became larger and more efficient, it absorbed the international trade of smaller Chesapeake towns, becoming to the upper Chesapeake what Philadelphia was to the Delaware Valley and New York was to the Hudson Valley.[11] Since neither Baltimore nor New York was notably more successful than Philadelphia before 1800, it appears that their merchants faced roughly the same array of problems and opportunities that confronted Philadelphia traders.[12]

7. Rhoda M. Dorsey, "The Pattern of Baltimore Commerce during the Confederation Period," *Maryland Historical Magazine*, LXII (1967), 119–134, esp. 126, 129; Paul Kent Walker, "Business and Commerce in Baltimore on the Eve of Independence," *Md. Hist. Mag.*, LXXI (1976), 296–309; Jane N. Garrett, "Philadelphia and Baltimore, 1790–1840: A Study of Intra-Regional Unity," *Md. Hist. Mag.*, LV (1960), 1–13; Rhoda Dorsey, "Comment," in David T. Gilchrist, ed., *The Growth of the Seaport Cities, 1790–1825: Proceedings of a Conference Sponsored by the Eleutherian Mills—Hagley Foundation March 17–19, 1966* (Charlottesville, Va., 1967), 62–67.

8. Stuart Weems Bruchey, *Robert Oliver, Merchant of Baltimore, 1783–1819*, Johns Hopkins University Studies in Historical and Political Science, 74th Ser., no. 1 (Baltimore, Md., 1956), 261–334; Robert C. Alberts, *The Golden Voyage: The Life and Times of William Bingham, 1752–1804* (Boston, 1969), 114–115, 224–226.

9. Walker, "Business and Commerce," *Md. Hist. Mag.*, LXXI (1976), 304.

10. See Dorsey, "Pattern of Baltimore Commerce," *Md. Hist. Mag.*, LXII (1967), 119–134; Geoffrey Neal Gilbert, "Baltimore's Flour Trade to the Caribbean, 1750–1815" (Ph.D. diss., Johns Hopkins University, 1975).

11. Bruchey, *Robert Oliver*, 101–102; Edward C. Papenfuse, *In Pursuit of Profit: The Annapolis Merchants in the Era of the American Revolution, 1763–1805*, Maryland Bicentennial Series (Baltimore, Md., 1975), 133–168, 225.

12. The general assumption of the extensive literature on American merchants before 1815 is that the basic experience of merchants did not differ radically from port to port. See, for example, Stuart Bruchey, ed., *The Colonial Merchant: Sources and Readings* (New York, 1966), 169–173; and "Success and Failure Factors: American Merchants in Foreign Trade in the Eighteenth and Early Nineteenth Centuries," *Business History Review*, XXXIII (1958), 272–292; Glenn Porter and Harold C. Livesay, *Merchants and Manufacturers: Studies in the Changing Structure of Nineteenth-Century Marketing* (Baltimore, Md., 1971), 5–7. Although it is dangerous to overlook the differences from port to port and decade to decade, the general climate of adversity undoubtedly existed in every port.

New England, as usual, was different. In the first place, overseas commerce was not concentrated in a single voracious port that swallowed up commercial activity within a large area. At various times between 1750 and 1840, Boston had to share New England trade with a host of small but tenacious rivals—Newburyport, Marblehead, Salem, and New Bedford in Massachusetts; Newport and Providence in Rhode Island; and Portsmouth in Maine. Competition from these towns and the general stagnation of the New England economy limited the population growth of Boston to a mere 20 percent between 1740 and 1790, and this slow growth, in concert with the insular, ethnically homogeneous character of New England society, made the area unappealing to foreigners.[13] In contrast to the Middle Atlantic ports, therefore, New England's business talent—apart from the iconoclastic town of Newport—was homegrown. There was, however, no shortage of local talent from which merchants could be drawn, for living in or near New England's port towns were thousands of people—shopkeepers, artisans, traders, and mariners—who possessed good education, relevant business skills, and the Puritan's commitment to his calling. Like merchants to the south, these people had access to European credit; established Boston traders echoed the complaints of wealthy New Yorkers and Philadelphians that there were an excess of shopkeepers, auctioneers, and imported merchandise and a dearth of profits.[14]

If the mechanism of merchant recruitment was somewhat distinctive in New England, the economic conditions in which the Yankees operated differed profoundly from those found in the middle colonies. For the adversity that shaped mercantile behavior throughout America was particularly acute in New England. The reason was simple: New England, unlike the middle colonies, produced no agricultural staple for export. To be sure, cod and pine could partly take the place of flour and pork, but the market for such products was smaller and less buoyant than the demand for breadstuffs. Between 1768 and 1772, for example, Pennsylvania's exports of breadstuffs to the West Indies and southern Europe were worth £1,116,182, while Massachusetts' exports of fish to these markets totaled only £655,186.[15] But it was not just that New England could not *export* breadstuffs: unable to feed itself, the region had to *import* large quantities of flour from the Middle Atlantic region.

13. Price, "Port Towns," *Perspectives in Am. Hist.*, VIII (1974), 143.

14. John W. Tyler, "The First Revolution: Boston Merchants and the Acts of Trade, 1760–1774" (Ph.D. diss., Princeton University, 1980), 182–188, 195.

15. James F. Shepherd, "Commodity Exports from the British North American Colonies to Overseas Areas, 1768–1772: Magnitude and Patterns of Trade," *Explorations in Economic History*, 2d Ser., VIII (1970–1971), 30, 31, 33, 39, 42.

The value of food imports into Massachusetts between 1768 and 1772 amounted to 65 percent of its foreign fish exports, obviously a heavy drain on the colony's balance of payments.[16]

Lacking an adequate base of exportable commodities, New England merchants, even more than their compatriots to the south, had to scramble and scrape to earn foreign exchange with which to pay for imports. New England's economic predicament was well understood by the Yankee whalemen who prowled the South Pacific around Desolation Island (near the Strait of Magellan) and composed these lines:

> Her officers are natives of old Cape Cod
> The place where there is nothing to eat on
> For the product of their land is mackerel bones and sand
> So they had to starve or go to Desolation.[17]

During the colonial period, New Englanders resorted to many expedients besides whaling to earn foreign exchange. They distilled rum, produced spermaceti candles, built ships for export, engaged in the carrying trade, and reexported imported manufactures.[18] The spirit of the region was exemplified by the thriving town of Newport, whose economic position, according to Jacob Price, was "entirely artificial." As Price has noted, Newport's prosperity in the late colonial period was "based upon no geographical imperative," but, rather, upon the capital and the business and technical skills that were concentrated there. In important respects, Newport was a "reduced and somewhat bizarre version" of Boston, whose hinterland produced little of value.[19]

Thus New England, as an eighteenth-century writer shrewdly observed, was the Holland of America—an area whose primary resource was not mineral wealth, agricultural potential, geographical advantages, or other natural endowments, but, rather, the enterprise of its citizens. Entrepreneurial excellence was not merely a fortuitous replacement for but a necessary response to the absence of remunerative resources. Although this pattern characterized all of the northeastern ports, it was most plain in New England, the land of "mackerel bones and sand." Sharpened by decades of adversity, New Englanders learned how to reap profits where others saw only danger and difficulty. They possessed the

16. *Ibid.*; David Klingaman, "Food Surpluses and Deficits in the American Colonies, 1768–1772," *Journal of Economic History*, XXXI (1971), 558.

17. Gale Huntington, *Songs the Whalemen Sang* (Barre, Mass., 1964), 38.

18. See Bernard Bailyn, *The New England Merchants in the Seventeenth Century* (Cambridge, Mass., 1955).

19. Price, "Port Towns," *Perspectives in Am. Hist.*, VIII (1974), 149–150 (on Newport), 140–148 (on Boston).

capacity to endure great hardship, take great risks, and even disregard conventional ethical standards in their pursuit of wealth. The stereotype of the sharp Yankee was no artifact of the antebellum South. One Philadelphia merchant who had been in America for about fourteen years remarked in 1774, "I have so indifferent an opinion of the integrity of the New England People in general, having seen a good deal of their conduct, that for my own part I would not be fond of trusting any of them unless they had Capitals or were guaranteed by those that had."[20] This prejudice was confirmed in the marketplace, where it was said, "Bills of exchange on New England do not enjoy very good credit here, as the people of that region are somewhat given to sharp practices."[21]

The full economic significance of the Yankee spirit of enterprise did not emerge until the constraints of the British Empire were lifted and the talents of New England merchants were given free rein. In the decades after 1783 her merchants and mariners pushed into many unfamiliar commercial spheres—the spice trade with the East Indies, the China trade, the California hide trade, international whaling, the neutral carrying trade, the Baltic trade, and the cotton trade. As Oscar Handlin has noted, such commerce was highly fragile because "Boston was never more than an entrepôt." "All the essential commodities of this trade were drawn from far-off ports as accessible to other cities as to Boston. Based upon the enterprise and initiative of Boston merchants rather than upon the city's advantageous position or natural resources, this commerce had no permanent or durable roots."[22] Fragile or not, these trades were lucrative while they lasted, and New Englanders shrewdly invested their winnings in manufactures. By the antebellum period New England was America's most heavily industrialized region and, with a per capita gross national product that was 41 percent above the national average in 1860, the most prosperous as well.[23]

The example of New England powerfully reinforces the argument I have made for the economic significance of the "fabric of adversity." According to the conventional canons of economic analysis, which focus on quantifiable variables rather than on such murky matters as national

20. William Pollard to Benjamin and John Bowers, Dec. 13, 1773, Pollard Letterbook, 1772–1774, 317, HSP.

21. Stephen Girard to John Girard, n.d., Girard Papers, 2d Ser., Reel 480. All references to the Girard Papers are to the microfilm collection in the American Philosophical Society (hereafter cited as APS).

22. Oscar Handlin, *Boston's Immigrants, 1790–1865: A Study in Acculturation* (New York, 1976), 3–5.

23. Robert William Fogel and Stanley L. Engerman, *Time on the Cross: The Economics of American Negro Slavery*, 2 vols. (Boston, 1974), I, 248.

character, New England's prospects in 1790 were bleak indeed. Its land was stony and overcrowded with impecunious farmers who had recently revolted against burdensome taxes. The fishing industry was ruined by the Revolution and did not recover its 1775 volume until about 1795.[24] The region was unable even to feed its indigenous population, let alone generate surplus crops for export, and the region's merchants were undercapitalized and dependent on small, scattered markets. Moreover, New England's future in industry was clouded by a dearth of technical expertise, cheap labor, and capital resources. But this very adversity equipped New England merchants to seize opportunities throughout the world, and they rapidly built a dynamic, modern economy.

And what of the three great ports to the south of Boston? How did they fare during the four decades after 1790? New York boomed in spectacular fashion, as did Baltimore until 1820, while Philadelphia declined in comparison to the other ports, although she continued to grow quite rapidly (see table 22). It is this last phenomenon that is of particular interest here: How did it come about that Philadelphia lost its position of leadership of the eighteenth century? Not the least of Philadelphia's problems was its port. Situated one hundred miles up the shallow and treacherous Delaware, it required the services of expensive, specialized pilots, and during the winter the river froze up for two or three months. Even more serious was the constricted nature of Philadelphia's agricultural hinterland. By the 1790s the burgeoning city of Baltimore was draining off produce from Maryland's Eastern Shore and from western Pennsylvania, which was connected with the Chesapeake Bay by the Susquehanna River.

Since the decline of Philadelphia was relative rather than absolute, it was also a function of the rise of New York City after 1790. The fortunes of the city and the colony of New York as a whole were linked, and in the early years the colony lagged in population for a variety of reasons. New York's Dutch founders did not aggressively promote settlement; the Iroquois dominated the interior during the eighteenth century; and the presence of gigantic manors along the Hudson prompted many immigrants to settle in New Jersey and Pennsylvania instead.[25] Because of New York's sparse settlement, its breadstuff exports to the West Indies

24. United States Bureau of the Census, *Statistical History of the United States: Colonial Times to 1970*, 2 vols. (Washington, D.C., 1975), Ser. Z, 534–538, II, 1195. Raymond McFarland, *A History of the New England Fisheries* (Philadelphia, 1911), 131; Harold A. Innis, *The Cod Fisheries: The History of an International Economy* (New Haven, Conn., 1940), 224. I am indebted to Daniel Vickers for this information.

25. Sung Bok Kim, *Landlord and Tenant in Colonial New York: Manorial Society, 1664–1775* (Chapel Hill, N.C., 1978), 129–142, 235–242.

TABLE 22. *Population of the Four Largest United States Cities and Their Suburbs, 1790–1840*

	Population (Decennial Increase in Parentheses)					
City	1790	1800	1810	1820	1830	1840
Boston	18,320	24,937	38,746	54,024	85,568	118,857
		(36.1%)	(55.4%)	(39.4%)	(58.4%)	(38.9%)
New York	33,131	60,515	100,775	130,881	214,995	348,943
		(82.7%)	(66.5%)	(29.9%)	(64.3%)	(62.3%)
Philadelphia	44,096	61,559	87,303	108,809	161,271	220,423
		(39.6%)	(41.8%)	(24.6%)	(48.2%)	(36.7%)
Baltimore	13,503	26,514	46;555	62,738	80,620	102,313
		(96.4%)	(75.6%)	(34.8%)	(28.5%)	(26.9%)

Source: George Rogers Taylor, "Comment," in David T. Gilchrist, ed., *The Growth of the Seaport Cities, 1790–1825: Proceedings of a Conference Sponsored by the Eleutherian Mills–Hagley Foundation, March 17–19, 1966* (Charlottesville, Va., 1967), 39.

and southern Europe amounted to only 30 percent of Pennsylvania's during the late-colonial period.[26] But these sundry handicaps of colonial days were lifted during the Revolution; between 1780 and 1810 New York's population grew by 356 percent, compared to Pennsylvania's 148 percent.[27] The state's trade grew proportionally, and by the period 1803–1810 Philadelphia's exports were worth only 68 percent of New York's.[28] Philadelphia, however, continued to prosper by making a successful transition from maritime commerce to banking, manufacturing, mining, and coastal trade. The city remained America's second largest, fully 85 percent larger than Boston in 1840. But Philadelphia's days as the most dynamic port in North America were over.

Unremitting warfare and diplomatic intervention in trade heightened both the risks and rewards of commerce between 1793 and 1815, and thereafter recurrent financial panics continued to wipe out many traders. By 1820 leading American traders were far richer than they had been in 1790, but the hazards of trade were still extreme and

26. Shepherd, "Commodity Exports," *Explorations in Economic History*, 2d Ser., VIII (1970–1971), 32, 33, 41, 42.

27. Diane Lindstrom, *Economic Development in the Philadelphia Region, 1810–1850* (New York, 1978), 35.

28. *Ibid.*, 34.

the chances of failure high.[29] The dynamic interaction between social fluidity, economic adversity, and entrepreneurial innovation was still at work, driving merchants to diversify their operations, much as Philadelphians had done during the Revolutionary era. In the course of time, the process of diversification undoubtedly changed somewhat, because, as traders became wealthier, there was increased pressure to find an outlet for surplus capital. Nevertheless, the inherent risks of trade both prepared merchants psychologically to move into new activities and gave them an incentive for doing so. After 1820, much of this diversification centered on manufacturing. In their various roles as marketer, financier, and founding industrialist, merchants have rightly been called the catalysts of the Industrial Revolution in America.[30]

By building a national market for boots and shoes and then gradually mechanizing production, coastal merchants in New England created the gigantic shoe industry based in Lynn, Massachusetts. Further south, a famous group of merchants developed the Waltham-Lowell system of cotton textile production between 1815 and 1820. This industrial process combined under one roof all of the operations of cloth production—cleaning, carding, spinning, weaving, and dyeing—and captured a large share of the market for coarse cotton cloth. Because it was carried out so deftly and efficiently, this revolutionary innovation appears almost effortless and risk-free. But as George Rogers Taylor has noted, "None but wealthy men could have financed such a venture, and probably none but merchants used to the huge risks attendant upon foreign trade during the Napoleonic Wars would have had the initiative or courage necessary for a project involving such drastic innovations in the techniques of production and business organization."[31] In a penetrating analysis, Robert F. Dalzell, Jr., has shown that traders were driven to innovate in the cotton industry because they were seeking a refuge from the narrow, anxiety-ridden existence of the merchant.[32] In a representative comment on mercantile life, Amos Lawrence concluded, "Property acquired at such sacrifices as I have been obliged to make the past year costs more than it's

29. Dorsey, "Comment," in Gilchrist, ed., *Growth of Seaport Cities*, 66, writes, for example, "For Baltimore 1819–21 were lean years, and many houses that had managed to stay afloat through all the difficulties of the war years, the embargo, and the British blockade went under then."

30. Porter and Livesay, *Merchants and Manufacturers*, chap. 4.

31. George Rogers Taylor, *The Transportation Revolution, 1815–1860*, The Economic History of the United States, IV (New York, 1951), 230.

32. Robert F. Dalzell, Jr., "The Rise of the Waltham-Lowell System and Some Thoughts on the Political Economy of Modernization in Ante-Bellum Massachusetts," *Perspectives in Am. Hist.*, IX (1975), 227–268.

worth; and the anxiety in protecting it is the extreme of folly."[33] Industrialization offered escape from such cares. Once placed on a secure footing, the cotton manufacturing companies provided a remunerative but relatively relaxing alternative to overseas commerce. Rapid financial gain was no longer the uppermost concern of many of these industrialists; they were content to draw substantial dividends from earnings instead of reinvesting most of the profits to finance further growth.

Although tremendously important, these Boston Associates were hardly typical; most antebellum industrialists were undercapitalized operators who had to struggle to survive. Some were upwardly mobile mechanics, often European immigrants possessing advanced technical skills.[34] Others were former merchants whose reverses in trade encouraged them to test the waters of American industry. The technical ability and personal ambition of these fledgling industrialists often exceeded their capital resources, and after sinking funds into fixed plant they often had little left over to finance inventory, purchase raw materials, and meet the payroll. What they needed was a banker who could extend short-term loans to provide working capital, but commercial banks would have nothing to do with these weak borrowers. It was here that wealthy merchants could step in and make a critical contribution. As professional risk-takers and masters of the intricacies of commercial finance, merchants were willing to discount the commercial paper of manufacturers, while providing marketing services and general business advice. Such credit was not cheap; merchants earned 12–30 percent on their capital by discounting commercial paper. But their services were evidently worth the price and played, according to one prominent study, "an indispensable part in American industrialization."

Planters and Merchants

Although the specific economic patterns varied greatly, a single behavioral dynamic was at work throughout the northeastern seaboard, hastening economic development in all of the major ports. From Salem to Baltimore, the lure of social mobility and the prod of economic adversity encouraged aggressive diversification and innovation by local entrepreneurs. The risks were gigantic and the failures many, but under

33. *Ibid.*, 257.

34. See, for example, Herbert G. Gutman, "The Reality of the Rags-to-Riches 'Myth': The Case of the Paterson, New Jersey, Locomotive, Iron, and Machinery Manufacturers, 1830–1880," in Stephan Thernstrom and Richard Sennett, eds., *Nineteenth Century Cities: Essays in the New Urban History* (New Haven, Conn., 1969), 98–124.

the insistent, reckless, often ruthless urging of merchants and manufacturers, a backward agricultural economy was pushed into the onrushing currents of the Industrial Revolution. The important role played in this process by mobility and adversity can be suggested not merely through direct observation but also in a negative way—by showing that where these forces were less powerful, entrepreneurs tended to be cautious and economic development slow.

For that was the case in the American South. There is no greater paradox in the history of the United States than the failure of the South to maintain its early position of economic leadership. In the colonial era, Virginia, Maryland, and South Carolina offered the ambitious young immigrant an unexcelled field of enterprise. By 1774 the South contained nearly as many people as New England and the middle colonies combined, and it had much the highest level of per capita wealth if slaves are counted as wealth, and a level roughly equal to the colonial average if they are not.[35] Yet during the next half-century the southeastern states generally stagnated, becoming an economic backwater in comparison to the rapidly advancing northern states. The reasons for this startling reversal are numerous and complex, embracing not only contrasting patterns of entrepreneurship but also divergent labor systems, natural endowments, religious traditions, and settlement patterns.

To disentangle every strand of this causal web would here be impossible. But if we focus simply on the matter of entrepreneurship, we may see, tentatively and hypothetically, how the ultimate failure of the southern businessman was embedded in his initial success. Having established a lucrative niche in the Atlantic economy, the planter became trapped therein, unable or unwilling to move into new markets as economic conditions changed and new opportunities appeared.

This paradox rests on the fundamental reality of early American economic history: an abundance of land and a shortage of capital and labor. This unusual combination of factor endowments gave the nation a comparative advantage over Europe in the production of agricultural staples and a relative disadvantage in manufacturing finished goods, which required greater inputs of labor and capital.[36] Seventeenth-century Americans did not immediately appreciate this economic imperative, and for a while both Virginians and Puritans struggled gamely to produce manufactures before turning their attention to agricultural staples. But here

35. Alice Hanson Jones, *Wealth of a Nation to Be: The American Colonies on the Eve of the Revolution* (New York, 1980), 50–69, esp. tables 3.3, 3.5, 3.6, 3.9.

36. This formulation follows the Heckscher-Olin model of international trade, which is summarized in Richard E. Caves and Ronald W. Jones, *World Trade and Payments: An Introduction* (Boston, 1973), chaps. 8, 9.

the similarities between the two sections end. Fertile though it was, acreage north of Maryland was best suited to growing commodities that competed with foodstuffs produced on the European continent. As a result, the price of these commodities was simply not high enough to support the cost of buying both the land and the labor to work it. The tillers of northern lands, therefore, as a rule were the same people who owned them: the family farmers. Barred from the role of producer, northern businessmen had to concentrate on marketing and shipping—importing manufactures and tropical groceries and exporting foodstuffs. Although this was a difficult way to build an estate, with markets small, capital scarce, and competition intense, there was no alternative.[37]

In the South, by contrast, businessmen were able to specialize in the production of their colony's key export crops—tobacco in Virginia and Maryland; indigo and rice in South Carolina; sugar, coffee, and cocoa in the West Indies. Because these commodities commanded a world market but could grow successfully in a limited geographical area only, they fetched sufficiently high prices to allow businessmen to buy up large amounts of land and secure slave or servant labor. Within a relatively short period after the founding of their colonies, agriculturists from Maryland to Barbados had secured an economically logical and financially profitable niche in the Atlantic economy. The planters did have considerable difficulty surmounting capital and labor bottlenecks, and overproduction with attendant price depressions was a recurrent problem, but they nevertheless controlled a unique resource that produced commodities with worldwide demand. Not surprisingly, many planters became extremely wealthy men.

So long as southern planters were able to grow cash crops profitably, they prospered, no matter whether the crop was tobacco, rice, indigo, or cotton. But when the market for these commodities deteriorated, southern entrepreneurs had little to fall back on. Flexibility, innovativeness, and speculative drive—characteristics that any successful northern merchant had to possess to survive—were not much in evidence on the great southern plantations. Decade after decade of sowing and reaping had fixed blinders on the southern businessman. Having so long left marketing, finance, shipping, and manufacturing primarily to European and Yankee capitalists, the planter was not readily disposed to enter these fields when the profitability of agriculture waned. There were persuasive reasons, after all, for remaining in agriculture. It had been a successful avenue of enterprise for many decades and might have become one again if a profitable new crop—such as cotton in the 1790s—had been discov-

37. On the many problems of 18th-century American traders, see above, chap. 3.

ered. For the large landowner, agriculture was far less risky than trade or manufacturing, and plantation life offered an appealing balance between business and social activity. One could earn a living while enjoying the pleasures of rural life and serving in government at the local and state level. Though no longer lucrative, such an existence was at least honorable, safe, and familiar. Certainly it was preferable to moving to a strange city—perhaps even a foreign port—and plunging into an alien, risky field of enterprise. This cautious approach was particularly appealing to planters who had inherited their wealth and therefore tended to take it for granted. Like the landed gentlemen of the North, such men were likely to be drawn to politics, military service, or cultural pursuits, in preference to merely duplicating the economic achievements of their fathers and grandfathers.[38] Thus the political proficiency and economic lethargy of Revolutionary Virginia went hand in hand: the planter elite directed its energies in one direction instead of the other.

The predilection of planters to remain in agriculture was perfectly understandable, and rational within the terms of their outlook, but it was hardly conducive to rapid economic development. South Carolina is a case in point. When the price of cotton fell below remunerative levels in the 1820s, the state declined economically and proved unable to redirect its considerable stock of capital and labor to other pursuits.[39] The same could be said of the South as a whole. Although the section generally prospered while cotton demand soared during the first phase of the Industrial Revolution, worldwide production eventually ran ahead of supply, and prices plummeted. Unable to adjust to this adversity, the section remained primarily agricultural and by 1880 possessed a per capita income equal to only 36 percent of the Northeast's.[40] There was deep irony in this pattern. It was the very weakness of the northern entrepreneur's position that compelled him to diversify his activities as rapidly as possible, and it was the great strength and stability of the planter's business franchise that kept him inflexibly specialized in agriculture. Wracked by adversity at every turn, northern merchants were

38. It is vital to recognize that the ideal of gentility was not restricted to the South in the 18th and early 19th centuries. See above, chap. 1; Arthur M. Schlesinger, "The Aristocracy in Colonial America," Massachusetts Historical Society, *Proceedings*, LXXIV (1962), 3–21; Carl Bridenbaugh, *Cities in Revolt: Urban Life in America, 1743–1776* (New York, 1955), chap. 9.

39. William W. Freehling, *Prelude to Civil War: The Nullification Controversy in South Carolina, 1816–1836* (New York, 1965), 25–48. On the failure of manufacturing in antebellum South Carolina, see Alfred Glaze Smith, Jr., *Economic Readjustment of an Old Cotton State: South Carolina, 1820–1860* (Columbia, S.C., 1958), 112–134.

40. Lance E. Davis *et al.*, *American Economic Growth: An Economist's History of the United States* (New York, 1972), 52.

willing to leap into unfamiliar enterprises, while well-established planters remained satisfied with their traditional occupation.

Economic stagnation in the South, it must be stressed, was not the result of incompetence; many planters were shrewd and energetic managers of their estates. The wealthy Virginian Landon Carter filled a journal of over one thousand lengthy pages, covering twenty-six years, with the minutiae of day-to-day plantation management. No detail was too small to capture Carter's attention as he strained to maximize the productivity of his lands and slaves. "I am much pleased with my new Cow stalls," Carter commented. "They keep the cattle drye and warm enough and their Food drye and by the Conveniency of the roof over it a boy can fill the Cribs for 30 cattle in ten minutes." He noted that "flies contrary to observations eat the large plants and let the small ones alone." And with scrupulous precision he calculated that "it has taken 11 1/2 bushels to compleat those 4 fields equal to 46 pecks which contain 588,800 grains which at 3 grains to a hill is 196,266 hills."[41] Landon Carter's peers were no less attentive in managing their properties. Carter's own nephew, Robert, imaginatively experimented with new crops and original approaches to household manufactures on his estate, and he owned a substantial share in an ironworks as well.[42] During the early nineteenth century the highly differentiated workforce on John Tayloe's Mount Airy plantation was kept steadily employed in a "closely synchronized" set of tasks that shifted with the seasons, and Mount Airy slave families were routinely broken up to accommodate the needs of the plantation.[43] Recent studies of the antebellum economy suggest that such efficiency, and the terrible human costs that it entailed, continued to characterize plantation administration until the Civil War.[44]

This vigilant management was rewarded with a high level of agricultural productivity, and since America as a whole had a comparative advantage in farming, it was perfectly rational for planters to concentrate on this area while it remained lucrative. But one cannot therefore conclude, as some historians have concluded, that the economy of the South before the Civil War was a great success; for in the end, southern

41. Landon Carter, *The Diary of Colonel Landon Carter of Sabine Hall, 1752–1778*, ed. Jack P. Greene, 2 vols. (Charlottesville, Va., 1965), I, 195, 394, 401.

42. Louis Morton, *Robert Carter of Nomini Hall: A Virginia Tobacco Planter of the Eighteenth Century* (Williamsburg, Va., 1945), 139–185.

43. Richard S. Dunn, "A Tale of Two Plantations: Slave Life at Mesopotamia in Jamaica and Mount Airy in Virginia, 1799 to 1828," *WMQ*, 3d Ser., XXXIV (1977), 54–56. See also Raymond George Peterson, Jr., "George Washington, Capitalistic Farmer: A Documentary Study of Washington's Business Activities and the Sources of his Wealth" (Ph.D. diss., Ohio State University, 1970).

44. Fogel and Engerman, *Time on the Cross*, I, 191–223.

businessmen were quite unable to strike out into new enterprises when the time had come to do so.[45] Though competent *managers*, they were ineffectual *entrepreneurs*. Having prospered admirably in agriculture, they could not bring themselves to embark on new careers in trade or industry. Thus, the southern economy *grew* more readily than it *developed*; impressive quantitative performance, as measured by agricultural output, was not matched by qualitative improvements that would have raised economic efficiency.

So much for the substantial planters, who, after all, made up a small proportion of the population. Why, it may be asked, did not minor businessmen assume the risks shunned by their social superiors, as many upwardly mobile northerners did? Without pretending to dissect the entire social structure of the South, a partial answer may be offered. Many of the most capable people in the southern working class were slaves, and white mechanics and shopkeepers had few role models to inspire aggressive entrepreneurship outside of agriculture. Judging from the pattern of immigration, the very presence of slavery reduced the attractiveness of the South to ambitious outsiders, because the peculiar institution seemed to associate manual labor with servitude. Furthermore, the relatively small number of bankruptcies in established plantation regions created few openings in the elite for aspiring young planters.

Important, too, was the paucity of cities in much of the South. The historical reputation of American cities is tarnished at best, for they are often viewed as receptacles of disease, vice, and discontent, places where the heights of wealth and the depths of poverty coexist. This is true enough, but it is sometimes forgotten that cities are also caldrons of opportunity, in which vistas are broadened and ambitions sharpened. In a traditional, face-to-face society where transportation and communication speeds were exactly equal, opportunity was limited by physical distance. In a remote rural county the aspiring shopkeeper had limited access to education, to market information, to commercial credit, to the patronage and advice of a wealthy merchant. His career horizons were likely to be circumscribed, and he was at a distinct disadvantage when competing with wealthy, well-educated members of the local gentry who were in regular contact with London and Glasgow, New York and New Orleans. These disadvantages were diminished in a city, because markets were larger and more competitive and information was more freely available. If one bank would not provide a loan, there were many others to

45. *Ibid.*, 247–257; Richard A. Easterlin, "Farm Production and Income in Old and New Areas at Mid-Century," in David C. Klingaman and Richard K. Vedder, eds., *Essays in Nineteenth Century Economic History: The Old Northwest* (Athens, Ohio, 1975), 77–117.

try.[46] If local wholesalers would not sell goods on reasonable terms, one could attempt to order a shipment directly from London or Liverpool. If the European export merchants would not fill this order, one could obtain a letter of recommendation from a fellow trader whose name was trusted on the far side of the Atlantic. In a sparsely settled rural area it could be difficult to find a competitor who would perform this service, but it was possible in a large port containing many traders.[47]

Closely related to the importance of cities was the simple fact that economic power in the South was based on land, a finite resource that could be engrossed by an elite. In a long-settled area there was likely to be relatively little high-quality land that had not yet been taken up, and it was therefore difficult for an upstart agricultural entrepreneur to supersede established planters. Opportunities were greater in northern ports, because there the basis of economic activity was not land, but capital and credit—a highly expandable resource that cannot easily be monopolized. It was quite possible for an ambitious, impecunious businessman to outstrip his larger competitors by building a business with borrowed funds. This career pattern was vitally important, because it meant that fresh entrepreneurial blood was steadily being pumped into the arteries of the northern economy, replacing the anemic leadership of genteel heirs. Although only a minority of wealthy merchants began their careers in the middle class, such bounding adventurers as Thomas Hancock, John Jacob Astor, Stephen Girard, and Robert Morris set high standards of performance that their competitors had to meet.

A corollary of this analysis is that in the South social mobility and the spirit of enterprise were greatest in those areas where land was most freely available—on the frontier. Once the land in an area had been bought up, an entrenched elite was likely to materialize, and opportunities were likely to decline. In South Carolina, for example, the early settlers were clear-sighted entrepreneurs from Barbados who established highly profitable rice plantations.[48] But once the colony was settled, the chance for advancement in the low country evidently diminished. According to Carl Bridenbaugh, "By the middle of the [eighteenth] century

46. Lance E. Davis, "The Investment Market, 1870–1914: The Evolution of a National Market," *Jour. Econ. Hist.*, XXV (1965), 355–399, finds that interest rates in the South greatly exceeded those in New England and the Middle Atlantic states after the Civil War and attributes this to the poor quality and noncompetitive character of the southern banking system. See especially 375, 388–392.

47. On the mechanics of social mobility of entrepreneurs in Philadelphia, see above, chap. 1.

48. Peter H. Wood, *Black Majority: Negroes in Colonial South Carolina from 1670 through the Stono Rebellion* (New York, 1974), 13–62.

the inhabitants frankly admitted that 'the valuable land is chiefly engrossed by the wealthy.' "[49] The energetic resourcefulness of the colonial planters of the low country was not much in evidence among their descendants. As William H. Freehling writes of the early nineteenth century: "The crux of the matter was that lowcountry planters were very large capitalists who often despised the painstaking care and economy which a capitalistic enterprise requires. The more disdainful patricians never escaped the suspicion that enthusiastic plantation management smacked of Yankee practicality." As for the sons of these men, they "drank and idled away [their] time in Charleston."[50] By the 1830s, one had to go westward, to Texas and Arkansas, to find a southern society dominated by entrepreneurs as the Carolinas had been a century earlier. Eugene Genovese observes that the "rough parvenu planters of the Southwestern frontier—the 'Southern Yankees' " displayed more "crudeness and naked avarice" than did planters in older regions.[51] As the term "Southern Yankees" itself reveals, such men did not typify the southern businessman, because the frontier itself was transient. The northern city, by contrast, was a sort of permanent frontier—a place where the "rough parvenu" could make his mark generation after generation.

In a port, in sum, far more than in a rural area, opportunity, enterprise, and adversity reinforced each other. A young businessman could borrow money and move into trade, challenging the commercial position of older, more established merchants. His opportunity was, in effect, their adversity. Such intense competition prompted traders to work hard and to stay on the lookout for lucrative new business opportunities that might secure their fortunes. The great risks of trade, and the ease of entry by young traders, ensured that this spirit of enterprise did not ossify or stagnate after one or two generations. For if an upwardly mobile merchant became rich and left large legacies to his sons, they, too, would face the same fierce competition from young upstarts that their father's competitors had met. Despite the advantages that inherited capital and social position bestowed, they could expect to survive in business only through cunning, efficiency, and luck. Some heirs elected to follow their fathers down this treacherous path, but others pursued safer and more genteel careers in the professions, while investing their patrimony in relatively safe, income-producing investments. In this way, men of sub-

49. Carl Bridenbaugh, *Myths and Realities: Societies of the Colonial South*, 2d ed. (New York, 1976), 58.

50. Freehling, *Prelude to Civil War*, 34, 35.

51. Eugene D. Genovese, *The Political Economy of Slavery: Studies in the Economy and Society of the Slave South* (New York, 1965), 28, 29.

stantial wealth but meager talent were steadily flushed from the urban business system, to be replaced by keen young upstarts.

In plantation economies, by contrast, second- and third-generation wealth continued to dominate the economy by virtue of ownership of the land. From this simple fact, three important consequences followed. First, the quality of entrepreneurship suffered because many southern heirs (like northern ones) were not particularly able or energetic men. Second, engrossment of land restricted the upward mobility of capable farmers, artisans, and shopkeepers. And third, where upward mobility was restricted, so was competitive pressure on established planters. To this extent, the adversity that persistently prodded merchants to move into new fields of enterprise was absent in the South. Wealthy planters were securely ensconced in the same social and economic niche that their fathers and grandfathers had occupied. Though the relative economic stature of their part of the nation might decline, they remained at the top of the heap. If soil exhaustion or overcrowding eventually threatened the viability of their estate, they could move to the frontier to start again.

This analysis implies that the economic differences between North and South cannot be understood purely in terms of divergent labor systems. The economic history of the South is not simply a chapter in the history of slavery, and the contrast between the slave labor system and free labor may not even be the most germane difference between northern businessmen and southern planters in the formative period of American economic development, 1775–1820. For in these years the most influential group of northern entrepreneurs was not manufacturers, but merchants, who employed few workers of any kind. And such labor as they did employ, particularly before 1790 or so, was often bond rather than wage labor. In 1774, for example, 27 percent of Philadelphia's merchant community owned servants, 33 percent owned slaves, and 52 percent owned servants, slaves, or both.[52] Among the wealthiest traders, these proportions were even higher.[53] Before 1820 the most distinctive feature of northern entrepreneurs, in comparison with planters, was that their enterprise was based on the manipulation of capital rather than the ownership of land. Fixation on the contrast between a slave society and a free-labor society is, in an important sense, an anachronistic application of the categories of abolitionists and their opponents.[54]

52. See Appendix, tables A-14, A-15.

53. Of the wealthiest 98 merchants, 38% owned servants, 38% owned slaves, and 62% owned servants or slaves, or both.

54. Most of the influential literature on American slavery has focused on the antebellum period, for four reasons. (1) Historians have been interested in the social and economic

Recent discussion of the economic performance of planters has tended toward divergent extremes. On the one hand, certain writers have suggested that they were prebourgeois aristocrats who operated their plantations with an economically irrational labor system. The impulse of the planters to maximize profits was fundamentally compromised by their affective relationships with their slaves, and they were less interested in the steady, rational accumulation of profits than in the acquisition of slaves and land to secure their status in an agrarian society.[55] By contrast, other writers, many of them economists, suggest that not only were the planters bona fide businessmen but they were just as rational and effective, within the strictures of a slave society, as their northern counterparts. Some claim that the planters were successful because they achieved high levels of productivity in the field of enterprise where the South had a comparative advantage, namely, agriculture.[56] Still other economists dissent from this positive assessment, pointing out that the South failed to diversify economically and develop a strong manufacturing sector.[57] But this failure is attributed not to the character of the planters themselves, but, rather, to a host of handicaps that plagued any businessman operating in a slave society.[58] The skewed income distribution and scattered settlement patterns of southern society, it is said, de-

origins of the Civil War; (2) they have been drawn to the provocative and informative writings of such contemporary observers as Frederick Law Olmsted, George Fitzhugh, Cassius Marcellus Clay, and Hinton Rowan Helper; (3) economists have been attracted to the period 1830–1860 by the superior census data available for these years; and finally, (4) this tendency is part of a general neglect of the economic history of the period 1775–1815. Concentration on this period has obscured the intergenerational development of the plantation economy and has focused attention on a period when—thanks to the rapid economic development in the North between 1775 and 1820—the North had developed a huge lead over the South in the process of economic development and had in fact established the preconditions for industrialization. To focus only on the period after 1820 is to focus more on the results of the different developmental patterns of North and South, rather than its causes. Modern work on the economic history of the southern economy before 1820 promises to correct this problem.

55. Genovese, *Political Economy of Slavery*; and *The World the Slaveholders Made: Two Essays in Interpretation* (New York, 1969).

56. Fogel and Engerman, *Time on the Cross*, I, 247–257.

57. Gavin Wright, *The Political Economy of the Cotton South: Households, Markets, and Wealth in the Nineteenth Century* (New York, 1978), 109–121. Wright takes note (89) of the failure of the cotton South to industrialize after the Civil War. Fred Bateman and Thomas Weiss, *A Deplorable Scarcity: The Failure of Industrialization in the Slave Economy* (Chapel Hill, N.C., 1981).

58. A useful review is Bateman and Weiss, *Deplorable Scarcity*, 27–48. See also Stanley Engerman, "A Reconsideration of Southern Economic Growth, 1770–1860," *Agricultural History*, XLIX (1975), 343–361.

prived potential southern manufacturers of a sound local market. The capital of the planters was tied up in land and slaves, and these workers were less efficient than free white laborers in the North. The supply of labor in the Southeast was more limited than the labor supply of New England, because Yankee workers migrated westward less rapidly than southeastern slaves were sold to western planters during the cotton boom.[59]

None of these interpretations is completely persuasive. These irrational, prebourgeois aristocrats somehow managed to turn a vast wilderness area into one of the most successful centers of commercial agriculture in the world, an achievement that required massive investments of capital, the management of large estates, the production of crops for volatile international markets, and the acquisition and deployment of large platoons of workers. Many planters did not shy away from limited mercantile activity, such as retailing manufactures to local farmers or shipping flour to the West Indies. It is not difficult to understand why careful studies of these men describe them as "merchant planters," "planter capitalists," "entrepreneurs," and "businessmen."[60] To be sure, the "habit of command" encouraged indolence, and patriarchal, paternalistic attitudes modulated their relationship to their labor force. But such attitudes did not preclude a reasonably rational management of an estate. Several of the largest and most complex industrial installations in eighteenth-century America were ironworks in the Chesapeake region that relied on slave labor.[61] As for the conspicuous consumption of aristocratic planters, it did not exceed the riotous, sometimes ruinous, material display of the haute bourgeoisie of Federalist Philadelphia—the sumptuous banquets with a dozen wines and six meat dishes, the oversized town houses trimmed with intricately carved woodwork, the coaches accompanied by footmen in livery, the country seats surrounded by exotic trees.[62] Many of the aristocratic airs of the wealthy planter slaveowners were adopted by successful northern capitalists of the late

59. Wright, *Political Economy*, 117–120.

60. Aubrey C. Land, "Economic Behavior in a Planting Society: The Eighteenth-Century Chesapeake," *Journal of Southern History*, XXXII (1967), 475–476; Paul G. E. Clemens, *The Atlantic Economy and Colonial Maryland's Eastern Shore: From Tobacco to Grain* (Ithaca, N.Y., 1980), 134, 200; Lewis Cecil Gray, *History of Agriculture in the Southern United States to 1860*, 2 vols., Carnegie Institution of Washington Publication, No. 430 (Gloucester, Mass., 1958 [orig. publ. Washington, D.C., 1933]), I, 302.

61. See, for example, Charles B. Dew, "David Ross and the Oxford Iron Works: A Study of Industrial Slavery in the Early Nineteenth-Century South," *WMQ*, 3d Ser., XXXI (1974), 189–224; Robert S. Starobin, *Industrial Slavery in the Old South* (New York, 1970).

62. See above, chap. 1.

eighteenth century, and intermarriage between aristocratic northerners and southerners was not uncommon.[63]

To insist, however, that the planters were bona fide businessmen is not to equate them with the commercial and industrial leaders of the North, for the planters did not display the spirit of enterprise—the drive and flexibility, the tolerance for risk, the roving quest for new markets—that characterized northern businessmen. It is hardly surprising that historical economists have overlooked this fact, because the dismal science itself systematically ignores the social and psychological basis of economic behavior and uncritically assumes that all men habitually devote their lives to maximizing income. Proceeding from this unwarranted assumption, economists have had to explain the failure of the South to diversify by adverting not to the entrepreneurial deficiencies of planters, but to the special burdens that they faced.[64] These burdens were real and serious, but it is not so clear that they were insuperable. It is hard to understand, for example, why slave societies did not provide an adequate market for supporting indigenous manufactures, when they consumed huge quantities of northern and European manufactures that carried heavy duties and shipping charges. And if a skewed distribution of wealth did in fact depress consumer demand, it also increased the volume of investment capital by a proportional degree. Although slave labor was undoubtedly deficient in some respects, so was much of the unskilled labor of the North, and the success of scattered southern factories suggests that this problem was not insoluble. If planters did have a large proportion of their capital tied up in slaves and land, they could have used these assets to back loans with which to launch new enterprises, an opportunity many impecunious northerners would have seized. Nor should it be forgotten that some important business opportunities available to planters were commercial and did not require large amounts of slave labor.

In the end none of these explanations of the failure of the South to diversify withstands close scrutiny. The path to economic development is always steep and strewn with obstacles, and when the way is not negotiated successfully, it can be pronounced impassable. Yet much depends always on the energy and resolve of those making the ascent. If New

63. On the prominence of Maryland-based families in the Philadelphia upper class, see above, chap. 1. On the intermarriage of northern and southern families, see Schlesinger, "Colonial Aristocracy," Mass. Hist. Soc., *Procs.*, LXXIV (1962), 8.

64. Several economists have suggested that inferior entrepreneurship might have been a significant variable, but this has been treated as a residual hypothesis, to be called upon when other possibilities have been exhausted, and little has been said about its causes. See Bateman and Weiss, *Deplorable Scarcity*, 35–37.

England had failed to develop economically in the early nineteenth century, there would be no shortage of plausible explanations—scarce labor, inadequate capital, small markets, technological inferiority, ferocious competition from English manufacturers. We know that these handicaps could be overcome only because Yankee enterprise proved as much. One suspects that many of the problems confronting businessmen in the South were similarly reducible. One modern study of manufacturing in the slave South, based on an analysis of census data, observes: "Manufactures in almost every industry and state were earning high rates. . . . The average [rate of return] for all southern manufacturing was 28 percent in 1860, and 25 percent in 1850."[65] The study concludes: "The evidence is quite clear that the South had not attained its full industrial and economic potential, nor does it seem to have been laying an adequate foundation for postbellum transformation and industrialization."[66]

The Case of Virginia

Undoubtedly much, perhaps most, of this entrepreneurial failure may be ascribed to the corrosive effects of slavery and directly related factors. But also important, one suspects, was the absence in an agrarian business system of the powerful synergism of social mobility and economic adversity that generated a spirit of enterprise in northern ports. Although incapable of conclusive demonstration here, the plausibility of this argument can be suggested by reviewing the course of economic development in Virginia. Aside from its great intrinsic importance, the Old Dominion merits attention for the simple reason that it did not produce cotton. As a consequence, the attractive argument that "the South's lag behind the North in industrialization is fully consistent with the proposition that during the antebellum era the South's comparative advantage was in agriculture rather than in manufacturing" does not apply.[67] Unable to grow cotton, Virginia planters faced a bleak future as tobacco became less and less profitable during the second half of the eighteenth century. One can learn much about the dynamics of entrepreneurship in southern societies by seeing how Virginia met this challenge to its prosperity.

Virginia's leading seventeenth-century planters were agricultural buc-

65. *Ibid.*, 106.

66. *Ibid.*, 158.

67. Fogel and Engerman, *Time on the Cross*, I, 255.

caneers who kept their eye and their fist on the main chance. They were tough, grasping entrepreneurs who behaved "like anything but a planter of the genteel tradition," and they combined planting with such related enterprises as logging, retailing, land speculation, and moneylending.[68] Because they wisely acquired large amounts of land while it was still cheap, these pioneer planters were able to establish their sons on large estates and give them the education and training suitable for polished English gentlemen. They did their job well. In addition to constituting a superior governing elite for Chesapeake society, many members of the second and third generation were, as we have seen, capable estate managers who paid great attention to the efficiency of their slaves and the productivity of their lands. They were not, however, the aggressive entrepreneurs that their fathers and grandfathers had been, because they did not need to be.

By the second half of the eighteenth century, many decades of land engrossment and intermarriage had molded the Virginia gentry into an exclusive, tightly knit elite. Jackson Turner Main has carefully studied the background of the wealthiest one hundred planters in Virginia in 1787 and compared the paths of recruitment into this group with comparable patterns in northern ports. Of the one hundred, seventy-nine or eighty "inherited all of their wealth"; nine "started near the top, as sons of well-to-do but not wealthy men"; two "inherited part of their wealth and cannot be considered mobile"; and ten were truly "self-made."[69] Significantly, the few upwardly mobile Virginians tended to have mercantile or professional backgrounds and were concentrated in newly settled areas where land was still available. Virginia's rate of upward mobility, Main discovers, was much lower than that of northern ports: "Whereas in Virginia only one tenth of the men had achieved wealth primarily by their own efforts, in Philadelphia [in 1765] one third had accomplished this. About one seventh were entirely self-made."[70] Comparable figures for Boston and New York after the Revolution were higher still—between 40 percent and 50 percent. Main concludes: "The landed aristocracy (in Virginia at least) was virtually a closed group by the time of the Revolution, undoubtedly because most of the available

68. Land, "Economic Behavior," *Jour. So. Hist.*, XXXIII (1967), 475. The exploitive character of seventeenth-century Virginia society is vividly described in Edmund S. Morgan, *American Slavery, American Freedom: The Ordeal of Colonial Virginia* (New York, 1975), 108–249.

69. Jackson Turner Main, *The Social Structure of Revolutionary America* (Princeton, N.J., 1965), 184.

70. *Ibid.*, 192.

good land was occupied. . . . Commerce, on the other hand, was a comparatively open field."[71]

An important cause of this low mobility rate was that relatively few of the young Scottish merchants who came to Virginia as agents of British firms joined the elite. Suspicious of traders in general, and of shrewd, clannish Scots in particular, established planters viewed these outsiders with distaste—an attitude that increased with the volume of Virginia's transatlantic indebtedness.[72] Foreigners were kept on the fringes of Virginia society, and the few immigrants who were accepted often abandoned trade and became planters. This pattern contrasted markedly, of course, with the situation in the expanding cities of the North, where immigrants composed a substantial portion of the elite. There is little doubt that if Virginia had been able to nourish a large, cosmopolitan city, it would have attracted and retained many more enterprising foreigners. Unfortunately, the process of urbanization, to the extent that it occurred at all, was extremely decentralized. Although the wheat trade spurred the growth of Norfolk and Alexandria in the later eighteenth century, the abundance of rivers in Virginia, the fact that tobacco was less bulky than wheat, and the possibility of orchestrating the tobacco trade from entrepreneurial headquarters in Great Britain all militated against the formation of large cities and unified trading communities.[73] At the end of the colonial period, Alexandria was reliably reported to contain only twenty merchant firms—hardly enough for its traders to develop much social autonomy.[74]

Lacking an influx of new talent, Virginia's planter elite eventually lost much of its managerial vigor and financial acumen. Noting the economic decline of many great Virginia families during the late-colonial period, Emory Evans has observed that "the members of the rising generation

71. *Ibid.*, 195.

72. Robert W. Coakley, "Virginia Commerce during the American Revolution" (Ph.D. diss., University of Virginia, 1949), 60–61.

73. Coakley, "Virginia Commerce," 29–64; and Peter V. Bergstrom, "Markets and Merchants: Economic Diversification in Colonial Virginia, 1700–1775" (Ph.D. diss., University of New Hampshire, 1980), 183–192, provide good descriptions of Virginia's merchant community. The "indigenous" merchant community is not easily defined, because so many Virginia traders were Scots who were both factors for Glasgow tobacco firms and independent operators in the wheat trade. This is, of course, a major reason why Virginia's merchant group was socially weak, but given the absence of large ports and the presence of a powerful landed gentry, it was very difficult for this state of affairs to change. On the dynamics of urbanization in Virginia, see Price, "Port Towns," *Perspectives in Am. Hist.*, VIII (1974), 163–173; Carville Earle and Ronald Hoffman, "Staple Crops and Urban Development in the Eighteenth-Century South," *Perspectives in Am. Hist.*, X (1976), 5–78.

74. Coakley, "Virginia Commerce," 29.

among the gentry—those who came of age after the middle years of the century—were generally speaking not as capable as their fathers and grandfathers."[75] Declining tobacco prices and waning economic vigilance led many wealthy planters into a morass of debt to their British factors, and Evans concludes that by 1775 "a majority of the elite were in serious financial difficulties, and a not inconsiderable number were on the verge of bankruptcy."[76] Since these were the men who controlled Virginia's economy, it is hardly surprising that, as early as 1760, perceptive observers realized that Virginia was not living up to its economic potential. In contrast to the "habitually frugal, industrious, and parsimonious" inhabitants of Pennsylvania and New York, Virginians appeared to the Reverend Andrew Burnaby to be "indolent, easy, and good-natured; extremely fond of society and much given to convivial pleasures. In consequence of this, they seldom show any spirit of enterprise, or expose themselves willingly to fatigue."[77] Economically, the province was a paradox, for "though it produces great quantities of tobacco, and grain, yet there seem to be very few improvements carrying on in it." Few attempts were made, Burnaby noted, "to force a trade" to the West Indies and the Ohio Valley, even though Virginia had "everything necessary for such an undertaking, viz. lumber, provisions, grain, and every other commodity, which the other colonies, that subsist and grow rich by these means, make use of for exports." Despite the advantages presented by the Youghiogheny River (which flowed from the headwaters of the Potomac into the Ohio River basin), Virginia had failed aggressively to extend its trade with the Ohio Valley, "while the industrious Pennsylvanians seize every opportunity, and struggle with innumerable difficulties to secure it to themselves." Owing to such lassitude, Burnaby expected Virginia to remain poorly developed.[78]

Although somewhat exaggerated, Burnaby's analysis was penetrating

75. Emory G. Evans, "The Rise and Decline of the Virginia Aristocracy in the Eighteenth Century," in Darrett B. Rutman, ed., *The Old Dominion: Essays for Thomas Perkins Abernethy* (Charlottesville, Va., 1964), 70. This penetrating study describes a process of intergenerational financial decline: Thomas Nelson, Sr., built a fortune in the early 18th century, his sons continued to manage and develop the estate successfully, but his grandsons were ineffectual and irresponsible and squandered large amounts of property. Evans suggests that this pattern was quite common (see 70, 71, 73).

76. *Ibid.*, 75. On the causes of the great planters' indebtedness, see Emory G. Evans, "Planter Indebtedness and the Coming of the Revolution in Virginia," *WMQ*, 3d Ser., XIX (1962), 517–525.

77. Andrew Burnaby, *Travels through the Middle Settlements in North-America. In the Years 1759 and 1760. With Observations upon the State of the Colonies* (Ithaca, N.Y., 1960 [orig. publ. London, 1775]), 22, 80.

78. *Ibid.*, 27.

and prophetic. A century before the Civil War, half a century before the beginnings of the Industrial Revolution in America, at a moment when the commanding economic stature of Virginia was still unchallenged, Burnaby sensed incipient stagnation. More clearly than some historians, he understood the difference between economic growth and economic development—between mere quantitative output of agricultural commodities, and qualitative improvements in the economy. The colony was productive enough, but its people lacked the "spirit of enterprise" needed to "force a trade" with unfamiliar markets. This analysis underscores the danger of conceptualizing the problems of the southern economy simply in terms of the flexibility of its labor system. The reasons commonly adduced for the rigidity of a slave economy—the immobilization of capital in land and slaves, the low productivity of slaves, the danger of establishing manufacturing towns filled with slaves, the constricted internal market for manufactures—are quite beside the point in this instance. Virginia's economy was producing vast quantities of lumber, meat, and wheat, but her society was producing few aggressive entrepreneurs to sell these goods in the West Indies. To be sure, a small trading community had sprung up by the Revolution, but because it lacked the support of Virginia's powerful landed gentry, it was weak and ineffectual. Even George Washington recognized that "the Virginians were a People not so much engagd in Trade as the Pennsylvanians, &ca."[79]

Virginia's entrepreneurial anemia became starkly evident during the Revolution, when the Old Dominion let slip a superb opportunity to expand her commerce and fortify her economy. In 1775 the British merchants who had long dominated the colony's tobacco trade were expelled from America, and a business vacuum opened up. Thousands of European consumers remained addicted to nicotine, but the established commercial pipeline had ruptured. The entrepreneur who could buy up tobacco and ship it to France either directly or via the West Indies would be able to make a fortune.[80] Here was a splendid commercial opportunity, similar to the West Indies trade mentioned by Burnaby, that did not

79. Donald Jackson and Dorothy Twohig, eds., *The Diaries of George Washington*, II, *1766–1770* (Charlottesville, Va., 1976), 293. Washington made this comment to the Indians of the Pittsburgh area in order to explain why the Pennsylvanians traded with them more actively than did the Virginians. It would thus seem to bear out one of Burnaby's observations. For this reference I am indebted to James McClure, "The Ends of the American Earth: Pittsburgh and the Upper Ohio Valley to 1795" (Ph.D. diss., University of Michigan, 1983).

80. On the tobacco trade during and after the Revolution, see above, chap. 7.

require an elaborate redeployment of Virginia's labor force. What it did require was an abundance of initiative, imagination, and nerve. As it turned out, these virtues were readily available in Revolutionary Virginia—once merchants from New York, Philadelphia, Baltimore, and France appeared on the scene. Despite their intimate knowledge of tobacco, despite the gigantic advantage that lay with the trader who was on the spot, the planters of Virginia made little serious effort to market the tobacco crop themselves. Given their unfamiliarity with transatlantic trade, marketing would not have been easy, but the planters could have joined forces with outside merchants, as Carter Braxton, Benjamin Harrison, and a few other planters did.[81] Even this more limited involvement would have been extremely risky, as Braxton's bankruptcy illustrates, but this is precisely the point: after specializing for so many years in the relatively stable field of estate management, the planters were averse to risk. Virginia's indigenous merchants did what they could to profit from the wartime opportunities, but the chaos of war, combined with their small capital and lowly social position, largely undermined these efforts. The primary beneficiaries of the disruption of the tobacco trade were not Virginians, but northerners and Frenchmen. As Governor Benjamin Harrison ruefully observed in 1782, "Our poverty, our wants and our distresses originate with ourselves: the inattention to our trade and its protection has brought them all on us."[82]

By the 1780s, many Virginians recognized that their economy would be strengthened by the development of large ports. In a remarkable piece of social engineering, the House of Burgesses in 1784 passed a bill confining the maritime trade of Virginia to just five enumerated ports.[83] The chief sponsor of the bill, James Madison, actually wanted trade to be concentrated in just one or at most two ports (Norfolk and Alexandria), for he was "sensible of the utility of establishing a Philada or a Baltimore among ourselves."[84] Although Madison understood the value of encour-

81. See L. Tomlin Stevens, "Carter Braxton, Signer of the Declaration of Independence" (Ph.D. diss., Ohio State University, 1969).

82. Coakley, "Virginia Commerce," 351. Coakley's excellent study views the Revolution as a missed opportunity, a time when a strong merchant community might have taken root in Virginia society and given rise to a balanced, dynamic economy. He operates on the assumption, shared by most historians, that the planters themselves had no inclination to take control of the tobacco trade.

83. Drew R. McCoy, "The Virginia Port Bill of 1784," *Virginia Magazine of History and Biography*, LXXXIII (1975), 288–303.

84. *Ibid.*, 290; James Madison to James Monroe, June 21, 1785, in Robert A. Rutland and William M. E. Rachal, eds., *The Papers of James Madison*, VIII (Chicago, 1973), 307. See also Madison to Thomas Jefferson, Aug. 20, 1784, 103.

aging the growth of an indigenous trading class, this was not his chief purpose.[85] Rather, he wished to prevent the tobacco trade from being monopolized by British merchants, as it had been during the colonial period. By concentrating trade in a few major ports, the experienced British merchants would not have undue advantages over northern and continental European merchants in the trade. And if more merchants were attracted to Virginia, tobacco prices would be higher and the price of imported manufactures lower—a fact driven home to Madison during his stay in Philadelphia as a congressman.[86] Madison also thought that the separation of Virginia commerce into a wholesale trade centralized in large ports and a retail trade dispersed through the countryside would discourage the extension of injurious long-term credits to consumers, while fostering the growth of an indigenous group of retailers.[87]

First watered down and later repealed, Madison's farsighted port bill did not have the desired effect; Virginia remained a highly rural society, and her trade was largely dominated by outsiders. Alexandria and Norfolk did prosper between 1790 and 1812, but after 1815 their trade was ruined by diplomatic intervention in the West Indies trade and the withering competition of New York in the European trade.[88] In 1834 a Norfolk newspaper bitterly lamented, "Instead of being what its geographical position entitles it to be—the great southern seaport—it is reduced to the humiliating condition of waiting on the pampered aristocracy of New York. . . . Without foreign commerce Norfolk must dwindle to a village, and Virginia sink to the lowest scale in the Union, while New York, vampire-like, is sucking her blood to the last drop."[89] This dire assessment was not far wrong. For no urban center in the Old Dominion had generated enough entrepreneurial expertise and investment capital to spearhead a successful transition from maritime commerce to domestic manufactures. Virginia's planters were no more inclined to accept the risks involved in launching the Industrial Revolution in the Old Dominion than they had been to take over the tobacco trade during the Revolution. Unable to cash in on either the cotton boom or the Indus-

85. Madison was frustrated by the absence of a group of articulate indigenous merchants who could defend the port bill. Virginia's planters did not understand their true interest in commercial affairs and were swayed by the British merchants. See Madison to Thomas Jefferson, Aug. 20, 1785, *ibid.*, 344.

86. James Madison to Thomas Jefferson, Aug. 20, 1784, *ibid.*, 103.

87. Madison to Thomas Jefferson, Aug. 20, 1785, *ibid.*, 344. Madison stated: "Our internal trade is taking an arrangement from which I hope good consequences. Retail stores are spreadg all over the Country, many of them carried on by native adventurers."

88. On the rise and decline of Norfolk, see Thomas J. Wertenbaker, *Norfolk: Historic Southern Port* (Durham, N.C., 1931), 27–165.

89. Quoted *ibid.*, 154, 168.

trial Revolution, Virginia forfeited the economic preeminence of colonial days. Its agriculture no longer lucrative, thousands of slaves were sold off to the Deep South.[90] And despite some serious efforts to industrialize, Virginia's per capita output of manufactures in 1850, though higher than that of Mississippi or Alabama, was only 27 percent of New York's and 13 percent of Massachusetts'.[91]

It could be argued that this stagnation was caused less by the absence of an aggressive business elite in Virginia than by the presence of slavery. Planters and slaves, after all, were two parts of the same mechanism—the lock and the key that bolted the door to economic progress. What slave state, it may be asked, has ever successfully diversified its economy, leaping the chasm from plantation agriculture to modern industry? The answer: Maryland. During the eighteenth century, Maryland was considered an extension of Virginia, so far as economic and social structure were concerned. Andrew Burnaby said of the colony, "The character of the inhabitants is much the same as that of the Virginians; and the state of the two colonies nearly alike."[92] As to patterns of settlement, Baltimore was no larger than Norfolk on the eve of the Revolution, when one perceptive observer stated, "In all probability, from the multitude of rivers which, with their branches, intersect this country in almost every direction, Maryland will never abound with ports or establishments of any considerable magnitude."[93] And John Adams snorted derivisely in 1777:

> The manners of Maryland are somewhat peculiar. They have but few merchants. They are chiefly Planters and Farmers. The planters are those who raise tobacco and the farmers such as raise wheat, etc. The lands are cultivated, and all sorts of trades are exercised by Negroes, or by transported convicts, which has occasioned the planters and farmers to assume the title of gentlemen, and they hold their negroes and convicts, that is all labouring people and tradesmen, in such contempt, that they think themselves a distinct

90. On the agricultural decline of plantation economies in general, see Gray, *History of Agriculture*, I, 445: "In the South, on the other hand, westward expansion brought inevitable depression to the older regions." On Virginia in particular, see I, 271–276, 445, 494; II, 908–923.

91. Calculated from *American Industry and Manufactures in the Nineteenth Century: A Basic Source Collection* (Elmsford, N.Y., 1970 [reprint of the U.S. Census of Manufactures for 1850]), V, 143; U.S. Bureau of the Census, *Historical Statistics of the United States: Colonial Times to 1957* (Washington, D.C., 1960), 13.

92. Burnaby, *Travels*, 50.

93. William Eddis, *Letters from America*, ed. Aubrey C. Land (Cambridge, Mass., 1969), 47.

> order of beings. Hence they never will suffer their sons to labour or learn any trade, but they bring them up in idleness or what is worse in horse racing, cock fighting, and card playing.[94]

The labor systems of Maryland and Virginia were also very similar at the end of the colonial period. Though blacks claimed a smaller population share than in Virginia, Maryland's blacks were nevertheless numerous, amounting to over one-third of the total population in every census year before 1840.[95]

According to conventional paradigms of economic development, this combination of aristocratic planters and oppressed Negroes was a recipe for failure. Yet by 1850 Maryland's economic profile more nearly resembled that of the free-labor North than of the slave South. In that year her production of manufactured goods, measured on a per capita basis, was 85 percent of Pennsylvania's output and 271 percent of Virginia's.[96] How had slavery's barriers to economic development been hurdled in Maryland? This intriguing question requires much further study, but there is little doubt that a major part of the story lies in the port of Baltimore and its enterprising merchant community. Baltimore grew dramatically during the last quarter of the eighteenth century, for it benefited from the American Revolution, the wars of the French Revolution, and from the Napoleonic Wars as well. The city grew from about 6,000 in 1775 to 13,503 in 1790; it nearly doubled its population during the 1790s; and it expanded by 76 percent during the first turbulent decade of the nineteenth century. Growing by a more moderate 30 percent during each of the next three decades, Baltimore had by 1840 established itself as a large commercial city of 102,313 inhabitants that did not labor under the shadow of a suspicious, condescending planter elite.[97] This was a place where shopkeepers and artisans could borrow money and try to get ahead, where foreign merchants could come to establish themselves in the New World. It was an expanding beachhead of commercial enterprise in a stable plantation economy, a catalyst of innovation that helped to reshape Maryland in the image of Pennsylvania rather than of Virginia.

94. L. H. Butterfield *et al.*, eds., *Diary and Autobiography of John Adams*, II, *Diary, 1771–1781* (Cambridge, Mass., 1961), 183.

95. U.S. Bureau of the Census, *Historical Statistics: Colonial Times to 1970*, II, table a-195.

96. See n. 91, above.

97. See George Rogers Taylor, "Comment," 39, and Dorsey, "Comment," 62–67, in Gilchrist, ed., *Growth of the Seaport Cities*; Dorsey, "Pattern of Baltimore Commerce," *Md. Hist. Mag.*, LXII (1967), 119–134; Gilbert, "Baltimore's Flour Trade"; Richard W. Griffin, "An Origin of the Industrial Revolution in Maryland: The Textile Industry, 1789–1826," *Md. Hist. Mag.*, LXI (1966), 24–36.

Appendix

The Commercial World of Revolutionary Philadelphia

Social Organization

TABLE A-1. *Occupational Mobility of Merchants, 1756–1791*

Future Occupation	Base Year as Merchant: 1756 (N=74)	1756 (N=33)	1774 (N=109)	1785 (N=266)
	Prospective Year: 1774	1791	1791	1791
Still a merchant	59.5%	33.3%	42.2%	56.8%
Specialized merchant	2.7	0	11.0	5.6
Retailer	2.7	3.0	8.3	12.0
Mariner	1.4	0	0	1.1
Professional	1.4	0	0	.4
Artisan	8.1	9.1	2.8	3.8
Gentleman	18.9	42.4	26.6	12.4
Government official	1.4	6.1	4.6	3.4
Other	4.1	6.1	4.6	4.5

Sources: Hannah Benner Roach, comp., "Taxables in the City of Philadelphia, 1756," *Pennsylvania Genealogical Magazine*, XXII (1961–1962), 3–41; Transcript of the Assessment for the 1774 Provincial Tax for the City and County of Philadelphia, Pennsylvania Historical and Museum Commission; Clement Biddle, ed., *The Philadelphia Directory* (Philadelphia, 1791). Occupations for 1774 supplemented with Transcript of the Assessment for the 1772 Provincial Tax for the City and County of Philadelphia, microfilm copy at the Historical Society of Pennsylvania; and County Tax Duplicates, 1773–1775, for Philadelphia City and County, Philadelphia City Archives.

TABLE A-2. *Change in Ward of Residence of Merchants, 1756, 1774, 1789*

Base Year	Retrospective/ Prospective Year	*N*	Years Elapsed		Annualized Ward Change	
			No.	Rank	Rate[a]	Rank[b]
1756	1767	121	11	8	3.6%	8
1756	1774	96	18	4	2.7	5
1756	1789	27	33	1	1.6	1
1774	1756	104	18	4	2.6	4
1774	1767	214	7	9	5.1	9
1774	1789	110	15	6	3.0	6
1789	1756	21	33	1	1.9	2
1789	1767	69	23	3	2.6	3
1789	1774	121	15	6	3.3	7

Sources: Hannah Benner Roach, comp., "Taxables in the City of Philadelphia, 1756," *Pennsylvania Genealogical Magazine*, XXII (1961–1962), 3–41; Transcript of the Assessment for the 1774 Provincial Tax for the City and County of Philadelphia, Pennsylvania Historical and Museum Commission; County Tax Assessment Ledgers, for the City and County of Philadelphia, 1789, Philadelphia City Archives; Transcript of the Assessment for the 1767 Provincial Tax for the City and County of Philadelphia, Van Pelt Library, University of Pennsylvania.

[a]Percentage of merchants changing wards divided by number of years elapsed.

[b]Inverse ranking system: 1 = lowest annualized change; 9 = highest.

Shipping and Trade

TABLE A-3. *Merchant and Nonmerchant Firms Receiving Vessels*

	No. of Firms Receiving Vessels[a]		
Year	Merchant	Nonmerchant[b]	Total
1766	100	60	160
1767	108	54	162
1768	106	41	147
1769	100	40	140
1770	112	40	152
1771	99	46	145
1772	106	41	147
1773	116	41	157
1774	111	49	160
1775	101	32	133
Overall	238	244	482

Source: Tonnage Duty Book (see Bibliography).

[a]Vessels consigned to their masters are excluded from this analysis.

[b]Includes supercargoes, nonmerchant residents of Philadelphia, and Philadelphia merchants who could not be identified as merchants from tax lists.

TABLE A-4. *Prices of Vessels, 1757–1786*

Owner	Year	Cost (Pennsylvania Currency)	Measured Tons	Cost per Measured Ton
James and Drinker	1757	£2,256	129	£17.5
James and Drinker	1757	2,500	133	18.8
Thomas Riche	1758	5,034	226	22.3
John and Peter Chevalier	1760	2,000	80	25.0
Daniel Clark	1761	623	40	15.6
Mifflin and Massey	1761	500	27	18.8
Mifflin and Massey	1761	2,217	120	18.5
Mifflin and Massey	1761	1,503	133	11.3
Baynton, Wharton, and Morgan	1764	1,595	116	13.8
Orr, Dunlope, and Glenholme	1768	2,300	110	20.9
Richard Parker and Co.	1772	2,100	239	8.8
Thomas Clifford, Jr.	1784	6,448	200	32.2
James C. Fisher	1784	4,775	256	18.7
Stephen Girard	1784	2,940	193	15.2
Donnaldson and Coxe	1786	5,000	310	16.1

Note: These figures include the cost of the basic ship carpentry and all other construction expenses required to make a vessel seaworthy, including rigging, boats, ironwork, masts, and so forth. The cargo and, insofar as possible, provisions for the crew have been excluded.

Sources: Prices were taken from the manuscript sources listed, as were tonnages for some (indicated by MS). Other tonnages were calculated from registered tonnages appearing in the Ship Register of Pennsylvania, 1726–1776, Historical Society of Pennsylvania; and Inward and Outward Entries, 1784–1787, Customs House Papers, Historical Society of Pennsylvania. The conversion from registered to measured tons was based on the following formula: registered tons = .75 × measured tons. This ratio is based on an analysis of 78 vessels that appear in both the Tonnage Duty Book (see Bibliography) and the Ship Register of Pennsylvania.

James and Drinker (£2,256): MS; James and Drinker to Nehemiah Champion, Sept. 13, 1757, James and Drinker Letterbook, 1756–1759, 171, Henry Drinker Papers, Historical Society of Pennsylvania (hereafter cited as HSP). The cost and outfit of the vessel is stated as £2,255 10s.

James and Drinker (£2,500): James and Drinker to Henry Ash, Aug. 13, 1757, James and Drinker Letterbook, 1756–1759, 157.

Thomas Riche: Thomas Riche Journal, 1757–1761, Aug. 3, 1758, Thomas Riche Papers, HSP.

John and Peter Chevalier: John and Peter Chevalier Daybook, 1760–1766, March 18, 1760, HSP.

Daniel Clark: Daniel Clark Letterbook, 1759–1762, 78, HSP: an account of the cost of building the vessel, which totaled £1,130. From this the outfit costs were deducted as nearly as they could be identified.

Mifflin and Massey (£500): Mifflin and Massey Ledger, 1760–1763, fol. 280, HSP. In addition to the prime cost of £500, outfitting costs amounted to £218.

Mifflin and Massey (£2,217): Mifflin and Massey Ledger, 1760–1763, fol. 267, HSP. The vessel plus outfitting costs totaled £2,417; I deducted £200 for the cost of the provisions.

Mifflin and Massey (£1,503): Mifflin and Massey Ledger, 1760–1763, fol. 304. The vessel sold for £1,503.

Baynton, Wharton, and Morgan: MS; Baynton, Wharton, and Morgan Journal A, 1763–1766, Dec. 15, 1764, Baynton, Wharton, and Morgan Papers, Pennsylvania Historical and Museum Commission (hereafter cited as PHMC).

Orr, Dunlope, and Glenholme: Orr, Dunlope, and Glenholme to Wilson, Beath, and Anderson, Feb. 17, 1768, Orr, Dunlope, and Glenholme Letterbook, 1768–1769, HSP. The cost of building and outfitting the vessel is stated at £2,300.

Richard Parker and Co.: Richard Parker Will no. 133, 1772, Wills and Administrations, City of Philadelphia, Office of the Recorder of Wills, Philadelphia City Hall.

Thomas Clifford, Jr.: Clifford Papers, VII, 37, Clifford Correspondence, 1778–1785, HSP. An excellent account of the cost of building and outfitting a vessel, which ran to £6,683. From this were deducted the outfitting costs.

James C. Fisher: MS; James C. Fisher Journal, 1783–1787, fol. 269, Leonard T. Beale Collection, HSP. An excellent account of the cost of building and outfitting the vessel, which ran to £5,001 in all. From this figure were deducted certain items, such as the cost of provisions, that related only to the vessel's maiden voyage.

Stephen Girard: Stephen Girard Journal, 1783–1786, 36 (Nov. 10, 1784), Stephen Girard Papers, microfilm, 3d Ser., Reel 113, American Philosophical Society.

Donnaldson and Coxe: MS; Donnaldson and Coxe Journal, 1785–1786, 690 (Jan. 6, 1786), Baker Library, Harvard University Business School. The cost of the ship was £5,000 as she lay at "Messrs. Whitesides and Co. Wharf." Additional outlays were made for the outfit to Canton and the cargo itself. On the vessel's tonnage, see Jacob E. Cooke, *Tench Coxe and the Early Republic* (Chapel Hill, N.C., 1978), 74.

TABLE A-5. *Vessel Ownership by Firms Receiving Vessels*

Year	Did Not Own Vessels Handled	Owned All Vessels Handled	Owned Some Vessels Handled
1766	63	68	29
1767	63	68	32
1768	48	66	34
1769	45	61	35
1770	48	74	30
1771	43	70	33
1772	38	76	33
1773	40	85	32
1774	37	82	41
1775	22	83	28
Overall	159	171	152

Source: Tonnage Duty Book (see Bibliography).
Note. Includes both merchant and nonmerchant firms, but excludes captains to whom vessels were consigned.

TABLE A-6. *Distribution of Incoming Shipping Tonnage among Firms*

		Proportion of Firms Receiving Tonnage						
		Amount of Measured Vessel Tonnage Received						
Year	No. of Firms Receiving Vessels[a]	1–100	101–200	201–300	301–500	501–1,000	1,001+	Overall
1766	160	41.2%	21.9%	8.8%	9.4%	9.4%	9.4%	100.1%
1770	152	30.9	28.9	11.2	10.6	11.9	6.6	100.1
1774	160	31.9	17.5	11.9	16.3	15.1	7.5	100.2

Source: Tonnage Duty Book (see Bibliography).
[a]Includes both merchant and nonmerchant firms, but excludes captains to whom vessels were consigned.

TABLE A-7. *Shipping Received from Four Geographic Sectors, by Tonnage, 1772–1775*

Sector	Firms Receiving Vessels[a]	Proportion of Firms Receiving Amount of Measured Vessel Tonnage Received: 1–100	101–200	201–300	301–500	501–1,000	1,001+	Total
American coast	125	49.6%	20.0%	10.4%	4.8%	8.8%	6.4%	100.0%
Great Britain	75	8.0	38.7	9.3	14.6	13.4	16.0	100.0
Southern Europe	77	18.2	26.0	13.0	18.2	15.6	9.1	100.1
West Indies	146	37.7	20.6	8.2	10.3	11.6	11.6	100.0

Source: Tonnage Duty Book (see Bibliography).

[a]Includes merchant and nonmerchant firms, but excludes captains to whom vessels were consigned.

TABLE A-8. *Profile of Shipping Entering, 1766–1775*

Year	Vessels Entering: No.	Measured Tonnage	Mean Size (Tons)	Distribution of Tonnage: Owned by Consignee	Consigned to Captain	Consigned to and Owned by Captain
1766	724	59,728	82.5	46.0%	15.7%	25.6%
1767	666	54,806	82.3	52.7	16.9	32.0
1768	641	51,399	80.2	55.8	15.7	35.0
1769	710	58,927	83.0	60.6	12.8	48.4
1770	723	59,495	82.3	56.5	15.3	34.9
1771	666	55,359	83.1	64.8	15.8	43.8
1772	713	57,555	80.7	64.4	15.2	34.0
1773	751	62,143	82.7	64.9	15.4	29.2
1774	816	68,793	84.3	64.8	12.2	32.4
1775	511	46,742	91.5	75.0	9.1	36.7
Total	6,921	574,947	83.1	60.4	14.5	34.8

Source: Tonnage Duties on Incoming Vessels, November 1, 1765–August 30, 1775, 3 vols., Cadwalader Collection, Thomas Cadwalader Section, Historical Society of Pennsylvania.

TABLE A-9. *Value of Goods Received from Five Geographic Sectors, May 1785–December 1787*

Sectors	No. of Firms Receiving Goods[a]	Proportion of Firms Receiving Goods: Value of Goods Received, in Pounds					
		1–500	501–1,000	1,001–2,000	2,001–10,000	10,001+	Overall
American coast	393	62.3%	14.0%	11.5%	11.2%	1.0%	100.0%
Great Britain	422	34.8	17.8	12.5	24.4	10.5	100.0
Southern Europe[b]	117	50.4	13.7	8.6	21.4	6.0	100.1
Northern Europe[c]	184	45.1	19.6	10.9	21.2	3.3	100.1
West Indies	375	53.0	15.0	13.3	13.9	4.8	100.0
All sectors[d]	815	36.0	17.4	14.6	21.2	10.8	100.0

Source: Registers of Duties Paid on Imported Goods, 1781–1787, 6 vols., Record Group 4, Pennsylvania Historical and Museum Commission.

[a]Includes both merchant and nonmerchant firms receiving at least £300 in total imports, 1785–1787.

[b]Principally wine islands, Iberian Peninsula.

[c]Principally France, Holland, and Germany.

[d]Includes China.

TABLE A-10. *The Dry Goods Business of Stephen Collins, 1759–1788*

Year	Total Sales	Total Cash Sales	No. of Credit Customers	No. of Credit Transactions
1759[a]	£ 2,504	£1,271	54	104
1763	7,083	936	139	362
1768	3,221	342	76	209
1774	6,343	626	99	295
1784	18,817	1,181	97	253
1788	3,973	402	49	109

Source: Stephen Collins Papers, CXVII, CXVIII, CXIX, CXXXI, CXXXII, Library of Congress.

[a]In 1759 Collins was in partnership with Hudson Emlen.

Mercantile Estates

TABLE A-11. *Rental Properties and Ground Rents of Merchants, 1774*

Type of Property	No. of Merchant Owners: No. of Properties Owned: 1	2–3	4–5	6–11	12	Total	Owners as Portion of Merchants[a]
Rental properties	38	41	14	21	4	118	40%
Ground rents	16	13	10	4	6	49	17
Rental properties and / or ground rents[b]	36	36	18	20	15	125	42

Source: Transcript of the Assessment for the 1774 Provincial Tax for the City and County of Philadelphia, Pennsylvania Historical and Museum Commission.

[a]Property holdings of 296 merchants, more than 90% of the merchants in Philadelphia, were examined.

[b]Includes many merchants in first two categories.

TABLE A-12. *The Structure of the Estates of Selected Merchants, 1754–1790*

Merchant and Year	Land as % of Net Worth	Net Financial Assets as % of Net Worth	Financial Liabilities as % of Financial Assets	Cash	Business Inventories
John Baynton, 1754	68	18	65	£ 4	£ 299
Henry Drinker, 1784	63			1,662	
Joshua Fisher and Sons, 1770		89	12	57	3,379
Benjamin Fuller, 1789	19	45	43		
Stephen Girard, 1785	17	13	89		3,962
Stephen Girard, 1790	4	74	57	162	3,980
Levi Hollingsworth, 1782	41	45	73	369	648
Levi Hollingsworth, 1785	74	23	78	99	686
William West, 1770		88	55	732	

Sources: John Baynton Journal B, 1754–1759, 1–3, Baynton, Wharton, and Morgan Papers, Reel 7, Pennsylvania Historical and Museum Commission. Henry Drinker Ledger, 1776–1792, 1, and Journal, 1776–1791, 18–20; Joshua Fisher and Sons Ledger, 1769–1773, 104; Benjamin Fuller Journal, 1782–1789, 360–364, William West Account Books, 1769–1804, Historical Society of Pennsylvania (hereafter cited as HSP). Stephen Girard Journal, 1783–1786, Dec. 31, 1785, 1788–1790, Dec. 31, 1790, Girard Papers, 3d Ser., Reels 44, 113, American Philosophical Society. Levi Hollingsworth Journal, 1781–1782, 371–382, 1784–1785, 377–398, Hollingsworth Papers; William West Ledger, 1770–1777, 1, William West Account Books, 1769–1804, HSP.

Note: Net worth = (business inventories + furniture + land + financial assets) − (financial liabilities). Net financial assets = (cash + debts receivable + notes receivable). Financial liabilities = (debts payable + notes payable).

TABLE A-13. *Real Estate Holdings of Merchants, 1774*

Holding	Mean Annual Rental Value per Owner[a]	Mean No. Owned	No. of Merchant Owners[b]
Dwelling	£ 67 1s.	1.0	105
Country seat	27 4	1.0	34
Acres around country seat and/or other dwelling	—	56.5	23
Other acres in Philadelphia suburbs	—	36.8	42
Overall acres	—	48.9	60
City lots	4 9	2.7	32
Ground rents	79 5	5.9	49
Rental properties	98 7	3.6	118
Ground rents and/or rental properties	124 4	—	125

Source: Transcript of the Assessment for the 1774 Provincial Tax for the City and County of Philadelphia, Pennsylvania Historical and Museum Commission.

[a]Pennsylvania currency. All values are 100% of rental value regardless of how they appeared in original document.

[b]Total number of merchants studied was 296.

The Personal Property of Merchants

TABLE A-14. *Merchant Ownership of Slaves, Servants, and Livestock, 1774*

	Type of Property Owned					
No. Owned	Slaves	Servants	Slaves and Servants	Cows	Horses	Cows and Horses
	No. of Poorer Merchant Owners ($N=133$)					
1	29	24	36	4	37	34
2	9	3	19	0	5	7
3+	1	1	3	0	0	1
Overall	39	28	58	4	42	42
	No. of Lower-Middle Merchant Owners ($N=65$)					
1	15	9	20	6	18	15
2	5	4	8	0	2	6
3+	3	1	6	0	2	2
Overall	23	14	34	6	22	23
	No. of Upper-Middle Merchant Owners ($N=67$)					
1	14	14	17	12	21	14
2	7	6	13	0	7	11
3	3	2	8	1	5	4
4, 5	1	2	2	1	2	4
6+	1	0	2	1	1	4
Overall	26	24	42	15	36	37
	No. of Wealthy Merchant Owners ($N=31$)					
1	5	5	3	6	2	2
2	6	6	11	1	5	3
3	0	2	5	1	4	2
4, 5	0	0	0	1	2	4
6+	0	0	0	2	3	5
Overall	11	13	19	11	16	16
	All Merchant Owners ($N=296$)					
1	63	52	76	28	78	65
2	27	19	51	1	19	27
3	6	6	21	2	11	8
4, 5	2	2	3	2	4	9
6+	1	0	2	3	4	9
Overall	99	79	153	36	116	118

Source: Transcript of the Assessment for the 1774 Provincial Tax for the City and County of Philadelphia, Pennsylvania Historical and Museum Commission.

TABLE A-15. *Merchant Ownership of Slaves, Servants, and Livestock, 1789*

No. Owned	Slaves	Servants	Slaves and Servants	Cows	Horses	Cows and Horses
			No. of Poorer Merchant Owners ($N=103$)			
1	3	12	15	7	15	14
2	1	0	1	2	3	4
3+	0	1	1	0	0	2
Overall	4	13	17	9	18	20
			No. of Lower-Middle Merchant Owners ($N=107$)			
1	13	16	25	17	29	25
2	1	2	5	2	5	13
3+	1	0	1	0	0	3
Overall	15	18	31	19	34	41
			No. of Upper-Middle Merchant Owners ($N=77$)			
1	13	10	19	15	29	24
2	3	2	7	1	11	15
3+	0	0	0	0	0	5
Overall	16	12	26	16	40	44
			No. of Wealthy Merchant Owners ($N=23$)			
1	2	4	6	7	4	5
2	1	0	2	2	7	7
3	0	0	0	0	2	1
4+	2	2	2	0	0	3
Overall	5	6	10	9	13	16
			All Merchant Owners ($N=310$)			
1	31	42	65	46	77	68
2	6	5	15	6	26	39
3	1	1	2	0	2	10
4+	2	1	2	0	0	5
Overall	40	49	84	52	105	122

Type of Property Owned (column group heading spanning Slaves through Cows and Horses)

Source: County Tax Assessment Ledgers, for the City and County of Philadelphia, 1789, Philadelphia City Archives.

TABLE A-16. *Merchant Ownership of Plate, 1789*

		No. of Owners						
		Ounces of Plate Owned						
Merchant Class	*N*	1–5	6–10	11–20	21–50	51–100	101+	Overall
Poorer	103	1	5	10	10	4	0	30
Lower-middle	107	0	7	23	28	15	1	74
Upper-middle	77	1	4	16	27	12	4	64
Wealthy	23	0	1	1	5	10	3	20
Total	310	2	17	50	70	41	8	188

Source: County Tax Assessment Ledgers, for the City and County of Philadelphia, 1789, Philadelphia City Archives.

TABLE A-17. *Merchant Ownership of Carriages, 1789*

		No. of Owners					
		No. of Carriages Owned					
Merchant Class	*N*	1	2	3	4	5+	Overall
Poorer	103	10	0	0	0	0	10
Lower-middle	107	32	1	0	0	0	33
Upper-middle	77	28	6	0	0	0	34
Wealthy	23	10	3	1	0	1	15
Total	310	80	10	1	0	1	92

Source: County Tax Assessment Ledgers, for the City and County of Philadelphia, 1789, Philadelphia City Archives.

TABLE A-18. *Types of Carriages Owned by Merchants, 1789*

	No. of Owners				
	Merchant Class				
Type of Carriage	Poorer (*N*=103)	Lower-Middle (*N*=107)	Upper-Middle (*N*=77)	Wealthy (*N*=23)	Total (*N*=310)
Chair	9	28	23	8	68
Chaise	0	1	5	1	7
Phaeton	0	1	6	5	12
Chariot	0	1	1	7	9
Wagon	1	1	2	9	13
Coach	0	0	1	1	2
Other	0	2	2	0	4
Overall	10	34	40	31	115

Source: County Tax Assessment Ledgers, for the City and County of Philadelphia, 1789, Philadelphia City Archives.

Bibliography

Quantifiable Records

TAX LISTS

1756. Paving Tax, 1756, for the Lower Delaware, High Street, and North Wards of Philadelphia. Microfilm copy at the Historical Society of Pennsylvania, Philadelphia.

1756. Roach, Hannah Benner, comp. "Taxables in the City of Philadelphia, 1756." *Pennsylvania Genealogical Magazine*, XXII (1961–1962), 3–41.

1767. Roach, Hannah Benner, comp. "Taxables in Chestnut, Walnut, and Lower Delaware Wards, Philadelphia, 1767." *Pennsylvania Genealogical Magazine*, XXII (1961–1962), 170–185.

1767. Transcript of the Assessment for the 1767 Provincial Tax for the City and County of Philadelphia. Original, microfilm copy, and index. Rare Book Room, Van Pelt Library, University of Pennsylvania, Philadelphia.

1769. Transcript of the Assessment of the 1769 Provincial Tax for the City and County of Philadelphia. Pennsylvania Historical and Museum Commission, Harrisburg. Microfilm copy at the Historical Society of Pennsylvania, Philadelphia.

1772. Transcript of the Assessment for the 1772 Provincial Tax for the City and County of Philadelphia. Microfilm copy at the Historical Society of Pennsylvania, Philadelphia.

1773–1775. County Tax Duplicates, 1773–1775, for Philadelphia City and County. Philadelphia City Archives, Philadelphia City Hall.

1774. Transcript of the Assessment for the 1774 Provincial Tax for the City and County of Philadelphia. Pennsylvania Historical and Museum Commission, Harrisburg. Microfilm copy at the Historical Society of Pennsylvania, Philadelphia.

1781, 1783, 1786. County Tax Assessment Ledgers, for the City and County of Philadelphia, 1781, 1783, 1786. Philadelphia City Archives, Philadelphia City Hall. Incomplete for certain wards in certain years.

1782. Effective Supply Tax, County of Philadelphia, 1782. *Pennsylvania Archives*, 8th Ser. Edited by William Henry Egle. Harrisburg, 1894–1899. 30 vols. XVI, 91–521.

1789. County Tax Assessment Ledgers, for the City and County of Philadelphia, 1789. Philadelphia City Archives, Philadelphia City Hall.

All individuals described as a "merchant" on any of these tax lists, or in the city directories for 1785 and 1791 discussed below, were included in a master roster of merchants. This roster was used to identify merchants in the Pennsylvania Ship Register, Tonnage Duty Book, and Customs Records discussed below.

All of the 1,277 individuals on the roster were traced through the tax lists for 1756, 1767, 1774, 1782 and the 1791 city directory. The tax lists for 1774 and 1789 were also analyzed more closely in order to learn details about the estates of the merchants.

The 1756 tax list is difficult to use because the details of assessment procedures are hazy. It was drawn up in accordance with a provincial act passed on September 15, 1756, which simply directed the constables to list the "houses, lands, tenements, rent charges, bound servants, and negroes" held by all people liable to tax.[1] Exempt from the tax were all people rated under eight pounds, people released from apprenticeship or servitude within the past twelve months, and single men under the age of twenty-one. These assessment procedures differed greatly from those used for the provincial taxes levied in 1767, 1769, 1772, and 1774, and consequently the size distribution of taxable property is also divergent. Of the merchants on the 1774 list, 45 percent had assessments of under eleven pounds, and only 40 percent were rated at over thirty pounds; the comparable figures for the 1756 list are 2 percent and 82 percent. The 1756 list has other drawbacks. It provides occupational designations for only about 65 percent of the taxpayers listed and does not include Southwark or the Northern Liberties, and it provides no detailed information about the estates of taxpayers. Its main value, therefore, is to provide the names and wards of residence for 177 merchants living in the city in 1756 and to provide a very rough measure of their economic standing.

The provincial tax lists for 1767, 1769, 1772, and 1774 have the same format and are far more useful than the 1756 list. An index is available for the 1767 list, and one can use the massive name index in the *Pennsylvania Archives* as an index for the 1769 and 1774 lists.[2] However, the original lists (rather than the transcriptions in the *Pennsylvania Archives*, 3d Ser., XIV) should be used. In these lists, the occupation is not given for every taxpayer, but for the years just prior to the Revolution one can compile a nearly complete census of merchants because the coverage of occupations in the 1774 list is relatively complete and can be supplemented by names on the 1772 list and the County Tax Duplicates, 1773–1775.

The great advantage of the Provincial Tax Lists for 1767, 1769, 1772, and 1774 is that they group all the taxable property located in Philadelphia City and County under the name of the taxpayer who owned it. For a wealthy merchant, this can mean dozens of ground rents and rental properties scattered through many wards and townships, as well as the personal property that he kept at his dwelling or his country seat. The tax law stipulated the following rates for the principal types of property taxed:[3]

1. James T. Mitchell and Henry Flanders, comps., *The Statutes at Large of Pennsylvania from 1682 to 1801*, 16 vols. (Harrisburg, Pa., 1896–1911), V, 231.

2. William Henry Egle *et al.*, eds., *The Pennsylvania Archives*, 3d Ser., 30 vols. (Harrisburg, Pa., 1897–1899), XIV, XXVII–XXX.

3. Mitchell and Flanders, comps., *Statutes at Large*, VI, 355–358.

Sheep	£1
Horses above 3 years old	13s. 4d.
Horned cattle above 3 years old	13s. 4d.
Slaves, age 12–50	£4
Bound servants, age 15–50	£1 10s.
Meadow lands	£30–£90 per 100 acres, depending on quality
Unimproved land	£5–£15 per 100 acres, depending on quality
Houses, country seats, stables, shops, stores, whether used personally or rented out	60% of annual rental value
Ground rents (perpetual mortgages)	100% of annual rental value
Offices and posts	80% of annual income

The tax lists sum these various measures of personal and real property and deduct from them the full value of ground rents that the taxpayer paid on property that he owned. In essence, these lists indicate the holdings of certain relatively unimportant forms of personal property and provide a fair measure of holdings of real property in the Philadelphia area. Totally excluded are the major types of commercial property, including merchandise, book debts, cash, and ships. And if a merchant rented the house he lived in, as many did, this house also is not mentioned. Since many merchants did not own much real estate, the effect of these assessment procedures is to list for a surprisingly large number of merchants quite small amounts of taxable property. In 1774, for example, when top taxpayers were assessed at two hundred pounds or more, 45 percent of the merchants had assessments of less than eleven pounds. As mentioned in Chapter 2, these lists therefore do not provide a reliable measure of economic power. Taxpayers with high assessments were assuredly wealthy, but many taxpayers with low assessments were considerably more affluent than they appear. However, it is true that there is a strong statistical correlation between 1774 assessments and various measures of ship ownership or shipping activity (as measured by the Pennsylvania Ship Register and Tonnage Duty Book) for merchants who did handle or own ships.

Like the 1774 Provincial Tax list, the 1789 County Tax Assessment Ledger was used to analyze the estates of the merchants intensively. The two lists differ in important respects. A major drawback of the 1789 list is that not all of the properties of a given merchant are listed under his name: one must comb through thousands of individual property entries in every city ward in order to collect all of the urban properties owned by a given merchant. I decided that it was not worth the effort to tackle this mammoth task and contented myself with collecting the main residential entry on each merchant. This entry lists the horses, cows, slaves, servants, ounces of plate, and wagons or carriages owned by a merchant, as well as the dwelling and warehouses that he had at his place of residence.[4] Unlike the 1774 list, it also lists the value of the house he rented, if he did not own his own dwelling. Finally, an occupational assessment was also applied to each merchant. From this information we can get a good idea of the size of the house that a merchant lived in and the style of his life, but we have no measure of the amount of capital that he had tied up in real property. County Tax Assessment Ledgers are available for most years during the 1780s, but researchers should remember that the exact assessment procedures changed from year to year and that lists are not available for every ward in every year. The 1782 Effective Supply Tax was used only to determine whether individuals were in the city in that year. Researchers should be aware that many individuals appear in the document more than once.

CITY DIRECTORIES AND THE 1790 CENSUS

Biddle, Clement, ed. *The Philadelphia Directory*. Philadelphia, 1791.

United States Bureau of the Census. *Heads of Families at the First Census of the United States Taken in the Year 1790: Pennsylvania*. Washington, D.C., 1908.

White, Francis. *The Philadelphia Directory*. Philadelphia, 1785.

Philadelphia's first directory was a hurried job. Incomplete and only partially alphabetized, it was issued in September 1785 before the incessant migration of Philadelphians rendered it entirely obsolete. It nevertheless lists 514 merchants, 74 more than the 1791 directory. This surprisingly high number leads one to wonder whether the compiler, in his hurry to publish, denominated some retailers as merchants. The directory shows no evidence of such an error; a sample of 674 entries included 118 shopkeepers and grocers and 86 merchants. However, this sample does suggest that lower occupational strata are seriously underrepresented.

By contrast, the 1791 directory is admirably complete because it was compiled by Clement Biddle, a recently bankrupt merchant and friend of Washington who landed a job as marshal of the Pennsylvania district for the first United States census. The occupational listings in the directory are strikingly similar to those in the census, but the two documents are not identical. Of 506 people listed in the census, 40 were not in the directory, and at least 11 others had different occupations. Evidently Biddle took the trouble to update the census before capitalizing on it the following year. For this study the directory was used for most purposes, because its occupational listings are more complete and it is generally easier to use.

PENNSYLVANIA SHIP REGISTER

Declarations of British Registry, 1727–1776. 12 vols. Record Group 41. Pennsylvania Historical and Museum Commission, Harrisburg.

McCusker, John J., comp. "Ships Registered at the Port of Philadelphia before

4. *Ibid.*, XI, 470.

1776: A Computerized Listing." Historical Society of Pennsylvania, Philadelphia.
Ship Register of Pennsylvania, 1726–1776. Historical Society of Pennsylvania, Philadelphia.

The main body of the Pennsylvania Ship Register, covering the years 1727, 1730, 1736–1739, 1742–1761, 1765–1775, and parts of six other years, is in the Historical Society of Pennsylvania, Philadelphia. The important gap of January 1762–October 1764, hitherto overlooked by economic historians, is in the Pennsylvania State Archives, Pennsylvania Historical and Museum Commission, Harrisburg. The segment of the register that is in the Historical Society of Pennsylvania has been carefully analyzed by Simeon J. Crowther and John J. McCusker.[5] In addition, Professor McCusker has deposited at the Historical Society a very useful and accurate listing of vessels registered in colonial Pennsylvania, based on the register and other documents. I am very grateful to Professor McCusker for permitting me to check my data against his list.

I used the register to determine how many tons of shipping each merchant in my roster registered. Since the exact share of the vessel owned by each investor is not indicated, it was assumed that each investor owned an equal share. A vessel had to be reregistered if its build, name, or ownership changed, so where a merchant twice registered vessels of identical tonnage, year of construction, and place of construction, it was assumed to be the same vessel. In such cases, only the registration giving the merchant the larger share of the vessel was included. Where the two shares were the same, the earlier was selected. An elaborate literature on tonnage measurement has established that registered tonnage systematically understates the carpenter's tonnage by a significant but variable amount.

In interpreting the Ship Register, it is important to remember that it indicates the amount of shipping purchased by a merchant—not the amount actually owned at a given time. To eighteenth-century merchants a vessel was both a capital good and an article of commerce. Captains were routinely instructed to sell the ship at the end of a voyage, if they could get an attractive price. Some merchants bought and sold vessels at a rapid rate, but actually owned only one vessel at any given time. For such people, the ship register may create a misleading impression of great wealth, because it discloses only that the merchant purchased a great many vessels—not the fact that they were sold off just as rapidly.

THE TONNAGE DUTY BOOK

Register of Tonnage Duties, 1775–1776. Record Group 4. Pennsylvania Historical and Museum Commission, Harrisburg.

5. Simeon John Crowther, "The Shipbuilding Industry and the Economic Development of the Delaware Valley, 1681–1776" (Ph.D. diss., University of Pennsylvania, 1970); Crowther, "The Shipbuilding Output of the Delaware Valley, 1722–1776," American Philosophical Society, *Proceedings*, CXVII (1973), 90–104; John J. McCusker, "Sources of Investment Capital in the Colonial Philadelphia Shipping Industry," *Journal of Economic*

Tonnage Duties on Incoming Vessels, November 1, 1765–August 30, 1775. 3 vols. Cadwalader Collection, Thomas Cadwalader Section. Historical Society of Pennsylvania, Philadelphia.

In order to finance a lighthouse at the mouth of the Delaware River, the Pennsylvania Assembly in 1764 levied a tonnage duty of sixpence per measured ton on all vessels entering and leaving Philadelphia.[6] This law generated the Tonnage Duty Book, a valuable list of vessels entering Philadelphia between 1765 and 1776, which survives in the Historical Society of Pennsylvania. It records, for each vessel entering the port, her date of arrival, name, tonnage, master, duty owed, and—most important for our purposes—her consignee. Whether this consignee owned the vessel or was managing it for the owner who lived in a foreign port is also indicated. For the years 1772–1775, the vessel's port of origin is usually indicated.

Tonnage was computed, for single-decked vessels, by the formula

$$(\text{length} \times \text{depth} \times \text{breadth}) \div 95$$

and for two-decked vessels by the formula

$$(\text{length} \times \text{breadth} \times .5\ \text{breadth}) \div 95$$

This "measured" tonnage is far more precise than the figures in the Ship Register, which are usually multiples of 10 and were manipulated to reduce taxes.[7] The consignee of the vessel could fall into one of four categories. He could be (1) the vessel's master, (2) a supercargo aboard the vessel, (3) a Philadelphia resident appearing in my merchant roster of 1,277 Philadelphia merchants, or (4) a Philadelphia resident not appearing in my merchant roster. People falling into category 1 are identified as such in the document itself, and people in category 3 can be identified fairly easily. The document sometimes uses several designations for the same firm—Pollard and Heaton, Heaton and Pollard, Pollard and Co., for example—but it usually is not difficult to identify the firms and, with the help of the Ship Register, to identify the full names of the individuals in the firm. Categories 2 and 4 are very difficult to distinguish from each other and, therefore, have been grouped together in my analysis.

The relationship between incoming tonnage managed and the economic standing of the firm is variable. If the vessel was owned by the firm, earnings—or losses—would depend upon what share of the vessel they owned. This is roughly measured by the Ship Register, but not by the Duty Book. Furthermore, freight earnings are based on ton-miles covered in a voyage, not just the tonnage

---

History, XXXII (1972), 146–157; McCusker, "The Pennsylvania Shipping Industry in the Eighteenth Century" (1973), MS, Historical Society of Pennsylvania.

6. Mitchell and Flanders, comps., *Statutes at Large*, VI, 373–378.

7. James and Drinker to Nehemiah Champion, July 13, 1757. "We took out her Register the 11th Current at 65 Tons which was as low as we could make it." James and Drinker Letterbook, 1756–1759, 144, Henry Drinker Papers, Historical Society of Pennsylvania.

of the ship that entered the port. A one-hundred-ton vessel entering from London generated more revenue than one entering from Boston.

Merchants who were consigned vessels that they did not own earned commissions on the following:

1. Expenses of the vessel while in port, including repairs, pilots' fees, crews' wages, and provisions for the outward voyage.
2. Freight earnings of the inward voyage.
3. Sales of goods exported to Philadelphia by the ship's overseas owners and sold on consignment by the vessel's consignee.
4. Value of goods ordered by the owners to be purchased in Philadelphia and loaded for the outward voyage.

Item 1 would be affected primarily by the vessel's size but also by the length of the voyage; item 2 by the value of the cargo and length of the voyage; and items 3 and 4 by the value of the incoming and outgoing voyages, respectively.

CUSTOMS RECORDS

Registers of Duties Paid on Imported Goods, 1781–1787. 6 vols. Record Group 4. Pennsylvania Historical and Museum Commission, Harrisburg.

These customs records have been studied in the aggregate in two valuable dissertations, but they have not been used to study social history.[8] The duties for the mid-1780s applied to all goods entering the state, whether foreign or American, and were based on the goods' current value in Pennsylvania currency.[9] The duty books for the period May 1785–December 1787, which were analyzed for this study, list vessel and master; the type, value, and provenance of the goods; and the persons or firm to whom the goods were consigned. Unlike the Tonnage Duty Book, they do not state whether these goods were owned by the consignee. Often they were not, and even when they were, the goods in many cases were purchased on credit (especially if imported from Great Britain) and not paid for until months or years after receipt. Thus the customs books do not directly measure the property or profits of firms, but, rather, the scale of their importing business. Nevertheless, they are the single best measure of the economic stature of a firm—far better than the Tonnage Duty Book or Ship Register, because many firms did not handle or own shipping.

Broken down firm by firm, the customs books yield 1,800 different importers, many of them very trivial. To keep the study manageable, I analyzed only firms who had a partner in my merchant roster or who imported at least three hun-

8. Gordon Carl Bjork, "Stagnation and Growth in the American Economy, 1748–1792" (Ph.D. diss., University of Washington, 1963); Rezin Fenton Duvall, "Philadelphia's Maritime Commerce with the British Empire, 1783–1789" (Ph.D. diss., University of Pennsylvania, 1960).

9. Mitchell and Flanders, comps., *Statutes at Large*, XI, 262–265, 546–556; XII, 99–104, 146–147, 233–235, 403–409.

dred pounds over the thirty-two-month period. This was a very low cutoff point, equaling only half of one medium-sized cargo of lumber or grain. Nevertheless, this cutoff reduced the number of people studied to 856. The major technical problem was presented by people who imported both singly (on their own account, typically quite small quantities of goods, for personal use) and as part of a multipartner firm. Where possible, these people were eliminated, a procedure that reduced the sample to 815.

These lists were also analyzed for the years 1781 and 1782.[10] In these years commercial activity was heavily concentrated in the hands of a few dozen firms, some of whom imported very large cargoes of dry goods (see chap. 5). Although the monetary value of these dry goods imports was stated in the document, the value of generic commodities such as coffee, sugar, rum, and so forth was not. Consequently, the quantities of such goods had to be converted into values, using, where possible, Anne Bezanson *et al.*, *Prices and Inflation during the American Revolution.*[11] For the few commodities not dealt with in Bezanson, I used prices in the 1785 customs list and multiplied by a factor of 2.5. This method is obviously inexact, but fortunately it was used for commodities whose value, relative to the whole, was very small. Mindful of the difficulties involved in converting quantities into values, my own analysis of this document concentrated on the values of dry goods imports and the quantities—not the value—of the generic commodities.

PROBATE DOCUMENTS

Wills and Administrations, City of Philadelphia. Office of the Recorder of Wills, Philadelphia City Hall.

Documents relating to wills are available on microfilm and should be used in this form because they are more accessible to researchers and are far less fragile. Copies of the wills are also available in bound volumes. Documents relating to administrations must be used in the original. All values were reduced to Pennsylvania currency and based on the price level prevailing in the period 1774–1776. I analyzed only those merchants who died before 1796.

In view of the heavy use that social historians have made of probate documents, these records were disappointing. Partly because merchants were a transient group and many of the 1,277 traders on my roster were young men when they entered the city in the 1780s, the proportion of the total merchant group that was represented in the probate documents was not very large. Moreover, large segments of the decedents' estates were in most cases not listed in inventories and estate accounts. The coverage for various types of property was as follows:

10. See *ibid.*, X, 252–258.

11. Anne Bezanson *et al.*, *Prices and Inflation during the American Revolution: Pennsylvania, 1770–1790*, Industrial Research Department, Wharton School of Finance and Commerce, University of Pennsylvania Research Studies, XXXV (Philadelphia, 1951), 337–338.

Property Type	*% of 97 Probated Estates Stating Value of Property Type*
Land	6
Financial assets	36
Financial liabilities	14
Business inventories	35
Household inventory	85
Nonland net worth	16

Clearly, household iventories were the only parts of the estate that were adequately covered. Landholdings are seldom listed, and financial assets and liabilities are highly incomplete. There is a particular danger of overstating the wealth of a merchant by analyzing only his financial assets and failing to deduct his own debts, which often were considerable. Such financial data as are available tend to be uncertain. Book debts, for instance, are sometimes missing, and it is impossible to be certain whether the decedent had no debtors or—as seems more likely—they are missing. Other ambiguities arise in interpreting the financial component of estates. Administrators could take years to settle a large estate. Was a certain payment by them a legacy, a debt of the decedent, or a postmortem expense of the estate (for maintenance of property, support of dependents, and so forth)? Because of all these defects, probate records were used not as a systematic source of quantitative information, but, rather, as a valuable supplement to the manuscript evidence.

Manuscripts

AMERICAN JEWISH HISTORICAL SOCIETY. Waltham, Massachusetts.

Haym Salomon Papers.

AMERICAN PHILOSOPHICAL SOCIETY. Philadelphia.

Stephen Girard Papers. Microfilm. A gigantic and extremely informative collection. Virtually inexhaustible.

Nathanael Greene Papers. Extremely valuable.

Manuscripts Relating to Non-Importation Resolutions, Philadelphia, 1766–1775.

BAKER LIBRARY. Harvard University. Boston.

Andrew Clow Papers.

Donnaldson and Coxe Journal, 1785–1786.

Richard S. Smith Invoice Book, 1792–1811.

BUCKS COUNTY HISTORICAL SOCIETY. Doylestown, Pennsylvania.

Kuhn and Risberg Letterbooks. In Kuhn and Risberg Papers.

COLUMBIA UNIVERSITY LIBRARY. New York City.

William Pollard Letterbook, 1764–1768. Montgomery Collection.

ELEUTHERIAN MILLS HISTORICAL LIBRARY. Wilmington, Delaware.

Andrew Clow and Co. Papers, 1784–1836.
Morris Family Papers.

HISTORICAL SOCIETY OF PENNSYLVANIA. Philadelphia.

Thomas Armat Papers. In Loudoun Papers.
Bank of North America Papers. Extremely valuable.
John Batho Letterbook, 1765–1768.
Leonard T. Beale Collection. 9 vols. Includes material on Thomas Wharton and James C. Fisher.
Clement Biddle Letterbook, 1789–1792. Important information on securities speculation.
Clement Biddle Papers.
Thomas A. Biddle Collection.
William Bingham Letterbook, 1791–1793. Conveys the enthusiasm of a rich merchant in the early Federalist period.
Jasper Yates Brinton Collection. Includes material on John Steinmetz, Henry Keppelle, Sr., and Henry Keppelle, Jr.
James Burnside Letterbook, 1778–1779.
Joseph Carson Receipt Books, 1775–1791. 4 vols.
Chaloner and White Collection. An important collection.
John and Peter Chevalier Daybook, 1760–1766.
Daniel Clark Letterbook, 1759–1762. Short but informative.
Clifford Correspondence, 1778–1785. Vols. VI, VII. In Pemberton Papers.
Andrew Clow and Company Papers. In Gratz Collection.
Josiah and Samuel Coates Papers. In Coates and Reynell Collection.
Stephen Collins Letterbook, 1783–1792. Complements the Collins Papers in the Library of Congress.
Tench Coxe Papers. Available on microfilm.
Cramond and Phillips Papers. In Gratz Collection.
Customs House Papers.
Samuel Dilworth Invoice Books, 1783–1786, 1788–1792. 2 vols.
Henry Drinker Papers. Important on pre-Revolutionary trade and post-Revolutionary land speculation.
Joshua Fisher and Sons Ledger, 1769–1773. An excellent ledger.
Samuel and Miers Fisher Journal, 1792–1795.
Thomas, Samuel, and Miers Fisher Journal, 1784–1788, and Ledger, 1792–1796. 2 vols.
Thomas Fitzsimons Journal, 1781–1785.
William Forbes Account Book, 1768–1780.

Tench Francis Ledger and Invoice Book, 1759–1763.
Franklin and Marshall Collection. Includes material on Dutilh and Wachsmuth and Andrew Clow.
Benjamin Fuller Papers, 1762–1799. 5 vols. Very informative.
Fuller and Sinnickson Ledger, 1766–1782.
Gough and Carmault Letterbook, 1757–1761.
John Greeves Ledger, 1753–1757.
Robert Henderson Papers.
Michael Hillegas Letterbooks, 1757–1760, 1777–1782. 2 vols.
Hollingsworth Papers. A gigantic and important collection. See the special guide to this collection, available at the Society.
Owens Jones Papers.
Jones, Clarke, and Cresson Receipt Books, 1783–1797. 2 vols.
Jones and Wister Invoice Book, 1759–1762. Complements the Owen Jones Papers.
John Kidd Letterbook, 1749–1763.
Samuel McCall Journal, 1743–1749.
Christopher Marshall Bills of Lading. 1 vol.
Mendenhall and Cope Papers, 1789–1795. 4 vols.
Mifflin and Massey Ledger, 1760–1763. Valuable.
Mildred and Roberts, Accounts Current, 1775–1789. 1 vol.
Morris and Miercken Ledger E, 1783–1789.
Morris and Miercken Papers. Vols. CDXXI–CDXXXIX of the Hollingsworth Collection. Complements the Morris Family Papers in the Eleutherian Mills Historical Library.
Richard Neave, Jr., Account Book.
Samuel Neave Ledger, 1752–1756.
John Nicholson Letterbooks, 1795–1798.
Joseph Ogden Invoice Book, 1749–1755.
Orr, Dunlope, and Glenholme Letterbook, 1767–1769. Valuable.
Israel Pemberton Ledger, 1774–1779. Pemberton Collection. Much information on Pemberton's real estate holdings.
Philadelphia Merchant Day Book, 1770–1788. The Journal of Thomas Canby, a Flour Merchant.
Philadelphia Merchant Journal, 1774–1776, continued as Ledger, 1826–1833.
William Pollard Letterbook, 1772–1774. Valuable.
Reed and Forde Papers. Important.
John Reynell Invoice Book, 1758–1772. In Coates and Reynell Collection.
Thomas Riche Papers. 4 vols. Important.
Daniel Roberdeau Letterbook, 1764–1771. Important.
Cropley Rose Letterbook, 1779–1781.
John Ross Papers, 1776–1793.
Edward Wanton Smith Collection. Includes Charles Wharton material.
Sarah A. G. Smith Collection. 3 boxes. Includes material on Charles Wharton and Lamar, Hill, and Bisset.
William Smith Letterbook, 1771–1775.

Richard Sweetman Receipt Book, 1771–1780.
Joseph Turner Letterbook, 1753–1774. An important, little-used volume.
Claude W. Unger Collection. Includes material on Dutilh and Wachsmuth and on Andrew Clow.
Richard Vaux Diaries, 1779–1782. 3 vols.
Waln Collection.
John Warder Letterbooks, 1776–1778. 3 books bound in 1 vol.
William West Account Books, 1769–1804. 10 vols. Includes material on William West, Francis and John West, James West, and (in Vol. III) Benjamin Fuller.
Wharton Papers. Includes material on Charles, William, and Thomas Wharton.
Willing and Morris Letterbook, 1754–1761. Important.
Wister Papers.

LIBRARY OF CONGRESS. Washington, D.C.

James Abeel Letterbook, 1778. Informative.
William Bingham Collection, 1776–1801. A small but excellent collection.
Ephraim Blaine Collection. An important collection.
Stephen Collins Papers. An important collection.
Constable, Rucker, and Co. Papers.
Continental Army Returns, Container 53. Force Papers, Series 7-D.
John Davis Collection, 1755–1783. 11 vols. An important collection.
John De Neufville Invoice Book, 1779–1780.
William Dunbar Papers. Relate to the investments of John Ross in southern plantations.
Richard Harrison and Co. Ledger, 1779–1783. A few accounts relate to the Philadelphia tobacco trade.
John Holker Papers.
Mathew Irwin Journal, 1769–1784. Important on shipping business during the Revolution.
Nicholas Low Papers. Valuable correspondence concerning the tobacco trade conducted by Low of New York and John Wilcocks of Philadelphia.
John Lownes Letterbook, 1760–1769.
John Pringle Cash Book, 1780; Invoice and Sales Book, 1775–1785. All bound in 1 vol.
Samuel Smith Papers, 1772–1869. Part of this collection relates to Robert Morris's French tobacco contract.
Walter Stewart Papers, 1776–1783. Engaging correspondence of a merchant who served in the Continental army.
Woolsey and Salmon Letterbook, 1774–1784. A Baltimore firm that traded with John Pringle of Philadelphia.

MASSACHUSETTS HISTORICAL SOCIETY. Boston.

Timothy Pickering Papers. Available on microfilm.

MORRISTOWN NATIONAL HISTORICAL PARK. Morristown, New Jersey.

Manuscript Collection. A large collection of miscellaneous material, mainly letters, relating primarily to the Revolutionary war. Available on microfilm.

NATIONAL ARCHIVES. Washington, D.C.

Papers of the Continental Congress. Available on microfilm. See the extraordinary work compiled by John P. Butler: *Index: The Papers of the Continental Congress, 1774–1789*, 5 vols. (Washington, D.C., 1978).

NEW YORK HISTORICAL SOCIETY. New York City.

Enoch Hobart Papers.
Joseph Read Papers.

NEW YORK PUBLIC LIBRARY. New York City.

Constable Pierrepont Papers. Should be read in connection with William A. Davis, "William Constable: New York Merchant and Land Speculator, 1772–1803" (Ph.D. diss., Harvard University, 1955). Only the first four chapters of this dissertation were written, and they are available in the manuscript room of the New York Public Library.
Robert Henderson Day Book and Journal, 1779–1791.
Robert Henderson Letterbook, 1779–1784.
Collin McGregor Letterbooks, 1783–1794. 4 vols.
Thomas Pratt Papers. 3 vols. Quite valuable.

PENNSYLVANIA HISTORICAL AND MUSEUM COMMISSION. Harrisburg.

Bankruptcy File in Record Group 27. An important source.
Baynton, Wharton, and Morgan Papers. A large and valuable collection. A microfilm edition, which is extensive but not complete, is available.
John and Peter Chevalier Ledger, 1770–1781. A valuable volume, which I found only on microfilm.
John Mitchell Sequestered Papers. 6 boxes.
John Nicholson Papers. Correspondence available on microfilm.
Robert Usher Invoice Book, 1759–1761.

SOUTHERN HISTORICAL COLLECTION. University of North Carolina. Chapel Hill.

William Attmore Letterbook. In Benjamin Robinson Huske Collection.
William Attmore Papers.
Lenoir Family Papers.

UNIVERSITY OF PENNSYLVANIA. Philadelphia.

The Wetherill Collection. A massive collection, currently kept in the basement of Lippincott Library. Includes the James and John Cox Letterbook, 1786–1795. See the Research Report by Miriam Hussey, "The Wetherill Papers, 1762–1899," Industrial Research Department, Wharton School of Finance and Commerce, University of Pennsylvania (Philadelphia, 1942).

Doctoral Dissertations

(Titles with an Asterisk [*] of Particularly Great Value)

Alexander, John Kurt. "Philadelphia's 'Other Half': Attitudes toward Poverty and the Meaning of Poverty in Philadelphia, 1760–1800." University of Chicago, 1973.

*Baumann, Roland Milton. "The Democratic-Republicans of Philadelphia: The Origins, 1776–1797." Pennsylvania State University, 1970.

*Berg, Harry Dahl. "Merchants and Mercantile Life in Colonial Philadelphia: 1748–1763." State University of Iowa, 1941.

*Bjork, Gordon Carl. "Stagnation and Growth in the American Economy, 1784–1792." University of Washington, 1963.

*Brobeck, Stephen James. "Changes in the Composition and Structure of Philadelphia Elite Groups, 1756–1790." University of Pennsylvania, 1973.

*Carp, E. Wayne. "Supplying the Revolution: Continental Army Administration and American Political Culture, 1775–1783." University of California, Berkeley, 1981.

Chernow, Barbara Ann. "Robert Morris, Land Speculator, 1790–1801." Columbia University, 1974.

*Coakley, Robert Walter. "Virginia Commerce during the American Revolution." University of Virginia, 1949.

Coulter, Calvin Brewster, Jr. "The Virginia Merchant." Princeton University, 1944.

*Crowther, Simeon John. "The Shipbuilding Industry and the Economic Development of the Delaware Valley, 1681–1776." University of Pennsylvania, 1970.

DiStefano, Judy Mann. "A Concept of the Family in Colonial America: The Pembertons of Philadelphia." Ohio State University, 1970.

Duvall, Rezin Fenton. "Philadelphia's Maritime Commerce with the British Empire, 1783–1789." University of Pennsylvania, 1960.

*Egnal, Marc Matthew. "The Pennsylvania Economy, 1748–1762: An Analysis of Short-Run Fluctuations in the Context of Long-Run Changes in the Atlantic Trading Community." University of Wisconsin, 1974.

Franz, George William. "Paxton: A Study of Community Structure and Mobility in the Colonial Pennsylvania Backcountry." Rutgers University, 1974.

Gilbert, Geoffrey Neal. "Baltimore's Flour Trade to the West Indies, 1750–1815." Johns Hopkins University, 1975.
Grundfest, Jerry. "George Clymer, Philadelphia Revolutionary, 1739–1813." Columbia University, 1973.
*Ireland, Owen Stephen. "The Ratification of the Federal Constitution in Pennsylvania." University of Pittsburgh, 1966.
Klopfer, Helen L. "Statistics of Foreign Trade of Philadelphia, 1700–1860." University of Pennsylvania, 1936.
*Larsen, Grace Hutchison. "Profile of a Colonial Merchant: Thomas Clifford of Pre-Revolutionary Philadelphia." Columbia University, 1955.
McCurdy, Linda. "The Potts Family Iron Industry in the Schuylkill Valley." Pennsylvania State University, 1974.
Manges, Frances Mayo. "Women Shopkeepers, Tavernkeepers, and Artisans in Colonial Philadelphia." University of Pennsylvania, 1958.
Martin, Alfred Simpson. "The Port of Philadelphia, 1763–1776: A Biography." State University of Iowa, 1941.
Nuxoll, Elizabeth Miles. "Congress and the Munitions Merchants: The Secret Committee of Trade during the American Revolution, 1775–1777." City University of New York, 1979.
Oaks, Robert Francis. "Philadelphia Merchants and the American Revolution, 1765–1776." University of Southern California, 1970.
Parsons, William T. "Isaac Norris, II, The Speaker." University of Pennsylvania, 1955.
Paskoff, Paul Frederick. "Colonial Merchant-Manufacturers and Iron: A Study in Capital Transformation, 1725–1775." Johns Hopkins University, 1976.
Platt, John David Ronalds. "Jeremiah Wadsworth: Federalist Entrepreneur." Columbia University, 1955.
*Rasmusson, Ethel Elise. "Capital on the Delaware: The Philadelphia Upper Class in Transition, 1789–1801." Brown University, 1962.
Romanek, Carl Leroy. "John Reynell, Quaker Merchant of Colonial Philadelphia." Pennsylvania State University, 1969.
*Sachs, William S. "The Business Outlook in the Northern Colonies, 1750–1775." Columbia University, 1957.
Slaski, Eugene R. "Thomas Willing: Moderation during the American Revolution." Florida State University, 1971.
Thompson, Tommy R. "Marylanders, Personal Indebtedness, and the American Revolution." University of Maryland, 1972.
Tyler, John W. "The First Revolution: Boston Merchants and the Acts of Trade, 1760–1774." Princeton University, 1980.
Viles, Perry. "The Shipping Interest of Bordeaux, 1774–1793." Harvard University, 1965.
Walker, Paul Kent. "The Baltimore Community and the American Revolution: A Study in Urban Development, 1763–1783." University of North Carolina, 1973.

*Walzer, John Flexer. "Transportation in the Philadelphia Trading Area, 1740–1775." University of Wisconsin, 1968.
Webster, Jonathan Howes. "The Merchants of Bordeaux in Trade to the French West Indies, 1664–1717." University of Minnesota, 1972.
*Wilkinson, Norman B. "Land Policy and Speculation in Pennsylvania, 1779–1800." University of Pennsylvania, 1958.

Index